ONLINE CONSUMER PSYCHOLOGY

Understanding and Influencing Consumer
Behavior in the Virtual World

Advertising and Consumer Psychology
A Series Sponsored by the Society for Consumer Psychology

Aaker/Biel: *Brand Equity & Advertising: Advertising's Role in Building Strong Brands* (1993)

Clark/Brock/Stewart: *Attention, Attitude, and Affect in Response Advertising* (1994)

Englis: *Global and Multi-National Advertising* (1994)

Goldberg/Fishbein/Middlestadt: *Social Marketing: Theoretical and Practical Perspectives* (1997)

Haugtvedt/Machleit/Yalch: *Online Consumer Psychology: Understanding and Influencing Consumer Behavior in the Virtual World* (2005)

Kahle/Chiagouris: *Values, Lifestyles and Psychographics* (1997)

Kahle/Riley: *Sports Marketing and the Psychology of Marketing Communications* (2003)

Mitchell: *Advertising Exposure, Memory, and Choice* (1993)

Schumann/Thorson: *Advertising and the World Wide Web* (1999)

Scott/Batra: *Persuasive Imagery: A Consumer Response Perspective* (2003)

Shrum: *The Psychology of Entertainment Media: Blurring the Lines Between Entertainment and Persuasion* (2004)

Thorson/Moore: *Integrated Communication: Synergy of Persuasive Voices* (1996)

Wells: *Measuring Advertising Effectiveness* (1997)

Williams/Lee/Haugtvedt: *Diversity in Advertising: Broadening the Scope of Research Directions* (2004)

ONLINE CONSUMER PSYCHOLOGY

Understanding and Influencing Consumer
Behavior in the Virtual World

Edited by:

Curtis P. Haugtvedt

Ohio State University

Karen A. Machleit

University of Cincinnati

Richard F. Yalch

University of Washington

Routledge
Taylor & Francis Group
New York   London

Routledge is an imprint of the
Taylor & Francis Group, an informa business

Routledge
Taylor & Francis Group
270 Madison Avenue
New York, NY 10016

Routledge
Taylor & Francis Group
2 Park Square
Milton Park, Abingdon
Oxon OX14 4RN

© 2005 by Taylor & Francis Group, LLC
Routledge is an imprint of Taylor & Francis Group, an Informa business

Printed in the United States of America on acid-free paper
10 9 8 7 6 5 4 3
International Standard Book Number-13: 978-0-8058-5155-0 (Softcover)
Library of Congress Card Number 2004027585
Cover design by Kathryn Houghtaling Lacey

Library of Congress Cataloging-in-Publication Data

Online Consumer psychology : understanding and influencing consumer behavior in the
    virtual world / Editors Curtis P. Haugtvedt, Karen A. Machleit, Richard Yalch.
        p. cm.— (Advertising and consumer psychology)
    Includes bibliographical references and index.
    ISBN 0-8058-5154-2 (case : alk. paper)—ISBN 0-8058-5515-0 (pbk. : alk.paper)
    1. Consumer behavior. 2. Internet advertising. 3. Electronic commerce. I. Haugtvedt, Curtis P.,
    1958-   II. Machleit, Karen A.   III. Yalch, Richard.   IV. Series.
    HF5415.32.O55   2005
    659.14'4'019—dc22   2004027585

Visit the Taylor & Francis Web site at
http://www.taylorandfrancis.com

and the Routledge Web site at
http://www.routledge.com

Contents

PART V: DECISION MAKING

PART VI: RESEARCH TOOLS AND APPROACHES

About the Contributors

Anat Toder-Alon is a doctoral candidate in the Department of Marketing at Boston University School of Management. She holds a MA and a BA from Hebrew University in Jerusalem. She is currently finishing her dissertation entitled: "Rediscovering Word of Mouth: An Ethnomethodological Analysis of Word of Mouth Talk in the Context of Online Communities." She has presented her research at several international conferences and has published in the *Journal of Consumer Psychology.*

Barbara Bickart (Ph.D., University of Illinois at Urbana–Champaign) is interested in context effects on judgment and decision-making processes, how people retrieve and use information about others in answering survey questions, and developing methods for reducing measurement error in surveys via questionnaire design. She serves on the editorial boards of the *Journal of Marketing, Journal of Consumer Research,* and *Journal of Public Policy and Marketing.*

Frank Biocca (Ph.D., University of Wisconsin–Madison) is the SBC Chaired Professor of Telecommunication, Information Studies, and Media and Director of the Media Interface and Network Design (M.I.N.D.) Lab at Michigan State University. The M.I.N.D. Lab is an international, multi-university human-computer interaction and communication research lab with ten facilities spanning six countries (www.mindlab.org). His research interests focus on the interaction of media and mind, specifically how media form can be adapted to extend human cognition and enhance human performance.

David M. Boush (Ph.D., University of Minnesota) is Associate Professor of Marketing at the University of Oregon. Topics of his research include brand equity, response to advertising, and consumer trust. His articles have appeared in such outlets as the *Journal of Consumer Research* and the *Journal of Marketing Research.* He is a member of the American Marketing Association, the Association for Consumer Research, the Academy of Marketing Science, and the Society for Consumer Psychology. He is also a former marketing research analyst for Hallmark Cards. His visiting appointments include a stint at ESSEC, and a series of e-commerce classes for University of California–Berkeley extension. He currently serves on the editorial board of the *Journal of the Academy of Marketing Sciences.*

Noel T. Brewer (Ph.D., University of North Carolina–Chapel Hill) conducts research is the areas of health psychology and public health. His work examines how health cognitions inform decision-making. One focus of the research examines the relation of mental models of illness to health behaviors such as medication compliance and physician utilization. Another focus examines the influence of Internet use on health judgments and choices.

Frédéric F. Brunel (Ph.D., University of Washington) is an Assistant Professor of Marketing at Boston University School of Management. He holds an MBA from Illinois State University, and a BS from Ecole Supérieure des Sciences Commerciales d'Angers (ESSCA) Angers, France. He has lead professional education programs in the USA, Europe, Latin America, and Asia. His primary research interests include consumers' perceptions of product design and visual aesthetics, consumers' attitude and emotions, and socio-cultural, gender, and relationship issues in marketing. He has presented his research at numerous conferences. He has been published in forums like: *Journal of Consumer Research, Journal of Advertising, Journal of Consumer Psychology, Journal of the Academy of Marketing Science, Journal of Advertising Research, Psychology and Marketing, Business Strategy Review, Advances in Consumer Research, Developments in Marketing Science, Cross-Cultural Consumer and Business Studies, Gender, Marketing and Consumer Behavior* and in several books. Professor Brunel has also won several teaching, research, and service awards.

Jean Louis Chandon (Ph.D., Northwestern University) is Professor of Marketing at IAE of Aix en Provence and Academic Director of the MBA E-Business program. He worked as a media consultant for Nielsen, Emap, and Mediametrie. He has written several papers in the area of audience measurement, media planning, and service marketing.

Mohamed Saber Chtourou (Ph.D., University of Aix Marseille III) is a research assistant in EDHEC Business School. He is also an associate researcher at CEROG - IAE Aix en Provence, University of Aix Marseille III. His area of interest is Internet advertising persuasion process; especially understanding what makes the Internet a different media. In addition, he is interested in factors affecting ad effectiveness, potential complementarily between online and offline media, and issues related to Internet media planning. This paper is a part of a larger project he is conducting at Wanadoo Regie, a leading French Internet ad agency. Other papers have been presented to the French Marketing Association Congress, ESOMAR Conference, IREP Conference.

June A. Cline works as a research consultant and statistician with doctoral students at Wayne State University who are completing their dissertations. She also works with school districts and nonprofit organizations, planning and completing program evaluations on educational programs intended to improve student learning. Her research interests are varied, including education, nursing, psychology, political science, and sociology.

Janis J. Crow is a doctoral student completing her dissertation in consumer psychology at Kansas State University and is an instructor in the Marketing Department. Her research interests are in unstructured decision making where a clear alternative does not exist such as in customizing a product. She is interested in the use of technology to aid in making decisions. She has published in *Behavior Research Methods, Instruments, and Computers* and the *International Journal of Internet Marketing and Advertising.*

Paula Danskin (Ph.D., The University of Memphis) is Assistant Professor of Management in the Campbell School of Business at Berry College. Her current research interests include the validity of Internet-based approaches, knowledge management, and international entrepreneurship. Her work has appeared in several journals, including *Entrepreneurship Theory & Practice, Journal of Small Business Management, Journal of World Business,* and *Academy of Management Review.*

Terry M. Daugherty (Ph.D., Michigan State University) is an Assistant Professor in the Department of Advertising at the University of Texas at Austin. His research focuses on investigating consumer behavior and strategic media management, with work appearing in the *Journal of Advertising, Journal of Consumer Psychology, Journal of Interactive Advertising, Journal of Interactive Marketing,* and in the impending books *Advances in Electronic Marketing* and *Marketing Communication: Emerging Trends and Developments,* among others. Before joining the Department of Advertising at UT, he held a Post-Doctoral Fellowship with eLab in the Owen Graduate School of Management at Vanderbilt University, and has worked in advertising media.

María D. de Juan, Ph.D., is a Business Administration Professor at the Universidad of Alicante (Spain), where she lectures since 1991. De Juan has been a lecturer at the University of Florida (USA) and at the Southampton Institute (United Kingdom), as well as at several Spanish Business Schools, such as ESADE (Barcelona). She is the author of the books *Shopping Centre Attraction Toward Consumers, Sales Promotions,* and *Commercial Distribution: Channels and Retailing.* Her articles about distribution and consumer behaviour have been published or are forthcoming in several journals and edited books, including the *Journal of the Academy of Marketing Science and the Journal of Consumer Psychology.*

Basil G. Englis (Ph.D., Dartmouth College) is the Richard Edgerton Professor of Business Administration and Chair of the Department of Marketing in the Campbell School of Business at Berry College. His current research interests include lifestyle and product symbolism, consumer socialization, and online research issues. His research has appeared in several journals and other publications, including the *Journal of Advertising, Journal of Business Research, Journal of Personality and Social Psychology,* and *Journal of Experimental Social Psychology.* Professor Englis has consulted with numerous organizations, including E. I. DuPont de Nemours, eBay, and the Vanity Fair Corporation.

Barbara Fasolo (Ph.D., University of Colorado at Boulder) studies multi-attribute choice processes across different domains, ranging from consumer and medical decision making to food and mate choice. She is interested in the development of aids to assist these difficult decisions, particularly on the Internet. She has investigated how online consumer choices are affected by web-based decision aids (compensatory or non-compensatory) and the correlation among the choice attributes (positive or negative). She co-authored an *Annual Review of Psychology* chapter reviewing consumer web-based decision aids. After completing a post-doctoral fellowship at the Max Planck Institute in Berlin, she is now an Assistant Professor in the Department of Operations Research at the London School of Economics.

John Godek (Ph.D., University of Michigan) is Assistant Professor of Marketing at the University of Oregon. Professor Godek directs his research at identifying the influence of firms' individual level marketing efforts (customization and personalization) on consumers' decision processes and choices. His research has appeared in the *Journal of Consumer Research* and the *Journal of Consumer Psychology.*

Gerald Häubl (Ph.D., Wirtschaftsuniversität Wien) is Canada Research Chair in Behavioral Science, R. K. Banister Professor of Electronic Commerce, and Associate Professor of Marketing at the University of Alberta's School of Business. His primary research areas are consumer decision-making, human-computer interaction, and consumer behavior in electronic shopping environments, the construction of preference and value, consumer information search, bidding behavior in auctions, and the automated creation of personalized customer interfaces. His research has been published in *Marketing Science, Journal of Consumer Psychology, International Journal of Research in Marketing, Communications of the Association for Computing Machinery*, and other journals. He serves on the editorial boards of *Computational Intelligence* and *Journal of Interactive Marketing.*

Curtis P. Haugtvedt (Ph.D., University of Missouri–Columbia) studies attitude change and persuasion, personality variables in consumer behavior, and computer-mediated behavioral research methodologies. Professor Haugtvedt teaches undergraduate courses in Electronic Marketing, Consumer Behavior and Marketing Management, MBA courses in Consumer Behavior and Electronic Marketing, and Ph.D. seminars in Advanced Topics in Consumer Psychology. His research has appeared in the *Journal of Personality and Social Psychology, Journal of Consumer Research, Journal of Consumer Psychology, Communication Monographs*, and numerous book chapters. He serves as a frequent reviewer for the major psychology and marketing journals, and is a member of editorial boards of the *Journal of Consumer Research, Journal of Consumer Psychology, Journal of Interactive Advertising*, and *Quarterly Journal of Electronic Commerce*. He is former Associate Editor of the *Journal of Consumer Psychology* and was President of the Society for Consumer Psychology (1999–2000).

C. Edward Heath is Assistant Professor of Marketing at Xavier University. He is currently completing his Ph.D. at the University of Kentucky. His work has been published in *Advances in Consumer Research.*

Paul Henry (Ph.D., University of New South Wales) is Senior Lecturer at The University of Sydney. He was previously Strategic Planning Director at Ogilvy & Mather in New York City where he worked on numerous internet-related projects. This included interactive strategy development within a broader communication setting, evaluation of content and functionality needs, and site realization.

Melanie Jones (Ph.D., University of Cincinnati) is a law student at Loyola University, New Orleans. Her primary research interests include data protection issues on the Internet and international strategy as it pertains to consumer behavior. She has presented two papers at the Academy of International Business. She has an article in the *International Journal of Technology Transfer*, and has an upcoming publication in the *Loyola Law Review.*

Lynn R. Kahle (Ph.D., University of Nebraska–Lincoln) is the James Warsaw Professor of Marketing at the University of Oregon. Topics of his research include social adaptation, values, and sports marketing. His articles have appeared in such outlets as the *Journal of Consumer Research, Journal of Marketing, Sport Marketing Quarterly, and Public Opinion Quarterly, Journal of Personality and Social Psychology,* and *Child Development.* His books include *Attitudes and Social Adaptation, Social Values and Social Change, Marketing Management, Cross-National Consumer Psychographics,* and *Values, Lifestyles, and Psychographics.* He has served as President of the Society for Consumer Psychology, President of the City of Eugene Human Rights program, and Chair of the Department of Marketing at the University of Oregon.

Robert J. Kent (Ph.D., University of Cincinnati) is an Associate Professor of Marketing at the University of Delaware. His work looks at issues in advertising media, promotions, and memory for ads. This work has appeared in *Journal of Marketing, Journal of Marketing Research, Journal of Advertising, Journal of Advertising Research,* and other outlets.

Katharine A. Lange (BA, University of Colorado at Boulder) contributed to studies about everyday decisions made on the Web, in order to help users make better choices online, and to further understand decision processes in general. She is currently working in Marketing and Public Relations at a ski resort and is in charge of the resort's web page development and organization.

Hyung-Il Lee (MS in Marketing, Korea University) is currently a research associate at Kookmin University, Seoul, Korea. Previously, he worked as a marketing specialist at a major telecommunication company in Korea (SK Telecom) where he developed the Ring Back Tone Service and Color-Ring. His work has appeared in journals such as *Korean Journal of Consumer Studies.*

Hyun-Jung Lee is a doctoral candidate in marketing, Korea University, Seoul, Korea. She is currently working on her dissertation research, which investigates psychological processes underlying consumer investment decisions in online stock trading contexts. Her research area includes brand extensions, advertising effects, and consumer investment decision making, and her work has appeared in journals such as *Korean Journal of Consumer Studies.*

Aron M. Levin is Assistant Professor of Marketing at Northern Kentucky University. He earned his Ph.D. from the University of Kentucky. His research interests are in brand alliances and the impact of sport sponsorships on consumers. His work has been published in the *Journal of Consumer Psychology, Journal of Business and Psychology,* and *Journal of Current Issues and Research in Advertising.*

Irwin P. Levin is a professor of psychology and marketing at the University of Iowa. His research interests are consumer decision-making, information framing effects, and individual differences and risky decision-making. His work has appeared in the *Journal of Consumer Psychology, Journal of Consumer Research, Organizational Behavior and Human Decision Processes, Journal of Behavioral Decision Making,* and *Journal of Personality and Social Psychology.* He is past president of the Society for Judgment and Decision Making.

Regina Lewis holds a Ph.D. from the University of North Carolina at Chapel Hill and an MBA from Columbia University. Since cofounding Lewis, Mobilio & Associates, her internet-related communications research has spanned segmentation, usability, and brand health analyses. She also has successfully pioneered sampling research and consumer-modeling work to help large Internet advertisers make spending and targeting decisions.

Hairong Li (Ph.D., Michigan State University) is an Associate Professor of Advertising and Research Fellow at the M.I.N.D. Lab at Michigan State University. His research interests include consumer behavior in electronic commerce, with emphasis on consumer learning from virtual experience.

David Luna (Ph.D., University of Wisconsin–Milwaukee) is an Associate Professor of Marketing at Baruch College. He conducts research focusing on the effect of language on consumer information processing and marketing communications. His work has appeared in the *Journal of Consumer Research,* the *Journal of Consumer Psychology,* the *Journal of the Academy of Marketing Science,* the *Journal of Advertising,* and *Psychology and Marketing.*

Patrick D. Lynch (Ph.D., University of Delaware) is a Principal with North Star Leadership Group. A former Research Fellow at the Accenture Institute for Strategic Change, he specializes in research and consulting on organizational and consumer behavior. His work on customer relationships, leadership, and business strategy issues has been featured in the books *The Ultimate CRM Handbook*; *DoCoMo: Japan's Wireless Tsunami*; and *Got Game: How the Gamer Generation is Reshaping Business Forever*. His work on the psychology of the Internet, wireless consumer behavior, customer experience, usability and teams has appeared in *Forum, Outlook, Journal of Applied Psychology, Applied and Preventative Psychology, Journal of Advertising Research, Journal of International Business Studies.*

Karen A. Machleit (Ph.D., Michigan State University) is Professor of Marketing, University of Cincinnati. Her primary research interests are in the areas of affective responses in consumption contexts and measurement issues/scale development. Her recent research examines the effect of the online store atmosphere on shopper responses. Her work has been published in many forums including the *Journal of Marketing, Journal of Consumer Research, Journal of Consumer Psychology, Journal of Advertising, Journal of Retailing, Marketing Letters*, and the *Journal of Business Research*, among others. She has served the Society for Consumer Psychology as Secretary/Treasurer during 1999–2001.

Gary H. McClelland (Ph.D., University of Michigan) is Professor of Psychology and Professor of Marketing at the University of Colorado at Boulder. He has published two books on statistical methodology: *Data Analysis, A Model Comparison Approach* (with Charles Judd) and *Seeing Statistics* (www.seeingstatistics.com), a recently published web-based statistics textbook using Java applets to visualize statistical principles, in addition to numerous journal articles in the areas of judgment and decision making, methodology, and data analysis. He serves on the editorial board of *Psychological Methods*.

Raj Mehta (Ph.D. in Marketing, University of Utah) is Professor of Marketing, University of Cincinnati. His research interests include the influence of information technology on marketing, international marketing, new product development, and marketing models. He also has interests in the role of competition in sustainable development. His work has been published in leading marketing academic journals such as the *Journal of Marketing Research, Journal of Consumer Research, Journal of Marketing* and *Marketing Letters* among others.

Saurabh Mishra (MA in Economics, India; Masters in Business, Indiana University) is currently a doctoral candidate in the Marketing Department at the Kelley School of Business, Indiana University. His research interests lie broadly in investigating consumer behavior in online and conventional store environments.

Andrew Mitchell is the Patricia Ellison Professor of Marketing in the Rotman School of Management at the University of Toronto. He received his Ph.D. at the University of California at Berkeley and has published over 50 articles, including articles in the *Journal of Consumer Research, Journal of Marketing Research, Management Science*, and *Journal of Marketing*. His current research interests include the effects of memory on judgment and choice, brand evaluation processes, and the organization of brand information in memory.

Lynne Mobilio (Ph.D., University of Minnesota) focuses her research on mental simulations, coping strategies, goal formation, and planning processes. In 1999 she cofounded Lewis, Mobilio & Associates to investigate issues relating to the online environment. By examining cognition, attitudes, and motivations of consumers as they approach the Internet, she and her partner, Regina Lewis, have helped numerous clients develop Web site strategy.

Kyle B. Murray (Ph.D., University of Alberta) is an Assistant Professor of Marketing in the Richard Ivey School of Business at the University of Western Ontario. His research focuses on consumer judgment and decision making, with an emphasis on how consumers make choices in electronic environments. Dr. Murray's work in this area has been published in the *Journal of Consumer Psychology* and the *Communications of the Association for Computing Machinery*. The results of his research have also been featured in a number of book chapters, as well as the National Post's Business Edge. As an educator, Dr. Murray has developed and taught undergraduate, MBA, and executive level courses in marketing and e-commerce. He has also been active as a consultant for a variety of organizations in fields as diverse as oil and gas, manufacturing, financial services, retailing, and not-for-profit enterprises.

Michelle R. Nelson (Ph.D., University of Illinois at Urbana–Champaign) is Assistant Professor of Journalism and Mass Communication at the University of Wisconsin-Madison. Her research focuses on persuasion processes and consumer behavior. She has published in *Journal of Advertising, Journal of Advertising Research, Journalism and Mass Communication Quarterly, Advances in Consumer Research,* and numerous book chapters.

Christie L. Nordhielm is an Associate Professor of Marketing at the University of Michigan Business School. She is interested in the impact of repetition on cognitive and affective response in a consumer behavior context. She recently received the 2003 Ferber Award for best article based on a Dissertation published by the Journal of Consumer Research. In addition to her publications in academic journals, Nordhielm has published in the *Harvard Business Review*, and her work is also presented in her forthcoming book, *Marketing Management: The Big Picture* (Thomson-Southwestern). Nordhielm has received numerous teaching awards and recognition as an educator. In 2003, the Northwestern University's Kellogg School of Management student body recognized her with the highest honor given to a Professor for teaching excellence, the Lavengood Outstanding Professor of the Year award.

Prior to joining the faculty of the University of Michigan, Nordhielm was an Assistant Professor at the Kellogg School of Management at Northwestern University. She was also a Lecturer in Marketing at the University of Chicago Graduate School of Business, where she earned her PhD in Marketing and Behavioral Science in 1998.

Richard W. Olshavsky (Ph.D., Carnegie-Mellon University, *Professor of Marketing, Kelley School of Business, Indiana University, Bloomington, IN*) is primarily interested in consumer behavior with a special interest in the heuristics used in choice. Most of his published articles have appeared in the *Journal of Consumer Research, Journal of Marketing Research, Journal of Marketing, Journal of Consumer Psychology, Journal of the Academy of Marketing Science,* and *Journal of Consumer Satisfaction, Dissatisfaction, and Complaining Behavior.* His published proceedings articles have been mainly in *Advances in Consumer Research.*

Richard Omanson (Ph.D., University of Minnesota) is a Director at User Centric, Inc., a design and usability consulting company where he conducts user research and designs software and Web interfaces. He has a patent for creating linear experiences on the Web and his published work has appeared in such journals as *Discourse Processes, Cognition and Instruction, Reading Research Quarterly, and Journal of Memory and Language* and in numerous book chapters.

Jong-Won Park (Ph.D., University of Illinois at Urbana–Champaign) is Professor of Marketing, Korea University, Seoul, Korea. His primary research interest is in cognitive processes underlying consumer choices, advertising effects, and strategic brand management. Topics of his recent research includes decoy effects in preference reversals, priming effects on choices for self versus others, effects of goal orientation on self-regulatory depletion, superstar effects in advertising, and brand extensions in online and offline contexts. His work has been published in *Journal of Consumer Research, Journal of Consumer Psychology, Journal of Personality and Social Psychology, Journal of Consumer Satisfaction, Dissatisfaction, and Complaining Behaviors,* and *Advances in Consumer Research.*

Laura A. Peracchio (Ph.D., Northwestern University) is Professor of Marketing at the University of Wisconsin–Milwaukee. She is interested in how bilingual consumers process verbal and pictorial information and make decisions. She also studies visual persuasion and its impact on information processing on and off/line. She has published her research in the *Journal of Consumer Research* and *Journal of Marketing Research.*

Joseph E. Phelps (Ph.D., University of Wisconsin–Madison) holds the Reese Phifer Professorship in the Advertising and Public Relations Department at The University of Alabama. The two major thrusts of his research agenda are consumer privacy concerns relating to marketers' use of consumer information and integrated marketing communications. Phelps has published in a variety of marketing and advertising journals. He served as editor of volumes 1–3 of *Frontiers of Direct & Interactive Marketing Research.* He serves on the Editorial Review Boards of the *Journal of Interactive Advertising, the Journal of Advertising Education, the Newspaper Research Journal,* the *Journal of Current Issues & Research in Advertising,* and the *International Journal of Internet Marketing and Advertising.* In 1999, the Direct Marketing Educational Foundation selected Phelps as the Outstanding Direct Marketing Educator. He served as Head of the Advertising Division (2001–2002) of the Association for Education in Journalism and Mass Communication. In 2004, he served as the President of the American Academy of Advertising.

Elizabeth Purinton (Ph.D., University of Rhode Island) is an Assistant Professor at Marist College in Poughkeepsie, New York. Dr. Purinton is a fellow of the AMA-Sheth Foundation Doctoral Consortium. Dr. Purinton's research programs include web site design, high-tech marketing, and the marketing orientation with emphasis on TQM techniques, marketing channel partnership survival, and mature marketing relationships. Dr. Purinton's research is published in the *Academy of Marketing Science Review, Journal of Electronic Commerce in Organizations, the Journal of Business Research*, and several conference proceedings.

Niranjan "Nick" Raman (Ph.D., University of Texas at Austin) is Vice President at ImpactRx Inc. Nick's research interests include information processing and consumer behavior in electronic media, and his work has been published in the *European Journal of Marketing* and in *Advances in Consumer Research.*

Deborah E. Rosen (Ph.D., University of Tennessee–Knoxville) is an Associate Professor in the College of Business Administration, the University of Rhode Island. Dr. Rosen's research interests include Web site design, online word-of-mouth (mouse), inter-organizational relationships, and quality management. Her research has appeared in the *Journal of Business Research, Journal of Electronic Commerce in Organizations, International Journal of Services Industry Management*, and *Academy of Marketing Science Review* and in conference proceedings.

Robert M. Schindler (Ph.D., University of Massachusetts) is interested in consumer motivation and the psychological processes underlying the effects of marketing techniques. His current research concerns price promotions, 9-ending prices, word-of-mouth communication, and the effects of early experience on consumer tastes. His papers have appeared in a number of journals and other publications, including the *Journal of Consumer Research, Journal of Marketing Research, Journal of Retailing, Journal of Advertising,* and *Journal of Consumer Psychology.*

James Shanteau (Ph.D., University of California–San Diego) is a Commerce Bank Distinguished Graduate School Professor of Psychology at Kansas State University. He is received his doctoral degree in Experimental Psychology. His research interests include analysis of expertise in decision makers and studies of consumer choices. He is co-founder, executive committee chair, and past President of the Judgment/Decision Making Society. He served as Program Director of Decision, Risk, and Management Science Program at the National Science Foundation. Presently, he is the Director of the Judgment and Decision Making Laboratory at Kansas State University. His publications include over 63 articles in referred journals, 10 books, 60 book chapters, 6 encyclopedia entries, 7 monographs, 21 proceedings papers, 14 technical reports, and 3 computer programs. He has been a consultant to 38 organizations on issues related to consumer behavior, expert systems development, and behavioral research methodology.

Wendy Schneier Siegal (Ph.D., Ohio State University) received her MBA at the Ohio State University and a BA in Psychology from Tulane University. She was and Assistant Professor of Marketing at Boston University School of Management when this chapter was written. Her research focuses on managerial/consumer learning and the impact of situational and dispositional factors on information search, information use, and decision-making processes. She has published and presented research in leading marketing conferences and journals such as the *Journal of Consumer Research, Information Systems Research, Journal of Product Innovation Management,* and the *CASE International Journal of Educational Advancement.*

Eugene Sivadas (Ph.D., Marketing, University of Cincinnati) is Assistant Professor of Marketing, Rutgers Business School—Newark & New Brunswick, Rutgers, The State University of New Jersey. His research interests include electronic and other forms of direct marketing, interorganizational relationships, and health care marketing. His research has appeared in the *Journal of Marketing, Journal of Business Research, Journal of Interactive marketing,* and *Marketing Health Services.*

Michael R. Solomon (Ph.D., University of North Carolina at Chapel Hill) is Human Sciences Professor of Consumer Behavior at Auburn University. His research interests include symbolic consumption, fashion psychology, and online consumer research methodologies. His work has been published in such journals as the *Journal of Consumer Research, Journal of Marketing, Journal of Advertising, Journal of Personality and Social Psychology,* and *Journal of Retailing.* He serves as a consultant to numerous organizations on issues pertaining to consumer behavior and marketing strategy.

Barbara Stern is Professor II of Marketing and department chair at Rutgers Business School. Her research on consumer behavior in online auctions has appeared in the *International Journal of Electronic Marketing* and the *Journal of Advertising*. Her research on the application of gender and literary theory to the analysis of advertisements, consumer behavior, and marketing text consists of over 100 articles appearing in the *Journal of Consumer Research, Journal of Marketing, Journal of Advertising, Current Issues in Research on Advertising*, and others. She served as co-chair of the 1995 American Marketing Association Summer Educators' Conference, and was track chair for the "Netvertising" track in the American Marketing Association 2001 Winter Educators' Conference. She is editor-in-chief of *Marketing Theory*, and co-editor of the Routledge Press series on "Interpretive Marketing Research." She serves on numerous editorial boards, including the *Journal of Consumer Research, Journal of Advertising, and Current Issues in Research on Advertising*. She received the American Academy of Advertising Outstanding Contribution to Research Award.

Richard F. Yalch (Ph.D., Northwestern University) is Professor of Marketing at the University of Washington. He served for three years as Director of Computing Services for the School of Business. His current research focuses on Internet start-ups and consumer inferences. Recently, he served as associate editor of the *Journal of Consumer Research*, where he published several papers. He has also published papers in the *Journal of Marketing, Journal of Applied Psychology, Journal of Marketing Research, Journal of Business Research*, and numerous conference proceedings. Richard regularly consults with Northwest Research Group, a full-service marketing research firm.

J. Frank Yates (Ph.D., University of Michigan) focuses his research on judgment and decision processes (including emphases on cross-cultural variations); decision management; decision aiding (including special attention to cross-cultural collaborations as well as managerial, marketing, medical, and risk-taking decisions); judgment analysis and training; and applications of cognitive psychology. His research has appeared in many books and journals, including the *Journal of Experimental Psychology, Organizational Behavior and Human Decision Processes, Psychological Bulletin*, and the *International Journal of Forecasting*. He is the associate editor for the *Journal of Behavioral Decision Making*, a consulting editor for the *Journal of Cross-Cultural Psychology*, and a member of the editorial review board for *Organizational Behavior and Human Decision Processes*. His latest book is *Decision Management* (Jossey-Bass, 2003).

ONLINE CONSUMER PSYCHOLOGY

Understanding and Influencing Consumer
Behavior in the Virtual World

Introduction

Curtis P. Haugtvedt
Ohio State University

Karen A. Machleit
Universtiy of Cincinnati

Richard F. Yalch
University of Washington

This volume contains edited versions of papers that were presented at the 2001 Advertising and Consumer Psychology Conference in Seattle, Washington. This annual conference was sponsored by the Society for Consumer Psychology (Division 23 of the American Psychological Association) with sponsorship assistance from Accenture Institute for Strategic Change.

The conference and this book follow from the 1996 Advertising and Consumer Psychology Conference and subsequent publication, *Advertising and the World Wide Web* (Schumann & Thorson, 1999). This book contains definitions of Internet terms, historical presentations, discussions of theoretical foundations, the structure of Web advertising, public policy issues, and applications of the medium. This important volume served to better acquaint advertisers with the medium and the important research questions at that time. The authors challenged researchers to think about the potential advantages and disadvantages of the Web as an advertising medium. Specifically, the authors mentioned the need for greater use of theory as well as studies that take advantage of the unique situations created by the Internet. The present volume addresses many of these issues and goes beyond the topic of advertising and the Web to include topics such as customization, site design, word-of-mouth processes, and the study of consumer decision making while online. Some of the research methods employed by authors in the current chapters allow us to gain more insight into the consumer's thought processes while online. Many of the chapters move beyond research that is descriptive of consumer

1

activities. The theories and research methods employed by the present authors help provide greater insight into the processes underlying consumer behavior in online environments.

The book begins with a section on **Community**. One advantage of the Internet is the ability to bring like-minded individuals from around the world into one forum. Alon, Brunel, and Siegal examine the way in which ritual activities maintain and develop the culture of the community forum. Schindler and Bickart examine published word-of-mouth comments to determine the way in which product experiences and information are communicated from consumer to consumer within a community. People who pass-along emails to others are examined by Lewis, Phelps, Mobilio, and Raman; these authors provide some insight into the issue of viral marketing on the Internet. This section concludes with Boush and Kahle's discussion and research agenda for using online consumer discussion communities to understand products, companies, and brands.

The second section in the book examines issues related to **Advertising**. The first two chapters in this section examine the issue of click-through rates, albeit from different perspectives. Chandon and Chtourou examine factors that affect the rate at which individuals will click on a banner ad. Mitchell and Valenzuela consider the banner ads that are not clicked—and reason that even without a click through, banner ads will still influence consumer judgment and choice. The other two chapters in this section examine advertising content that is placed in a different content—first within the context of gaming online (Nelson's article on Advergaming) and next within the context of wireless networks (Lynch, Kent, and Srinivasan's chapter on mobile advertising).

Customization is the third section. Crow and Shanteau's chapter provides us with reasons why consumers customize products and the benefits of customization. Godek and Yates look at the role of customer perceptions of control in the personalization/customization process. Luna, Perrachio, and de Juan Vigaray examine Web site customization and the importance of adapting the site across cultures. Finally, Häubl and Murry examine electronic recommendation agents as one form of preference customization and construction.

The psychological effects of **Site Design** are considered next. Omanson, Cline, and Nordhielm's chapter demonstrates that visual consistency in the look and feel of Web sites will affect, among other things, brand attitudes of visitors to that site. Purinton and Rosen examine gender differences in processing Web site information and present both similarities and differences by gender. Finally, Fasolo, McClelland, and Lange examine the way in which the format that product decision sites use to present information to site visitors can affect the visitor's ability to make better decisions.

The Fasolo, McClelland, and Lange chapter overlaps with the next section—**Decision Making**. Henry begins by asking the question of whether the Internet empowers consumers to make better decisions? Similarly, Mishra and Olshavsky consider whether the increased availability of information technology (personal computers, the Internet, cellular technology) will allow consumers to make more rational decisions and examine how new technology affects the consumer decision making process. The chapters that follow become more specific in nature. For example, Park, Lee, and Lee examine decision making within the context of e-branding strategy. Levin, Levin, and Heath examine the advantages and disadvantages of online and offline shopping and discuss situations when strategic alliances between online and offline brands will benefit consumers. This section concludes with chapters that examine decision making in online auctions (Sivadas, Stern, Mehta, and Jones) and using the Internet to make better health care decisions (Brewer).

The book concludes with a discussion of **Research Tools and Approaches** that can be used online. This final section contains a discussion of the use of the virtual experience environment as a research tool (Daugherty, Li, and Biocca). Using the Web to create an online, interactive research space is proposed as a way to provide benefits throughout the research process (Englis, Solomon, and Harveston).

Clearly, there is much to learn when applying principles of consumer psychology to the online environment. We thank the chapter authors for their creative contributions to this book.

I. COMMUNITY

Ritual Behavior and Community Change: Exploring the Social-Psychological Roles of Net Rituals in the Developmental Processes of Online Consumption Communities

Anat Toder-Alon
Frédéric F. Brunel
Wendy L. Schneier Siegal
Boston University

Ask any Internet Entrepreneur about the secret to successful Websites and you'll likely hear the knee-jerk answer: content, commerce, community, the holy trinity of Web portaldom, with stress placed on community. . . . [W]hen you ask the same crowd about what makes a successful online community, you'll likely hear about the suite du jour of Internet communications tools. Tools do not a community make. It does not work that way in real life; it does not work that way online.
—Banks & Daus (2000, p. 317).

The objective of this chapter is to reach beyond existing theories and conceptual frameworks of communities' developmental processes in an attempt to search for new insights regarding the role of rituals in these processes. Although electronic communities (also called online communities, Internet communities, or virtual communities) are in their infancy, they are predicted to exercise significant power in the future (Bickart & Schindler, 2001; Hagel & Armstrong, 1997; Venkatraman & Henderson, 1998). Online communities are among the most trafficked Web sites. For example, statistics have shown that 6 of the 20 most trafficked Internet domains are primarily community based (Ward, 2000). Moreover, a study from McKinsey & Co and Jupiter Media Metrix (Brown, Tilton, & Woodside, 2002) found that one third of the visitors to e-commerce sites used community features such as chat rooms and bulletin boards. Furthermore, these users make two thirds of all purchases at e-commerce sites. Also, site visitors who contribute to community features are nine times as likely to come back to that site, and twice as likely to make a purchase. Even users who read, but don't participate in, the community sections of an e-commerce site tend to come back more often and buy more often than those who do not visit the community features at all. Thus, as the importance of online communities grows, one of the most profound challenges for marketers is to understand the dynamics of the relationships among community members and to develop appropriate mechanisms as part of their business strategies.

Indeed, in online communities, as in any other types of community, there is an ongoing process of change and development. However, little social science research has focused on dynamic and developmental processes, instead of the more common cross-sectional "snap-shots." The tendency to generate studies that focus on cross-sectional rather than longitudinal perspectives has been criticized by scholars from different fields, including marketing, organizational studies, and communication studies (e.g., Quinn & Cameron, 1983; Araujo & Easton, 1996; Hakan & Sharma, 1996; Barker et al., 2000). This "structuralist and static mode of explanation of social behavior" was mainly criticized as "poorly equipped to explain how structures are created, reproduced and transformed" (Araujo & Easton, 1996, p. 75). The typical artificial nature of the conventional studies' research context (i.e., lab environment), the lack of real value of the task to group members, and the cross-sectional nature of the research precludes meaningful study of how group relationships develop over time in natural settings (Barker et al., 2000). Consequently, group communication scholars have emphasized the need for a broader perspective incorporating naturalistic contexts (Poole, 1999), the necessity to widen the perspective beyond task processes and to renew the interest in relational communication in groups (Frey, 1996; Keyton, 1999; Poole, 1999), and particularly relevant to this research, the requirement to consider how specific contexts and forms of communication impact relational communication in groups (Barker et al., 2000).

Further, specifically within the marketing milieu, Bagozzi (2000) advocated research on the social aspects of consumer behavior, particularly as found in groups of consumers and manifested through group action. Moreover, later, Bagozzi and Dholakia (2002) articulated this appeal specifically to the context of online communities arguing for the distinctiveness of the "group intentions" concept by establishing its value for understanding individuals' participation in virtual communities. Likewise, following Belk's (1991) Consumer Behavior Odyssey, Catterall and Maclaran (2002) advocated the need for a new odyssey, one that focused on consumers in virtual worlds. The researchers stressed the value for studying online communities, emphasizing their many interactions that are continuously documented. Accordingly, it is suggested in this chapter that the context of online community provides an opportunity to unobtrusively observe and develop a theoretical understanding of relationship dynamics within consumers' communities.

Answers for the foundational question of what constitutes an online community are as many and varied as the researchers attempting to study the phenomenon (for a review of the different types of communities, see Hagel & Armstrong, 1997; Jacobs, 2000; Rayport & Jaworski, 2001; Mohammed, Fisher, Jaworski, & Cahill, 2002). The term "online community" has different meanings for different people and these meanings are often influenced by the discipline from which this term is being defined (Preece, 2000; Maloney-Krichmar & Preece, 2002). Rheingold defined online communities as "social aggregations that emerge from the Net when enough people carry on those public discussions long enough, with sufficient human feeling, to form webs of personal relationships in cyberspace" (Rheingold, 1993, p. 5). However, researchers and practitioners "are left in the dark as to when feelings will be sufficient to form webs of personal relationships and about the processes by which such communities will develop" (Wilbur, 1996, p. 7).

We propose that the performance and expression of Net-ritual activities play a significant social-psychological role in communities' transformational processes. Despite apparent interest in the field of consumer rituals, the relationship between rituals and intragroup processes within consumer communities has not yet been explored. Although scholars have examined consumption during ritual occasions, various rites of passage as forms of consumption, and the relationship between advertising and rituals, relatively few studies discuss the role that ritual activities play in maintaining the culture of a community (e.g., Muniz & O'Guinn, 2001; Schouten & McAlexander, 1995). In addition, although the dynamic nature of rituals is well accepted (Rook, 1985; Bell, 1997), there has been a lack of research addressing the role that these dynamics play in the developmental and transformational processes within a community's life cycle. The objective of this chapter is to address these important issues.

In the first part of this chapter, literature on the nature and characteristics of online communities, communities' developmental processes, and ritual behavior is selectively reviewed and interpreted. This review intends to familiarize the readers with the conceptual foundations of the subsequent analysis and to identify the gaps in the literature. In the second part, we briefly present an illustrative case study that was used to ground and illustrate the theories, frameworks, and processes presented in the rest of the chapter. This part is concluded by a presentation of several research questions. In the third section, we develop a typology of ritual behavior. Employing this typology, in the forth section we develop an integrative model that connects Net-ritual expression with a community's developmental stages. Finally, we conclude the chapter by discussing conceptual and practical implications and suggestions for future research.

FOUNDATIONS

The objective of this chapter is to reach beyond existing theories and conceptual frameworks of communities' developmental processes in an attempt to search for new insights regarding the role of rituals in these processes. It is first necessary, then, to outline the current status of the literature in order to establish the foundations on which this project develops. Thus, in this section, a review of the literature on the nature and characteristics of online communities is provided. In addition, the pivotal importance of reaching beyond the traditional stages models is stressed. Finally, the notion of ritual dynamics is developed, granting license to pursue ritual-oriented analysis.

Online Communities—Exploring the Distinction Between Virtual and "Real" Communities

Hagel (1999) stated that Internet-based communities started as "spontaneous social events on electronic networks, gathered around common areas of interest, engaging in shared discussions that persist and accumulate over time, leading to a complex network of personal relationships and an increasing identification with the group as a community" (p. 55). Within the context of electronic communities, the virtual spaces where relationships can be formed include chat areas where people can speak in real time to others about their topics of interest, bulletin board services that enable people to exchange information, special debate forums where members can communicate their views, product and service reviews where members can post their evaluations about products and services, and so on. The nature of the relationship varies: Participants may be seeking advice, giving advice, or both; exchanging technical information; exchanging gossip about others in the community; giving or receiving moral support in a time of crisis; sharing affections; or sharing secrets (Galaskiewicz, 1996).

An attempt to understand what "community" means brings right from the start a sense of the complexities of this term. Bell and Valentine (1997) elaborated on this: "'Community.' It's a word we all use, in many different ways, to talk about. . . . what? About belonging and exclusion, about 'us' and 'them.' It's a common-sense thing, used in daily discussions, in countless associations, from 'care in the community' to the Community hall; from 'community spirit' to the 'business community.'. . . The term community is not only descriptive, but also normative and ideological; it carries a lot of baggage with it" (p. 93).

Undoubtedly, studies and definitions of communities have typically emphasized the concept of a physical place where social scientists can engage in participant observation (Jones, 1998). Clearly this place-centered notion of community does not seem readily applicable in cyberspace. Hence, although a few scholars have questioned the appropriateness of imposing the community metaphor onto the social relations emanating from cyberspace (e.g., Foster, 1996; Lockard, 1996), others believe that if "we embrace the symbolic form of community (that is, not the physical manifestation of the term community but, rather, a community of substance and meaning), concerns of the 'real' juxtaposed against the 'virtual' are of less importance" (Fernback, 1999, p. 213). Moreover, it has been argued that any sizeable community is to a large extent imagined, because each community member owns a mental image of his or her communion with the group. Therefore, a community's reality should be evaluated based on how it is imagined and not on the space in which it exists (Anderson, 1983).

Thus, it can be argued that if consumers log on, form relationships in cyberspace, and believe they have found communities, these must be "real" for them (Fernback, 1999). This fact is illustrated in our observation of the BabyCenter.com community. This community is actually very "real" to its members, and they truly believe that they have found and joined a strong and supportive community. The following quote is a vivid illustration of this point:

> Thank you very much. I feel like your Web site saved my life (OK, maybe I am being a bit dramatic—it's the hormones), but really . . . I was feeling very alone in my pregnancy. My husband is amazing but just can't understand what I'm going through. I was having a bit of a problem with my weight gain thus far, but after using your chat room and posting my concerns on the bulletin boards, I have talked to a lot of women who feel the same way as me. It is so nice to know that I am not alone. I plan to visit your site daily and tell everyone I know about it. You are doing more than you will ever know for me and I am sure tons of other women.
>
> [—Babycenter.com feedback archive]

It is important to recognize, however, that not all online social gatherings are communities. When Internet forums lack individual commitment and closeness between members they are just "a means of communication among people with common interests" (Fernback, 1999, p. 216).

Community Development—Beyond Levels-by-Stages Models

Our analysis emphasizes the need to think of a community as a continuous process, thus concentrating on the dynamic of communicative practices among members of the group. This notion rejects communities as ontologically real entities and argues that what is ontologically real are the relationships among the members of the community (Tuomela, 1995). Accordingly, this exploratory study sees community life "a continually-evolving entity, an entity experiencing on-going growth, change, and redefinition" (Fournier, 1994, p. 34). The emerging question is how to explore the social interactions within a community, that is, how are we going to develop an understanding of the way interactions evolve and change over time?

Across disciplines, various conceptual frameworks have been proposed to capture the dynamic nature of community development and the reasons for growth and change. Most theories of community relationship development have adopted a life-cycle conceptualization or what Brent (1984) referred to as the levels-by-stages model. A variety of levels-by-stages models have been proposed in the interpersonal relationships literature (e.g., Davis, 1973; Scanzoni, 1979; Levinger, 1983) and in the communication and organizational behavior literature (e.g., Bales, 1951; Lacoursiere, 1980; Tuckman, 1965; Tuckman & Jensen, 1977).

Although these models are appealing because of their parsimony and linear structures, one should keep in mind that communities are complex and dynamic systems. As such, the basic assumption that stages in a community life cycle occur as a hierarchical progression, with each stage appearing as more "evolved" than its preceding stage, is somewhat problematic. Thus, although groups follow some of the same stages or phases, the exact composition, number, and ordering of stages involves more particularity (Poole, 1981; Cissna, 1984). As Cissna (1984) stressed, the core problem is that: "Every group is like *all* group in some respects, like *some*—or even *most* groups in some respects, and like *no* groups in other respects" (p. 25). In addition, in general, the models mentioned here are primarily descriptive. They do not provide specific insights into the drivers of community change or the psychological and social meanings that characterize each stage.

Furthermore, exploring social interactions within a community and understanding the way interactions evolve and change over time is particularly challenging for researchers who attempt to explore the development of the relationship within the context of an online community. In the absence of direct control on who reads or writes to the community, it is critical to distinguish between the participants who are really members of the community and others who are not (Tepper, 1996). This distinction has to be based on "asynchronous textual production, with none of the verbal or visual cues that are so crucial to traditional notions of subcultural formation" (Tepper, 1996, p. 45).

Considering these unique features, we believe that a ritual-oriented analysis provides a more useful framework for making sense of the sort of activities that is happening. The importance of studying rituals in the context of online communities is further underscored in the premise that rituals are perceived as a means to regulate and stabilize the life of a community, adjust its internal interactions, maintain its group ethos, and restore a state of harmony after any disturbance (Bell, 1997). However, rituals may also exaggerate conflicts that exist in relationships (Bell, 1997). In, fact, Gluckman (1963) argued that rituals are actually the expression of complex social tensions rather than the sole affirmation of social unity. Thus, rituals do not simply restore social equilibrium, they are part of the ongoing process by which a community is continually redefining and renewing itself (Turner, 1974).

It is important to understand that a ritual-oriented analysis shifts the focus from issues such as the nature and degree of relationship among community members that typify levels-by-stages models to the purpose of the communication and its regularities of form and substance. As Erikson (1997) emphasized, online discourse may be useful and engaging to its participants even if the participants form no lasting relationships. What is important is the communication itself—the shared informational artifact that is created by the participants—rather than a real or perceived bond among the participants in the communication (Erikson, 1997). Thus, a ritual-oriented analysis is useful because it shifts the focus from the participants and the putative relationships among them to shared artifacts (i.e., rituals) and the way these artifacts are typically interpreted and used.

Rituals as Adaptive Phenomena

Over the last 20 years, researchers from diverse fields have turned to rituals as a window on the cultural dynamics by which people make and remake their worlds (Bell, 1992). Although scholars differ regarding the precise definition of this rich concept, there is a general agreement that a ritual consists of some form of symbolic action with some degree of repetition, regularity, and routine (Lipari, 1999).

Within consumer behavior research, Rook's (1985) definition of ritual is widely accepted. Rook defines ritual as "a type of expressive, symbolic activity constructed of multiple behaviors that occur in a fixed, episodic sequence, and that tend to be repeated over time. Ritual behavior is dramatically scripted and acted out and is performed with formality, seriousness, and inner intensity" (p. 252). Hence, several characteristics of ritual activities are noteworthy: (1) episodic string of events, (2) repetition and invariance, (3) performance, (4) symbolism, and (5) formalism. Besides these descriptive characteristics, Rook (1985) suggested that ritual experience relies on four key elements: (1) ritual artifacts, (2) ritual script, (3) ritual performance role(s), and (4) ritual audience. Accordingly, ritual activities involve the use of artifacts (i.e., objects that are used in a ritual context). Artifacts often communicate specific symbolic messages that are integral to the meaning of the total experience. The script identifies the artifacts to be used, their behavioral sequence, and by whom they will be used. Ritual scripts are performed by individuals who occupy various ritual roles. These roles may be explicitly scripted, as in weddings, or alternatively, on other occasions individuals have a great deal of freedom in ritual-role enactment. Finally, a ritual may be aimed at a larger audience beyond those individuals who have a specified ritual-performance role.

Not all scholars agree, though, that specific rules and features are necessary criteria for defining rituals (Lipari, 1999). Bell (1992) rejected the notion of a formal-feature definition of rituals and avoids proffering a restrictive definition for rituals because of their great diversity of forms and purposes across cultures. Overall, whether one recognizes a formal definition of rituals, it is important to highlight that rituals can be indeed context, rather than purely content, dependent. These considerations seem directly applicable and relevant to our present effort, and allow us make a case for how rituals can be evidenced and enacted in the context of online communities.

Ritual activities generally tend to give the impression of being old and immutable. However, there is much evidence that like most marketplace products, rituals are also subject to life-cycle forces (Bell, 1997; Rook, 1985). For instance, some scholars have made an attempt to connect ritual expression with individuals' stages of maturation within the human life cycle (Gennep, 1908; Erikson, 1982).

TABLE 1.1

Classification of Ritual Activities Within Consumer Behavior Literature

	Focus of Experience	
Nature of Inquiry	Personal Activity	Dyadic/Group Interactions
Ritual as a stable phenomenon	Rook (1985)	Sherry (1983)
	Belk, Wallendorf, & Sherry (1989)	Caplow (1984)
	O'Guinn & Belk (1989)	Sherry, McGrath, & Levy (1993)
	Hirschman & LaBarbera (1989)	Ruth, Otnes, & Brunel (1999)
	Sherry & McGrath (1989)	Ritson & Elliot (1999)
	Schouten (1991)	Muniz & O'Guinn (2001)
	Otnes & Lowrey (1993)	
	Lowrey and Otnes (1994)	
Ritual as an adaptive phenomenon	Belk (1989)	Wallendorf & Arnould (1991)
	Otnes & Scott (1996)	Fischer & Gainer (1993)
		Schouten & McAlexander (1995)

Nevertheless, despite many demonstrations that the context of communities can generate a variety of changes in the structures, symbols, and interpretations of ritual activities, scholars have not addressed the connections between ritual expression and communities' developmental and transformational processes.

Because the focus of this research is on the dynamic roles that rituals play in the developmental processes of online communities, we reviewed various studies that appear within the consumer behavior field and characterized them along two dimensions: (1) the focus of ritual experience: whether the ritual was viewed from a personal point of view (e.g., grooming) or as part of a dyadic or group interactions (e.g., gift giving) and (2) the nature of inquiry: whether the research explored ritual practices as a dynamic phenomenon that adapts and transform as conditions change, or as a stable and static activity at a specific point in time (see Table 1.1).

As shown in Table 1.1 and to our best knowledge, the number of studies that have focused on rituals as an adaptive phenomenon is very limited. More importantly, although a few exceptions do exist, this analysis illustrates the paucity of consumer behavior research addressing the dynamic nature of rituals within the context of group interactions. Bearing in mind that rituals are always embedded in a thick context of traditions, changes, and tensions (Bell, 1997), a community's ritualistic activities should be considered to be inseparable from its worldview. Thus, it is clear that rituals are prone to change as the conditions of the community change.

AN ILLUSTRATIVE CASE STUDY

This chapter employs what Kozinets (2002) refers to as netnography technique: "a new qualitative research methodology that adapts ethnographic research techniques to study the cultures and communities that are emerging through computer-mediated communications" (p. 62). Netnography, also called online ethnography or cyber ethnography (Fox & Roberts, 1999), has emerged as a methodology only within the past decade. Text data was used from the discourse of bulletin boards within a selected Internet community, BabyCenter.com. This is a site on the Internet for new and expectant parents. The community section within the site includes bulletin boards, chat areas, special events (usually chat with special guests), and great debates. In order to participate in chats and to post messages on the community's bulletin boards, a participant has to become a member of BabyCenter.com. Once registered (which is free of charge), a member can get to the bulletin boards. A participant can decide on which board to post by defining the topics that she is most interested in. Once a participant found her niche, she may see many "topics" on each board. These are also referred to as "threads." She can post a response on someone's topic, or start one of her own. Most messages expire in 30 days on most boards (if the topic is no longer active).

In an attempt to explore the complex roles that online rituals play within the different phases of a community's life cycle, and the relationships between ritual expression and intragroup processes, we used threads from the Birth Clubs bulletin boards. The fact that the Birth Clubs bulletin boards are organized according to "due date" enables us to analyze changes and trends within the community from inception to decline because new boards are "born" every month. The unit of analysis was the verbatim thread transcripts, which was operationalized as a post (seed) with all replies.

We collected messages on five different bulletin boards (cross-sectional) in two points of time (longitudinal). The complete text of all messages of each bulletin board was captured for a one-month period during both September 1999 and November 2000. Our data contain the following: two bulletin boards that are around 6 months old (parents during pregnancy), two bulletin boards that are about 1 year old (parents with newborn), two bulletin boards that are approximately a year and a half old (parents with infant), and two bulletin boards that are more than 2 years old (parents with toddler).

This research adheres to theory-grounding guidelines articulated by Strauss and Corbin (1998). As Charmaz (1990) suggested: "by starting with data from the lived experience of the research participants the researcher can from the beginning attend to how they construct their worlds" (p. 1162). In this process, we read through the entire set of threads, enabling the development of notions regarding substantive content areas. These initial areas were aggregated into meaning categories. The threads were then reanalyzed to further develop thematic categories and to identify holistic relationships among the meanings and categories members used in their messages.

In analyzing the transcripts, our interpretations addressed the following issues:

1. Can we identify consumption rituals in a virtual space, where the typical, established characteristics of rituals are not found?

2. Can we identify distinct phases in an online community's life cycle? Can we distinguish different Net rituals that characterize each phase?
3. What symbols are invoked in the different rituals? Can we identify any relationship between these symbols and shifts in members' identity orientation? What is the primary function that Net ritual activities serve within each phase? Can we identify any relationships between rituals' symbolic systems and shifts in rituals' primary function?

Because of the conceptual nature of this chapter and also because of space and scope constraints, we do not systematically report on all the findings of the grounding case study. Rather, the findings were used first as foundations for the models and frameworks that we present, and second as illustrations of some selected points of our argument.

TOWARD A DYNAMIC TYPOLOGY OF RITUAL BEHAVIOR

Rituals in an Online Setting

Our exploratory, theory-grounding study confirmed that many of the characteristics of ritual activities discussed earlier can be empirically observed in online communities, albeit without the physical manifestation typically present in traditional settings. An examination of the primary characteristics and principal elements (cf. Rook, 1985) of ritual behavior as they appeared in the exploratory study of online communities is provided in Table 1.2.

First, although ritualistic message exchanges on the Internet do not have a formal script and unquestionably allow for spontaneous variation, we were able to observe evidence of emergent or casually stereotyped script. Messages that we considered as rituals tended to be posted with virtually the same content and structure each time they appeared. For example, messages that were concerned with the creation of communities' daily routines were very short and formal in style. It seems that these messages serve as symbolic community markers. Thus, we presume that, in this context, ritualistic messages function as mnemonic devices that elicit specific thoughts and sentiments from the individual (Mead, 1956).

Second, individuals who occupied various ritual roles performed ritualistic message exchanges. For example, the typical roles we observed in word-of-mouth messages include a word-of-mouth seeker and a word-of-mouth provider. As suggested by Rook (1985), ritual roles can be either active or passive. Hence, although the initiator of the ritualistic message (i.e., the person that posts the seed message) occupies an active role, as do the various members that post replies, there can be many other readers that actually participate in the ritual although not in any active way. Thus much like any other ritual activities, online ritualistic message exchange

TABLE 1.2
Rituals in an Online Setting

		Net Ritual Description
Ritual Elements	Artifacts	No physical artifacts. Community-specific shorthand communication. Verbal and graphic artifacts.
	Script	Casual script. Similar content of messages.
	Performance role(s)	Various active and passive roles. Freedom in ritual role enactment.
	Audience	Members of the bulletin board and members of other bulletin boards.
Ritual Characteristics	Episodic string of events	Simple string.
	Repetition and invariance	Messages with similar content are posted in different bulletin boards.
	Performance	No bodily action. One sensory level (through reading).
		Ritual-like messages have the ability to shape member's experience.
	Symbolism	Messages facilitate interpersonal interactions.
		Message differentiate the "community" from others.
	Formalism	Low formalism, possibility of spontaneous variation.

may be aimed at a larger audience beyond those individuals who have a ritual role. The audience may include not only other members of the community that read the thread, but also members of other communities that happen to lurk in the bulletin board.

Finally, although online ritualistic message exchanges lack physical artifacts to accompany the ritualistic activity, they can be classified as a verbal rituals (Douglas & Isherwood, 1978) in which the material exchange of a physical good is replaced by the exchange of a verbal artifact in the form of message interpretation (see Ritson & Elliot, 1999). In many ways, one could interpret the specific shorthand and visual signs that community members develop as a type of verbal or visual artifact that is used to signal that one is familiar with the group's rituals and belongs there. It thereby reinforces the separation between members and nonmembers. Multiple exemplars of observed Net rituals are presented in the later part of this chapter.

Although one could argue that all the messages that are posted on bulletin boards contain certain roles (e.g., advice seeker, advice giver, joker, etc.), audience, and some kind of simple script, it should be emphasized that it is the *symbolic meaning* that occurs when messages are repeatedly written and perceived by community's members that establishes these messages as Net rituals. Hence, we would consider message exchanges as Net rituals as long as they can be interpreted as a means for regulating social behavior of community members and as long as they generate and express the significance of key symbols within that particular community.

A Typology of Ritual Behavior

The tremendous variety of rhetorical ritual observed in the data calls for an attempt to organize them in some meaningful way. Almost all the theories of ritual behavior come with their own classification systems for analyzing ritual activities. Although the existing typologies delineate common elements that can be observed among very different ritual experiences, we argue that their main drawback lies in the fact that they cannot guide our understanding of why ritual activities transform over time.

Based on our review of the literature and our exploratory analysis, we have developed a two-dimensional typology of ritual behavior. The main advantage of this typology is that it enables us to develop a deeper understanding of the sources of shifts in ritualistic messages and of the ways these dynamics inspire communities' transformational processes. The two dimensions are: (1) *identity orientation* (i.e., the focus of ritual messages) and (2) *patterns of interaction* (i.e., the functions that ritual messages serve) (see Fig. 1.1).

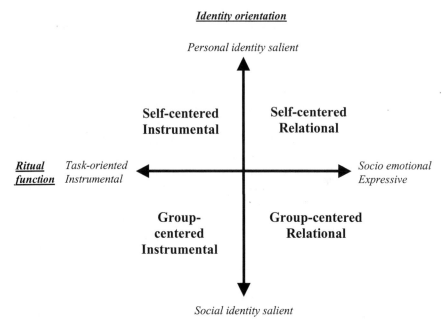

FIG. 1.1　A typology of ritual behavior.

Identity Orientation—The Focus of Ritual Activities. Of special interest to our conceptual framework is social identity theory (Tajfel & Turner, 1986) and self-categorization theory (Turner, 1987). The central tenet of these theories is that belonging to a group (whatever size and distribution) is largely a psychological state that is distinct from being a unique and separate individual. As such, it confers social identity: a shared, collective representation of who one is and how one should behave (Turner, 1982). Interindividual attraction, which is grounded in group membership and is generated by the process of self-categorization, is responsible for psychological group belongingness. The notion that social identity and group belongingness are inextricably linked is based on the perception that one's conception or identity is largely composed of self-descriptions in terms of the defining characteristics of social groups to which one belongs (Hogg & Abrams, 1998).

Social identity theory and self-categorization theory provide the foundations for our ritual activities typology in advocating that the self is not a fixed entity, but is socially defined in the context. Hence, there are different possible identities that participants can assume within the same interactive context. As Schegloff (1995) emphasized, "The number of parties into which those participants may be seen to be organized (because they see themselves so to be organized and to embody that stance in their conduct) can change continuously as to contingencies of the talks change, contingencies most centrally supplied by the participants themselves and the nature of the talk which they undertake with one another" (p. 35). Accordingly, the choice about what possible self to show is driven by individuals' perceptions of how the social situation is characterized and what features could be more relevant and more effective in a given situation.

Furthermore, identities built during the interaction are not only depending on what each one decides to show about her or his self in that context, but also the context itself plays an active role in guiding and modeling the possible choices. In fact, the context gives salience to some specific characteristics of each person, according to what is happening in that community. Correspondingly, the way people use identity during discourse in interaction shows that identity is occasioned (i.e., the specific context shapes the way participants choose to negotiate their identity) and indexical (i.e., participants choose to give salience to specific aspects of the self according to their goals in that specific interactive moment) (Sacks, 1992). Ellemers, Kortekaas, and Ouwerkert (1999, p. 372) suggested that members of a group achieve a social identity that is manifest in: (1) a cognitive component made up of self-awareness of membership, (2) an affective component consisting of attachment or feelings of belongingness, and (3) an evaluative component inherent in collective self-esteem.

Social identity and self-categorization theories assume that there are two types of self-regulation: as a group member (called "social identity salient") and as an individual (called "personal identity salient") (Reicher, 1987). The mechanisms by which these self-definitions are selectively deployed are central to the predictions of our theory. The extent to which a categorization is applied at a particular level is referred to as its *salience*. Importantly, salience relates not just to the general relevance of a group membership but refers to a selective change in self-perception whereby people actually define themselves as unique individuals or as members of groups. When they define themselves as members of a group they perceive themselves to be *interchangeable* with members of that group, and distinct from members of other groups. Further, this theory acknowledges that the nature of behavior changes when different self-images become salient (Brown & Turner, 1981; Hogg & Abrams, 1998).

It has been suggested that the Internet represents a kind of "middle landscape" that allows individuals to exercise their impulses for both separation and connectedness (Healy, 1996). As such, online communities operate as sites where centrifugal and centripetal forces must meet (see Miller, 1994). Actually, an important technical reality of the Internet is that although it connects people, it also isolates them physically. This dual identity has interesting and contradictory effects. Similarly, specifically developed for the context of the Internet is the SIDE model (the Social Identity model of Deindividuation Effects: Spears, Lea, & Postmes, 2000), which attempts to predict the form and direction of behavior deriving from the level and content of identity. According to this approach, deindividuation caused by immersion and anonymity in the group does not result in loss of identity or reduced self-awareness (as proposed by classical deindividuation theory). Rather this results in a shift of self-focus from personal to group identity.

In the same vein, we argue that the expression and nature of rituals within Internet communities change as a result of members' contrasting struggle between social identity and personal identity. Self-definition as either an individual or as a group member influences the expression of ritualistic messages and consequently it is through this dynamic nature of rituals that communities develop and transform. In other words, online communities' communicative practices are codetermined by the simultaneous and dynamic forces of members' desires for involvement (i.e., social identity or commitment) and independence (i.e., personal identity or individualism). The dynamic characteristics of these contradictory desires contribute to the dynamic nature of rituals. Net rituals serve as the means for acting out the struggle between the desire for involvement and independence. Accordingly, Net ritual experiences can be classified as focusing either on the individual or on the group.

Ritual messages that focus on the individual (i.e., personal identity salient) are concentrated in the individuals' emotions, needs, and goals. Theses ritual activities can act as means for a healthy accommodation of the repression of desire (Bell, 1997, p. 15), provide a defense against impulsiveness (Freud, 1962), or contribute to a person's individuation (Jung, 1958).

By contrast, ritual activities that focus on the group (i.e., social identity salient) serve as means for regulating group's interactions. Generally, ritual activities belong to this group to the extent that they demarcate or celebrate a community's deepest and most closely held values; assert and invoke particular norms, standards, and values (Lipari, 1999); invoke, foster, and reinvigorate attachments to social groupings; and communicate affections and sentiments. Following the conceptualizations of social identity theory and self-categorization theory, we suggest that when members of a community define themselves as members of a group (i.e., social identity salient) they discover a world of meanings and transform some of these meanings to a shared organization of meanings, thus, forming a social entity and a world of meanings of and for themselves. This practice provides members who act in line with this shared organization of meanings a sense of security and common understanding of their belongingeness to a particular, distinguished group.

Patterns of Interaction—Functions of Ritual Activities. We have already stressed that messages that we considered as rituals tended to be posted with virtually the same content and structure each time they appeared and served as symbolic community markers. As such, rituals can be conceptualized as social knowledge structures that are organized and stored in memory in the form of particular scripts. It is proposed that these ritual scripts are "shared social schemas" that contain expected sequences of communicative practices to reach certain goals or to behave appropriately in certain settings (e.g., a roll call may be perceived as a script for the creation of acquaintance between members of an Internet community). Because ritual activities are shared cognitive structures, it is important to appreciate that members of online communities may create or act out rituals for specific functions. Thus, rather than viewing rituals as motivationally vacuous, we assume that rituals serve and therefore reflect important social and personal needs and goals.

Specifically, drawing on the seminal work of Bales (1951, 1970) on regularities in group interaction, we propose that Net rituals represent two overarching and conceptually distinct interaction patterns: an informational/instrumental/task-oriented communicative act and a symbolic/expressive/socioemotional communicative act. Bales believed that groups have a natural tendency toward equilibrium and, therefore, move through cycles of instrumental and expressive behavior. Accordingly, he developed a coding system for the systematic observation and analysis of verbal interactions in a group, called Interaction Process Analysis (IPA). IPA classifies every communicative act occurring in a group discussion according to socioemotional categories (e.g., shows solidarity/seems friendly, shows tension and shows antagonism/seems unfriendly) as well as task categories (e.g., gives suggestions, opinions, or orientation/information, asks for orientation/information, opinions, or suggestions).

Following this conceptualization, we suggest that Net ritual activities are instrumental or task oriented to the extent that they attempt to accomplish something, and to the extent that they serve as means for gaining information about the world (see also the notions of knowledge and utilitarian functions suggested by Katz, 1960; and, Smith, Bruner, & White, 1956). The information can be aimed either for individual needs (i.e., rituals that serve as means for organizing individual's personal life) or for community needs (i.e., rituals that serve as means for organizing community life).

Alternatively, Net ritual activities are relational or socioemotional to the extent that they act to sustain or weaken interpersonal relationships within the group. As Keyton (1999) suggested "relational communication in groups refers to the verbal and nonverbal messages that create the social fabric of a group by promoting relationships between and among group members. It is the affective or expressive dimension of group communication, as opposed to the instrumental, or task-oriented, dimension" (p. 192). Employing Bales's (1951, 1970) conceptualization these type of ritualistic messages will include interactions that show solidarity, release tension, or indicate acceptance, or alternatively interactions that show disagreement, tension, and antagonism (see also Katz's [1960] value-expressive and ego-defense functions, as well as Smith, Bruner, & White's [1956] social-adjustment function, and Herek's [1986] expressive functions).

To sum up, utilizing this typology, throughout the analysis of the data from the BabyCenter.com bulletin boards, for each conversation that appeared in the bulletin boards we analyzed its focus and purpose and its regularities of content and form, confirming that there are different ritualistic practices that have rather different focuses and support rather different functions.

A PROPOSED MODEL FOR ONLINE COMMUNITY TRANSFORMATIONAL PROCESSES

The exploratory, theory-grounding inquiry brought a whole new insight concerning the evolution of the relationship within the community, proposing a new way to conceptualize group development. This novel perspective perceives the community development as a continuous process of reciprocal social construction. As such, it provides guidance on the interplay between communities' development and circumstantial events, on triggers of change, and on the mechanisms that cause a community to remain in any stable phase. It is important to understand that although in the subsequent netnographic investigation we have arbitrarily separated ritualistic communicative practices into several states, the actual process is fluid and unexpected. At any moment, the community can reverse direction and move back into a previous communicative ritual or suddenly switch to a whole new communicative ritual. Yet for the purpose of this analysis and for simplicity and clarity, throughout this netnographic account we concentrate on the major milestones in the communities' interaction processes (see Table 1.3).

TABLE 1.3

Integrative Model: Net Ritual Expression and Online Community Relationships

States	Ritual Themes	Ritual Function	Ritual Orientation	Ritual Type	Examples of Ritual Activities
Acquaintance	Anarchism, Impulsiveness, Opportunism	Task-oriented Informational Instrumental	Personal identity salient	Self-centered Instrumental	Roll calls
Construction	Planning, Coordination, Structuring	Task-oriented Informational Instrumental	Social identity salient	Group-centered Instrumental	Web page, email list
Intimacy	Affiliation	Socioemotional Relational Symbolic	Personal identity salient	Self-centered Relational	Confessions Secrets
Routine	Intragroup relationship	Socioemotional Relational Symbolic	Social identity salient	Group-centered Relational	Setting rules, Mechanisms for conflict resolution
Disconnection	Pragmatism	Task-oriented Informational Instrumental	Personal identity salient	Self-centered Instrumental	Advice seeking

Comparison of the textual discourse of communities in different developmental phases suggested that shifts in identity orientation over a community's life span do not follow a linear pattern but rather are more cyclical in nature. In other words, members' contrasting struggle between social identity and personal identity was not solved in one particular phase in one direction or the other, but rather self-definition as either an individual or a group member alternated from phase to phase.

State 1—Acquaintance

The first state is the creation of the online community. In this initial state a group of people who share some common interest decide to construct a new subcultural configuration. This state contains Net rituals that aim to generate and increase the acquaintance between members of the community. Because this state is typified by little, if any, formal structure, and little coordination, Net ritual activities that characterize this state typically belong to the self-centered instrumental quadrant (see Fig. 1.1). Members engaged in ritual activities that were instrumental in nature and that were typically focused on the individual.

Examples of Net rituals identified in our exploratory research that appeared in this state are roll calls. Different types of roll calls are possible, including generic roll calls (e.g., "Who's who?"), more detailed roll calls (e.g., "Anyone want to say where they are from or what kind of weather they are having?"), or even personal roll calls (e.g., "Where did you and your significant other meet?"). Roll calls serve many instrumental purposes in this phase, including getting to know each other, allowing members who lost track for a while to catch up, and giving newcomers who are excited to join the bulletin board the opportunity to become part of the community. It is interesting to note that at this early phase members have tended to participate in roll calls, writing about themselves with no evidence for any interest in what others write about themselves or of even reading others' messages. Thus, although roll calls may be initiated as a group activity, in fact, in this phase messages that appeared in roll calls focused mostly on individuals (i.e., personal identity salient).

Hence, in many ways, in the first state the bulletin board seems to be like a public square, with people joining and leaving regularly. Appropriately, most of the messages at this phase focused on individuals' needs and experiences (i.e., personal identity salient). Thus, in this first discontent state (see Worchel's [1994] cyclical stage model for a similar conceptualization) members still feel alienated from the group, and centrifugal forces are dominant.

State 2—Construction

The second state is concerned with the establishment of an organized online community with certain signals and symbols that differentiate the community from others. These symbols aim to promote community pride, sense of collectivity, and cohesiveness. In this state we observed rituals that invoke symbols of unity, for instance, by making explicit references to "our bulletin board." Also, ritual activities emphasize the differences between "us" and "others":

> I am so glad our board is up and healthy and ready for the holidays (cause with my in-laws, I know I'm gonna need lots of support round that time).

> What a wonderful bb [(bulletin board)] we have where women give each other such strong, supportive comfort ... it is the best board here and has been nothing but information.

Net ritual activities that characterize this state typically belong to the group-centered instrumental quadrant (see Fig. 1.1). Members were engaged in ritual activities that are task oriented (i.e., instrumental or informational) and that are typically focused on the group. Other examples of Net rituals that appear in this stage include messages that relate to the creation of a community Web page, community photo album, or community's email list. Most of these posts were very short and formal in style. Also in this state individual participants were starting to perform specific roles within the community, thus, participants were organizing specific threads and a community's host was nominated.

It is important to emphasize that although these messages were focused on the group they were mainly instrumental (i.e., concerned with the establishment of an organized online community with certain signals and symbols). At this state, members of the group were able to counter the forces that pull participants away from the group by maintaining a minimum of group cohesion through group-focused task-oriented interactions (i.e., organization and coordination of group activities).

State 3—Intimacy

The third state is concerned with the establishment of commitment and cohesion. This state is typified by informal communication. We observed Net rituals that invoke symbols of unity by implicitly increasing intimacy between members of the community. Ritual activities that characterize this state typically belong to the self-centered relational quadrant (see Fig. 1.1). Members were engaged in ritual activities that are socioemotional in nature and that are typically focused on the individual.

Typical demonstrations of intimacy that we observed were ritualized messages in which members relate to other members of the community as close friends:

> I am sitting here wishing I had someone to call and talk to and thought of you guys. I cannot call my sisters because I will get the I told you so. ... Thank you all for listening, you are great.

Another example for ritualistic practices that appear in this state were messages that contain confessions or sharing secrets with members of the community while keeping them hidden from others outside the community:

> Hi ladies. I hope you are all doing better than I am in the child care area. I thought we had our situation all figured out until my mil [mother in law] told us that she would not mind watching the baby. Don't get me wrong I am happy she offered but she made a comment about having to start all over again raising children. . . . Anyway what kind of questions do you ask a relative? . . . I don't want to hurt my mil [mother in low] feeling and that can be done easy with her. . . . I would say email but dh [dear husband] checks my email and I certainly do not want to get him mad at me.

It should be emphasized that although messages in this state serve symbolic functions by alignment of oneself with other members of the community, Net rituals here were concentrated in the individuals' emotions, needs, and goals and not in the group's concerns per se. Accordingly, these Net ritual practices typically fit in to the self-centered relational quadrant.

State 4—Routine

The fourth state is characterized by stable structures, formalization of rules, and emphasis on norms and procedures. Accordingly, we observed ritualized messages that were socioemotional in nature and that were concerned with the community's intrarelationships (i.e., focused on the group). Ritual activities that characterize this state typically belong to the group-centered relational quadrant (see Fig. 1.1). This type of ritualistic messages focuses on the group and consists of interactions that show solidarity, release tension, or indicate acceptance, or alternatively interactions that show disagreement, tension, and antagonism.

Typically, in this state, the relationships between members of the online community were dynamic, characterized by positive and negative interactions and feelings:

> Hi, I know you are hurt by some of the comments made to you on your post but this has been a very hot topic here in this board. Literary people were fighting with each other with hateful words. I know that you did not know this and no one should criticize anybody's parenting. Like we have said it before if you don't like the posting posted don't read it. Please don't feel like you don't have a support group here because you do.

The ups and downs within the community's intrarelationships commonly result in the development of norms and coping strategies for dealing with conflict among members. Also, often members demonstrate involvement and appreciation of their intrarelationships as illustrated in the following message:

I hope our board can make it through this—I visit every day and count on the support I receive here. If I see a post that seems to be personal rather than practical, I just don't read it. But I count on the input from more experienced moms and I hope that resource won't go away. Let's all try and get back to the supportive environment we all want to create.

Despite the conflictual nature of numerous messages in this state, it seems that the fact that these messages were essentially focused on the community, its importance, and its goals, sets in motion a whole new atmosphere with a much more cohesive community. At this time, the centripetal forces were getting stronger and the attention of group members was focused on the bond between themselves and the group. Participants discussed numerous issues that were concerned with the community's intrarelationships, including the content of the topics that should be discussed in the board; procedures to participate in conversations and, ultimately, to prevent conflict; the role of the community's hosts in monitoring group's conversations; and plentiful statements on the importance, the value, and the uniqueness of the board.

Indeed, groups often develop their conflict-handling norms "on the fly," settling on norms by trial and error and often with considerable turbulence (Arrow, McGrath, & Berdahl, 2000). As Keyton (1999) suggested: "these powerful regulations of group members' behavior generally develop slowly, often implicitly, and typically unconsciously from social pressures exerted in group interaction" (p. 206).

State 5—Disconnection

The fifth state is characterized by adaptation and decentralization. Typically, we would expect a disappearance of original community patterns. The focus in this state is on pragmatic issues. Consequently, relationships in this state would typically be instrumental or informational in nature, focusing on the needs of individuals. Accordingly, our observations demonstrate that Net rituals in this state were usually in the form of "seeking advice" or "giving advice." In fact, members did not demonstrate much attention to others' posts. Thus, during this time many participants were starting to feel that their threads go unnoticed, causing them to experience such feelings as alienation, disengagement, and disconnection. Accordingly, ritual activities here resembled in a sense ritual activities that had appeared in the first state, albeit without the excitement that characterizes that state.

CONCLUSION

In a nutshell, the netnographic analysis mentioned here is original in emphasizing the role that ritual practices play in communities' evolution. Moreover, this analysis calls attention to the fact that complex systems of the sort of online communities never settle to a fixed state. On the contrary, these systems are subject to constant perturbation, which drives bursts of transient behavior. Definitely, change events vary in how much and how directly they perturb a group's communicative rituals. It is important to understand that "groups do not respond to change as a generic event. Different kind of change has different meanings to group members and different implications for group coordination and development. The same event can evoke different responses from different groups or from the same group at different time" (Arrow, McGrath, & Berdahl, 2000, p. 195).

IMPLICATIONS AND FUTURE DIRECTIONS

Consumer researchers have often ignored the "embeddedness of psychological processes in larger schemes of relations such as culturally shared and socially communicated Networks of reasoning" (Ward & Reingen, 1996, p. 305). From its outset, consumer research has relied heavily on cognitive psychology (Wells, 1993; Costa, 1995; Ward & Reingen, 1996). Research inspired by the lens of cognitive psychology regards the internal "information processing" actions of individuals as the focal phenomena (Ward & Reingen, 1996). Actually, much of the traditional social psychology is individualistic in nature, in that it "explains the social group in terms of properties of the individual" (Hogg & Abrams, 1998, p. 12). Consequently, despite the importance ascribed to the idea of communal consumption, consumer research has largely neglected the sociocultural settings that contextualize consumers' communities.

Therefore, this chapter should not be seen as just another example of the growing interest in ritual activities within consumer behavior studies. Unlike past research that was mainly interested with theories on the role of rituals in various events within consumers' lives and activities, this chapter portrays rituals as a system of contextually generated meanings whose nature is, in and of itself, worthy of investigation. Moreover, from a thematic point of view, this chapter is interested with how members of communities use rituals as means to symbolically create an ordered world. Also, meeting Porter's (1996) appeal, this chapter provides new insights into the ways the Internet affects our understanding and experience of community as well as the sociology of virtual communities and the precise nature of the communality they claim to embody.

The goal of this chapter is also to provide direction for better managing and facilitating consumer-to-consumer interactions on the Internet. By understanding the processes by which communities develop, marketers will be able to identify the needs and interests of community members in different states within the community lifespan. This will enable them to make the experience in the community more compelling for members. Through this research, it is hoped that marketers will be able to leverage the unique asset of member-generated content. First, emphasis should be placed on creating incentives for members to spend increasing time in the community. It is assumed that the more satisfactory the experience, the less likely consumers are to switch to a competing community and the more likely they are to spend more time on each visit. Understanding the drivers of community change can aid in the design of sites most likely to attract consumers. Second, efforts should be aimed at facilitating personal relationships and sense of belongingness. By designing sites that incorporate the psychological and social meanings that characterize phases in a community's life cycle, marketers will be able to promote the salience of the community for its members.

Future empirical research should attempt to explore further the role that rituals play within the different phases of a community life cycle and the relationship between ritual expression and intragroup processes in other types of communities. Because we recognize that most of the participants in the BabyCenter.com are women, gender issues may limit the generalizability of this research. And providing that gender has been shown to affect communication styles (Tannen, 1990), this might be also relevant to online communication. Future research should attempt to explore whether and how relationship building is affected by gender in different types of communities. Moreover, the use of baby-oriented community enables us to observe the life cycle of a community in a somewhat definite way. It would be interesting for future research to explore communities' life cycles in a more fluid community, when the phases are not so clear and people are constantly joining and leaving the community. We believe that the investigation of the characteristics of ritual activities in such a naturalistic setting as virtual community can make a substantial contribution to the consumer literature on both ritual and virtual communities. Using both longitudinal and cross-sectional text data from the discourse of bulletin boards, researchers may further examine the preliminary model presented earlier, with the intent of lending support to the contention that social identity, as reflected in expressions of community ritual, is differentially reflected in different communities.

REFERENCES

Anderson, B. (1983). *Imagined community: Reflections on the origin and spread of nationalism.* London: Verso.

Araujo, L., & Easton, G. (1996). Networks in socioeconomic systems: A critical review. In D. Iacobucci (Ed.), *Networks in Marketing* (pp. 63–107). London: Sage.

Arrow, H., McGrath, J. E., & Berdahl, J. L. (2000). *Small groups as complex systems: Formation, coordination, development, and adaptation.* Thousand Oaks, CA: Sage.

Bagozzi, R. P. (2000). On the concept of intentional social action in consumer behavior. *Journal of Consumer Research, 27*(3), 388–396.

Bagozzi, R. P., & Dholakia, U. M. (2002). Intentional social action in virtual communities. *Journal of Interactive Marketing, 16*(2), 2–21.

Bales, R. F. (1951). *Interaction process analysis: A method for the study of small groups.* Cambridge: Addison-Wesley.

Bales, R. F. (1970). *Personality and interpersonal behavior.* New York: Holt, Rinehart & Winston.

Banks, D., & Daus, K. (2000, June). Are We There Yet? The long and winding road to online community, *Business 2.0.*

Barker, V. E., Abrams, J. R., Tiyaamornwong, V., Seibold, D. R., Duggan, A., Park, H. S., & Sebastian, M. (2000). New context for relational communication in groups. *Small Group Research, 31*(4), 470–503.

Belk, R. W. (1989). Materialism and the modern U.S. Christmas. In E. C. Hirschman (Ed.), *Interpretive consumer research* (pp. 115–135). Provo, UT: Association for Consumer Research.

Belk, R. W. (1991). *Highways and buyways: Naturalistic research from the consumer behavior odyssey.* Provo, UT: Association of Consumer Research.

Belk, R. W., Wallendorf, M., & Sherry, J. F. Jr. (1989, June). The sacred and profane in consumer behavior: Theodicy on the odyssey. *Journal of Consumer Research, 16,* 1–38.

Bell, C. (1992). *Ritual theory, ritual practice.* New York: Oxford, UK University Press.

Bell, C. (1997). *Ritual perspective and dimensions.* New York: Oxford, UK University Press.

Bell, D., & Valentine, G. (1997). *Consuming geographies: We are where we eat.* London: Routledge.

Bickart B., & Schindler, R. M. (2001). Internet forums as influential sources of consumer information. *Journal of Interactive Marketing, 15*(3), 31–40.

Brent, S. (1984). *Psychological and social structures.* Hillsdale, NJ: Lawrence Erlbaum Associates.

Brown, R. J., & Turner, J. C. (1981). Interpersonal and intergroup behavior. In J. C. Turner & H. Giles (Eds.), *Intergroup behavior* (pp. 33–64). Chicago: University of Chicago Press.

Brown, S., Tilton, A., & Woodside, D. (2002). The case for online communities. *The Mckinsey Quarterly,* 2002 (1). Retrieved February 25, 2003, from www.mckinseyquarterly.com.

Caplow, T. (1984). Rule enforcement without visible means: Christmas gift giving in Middletown. *American Journal of Sociology, 89*(6), 1306–1323.

Catterall M., & Maclaran, P. (2002). Researching consumers in virtual worlds: A cyberspace odyssey. *Journal of Consumer Behavior: An International Review, 1*(3), 228–237.

Charmaz, K. (1990). Discovering chronic illness: Using grounded theory. *Social Science and Medicine, 30,* 1162–1172.

Cissna, K. (1984). Phases of group development. *Small Group Behavior, 15*(1), 3–32.

Costa, J. A. (1995). The social organization of consumer behavior. In J. F. Sherry (Ed.), *Contemporary marketing and consumer behavior.* (pp. 213–244). London: Sage.

Davis, M. S. (1973). *Intimate relations.* New York: The Free Press.

Douglas, M., & Isherwood, B. (1978). *The world of goods: Towards an anthropology of consumption.* London: Allen Lane.

Ellemers, N., Kortekaas, P., & Ouwerkerk, J. W. (1999). Self-categorization, commitment to the group and group self-esteem as related but distinct aspects of social identity. *European Journal of Social Psychology, 29,* 371–389.

Erikson, E. H. (1982). *The life cycle completed.* New York: Norton.

Erickson T. (1997). Social interaction on the Net: Virtual community as participatory genre. In J. F. Nunamaker, Jr. & R. H. Sprague, Jr. (Eds.), *The Proceedings of the Thirtieth Hawaii International Conference on Systems Science* (Vol 6, pp. 23–30), IEEE Computer Society Press: Los Alamitos, CA.

Fernback, J. (1999). There is a there there: Notes toward a definition of cybercommunity. In S. Jones (Ed.), *Doing Internet research: Critical issues and methods for examining the Net* (pp. 203–220). Thousand Oaks, CA: Sage.

Fischer, E., & Gainer, B. (1993). Baby showers: A rite of passage in transition. In L. McAlister & M. L. Rothschild (Eds.), *Advances in consumer research,* 20 (pp. 320–324). Provo, UT: Association for Consumer Research.

Foster, D. (1996). Community and identity in the electronic village. In D. Porter (Ed.), *Internet culture* (pp. 23–37). New York: Routledge.

Fournier, S. (1994). *A consumer-brand relationship framework for strategy brand management.* Unpublished doctoral dissertation, University of Florida.

Fox, N., & Roberts, C. (1999). GPs in cyberspace: The sociology of a virtual community. *The Sociological Review, 47*(4), 643–671.

Freud, S. (1962). *The neuro-psychoses of defense. The standard edition of the complete works of Sigmund Freud.* London: Hograrth Press and the Institute of Psycho-Analysis.

Frey, L. R. (1996). Remembering and "re-membering": A history of theory and research on communication and group decision making. In R.Y. Hirokawa & M. S. Poole (Eds.), *Communication and group decision making* (2nd ed; pp. 19–51). Thousand Oaks, CA: Sage.

Gennep, A. V. (1908). *The rites of passage* (M. B. Vizedom & G. L. Caffee, Trans.). London: Routledge & Kegan Paul.

Gluckman, M. (1963). *Order and rebellion in tribal Africa.* New York: The Free Press.

Hagel, J. III (1999, Winter). Net gains: Expanding markets through virtual communities. *Journal of Interactive Marketing, 13*, 55–65.

Hagel, J. III, & Armstrong, A. G. (1997). *Net gains: Expanding markets through virtual communities.* Boston: Harvard Business School Press.

Hakan, H., & Sharma, D. D. (1996). Strategic alliances in a network perspective. In D. Iacobucci (Ed.), *Networks in marketing* (pp. 108–124). London: Sage.

Healy, D. (1996). Cyberspace and place: The Internet as middle landscape on the electronic frontier. In D. Porter (Ed.), *Internet culture* (pp. 55–68). New York: Routledge.

Herek, G. M. (1986). The instrumentality of attitudes: Toward a neofunctional theory. *Journal of Social Issues, 42*(2), 99–114.

Hirschman, E. C., & LaBarbera, P. (1989). The meaning of Christmas. In E. C. Hirschman (Ed.), *Interpretive consumer research* (pp. 136–147). Provo, UT: Association for Consumer Research.

Hogg, M. A., & Abrams, D. (1998). *Social identifications: A social psychology of intergroup relations and group processes.* London: Routledge.

Jacobs, J. (2000, October 4). Online communities the lifeline for Net services. *Business Times,* 5.

Jones, S. (1998). Information, Internet and community: Notes toward an understanding of community in the information age." In S. Jones (Ed.), *Cybersociety 2.0* (pp. 1–34). Thousand Oaks, CA: Sage.

Jung, C. G. (1958). *Psyche and symbol* (V. S. de Laszlo, Ed.). Garden City, NJ: Doubleday.

Katz, D. (1960). The functional approach to the study of attitudes. *Public Opinion Quarterly, 24*, 163–204.

Keyton, J. (1999). Relational communication in groups. In L. R. Frey, D. S. Gouran, & M. S. Poole (Eds.), *The handbook of group communication theory and research* (pp. 192–222). Thousand Oaks, CA: Sage.

Kozinets, R. V. (2002). The field behind the screen: Using netnography for marketing research in online communities. *Journal of Marketing Research, 39*(1), 61–73.

Lacoursiere, R. B. (1980). *The life cycle of groups: Group development stage theory.* New York: Human Science Press.

Levinger, G. (1983). Development and change. In H. H. Kelley, E. Berscheid, A. Christensen, J. Harvey, T. Huston, G. Levinger, E. McClintock, L. A. Peplau, & D. Peterson (Eds.), *Close relationships* (pp. 315–359). New York: Freeman.

Lipari, L. (1999). Polling as ritual. *Journal of Communication, 49*(1), 83–102.

Lockard, J. (1996). Progressive politics, electronic individualism and the myth of virtual community. In D. Porter (Ed.), *Internet culture* (pp. 219–231). New York: Routledge.

Lowrey, T. M., & Otnes, C. (1994). Construction of a meaningful wedding: Differences between the priorities of brides and grooms. In J. Costa (Ed.), *Gender and consumer behavior* (pp. 164–183). Beverly Hills, CA: Sage.

Maloney-Krichmar, D., & Preece, J. (2002). The meaning of an online health community in the lives of its members: Roles, relationships and group dynamics. *Social implications of information and communication technology. 2002 international symposium on technology and society ISTAS'02,* 20–27.

Mead, G. H. (1956). *On social psychology* (A. Strauss, Ed.). Chicago: University of Chicago Press.

Miller, C. R. (1994). Rhetorical community: The cultural basis of genre. In A. Freedman & P. Medway (Eds.), *Genre and the new rhetoric* (pp. 67–78). London: Taylor & Francis.

Mohammed, R. A., Fisher, R. J., Jaworski, B. J., &. Cahill, A. M. (2002). *Internet marketing: Building advantage in a networked economy.* New York: McGraw-Hill/Irwin.

Muniz, A. M. Jr., & O'Guinn, T. C. (2001). Brand community. *Journal of Consumer Research, 27*(4), 412–432.

O'Guinn, T. C., & Belk, R. W. (1989, September). Heaven on earth: Consumption at heritage village, USA. *Journal of Consumer Research, 16,* 227–239.

Otnes, C., & Scott, L. M. (1996, Spring). Something old, something new: Exploring the interaction between ritual and advertising. *Journal of Advertising, 25,* 33–50.

Otnes, C., & Lowrey, T. M. (1993). Till debt do us part: The selection and meaning of artifacts in the American wedding. In L. McAlister & M. L. Rothschild (Eds.), *Advances in consumer research, 20* (pp. 325–329). Provo, UT: Association for Consumer Research.

Poole, M. S. (1981). Decision development in small groups I: A comparison of two models. *Communication Monographs, 48,* 1–24.

Poole, M. S. (1999). Group communication theory. In L. R. Frey, D. S. Gouran, & M. S. Poole (Eds.), *The handbook of group communication theory and research* (pp. 88–165). Thousand Oaks, CA: Sage.

Porter, D. (Ed.). (1996). *Internet culture.* New York: Routledge.

Preece, J. (2000). *Online communities: Designing usability, supporting sociability.* Chichester, UK: Wiley.

Quinn R. E., & Cameron, K. (1983, January). Organizational life cycles and shifting criteria of effectiveness: Some preliminary evidence. *Management Science, 29,* 33–51.

Rayport, J. F., & Jaworski, B. J. (2001). *e-commerce.* New York: McGraw-Hill/Irwin.

Reicher, S. D. (1987). Crowd behavior as social action. In J. C. Turner, M. A. Hogg, P. J. Oaks, S. D. Reicher, & M. S. Wetherell (Eds.), *Rediscovering the social group: A self-categorisation theory* (pp. 171–202). Oxford, UK: Blackwell.

Rheingold, H. (1993). *The virtual community: Homesteading on the electronic frontier.* Reading, MA: Addison-Wesley.

Ritson, M., & Elliot, R. (1999, December). The social uses of advertising: An ethnographic study of adolescent advertising audiences. *Journal of Consumer Research, 26,* 260–277.

Rook, D. (1985, December). The ritual dimension of consumer research. *Journal of Consumer Research, 12,* 251–264.

Ruth, J. A., Otnes, C. C., & Brunel, F. F. (1999, March). Gift receipt and the reformulation of interpersonal relationships. *Journal of Consumer Research, 25,* 385–402.

Sacks, H. (1992 [1972]). *Lectures on conversation* (G. Jefferson, Ed.). Cambridge, MA: Blackwell.

Scanzoni, J. (1979). Social exchange and behavioral interdependence. In R. L. Burgess & T. L. Huston (Eds.), *Social exchange in developing relationships* (pp. 61–98). New York: Academic Press.

Schegloff, E. (1995). Parties and talking together: Two ways in which numbers are significant for talk-in-interaction. In P. ten Have & G. Psathas (Eds.), *Situated order: Studies in social organization and embodied activities* (pp. 31–42). Washington, D.C.: University Press of America.

Schouten, J. W. (1991). Selves in transition: Symbolic consumption in personal rites. *Journal of Consumer Research, 17*(4), 412–425.

Schouten, J. W., & McAlexander, J. (1995). Subcultures of consumption: An ethnography of the new bikers. *Journal of Consumer Research, 22*(1), 43–61.

Sherry, J. F. Jr. (1983). Gift giving in anthropological perspective. *Journal of Consumer Research, 10,* 157–168.

Sherry, J. F. Jr., & McGrath, M. A. (1989). Unpacking the holiday presence: A comparative ethnography of two gift stores. In E. C. Hirschman (Ed.), *Interpretive consumer research* (pp. 148–167). Provo, UT: Association for Consumer Research.

Sherry, J. F. Jr., McGrath, M. A., & Levy, S. J. (1993). The dark side of the gift. *Journal of Business Research, 28*(3), 225–245.

Smith, M. B., Bruner, J. S., & White, R. W. (1956). *Opinions and personality*. New York: Wiley.

Spears, R., Lea, M., & Postmes, T. (2000). Social psychological theories of computer-mediated communication: Social pain or social gain? In P. Robinson & H. Giles (Eds.), *The handbook of language and social psychology*. Chichester: Wiley.

Strauss, A., & Corbin, J. (1998). *Basic of qualitative research*. Newbury Park, CA: Sage.

Tajfel, H., & Turner, J. C. (1986). The social identity theory of intergroup behavior. In S. Worchel & W. G. Austin (Eds.), *Psychology of intergroup relations*. Chicago: Nelson-Hall.

Tannen, D. (1990). *You just don't understand: Women and men in conversation*. New York: Morrow.

Tepper, M. (1996). UseNet communities and the cultural politics of information. In D. Porter (Ed.), *Internet culture* (pp. 39–54), New York: Routledge.

Tuckman, B. (1965). Developmental sequence in small groups. *Psychological Bulletin, 63*, 384–399.

Tuckman, B. W., & Jensen, M. A. C. (1977). Stages of small group development revisited. *Group and Organizational Studies, 2*, 419–427.

Tuomela, R. (1995). *The importance of us: A philosophical study of basic social notions*. Stanford, CA: Stanford University Press.

Turner, J. C. (1982). Towards a cognitive redefinition of the social group. In H. Tajfel (Ed.), *Social identity and intergroup relations*. Cambridge: Cambridge University Press.

Turner, J. C. (1987). A self-categorisation theory. In J. C. Turner, M. A. Hogg, P. J. Oakes, S. D. Reicher, & M. S. Wetherell (Eds.), *Rediscovering the social group: A self-categorisation theory*. Oxford, UK: Blackwell.

Turner, V. (1974). *Dramas, fields, and metaphors: Symbolic action in human society*. Ithaca, NY: Cornell University Press.

Venkatraman, N., & Henderson, J. C. (1998). Real strategies for virtual organizing. *Sloan Management Review, 40*, 33–48.

Wallendorf, M., & Arnould, E. J. (1991, June). We gather together: Consumption rituals of Thanksgiving day. *Journal of Consumer Research, 18*, 13–31.

Ward, H. (2000). *Principles of Internet marketing*. Ohio: South-Western College Publishing, Thomson Learning.

Ward, J. C., & Reingen, P. (1996). A network perspective on crossing the micro-macro divide in consumer behavior research. In D. Iacobucci (Ed.), *Networks in marketing* (pp. 303–324). London: Sage.

Wells, W. D. (1993, March). Discovery-oriented consumer research. *Journal of Consumer Research, 19*, 489–504.

Wilbur, S. P. (1996). An archaeology of cyberspaces: Virtuality, community, identity. In D. Porter (Ed.), *Internet culture* (pp. 5–22). New York: Routledge.

Worchel, S. (1994). You can go home again: Returning group research to the group context with an eye on developmental issues. *Small Group Research, 25*, 205–223.

CHAPTER TWO

Published Word of Mouth: Referable, Consumer-Generated Information on the Internet

Robert M. Schindler
Barbara Bickart
Rutgers University, Camden

Verbal consumer-to-consumer communication, often referred to as simply "word of mouth" (WOM), has long been recognized as an important factor in consumer behavior (e.g., Whyte, 1954). The development of the Internet has led to the appearance of new forms of word-of-mouth communication (Granitz & Ward, 1996). Using the Internet, consumers can now easily publish their opinions, providing their thoughts, feelings, and viewpoints on products and services to the public at large. For example, on a message board at www.oxygen.com, consumers exchange opinions about good (and bad) shopping sites on the Web. Likewise, "Style Chat" at www.leftgear.com provides users with an opportunity to discuss fashion and design. Sites such as www.consumerreviews.com and www.epinions.com allow consumers to post their reviews of products and services in a number of different categories, as do many major online retailers. This type of information is already playing a role in marketing, and promises to do so much more in the future.

The importance of online WOM increases as access to and usage of the Internet continues to grow. For the last week of August 2004, Nielsen/NetRatings estimated that the average user in the United States logged onto the Internet nine times, and visited 22 unique sites. Nielsen estimates that the active digital media universe in the United States during this period was over 106 million (Nielsen/NetRatings, 2004).

This large number of users gives Internet WOM significant potential power for marketers. Anecdotal evidence of the power of Internet WOM abounds. For example, after the success of the use of Internet buzz in promoting the movie *The Blair Witch Project*, studios are increasingly relying on online WOM to develop interest in new films. In promoting the trilogy of films based on *The Lord of the Rings*, New Line Cinemas encouraged the development of unofficial Web sites about the movies, providing these sites with interviews with the film's director in order to generate discussion and excitement about the movies (Brinsley, 2000). Likewise, students hired to post questions and comments on teen-oriented chat rooms and bulletin boards generated discussion and interest in pop singer Christina Aguilera (White, 1999). Epinions.com estimates that it gets one million unique visitors per month (Schoenberger, 2000). And consumer stories posted on Oxygen Media boost traffic to the site by 14% (Stepanek, 2000).

Our earlier research (Bickart & Schindler, 2001) provides some empirical evidence regarding the power of one form of Internet WOM—the online forum. As part of a weekly class assignment, we randomly assigned students to look at either corporate web pages or consumer forums for information about specific product categories such as nutritional supplements or biking. At the end of the semester, students' interest in the assigned product categories was measured. We found that interest in the product category was higher for students assigned to view forum information on the topic than for those assigned to look at marketer-generated information. We suggest that the discussion forums are more successful in generating product interest because the content posted on such sites is thought to be more relevant and credible and is able to generate greater empathy among readers.

Our primary goal in this paper is to explore in more depth the potential power of online WOM. Under what circumstances do consumers find such information to be most useful? What are consumers' motives for searching for online consumer information? What kinds of online WOM do consumers look for and how do they evaluate it? How does it affect their buying decision processes? In addressing these issues, we first describe what is unique about Internet WOM. Then, we briefly review the relevant literature. Together with qualitative depth interviews, we use this literature to gain insights into the questions described above. Finally, we discuss the key findings and some directions for future research.

WOM Communication on the Internet

Studies of consumer information search have consistently found WOM to be particularly powerful in affecting the consumer. Katz and Lazarsfeld (1955) found WOM influence to be far more important than advertising or personal selling. Alreck and Settle (1995) found that, for a service product, advice from other consumers had a greater influence on consumers than the effects of all marketer-generated sources of information combined. WOM has been shown to be important in the diffusion of new products (Rogers, 1983) and to influence consumer decisions in a wide range of product categories (e.g., Arndt, 1967; Feldman & Spencer, 1965; Gitelson & Crompton, 1983; Swan & Oliver, 1989). WOM is a major influence on consumer behavior and affects a substantial proportion of the United States economy (Dye, 2000).

Consumer researchers are beginning to address the issue of WOM on the Internet (e.g., Bussiere, 2000; Chatterjee, 2000; Granitz & Ward, 1996; Lewis, Phelps, Mobilio, & Raman, 2005; Okleshen & Grossbart, 1998). In particular, Granitz and Ward (1996) propose a typology of comments based on Usenet discussion groups. A content analysis of a specific Usenet group suggested that the majority of comments were related to recommendations, how-to advice, and explanations. Granitz and Ward note that Internet WOM differs from traditional WOM in that the participant's identity is not "constrained by circumstances of their background, appearance, status, neighborhood, and workplace" (p. 165; see also Fisher, Bristor, & Gainer, 1996). In other words, the Internet provides consumers with a large and diverse set of opinions about products and services from individuals with whom they have little (or no) prior relationship.

Thus a key difference between traditional WOM and online WOM is the strength of the ties between the consumers who are exchanging information. Granovetter (1973) suggests that the strength of a tie between two individuals is a function of the amount of time spent together, the emotional intensity and degree of intimacy in the relationship, and the extent to which reciprocal services are provided by the dyad members. He further suggests that weak ties are particularly important in serving as bridges across cliques of strong ties, and thus are central to diffusion processes (see also Brown & Reingen, 1987). In the context of online WOM, weak ties provides three possible benefits to consumers. First, the presence of weak ties allows for more potential input to a decision (Friedkin, 1982). Second, consumer information distributed via the Internet should be more diverse than that which would be obtained via strong ties (Constant, Sproull, and Kiesler, 1997). Finally, using online WOM can enable consumers to obtain higher quality input into a decision—that is, it can provide access to people with greater expertise on a topic (Constant et al., 1997). In fact, in an organizational context, Constant et al. (1997) found that employees were able to receive useful technical advice from relative strangers via a firm's computer network. In this context, the primary benefit seemed to come from the superior resources of the information providers (i.e., technical knowledge), rather than the amount of information received. Along with these benefits of potentially providing more and better information to consumers, relying on weak ties may present difficulties. In particular, weak-tie sources may make it harder for consumers to assess the quality of the WOM information they are receiving (Constant et al., 1997). Consumers do not know the motives of the informant for providing information, and it may be difficult to assess this person's background and expertise on the topic.

Of course, the relative strength of these ties varies between and within the different forms of Internet WOM. For example, one might expect to find both strong ties (e.g., old friends) and weak ties (e.g., email acquaintances) among email WOM exchanges. This brings up the important point that there are a number

TABLE 2.1
Characteristics of Seven Sources of Internet Word of Mouth

	Information Flow	Timing of Interactions	Interacting With	Referability
Posted reviews	One-way			Constant
Mailbags	Two-way	Delayed	Sellers	Constant
Discussion forums	Two-way	Delayed	Consumers	Constant
Electronic mailing lists	Two-way	Delayed	Consumers	Limited
Personal email	Two-way	Delayed	Consumers	Limited
Chat rooms	Two-way	Immediate	Consumers	Limited
Instant messaging	Two-way	Immediate	Consumers	Limited

of ways in which WOM messages are communicated on the Internet. They can be divided into the following seven categories (see Table 2.1):

1. *Posted reviews.* Includes consumer opinions published on the Internet by online merchants, by commercial Web sites that specialize in posting consumer opinions, and by consumers who publish their product opinions on their own Web sites, including "revenge" sites.
2. *Mailbags.* Includes customer and reader comments and feedback posted on the Web sites of such organizations as consumer products manufacturers, service providers, magazines, and news organizations.
3. *Discussion forums.* Includes bulletin boards, Usenet groups, and published ongoing discussions on specific topics.
4. *Electronic mailing lists.* Includes consumer opinions sent by email to the members of an email list.
5. *Personal email.* Includes messages sent by one person directly to another (or a group of people).
6. *Chat rooms.* Includes real-time conversations over the Internet between groups of people, often based on a particular topic.
7. *Instant messaging.* Includes one-on-one real-time conversations over the Internet.

One dimension on which these forms of Internet WOM differ is the degree to which their information can be easily accessed by a large number of people. This will be termed the *referability* of the WOM information (see also Boush & Kahle, 2001). Posted reviews are often maintained on Web sites for a year or more. Each message is available to the general public for a relatively long period of time. Thus, the WOM information in posted reviews would be considered highly referable. Similarly, consumer opinions in mailbags and discussion forums are usually publicly available for a considerable period of time. Because they are published on the Internet, these three types of Internet WOM—posted reviews, mailbags, and discussion forums—are accessible to a large number of people for a relatively long time. This makes them highly referable forms of WOM.

By contrast, the other four forms of Internet WOM are not published on the Internet and thus are less referable. Although managers of electronic mailing lists usually archive the distributed messages, these archives are not usually easily available to the general public. The WOM messages communicated by electronic mailing lists and personal email are accessible to only a relatively small number of people and only for a limited time. Unless recipients habitually store their email, receiving an email message (either directly from another consumer or via a electronic mailing list) will not result in their having a bank of WOM information to which they can refer. WOM messages exchanged in chat rooms are publicly available but only for the time they are being transmitted; chat room conversations are only rarely archived. Messages communicated by instant messaging are neither publicly available nor are they archived. Thus, instant messaging is the least referable form of WOM transmitted over the Internet.

The referability dimension is important because it affects the degree to which consumer product communication over the Internet increases the possibility of weak-tie WOM. Less referable forms of Internet WOM, being available to only a limited number of people and/or for only a limited time, offer few opportunities for a consumer to make contact with unfamiliar others who might have particularly powerful or useful information. More referable forms—those forms of WOM communication that are *published* on the Internet—offer many opportunities for consumers to gain beneficial information from weak-tie sources. For this reason, we focus our investigation primarily on these referable forms of consumer-generated Internet information: WOM published as posted reviews, in mailbags, or in discussion forums. (See Chapter 3 by Lewis et al. for a discussion of the motives and behaviors associated with email WOM.)

Framework of Investigation

As a starting point in understanding the role played by Internet WOM, we have carried out an investigation of the consumer's usage of this information. This investigation is guided by a framework based on the research literature on WOM effects. The framework leads us to first consider the consumer's motives for using published WOM information. Then we examine how the consumer evaluates the information obtained in this manner. Finally, we look at the ways in which published WOM information can influence the consumer decision process.

Motives for Using Published WOM. Perhaps the most basic motive for a consumer's attention to WOM messages is the expectation of receiving information that may decrease decision time and effort and/or contribute to the achievement of a more satisfying decision outcome (Schiffman & Kanuk 2000, p. 398). Information motives may be particularly important for the use of WOM published on the

Internet because such weak-tie sources seem favored by consumers who are interested in specific product information as opposed to affective product evaluations (Duhan, Johnson, Wilcox, & Harrell, 1997).

A second motive for using WOM concerns the consumer's desire to decrease dissonant cognitions and increase cognitive consistency (Cummings and Venkatesan, 1976; Festinger, 1957). It has been found that consumers' receptivity to WOM depends on the fit of this information with their prior beliefs (Wilson & Peterson, 1989). This suggests that consumers may use WOM to reinforce their decisions or to increase their confidence in the views that they already have.

Consumer Evaluation of Published WOM.   Consumers may evaluate a published WOM message on the basis of the content itself. For example, the presence of negative information along with positive information has been found to increase message credibility (Crowley & Hoyer, 1994; Pechmann, 1992). The presence of negative comments in the content of an Internet WOM message could give it an enhanced believability. Also, it has been observed that WOM information is likely to be based on memories of salient product experiences (Dichter, 1966). It is possible that published Internet WOM content that is perceived by readers as being based on first-person consumer experience might further contribute to the believability of the message.

In addition to using the content of a published WOM message to evaluate the message, consumers are also likely to use information about the source, or writer, of the message. The perception that the source of a message is similar to the reader can lead to a greater persuasive effect (Hass, 1981; McGuire, 1969; Price, Feick, & Higie, 1989). If the writer of a WOM message is more well-known to a reader, then that message is likely to have more influence (Brown & Reingen, 1987). Cues that give a source the appearance of expertise, such as credentials and past achievements, are also capable of increasing a message's persuasive effect (Ratneshwar & Chaiken, 1991). Finally, information from a source that is perceived to be more trustworthy can lead to a greater persuasiveness of that information (Hovland & Weiss, 1951; Wilson & Sherrell, 1993). The audience's attributions of a source's intentions are a key factor in the perception of trustworthiness (Eagly, Wood, & Chaiken, 1978).

Effects of Published WOM on the Consumer Decision Process.   Typically, WOM is considered as one of the external sources of information that consumers acquire during the information-search stage of the decision process (e.g., Claxton, Fry, & Portis, 1974; Westbrook & Fornell, 1979). However, there has been little examination of the processes by which WOM can have an impact on this decision-process stage (for an exception, see Price and Feick, 1984). It has been shown that an important outcome of predecision information search is a set of alternatives that will be further considered, often referred to as the *consideration set* (Nedungadi, 1990; Shocker, Ben-Akiva, Boccara, & Nedungadi, 1991). WOM input may add items to a consumer's consideration set by presenting interesting ideas and may cause the deletion of items from the set by presenting negative information about the items.

The commonly used model of the consumer decision process includes several stages other than information search (see Engel, Blackwell, & Miniard, 1995, p. 154), and each of these stages could be influenced by WOM (Price & Feick, 1984). For example, product awareness created by WOM could create a discrepancy between a consumer's ideal and actual states and, thus, cause problem recognition. WOM could suggest attributes that should be attended to during the alternative-evaluation stage, could help a consumer decide where an item should be purchased, and could influence postpurchase evaluation either by helping decrease dissonant cognitions (as mentioned above) or by other means.

All of these possible effects of WOM on the consumer decision process could also occur for WOM published on the Internet. Indeed, the referability of published online WOM may enhance the strength of these effects and/or the likelihood that they can be reported because the information can be accessed when most needed and can be absorbed by the consumer at the consumer's own pace.

METHOD

Data Collection

Given the exploratory nature of the research objectives, we used depth interviews to help provide insight into consumers' motives for using online WOM, how they evaluate this information, and the effects it has on their decision processes. We recruited 19 consumers who claimed they "frequently shop online" to participate in the study. For their participation, informants received a $10 gift certificate from Amazon.com. Informants ranged in age from 15 to 56, with 8 males and 11 females. The informants were generally quite experienced with the Internet— approximately half of the informants spent more than 7 hours per week on the Internet. All of the informants reported that they checked their email daily. Among the informants, the most common uses of the Internet included obtaining news, information search for school or work, checking financial information, and shopping. Approximately half of the informants reported that they never participated in chats/forums or played games online. Younger informants were more likely to participate in chats and play games online.

Both authors and a trained research assistant conducted interviews that lasted approximately 45 to 60 minutes. Interviews were audio-recorded and transcribed for later analysis. We began the interviews by asking informants to describe several recent situations in which they had shopped for a product or service online. We probed to learn about the different sources of online WOM that were obtained during the shopping experience. If online WOM was obtained, we explored how participants found the information, what they expected to learn from this information and how this information was used in their decision process. We also asked if they provided feedback or interacted with the information provider. We then probed for the use of sources of online WOM not spontaneously mentioned in the descriptions of the shopping experiences. Specifically, we probed for the use of posted reviews, mailbags, discussion forums, electronic mailing lists, personal emails, chat-rooms, and instant messaging. If an informant had not used a particular source of online WOM, we asked why not. We also asked for impressions of the types of people who would use such information sources.

Data Analysis

The analysis was exploratory and descriptive in nature, with the goal of better understanding how consumers use Internet WOM. Each of us individually reviewed the transcripts of the interviews. We looked for statements or comments that were related to (a) motives for using Internet WOM, (b) evaluation of the content of online WOM messages, and (c) the influence of this information on consumer decision-making. Individually, we attempted to identify consistent themes that emerged within each of these general areas, along with supporting comments made by the informants. We then compared the themes that we had separately identified, as well as the supporting comments for each theme. We resolved differences through discussion and repeated this process until we felt that (a) we had identified the major issues related to each topic and (b) that these issues were supported by the interviews.

RESULTS

Overview of the Types of Internet WOM Information Used

Of our 19 informants selected for being frequent Internet shoppers, all but one had experiences using online WOM. In general, the informants appreciated the convenience of having consumer input available on the Internet. In particular, they mentioned that online information search was more efficient than other forms of information search and that the referability of the online information was a great convenience. Toward the end of each interview, we asked informants specifically about their use of each of the seven sources of online WOM that we have described above.

Among our informants, the most frequently used source of online WOM was consumer reviews. Informants often spontaneously mentioned that they referred to consumer reviews as one piece of input when making a specific purchase decision. Most of our informants used reviews that were provided by the retail site on which they were shopping. For example, many informants mentioned using reviews when purchasing books or toys on Amazon.com. For these kinds of product categories, checking reviews appears to have become part of the "script" for online shopping. Unless the purchase was very important or involving, informants were not likely to seek out reviews at other independent sites.

What we defined as mailbags were viewed similarly to posted consumer reviews by our informants. Informants rarely mentioned seeking out mailbags on the Internet. When prompted, however, informants thought that this kind of information might be useful if it was "not controlled" by the company, and several could imagine providing information to others via this format. In particular, informants were interested in posting negative stories and experiences with products and services in a mailbag-type setting, but not on the manufacturer's Web site.

Online discussion forums and electronic mailing lists were less likely to be used than consumer reviews, although usage of these sources was quite high among a small number of our informants. (Two or three of our informants were active members of online communities, while several others lurked or participated occasionally.) Discussion forums and electronic mailing lists were perceived to be similar, but the use of forums was much more extensive than that of electronic mailing lists. Electronic mailing lists require an effort to join (the user must send an email to subscribe), which implies a longer-term commitment to the group. In contrast to consumer reviews, informants tended to seek out discussion forums for more general issues or questions (versus to obtain specific product information). For example, informants visited forums when they were looking for community or support related to a product they had already purchased (such as a car) or for an enduring interest (such as a rock band). In these situations, reading and participating in forums helped informants become better consumers of the product. Likewise, an important, highly involving decision or situation, such as a serious medical condition, served as a catalyst to seek out information on a forum or electronic mailing list (see Chapter 1 by Alon, Brunel, and Siegal, 2005). Informants viewed participants in discussion forums and electronic mailing lists as knowledgeable and as good resources.

In contrast to the information-seeking motives for visiting online forums, the motives for using chat rooms, email, and instant messaging seemed primarily social. Informants used email and instant messaging as an efficient way to communicate with friends. Only a few of our informants mentioned participating in chat-room discussions. Most informants were quite leery of chat rooms, perceived them to be a waste of time, and held negative perceptions of chat participants. The few informants who did participate seemed to enjoy being an information resource to others on a specific topic.

Motives for Using Internet Word of Mouth

Why do people seek out consumer input on the Internet? Previous research has suggested that consumers use WOM to facilitate the decision process (i.e., provide specific input to a decision) and to help reduce dissonance related to a decision (i.e., postdecision support). Among our informants we found evidence for both of these motives, but other reasons for seeking out consumer information also came up frequently. In the discussion that follows, we broadly group motives into three categories: information, support and community, and entertainment.

Information Motives. Informants used online WOM as input to a variety of purchase decisions, including both large and small purchases, with both utilitarian and hedonic objectives. When specific information was sought, consumer reviews were the most frequently mentioned source of Internet WOM. Informants with information-seeking motives tended to appreciate seeing direct comparisons between brands or products. Also, they often seemed especially interested in negative information about a specific alternative. For example:

> I would think, based on the ones I had read before on the digital camera, the ones I read the people had used them for a period of time and I would want to know something about glitches or any bugs that were in them or problems, for instance, with scanning or the speed of the scanner or reliability of it. (female, age 56, retired high school teacher)
>
> Technical reviews of a technical book . . . . were there a lot of errors in the books and stuff like that . . . you know the people who actually purchased the books and they read the books so I look for whether they said that in this book the author makes a lot of technical errors. That would be a good determinant. (male, age 29, systems administrator)

This kind of content is frequently provided in consumer reviews. As would be expected, informants were most likely to mention referring to online WOM as an information source when the decision was risky or important:

> Well, I was planning a special dinner and I wanted it to be a success. I wanted to go to a restaurant that I had never eaten at but I wanted to try to make the most informed choice I could make because it was a one-shot deal. And I knew about the Digitalcity restaurant site because I had looked at it before. (female, age 45, horticulturist)

One particularly interesting idea that emerged from the interviews was that consumers rely on Internet WOM when input from friends and family (or other strong-tie sources) is not available. For example, informants were more likely to mention using online WOM for products or services that were new or infrequently purchased. For example:

> I've been searching for a new camera. And I'm trying to decide whether I want to buy a point-and-shoot 35 mm camera or they have this new format out called APS and I really don't know too much about it so I've been searching the Internet a lot trying to find what people are saying about the APS format versus the 35 mm format.

I have found a lot of information on the Internet about that subject. (male, age 42, operating engineer)

Because this is a new product, strong-tie sources of information may be more difficult to locate. The comment reflects the vast amount of weak-tie information made accessible by the Internet. Another similar situation in which online WOM was sought was for travel decisions. In this case, the consumer is seeking information about a faraway place for which it may be difficult to find strong-tie sources of consumer input. In addition, the nature of the service makes consumer input particularly diagnostic in this context.

> Recently I decided with my husband that we would like to take a vacation to a place that we had never been and I didn't really feel that I was getting information from typical sources. I called the travel agent and they were vague and not very friendly and not very informative. So I thought I would go online and try to research where we might want to go. I had some idea but I wasn't real sure because I'm planning a vacation to a place where we had never been so I went online. I looked at several different travel sites that had links and consumer opinions and stuff like that and I read as much consumer information as I could about these different places. (female, age 45, horticulturist)

Finally, a number of informants used online WOM when purchasing gifts. Gift givers are motivated to give items that are considered appropriate for the relationship but that also reflect an understanding of the recipient's needs and pleasures (Ruth, Otnes, & Brunel, 1999). In this situation, the person likely to be the best source of WOM—the gift recipient—is unavailable. Online WOM can serve as an effective surrogate information source. For example:

> Actually I was buying cooking books for my mother. And I really don't know too much about them. I read the reviews to see what the people who actually used them would think of them. (female, age 26, undergraduate student)

Support and Community Motives.   Another motive for using online WOM was to obtain support for a decision already made and to seek out a community related to the product or service. Informants mentioned seeking out positive information to support or confirm a previously-made decision. For example:

> The movie I recently purchased, *The Perfect Storm* . . . is a movie that [my wife] really wanted to see and we couldn't get to the movies before it went off. I thought I should get that movie for her. But being my cheapskate self [and needing to think about it] . . . I went out and I reviewed some customer feedback on the movie. I found some things that were appealing to me. It was action-packed, there was some drama, you didn't really know how it was going to come out during the movie and I love movies where I can't figure them out till the end. (male, age 46, account manager)

Likewise, the following informant sought confirmation of her decision to spend a semester abroad in London by querying (random) London residents using instant messaging:

> It helped just reaffirm what I wanted to do. I wanted to go to London but I wasn't sure if the city was a totally safe city. After talking to a couple of people, I found out it's a safe city. . . . I should definitely go through with it. (female, age 20, undergraduate student)

Informants also mentioned using discussion forums to find a community of consumers with similar concerns and product interests. The following informant participated in a discussion forum for Volvo owners. As reflected in the quote, this group bonded together to help each other solve product-related problems.

> Other people talk about the electronic brakes in this thing take some getting used to. People were giving each other tips on that . . . They are very sensitive brakes. A lot of people were having trouble and saying "what's wrong with my brakes" . . . One person wrote in. "I think I'm going to have to take this car back. I can't possibly deal with this." So we wrote, "go to the parking lot and practice stopping and get used to exactly where the brakes start to catch." (male, age 41, investment fund manager)

In fact, consumers often seek "stories" recounting the product experiences and usage of fellow consumers. Although these kinds of stories are more likely to be found in discussion forums, they can be also be found in posted reviews. For example, for the following informant, one relevant story seemed to call for another:

> One of the [golf] courses one of the people had a fairly negative comment but they said they had played the course another time and had a much better experience so they didn't know if it was just an off day. And I almost wanted to contact them and say was your other experience considerably more pleasant? (female, age 56, retired high school teacher)

Entertainment Motives. A number of informants mentioned that they read online WOM for fun. Discussion forums were the most popular source of entertainment. Informants found extreme viewpoints and debates to be particularly interesting, as reflected in the following quote:

> I didn't participate [in discussions]; I basically read. They were interesting. One of the ones that was funny. I was also looking at minivans. Although we had already bought our minivan, it was interesting to see what people had to say about my minivan. You either have people who hate the Chryslers or love the Chryslers, so they have the comparisons of the Chrysler minivans and the Honda Odyssey. . . . You'd have the people talking about what they loved and hated about each. . . . It was interesting to see what people said about their new cars. (female, age 43, homemaker)

They also enjoyed humorous stories or exchanges on discussion forums.

> A very humorous thing that I did post in recently is someone complaining that they
> were disappointed with the gas mileage in the car. Well it's a six-cylinder engine as
> opposed to a five-cylinder in the old one. Someone had written in to say that you
> can coast up to a red light and this gives you two miles per gallon more. One person
> answered that you can't do that in Texas—the person behind you is likely to shoot
> you. You have to drive the speed limit right up to the stoplight. Then we had this
> long humorous discussion about what it must be like to drive in Texas. (male, age
> 41, investment fund manager)

It is important to note, however, that while informants found these exchanges
amusing, they were also learning about the product or service being discussed. Information obtained in this passive manner may affect future decisions or behavior.

> I even read people's opinions about different stocks and stuff. Not that I'm really into
> the stock market or whatever, but I find it interesting to read the opinions of other
> people although the opinions of other people are not necessarily expert opinions. They
> do offer some insight into other people's experience that you may not otherwise have
> access to. (female, age 45, horticulturist)

Evaluation of Internet WOM Content

In evaluating online information from consumers, our informants appeared to be
concerned with two types of potential problems. One is that the information may
be untrustworthy or biased. Biased information could be due to the writer of
the message not being the fellow consumer that he/she appears to be or simply
because genuine consumer messages are selectively filtered by the Web site's
owner. The other potential problem is that the message may contain so little valid
or accurate information that it may not be worthy of the reader's attention.

Cues for Bias. One cue our informants used for determining bias is simply the
owner of the Web site on which the consumer comments are posted. For example,
when asked about consumer reviews found on a manufacturer's Web site, one
informant responded:

> I think that [the site] had testimonials from people but again I think this is just
> advertising and doesn't really help me become a more informed consumer. Anything
> that is posted by the manufacturer is pretty much going to be self-promoting so I
> don't think it helps me become a better consumer. (female, age 45, horticulturist)

It appeared that this informant questioned the credibility of the consumer postings
simply because they were found on a manufacturer's Web site. Another informant
felt similarly about comments found on the Web sites of retailers:

> The book reviews on Amazon tend not to have the credibility to me. On the other hand, the voluntary ones on Yahoo—it's independent and it was set up by drivers for themselves. It clearly had that independent kind of feeling. They were talking about, we all hate this feature how do we make Volvo change it? Who do we write to? Who do we call? How many members do we have on this board? Can we all get signatures and send it to them? Tell them we're 200 S80 owners who don't like this: change it next time. It had a different kind of independent feeling than things posted at Amazon at Amazon's discretion. (male, age 41, investment fund manager)

Note that for this latter informant, it was not just the independence of the Yahoo sites that gave them credibility. The belief that these sites really are independent was apparently reinforced by the presence of negative information about the product, such as the features that are disliked by Volvo owners. The use of this second cue for bias—the lack of negative information—was sometimes mentioned explicitly:

> The thing you have to be careful about on the Internet is if you don't know what you're doing, you can be misled very, very quickly by the testimonials of people who are way biased on stuff. For instance, like Amazon.com if I recall you can go look at testimonials about a specific product. It will give it a one- to five-star rating and then someone will type in a little note about what they thought about this product. I think ninety percent of what you see out there is like four stars plus and every once in a while you get one dissenting opinion on a product. (male, age 46, account manager)

A third reported cue for assessing bias was a sense of whether the posted comment was based on authentic first-person experience. If a comment involves "I" statements or otherwise evokes real personal experience, then its credibility is enhanced. On the other hand, if a consumer comment seems forced, stilted, or otherwise lacks verisimilitude, then the credibility of the comment is questioned. For example:

> [I value] questions and replies from consumers. You are able to get a good feel of what the consumer was experiencing with each and every product that they had and it wasn't—you know the postings weren't controlled by the manufacturer. They didn't censor anything so you were able to get a good feel for what the product was. (male, age 42, operating engineer)
>
> I went out to the Aiwa site . . . and I saw a lot of testimonials about the various surround-sound systems and other audio equipment that they had. It just sounded like something you would hear on television—a testimonial that you hear on television that you know is scripted. Maybe these weren't scripted, but again, I found that these people—the way they expressed themselves and what they talked about—was more hype than substance. I rejected it out of hand. (male, age 46, account manager)

Cues for Validity. One of the most commonly mentioned aspects of a consumer posting that appeared to serve as a cue for its validity, or usefulness, was the presence of specific details in the posting. For example:

> [I look for]...if they have more specifics—like say if it was on the options book they said things like "this book increased my knowledge of cover call options and I was able to make thirty percent in a year" or whatever. If they can give some definite things of what the book accomplished for them, I think that would help more than "this book was a complete waste of time," "the money wasn't spent well at all." If it's just their strict opinion it doesn't really help, but if they put up some logic and some facts to back it up I think I would definitely take it more seriously. (male, age 22, graduate student)
>
> "This is the best stereo system I've ever owned, you got to buy one." "It even looks better on my bookshelf than I thought it would." I don't care about that stuff. I want substance. (male, age 46, account manager)

The words of another informant suggests that cues are often used together. She wanted not only details, but those details to come from the writer's first-person experience:

> A really good review would definitely have obviously some kind of personal reference to what you were talking about like "this song on this side," or "I feel the reason that this product doesn't work well is because of...the wheels on it don't rotate right," or something like that. Something that would be very detailed. Something that would be very general I would be like, did you really take the time to use it? (female, age 26, undergraduate student)

A second aspect of consumer comments that served as a cue for validity was the presence of some degree of consensus among reviewers. It appeared that consumer opinions were used to validate other consumer opinions:

> I would trust consumers but I wouldn't trust one consumer. I would want a consensus. I think again if it's only one person's opinion...so I would look for averages. (male, age 29, systems administrator)
>
> If the majority of the people who have submitted reviews say that it is good or bad or whatever, as long as the majority agrees on it, then I would trust the information. (male, age 15, high school student)

As one might expect, information about the identity of the consumer who posted some information was also used as a cue for the validity of that information. This is a third type of validity cue. Sometimes the informants used the information about the consumer posting the review that is provided by the site explicitly as a means of helping readers evaluate comments. For example, a student looking at software reviews posted by other students used the names of the school that the writers attended as a means of judging the value of the comments:

> For the Dreamweaver and the FrontPage [reviews] I just scrolled down to look at the university name so whatever university I know of, I just click on that one. *Interviewer: So you went to schools that you respected?* Yes, respected—NJIT, Lehigh, and some others. *Interviewer: What schools did you avoid?* Some like, I think there's one called something about Bowling Green or something. I avoided that one. I didn't know that much about that one so I just avoided that one. (male, age 23, undergraduate student)

At other times, source identity cues were gleaned from the text of the consumer comment:

> Sometimes they [the reviewer of a golf course] will tell you, for instance, I'm a 9 handicap or I'm a 25 handicap or whatever, which gives you at least some comparison in terms of their comments. (female, age 56, retired high school teacher)
>
> What I would do if I read the reviews and they said this song bla bla bla is really good. I might start with that first and then they say this song wasn't that great and I might listen to that one and see what I thought about it to judge whether I think the same as their opinion . . . good enough to judge on. (female, age 26, undergraduate student)

In this latter statement, the informant was saying that in evaluating a reviewer's comment about a new song or album, she would first listen to other songs (via the retailer's Web site). She would then use the writer's opinions of these accessible songs to calibrate her assessment of the writer's opinion about the other music by the artist.

A fourth type of validity cue that our informants reported involves the wording used in the posted comment. This is interesting because wording is a factor that may have become more important, or at least more noticeable, because online comments are written rather than spoken and can be examined more carefully. Wording cues could be based on particular kinds of words, such as inexpressive slang or words suggesting a cursory, emotional reaction, or they could involve the use of wording to judge the degree to which the writer is sensible or reasonable. For example:

> [I would not trust a comment] if they use an extreme word like this: "don't buy it," or "this product really sucks," or something like that. (male, age 29, systems administrator)
>
> I kind of use my senses of if that person sounds similar to me. I know someone who's different from me can have a valid opinion. I kind of judge like if that sounds like something I would say then I might enjoy the book if they enjoyed it. (female, age 22, undergraduate student)

Effect of Internet WOM on Consumer Decision Processes

Examination of our informants' descriptions of their uses of Internet WOM in the context of the consumer decision process showed that it can exert influence in a number of decision-process stages. For example, one informant learned about the existence of a book that appeared to have the effect of initiating a decision process:

> I learned about the prequel to *Divine Secrets*, which is called *Little Altars Everywhere*. And I learned about the author of the book and I think I'll probably purchase the prequel just because I'm interested. (female, age 17, high school student)

On the other hand, information from online consumer reviews also appears able to terminate a consumer's decision process:

> One of the things that I had looked at was this walking tour of Philadelphia. Was it a fun experience for people? Was it something I wanted to do? I was able to read the opinions of several people and it was just a small little thing—a little walking tour—but did I want to spend the time and money to go on this walking tour or not. After reading the reviews I decided that maybe I don't want to do this because although the consumers seemed to enjoy it, they weren't raving about it that it was the greatest, most fun thing to do. I chose not to do it based on just a couple of reviews by maybe three different people. (female, age 45, horticulturist)
>
> Actually, I was going to buy the new Back Street Boys album but I read a review on it and they were customer reviews of people who had bought this album, and four out of five people said it wasn't as good as the other ones so I decided to hold off and see if I get it for Christmas. (female, age 26, undergraduate student)

Consistent with our expectations, our informants reported that Internet WOM information affected the content of their consideration sets. Online consumer information could lead to additions to a consideration set:

> I definitely would look at what other people had recommended and what they felt was a good bike. I'd look through to see if a certain bike keeps popping up again as being a good bike. I'd definitely take a look at that more strongly than if I saw a bike and there were no reviews on it. That would definitely help me out. If they kept saying that this bike is a real good bike, if I kept reading a whole bunch of reviews about a specific bike, like maybe Cannondale, I would be more inclined to take a look into that bike if more people are raving about it. (female, age 20, undergraduate student)

It could also lead to items being removed from the informant's consideration sets:

> One of the [golf] courses that I looked at, every review I read said that play was very slow and they didn't marshal play. It took them a considerably longer time to play

the course. It was nice, but it was a long day. So I didn't even consider that course. (female, age 56, retired high school teacher)

I was researching Palm Pilots because I was thinking of getting one of those, and several of the reviews for different brands were horrible. They said get the other brand, it's much better. I said well I won't even consider getting that one. (male, age 15, high school student)

And it appeared that sometimes the Internet WOM information could have both effects:

They had a whole bunch [of reviews about video games for a child] and they had the most recent ones out and I read through those. And I used certain things to decide ahead of time I'm not going to buy that at all. If the name sounded too violent, like ninja something, I was not going to get that one. If it was a Bugs Bunny thing—anything cartoony—I read all of that. (female, age 26, actuary and graduate student)

The reports of a number of informants indicated that Internet WOM affected the alternative-evaluation stage of their decision processes by suggesting to them a new attribute that should be considered. For example:

The [online bulletin] boards helped me understand a little bit about what I should look for when I was test driving. If someone says "I hate this feature," well maybe I wouldn't. Maybe I would actually like that. I've got to remember when I get into the new super large Camry I have to check the seat controls and make sure I can actually see all the dials and gauges when I've adjusted the seat. (male, age 41, investment fund manager)

It [reading Internet forums] told me of a recall on the Accord, which I didn't know about. The year 2000 Accords that were built at the very beginning of the 2000 model year had a particular problem.... It had something to do with the transmission. It said you want to look at the date the car was manufactured if we decide on a Honda because if it was made before this date ... I did learn that. Practically everybody who was talking about the Hondas said that they were noisy, the wind noises, and that was never something we thought about. (female, age 43, homemaker)

In addition, there were also reports of alternative evaluation being affected by useful comparative information on how the various alternatives rated on attributes that the informant had already recognized as important. For example:

They [the commenting consumers] compared it to other games. They had Ninja 1, Ninja 2, and Ninja 3 so they compare it, that kind of thing. They talked about comparisons at different levels. I remember one particular game had more levels and was more challenging, more exciting, and that the scenes were nicer, and stuff like that. (female, age 26, actuary and graduate student)

An interesting possible downside of the ability of online consumer information to make a buyer aware of new relevant features is that this information could also have the capacity to impair postpurchase satisfaction. For example, one informant appeared unsure of the value of having learned about a possible problem with a new car that he had recently purchased:

> I finally figured out what they meant by the clunk in the steering wheel and I wrote back "it's such a tiny thing. If you hadn't made me so paranoid I never would have noticed it." (male, age 41, investment fund manager)

Given the large amount of online consumer information available about most products, it is not surprising that many of our informants reported using heuristics to simplify the information and help them absorb it with minimal effort. One interesting example of this is the use of "flash points"—each flash point being a single piece of information that in itself could cause rejection of an alternative. For example, one informant, searching for an authentic Italian cookbook as a gift for her mother, rejected an alternative as soon as she read about the book's suggested source of cheese:

> One of them [books being considered] was about the fresh ingredients you have to get, the most virgin olive oil. The other one was, you can get the mozzarella from the deli department. And I thought I definitely don't want this book! (female, age 26, undergraduate student)

For another informant, the flash point for an alternative was the WOM alert that the new, more expensive game was just like the previous year's version:

> People's reaction to the game in terms of the level of challenge, if they thought it was too easy, if they thought it was too violent, if it was similar to another game that they had put out before and probably was cheaper. One of the games I was about to buy—actually somebody said it was just like something they had out before and that it would be pointless to spend the extra $5 or $10 for this new game because it's exactly like a game that was put out last year. That's the kind of information I wanted to get. (female, age 26, actuary and graduate student)

DISCUSSION

Our empirical work examined consumers' motives for seeking out Internet WOM, the criteria used to evaluate online WOM, and the effects of online WOM on consumer decision processes. Many of our findings are consistent with earlier consumer research on WOM processes. Our depth interviews, however, suggest several new insights and possibilities regarding how WOM operates, both on the

TABLE 2.2
Summary of Motives to Use Internet Word of Mouth

Motive Type	Prominent Examples	Common Types of IWOM Used	Types of Content Favored
Information	Risky purchases Infrequent purchases Distance-related Gifts	Posted reviews (convenience is key)	Negative information, comparisons
Support and community	Relieving dissonance Dealing with problems	Discussion forums	Positive information, stories
Entertainment	Views of enthusiasts How own views compare with those of others	Discussion forums, chats, instant messaging	Extreme viewpoints, humor, photographs, etc.

Internet and in other settings. We now review our key findings, highlighting emergent issues, integrating our results with the consumer research literature, and discussing possible managerial implications.

Usage Motivation and Internet WOM Content

As summarized in Table 2.2, we identified three motives for seeking Internet WOM. First, consumers seek out Internet WOM as an *informational input* to specific purchase decisions. Online WOM seems particularly useful for decisions that are risky, important, or infrequent and is a good surrogate when stronger-tie sources of WOM are not available, such as for travel and gift decisions. Consumers with information motives often rely on posted consumer reviews. Such reviews are typically more specific in focus than other types of Internet WOM. When information is the motive, there seems to be particular interest in negative comments. Negative information is given more weight by consumers (Mizerski, 1982; Weinberger & Dillon, 1980). Further, given the relative anonymity of communication on the Internet (Fisher et al., 1996; Granitz and Ward, 1996), people may tend to act in a freer, less constrained manner in this environment. This anonymity might have the effect of increasing the amount of negative WOM information that could be found published on the Internet and may thus make Internet WOM particularly able to satisfy consumer informational motives.

A desire for *support and community* was another motive for seeking out online WOM. For example, informants appeared to look for positive information to help reduce dissonant thoughts related to a specific purchase decision (Cummings & Venkatesan, 1976; Festinger, 1957). In addition, our informants sought out solutions to specific product problems and guidance on how to consume products or services. Consumers with support and community motives often appear to rely on discussion forums and particularly seem to value dialog. Participants in these forums exchange stories about their product experiences, helping others deal with common problems and building a community among product owners, users, or enthusiasts (Muniz & O'Guinn, 2001). Seeking out this kind of support and community also appears to be related to facing a new, unfamiliar situation with many associated decisions. For example, one popular discussion forum is for pregnant women, with groups organized around due dates. Participants provide each other with feedback, decision input, and personal stories. As a group of women continue to exchange information over the course of their pregnancies and after the birth of their babies, a community, with its associated rituals, will begin to form (see Chapter 1 by Alon, Brunel, and Siegal).

Finally, some consumers read online WOM purely for its *entertainment* value. Consumers with entertainment motives seem to enjoy seeing the views of enthusiasts and comparing their own opinions and experiences with those of others. This is consistent with Holt's (1995) notion of consuming as play. Because consumers with entertainment motives are often interested in dialogue, discussion forums and chats are common types of Internet WOM used in this situation. Entertainment-seeking consumers appear to particularly value content presenting extreme viewpoints and humorous exchanges. In addition, consumers with entertainment motives may be more interested in special features of Internet WOM sites, such as photographs. Previous research has shown that consumers in a recreational shopping mode are more highly involved with the product category, engaging in ongoing search, and ultimately spending more money in the product class (Bloch, Sherrell, & Ridgway, 1986). In addition, these consumers tend to be opinion leaders (Bloch, Ridgway, & Sherrell, 1989). Thus, marketers may want to develop Internet WOM sites that are attractive to these entertainment-seeking consumers. For example, Schlosser and Kanfer (2002) show that for consumers with hedonic browsing motives, Internet WOM sites that incorporate web features such as product interactivity may be more effective in influencing attitudes and purchase behavior.

Toward Building Better WOM Web Sites

Past research has indicated that consumers are likely to evaluate a WOM message based on the content of the message as well as the message's source. Our results not only provide evidence for both of these means of message evaluation, but also give us some insights into how they are accomplished. Our informants used message content for evaluating bias and validity by:

- Looking for the presence of negative information
- Determining whether there is a consensus among reviewers
- Noting the presence of details in reviews
- Using wording cues such as inexpressive slang or extreme emotion words to judge the degree to which the review reflects a careful, thoughtful analysis
- Paying attention to whether the reviews plausibly result from authentic first-person experiences

Our informants used information about the message source to evaluate a message by:

- Noting the owner of the Web site on which the message is found
- Examining explicit identity information about the writer

We are currently more systematically investigating these evaluative cues by using a detailed content analysis to compare online reviews that consumers consider to be very useful with those that consumers consider not useful. The perceived usefulness as well as the importance of specific cues is likely to vary by the motive driving the information search.

The identification of the cues consumers use to evaluate Internet WOM could be used to aid in the development of Web sites that are more effective in providing information that consumers perceive as useful. Consumers considering posting reviews on a Web site could be given information on how readers tend to evaluate reviews and could be encouraged, for example, to emphasize detailed description of their personal experience with the product. Web sites that specialize in consumer reviews, such as Epinions.com, often provide an information page containing a reviewer's personal information and often a photograph. These sites could encourage the posters to submit a set of selected personal facts or doing so could even be made a requirement for the posting of a product review. On the downside, these kinds of requirements could limit the number of consumers willing to provide WOM comments due to concerns about privacy.

Our research suggests that manufacturer or retailer Web sites that display WOM messages must also deal with consumer concerns that the selling intent of these sites leads to biases in this WOM information. Owners of such sites could meet these concerns by establishing an explicit general policy on the posting of consumer reviews and making it easy for a consumer to test this policy by posting a review. More permissive general policies—such as promising to publish every received comment that avoids obscene language and content offensive to any particular person or social group—would lead to greater perceived credibility than more restrictive general policies. The challenge for management would be to maintain some control of message content while at the same time showing a willingness to publish both positive and negative information.

Our research also suggests that there may be entrepreneurial possibilities regarding Internet WOM. The numerous benefits of online WOM detailed by our informants suggests that there would be consumer interest in making such information easier to obtain. For example, access to consumer reviews, discussion forums, and other forms of published Internet WOM could be facilitated by the development of search sites that selectively index consumer-to-consumer postings. Further, consumers are looking for venues in which to exchange brand- and product-related information. Our research highlights the importance of using the Internet to build brand- and product-based communities (McAlexander, Schouten,

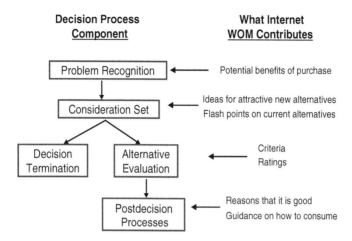

FIG. 2.1   The impact of Internet WOM on consumer decision-making processes.

& Koenig, 2002; Muniz & O'Guinn, 2001). Applying our findings on the motives for using online WOM, such search sites could promote their entertainment value as well as their usefulness in aiding consumer purchase decisions.

WOM Information and the Consumer Decision Process

The results of our interviews indicate that the influence of Internet WOM information may be broadly spread throughout the decision process (see Fig. 2.1). A fellow consumer's mention of a product or a potential product benefit could stimulate problem recognition. Other consumers could provide ideas that would lead an alternative to be included in a consumer's consideration set or information that could lead to an alternative being removed from the consideration set. If after consideration of the WOM information there were no viable alternatives remaining, then the information would have contributed to decision termination. If more than one viable alternative remains, then online WOM suggesting important attributes could influence the criteria by which these alternatives are compared. Information from other consumers concerning how the alternatives rate on important attributes could also affect alternative evaluation. After a purchase has been made, online WOM could increase the consumer's satisfaction with the choice by providing reassuring positive information and by helping to resolve consumption-related problems. Finally, while this figure focuses on medium- and high-involvement decision-making situations, it is clear from our research that Internet WOM also affects low-involvement decision-making. In particular, consumers are passively exposed to Internet WOM when browsing or searching for information with an entertainment motive. This information is likely to affect subsequent low-involvement decisions.

Each of these decision-process influences could be considered separate effects, and each could constitute a productive topic for further research. For example, the observation that a decision alternative can be removed from further consideration by only a single piece of online WOM information may provide an approach to investigating this form of heuristic processing in consumer decision-making. Future research could focus on what types of attributes are likely to serve as such "flash points" and in what decision situations are flash points most likely to be used. This line of investigation could potentially provide insight into the mechanisms by which consumers manage their consideration sets in an increasingly information-rich environment.

Conclusions

The Internet has made it possible for consumers to easily discuss product-related information and experiences with other people. This ease of information exchange greatly enhances the potential impact of WOM on the consumer. Our study examines this increasingly important phenomenon, reinforcing findings from earlier research on WOM effects and identifying new possibilities for WOM effects within the online environment.

Our research provides direction for better managing and facilitating consumer-to-consumer interactions on the Internet. Understanding consumers' motives for seeking out information can aid in the design of sites most likely to attract consumers with specific information needs. Understanding how consumers evaluate WOM content can provide guidance in eliciting posted reviews (forms to use, how much personal information to provide, etc.), as well as disclosure policies to help assure the validity of reviews. Finally, understanding the impact of WOM on decision-making processes can help marketers to better utilize online WOM to encourage purchase and consumption. For example, marketers may want to target those consumers most likely to post reviews or participate in discussion forums since, through such behaviors, these consumers serve as opinion leaders. In addition, marketers may be able to apply what we have learned about effective WOM messages to help motivate desirable but difficult behaviors, such as weight loss or exercise.

This research program not only has practical implications, but can also help us better understand the mechanisms by which WOM communication exerts its powerful effects on consumer behavior in other (offline) contexts. For example, the criteria used to evaluate online WOM are also likely to be used in other contexts. Earlier research on WOM has had limited access to the actual dialog between the information provider and the seeker. Future research can take advantage of the "frozen chunks" of WOM exchanges saved on the Internet to more effectively study what makes a persuasive message and the effects of such messages on buyer behavior.

ACKNOWLEDGMENTS

This research was supported by the Rutgers University, School of Business-Camden Dean's Fund. We would like to thank Frederic Brunel, Joe Phelps, and Julie Ruth for their constructive input on an earlier draft of this manuscript, and Erica Cretarolo for her assistance with this research.

REFERENCES

Alon, A., Brunel, F., & Siegal, W. S. (2005). Ritual behavior and community change: Exploring the social-psychological roles of net rituals in the developmental process of online consumption communities. In C. P. Haugtvedt, K. A. Machleit, & R. F. Yalch (Eds.), *Online consumer psychology: Understanding and influencing consumer behavior in the virtual world* (pp. 7–34). Mahwah, NJ: Lawrence Erlbaum Associates.

Alreck, P. L., & Settle, R. B. (1995). The importance of word-of-mouth communication to service buyers. In D. W. Stewart & N. J. Vilcassim (Eds.), *1995 AMA Winder Educators' Proceedings* (pp. 188–193). Chicago: American Marketing Association.

Arndt, J. (1967). Role of product-related conversations in the diffusion of a new product. *Journal of Marketing Research, 4*(August), 291–295.

Bickart, B., & Schindler, R. M. (2001). Internet forums as influential sources of consumer information. *Journal of Interactive Marketing, 15*(Summer), 31–52.

Bloch, P. H., Ridgway, N. M., & Sherrell, D. L. (1989). Extending the concept of shopping: An investigation of browsing activity. *Academy of Marketing Science Journal, 17*(Winter), 13–22.

Bloch, P. H., Sherrell, D. L., & Ridgway, N. M. (1986). Consumer search: An extended framework. *Journal of Consumer Research, 14*(December), 119–127.

Boush, D. M., & Kahle, L. (2001). What, and how, we can learn from online consumer discussion groups. Unpublished Manuscript, University of Oregon, Eugene, OR.

Brinsley, J. (2000, September 4). Hobbit hype. *Los Angeles Times Business Journal*, p 1.

Brown, J. J., & Reingen, P. H. (1987). Social ties and word-of-mouth referral behavior. *Journal of Consumer Research, 14*(December), 350–362.

Bussiere, D. (2000). Evidence and implications of electronic word of mouth. In H. E. Spotts & H. L. Meadow (Eds.), *Proceedings of the Annual Conference of the Academy of Marketing Science*, 23, (pp. 361).

Chatterjee, P. (2000). *Online consumer reviews: Do consumers use them?* Paper presented at the 2000 Association of Consumer Research Annual Conference, Salt Lake City, UT.

Claxton, J. D., Fry, J. N., & Portis, B. (1974). A taxonomy of prepurchase information gathering patterns. *Journal of Consumer Research, 1*(December), 35–42.

Constant, D., Sproull, L., & Kiesler, S. (1997). The kindness of strangers: On the usefulness of electronic weak ties for technical advice. In S. Kiesler (Ed.), *Culture of the Internet* (pp. 303–321). Mahwah, NJ: Lawrence Erlbaum Associates.

Crowley, A. E., & Hoyer, W. D. (1994). An integrative framework for understanding two-sided persuasion. *Journal of Consumer Research, 20*(March), 561–574.

Cummings, W. H., & Venkatesan, M. (1976). Cognitive dissonance and consumer behavior: A review of the evidence. *Journal of Marketing Research, 13*(August), 303–308.

Dichter, E. (1966, November/December). How word-of-mouth advertising works. *Harvard Business Review*, 147–166.

Duhan, D. F., Johnson, S. D., Wilcox, J. B., & Harrell, G. D. (1997). Influences on consumer use of word-of-mouth recommendation sources. *Journal of the Academy of Marketing Science, 25*(4), 283–295.

Dye, R. (2000, November/December). The buzz on buzz. *Harvard Business Review*, 139–146.

Eagly, A. H., Wood, W., & Chaiken, S. (1978). Causal inferences about communicators and their effects on opinion change. *Journal of Personality and Social Psychology, 36*(April), 424–435.

Engel, J. F., Blackwell, R. D., & Miniard, P. W. (1995). *Consumer behavior* (8th ed.). Fort Worth, TX: The Dryden Press.

Feldman, S. P., & Spencer, M. C. (1965). The effect of personal influence in the selection of consumer services. In P. D. Bennett (Ed.), *Proceedings of the Fall Conference of the American Marketing Association* (pp. 440–452). Chicago: American Marketing Association.

Festinger, L. (1957). *A theory of cognitive dissonance.* Stanford, CA: Stanford University Press.

Fisher, E., Bristor, J., & Gainer, B. (1996). Creating or escaping community? An exploratory study of Internet consumers' behavior. In K. P. Corfman & J. G. Lynch, Jr. (Eds.), *Advances in consumer research* (Vol. 23, pp. 178–182). Provo, UT: Association for Consumer Research.

Friedkin, N. (1982). Information flow through strong and weak ties in intraorganizational social networks. *Social Networks, 3*, 273–285.

Gitelson, R., & Crompton, J. L. (1983). The planning horizons and sources of information used by pleasure vacationers. *Journal of Travel Research, 21*(Winter), 2–7.

Granitz, N. A., & Ward, J. C. (1996). Virtual community: A sociocognitive analysis. In K. P. Corfman & J. G. Lynch, Jr. (Eds.), *Advances in consumer research*, (Vol. 23, pp. 163–166). Provo, UT: Association for Consumer Research.

Granovetter, M. S. (1973). The strength of weak ties. *American Journal of Sociology, 78*(May), 1360–1380.

Hass, R. G. (1981). Effects of source characteristics on cognitive responses and persuasion. In R. E. Petty, T. M. Ostrom, & T. C. Brock (Eds.), *Cognitive responses in persuasion* (pp. 141–172). Hillsdale, NJ: Lawrence Erlbaum Associates.

Holt, D. B. (1995). How consumers consume: A typology of consumption practices. *Journal of Consumer Research, 22*(June), 1–16.

Hovland, C. I., & Weiss, W. (1951). The influence of source credibility on communication effectiveness. *Public Opinion Quarterly, 15*(Winter), 635–650.

Katz, E., & Lazarsfeld, P. F. (1955). *Personal influence: The part played by people in the flow of mass communication.* Glencoe, IL: Free Press.

Lewis, R., Phelps, J. E., Mobilio, L., & Raman, N. (2005). Understanding pass-along emails: Motivations and behaviors of viral consumers. In C. P. Haugtvedt, K. A. Machleit, & R. F. Yalch (Eds.), *Online consumer psychology: Understanding and influencing consumer behavior in the virtual world* (pp. 63–100). Mahwah, NJ: Lawrence Erlbaum Associates.

McAlexander, J. H., Schouten, J. W., & Koenig, H. F. (2002). Building brand community. *Journal of Marketing, 66*(January), 38–54.

McGuire, W. J. (1969). The nature of attitudes and attitude change. In G. Lindzey & E. Aronson (Eds.), *The handbook of social psychology* (Vol. 3, 2nd ed., pp. 136–314). Reading, MA: Addison-Wesley.

Mizerski, R. W. (1982). An attribution explanation of the disproportionate influence of unfavorable information. *Journal of Consumer Research, 9*(December), 301–310.

Muniz, A. M., Jr., & O'Guinn, T. C. (2001). Brand community. *Journal of Consumer Research, 27*(March), 412–432.

Nedungadi, P. (1990). Recall and consumer consideration sets: Influencing choice without altering brand evaluations. *Journal of Consumer Research, 17*(December), 263–276.

Nielsen/NetRatings (2004). United States Weekly Web Usage Data, Retrieved Sept. 2004 from http://nielsen-netratings.com

Okleshen, C., & Grossbart, S. (1998). Usenet groups, virtual communities, and consumer behaviors. In J. W. Alba & J. W. Hutchinson (Eds.), *Advances in consumer research* (Vol. 25, pp. 276–282). Provo, UT: Association for Consumer Research.

Pechmann, C. (1992). Predicting when two-sided ads will be more effective than one-sided ads: The role of correlational and correspondent inferences. *Journal of Marketing Research, 29*(November), 441–453.

Price, L. L., & Feick, L. F., (1984). The role of interpersonal sources in external search: An informational perspective. In T. C. Kinnear (Ed.) *Advances in consumer research* (Vol. 11, pp. 250–255). Ann Acbov, MI: Association for Consumer Research.

Price, L. L., Feick, L. F., & Higie, R. A. (1989). Preference heterogeneity and coorientation as determinants of perceived informational influence. *Journal of Business Research, 19*(November), 227–242.

Ratneshwar, S., & Chaiken, S. (1991). Comprehension's role in persuasion: The case of its moderating effect on the persuasive impact of source cues. *Journal of Consumer Research, 18*(June), 52–62.

Rogers, E. M. (1983). *Diffusion of innovations.* New York: Free Press.

Ruth, J. A., Otnes, C. C., & Brunel. F. F. (1999). Gift receipt and the reformulation of interpersonal relationships. *Journal of Consumer Research, 25*(March), 385–402.

Schiffman, L. G., & Kanuk, L. L. (2000). *Consumer behavior* (7th ed.). Upper Saddle River, NJ: Prentice Hall.

Schlosser, A., & Kanfer, A. (2002). *Impact of product interactivity on searchers' and browsers' judgments: Implications for commercial Web site effectiveness.* Paper presented at the 2001 Online Consumer Psychology Conference, Seattle, WA.

Schoenberger, C. R. (2000, September 4). The opiners. *Forbes,* p. 123.

Shocker, A. D., Ben-Akiva, M., Boccara, B., & Nedungadi, P. (1991). Consideration set influences on consumer decision-making and choice: Issues, models, and suggestions. *Marketing Letters, 2*(3), 181–197.

Stepanek, M. (2000, May 15). Tell me a (digital) story: Companies build brand by allowing their customers to share tales online. *Business Week,* p. EB90.

Swan, J. E., & Oliver R. L. (1989). Postpurchase communications by consumers. *Journal of Retailing, 65*(Winter), 516–533.

Weinberger, M. C., & Dillon, W. R. (1980). The effects of unfavorable product information. In J. C. Olson (Ed.), *Advances in Consumer Research* (Vol. 7, pp. 528–532). Ann Arbor, MI: Association for Consumer Research.

Westbrook, R. A., & Fornell, C. (1979). Patterns of information source usage among durable goods buyers. *Journal of Marketing Research, 16*(August), 303–312.

White, E. (1999, October 5). Chatting' a singer up the pop charts. *The Wall Street Journal,* p. B1.

Whyte, W. H., Jr. (1954). The web of word of mouth. *Fortune, 50*(November), 140–143.

Wilson, E. J., & Sherrell, D. L. (1993). Source effects in communication and persuasion research: A meta-analysis of effect size. *Journal of the Academy of Marketing Science, 21*(Spring), 101–112.

Wilson, W. R., & Peterson, R. E. (1989). Some limits on the potency of word-of-mouth information. In T. K. Srull (Ed.), *Advances in Consumer Research* (Vol. 16, pp. 23–29). Provo, UT: Association for Consumer Research.

CHAPTER THREE

Understanding Pass-Along Emails: Motivations and Behaviors of Viral Consumers

Regina Lewis
Lynne Mobilio
Lewis, Mobilio & Associates

Joseph E. Phelps
The University of Alabama

Niranjan (Nick) Raman
ImpactRx Inc.

Whether one agrees or disagrees with Godin's (2000) claim that permission marketing and one-to-one marketing are passé, it is clear that the marketing communications landscape is at the threshold of dramatic change. Marketers are at the center of the old landscape—and within this landscape, communication flows primarily from the marketer out to targeted groups of consumers. In contrast, in the new networked age, consumers will be at the center and information will flow more freely in all directions (from consumer to consumer, from consumer to business, and from business to consumer). Of course, the biggest change occurring is in the increased amount of consumer-to-consumer communication possible now that so many people are online. This change holds tremendous opportunity for marketers willing to adapt and to develop messages that consumers are then willing to share with one another.

In the online world, turning your customers into your marketing force means having customers that will initiate and pass along positive email messages about your product or service to others. By definition, viral consumers are much more likely than non viral consumers to share their opinions and information with a wide range of people. Despite the potential power viral consumers exercise via these electronic word-of-mouth activities, almost nothing is known about the motivations, attitudes, and behaviors associated with creating and passing along email to others. This lack of understanding is surprising as the ability to encourage and/or generate such pass-along activity constitutes an essential component of any viral marketing strategy.

In a recent program of research, the authors of this chapter traveled the country to conduct focus group sessions with potential viral consumers; they also became included on these consumers' email lists for a month. The overall goal of the research was to better understand the attitudes, motivations, and behaviors of people receiving and forwarding pass-along email. It is only by understanding these motivations and behaviors that marketers can hope to tap into this rich vein of communication and advocacy.

Viral Marketing and Research Backdrop

According to a report of The Pew Internet & Life Project (2000), emailing is the number one Internet activity. Ninety-one percent of the respondents to their tracking poll reported sending email. Projecting their findings, they estimate that some 48 million Americans, or 87% of Internet users who access the Internet on a given day, send and read email each day. Furthermore, they report that 84 million Americans have used email, and that Americans send more than 285 million emails on a typical day.

While individuals are using email to communicate with family, friends, and co-workers, marketers are using email to communicate with customers and prospective customers. The growth projections for email marketing are staggering. According to a leading Market research firm, Forrester Research, the average household will receive nine email marketing messages a day (that is, 3,285 a year) in 2004 (Priore, 2000). Among the forces driving the growth of email marketing are the low cost (to the marketer), the ability to selectively target messages, and high response rates relative to other forms of direct consumer communication. However, as the field and consumers' electronic mailboxes become more crowded, response rates are likely to fall. In fact, email saturation and misuse (spam) of the medium may already be depressing response rates (Priore, 2000). Consumers often are quick to hit the delete key when they know the message is from a marketer.

Consumers are much more reluctant, however, to delete a message from a person they know—and it is difficult to contest the argument that "buzz" plays a critical role in the purchasing process for many products. This is perhaps most clearly expressed by Rosen (2000) when he says, "[Purchasing] is part of a social process.... It involves not only a one-to-one interaction between the company and the customer but also many exchanges of information and influence among the people who surround the customer" (p. 6) Rosen posits that important invisible networks comprise hubs (people well-positioned to share information), clusters (areas of dense connections), and connections among clusters. Within these networks, he says, "You notice a constant flow of green sparks between certain nodes. These are comments. This is buzz" (Rosen, 2000, p. 8).

We, the authors of this chapter, view viral marketing as the process of encouraging honest communication among consumers, across their networks; we focus on the use of email as the channel of communication.

Our focus developed based upon the following considerations. First, consumers are influenced by information they receive from other consumers. For example, the diffusion literature (e.g., Rogers, 1995) would suggest that persuasion is more likely to be accomplished via interpersonal communication, such as consumers communicating through email, than via typical mass media advertising and promotional activities. Given what is known about source effects, such a statement is not surprising. Over the years, a number of studies (such as Price & Feick, 1984; Udell, 1966) have endorsed the influence of interpersonal sources and the impact of this communication on choices (Arndt, 1967). However, advertisers tapping viral efforts are hoping that such consumer-to-consumer communication also will prove effective at building knowledge and awareness for their products and services. The hope is that by encouraging this communication among consumers, important perceptions about products—as well as compelling triggers for purchase—will spread quickly and widely, thereby achieving mass reach a few people at a time. Put differently, marketers strive to accomplish what Gladwell (2000) has labeled the tipping point, that moment when any social phenomenon reaches critical mass, through the efforts of a handful of exceptional influencers; the stickiness factor, or specific ways in which a contagious message is made memorable; and environmental circumstances and conditions that encourage a virus to be unleashed.

If they are to accomplish viral marketing goals, however, marketers will need to understand which consumers are most likely to help pass these messages along and what motivates them to do so. In short, they need to understand the viral consumer. Feick and Price (1987) suggest that such consumers may be motivated to spread the word for use in social exchanges and to benefit family, friends, and acquaintances. Thus, while the diffusion literature provides useful insights regarding the identification of, and the role played by, opinion leaders, uses and gratifications research may provide insights into the motivations of and rewards experienced by consumers sending and receiving email. For those interested in examining potential theoretical foundations of the viral marketing topic, scholarly research in such areas as social and communication networks, opinion leadership, uses and gratifications, and diffusion of innovations, to name just a few areas, can provide insights.

Second, there are a number of ways in which word of mouth can spread via the Internet. For a review of what is known about Internet word of mouth and a discussion about how consumers find and use this marketplace information, see Chapter 2 by Schindler and Bickart. We decided to examine interpersonal communication via email because it has become, like postal mail and the telephone had earlier, a common channel for interpersonal communication. Importantly, there are also some uncommon characteristics of email that played a role in its selection. For example, a person can communicate with a larger number of others, more quickly and more easily, via email than many of the other channels. Passing along an email message is even easier than writing one's own comments. Furthermore, pass-along email seems particularly well-suited for the spread of images and/or verbal content that is too detailed to be spread in what has traditionally been known as word of mouth.

A Series of Three Studies

To better understand the attitudes, motivations and behaviors associated with pass-along email, we conducted three interrelated studies. In this section of the chapter, we briefly describe each study. Later, we present findings.

First, focus groups helped us to identify and assess participants' rational and emotional connections with pass-along email and senders of those messages and the reactions pass-along email evoke. Trained moderators spoke with 66 individuals in a total of eight focus groups conducted in Atlanta (GA), Cincinnati (OH), Buffalo (NY), and Los Angeles (CA). Potential recruits, all of whom spend at least 4 hours online per week, were asked the following question:

> Some people send jokes, stories, or other information to groups of people they have organized into email lists. Do you ever *receive* this kind of "group" email from your friends or colleagues?

Those who affirmed receipt of group email were asked further questions to determine whether they received and sent pass-along email frequently—therefore falling into a group we called "Viral Mavens"—or whether they are less avid about sending these emails along—therefore falling into a group we termed "Infrequent Senders." Importantly, all participants in our study expressed clear understanding of the concept of pass along, or viral, email. To absolutely ensure this understanding, however, we emphasized that by pass-along email, we mean email that you receive from someone you know, which that person most likely has received from someone they know, and so on and so on. Fig. 3.1 helps explain what we mean a little better.

In the second phase of our study, we requested that focus group participants invite us into their actual email "living rooms." At the close of all Viral Maven groups and one Infrequent Senders group, participants were offered the opportunity to participate in the empirical phase of this research.

FIG. 3.1   Basic anatomy of a pass-along email.

To ensure understanding, we conducted training sessions in which participants were asked to send us every pass-along email that they received over the course of a month—both those emails that they passed on to others as well as those messages that they decided to quash. Participants were urged to pass along all emails that they received—even those that may be salacious in content or tone. (From the number of people who sent quite risqué emails, it would appear that participants did not hesitate out of concern for how they would be perceived by study leaders!) Thirty-four people participated in the 4-week study and we received 1,259 pass-along emails.

Finally, in-depth interviews with these same participants provided communication motivation data to better understand potentially viral consumers. Of the 34 people who participated in the second study, we were able to personally interview 23 individuals by phone or by email.

Many findings we consider both interesting and important are covered in the pages that follow. We begin by providing background information about our respondents' attitudes toward email in general as well as their email practices. Next, we take a phenomenological approach by adopting the perspective of a viral consumer and detailing the events, decision points, and emotional reactions that unfold during one full pass-along email episode. Finally, we discuss how pass-along email meshes with broader American archetypes, as well as the impending and critical implications viral marketing has for marketers.

Email's Life-Changing Impact

It was no surprise, given their length of time online, that our respondents were not new to email. Our Viral Mavens are avid users; almost all spend at least one hour on email a day, with many spending upwards of four hours or more. Our Infrequent Senders also use email fairly extensively; about half said they are online at least one hour per day.

Viral Mavens believe that email brings great value to their lives; all, without exception, agreed with the statement "Would you say email has changed your life?" The bulk of respondents' answers to this question revolved around themes of maintaining contact with family and friends. In fact, the one self-admitted introvert in the groups stated that email "compensates for my introversion." Other comments included the following:

> "Friends who are far away are suddenly close . . . It brings everything closer."
>
> "I'm able to keep in touch with family and friends on a much more casual basis. It used to be the every Sunday call to my father. Now it's drop him 4 lines a few times a week. I feel much more in touch with my family and friends than with 5 cent Sundays."

In addition, Viral Mavens feel that they are able to pursue friendships that would not flower without email—either because they meet a new circle of friends in the online space or because it deepens connections that they have initially made in the offline world. As one participant stated: "[Email has] brought us in touch with people we'd thought about calling, but it's easier now."

These viral consumers also see great advantages to email in the work context, of course. Several stated that email renders their days more efficient and lends accountability that was absent in the pre-email work context. For example: "I like the fact that I don't get caught in long telephone conversations when it's business." "Great for setting up meetings."

When we asked the Infrequent Senders whether they felt email had changed their lives, we again were met, for the most part, with affirmative nods. Voicing similar themes, these study participants indicated email had made them more productive and efficient (by allowing them to get through to others) and brought them closer to their families.

> "[With email] You can achieve a new level of communication—I just feel a lot more efficient."
>
> "I keep in touch with people more now . . . I've found it to be a great tool—good when you don't really want to talk with people."
>
> "[Email] keeps you in touch with people who are sort of in your life . . . you wouldn't bother to call or send a letter but you email."
>
> "[With email, you] can communicate with family and friends easier, on your own time. You can send when you want and they respond when they want."

To better understand spheres of email influence, we asked whether consumers had address books set up at home and at work. The great majority of participants had address books either at home or at work, or in both places. Viral Mavens appear to have larger address books than do Infrequent Senders. When asked how many names their address books contained, Infrequent Senders provided numbers that appear relatively low. Three fourths of these respondents from whom we collected precise counts said they have 25 names or fewer in their address books; in many cases these counts were for home and work combined. No one reported having more than 40 names in total. (The only exception was where their employers had provided them with large company-wide lists.) In contrast, home address books of Viral Mavens typically include between 25 and 50 names. Participants who were especially viral—those who spend several hours a day on email and send multiple pass-along messages each day—reported having even more names in their address books.

Standing in the Shoes of a Viral Consumer

There is no doubt that wired consumers are passionately connected to email—this mode of communication has produced powerful repercussions throughout their personal and professional lives. What we were interested in, more specifically, were consumers' connections to a particular specie of email—pass-along email. To ensure that we were using intuitive terminology around this pass-along email

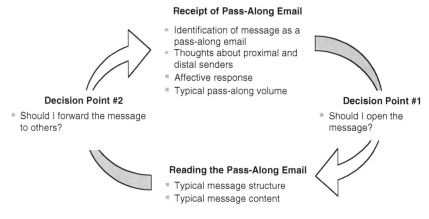

Receipt of Pass-Along Email

* Identification of message as a pass-along email
* Thoughts about proximal and distal senders
* Affective response
* Typical pass-along volume

Decision Point #2

* Should I forward the message to others?

Decision Point #1

* Should I open the message?

Reading the Pass-Along Email

* Typical message structure
* Typical message content

FIG. 3.2   Typical email episode.

topic, we asked people "What words would you use to describe the different pass-along messages we've been talking about?" Respondents had a few suggestions, including "Forwards," "Chain," "Junk mail," "Mass email," "Spam," and "Forwarded email," but the pass-along terminology seemed to be clear and intuitive.

In this section, we detail our findings throughout a pass-along email episode—from the realization that one has received a pass-along email, to the decision to open the email, to content and features of typical viral messages, through to the decision whether to forward the message to others. (see Fig. 3.2).

The Beginning—Receipt of a Pass-Along Email

Upon logging into his or her email account, the typical pass-along email participant finds it quite easy to distinguish pass-along email from other types of messages by virtue of a quick scan of the email queue. The typical viral consumer will identify an email as of the pass-along variety if they recognize the subject line and have received the message before; or if they see Fwd: Fwd: Fwd: in the subject line; or if they recognize the particular sender of the email. These immediate cues of sender and subject line can quickly inform consumers that they have received a pass-along email before they even open the message.

People's Perceptions of Pass-Along Senders.   Senders are perhaps most salient to viral consumers when they scan their email inboxes. When we explored the motivations that people attribute to these senders of pass-along emails, Viral Mavens and Infrequent Senders alike attributed largely positive motivations to the senders; the most frequent motivation mentioned, as illustrated in the comments below, was desire to connect and share with others.

"Sometimes people have specifically thought of me, for some reason."
"It's like conversation . . . it lifts somebody up."

"Ideally it's people who know you well enough to know that you'd appreciate something."

"I think for some people it's a way to share a part of themselves."

Other motivations ranged from the evangelical, to the superstitious, to the mundane. These categories include:

- Desire to humor others: "I think my one friend just loves to make people laugh."
- Evangelical: "They really want to spread the message."
- Superstition: "People may not know much about the Internet yet—they pass it along just in case."
- Altruistic desire to save others from harm: "Because they're concerned [about the product warnings]." "Because they believe a hoax or warning."
- Impression-management concerns: "People want others to know that they know things."
- Entertainment: "People have too much time on their hands." "Sometimes it's fun to pass them on."
- Desire to comfort self or others: "I have other friends who just send if they know I'm going through a stressful time, to lift my spirits." "I think it is therapy for some people."

It is intriguing that the motivations attributed to senders were so positive, even though the experience of receiving pass-along emails can be negative at times. Consumers truly seem to separate the intended effect of pass-along email—viewed largely as positive—from its sometimes negative reality.

People's Perceptions of the Origin of Pass-Along Email. If viral consumers know the senders of their pass-along email quite well, it may be easy to determine why a sender forwarded a particular message. We were interested in consumers' perceptions of senders that were several generations (by generations we mean the number of send and receive cycles visible in the text of the message) removed from the known individual. We asked our focus group participants to brainstorm where pass-along emails originate. The immediate response in all groups—viral and non-viral alike—was a variant of "people with too much time." Others stated that the genesis for many of these emails is the Internet itself—Joke of the Day sites, for example, or other Web sites dedicated to humorous material. Still other mentions included "somebody with a lot of friends," "somebody with a political cause," "somebody in the church who wants to do lessons on the Internet," and someone who truly had experienced a trauma ("that letter . . . about the kidnapped girl was started by her father").

To probe perceptions of senders of pass-along email a bit differently, we asked Infrequent Senders to paint us a portrait of the type of person they picture when thinking about pass-along senders. People in Atlanta and Los Angeles communicated surprisingly positive descriptions. In particular, Infrequent Senders in these cities viewed pass-along email senders as outgoing, gregarious, jovial, intelligent, generous, giving, and passionate. "[They are] real nice people and they're doing it so I'll feel good . . . I have a real positive outlook on who sends me these group things because they're trying to help me."

Cincinnati and Buffalo participants also mentioned positive traits in their descriptions, but they were more likely to see senders as somewhat insecure and hermit-like, as busybodies, as the class clown, or perhaps too busy to keep in touch in a more personal manner.

How Receiving Pass-Along Emails Makes People Feel.   Not only does reception of a pass-along email spark thoughts about the sender but emotions are elicited as well. An important objective of all focus group sessions was to gain insight into people's emotional reactions to receipt of pass-along emails. To accomplish this, moderators asked participants how they feel when pass-along emails are forwarded to them.

Certainly, the affective experience of receiving pass-along email is mixed, with people reporting both positive and negative emotions. We found, however, that the emotions—and their stimuli—are markedly similar between Viral Maven and Infrequent Sender groups. Figures 3.3 and 3.4 show the types of emotion mentioned by research participants, as well as the conditions under which they experience commonly mentioned emotions.

Most interesting here, perhaps, is that many respondents—viral and non-viral—talked about their reaction to pass-along email in the context of their own moods/mindsets. If they feel rushed or if they are having a bad day at work, they report frustration or annoyance. Moreover, many people were quick to state that the negative feelings that they do experience do NOT color their perceptions of the senders.

> "If you're in a bad mood and get something like that then you're like aaarrrhhhh . . . it makes it worse."
>
> "It depends where you are: If I'm at work, I feel disrupted . . . if I'm at home I'm glad to get the email from my friends . . . I'm glad to get the email if I'm doing it on my time."
>
> "[Good emotions apply] when I have some free time and I'm not stressed out."

One interesting trend among Viral Mavens was that some participants described negative emotions that they would experience in the absence of pass-along email.

> "If I had ever gone and I didn't have any emails, I would be upset because I'm so used to being in that circle . . . that's acceptance, that's you know I'm in there, let's do this.

Viral Mavens	Infrequent Senders
Good	Good
❏ someone is thinking about me	❏ someone is thinking about me
❏ when I'm not too busy	❏ I'm staying in touch
❏ when it's sent to you personally	❏ when I have free time
Happy / Brightens my day	Happy / Brightens my day
❏ when it's someone I haven't heard from	❏ when it's someone I haven't heard from in a while
Excited	❏ when the message is a good joke, is inspirational,
❏ "It's like seeing a letter in the mail …	contains helpful advice
you look at the top left-hand corner and	Curious
you're excited to see who it's from"	❏ about new or infrequent senders
Connected	❏ will the message be good?
❏ even though we don't have an opportunity to talk	Relief
Rewarded	❏ relief of tension at work
❏ when I get something from church	❏ makes me laugh
❏ when I get certain "pictures"— meaning sexual	Glad
content	❏ if the content is good
Anticipation	❏ if I'm anxious to hear from the sender
Inspired	Anticipation
Makes me feel special	Interested

FIG. 3.3   Positive emotional responses to receiving pass-along email.

"If she didn't send me one day, I would say, What's going on?"

"[When you return from vacation, you wonder] what have you missed? Who's talking to you? When you go away, you're more inclined to sit there and reply to all of those because you're basically trying to communicate. You're anxious to find out what's on there. You want to keep up that conversation."

The Sheer Number of Pass-Along Emails.   Thankfully for those who dread the absence of pass-along email, we found that—for Viral Mavens especially— receipt of pass-along email was quite frequent. During the empirical phase of our research, we received 1,259 pass-along messages, which averages to more than one pass-along message a day from each person. There was, however, incredible variety in the volume of email received across our participants. One individual received (and forwarded) 177 messages during the month; a total of three participants sent more than 100 messages each during the course of the study. At the low end, we had three participants who sent just one message during the same 4-week time

Viral Mavens	Infrequent Senders
Irritated	Irritated
❑ when the message is irrelevant	❑ that I'm one in a crowd
❑ when it feels like it's wasting my time	❑ when I've had a bad day
❑ by too much "spiritual stuff"	❑ when I've asked to be taken off the list
❑ by too many messages from one person	❑ when it's been months since I've received
Angry	a personal message from the sender
❑ when I've asked to be taken off a list	Aggravated
❑ when content is offensive or shocking	❑ when I receive the same message repeatedly
Disappointed	❑ when one person sends too many messages
❑ when I want a personal note from someone	Frustrated
Skeptical	❑ that I don't have the time to read a message
❑ about an offer that is too good to be true	Obligated
Burdened	❑ too much hassle to pass it on
❑ when I have too much work	Disgusted
❑ when I feel overwhelmed	❑ at "wrong" kinds of jokes
❑ when I feel obligated to answer	Stressed
Overwhelmed	Disrupted
❑ when I'm spending too much time	
on email	
Uninterested	

FIG. 3.4 Negative emotional responses to receiving pass-along email.

span; two of these were in the Infrequent Senders group. Figure 3.5 illustrates the volume of email the research team received from each of the 34 participants as well as the number forwarded by each participant.

Viral Mavens received many more messages than did Infrequent Senders. On average, Viral Mavens received almost twice as many pass-along emails (42 messages) than Infrequent Senders received (22 messages). This finding, based on actual behavior, validates the respondents' subjective self-evaluation. In other words, their behavior matches the verbal reports offered in the focus groups.

It is important to note that, if anything, this volume may underestimate the volume of email typically received by Viral Mavens; one third of people in the follow-up interviews stated that their email volumes were abnormally low during the course of the study. The LoveBug virus scare took place during this phase of data collection, and pass-along activity from respondents slowed down for a little over a week before rebounding.

Number of Pass-Along Emails Received vs. Sent By Each Participant

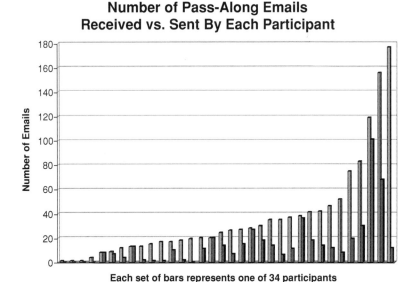

FIG. 3.5 Pass–along emails received and forwarded.

Decision Point #1: To Open or to Delete?

The fact that people receive pass-along email messages does not necessarily mean that they open all of them. During the focus groups, at least one third of each viral group said that, at times, they automatically delete messages without opening them. Infrequent Senders also reported deleting messages without viewing content.

Sender name was most commonly cited as the determinant of whether a pass-along email was opened or immediately deleted. Respondents commonly open emails only if they are from somebody they know. However, knowing the source can also trigger the automatic delete decision if the sender is perceived as someone who sends too many messages or who sends low-quality messages.

Aspects of the message itself also cause respondents to delete pass-along emails without opening them. For example, if the receiver recognizes the subject line and have received the message before or if see Fwd: Fwd: Fwd: in the subject line, they may delete the message. Emails containing attachments drove deletions for two reasons: respondents suspected they carried viruses and respondents anticipated long download times.

In addition to these cues, which center on characteristics of the sender and of the message itself, respondents also commonly make the decision to open or delete based on their own states of mind and their own contexts. For example, respondents are apt to delete a message without reading it if they are pressed for time or if it appears that the content is inappropriate.

"[I delete it] if it is obvious it is a chain letter . . . or I don't have time to deal with it. It depends on my mood."
"[I open it] if it's someone I know . . . it depends on how much time I have that day or how busy I am."
"If it's short I'll look at it. It depends on whether I'm in the mood for a joke at that time . . . if I'm not, I'll just delete it and move on."
"[I delete] when I'm tired and I don't want to read 'em anymore."

Reading the Email—Typical Message Structure and Content

Much pass-along email makes it to the opening stage so that receivers actually peruse the content of the message. Our examination of message structure showed that the average pass-along email contained three generations and included the email addresses of 26 individuals throughout the message. There was no difference between the emails of Viral Mavens and Infrequent Senders on these two dimensions.

In all focus groups, the first type of pass-along email mentioned was jokes. To consumers, jokes represent the prototype of pass-along email; jokes seem to be the type that people receive most frequently, and the type that they are most apt to pass along. Also among all groups, however, there was unaided mention of multiple other message strains—virus alerts, inspirational (lesson learned) and religious stories, requests to vote on certain issues, lost children notices, chain letters, poems, animated clips, pass-along emails with links to specific Web sites, and urban legends. In terms of this last strain, respondents specifically mentioned receiving emails that were purportedly from the GAP, a clothing retailer with a focus on youth. These emails promised GAP gift certificates, worth from $25 to $35 depending on the version of the hoax, to those who would forward the email to seven friends. The GAP hoax was one of many that fall into the urban legend strain. For example, respondents mentioned receiving other hoax emails that were purportedly from or about other corporate interests such as KFC, Coke, Pokemon, and Bill Gates. They also mentioned receiving similar hoax emails concerning health warnings, such as the flesh eating banana and tampon warnings. Reactions to this strain vary in positivity:

"I think of things that make me laugh; that's one thing I like about it . . . one way [email] has changed my life."
"I also got the KFC ad; it changed my life in that I'm totally into my health and so I stopped eating it because I just wasn't sure; I just think it can go both ways, but like, you never know what's authentic."
"[I get] those stupid emails that say if you call this company you get this amount of money."

"I got one saying Pokemon was a tool of Satan. I didn't read it...I said 'come on!'"

"They're just a waste of time, some of them."

It is interesting to note that many of the specific emails mentioned in groups were referenced in more than one city, witness to how pass-along email can permeate geographic boundaries.

All emails that respondents received during the 4-week study were coded into content categories. To develop these categories, the research team first reviewed all of the focus-group tapes to ensure all types of messages that were mentioned were represented in the coding scheme. Then, the team did an initial examination of all of the messages received during the empirical research period. As a result of these reviews, we created 16 general categories, 7 of which were broken into more specific subcategories. To maximize consistency, the research team trained one primary coder who was responsible for sorting all 1,259 messages into their appropriate categories. As part of the training process, multiple coders sorted random subsets of messages to ensure that inter-rater reliability would be adequate. In addition, throughout coding, spot checks were done to ensure that coding continued to be accurate.

As shown in Table 3.1, almost half of the emails received in our research email box were joke emails. Chain letters were also common, representing about one of every five emails received. The table shows percentage of emails passed along by category and also provides more specific information about how messages sorted. General jokes were most common, followed by jokes of a sexual nature. Interestingly, a very low number of emails were overtly about products and/or companies (1.2%). This finding suggests that either advertisers are not exploiting this method of communicating with consumers or that their messages are not meeting the pass-along threshold. Implications and suggestions related to this, and other findings, are discussed later in this chapter. Although product warnings were a salient and memorable category to focus group participants, no messages fell into this category during the data collection period.

Our results shows that Viral Mavens received 4 times as many warnings (e.g., computer virus warnings) and almost 10 times as many naked pictures, than did Infrequent Senders. Although money chain letters and emails about entertainment/events were relatively rare, Mavens also were significantly more likely to receive these types of pass-along messages than were Infrequent Senders.

Women and men displayed some differences in the types of emails that they received. For example, women were 3 times more likely to receive chain letters than were men. Women also were significantly more likely to receive games than were their male counterparts.

In addition to examining message content, our research team analyzed the structure of pass-along emails received. We coded messages into seven major

TABLE 3.1
Percentage of Messages Received in Each Content Category

General Content Categories	%	Content Subcategories	%
Jokes	48.8	General	20.8
		Sexual	14.5
		Gender issues	6.2
		Work or computer related	3.3
		Current Events	1.9
		Political	1.9
		Poem	0.2
Chain letters	17.7	General	8.4
		Religious	4.3
		Inspirational	2.1
		Luck	1.6
		Free stuff	0.8
		Money	0.4
Inspirational	8.4	Thought for the day	6.4
		"Feel good" pictures	2.0
Religious messages	4.8		
Information	4.4	Current events	2.2
		Entertainment and events	1.0
		Helpful tips	0.9
		Recipes	0.2
Warnings	3.5	Computer virus	2.6
		Crime	0.9
		Product	0.0
Naked pictures	2.8	Naked pictures	2.1
		Altered naked pictures	0.7
Email digests	1.3		
Comment about a company	1.2		
Free stuff	1.2		
Games	1.1		
Company-originated messages	0.3		
Missing children	0.3		
Political message	0.2		
Good deeds	0.1		
Other type of message	4.0		

categories: text messages (74.7%), static pictures (10.1%), cartoons (6.1%), URLs (5%), animated cartoons (2.9%), movies (0.6%), and other (0.5%).

Almost 23% of pass-along emails received in our research email box contained some type of attachment. We examined the types of these attached files and found that .jpg files and .gif files were most common, representing almost 70% of the attachments participants received.

The Dark Side of Pass-Along Email. Although Viral Mavens had a difficult time thinking of a dark side to pass-along email, Infrequent Senders expressed a bit more concern about viruses and having their addresses floating around. Infrequent Senders also expressed a sense that pass-along email was sham communication that made them feel like they were communicating with somebody when they really were not. One female Infrequent Sender said, "For me, the dark side is that it makes me feel like you're communicating with somebody when you're not really communicating with anybody." A gentleman in the Viral group echoed her sentiments; common parlance in his social circle is "Do you talk to that person? No, I just get forwards." He also related feeling disappointed when he had been looking forward to receiving a personalized email from a certain individual but received a pass-along email instead.

Suspicion rarely emerged in participants' open-ended lists of emotions they experience in response to pass-along emails. When asked directly, however, whether they ever are suspicious of pass-along emails, most people chimed in with strong assent. Much of the suspicion revolves around addresses they do not recognize. If there is an attachment to messages from unknown senders, suspicion increases due to concern about computer viruses; this spurs an immediate delete reaction. People also reported being suspicious of what they termed "pyramid schemes," and warnings about harmful products also pique suspicion in some.

To deal with suspicion, most participants reported taking one of two approaches. Some rely solely on their common sense and good judgment. The second approach to determining legitimacy appears to involve checking other sources. Some respondents turn to other people, the Centers for Disease Control (CDC) or law officers. Still others actually have written emails to companies who are reportedly offering free "stuff" to determine whether those offers are valid.

Decision Point #2: To Send or to Quash?

Once consumers have opened a pass-along email message and scanned its content, consumers typically decide whether to pass the message to others, to quash it, or to take some other action. From our focus group discussion, it appears that Viral Mavens pass email along if it seems important, the other person would like it, they are in the right mood or they have the time.

Also, several viral consumers communicated a strong sense of responsibility to send along forwarded email. These individuals believe that sending forwarded messages is one's duty. It is interesting to consider that, to consumers who are particularly involved in pass-along email, this pass-along email may be a new type of social contract. Social contracts apply to all areas of life: relationships, business, information sharing, and so on. The fuel to these contracts is the reciprocity norm: if someone does something for you, you are obligated to return a favor. Indeed, this dynamic appears alive and well among Viral Mavens, as these quotes attest:

"Because I get great jokes, and I *must* share, and I *must* respond, and then I get more and more."

"If you don't send, people won't send to you."

"I've done my job [when I send a pass-along email]."

"People keep feeding you, so you got to feed back."

"Feeling like you're left out ... like if you don't send them something back when they send you stuff all the time, they may not send it again."

An important part of monitoring social contracts is identifying "cheaters"—those individuals who don't "make good" on their end of the bargain. Pass-along email—at least to some Viral Mavens—appears to be no exception. Some expressed a mild sense of retribution when someone was frequently nonresponsive; Mavens retaliate for the nonresponse by taking the individual off of their email lists.

In general, Infrequent Senders appear more leery of sending pass-along email than are Viral Mavens, and they do so much less frequently. As one Infrequent Sender stated, "You don't want to be identified by people as someone who is 'input trash, output trash.'" Some Infrequent Senders do pass on, though, if the message meets their standards for quality or relevance. Indeed, a major reason that Infrequent Senders opted not to forward messages in the behavioral study was because the content doesn't meet their threshold. "If it really makes me laugh, or if it's really good information, or really inspirational to me ... but it's got to be special."

Infrequent Senders also send along email in a particular way. As the comments below indicate, they tend to be a bit more selective in choosing the people to whom they'd pass messages:

"I send them selectively ... I don't batch send."

"You got to be real careful when you start transferring things along."

"I don't just broadcast."

"If I can't prove that it's true, then I'd be kind of worried someone else would believe it."

"If I don't see any reason for people to like it, I don't pass it on."

What Makes a Pass-Along Email Virus Spread?

It is good news for potential viral marketers that participants passed along almost 40% of the messages that they received over the four-week study period. However, the tendency to pass-along email was extremely variable (from 0% to 100%) across participants.

Not surprisingly, Viral Mavens sent more than two and a half times as many messages as did Infrequent Senders. Not only did they send a greater number of pass-along emails, they also were 50% more likely to forward a pass-along email that they received than were Infrequent Senders. Interestingly, however, there were gender differences for the propensity to forward email; although there were no differences in the number of pass-along emails that men and women *received*, women were significantly more likely than were men to pass these messages along to others.

It also is important to note that not only did Viral Mavens forward a greater proportion of messages than did Infrequent Senders, they also reported having significantly wider circles of influence. Specifically, Viral Mavens appear to have circles of influence that are 3 times more extensive than are circles of Infrequent Senders. Whereas Infrequent Senders listed between one and two people on each forwarded email, Viral Mavens listed four intended recipients, on average. Not only are Viral Mavens sending more messages, they're sending these messages to more people.

To identify those message types that compelled a pass-along response, we compared the number of emails received within each category to the number of emails sent in each category. Table 3.2 ranks message types in terms of their viral potential. More than half of all messages containing naked pictures, jokes about gender, jokes about work or computers, crime warnings, games, and luck-oriented chain letters were passed on.

To better understand the decision to pass a message along, the research team administered the Interpersonal Communication Motives Scale (Rubin, Perse, & Barbato, 1988) during 30-minute phone interviews. This scale consists of 28 reasons for communicating. The instructions for this scale were altered slightly by asking respondents about their reasons for communicating with others via pass-along email. Interviewees stated how much each reason matched their own motivations on a scale from 1 ("not at all like my reason") to 5 ("exactly like my reason").

As shown in Table 3.3, four of the six top-rated reasons had to do with enjoyment and entertainment. The other two top reasons had social motivations at their core—a motivation to help and a motivation to communicate caring.

Interviewee's open-ended comments supported this emphasis on fun and on social connection.

"[I participate] mostly for entertainment."

"[I participate] to help other people, for information, and support. Kind of a socially correct hug to a coworker who's a good friend at work only."

"I don't pass along everything, nor do I read everything I receive. There is no one reason because I pick and choose what goes to whom. It is a five second way of letting someone know I'm thinking about them. And I don't do that often enough for some people. It can also let me express a sincere and deep emotion for someone that I would hesitate to actually say/do."

As one respondent noted, "If I'm too busy to write a note, I'll select a specific thing to say 'I'm thinking of you, but I don't have time to write.'" Other respondents had very pragmatic reasons for keeping up with the flow of pass-along email—one insurance salesman sends pass-along email because he believes

TABLE 3.2

Percentage of Email Forwarded by Category

Message Type	Percent
Good deed (small number of emails!)	100.0
Naked pictures	60.0
Joke, gender issues	56.0
Joke, work, or computer	55.0
Warning, crime	54.5
Games	53.8
Chain letter, luck	52.6
Other	51.2
Cute, feel good picture	50.0
Missing children	50.0
Free stuff, general	46.7
Information, helpful tips	45.5
Joke, sexual	43.8
Joke, current events	43.5
Joke, political	43.5
Chain letter, religious	42.3
Chain letter, general	40.2
Chain letter, money	40.0
Warning, computer virus	38.7
Inspiration, chain letter	38.5
Joke, nonspecific	37.3
Inspiration/thought for the day	36.4
Information, recipes	33.3
Free stuff, chain letter	30.0
Altered naked pictures	25.0
Company sent it	25.0
Information, entertainment	25.0
Religious	24.1
Company or product in positive way	20.0
Information, current events	18.5
Digest	0.0
Joke, poem	0.0
Political	0.0
Product warnings	0.0

that keeping his name top-of-mind increases his business. "[To me] the perfect reason for participating in pass-along email [is] to stay in contact with folks." And still others reiterated a feeling of obligation that we heard throughout focus group discussions—"I have an obligation to pass it along ... It's what you're supposed to do with it."

Although their behavioral patterns differed in many ways, Infrequent Senders and Viral Mavens reported similar motivations for and emotional responses to forwarding pass-along email. These included:

TABLE 3.3
Motives for Sending Pass-Along Email

Item	Mean	Std. Dev.
Because it's fun	3.91	1.12
Because I enjoy it	3.61	1.34
Because it's entertaining	3.48	1.12
To help others	3.48	0.85
To have a good time	3.39	1.31
To let others know I care about their feelings	3.39	1.03
To thank them	3.09	1.24
Because it peps me up	2.74	1.14
To get away from what I'm doing	2.74	1.39
To show others encouragement	2.70	1.22
Because it allows me to unwind	2.70	1.26
Because it's exciting	2.65	1.11
Because it relaxes me	2.48	1.24
Because it's stimulating	2.48	1.08
To get away from pressures	2.48	1.24
To get something I don't have	2.48	2.35
Because it's a pleasant rest	2.43	1.08
Because I'm concerned about them	2.43	1.16
Because it makes me feel less tense	2.35	1.15
To put off something I should be doing	2.35	1.30
Because I have nothing better to do	2.26	1.25
Because it's reassuring to know someone's there	2.13	1.32
Because I want someone to do something for me	2.00	1.17
Because it's thrilling	2.00	1.13
Because I just need to talk	1.83	1.07
To tell others what to do	1.83	1.19
Because I need someone to talk to	1.65	0.83
Because it makes me feel less lonely	1.48	0.79

- To amuse
- To inform
- To inspire
- To keep someone from being left out of a group

- To help someone
- To do a good deed
- To comfort someone
- To touch a person

Based on respondents' answers to these items, we were able to tentatively sort people into three very differently motivated subgroups. These subgroups are described below:

Subgroup #1: The Pleasure and Inclusion Seekers
These participants engage in pass-along email because they view it as fun (it represents a source of entertainment for them) and because it makes them feel less lonely and reassured.

Subgroup #2: The Control, Escape and Relaxation Seekers

These participants participate in pass-along email because of what it allows them to do. They are seeking to "tell others what to do" or to "get something I don't have" or to "put off something I should be doing" or to "get away from pressures and responsibilities." They also are seeking pleasure from pass-along activity but they are more likely seeking relaxation (which makes sense given their desire to escape).

Subgroup #3: The "Casual Joes"

This final group we have dubbed the "Casual Joes," because they are not as passionate about pass-along email as the other groups are. However, they, too, participate for the entertainment pass-along email provides.

How To's of Sending Pass-Along Email. Once a decision has been made to forward a pass-along email to others, for whatever reason, there are several ways in which the sender can alter the message in order to give it a personal touch. In fact, our focus group discussions revealed that a strong understanding of pass-along email etiquette exists, and Infrequent Senders seem to adhere to these rules more than do Viral Mavens. A list of appropriate rules of etiquette might include the following:

1. Be wary of sending off-color jokes or other inappropriate content to your whole email list. Make sure that the content you send is appropriate for all recipients on the list. If not, do not include the recipient.
2. Do not send salacious content to people at work.
3. Add a personalized note before passing it on.
4. Delete the other forwards contained in the email so that people can find the content easily.
5. Fix any spacing that renders the message difficult to read.
6. Send your messages selectively, keeping in mind relevance of the message to the recipient.

Our behavioral data further supported the idea that Infrequent Senders keep a closer eye on the niceties of pass-along email. Analysis suggests that Infrequent Senders include personalized notes more often, they send to a smaller number of people at one time, and they are more likely to avoid passing content that they view as inappropriate. However, the findings of the content analysis differ from the focus group responses in one area. Neither Infrequent Senders nor Viral Mavens typically "clean up" messages by deleting earlier generations, even though this was a strong theme during the focus groups.

Is It Personal? Personalization can come in three forms in pass-along email. A message can be personalized if it is sent to one individual at a time, by the inclusion of a note written by the sender, and if the sender simply changes the subject line.

The results of the content analysis match up very well with focus groups' responses relating to personalization. Interestingly, Viral Mavens felt that pass-along emails can be personal even if the email is not sent to the one person alone. Despite the number of other names on the list, they feel personally touched as long as the content is relevant to their interests.

Although 75% of the content analysis participants crafted at least one person-alized note, on average, just one third of forwarded messages contained a per-sonalized note. The content analysis also confirmed that Infrequent Senders are marginally more likely to add personalized notes than are Viral Mavens; half of Infrequent Senders' pass-along emails contained a note (51%), as compared to less than one third of Viral Mavens' pass-along emails (29%).

In addition to assessing the frequency of adding personalized notes, we exam-ined the types of notes that participants included. When people bother to include a note, they appear most likely to write a note to motivate readership. (Again, the reader should consider this finding good news for viral marketers.) Over half of the notes received could be coded into this category (56%). And interestingly, women appear marginally more likely to add disclaimer notes than are men.

Finally, content analysis results suggested that subject lines of pass-along emails rarely are changed. Only 19% of the participants changed any of the subject lines of the messages that they passed along and even those who did alter subject lines did so for less than 10% of the emails they forwarded to others.

How Passing Along Emails Makes People Feel.   In light of the high percentage of people who pass along email, it is no surprise that people find the activity reinforcing. Whereas their emotional reactions to receiving pass-along email were mixed, people reported experiencing largely positive emotions—excited, helpful, happy, satisfied—when they sent pass-along emails. Relevant statements include:

> "Good. You think you've inspired someone or have given them information that may be beneficial to them."
> "Hopeful that you've connected or helped."
> "For a brief period in time, you're on the same page."
> "You've reached out and touched."
> "You feel a sense of belonging."
> "It makes the joke funnier to think that someone else is going to enjoy it too."

The only somewhat negative emotion that emerged was voiced by one woman, who said that she felt "Like I'm being a bother" when she sends along forwarded email.

People do report hearing back from individuals to whom they've sent pass-along emails. Inspirational stories and jokes, in particular, will motivate a recipient to call the sender to share his or her reaction to the note. One gentleman appreciated this reaction, stating that "By sending an email, you get 'real communication.'" The positivity of these reactions definitely impact the frequency with which Viral Mavens send messages to particular individuals. One woman sees this feedback as critical to whether she retains the individual on her list—she views recipients as shirking their duties if they do not respond with a voice message or with pass-along emails of their own.

People were understandably reluctant to talk too much about "backlash" that they had experienced. Some did share the experience when someone to whom they'd sent a pass-along email asked that they be removed from the list. All complied with the request, although they did feel negative emotion surrounding the experience.

Why People Quash Pass-Along Emails. To this point we have concentrated on the decision, actions, and consequences of actually continuing the chain of a pass-along email. Of course, many individuals opt instead to quash pass-along email that they receive. To understand pressures leading to this choice, we asked focus group participants why they choose NOT to forward pass-along emails that they have received. General reported reasons for NOT passing email along include:

- "If it's inappropriate and kids may be sitting on the computer."
- "I don't send my religious propaganda to my heathen friends."
- "If I think that everyone in the group has seen it already."

Recall that we also asked participants in the empirical phase of this research to send us messages they received they opted NOT to pass on to others. We, of course, were interested in better understanding their actual reasons for breaking the pass-along chain. For each unforwarded message that participants sent to us, they were asked to provide a reason for not forwarding it to others. These reasons were sorted into the 6 categories listed in Table 3.4. The number one reason for quashing a message was the sense that the content was old. This reason was particularly salient

TABLE 3.4
Reasons for Not Forwarding Email

Reasons	Percent
Old message/all have seen it	21
Uninteresting/stupid content	20
Not appropriate/offensive	10
Not enough time	8
Cute content, but doesn't meet threshold	7
Other	33
Total	**100**

to Viral Mavens, who were significantly more likely to quash emails because they viewed the message as old, as compared to Infrequent Senders. Viral Mavens were also significantly more likely to quash emails due to content that seemed uninteresting or stupid.

There were also some regional differences in the reasons people attributed to blocking email. Residents of West Coast and East Coast cities were more likely to stifle email due to lack of time; Cincinnatians and Los Angelenos cited this reason significantly more than did residents of Buffalo and Atlanta. Residents of the arguably more conservative cities in our sample were somewhat more likely to stifle a pass-along email because of concern that the content was inappropriate or offensive.

The Effect of Computer Virus Scares on Pass-Along Behavior

External events definitely impact consumers' decisions to forward pass-along email, computer virus scares being one of the most vivid and relevant of these external events. Fortuitously, for the researchers in this study anyway, the [Love Bug virus] hit in the middle of data collection, an event that afforded us the opportunity to track email flow before and after the virus attack. The week following the Love Bug contagion, we observed a 58% drop in pass-along emails as compared to the number received the week preceding the Love Bug virus. This drop in email volume was noticeable to our participants, even though only one had actually gotten infected by the virus. During follow-up interviews, participants noted:

"The flood became a trickle. There had been a decrease for a week or so just before that due to the Easter holiday—people out of town or busy—but the virus definitely dropped it way down. (It's pretty much back to normal now.)"

"I would venture to say that there were some changes in receiving and reviewing emails on my part. Once we were up and running, there was about a three day period where I did not receive the usual numbers. But once the scare was over, it was business (play) as usual. Also, I would not open an email if it were not from one of my circle of users."

"In the beginning of the study, I experienced a few problems as a result of the widespread Love Bug virus, which affected most companies. But once that problem was resolved, it was pass-along emails as usual."

During follow-up interviews, people reported having been somewhat more cautious when opening emails and attachments in the aftermath of the virus. This timidity, however, did not seem long lived. Email behavior was back to normal relatively soon, so they said; "business as usual" was a common theme in participants' responses. This is heartening, as it suggests that people's willingness to engage in pass-along email is resilient to virus disturbances.

Other Actions

Independent of individuals' choice to send along or stifle a pass-along email, it was clear through focus group discussion that pass-along email spurs a wide range of behavior. We asked respondents if they have ever done anything, offline, as a direct result of having an email forwarded to them. (Obviously, this information is important for marketers!) It appears both Viral Mavens and Infrequent Senders *do* take action as a result of receiving pass-along emails. Our respondents often research virus alerts by asking their Information Systems (IS) departments. A few have taken the time to contact their congressional representatives in response to pass-along emails, and others have visited the Web sites featured in animated pass-along items. In response to health warnings (like the tampon/asbestos scare and the antiperspirant/cancer scare), some participants reported having called their doctors.

Pass-along emails also appear to leave the electronic space with some frequency. Most Viral Mavens said that they end up talking about pass-along jokes or other emails with other people. Some senders actually will call a recipient to ask whether the individual has received a particular pass-along and to discuss that message. Other senders retell jokes in person or on the phone that they have received via email. At times, pass-along emails are converted to paper so that the message is disbursed even further; Viral Mavens especially report printing out emails so they can paste them up in the office or pass them along to those who are not online.

Is It Cultural?

Often, ideas and technologies that are particularly powerful and popular take hold because they mesh with important American cultural patterns. The Internet is a prime example. The web has achieved high adoption rates largely because it fits with fundamental American value systems. The gratifications that the web provides are in sync with the American need for large space, balanced by the need to feel safe and "at home"; immediacy; adventure, opportunity, freedom, and magic; continual self-exploration, married with a sense of progress; rewards and recognition, balanced with a need to maintain individualism and to avoid commitment.

Our follow-up interviews provided an opportunity to see whether viral marketing has evolved with force and furor partly because it, too, meshes with American cultural patterns. To see how pass-along emails fared, we presented interviewees with eight statements that described pass-along email in disparate ways. Participants were asked to report how much they thought each phrase described pass-along email on a scale from 0 to 6, where 0 meant the phrase did not describe pass-along email at all, and 6 meant the phrase described pass-along email very well. The mean score for each of the phrases are shown in Table 3.5.

Participants saw two phrases in particular as somewhat descriptive of pass-along email: "It's like a wide open field," and "It's like being in a neighborhood

TABLE 3.5
Descriptions of Pass-Along Email

Item	Mean	Std. Dev.
It's like a wide-open field	3.52	2.04
It's like a neighborhood I know	3.48	1.78
It's like an amusement park	2.52	2.04
It's like being a teenager again	2.22	2.07
It's like a friend's birthday party	2.11	2.16
It's like being my own boss	1.91	2.11
It's like starting off on a vacation	1.39	1.59
It's like acting lessons	0.91	1.08

I know." When they were asked to explain especially high ratings they had given, they provided us with the quotes recorded below:

It's like a wide open field

Themes of control and opportunity emerge in respondents' explanations of the "wide-open field" phraseology. This freedom and absolute personal choice certainly resonate with American ideals.

"I have no control over what comes in but I can and do exercise complete control over what goes out. I have a lot of options to choose from. And I can always start something myself if what comes in doesn't suit the need."

"You could pass it along and nobody would ask me about it. Freedom."

"There's a lot to explore and to tell people. It's wide open . . . ready to be walked on."

"Because you can pick and choose . . . it's up to your judgment . . . what you receive is up to you . . . you're the judge."

"Because it's open to the whole world. . . . You can email anyone from anywhere."

It's like a neighborhood I know

Reknitting the social fabric also emerges as an important association with pass-along email. Email situates senders and receivers within a community of familiar others. This feature also, of course, primes the pump for viral marketing, as consumers will likely attend more to the opinions of people they know and respect than to opinions of relative strangers.

"It's everybody that I know very well."

"I'm in contact with old friends. It's very personal. We know one another. Everyone's entertainment."

"Almost all [of my pass-along email is] from one friend, and I know her, and I like her. That's kind of like being in a neighborhood. . . . Just gives me a good feeling."

"So much of [the content] is familiar to me."

"Because you don't get too much email that isn't solicited . . . that isn't from people you don't know. And I'm very cautious if it's from someone I don't recognize . . . so it's like a neighborhood you know because you can choose to say hello to someone or not. No risk of being rude."

"I just think it's fun to communicate with people you know in a quick, fun way."

It's like a friend's birthday party

Associating with similar others in a friendly setting is also related to pass-along email.

"It's a group of people . . . a bunch that sits together, tells jokes . . . a small group of people that you pass along."

"It doesn't matter what you send. It's a fun thing."

"My friends are my age, entertaining, provocative, thrilling, enjoyable."

"It's fun to just shoot the shit with your friends. Being together when you're all in different states."

It's like an amusement park

For some, pass-along email also jibes with the classic American pasttime—the county fair or the amusement park.

"You see interesting things. You laugh and have a good time, and I get that with email. I get funny cartoons, you know. I always laugh."

"It's like an amusement park because it's full of fun."

"Because it all is amusing. There are so many people; it's so crowded."

It's like being a teenager again

Pass-along email may also remind some consumers of their teenage years, when life held fewer responsibilities and was more carefree.

"Just because it's like when you pass notes in school."

"When you're doing emails, it is uninhibiting, fresh, new, wild."

It's like being my own boss

And, of course, pass-along email allows everyone executive privileges.

"I have control over whether or not it stops with you or continues."

"You're in complete control. You manage what you want to say and do at your own convenience."

"Because you choose what you're going to do with it."

"I don't have to listen to anyone. I'm in charge. It's up to me."

Those who did not assign high ratings to the metaphors listed were asked to provide their own associations with pass-along email. From what one gentleman said, it appears that pass-along email has become an ingrained habit. "It's like brushing my teeth because you do it everyday and you don't think about it unless you have to pass along." Several others emphasized the informational aspect to pass-along email.

"It's just a quick information exchange."

"It is a chance to interact with friends while sharing a laugh or interesting fact."
"It's like having a funny thought for the day, or it's an important pass-along email,
it's like being warned about something to be aware of, like news."

These individuals may be particularly fertile ground for viral marketing if they
are closely tuned to exchanging information about products and services. It will
be important to identify these individuals to see whether they treat informational
messages as particularly deserving of a pass along.

Viral Mavens and Infrequent Senders: How They Are Alike . . .

All in all, Viral Mavens and Infrequent Senders were quite similar in terms of their
online histories, online habits, and the importance they attribute to email. Many
of their reactions to pass-along email also had a similar flavor. In particular, Viral
Mavens and Infrequent Senders were alike in the following ways:

- As people are running faster and faster with little or no time to maintain
connections face-to-face, email is certainly a way to maintain closeness with others.
When time becomes too precious, people consider pass-along email to be a generic
way to touch someone, to tell them that you care. There is a definite sense that
people are tied together through the pass-along email link . . . that for a short time,
the sender and recipient are "on the same page."
- They experience a host of positive and negative emotions when they receive
pass-along email, ranging from excitement and happiness to anger and frustration.
Many of the negative emotions are prompted by the recipients' own temporary
mood or state—irritation is reported when people don't have time to read pass-
along emails, for example. What is interesting is that this emotion is *not* transferred
to the sender. In fact, Mavens and Infrequent Senders attribute largely positive
motivations to senders of pass-along email. They believe others send pass-along
email to amuse, to inspire, to make social contact and to comfort the recipients,
among other reasons.
- Messages that spark strong emotion—either humor, fear, sadness, or
inspiration—seem to be those messages that are most likely to be forwarded.
Very humorous jokes, frightening virus alerts or product warnings, touchingly sad
stories, and particularly apt inspirational messages are those emails that meet even
most Infrequent Senders' thresholds for passing.
- People take action in response to these messages, they call experts to check the
legitimacy of product warnings, they call to thank senders for especially touching
or humorous messages, they change their behavior in order to avoid negative
consequences after reading a health warning, and so on.
- Pass-along emails leave the electronic realm rather frequently. People reported discussing pass-along emails with others, printing out these emails to post
in public places, mailing paper copies to other people, and so on.

... and How They Differ

Despite the many similarities between viral and non-viral consumers, there were differences in the sheer quantity of their pass-along email habits. In comparison to Infrequent Senders, Viral Mavens:

- received twice as many pass-along emails;
- received more warnings, naked pictures, chain letters, and informational emails;
- sent three times as many messages;
- have spheres of influence that are three times greater.

Also, in comparison to Infrequent Senders, Viral Mavens were more likely to:

- feel a sense of social obligation and responsibility to forward messages along;
- consider these emails to be "personal"—and to satisfy relationship mainte-nance goals—even if they are sent to numerous people at one time (what is critical is the relevance of the message, not the number of people to whom it was sent);
- view forwarding messages as important to remaining "in the loop" and to maintaining relationships with those who send messages to them.

Finally, when Infrequent Senders decide to forward a pass-along message, they tend to do so more sparingly and selectively than do Viral Mavens. For example, Infrequent Senders are more likely to:

- forward messages to one person at a time;
- add personalized notes to messages to motivate recipients to read the message;
- follow pass-along email etiquette more stringently.

What It All Means for Marketers

We were, of course, interested when companies were named in conjunction with pass-along emails. There were two cases in which companies were spontaneously mentioned: as providers of "free stuff" and in conjunction with product warnings. With respect to the first category, individuals mentioned free stuff emails that were purportedly from the Gap, Microsoft, and Bath & Body Works but actually were hoaxes. In these cases, there appears little potential for negative emotion to rub off on brands mentioned in free stuff emails. People don't hold these companies accountable for the emails that circulate and they seem to understand that the companies hold no responsibility for their genesis. As one gentleman thoughtfully said: "It's like getting mad at somebody's words instead of the person." People indicated that these hoaxes reflect more on the media than on the companies named in the emails—"It reminds you to be skeptical of what you read."

In the case of product warnings, there appears to be greater potential for companies to be viewed negatively, and this link may even be indirect. For example, many people mentioned seeing emails about tampons and asbestos, and antiperspirants and cancer. Although they did not mention negative views of tampon or antiperspirant manufacturers or retailers, people may be more wary toward the category as a whole as a result of having read these emails. When a company was mentioned in conjunction with a product warning (e.g, tainted orange juice), people found it difficult to remember the brand with which the warning was linked. People knew to which brands the note did NOT apply—perhaps because they don't drink the brand cited and decided that the warning was not applicable. In any case, these product warnings do hold potential for more negative perceptions of the brands. It bears repeating, however, that although these emails are salient to participants, not one product warning email was received during the course of the study.

It is important that we be clear: Participants did communicate much irritation at the unsolicited emails that they receive from companies. They are frustrated at the sheer volume of junk email that they receive, and they usually delete these messages without opening them. Recall that emails that originate directly from a company and not from a known individual are viewed as spam.

However, when probed, individuals said that they did not consider information about a company junk if it came from a person that they know. They would assume that the product is of value, and that the individual passed on the information for a good reason. Of course, pass-along email presents this positive word-of-mouth opportunity on an incredibly large scale. It is critical that companies carefully identify viral consumers and opinion leaders, sending original messages just to them so that the number of people who receive email direct from the company is minimized.

Important Pass-Along Consumer Profiles

The examination of pass-along email receipt and sending patterns revealed four separate pass-along email profiles: those who neither received many pass-along emails nor forwarded many of those they received; others who did not receive many pass-along emails, but forwarded a large percentage of those that they did get; still others who received many messages and sent many messages; and those consumers who received many pass-alongs but passed on virtually none of them (see Table 3.6).

Obviously the Viral Mavens are important to advertisers, as they receive large quantities of pass-along email and send a large percentage of those that they receive. However, another potentially overlooked but valuable conduit for marketing messages are the Infrequent Senders in the upper right quadrant of the figure. Although these individuals send a relatively low volume of pass-along email, the main problem appears to be the low numbers of email that they actually receive; they appear willing and eager to pass messages along, as long as they get them.

TABLE 3.6

Pass-Along Profiles

		Receiving Pass-Along Emails	
		Many	*Few*
Sending Pass-	Large %	Viral Mavens	Infrequent Senders
Along Email	Small %	Infrequent Senders	Infrequent Senders

If advertisers can access these individuals and present them with relevant and/or interesting information, they could develop into more influential market members. Indeed, Infrequent Senders may wield an especially noteworthy impact due to their more targeted, personalized, and motivating approaches to sending emails to their network members.

Simply identifying and contacting Viral Mavens and Infrequent Senders is not enough, however; hopefully, the research reported here provides advertisers with interesting insights about how to consider and approach viral marketing efforts.

Implications for Target Selection and Message Creation

The current study illustrates the importance of selecting targets that will find the advertiser's information relevant enough to pass along. Both Viral Mavens and Infrequent Senders will quash email that they judge to be irrelevant or uninteresting. Thus, initially targeting the right people is essential for any viral effect to occur. Finding people who are interested in what the company/organization has to say is easier if the company has an internal list of consumers that have opted in for email updates. In this sense, viral marketing has been compared with activating an affinity group where you are reaching people who are ready to hear your message (Parker, 2000). Once the affinity group is contacted (and hopefully activated), they are in total control. It is up to them to circulate the message. Fortunately, pass-along emails are an established part of people's communication patterns, and the current study found multiple positive motivations for and gratifications of participating in pass-along email. Perhaps most importantly, the observed frequency of pass-along email and consumers' apparently large influence spheres suggest consumers definitely do and will share with one another if the message initially reaches the right people.

Another finding reported here that is rife with implications is the conclusion that people really do distinguish between unsolicited mail they get from companies and mail they get from people they know. It is important to reiterate that our research respondents did communicate much irritation at the unsolicited emails that they receive from companies. They are frustrated at the sheer volume of spam they get, and they usually delete these messages without opening them. However, upon probing, individuals said they did not consider information about a company junk if it came from a person that they know. They would assume that the product is of value, and that the individual passed on the information for a good reason. Thus, it is critical that companies carefully identify viral consumers and opinion leaders that are truly interested in the information, sending messages to as few as necessary so that the number of people who receive email direct from the company is minimized. If the information meets the viral consumers' thresholds for relevance, it has a better chance of being passed along—and now they become the source of the message. Furthermore, if the company contacts only those people who have expressed an interest in receiving information, the email is no longer unsolicited and, in fact, may be welcomed. According to Parker (2000), an email campaign for the band Nsync proved so powerful that one girl forwarded the message to 500 friends because it contained video messages from band members that were not available elsewhere.

The example above illustrates the impact of reaching the right viral consumers and it also illustrates the importance of understanding these consumers well enough to create relevant information that the target will find interesting. This point is also illustrated by one of the efforts Nike used to activate electronic word of mouth for its Presto line of shoes. Nike encouraged teenagers to select psychedelic Presto graphics from its Web site, pair the graphics with music, and then email their creations to their friends (White, 2001).

Although it is impossible to offer creative advice for any specific marketing effort, the present study does offer general insights regarding the creation of viral messages. Perhaps most importantly, as was noted above, it reinforces the notion that buzz marketing can only work if the targets are known by the senders *and if they receive something they merit worthy of passing along.* For example, a recent online Lee Dungarees campaign, that targeted young males from a list of Internet surfers, worked because it both understood young web users and offered them humor along with an ensuing game that appealed within the fabric of America's youth culture (Khermouch & Green, 2001). Lee offered these young men the opportunity to create quick flicks and the ability to pass along their creations to their friends. This is a different, and we argue more beneficial, way to create buzz than trendsetters hired by Ford to be seen in Focus cars and give out trinkets because such trendsetters may be recognized as subversive (even hired) corporate help (Khermouch & Green, 2001).

Message developers should note that messages that spark strong emotion—humor, fear, sadness, or inspiration—are most likely to be forwarded. They should consider crafting messages consistent with those particularly viral strains that are most appropriate to their cause. Very humorous jokes, touchingly sad stories, and particularly apt inspirational messages are those emails that meet even most Infrequent Senders' thresholds for passing. Interestingly, results of this study indicate emails about free stuff and helpful tips are passed along almost half of the time; companies surely are not yet maximizing opportunities for "seeding" buzz among key targets through use of these mechanisms.

In addition, advertisers should match messaging to consumers' motivational bases for participating in pass-along email. More specifically, they should consider appealing to consumers' clear desires for fun, entertainment, and maintenance of connections with others. Charitable organizations, or those with public service goals, may want to pay special attention to the important role that social motivations play in pass-along email behavior. For example, Viral Mavens and Infrequent Senders were motivated by their desire to help someone, to do a good deed, and so forth. Such motivations suggest that viral marketing efforts hold considerable promise for the marketing of social causes. Thus, the present research has applications with regard to profit and nonprofit oriented organizations. Future research could explore the influence of social motivations with regard to commercial versus charitable marketing efforts. Perhaps even more interesting would be an examination of cause-related marketing efforts in which commercial entities and charitable organizations work together as partners.

On the tactical front, marketers should never underestimate the power of their chosen subject lines: since these tend to be retained throughout the life of a pass-along email chain, they had best be powerful.

Finally, advertisers must be savvy in sparking viral marketing among online networks of women. Based on content analysis in this study, it appears women are more likely than are men to pass along email messages. Marketers must, given women's great purchasing power in the household and their rapidly increasing representation in the online population, tailor message strains and dialogue to women's interests and needs.

The enhancement of viral marketing efforts does not represent a risk-free opportunity for organizations. Although our respondents did not indicate that they hold companies accountable for annoying emails that circulate, they did indicate product warnings may potentially contribute to more negative perceptions of brands. Advertisers should tap into viral marketing possibilities while, at the same time, proceed with due caution. Consumer-to-consumer interaction is a two-way street, and bad news travels just as fast, if not faster, than good news. Paraphrasing Shirky (2000), viral marketing is the scourge of the stupid and the slow because it only rewards those that offer great service and have the guts to encourage their customers to publicly pass judgment on that service every single day.

Wrap Up: Top 10 Implications for Marketers

In summary, here's a list of 10 implications to whet the appetite for further viral marketing consideration:

1. Buy into Malcolm Gladwell's (2000) idea of placing consumers at the center. The frequency of pass-along emailing by Viral Mavens, and their spheres of influence, clearly support the fact that consumers will share with one another.

2. Match messages to consumers' motivational bases for participating in pass-along email—appeal to their desire for fun, entertainment, escape, and, importantly, to maintain connections with others.
3. Think about whether there is an intersection between your brand and the fact that (according to lifestyles and values data collected from respondents but not reported in the present study) Viral Mavens appear more likely to follow trends and fashions, consider themselves intellectuals, like trying new things, and so on.
4. Take advantage of the cultural "sweet spots" identified in the study—the freedom of the open field, the close-knit community of familiar others, seizing executive privileges, and so on. Ensure that messaging is at least consistent with these themes.
5. Don't neglect the Infrequent Senders who, nonetheless, send a high portion of the pass-along emails that they receive. Seek out this group, as they may wield a bigger impact than Viral Mavens, because their sending of messages is more targeted and personalized.
6. Consider crafting messages that are consistent with those strains that were identified as particularly viral—jokes about work, computers, games, and gender issues may be safest (as opposed to the naked picture category!).
7. Avoid recycling old content—remember that Viral Mavens' number one reason for quashing emails was because the content appeared old.
8. Don't worry about the effects of viruses like the Love Bug virus on pass-along email. Although email volume dropped right after the infection, consumers seem resilient.
9. Wondering how much control you'll have over mutations in your message? Your subject line has a good chance of being retained throughout the pass-along email chain. Make sure it's a good one!
10. In terms of personalized notes, the people who are least likely to pass-along your message are, in fact, most likely to attach a note to motivate the recipient to actually read the message. Another reason to target those Infrequent Sender prospects.

Of course, marketing ethics remain of paramount importance whether one is considering traditional or buzz efforts. Although corporate technology is close to allowing firms to track HTML-based email links and, therefore, identify individual viral influencers, individual privacy must be respected. Also, trickery not only is quickly recognized as manipulation by consumers but also represents fundamentally inappropriate business practice. Good creation of online word-of-mouth advertising—or viral seeds that truly offer consumers benefits—represents perhaps the greatest creative challenge the marketing field has faced to date.

Limitations and Suggestions for Future Research. As with all exploratory research, the present study has limitations that must be considered. Within this section, we identify some of these limitations and offer suggestions for how future research may address these deficiencies. First, although multiple research methods were used, participants for each research phase were drawn from the initial focus group sample. While recruiting the content analysis and in-depth interview participants from the focus groups provided the opportunity to compare verbal claims regarding pass-along email with actual behavior, the generalizability of our findings would be enhanced by having different and more participants in each phase. Larger studies, replicating each phase of this research project, are needed.

Another limitation of the current study is that it does not offer enough information regarding who the Viral Mavens and Infrequent Senders really are. It is critical that future research more specifically profile types of viral participants and members of all relevant (and reachable) subtypes. If detailed behavioral and psychographic profiles are developed, it will be much easier for advertisers to target those valuable Viral Mavens and Infrequent Senders. Of particular value would be a large-scale psychographic segmentation study that used consumers' attitudes and motivations to predict actual infection rates for varying message strains.

Directly related to the above is that the design of the present study does not allow for actual testing of marketer-produced viral attempts. Specific message strain testing among identified targets is required for successful viral message seeding. Clearly, a well-designed experiment would bring researchers much closer to understanding how to trigger online (and offline) behavior through viral marketing. However, such an experiment would raise a number of ethical concerns, the most important of which relate to consumer privacy. For an experiment of this type to be truly useful, one would have to have the capability to track the email message from origination through each successful pass-along phase. Furthermore, it would be difficult to fully inform the participants of this tracking without having that knowledge alter their behavior and render the experiment useless. Although carrying out this experiment without the consumers' knowledge and consent may sound innocent enough, consumers have expressed outrage over perceived privacy invasions on numerous occasions and seem especially concerned about privacy with regard to the online environment (Fox, Rainie, Horrigan, Lenhart, Spooner, & Carter, 2000). Consumer discovery of such research could prove costly to the sponsoring organization and/or scholar. If, however, pretests suggest that consumers continue to react normally after being fully informed of the tracking mechanism and a method is developed to also inform each pass-along recipient, then the ethical concerns have been addressed and much could be learned from this work.

Of course, more public word-of-mouth information is available on the Internet and Schindler and Bickart's chapter 2 in this book proposes a framework for how consumers use this type of information. Furthermore, monitoring of chat rooms and newsgroups already takes place. Researchers such as Newman (1999) have outlined methods for analyzing word-of-mouth exchanges unobtrusively. These types of approaches also could be fruitful in email research as long as the ethical concerns mentioned above are addressed.

Regardless of how much is learned about what works, a fuller understanding of viral marketing will only come about when scholars can provide theoretical explanations for why and how it works. As stated earlier, a number of research streams could prove extremely helpful in these efforts. Perhaps the largest stream of research that could be applied comes from the work of Rogers and countless others on the diffusion of innovations. Most recently, Rogers (2000) published a summary of the diffusion of information research that could prove helpful.

Furthermore, a key tenet of viral marketing is the belief that consumer-to-consumer communication is open and honest. In contrast to traditional advertising messages, viral messages may be perceived as more credible because the communicator's motivation is more likely prosocial (to educate or to help) than probusiness (to acquire new customers). The persuasive power of a viral marketing message hinges on recipients' attributions that the message is credible because the communicator is prompted to speak by the quality of the product or service and not for reasons that would undercut the recommendation. Clearly research examining the influence of source characteristics could prove useful here.

It is interesting that some companies have begun offering incentives to spark viral marketing. Consumers are paid, for example, if they convert new customers based on their recommendations. Or, they receive discounts if they send a certain number of emails to friends. This practice of reimbursing consumers for spreading the word likely jeopardizes the honesty that should be inherent in consumer-to-consumer marketing. Compensation would seem to introduce a source of bias and would dilute the power of the recommendation if recipients were aware of the hidden rewards. Future work might focus on the effects of such rewards on variables such as the trustworthiness dimension of source credibility that are important to persuasion—so that marketers more accurately can weigh the benefits of sparking buzz against the dilution of source credibility.

Finally, it may be noted that consumers who are particularly involved in pass-along email may be adhering to a new type of social contract. Fueling these contracts is the reciprocity norm, which dictates that if someone does something for you, you are obligated to return a favor. Clearly, associations between pass-along emailing and adherence to social contracts are too complex to have been covered within the scope of the research reported here. However, because this dynamic appears alive and well—particularly among Viral Mavens—it also merits further examination.

Obviously, there are many unanswered questions regarding viral marketing. However, the exploratory work presented here offers an initial assessment of the motivations and behaviors of viral consumers. For marketers, the key implications of the current research relates to the targeting and creation of viral messages. For scholars, it is hoped that this work provides a useful first step on the path to better understanding the viral phenomenon, and that the suggestions for future research provide fruitful avenues for scholarly investigation.

REFERENCES

Arndt, J. (1967). Role of product-related conversations in the diffusion of a new product. *Journal of Marketing Research, 4*(August), 291–295.

Feick, L. F., & Price L. L. (1987). The market maven: A diffuser of marketplace information. *Journal of Marketing*, 51(January), 83–97.

Fox, S., Rainie, L., Horrigan, J., Lenhart, A., Spooner, T., & Carter, C. (2000). Trust and privacy online: Why Americans want to rewrite the rules. *The Pew Internet & American Life Project*. Retrieved September 11, 2000, from www.pewinternet.org/.

Gladwell, M. (2000). *The tipping point: How little things can make a big difference*. New York: Little, Brown and Company.

Godin, S. (2000). *Unleashing the ideavirus*. New York: Do You Zoom, Inc.

Khermouch, G., & Green, J. (2001). Buzz marketing [Electronic version]. *Business Week*. Retrieved July 24, 2001, from www.businessweek.com:/print/magazine/content/01_31/b3743001.html? mainwindow

Knight, C. (1999). Viral marketing. *Boardwatch Magazine*. Retrieved September 4, 2000, from www.boardwatch.com/mag/99/nov/bwm50.html.

Newman, Peter J., Jr. (1999). When windows replace walls: Investigating virtual word of mouth exchanges and constructing multilogue profiles. *Advances in Consumer Research, 26*, 653.

Parker, P. (2000). Achoo! Getting viral with rich media. Retrieved September 4, 2000, from www.turboads.com/richmedia/2000rmn/rmn20000822.shtml

Price, L. L., & Feick, L. F. (1984). The role of interpersonal sources in external search: An informational perspective. In T. C. Kinncar (Ed.), *Advances in consumer research* Vol. 11, (pp. 250–253). Ann Arbor, MI: Association for Consumer Research.

Priore, T. (2000, September 4). The fall, rise of e-mail response rates. *Direct Marketing News, 22*(33), 22.

Rogers, E. M. (2000). Reflections on news event diffusion research. *Journalism & Mass Communication Quarterly*, 77(3), 561–576.

Rogers, E. M. (1995). *Diffusion of innovations* (4th ed.). New York: The Free Press.

Rosen, E. (2000). *The anatomy of buzz: How to create word-of-mouth marketing*. New York: Doubleday.

Rubin, R. B., Perse, E. M., & Barbato, C. A. (1988). Conceptualization and measurement of interpersonal communication motives. *Human Communication Research, 14*, 604–628.

Shirky, C. (2000, July 25, 2000). The toughest virus of all. *Business 2.0*, p. 87.

The Pew Internet & Life Project. (2000). *Tracking online life: How women use the Internet to cultivate relationships with family and friends* . Retrieved September 25, 2000 from, www.pewinternet.org

Udell, J. G. (1966). Prepurchase behavior of buyers of small electrical appliances. *Journal of Marketing*, 30(October), 50–52.

White, E. (2001). Word of mouth, Creative advertising make nike slip-on sneakers take off. Retrieved June 7, 2001 from, http://interactive.wsj.com

CHAPTER FOUR

What, and How, We Can Learn From Online Consumer Discussion Groups

David M. Boush
Lynn Kahle
University of Oregon

Ever since the prohibition against commercial use of the Internet was lifted in 1994, consumers have been exposed to an escalating barrage of product advertising (Hanson, 2000). As the number of banners, buttons, and commercial emails has grown, so has the volume of discussion among consumers themselves. Every day, 24 hours a day, people around the world are sharing information online that influences product purchase. Consider this posting to a Usenet group from a participant who became angered when a Baltimore Burger King franchise gave out discount coupons with the name of a gun store on the back.

> "I tried to email Pepsico, the parent of Burger King (as well as Kentucky Fried Chicken, Taco Bell, Frito Lay, Pizza Hut, Pepsi, etc.... all of which I LOVE) but they do not have a home page. I think we should all express how unhappy we are about it and perhaps propose a boycott of some sort. This may sound drastic, but it will send a message if they know how mad we all are."

A boycott of Pepsico brands did not materialize when this posting was made in 1996. It would have been especially unfair as Burger King was a subsidiary of Pillsbury (actually owned by Grand Metropolitan PLC), not Pepsico (Burger King, 2001). However, those who follow Usenet groups are probably aware that boycotts of Burger King and other companies are regularly encouraged, for reasons that range from environmental practices to offensive advertising jingles (Boush

& Kahle, 2001; Kozinets & Handelman, 1998). The following exchange between two mothers of young children in a parents' discussion group illustrates a more positive kind of communication among consumers. Note how one mother's recommendation streamlines the decision process for the other and facilitates a purchase.

"I'm looking for an outdoor playset for Angela, but only part of it, I think . . . I mainly just want a slide that I can bring indoors when needed so these thief neighbors don't take off with it . . . just one of those plastic ones . . . hard to describe . . . would like to get it for her b-day." TIA

"Try this site. This is the Web site for Little Tikes toys and they have a toy finder by State and closest city.

http://www.littletikes.com/toyfinder/default.asp?URL=/toyfinder/toyfinder.asp? C=TF"

The two conversation fragments above represent both positive and negative word of mouth (WOM), or what Granitz and Ward (1996) called word on line (WOL). The first posting shares a feeling of discontent and invites fellow participants to act collectively; the second quickly solves a consumer problem by sharing a Web site. The two examples above also illustrate fundamentally different ways that online communities are relevant to marketers. In the first example, the call for a boycott was relevant only because of its effect on offline purchase behavior. In the second example, much of the decision and purchase behavior occurred online. Online communities affect the physical world; they also have a reality of their own for consumers. The two fragments are also different in that one conveys useful information, the other, misinformation. We will return to both discussions later in this chapter.

Online discussion groups allow people whose social or physical separation previously kept them from communicating to form groups to discuss mutual interests, entertain each other, and work collectively (Jones, 1995). As we saw above, some of these online discussions can directly influence the purchase of products and services. In spite of its potential importance, previous research on bulletin boards (an electronic message database where people can log in and leave messages) has been rare in consumer research for an exception (see Granitz & Ward, 1996) and there has been no attempt to integrate the streams of existing research that might guide the use of bulletin boards in consumer research.

The purpose of this paper is to answer two questions: what can we learn from bulletin board discussion groups and how best can we learn it? The first step toward answering those questions may be found by asking a fundamental question related to the Internet, namely, "how is this really new?" We begin, therefore, by comparing online discussions with other media, online and offline. We examine characteristics of online discussion that make it special both to participants and to researchers, and then summarize the unique capabilities and challenges of discussions as data. Contributions from sociology, conversation analysis, and content analysis are reviewed and applied to bulletin boards. We conclude by presenting a research agenda for online discussion groups. The focus throughout will be the online text bulletin board, also known as an online discussion forum, whose best-known form is the Usenet group.

ADVANTAGES AND DISADVANTAGES OF ONLINE BULLETIN BOARDS

Differences Among Discussion Media

The various ways in which two or more consumers can converse differ according to a number of attributes as shown in Table 4.1. Our description will proceed by attribute across communication type. Previous researchers have characterized online discussions as a hybrid of interpersonal and mass communication as well as oral and written language (Baym, 1996). We will argue that, while online discussions are not unique on any single attribute, they present a unique combination of attributes.

Time to respond refers to the interval between communications among participants. Three of the seven media shown in Table 4.1—face-to-face, telephone, and chat—occur in real time. There is usually only a brief pause between comments, and occasionally participants' comments overlap in time. As we will see, the potential for interrupting one another introduces problems that conversation participants work hard to solve. In synchronous communications there is no opportunity for the communicators to edit their messages. Real-time communication is therefore more spontaneous but also more prone to error. Email and discussion forums are slower than real time but faster than a letter, as participants may communicate many times during a single day. It is also possible for some members of a community to carry on a discussion through a publication forum such as letters to the editor of a newspaper or a forum in a medium like television or radio (e.g., *Cartalk*). This method is often not only slow but, more importantly, undependable as a conversation among audience members because editors or hosts only publish

TABLE 4.1

Characteristics of Consumer-to-Consumer Communications

	Time to Respond	Physical Proximity	Anonymity	Scale	Research Access	Archive
Face to face	Real time	Yes	Low	Small	Low	No
Telephone	Real time	No	Some/rare	Small	Low	No
Letter	Slow	No	Some/rare	Small	Low	Yes
Email	Fast	No	Some/rare	Small	Moderate	Yes
Online chat	Real time	No	High/often	Small	Access	No
Online discussion	Fast	No	High/often	Large	High	Yes
Publication forum	Slow/ Never	No	Some/rare	Large	High	Yes

(or air) a small number of communications. This shortcoming makes such forums inefficient for communication among community members. We include them here because they share other characteristics with online bulletin boards.

Of the seven media compared in Table 4.1, only face-to-face requires *physical proximity*. We should note, however, that telephone and conventional mail are affected by distance; mail is slower as distance increases and telephone usually is more expensive (as is international mail). A major advantage of online media is that physical distance is unimportant.

Anonymity refers to the extent that discussion participants can withhold their identity from each other. It is important to consider both the potential for anonymity and the norms concerning disclosure in each medium. Face-to-face communication has the least anonymity. In some situations strangers may converse without introductions; however, such things as gender, age, and race, are directly observable. Telephone, letter, and email all permit a higher level of anonymity, however, it is generally one-sided. The sender of the message can withhold identity more easily than the receiver, although increased use of caller identification is changing telephone anonymity. Perhaps most importantly, the norms for communicating by phone, letter and, email militate against anonymity. If callers will not disclose their identity, or the identity of the organization they represent, message receivers are highly skeptical. Anonymous letters have little credibility. Contributors to a publication forum such as letters to the editor usually reveal their name and town. In contrast, it is common for participants in an online chat room or discussion forum to reveal only as much of their identity as they want, or even to change identities. Norms of identification vary across different discussion groups, however, and these differences have important implications for group communication.

Scale refers to the maximum number of people who can communicate with each other in a particular discussion. Telephone and chat rooms become cumbersome with more than a handful of participants because it is difficult to track who is speaking or which thread of the conversation is active. Participants in a chat room have difficulty addressing each other and keeping the discussion focused. Conventional mail is appropriate for large scale communication only as a one-to-many medium. For example, a newsletter is more suited to communicating about a group than between individual group members. Face to face, in the form of a focus group, is effective for groups of up to nine or so (Stewart & Shamdasani, 1990). In a less interactive form, such as a town meeting, perhaps as many as 100 people can participate at some level. Email, in the form of an electronic mailing list, also permits moderately large groups to converse, sometimes facilitating a community (Sheldon, 1999). However, as members of a large electronic mailing list group can attest, too many messages are uninteresting and necessitating some form of hierarchy and control. By providing a central location to post and a way to organize and track discussion threads, a discussion forum scales best.

The remaining attributes in Table 4.1, *research access* and *archive*, view the media from the standpoint of the researcher rather than the participant. Research access is the ability of researchers to see or listen to a discussion so it is nearly the opposite of privacy. Research access to conversations conducted face to face, by telephone, and by letter is generally low. Access to email is higher, due to the ease with which email can be passed along. Research access is quite open to online chat, online discussions forums, and publication forums. Letters, email, discussions forums, and publication forums all leave a trace, or archive. There is no naturally occurring archive for face-to-face conversation, telephone, or chat.

Why Online Bulletin Boards Are Unique

To summarize Table 4.1, online bulletin boards combine a set of characteristics that make them uniquely valuable both to participants and researchers. They bring together people who would not be able to communicate in the same way in any other medium. In contrast to a town hall or focus group, online discussions render geographic location irrelevant. Unlike a print forum, such as the letters to the editor, online discussions permit an interaction between contributors with little selection or intermediation. Messages can be edited, but delays are much shorter than when writing conventional letters. Unlike chat or email, online discussions permit very large-scale interaction. Consumers are more sheltered by anonymity than in any other medium except the chat room. This anonymity provides both a benefit and a potential for abuse, as participants are often free to take aim at others without fear of reprisal. From the researcher's perspective, online text discussions provide particular advantages over the usual spoken conversation. First, a written text record of online forums exists after the conversation ceases. This text eliminates the need for transcription, which is both effortful and error prone. Second, online conversations are often extremely accessible. Opinions from diverse groups all over the world are readily and publicly available. Bulletin boards, like overheard conversations, can provide a window into what people are really saying without contamination from the researcher. As with focus groups, bulletin boards provide a means of learning about how people think about the dimensions of a problem independent of the researcher's cognitive structuring of the issues.

HOW WE CAN LEARN FROM BULLETIN BOARDS: THREE PERSPECTIVES

The study of online bulletin boards may be informed by at least three perspectives: bulletin boards as communities, as conversations, and as text. Dividing the research terrain in this fashion is not without dangers. The research literatures suggested by each perspective, sociology, conversation analysis, and content analysis often overlap. Of the three, content analysis stands out as a group of methods rather than a point of view. The sociology literature is very diverse, encompassing sociocultural, sociocognitive, and interpersonal communications studies among others. However the three perspectives highlight different aspects of online bulletin boards and therefore merit separate treatment. The next section discusses each perspective and some of the major concepts that might apply to the study of online bulletin board discussions.

Online Bulletin Boards as Communities

The concept of online community is sufficiently compelling that research involving online bulletin boards has approached the subject almost exclusively from a sociological perspective (Granitz & Ward, 1996; Kozinets 1998, 2002; Kollock & Smith, 1999; Rheingold, 1993). Some of the main areas of inquiry are group hierarchy, identity (especially gender identity), and online relationships. The overarching question seems to be, "What kind of community is an online community?" There is even dispute over whether community can exist online at all. Critics charge that an online environment lacks the requisite context, continuity, and cohesiveness to be a real community (Sardar, 1996). Kolko and Reid (1998) discuss the failure of online communities, focusing especially on the way fragmented and falsified personal identities inhibit the formation of real interpersonal relationships. The nature of online language is also new. "Language, as the building block of what occurs in cyberspace, is more ephemeral than the written word and more fixed than the casual spoken word" (Kolko & Reid, 1998, p. 213). The inflexibility of positions taken online provides a counterpoint to the flexibility of identity. People can be inflexible online in that they can become committed to the precise wording of a position (Reid, 1992).

Although certainly not every online discussion represents a meaningful community, a number of studies have described ways in which a discussion mirrors a community. For example, Fox and Roberts (1999) conducted a kind of cyber-ethnography based on postings to an online forum for physicians in the United Kingdom. They found that the online community had a distinct social order reflected in social norms, strategies used to establish identity, and agreement about professional values. They also reported that participants went through a series of stages as they were integrated into membership. Fox and Roberts (1999) found evidence of "a spirit of mutual trust, responsibility, and ongoing commitment on the one hand; on the other the petty spats and flaming which also mirror the tensions which arise in face to face engagements" (p. 666). Comparison between real and online communities was also the focus of Harrington and Bielby's (1995) study of bulletin board gossip regarding television soap operas. They found that interaction online was indeed different from face-to-face interaction, especially in the mechanisms used to establish trust. Because intimate social bonds were unavailable, interactants relied on source characteristics such as personal knowledge or claims to a direct connection to inside information. For example, they sometimes claimed to know an actor or director connected with a show. Harrington and Bielby (1995) also found that trust emerged over time and preceded, rather than resulted from, insider status. These studies seem to argue that online community does indeed exist, but in a somewhat different form from the offline world, and often in a way that augments or mirrors existing communities. An interesting application of community for marketers is the notion of a brand community (Muniz & O'Guinn, 2001).

An online bulletin board can also be viewed as a community information network (Festinger 1949). The pattern and content of such communication is important to marketers because research has shown that word of mouth is an extremely influential source of product information (Arndt, 1967; Engel, Blackwell, & Kegerreis, 1969; Katona & Mueller, 1955). Online word of mouth also seems to have advantages over commercial sources. Bickart & Schindler (2001) had consumers gather product information online from either discussion groups or from marketer-generated sources such as corporate web pages. At the end of a 12-week period, consumers who had used discussion forums were more interested in the topics than consumers who acquired information from marketer-generated sources.

Issues that arise in social network analysis include the relative centrality of network members and the cliques that form within the larger community. In the only application of social network analysis to online consumer discussion groups to date, Granitz and Ward (1996) examined interactions among members of a Usenet group that discussed coffee. They found that experts, as measured by the type and quality of their postings, were more central within the network. That is, experts interacted more with other network members. Interestingly, Kozinets (2002) also uses a coffee user group as an example of netnography (online ethnography).

Online Bulletin Boards as Conversation

During the 1970s the sociologist Harvey Sacks gave a series of lectures concerning the way interactions are organized within spoken conversation (Sacks, 1992). The research approach that emerged, known as conversation analysis (CA), essentially is about the organization of interaction (Arminen, 1999; Hutchby & Wooffitt, 1998). Conversation analysis involves what an utterance does in relation to the preceding one(s) and the implications it poses for the next one(s). The basic unit of analysis therefore is a "turn of talk," a piece of conversation in context. The emphasis in CA is on understanding the meanings conveyed in the conversation itself, as it takes shape between or among participants. The context is critical, but it is assumed to be supplied by the conversation itself. Therefore talk is considered to be context renewing (Silverman, 1998).

The overarching question of CA is how social tasks are accomplished in interaction. This makes the purpose of a conversation extremely important, as it is assumed that participants are working toward that purpose as they converse. Some of the more specific issues in CA include the techniques that speakers use for various purposes, for example, to preempt the skepticism of the message recipient. CA studies are characterized by analysis of conversation at a very micro level—looking for the use of particular words, intonations, and gaps in conversation. For example, Atkinson (1984) noted the preference for three-part lists (an example of which can be found at the end of the preceding sentence). A three-part list lets the hearer know when a point has likely been made and the speaker can be interrupted. This phenomenon suggests another area of inquiry, turn-taking, or how speaking time is allocated. An important purpose of taking turns in conversation is to be polite, which brings us to a related area of inquiry known as politeness theory (Brown & Levinson, 1978, 1987).

Politeness, according to Brown and Levinson (1987), is the phrasing of one's remarks so as to manage the face, or public identity (Goffman, 1967), of each participant in the conversation. It is assumed that everyone wants to protect their face from others (negative face) and to connect or be close with others (positive face). Many acts threaten the positive or negative face (or both) of participants. For example, requests threaten the hearer's negative face by imposing on him or her, and disagreements threaten the hearer's positive face by jeopardizing closeness. Acts threatening the face of a participant can be made less face threatening by performing them with one of Brown and Levinson's (1987) politeness super strategies. These strategies, ordered in terms of increasing politeness, are positive politeness, negative politeness, and off-record politeness. Positive politeness is conveyed by appealing to the other's positive, rather than negative, face (Holtgraves, 1997). For example, a speaker can convey positive politeness by emphasizing intimacy or commonality with the other. Brown and Levinson (1987) outline three broad strategies for conveying positive politeness: claiming common ground, conveying that the participants are cooperators, and fulfilling the hearer's wants. These three strategies can be carried out by 15 more specific mechanisms. For example, one can claim common ground by emphasizing in-group identity or by joking; cooperation can be conveyed by asserting reciprocity or by promises or offerings; fulfilling the hearers' wants can be achieved by giving them gifts. The microanalysis of conversational techniques may be especially interesting for online discussions because of the particular challenges to building trust and community online.

Conversation Analysis Applications. Because online discussions are interactive, applications from CA are plausible. However, as we have noted, online bulletin boards combine characteristics in ways that make them unique. For example, managing face in online bulletin boards is different from face-to-face interactions in at least two ways. First, participants may disclose more or less of their identity online. Second, the nature of interactions in very large groups probably changes the nature of face threats. For example, posing a question to a bulletin board seems more likely to threaten the negative face of the speaker, by exposing a potential lack of knowledge, than of the multiple hearers, who have no obligation to respond. (It would be interesting to explore the reactions of those whose questions go unanswered.) Taking turns is also different online than in face-to-face conversation, because there is no possibility of interrupting in the middle of a posting (except for chatrooms). Instead, the number and length of postings constitutes the allocation of speaking time. Interruption of a conversation can occur by an off-topic posting (sometimes designated as OT) in a particular thread. It is interesting in that context to consider the resultant new norms of conversation. It seems likely that a major component of these norms is to avoid wasting the time and effort of other participants.

In the case of the first posting at the beginning of this chapter, conversation analysis would perhaps be most interested in the dynamics of the conversation regarding a possible boycott of Pepsico. What is the structure of the thread, and how does each posting play off of and set up the next?

Online Bulletin Boards as Text

Bulletin boards also can be viewed as records of written text, a perspective that directs our attention to the literature on content analysis. This literature is especially appropriate for answering this paper's second question, namely, how best can we learn from online bulletin boards? The use of content analysis in the social sciences is extremely widespread; from 1965–1994 content analysis was used as the primary method in approximately one fifth of the articles published in mainstream media journals (Cooper, Potter, & Dupagne, 1994; Evans, 1998). Content analysis also has a long tradition in consumer research (Ferber & Wales, 1958; Kassarjian, 1977; Kolbe & Burnett, 1991). There are at least four characteristics of content analysis that make it advantageous as a research technique: it is unobtrusive, it accepts unstructured material, it is sensitive to context, and it allows for large volumes of data (Krippendorff, 1980). All of these virtues seem especially relevant to online bulletin boards.

As we said earlier, content analysis is more a group of methods than a theoretical perspective, so our discussion will focus on the distinctions among methods and their applications to online bulletin boards. The first distinction to note is between qualitative analysis, also associated with grounded theory, and quantitative analysis, sometimes called classical content analysis (Bernard & Ryan, 1998).

Qualitative content analysis is more conventionally used in the discovery of hypotheses; consequently, the method accommodates a great deal of flexibility. In the grounded theory approach, analysis of a text begins by reading through a small part of it line by line to identify potential themes. Sandelowski (1995) recommends proofreading texts and simply underlining key phrases because they may not make enough sense at first to categorize. These themes are coded inductively and then linked together to build theoretical models. As a model takes shape, researchers look for examples that do not fit the pattern. These negative cases may either disconfirm parts of the model or suggest new linkages (Miles & Huberman, 1994). A number of computer software packages have been developed to aid in grounded theory development, of which perhaps the best known is NUD*IST (Richards & Richards, 1991). The building of a model is best considered as a step in the research process to be followed by validating the model using an independent sample of data (Glaser & Strauss, 1967).

Online discussions may be useful to marketing practitioners and academics for generating hypotheses and for providing thick description, however, as with focus groups, online discussions have the potential to lead in the wrong direction if vivid descriptions are substituted for quantitative analysis. Quantitative text analysis involves drawing statistical inferences from samples of text and transcripts. All such analysis involves two steps, sampling text units and projecting sampled texts into a two-dimensional unit-by-variable data matrix. The variables in this matrix reflect the extent to which it is important to understand relations among the concepts that are being counted. Therefore, text analysis can be classified in order of increasing attention to relations among the text units (Roberts, 1997). Thematic text analysis is concerned with occurrences (or counts) of concepts, for example, the use of brand names. Semantic-text analysis maps relations among concepts or themes, for example, the frequency with which brand names are described as high quality. Network text analysis maps relations among statements, for example, the frequency with which statements indicating brand quality are associated with statements indicating brand price. Online discussion content analysis can quantify these terms and topics using commercially available software for which extensive reviews are available (Popping, 1997). Classification of software programs follows the distinction outlined above between thematic, semantic, and network analysis. McMillan (2000) identified particular challenges for using content analysis on the World Wide Web (WWW). Her study reviewed content analyses of Web sites rather than bulletin boards but her results apply equally well to bulletin boards. Sampling and coding were especially problematic, creating difficulties for making any generalizations.

It is impossible to analyze all online discussion group content on any subject, so some sampling decisions are necessary. The population from which the sample is taken will be dictated by the purpose of the research. If discussion groups are organized by interest area, they may not correspond to a target-market profile. The sampling process itself will probably involve multiple stages. Some subset of discussion groups will be chosen and then some subset of discussion content or threads will be chosen. Choice of discussion groups may begin by choosing search engines, so the limitations and biases of these search engines must be understood as well. It appears that, both analytically and from published research (McMillan, 2000), sampling is the Achilles' heel of online research. That is, it is extremely difficult to draw a sample of online phenomena (individuals, discussions, Web sites, and so forth) that is representative of a population that corresponds to the physical world. There are several possible ways around this problem. Marketers can improve the quality of discussion data by creating online panels whose members have known real world characteristics. Commercial Web sites might accomplish this goal by encouraging membership in particular discussions. Similarly, research firms can create intranets with expert participants or samples selected based on the physical world. These samples would be more representative of real-world populations but would lack the advantage of being able to observe real discussion unobtrusively. Therefore, an alternative approach would be to sample from an online population making no statement about inferences to the offline world.

The analyses of online content will be dominated by the comparisons that are made. In our first example, if the purpose is to determine whether attitudes toward Burger King are worsening, the comparison would be across time. For example, we could examine whether there is a trend in the incidence of negative statements about Burger King. Similarly, a comparison may be made in response to a particular event, such as a media report or public demonstration. More general comparisons of interest to academics include comparisons across levels of analysis (organizations vs. issues), comparisons between consumer groups, and comparisons between discussion groups and different media, such as Web sites or search engine results).

A DESCRIPTIVE FRAMEWORK FOR BULLETIN BOARD ANALYSIS

The analysis of an online discussion could be guided by the characteristics shown in Table 4.2 below. Table 4.2 is organized by the levels of analysis in an online bulletin board, community (group), participant (individual), and message (text). These three levels partially map on to the three perspectives discussed above. Community characteristics and their relation to individual participant characteristics have been addressed in the sociology literature; message characteristics come from conversation analysis and content analysis.

In the following description of the characteristics in Table 4.2 we will draw on the two conversation fragments with which we began this paper. The first example, from a Usenet group, suggested a possible boycott of Burger King. The second example was a question and answer exchange between two women who are members of a discussion group for parents of children born in the same month.

Community Characteristics

Purpose. Our Usenet example is convened for the purpose of talk alone. It is the sort of group that really has no counterpart in face-to-face interaction because just talking about politics would require a political agenda, tavern, or other justification. The parents' discussion is essentially an online "Birth to Three" group.

TABLE 4.2
Characteristics to Analyze in an Online Bulletin Board

Community Characteristics	Participant Characteristics	Message Characteristics
Purpose	Demographics	Structure
Organization & structure	Attitudes & values	Tone
Membership rules	Knowledge & expertise	Formality
Norms		Conflict
Cohesion	Personal Disclosure	Politeness
Continuity	Motivation	Emotion
Context	Role	Content

There is sharing of information of mutual interest to young parents, primarily women. However, most of all it is a support group.

Structure. Communities differ according to their level of organization, the presence of hierarchies, and the formation of subgroups or cliques. In our example, the Usenet group is equipped with software that allows participants to follow a thread. There is the possibility that subgroups can be formed naturally because of the pattern of postings. However, no one is in charge of the group, and no one has responsibility for it. In contrast, the parents' discussion has a very formal hierarchy with several layers. The discussion group has two community leaders.

Membership Rules. Online discussions can have rules for participation and management that make them different from both print media and spoken conversation. Communities differ greatly in the rules of participation, the most basic of which is who participants can be. Some online communities require professional licensing, such as in a particular health care profession, which enables all participants to trust the information provided. For example, discussions among physicians generally require participants to register by email with a discussion administrator, who then issues a password. Most online groups are open to all participants and are defined by interest only, however, even when participation is open, some groups actively discourage unwanted members (MacKinnon, 1995). An example of this discouragement is the hostility expressed toward America Online members in some Usenet discussions, presumably because an aol.com email address indicates ignorance or "newbie" status. Generally, stronger membership rules yield stronger communities. In our example, the parents' group has rules against flaming and against commercial purposes. Usenet groups have essentially no rules. Communities differ according to how tightly they are managed, and more centralized management usually accompanies more stringent rules. Discussions on parents' groups typically are overseen by several layers of management, beginning with the community leader. Offensive or commercial postings are deleted and are not part of the archive. Usenet bulletin boards have essentially no central administration. One caveat of controlling a discussion is that it tends to imply some responsibility for content. A site that posts messages through some kind of central authority confers an implied acceptability for the postings, much like when a newspaper publishes a letter to the editor. Therefore, managing a discussion can threaten a company or organization's reputation if it is not done carefully. Although an organization promotes a stronger community by managing the postings they are also assuming a risk.

Norms. Communities have norms for behavior in a variety of areas: how others are treated, the kinds of topics that can be addressed, the extent that postings can vary from thread topics, the level of personal disclosure, and so forth. Groups can also proscribe certain kinds of behavior, such as shouting (typing in all caps) or flaming (insulting other participants).

Cohesion. The cohesion characteristic refers to how closely members of the community identify with it. Cohesion has often been related to how much members like each other, however, Hogg and Hains (1996) argue that members of a cohesive group like each other not as individuals but as embodiments of the group. In our example it is difficult to see how a Usenet group can be very cohesive, but we might expect that members of a parents' support group could have a group identity. Women with children born in the same month have a lot in common and there are many reinforcements for sharing online experiences.

Continuity. This standard, which is refers to the extent that the community is ongoing in time, probably most closely related to the stability of community membership and the degree to which community history is archived. In our example, Usenet discussions are archived, creating some continuity, however, other forms of social glue are absent.

Context. There is generally little relationship between Usenet postings and the real-world lives of participants. In contrast, discussions among parents' groups are richly contextualized. There is often extensive personal disclosure, strong enforcement of group norms, and an ongoing, stable relationship with a relatively small number of people who are at the same stage in life. Sometimes group members post pictures of their families, and particular members contact each other personally by email and even meet in person.

Participant Characteristics

Content analysis has frequently been guided by examining who said what to whom with what effect (Lasswell, 1948). The same examination of source and message characteristics can be applied to the analysis of online discussions. Because online discussions cast participants as both source and audience, participants may be described in both those roles. As discussed above, characteristics of forum participants are critical in assessing the meaning of online discussions.

Demographics. In spite of the hopes expressed by early writings on online community, gender, race, ethnicity, socioeconomic status "SES", and occupation all influence participants' contributions. For example, Herring (1996) demonstrates that women and men have different values toward harmonious and agonistic debate, which are reflected in different discussion forum posting styles. Simply put, men are less polite than women (cf. Tannen, 1996). They flame more; they support each other less. The relationship between demographics and message content has also been discussed in relation to other media. For example, Evans (1998) suggests a need to model more rigorously the relationships between news content and audience characteristics. An important element of context in our examples is that the Usenet group is male dominated and the parents' group is overwhelmingly female.

Attitudes and Values. Participants bring the same biases online that exist in the real world (cf. Kahle 1996). If content analysis is used, it may be necessary to examine a number of postings over time to assess stable attitudes. Attitudes and values also could be measured by contacting discussion participants by email and administering an online questionnaire.

Knowledge and Expertise. Participants can establish expertise by their use of such signs as terminology, abbreviations, and so forth. Usenet hacker group participants provide a hack in their messages to demonstrate expertise. A reputation for expertise can be established over time. As Granitz and Ward (1996) found, expertise can be related to how central a participant is in the network.

Personal Disclosure. It is possible to disguise online identity completely or to divulge a great deal. Domain names can indicate whether the participant is from a particular university or company. Hotmail accounts reveal little, and some services (remailers) strip all identification and allow complete anonymity for the sender. An aol.com address inadvertently reveals new user status. Actual names—John Smythe rather than handles such as nospamJohn—provide the same identity online as in the physical world. In our examples the author of the Usenet posting appeared to provide a real name (we did not print it here). The two women in the parents' group signed their first names only, but registration on this parents' group would permit others to see their first names along with the city and country they live in and other personal details including their spouses first names, occupations, and names of their children. In some cases other hobbies and interests are disclosed. Perhaps more importantly, the nature of postings in that group reveals many details of participants' real lives. Support group discussions also frequently involve questions posed to all members of the community such as "what is your favorite song, television show, or movie?"

Motivation for Response. It is useful to consider what participants personally want out of the discussion. They may want to be entertained or to feel a part of a group. They also may be motivated to persuade, to win, to dominate, or to vent their emotions. These motivations may be analyzed at the level of individual postings since participants may want to accomplish different things at different times. In our Usenet example, it first appears that the motivation is to persuade others to boycott Burger King however, it may be just as likely that the real motive is to validate the sender's opinion. In other words, the question is not "won't someone out there help me take action?" so much as "does anyone out there agree with me?"

Role. In any particular posting, contributors assume a role that closely ties to their motivation. Examples (some of which overlap) include providing information, initiating a topic, asking a question, answering a question, clarifying an answer, corroborating an answer, and emotionally supporting a participant. Over time it may be observed that participants consistently assume the same role. In Usenet all roles are self-designated; in the parents' group there are community leaders. In our examples, the roles assumed are, respectively, initiating a topic, asking a question, and answering a question.

Message Characteristics

Structure. In a bulletin board discussion a thread is a more- or less-continuous chain of postings on a single topic. To "follow a thread" is to read a series of postings that share a common subject or (more correctly) that is connected by reference headers (FOLDOC, 2000). Within each thread are individual postings. Both threads and postings can be considered units of conversational analysis. Applying content analysis to a discussion may begin by simply quantifying the number of participants, number of levels in the thread, number of entries per participant, and length of each entry. A critical decision in content analysis would also be the choice of whether to sample threads, postings, or participants. More than one unit of analysis is possible, for example, Granitz and Ward (1996) analyzed a matrix of postings by participants to determine how central each participant was in the discussion network. Applying conversation analysis to the discussion would involve treating each posting as a "turn of talk." The analyst would concentrate on the meaning of each turn in context.

Message Tone. Tone refers to the participants' attitudes toward other participants and toward the subject matter. Tone is often a direct reflection of the motivation of participants. Consistent with the kind of microanalysis used in conversation analysis, tone may be characterized further. Formality reflects the amount of social distance implied in the communication. Referring to other members by their first names, using slang, or incomplete sentences, for example, indicate a less formal tone. Conflict refers to clear differences of opinion and threatens positive face. Independent of whether conflicting views are expressed, messages differ in the extent to which other members are treated with respect. Lack of civility threatens positive face. At the extreme negative end of the spectrum, participants may engage in deliberate insults known as "flame wars." (An example can be found in the Usenet group rec.ski.alpine, and contributors are strongly cautioned to use a remailer.) Online emotion is generally expressed through word choice, and it can be confounded with civility. Exclamation points and other expressions, such as ☺ ☹, can be used to substitute for voice inflection. In our examples both discussion fragments seem relatively informal, and they address others politely with little threat to anyone's face.

Content. Perhaps most importantly, discussions can be characterized by the particular terms used and points made. These terms are used to compile a dictionary that can be used in content analysis. In our examples, such terminology might include the names of specific companies or brands, and phrases that link them in a positive or negative way.

SUMMARY AND RESEARCH AGENDA

Online bulletin boards can provide a window into consumers' minds, showing us the kinds of things they find important about products and the language they use. However, the most important thing that we need to understand about online discussions is how the discussions themselves work. Research concepts and methods for examining online forums are suggested by considering them as communities, as conversations, and as text. The online world has both a life of its own and an impact on the physical world. An online discussion gives consumers a new communication medium with different strengths and weaknesses than other media, and therefore suggests new questions:

• What factors increase the trust that people place in product information from online discussion groups? This is perhaps the most important overarching question. It subsumes issues related to characteristics of individuals, of their discussion groups and of the discussions themselves. Our examples in this chapter suggest that the characteristics of the community itself, particularly strong discussion rules and management, provide a place where trust is more likely to take hold.
• What kind of information from online discussion groups do people believe more (for example, positive vs. negative information, recommendations vs. offhand comments)? Previous research has shown that negative information is given more weight than positive information. However, in one of our examples, a positive recommendation for a swing set directed a consumer to a Web site at the click of a mouse. Online recommendations may be especially powerful because of this short circuiting of the decision process.
• How much do discussion group participants trust information from the discussion group compared with information from other sources? Word on line is not exactly word of mouth. Online discussions take place among people who usually have never met face to face. However, some discussion group members have long-standing online relationships. They may also have established reputations for expertise. Online discussions are more interactive than print or broadcast media, however, credibility signals, such as might exist under a seal of approval or Consumer Reports rating are absent. Bickart and Schindler (2001) reported results from an experiment indicating that there is greater interest in products when the product information comes from online discussions rather than from marketer-generated sources such as Web sites. Does such interest translate into trust?

• What are the characteristics of people who persuade others or make online recommendations? Are there differences between people who are opinion leaders in online versus face-to-face interactions? Online forums are different from face to face interactions in the way participants project their identity and present cues. Online forums also remove physical barriers of space and time. This may provide the opportunity for a greater leadership role to be assumed by those whose physical limitations or geographic location preclude such a role in face-to-face interactions. Similarly, how generalizable is online opinion leadership? (Across different products? Other domains like sports or politics?) What are the characteristics of those who adopt other online roles, such as asking questions or just "lurking?"

• How do the conventions of online product discussions differ from talk face to face or by telephone? This question could be addressed by conversation analysis and brings up issues of politeness and of allocating talk among speakers. Participants in an online discussion are less constrained by time than in real-time conversation modes. There are no possibilities to interrupt each other, and long tirades can be easily skipped or read quickly. Therefore, we should expect greater tolerance for long postings than for long monologues and greater variation in the length of a turn of talk online than in face-to-face or telephone conversation.

• How do online discussions influence different stages in the purchase process? Online question and answer sequences seem naturally directed toward early stages in the decision process. However, we have seen that posting a Web site can facilitate a purchase and eliminate stages, or compress, such as alternative evaluation. Online word of mouth has the potential to fundamentally change the buying process.

• How might research explore the extent to which marketers are currently employing techniques to use or encourage online word of mouth?

A POST SCRIPT ON RESEARCH ETHICS

There is some disagreement over the obligations of researchers who use online bulletin boards as data. Despite the fact that such postings may already be available to everyone on the Internet, their publication in another medium involves issues of privacy, deception, and invasiveness. King (1996) notes that human subjects' committees generally exempt publicly accessible forums from the requirement to obtain informed consent. However, King and others (Waskul & Douglass, 1996) have argued that researchers should distinguish between accessibility and dissemination. Although participants in an online forum may be aware that many other people can read their postings, they may not expect them to be widely disseminated. There even may be a high level of perceived privacy. In cases where there is a sense of perceived privacy, researchers should be especially careful not to reveal either the identity of participants or of the particular forum.

There remains some question over issues related to gaining permission from a group whose postings are being studied. Kozinets (2002) states that netnographers should: disclose their presence, affiliations, and intentions to community members; insure confidentiality and anonymity to informants; seek and incorporate feedback from members of the community; and obtain permission for stories or specific quotations. However, in the case of a close community, the request for informed consent may be disruptive in itself (Waskul & Douglass, 1996). Informed consent of anything other than quoting particular messages would require that researchers make their presence known frequently, which would be even more disruptive.

Despite gray areas, there is a consensus on several points. The first, overarching principle is that researchers should endeavor to do no harm. Second, researchers should not misrepresent themselves to bulletin board participants or managers. Third, researchers should err on the side of masking the identity of participants and of bulletin boards. Fourth, researchers should be sensitive about possible disruption to genuine online communities. Adhering to these guidelines calls for common sense regarding the varying sensitivity of groups and of postings. The possibility for harm is greatest when groups are closely knit and/or the topic is personal. In our examples, the call for a boycott of Burger King in a public Usenet group does not warrant much concern over doing harm by doing research. The contributor does not exhibit any sense of perceived privacy (he makes a public call to action) and neither the bulletin board nor the topic is private. The group itself has virtually no context or cohesion and no community to disrupt. This posting is much more like a letter to the editor than it is a private conversation fragment.

In contrast, research on the postings to an online parents' group warrants more sensitive treatment. Although the particular postings described here are not sensitive, they may imply a sense of perceived privacy. Other individual contributions to the parents' group are more self-revealing. There is also a threat of disrupting their collective sense of community despite the public accessibility of the bulletin board. Therefore both the group and its participants probably should be kept anonymous, and the researcher probably should not contact members of this group to request informed consent because such contact may be disruptive in itself. Research concerning postings to a group that shares more personally sensitive information, such as an online support group for sexual assault survivors, would warrant even more concern for respecting privacy and avoiding invasiveness. Besides maintaining anonymity of both group and participants, it would seem best not to publish any verbatim quotations from such a group.

REFERENCES

Arminen, I. (1999). Conversation analysis: A quest for order in social interaction and language use. *Acta Sociologica, 42,* 251–257.

Arndt, J. (1967). Role of product-related conversations in the diffusion of a new product. *Journal of Marketing Research, 4*(August), 291–295.

Atkinson, J. M. (1984). *Our masters' voices: The language and body language of politics.* London: Metheun.

Baym, N. (1996). Agreement and disagreement in a computer-mediated group. *Research on Language and Social Interaction, 29,* 315–346.

Bernard, H. R., & Ryan, G. (1998). Qualitative and quantitative methods of text analysis, In H. R. Bernard (Ed.), *Handbook of method in cultural anthropology.* Walnut Creek, CA: AltaMira Press.

Bickart, B., & Schindler, R. M. (2001). Internet forums as influential sources of consumer information. *Journal of Interactive Marketing, 15*(3), 31–40.

Boush, D. M., & Kahle L. (2001). Evaluating negative information in online consumer discussions: From qualitative analysis to signal detection, *Journal of Euromarketing, 11*(2), 89–105.

Brown, R., & Levinson, S. (1978). Universals in language usage: Politeness phenomena. In E. Goody (Ed.), *Questions and politeness* (pp. 256–324). Cambridge, UK: Cambridge University Press.

Brown, P., & Levinson, S. (1987). *Politeness: Some universals in language usage.* Cambridge, UK: Cambridge University Press.

Burger King. (2001). Company timeline history. Retrieved September 14, 2001, from http://www.burgerking.com/company/timeline.htm.

Cooper, R., Potter, W. J., & Dupagne, M. (1994). A status report on methods used in mass communication research. *Journalism Educator, 48,* 54–61.

Engel, J. E., Blackwell, R. D., & Kegerreis, R. J. (1969). How information is used to adopt an innovation. *Journal of Advertising Research, 9*(December), 3–8.

Evans, W. (1998). Content analysis in an era of interactive news: Assessing 21st century symbolic environments. In D. L. Borden & K. Harvey (Eds.), *The electronic grapevine: rumor, reputation and reporting in the new on-line environment* (pp. 161–172). Mahwah, NJ: Lawrence Erlbaum Associates, Inc.

Ferber, R., & Wales, H. G. (1958). *Motivation and market behavior.* Homewood, IL: Irwin.

Festinger, L. (1949). The analysis of sociograms using matrix algebra. *Human Relations, 2,* 153–158.

Fox, N., & Roberts, C. (1999). GPs in cyberspace: The sociology of a virtual community. *The Sociological Review, 47*(November), 643–671.

Free Online Dictionary of Computing (FOLDOC). (Updated July 12, 2000). Retrieved September 14, 2001, from http://foldoc.doc.ic.ac.uk/foldoc/index.html.

Glaser, B. G., & Strauss, A. (1967). *The discovery of grounded theory: Strategies for qualitative research.* New York: Aldine.

Goffman, E. (1967). *Interaction ritual: Essays on face-to-face behavior.* Garden City, NY: Anchor Books.

Granitz, N. A., & Ward, J. C. (1996). Virtual community: A sociocognitive analysis. *Advances in Consumer Research, 23,* 161–166.

Hanson, W. (2000). *Principles of Internet marketing.* Cincinnati, OH: Southwestern College Publishing.

Harrington, C. L., & Bielby, D. D. (1995). Where did you hear that? Technology and the social organization of gossip. *Sociological Quarterly, 36*(3), 607–628.

Herring, S. (1996). Posting in a different voice: Gender and ethics in computer-mediated communication, in C. Ess (Ed.). *Philosophical perspectives on computer-mediated communication.* (pp. 115–145). Albany, NY: State University of New York Press.

Hogg, M. A., & Hains, S. C. (1996). Intergroup relations and group solidarity: Effects of group identification and social beliefs on depersonalized attraction. *Journal of Personality and Social Psychology, 70*(2), 295–309.

Holtgraves, T. (1997). Yes, but … positive politeness in conversation analysis. *Journal of Language and Social Psychology, 16*(2), 222–239.

Hutchby, I., & Wooffitt, R. (1998). *Conversation analysis: Principles, practices, and applications.* Cambridge, UK: Polity Press.

Jones, S. G. (1995). Understanding computers in the information age. In S. G. Jones (Ed.), *Cybersociety: computer-mediated communication and community*, London: Sage.

Kahle, L. R. (1996). Social values and consumer behavior: Research from the List of Values. In C. Seligman, J. M. Olson, & M. P. Zanna (Eds.), *The psychology of values: The Ontario Symposium* (Vol. 8, pp. 135–151). Mahwah, NJ: Lawrence Erlbaum Associates, Inc.

Kassarjian, H. H. (1977). Content analysis in consumer research. *Journal of Consumer Research, 4*(June), 8–18.

Katona , G., & Mueller, E. (1955). A study of purchase decisions, In L. H. Clark (Ed.), *The dynamics of consumer reaction* (pp. 30–87). New York: New York University Press.

King, S. A. (1996). Researching Internet communities: Proposed ethical guidelines for the reporting of results. *The Information Society 12*, 119–127.

Kolbe, R. H., & Burnett, M. S. (1991). Content analysis research: An examination of applications with directives for research reliability and objectivity. *Journal of Consumer Research, 18*(2), 243–250.

Kolko, B., & Reid, E. (1998). Dissolution and fragmentation: Problems in online communities. In S. G. Jones (Ed.) *Cybersociety 2.0: Revisiting computer mediated communication and communities* (pp. 212–230). Thousand Oaks, CA: Sage.

Kollock, P., & Smith, M. A. (1999). Communities in cyberspace. In M. A. Smith & P. Kollock (Eds.), *Communities in cyberspace* (pp. 3–25) London: Routledge.

Kozinets, R. V. (1998). On netnography: Initial reflections on consumer research investigations of cyberculture. In J. Alba & W. Hutchinson (Eds.) *Advances in Consumer Research* Vol. 25, pp. 366–371. Provo, UT: Association for Consumer Research.

Kozinets, R. V., (2002). The field behind the screen: Using netnography for marketing research in online communities. *Journal of Marketing Research, 39*(February), 61–72.

Kozinets, R. V., & Handelman J. (1998). Ensouling consumption: A netnographic exploration of the meaning of boycotting behavior. *Advances in Consumer Research, 25*, 475–480.

Krippendorff, K. (1980). *Content analysis: An introduction to its methodology.* Beverly Hills, CA: Sage Publications.

Lasswell, H. D. (1948). The structure and function of communication in society. In L. Bryson (Ed.), *The communication of ideas* (pp. 37–51). New York: Harper and Rowe.

MacKinnon, R. C. (1995). Searching for the leviathan in Usenet. In S. Jones (Ed.). *Cyber society: Computer mediated communication and community.* Thousand Oaks, CA: Sage Publications.

McMillan, S. J. (2000). The microscope and the moving target: The challenge of applying content analysis to the World Wide Web. *Journalism & Mass Communication Quarterly, 77*(1), 80–98.

Miles, M., & Huberman, A. M. (1994). *Qualitative data analysis* (2nd ed.). Thousand Oaks, CA: Sage Publications.

Muniz, A. M., Jr., & O'Guinn T. C. (2001). Brand community. *Journal of Consumer Research, 27*, 412–432.

Popping R. (1997). Computer programs for the analysis of texts. In C. W. Roberts (Ed.). *Text Analysis for the Social Sciences: Methods for Drawing Statistical Inferences from Texts and Transcripts*, (pp. 209–221). Mahwah, NJ: Lawrence Erlbaum Associates, Inc.

Reid, E. M. (1992). Electropolis: Communication and community on Internet relay chat. *Intertek, 3*(3), 7–15.

Rheingold, H. (1993). *The virtual community.* New York: Addison-Wesley.

Richards, T., & Richards, L. (1991). The NUDIST qualitative data analysis system. *Qualitative Sociology, 14*, 307–325.

Roberts, C. W. (1997). A theoretical map for selecting among text analysis methods. In C. W. Roberts (Ed.), *Text analysis for the social sciences: Methods for drawing statistical inferences from texts and transcripts* (pp. 275–283). Mahwah, NJ: Lawrence Erlbaum Associates, Inc.

Sacks, H. (1992). *Lectures on conversation.* G. Jefferson vols. I and II. Oxford: Blackwell.

Sandelowski, M. (1995). Qualitative analysis: What it is and how to begin. *Research in Nursing and Health*, 18: 179–183.

Sardar, Z. (1996). Alt.civilizations.faq: Cyberspace as the darker side of the west. In Z. Sardar & J. R. Ravetz (Eds.), *Cyberfutures: Culture and politics on the information superhighway.* London: Pluto Press.

Sheldon, P. (1999). Green and gold blood on the information superhighway: An ethnographic log onto the Green Bay Packer listserver newsgroup. *Advances in Consumer Research, 26,* 652.

Silverman, D. (1998). *Harvey Sacks—Social sciences and conversation analysis.* Cambridge, UK: Polity Press.

Stewart, D. W., & Shamdasani, P. N. (1990). *Focus groups: Theory and practice.* Newbury Park, CA: Sage.

Tannen, D. (1996). *Gender and discourse.* New York: Oxford University Press.

Waskul, D., & Douglass, M. (1996). Considering the electronic participant: Some polemical observations on the ethics of online research. *The Information Society, 12,* 129–139.

II. ADVERTISING

CHAPTER FIVE

How Banner Ads Affect Brand Choice Without Click-Through

Andrew Mitchell
University of Toronto

Ana Valenzuela
San Francisco State University

According to conventional wisdom, Internet advertising differs from traditional advertising in that it is customized, nondisruptive and allows for sales-based efficient tracking via click-through rates (The Economist, 2001). However, click-through rates (i.e., the number of clicks on a banner relative to the total number of displays), are generally very low (seldom tops one percent), and consumers have even learned not to look at the banner ads (Wall Street Journal, 2001). Therefore, it has been concluded that banner ads on the Internet are of little value. For this and other reasons, the revenue from banner ads has declined recently (Green and Elgin, 2001) creating problems for Internet firms which rely heavily on advertising revenue (e.g., Yahoo, DoubleClick). The question remains whether banner advertisements have positive effects on consumer behavior other than click through. If so, click-through rates are used incorrectly as an absolute measure of success.

Clicking on a banner ad is considered a short-term response equivalent to returning a coupon after seeing a print ad or impulse buying after seeing a point-of-purchase ad (Chandon & Chtourou, 2001). Because most advertising does not always have a short-term response, industry specialists suggest that marketers should look beyond click though and institute performance measures that are more indicative of an Internet banner ad's effect on consumer behavior (Kumbil, & Nums, 2001). A number of industry studies have examined the effect of banner ads on advertising awareness, brand awareness, and probability of purchase (Gilliam, 2000; Hofacker & Murphy, 2000; Internet Advertising Bureau, 1997).

All these studies have found positive effects of exposure to an Internet ad on the probability of purchasing the advertised brand.

Consequently, there is some evidence that banner ads affect consumer behavior without click through. In this chapter, we argue that simple banner ads that only mention the brand name and logo may have both a direct effect on the probability of purchasing the advertised brand and an indirect effect on competing brands. The direct effects occur because the banner ad increases both the accessibility of the advertised brand in memory and the perceptual fluency experienced when the brand is next encountered. The indirect effects occur because the advertised brand is more likely to be retrieved when making judgments about competing brands, thereby biasing these judgments. We discuss theoretical reasons why this may occur and present the results of two experiments that demonstrate these effects.

In the next sections, we first briefly discuss a model of memory-based choice and then use this model to discuss how exposure to a simple banner ad may create direct and indirect effects on memory-based choice by increasing brand accessibility. Then, we extend the model to a constrained choice setting where consumers choose between a subset of brands from a product category. Again, we discuss the direct and indirect effects that may occur from exposure to a banner ad. Next we present the results of two experiments that demonstrate these effects. Finally, we discuss the implications of these findings.

THEORY

There are two streams of research in psychology that are relevant to understanding the effects of banner advertisements on consumer behavior. The first of these streams is the literature on priming effects on judgment. The basic idea behind these studies is that prior exposure to a stimulus (e.g., word) activates the representation of the stimulus in memory, and this activation influences judgments that are made about a person or object (called the target). In these studies the priming stimulus and target judgment are disguised as separate studies to eliminate demand effects.

The initial studies in this stream found that priming attributes created assimilation effects (the target is perceived to be similar to the prime) on judgments about individuals when the information available about those individuals is ambiguous (e.g., Higgins, Rholes, & Jones, 1977). For instance, when presented with information about a person who enjoyed participating in dangerous activities that person would be judged more favorably if adventurous is primed than if reckless is primed. Later research found that priming moderate exemplars (an example of a moderately non-hostile exemplar is Robin Hood) also produced assimilation effects when the target of judgment was ambiguous, however, contrast effects (the target is perceived to be different from the prime) would occur if the prime is extreme (an example of an extreme nonhostile exemplar is Santa Claus) (Herr, 1986). Contrast effects were also found to occur with both moderate and extreme primes if the target is unambiguous. Current models of these effects posit that when the target is ambiguous the primed exemplars are used to interpret the target, however, when the target is unambiguous the primed exemplars are used as standards of comparison in making judgments about the target (Schwarz & Bless, 1992).

The second relevant stream of research in psychology is the fluency literature (e.g., Jacoby, Kelley, & Dywan, 1989). In these studies, subjects are first exposed to a stimulus (e.g., word) and, after a short delay, see the stimulus again and make a judgment about it. It is argued that it is easier to process a stimulus during the second exposure and this ease of processing creates a feeling of familiarity, which may bias judgments about the stimulus. Perceptual fluency has been found to affect recognition judgments (Jacoby & Dallas, 1981), whether an individual is judged to be famous or not (Jacoby, Kelley, Brown, & Jasechko, 1990), whether a stimulus is liked or not (Mandler, Nakamura, & Van Zandt, 1987), and whether it is perceived as being light or dark (Mandler, Nakamura, & Van Zandt, 1987). A number of studies have manipulated perceptual fluency by exposure time (Witherspoon & Allan, 1985) and background noise (Jacoby, Allan, Collins, & Larwill, 1988) and found that prior exposure to the stimulus biased the subjects' perception of the actual exposure duration and background noise, respectively.

In summary, the priming literature indicates that prior exposure to a stimulus will make that stimulus more accessible in memory and will influence judgments made about both ambiguous and unambiguous stimuli from the same category. The fluency literature indicates that prior exposure to a stimulus will create perceptual fluency, or a feeling of familiarity, if the individual encounters the stimulus again. This perceptual fluency may also influence the judgments the individual makes about the stimulus.

Memory-Based Choice

The standard model of memory-based choice contains three stages (Fig. 5.1). In the first stage, brand retrieval, a set of brands are retrieved for a specific purchase

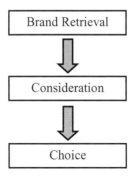

FIG. 5.1   Memory-based choice.

situation. Usually, these brands will be from one product category or subcategory, however, in some purchase situations the brands may be from different product categories (Ratneshwar, Pechmann, & Shocker, 1996). The retrieved brands may be screened prior to retrieval for appropriateness given the purchase situation or they may be screened after retrieval to form a consideration set. Current evidence suggests that the former may occur (Hutchinson, Raman, & Mantrala, 1994), however, we do not have a good understanding of which variable or variables will be used to screen out inappropriate brands. After this screening process, a consideration set is formed and a brand is chosen from the consideration set for purchase. Current research (e.g., Sanbonmatsu & Fazio, 1990; Fazio & Towles-Schwen, 1990; Mantel & Kardes, 1999) suggests that brand attitudes will be used to select a brand from the consideration set when consumers expend little effort in making a choice (e.g., motivation and opportunity are low, i.e., there are minor consequences from a wrong decision and little ability to make an informed decision) and brand related information (e.g., product attributes) may be used when consumers expend considerable effort in making a choice (e.g., motivation and opportunity are high). In these studies, however, subjects choose between only two alternatives, which are highly accessible in memory.

We have found that when subjects have to choose between more than two brands and the brands are not highly accessible in memory, brand accessibility has the strongest effect under low motivation and opportunity conditions, while attitude accessibility has the strongest effect under high motivation and opportunity conditions (Mitchell, 2002). In these studies, brand and attitude accessibility were manipulated on the brand with the second highest attitude, not the highest. Consequently, increases in brand and attitude accessibility increased choice of a less preferred brand. This means that these increases in accessibility compensated for a less favorable evaluation in choice. Finally, the accessibility/diagnosticity framework (e.g., Feldman & Lynch, 1988) suggests that what brand information (e.g., attitudes, attributes) is used in making a choice depends on the objectives to be achieved and the accessibility and diagnosticity of the brand information for the retrieved brands.

Effects on Banner Ad Brands. Increasing the accessibility of a brand will have a direct effect since it will increase the probability that the brand will be retrieved in a purchase situation, which, in turn, increases the probability it will be considered and chosen (Nedungadi, 1990). Since exposure to a banner ad will increase the accessibility of the advertised brand, it will also increase the probability that it will be chosen. It is important to note that in a memory based choice situation, if a brand is not retrieved, it cannot be chosen.

Effects on Competing Brands. Indirect effects can occur in two different ways when a consumer is evaluating a competing brand. First, if very little is known about the brand and very little information is available about it in the immediate environment (e.g., the brand is ambiguous), the activated brand in memory will be used to provide an understanding of the brand. Under these conditions, the brand being evaluated will be perceived as being similar to the activated brand, thereby creating assimilation effects (as long as the activated brand is not an extreme exemplar of the product category). For instance, priming Ford Thunderbird will cause an unknown automobile brand to be judged to be more expensive than if Ford Escort were primed (Herr, 1989).

Second, if the consumer has a good understanding of the brand that is to be evaluated, either from information stored in memory or available information in the environment (e.g., the brand is unambiguous), highly accessible brands will be used as standards of comparison that are then used to evaluate the brand. Under these conditions, the evaluated brand will be perceived as being further away from the accessible brand, thereby creating contrast effects. For instance, if Mercedes Benz is primed, a Honda Accord will be judged to be less expensive than if a Volkswagen Beetle is primed (Herr, 1989). As mentioned previously, there are a large number of empirical studies in both psychology and consumer behavior that support these two types of indirect effects (e.g., Herr, 1986, 1989; Stapel, Koomen, Van der Pligt, 1997; Yi, 1990, 1993).

Constrained Choice

Constrained choice is a special case of mixed choice. In mixed choice, some information about alternative brands is available in the external environment, while other information is stored in memory. Mixed choice is typically thought of as situations where consumers visit different stores when buying a major appliance. Since different stores carry different brands, information about some of the brands is available in the environment while information about others must be retrieved from memory when making a choice in a store (e.g., Biehal & Chakravarti, 1986). In constrained choice, consumers must choose between a subset of brand names from a product category that are presented to them. This type of choice occurs when consumers select a product from a vending machine or when they select a product in a self-service store based only on the brand name or package design.

The primary difference between constrained and memory-based choice is that instead of retrieving the alternative brands from memory as in memory-based choice, the consumer must recognize and focus attention on specific brands in the environment for constrained choice. Consequently, by replacing brand retrieval with brand recognition in Fig. 5.1, we have a model of constrained choice.

Effects on Banner Ad Brands. When consumers have been previously exposed to a brand name, possibly from a banner ad, perceptual fluency will be created when the consumer is exposed to the same brand name again in a constrained choice situation. For this to occur, the brand name in the banner ad and the constrained choice situation have to be identical perceptually (e.g., same type face or logo) to create the maximum amount of perceptual fluency. Previous research indicate that perceptual fluency affects recognition (e.g., Jacoby & Dallas, 1981) and also causes individuals to focus attention on the previously seen stimuli (e.g., brand name). Consequently, when consumers expend little effort in a constrained choice situation, perceptual fluency will affect choice (Chung and Mitchell, 2004).

Previous research has also indicated that individuals will tend to focus their attention on objects for which they have highly accessible attitudes (Roskos-Ewoldsen & Fazio, 1992). Therefore, under low motivation and opportunity conditions, Chung and Mitchell (2004) found that attitude accessibility affects choice. As might be expected, since both perceptual fluency and attitude accessibility affect the brands consumers focus their attention on, they have independent effects under these conditions. When motivation and opportunity were high, however, only attitude accessibility affected constrained choice. Consequently, we would expect banner ads to have a direct effect on constrained choice only when motivation and opportunity are low. Finally, it should be noted that these effects were found on the brand with the second-highest attitude, not the highest. This indicates that creating perceptual fluency and increasing attitude accessibility compensates for a less favorable attitude.

Effects on Competing Brands.   Banner ads may also have an indirect effect for the same reason they had an effect in memory-based choice although this has not been tested empirically. If the brand being evaluated is ambiguous, the activated brand may be used to interpret the target brand. If the brand being evaluated is unambiguous, the activated brand may act as standards of comparisons when individuals make judgments about another brand from the same product category.

RESEARCH METHODS

We now discuss the results of two experiments designed to test the proposed framework of the direct and indirect effects of banner ads on judgment, consideration set formation, and choice. To avoid demand effects, the experiments were disguised as four different studies each with a different purpose. The subjects were undergraduate business students at a major university in the western United States.

During the first study, the subjects were exposed to banner ads that contain only the logo and brand name for two different airlines that varied in quality. Based on pretests, Southwest Airlines was selected as the high quality brand and TWA was selected as the low quality brand. Additionally, there was a control condition in which subjects were not exposed to any airline banner ads.

During the second study, the subjects received information about Vanguard Airlines, a new airline recently launched in the market, and made judgments about it. Pretests indicate that our subject population had very little knowledge about this brand other than it existed. Finally, during the fourth study the subjects were asked to quickly select an airline for a trip they were planning.

Experimental Procedure

As subjects entered the lab, they were randomly assigned to different personal computers, which contained programs for the different banner ad conditions. At that time, the subjects were told that they would be participating in four different studies. In the first study, the subjects were told that the purpose of the study was to learn how different presentations of the same information would affect the learning of the information. For this study, they read information about online auctions and then answered a series of questions about the material. While they read the material, either no airline banner ads, or a banner ad either for Southwest or TWA appeared on the computer screen. After answering the questions about online auctions, the subjects were told that this was the end of the first study.

In the second study, the subjects were told that the purpose of the study was to evaluate a number of advertisements for some recently introduced new products. They then saw advertisements for three new products. One of the new products was Vanguard Airlines. While viewing the advertisements, they were asked a number of questions about it, including in some cases, an evaluation of Vanguard Airlines. After viewing the three advertisements and answering questions about them, the subjects were told that this was the end of the second study.

The third study was a filler task, which took approximately 15 minutes. For the fourth study, subjects were given a series of purchase situations that required them to choose a brand from a number of different product categories. One of these purchase situations required the choice of an airline. In the memory-based choice situation, they were told to quickly write the names of the brands they would consider purchasing and indicate which brand they would purchase. In the constrained choice situation, they were given a list of brands and were told to quickly click on the brands they would consider and then quickly click on the brand they would choose.

According to the theoretical framework presented earlier, if consumers are exposed to a Southwest or TWA banner ad, we should expect to find the following results for **memory-based choice**:

• Effects on Banner Ad Brands. If Southwest Airlines or TWA appear in a banner ad, the accessibility of that brand increases. Consequently, the brand featured in a banner ad should have a higher probability of being in the consideration set and being chosen than if it were not featured in a banner ad.

• Effects on Target Brands. If little is known and little information is provided about a particular brand, that brand will be perceived as similar to the brand that appeared in the banner ad. As a result, judgments and evaluations of Vanguard Airlines would be more positive when subjects are exposed to the banner ad for

Southwest Airlines than when they are exposed to a banner ad for TWA or no banner ad at all. If consumers evaluate Vanguard Airlines more positively, then the probability of that brand being included in the consideration set and chosen is higher as well.

We should expect to find the following results for *constrained choice:*

• Effects on Banner Ad Brands. In this case, the consumer has to choose between a limited set of brand names, which are presented to him or her. When opportunity and motivation are low, perceptual fluency will increase the probability of considering and choosing Southwest or TWA if subjects have been exposed to that brand before in a banner ad.

• Effects on Target Brands. If the target brand is ambiguous, it will be perceived to be similar to the brand featured in the banner ad. In that case, Vanguard Airlines will be evaluated more positively if the subjects are exposed to a high quality brand in the banner ad (Southwest Airlines). This higher evaluation will increase the probability of Vanguard Airlines being considered and chosen.

RESULTS

In presenting the results, we first examine the effects on the brands in the banner ads and then examine the effects on the target (ambiguous) brands.

Banner Ad Brands

According to our hypotheses, the brands featured in the banner ads should have a higher probability of being considered and chosen than if they were not featured in the banner ads. This hypothesis is supported in both the memory-based and the constrained choice situations.

The effects for TWA are very dramatic since the probability of being considered and chosen is very low when it is not featured in a banner ad. When TWA is not featured in a banner ad, it is included in a consideration set only 7.5% and 3.5% of the times, respectively, for the memory-based and constrained choice condition. However, as indicated in Fig. 5.2, when subjects are exposed to TWA in a banner ad, it is included in the consideration set 5 times more often in both the memory-based and the constrained choice situation.

The results of a logistic analysis indicate that the probability that subjects include TWA in their consideration set if they are exposed to a TWA banner ad is significantly higher for both memory-based choice ($\chi^2(1) = 18.50$; $p < 0.01$) and constrained choice ($\chi^2(1) = 12.25$; $p < 0.01$). When TWA is featured in the banner ad, the ratio of the odds of TWA being included in the consideration set to not being included in the consideration set increased seven times on average for both conditions.

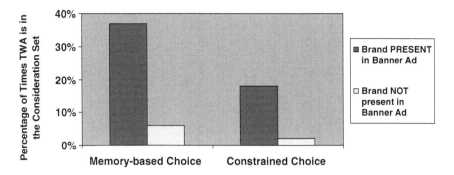

FIG. 5.2   The effect of exposure to a Banner Advertisement for low prestige brand (TWA) on the probability of it being in the consideration set.

For Southwest Airlines (not shown in graph), the likelihood of it being considered, also increased if it appeared in a banner ad, however, the increases are much smaller since Southwest was included in the consideration set around 73% of the time when subjects did not see a banner ad for it. Southwest is included in the consideration set 10% more often when subjects were exposed to the brand in the banner ad in the memory-based choice condition and 3% more of the time in the constrained choice condition. These differences are not significant ($\chi^2(1) = 1.12$, p > 0.2 for memory-based choice, and ($\chi^2(1) = 0.41$, p > 0.5 for constrained choice).

Similar effects are found for choice. When TWA is not featured in a banner ad, it is only chosen 2.1% of the time in memory-based choice. As indicated in Fig. 5.3, in this choice situation, TWA was chosen seven times more often when it appeared in a banner ad than when it didn't. In the constrained choice situation, TWA is chosen by only 1.6% of the subjects when they are not exposed to a TWA banner ad, however, the percentage of subjects choosing TWA is 5 times greater when they are exposed to the brand in the banner ad.

The results of a logistic analysis indicate that whether TWA is featured in the banner ad or not increases the odds of TWA being chosen significantly for both the memory-based choice situation ($\chi^2(1) = 8.48$; p < 0.01) and the constrained choice situation ($\chi^2(1) = 6.62$; p < 0.01). When TWA is featured in the banner ad, the ratio of the odds of TWA being chosen to not being chosen increase 7.5 times on average for memory and constrained choice conditions.

While not as great, choice of Southwest also increases when it is featured in the banner ad (not shown in graph). The percentage of subjects who chose Southwest when it was not in the banner ad was 45.2% in memory-based and 51.6% in constrained choice situations. Choice of Southwest increased 33% of the time with memory-based choice and 24% with constrained choice when subjects saw it in a banner ad as opposed as when they did not see it.

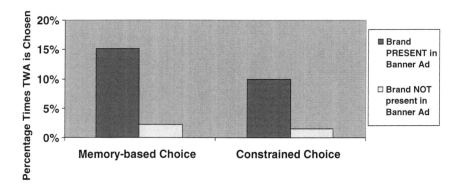

FIG. 5.3   The effect of exposure to a Banner Advertisement for low prestige brand (TWA) on the probability of choosing Vanguard Airline.

The results of a logistic analysis indicate that the difference in the probability of Southwest being chosen if Southwest is featured in the banner ad is marginally significant for both memory-based choice ($\chi^2(1) = 2.88$; $p < 0.1$) and constrained choice ($\chi^2(1) = 2.33$; $p < 0.1$). When Southwest is featured in the banner ad, the ratio of the odds of Southwest being chosen to not being chosen increase 1.7 times on average for the memory and constrained choice conditions.

Interestingly, the probability of considering TWA is significantly lower in constrained choice relative to memory-based choice ($\chi^2(1) = 4.81$, $p < 0.02$). This occurs whether or not TWA appears in a banner ad. When the subjects were made aware of other airlines, as they are in the constrained choice situation, they were much less likely to consider TWA. For Southwest, however, the probability of being considered is higher in the constrained choice situation, but these differences are not significant ($\chi^2(1) = 0.023$, $p > 0.8$). This occurs whether or not Southwest appears in a banner ad.

Target Brand

According to our hypotheses, judgments and evaluations of an ambiguous target brand should be more positive when subjects are exposed to the banner ad for Southwest Airlines than when they are exposed to a banner ad for TWA or no banner ad at all.

We first examine the effect of the banner ads on the evaluation of Vanguard by combining the memory-based and constrained choice conditions since the experimental conditions in both studies were identical up to this point. Overall there is a significant effect due to the banner ad manipulation on the evaluation of Vanguard ($F(2,17) = 23.30$, $p < 0.01$). Vanguard Airlines is evaluated significantly more positive when subjects are exposed to the Southwest banner ad as opposed to the

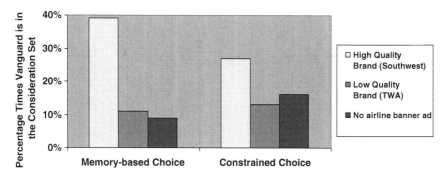

FIG. 5.4 The effect of Quality of the brand in banner ad on the probability of Vanguard Airline, being included in consideration set.

TWA banner ad (4.72 vs. 3.49; t(107) = 6.24, p < 0.01) or no airline banner ad at all (3.56; t(119) = 7.30, p < 0.01).

As indicated in Fig. 5.4, the probability of Vanguard Airlines being in the consideration set increases significantly when consumers are exposed to the Southwest Airlines banner ad than when they saw the TWA banner ad or no airline banner ad at all. This effect is larger with memory-based choice than with constrained choice. Vanguard Airlines was included in the consideration set twice as often when consumers were exposed to the Southwest Airlines banner ad than when they saw the TWA banner ad or no banner ad in constrained choice and almost four times more in memory-based choice.

The results of a logistic analysis indicate that the type of banner ad to which subjects were exposed (high quality brand in banner ad, low quality brand in banner ad, No banner ad) has significant effects on the probability of Vanguard being considered in memory-based choice ($\chi^2(2, 141) = 17.93$; p < 0.01). When Southwest is featured in the banner ad, the ratio of the odds of Vanguard being included in the consideration set to not being included in the consideration set increased 7.1 times compared to when subjects are not exposed to any banner ad. The difference in this probability ratio when TWA is featured in the banner compared to having no airline banner ad is not significant (Wald (1, 143) = 0.15, p > 0.7).

For constrained choice the effect of the type of banner ad on the probability of Vanguard being considered is marginally significant ($\chi^2(2, 191) = 5.31$; p < 0.07). When Southwest is featured in the banner ad, the ratio of the odds of Vanguard being included in the consideration set to not being included in the consideration set increases two times compared to when subjects are not exposed to any banner ad. The difference in these probability ratios when TWA is featured in the banner ad compared to not being exposed to any banner ad is also not significant (Wald (1, 143) = 0.25, p > 0.6).

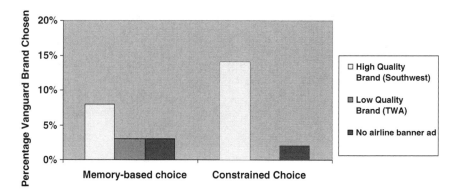

FIG. 5.5   The effect of the quality of the brand in banner ad on the probability of Vanguard being chosen.

Finally, for the choice measures, Vanguard Airlines is chosen more than twelve times more often when subjects are exposed to the Southwest banner ad than when they saw the TWA banner ad or no banner ad in memory-based choice (Fig. 5.5). In constrained choice, however, TWA is only chosen two times more often.

The results of a logistic analysis indicate that the type of banner ad to which subjects were exposed (high quality brand in banner ad, low quality brand in banner ad, No banner ad at all) significantly influenced the probability of Vanguard being chosen for memory-based choice ($\chi^2(2, 141) = 11.5$; $p < 0.01$). When Southwest is featured in the banner ad, the ratio of the odds of Vanguard being chosen to not being chosen increased 7.5 times compared to when subjects are not exposed to any banner ad. However, the difference in this probability ratio when TWA is featured in the banner ad compared to not being exposed to any banner ad is not significant (Wald $(1, 143) = 0.05$, $p > 0.9$). The effect of the type of banner ad is not significant ($\chi^2(2, 191) = 1.94$, $p > 0.3$) for constrained choice.

It is interesting to note that the differences in evaluation, consideration, and choice for Vanguard between the no airline banner ad condition and the TWA banner ad condition are very similar. This suggests that the information that the subjects had about TWA relative to their knowledge about Vanguard had very little impact on their evaluation of Vanguard and whether they would consider and choose it.

These findings clearly demonstrate that banner ads can have both direct and indirect effects. The direct effects on the brands advertised in banner ads increased the probability of those brands being included in the consideration set and chosen. The indirect effects, which occur on ambiguous target brands, caused them to be evaluated more highly when subjects are exposed to a high quality brand in the banner ad than when they see a low quality brand or no banner ad at all. A more positive judgment about the ambiguous brand results is a higher probability of that brand being included in the consideration set and chosen.

NECESSARY CONDITIONS

In the two studies, we demonstrated that banner advertisements may have both direct and indirect effects in judgments and choice. In these studies we used actual brands, so it may not be obvious what conditions must hold in order to obtain these effects. Here we will discuss these conditions, first for direct effects and then for indirect effects.

Direct Effects

The direct effects occurred for the two airlines featured in the banner advertisements—Southwest Airlines and TWA. The former airline is evaluated highly by our subject population, while the latter airline was not evaluated as positively. Importantly, our subjects had considerable knowledge about each airline (the familiarity ratings were 5.2 and 4.6 on a 7 point scale for Southwest and TWA respectively, compared with only 1.5 for Vanguard) and probably had an evaluation of both airlines stored in memory. The question, of course, is exactly what knowledge about a brand is required in order to obtain direct effects with banner ads. We will initially consider three types of knowledge. The first is the product category or subcategory to which the brand belongs. Clearly, it must be known that the brand is an airline and it may also be important to know that it is a national airline as compared to a smaller regional airline. The second concerns other knowledge about the brand that may be thought of as associations with the brand. These associations may include product attribute information, user and usage information, advertisements, experiences, and feelings (Keller, 1993). The third type of information is an attitude toward the brand, the favorability of the attitude and its accessibility. Previous research indicates that choices in memory-based and constrained choice situations may be based on favorable brand attitudes and the accessibility of these attitudes under both low and high motivation and opportunity conditions.

In summary, consumers must have a considerable amount of knowledge about the brand before increasing the accessibility of the brand or the perceptual fluency of the brand name affects choice. Then, the effect of banner ads will be highly dependent on the accessibility of the brand and the amount of perceptual fluency in the target population. Since the less preferred brands generally will be less accessible and have less perceptual fluency because they spend less on advertising, banner ads for these brands will tend to have a greater effect on sales than highly evaluated brands. As we saw in the two studies, the banner ads had a much greater effect on the consideration and choice of TWA than Southwest.

Indirect Effects

The indirect effects occurred for a new airline, Vanguard Airlines, that subjects knew very little about. In this situation, the brand in the banner advertisement was used to interpret this brand. Consequently, when subjects evaluated Vanguard Airlines after being exposed to the banner ad for TWA, they evaluated it less favorably than when they were exposed to the banner ad for Southwest Airlines. Previous research indicated that these effects occur shortly after exposure to the banner ad, as they did in the studies reported here. The question is whether they will occur after a longer delay. A partial answer is provided by Wyer and Srull (1981), who varied the amount of priming of an attribute and the delay between the prime and the measures. They found that the effects of the prime decayed after the priming of the attribute and had essentially disappeared after two days. It should be noted, however, that the primes were attributes, not exemplars. It is possible that highly accessible exemplars will always be used when evaluating an ambiguous target.

It should also be noted that these effects have been obtained even when the priming stimulus is only in the parafoveal region of attention, that is, when the banner ad is outside the area of the focus of attention (e.g., Bargh & Pietromonaco, 1982; Bargh & Chartrand, 2000; Shapiro, MacInnis, & Heckler, 1997). Consequently, consumers do not have to focus their attention on the banner ad in order for it to have an effect. If the banner ad is in their peripheral vision, it will still have an effect. The effect, however, may not be as great as it would have been if it were the focus of attention.

Finally, these effects were found with an ambiguous target. As mentioned earlier, indirect effects have also been found with an unambiguous target, however, under these conditions the primed exemplars are used as standards of comparison, so contrast effects occur. Dacin and Mitchell (2001) have proposed and tested a model of brand evaluation formation where subjects generate alternative brands from memory and use them to form standards of comparison when evaluating an unambiguous target. Consequently, if the banner ads increase the accessibility of a brand so that it would be generated when evaluating a competing brand, the resulting effect should occur over much longer time periods. In one of their studies, they found contrast effects remained two days after the presentation of a new competing brand to the subjects.

BANNER ADS AND ADVERTISING STRATEGY

It is important to understand the role of banner ads in the development of advertising strategy. In order to do this, we must understand what affects purchase behavior under different choice conditions.

As discussed earlier, in order for consumers to purchase a brand under memory-based or constrained choice conditions, two elements must be in place. First, a representation of the brand must exist in memory. Second, the consumer must have knowledge about what product category or subcategory the brand belongs to and its unique characteristics that differentiate it from competitors. These differentiating characteristics may be based on the type of consumers who use the brand; the usage situations for which the brand is appropriate; and experiences, feelings, or benefits provided by the brand (e.g., Keller, 1993). Ideally these differences should be such that at least one segment of the market evaluates it favorably relative to competing brands, however, as indicated in the experiments presented here, this is not a necessary condition.

This knowledge about the brand is generally created with traditional media advertising, however, it can also be created with click through from banner advertisements. Initially, large expenditures on media advertising are needed to ensure that consumers acquire this knowledge, however, once this knowledge is acquired only maintenance levels are needed.

Once the consumer obtains the appropriate knowledge about the brand, the brand must be made accessible in memory as well as its attitude. If the brand is purchased in a constrained choice situation, then perceptual fluency must also be created. The accessibility of the brand and its attitude as well as its fluency can be increased with repetition in traditional media advertising (e.g., Nedungadi, Mitchell, & Berger, 1993; Berger & Mitchell, 1990). Repetition with simple banner ads or signs will increase brand accessibility and create perceptual fluency.

If the brand tends to be purchased under memory-based conditions, and the consumer spends little effort in making a choice, the brand would benefit from being highly accessible in memory. On the other hand, if the consumer were to spend considerable time and effort in making the choice, the brand would be more likely to be chosen if there is a favorable attitude that is highly accessible.

If the brand is chosen under constrained choice conditions, the likelihood of choosing it also increases if the consumer has a favorable attitude about the brand that is highly accessible. Additionally, if it is purchased under low motivation and opportunity conditions, and consumers have seen the brand name recently (maybe in a banner ad), exposure to the brand name at point of purchase should create fluency, thereby increasing the likelihood that it will be considered and chosen.

In summary, advertising strategy can be decomposed into two components. First, advertising must communicate what the brand is (what product category or subcategory it is a member of) and information about the brand (e.g., attributes, feelings, etc.), so it will be evaluated favorably. Media advertising is usually used to transmit this information to consumers, however, the Internet might also be used. Once consumers acquire this knowledge, some media advertising will be required to reinforce it and create highly accessible attitudes. Second, brand accessibility and perceptual fluency must be at high levels. As the research presented here indicates, high levels of brand accessibility and perceptual fluency will induce purchase even if the brand is not the most preferred brand on the market. In fact, since brand accessibility and perceptual fluency are subject to more rapid decay, they must be continually reinforced. Luckily this can be done with banner ads, which are less expensive than traditional media advertising. This seems to be a more effective use of banner advertisements.

Finally, this discussion of the role of banner ads in advertising strategy is based on relatively simple banner advertisements that mention only the brand name and logo. As the number of consumers with high speed Internet connections increases, banner ads will become more complex and will also be able to communicate brand-differentiating information.

SUMMARY

Although there is a general belief in the industry that banner advertisements are not effective unless there is click through, industry studies have presented evidence that this may not be true. In this chapter, we have presented theoretical reasons, based on research in psychology, as to why simple banner advertisements without click through will influence consumer judgment and choice. This influence may directly affect the brand in the banner advertisement (direct effects) or may influence judgments made about competing brands (indirect effects). We presented the results of two experiments that examined and demonstrated these effects in memory-based and constrained choice. We then discussed the conditions necessary for these effects to occur and the role that banner advertisements should play in the development of advertising strategies.

ACKNOWLEDGMENTS

We would like to thank UC Berkeley's Center for Marketing and Technology for their research grant and Diane Huang for her help as Research Assistant in this project.

REFERENCES

Kumbil, A., & P. F. Nums (2000). Measuring advertising effectiveness. *Research Note*, Accenture Institute for Strategic Change, July 24, 2000, p 1–2.

Gillam, J. (2001). Proving branding effect of Web advertising. Atlas Institute *Digital Marketing Insights.* p 1–2.

Bargh, J. A., & Chartrand, T. (2000). The mind in the middle: A practical guide to priming and automaticity research. In H. T. Ries, and C. M. Judd, (Eds.), *Handbook of research methods in social and personality psychology* (pp. 286–312). Cambridge, UK: Cambridge University Press.

Bargh, J. A., & Pietromonaco, P. (1982). Automatic information processing and social perception: The influence of trait information presented outside of conscious awareness on impression formation. *Journal of Personality and Social Psychology, 43*, 437–449.

Berger, I. F., & Mitchell, A. A. (1990). The effect of advertising on attitude accessibility, attitude confidence, and the attitude-behavior relationship. *Journal of Consumer Research, 16*, 269–279.

Biehal, G., & Chakravarti, D. (1986). Consumer's use of memory and external information in choice: Micro and macro perspectives. *Journal of Consumer Research, 12*, 382–405.

Briggs, R., & Hollis, N. (1997). Advertising on the Web: Is there response before click-through? *Journal of Advertising Research*, March-April, 33–45.

Chandon, J. L., & Chtourou, M. S. (2001). *Factors affecting click-through rate.* Unpublished manuscript, University of Aix Marseille III, BP 33, Clois Guiot, 13540 Puyricard, France.

Chung, S., & Mitchell, A. A. (2004). *The effects of fluency, attitude, and attitude accessibility on constrained choice.* Unpublished manuscript, Rotman School of Management, University of Toronto, Toronto, ON, M5S 3E6.

Dacin, P. A., & Mitchell, A. A. (2002). *A model of brand evaluation formation with memory based context effects.* Unpublished manuscript, Rotman School of Management, University of Toronto, Toronto, ON, M5S 3E6.

The Economist. (2001, March 2). Business: Banner-ad blues. London: Feb. 24, 2001, Vol, 358, Iss. 8210 p. 63.

Fazio, R. H. (1990). Multiple processes by which attitudes guide behavior: The MODE model as an integrative framework. In M. P. Zanna (Ed.), *Advances in experimental social psychology* (Vol. 23, pp. 75–109). San Diego, CA: Academic Press.

Fazio, R. H., & Towles-Schwen, T. (1990). The MODE model of attitude-behavior processes. In S. S. Chaiken & Y. Trope (Eds.), *Dual-process theories in social psychology* (pp. 97–116). New York: The Guilford Press.

Feldman, J. M., & Lynch, J. (1988). Self generated validity and other effects of measurement on belief, attitude, intention, and behavior. *Journal of Applied Psychology, 73*, 421–435.

Green, H., & Elgin, B. (2001 January 22). Do e-ads have a future? The ruce is on to find ways to increase advertising effectiveness. *Business Week*, New York, January 22, 2002, Iss. 3716, p. 46.

Herr, P. M. (1986). Consequences of priming: Judgement and behavior. *Journal of Personality and Social Psychology, 51*, 1106–1115.

Herr, P. M. (1989). Priming price: Prior knowledge and context effects. *Journal of Consumer Research, 16*, 67–75.

Higgins, G. T., Rholes, C. R., & Jones, C. R. (1977). Category accessibility and impression formation. *Journal of Experimental Social Psychology, 14*, 141–181.

Hofacker, C. F., & Murphy, J. (2000). Clickable World Wide Web banner ads and content sites. *Journal of Interactive Marketing, 14*, 49–59.

Hutchinson, J. W., Raman, K., & Mantrala, M. K. (1994). Finding choice alternatives in memory: Probability models of brand name recall. *Journal of Marketing Research, 31*, 441–461.

Internet Advertising Bureau. (1997). *Online advertising effectiveness study.* San Francisco, CA: Millward Brown Interactive.

Jacoby, L. L., Allan, L. G., Collins, J. C., & Larwill, L. K. (1988). Memory influences subjective experience: Noise judgments. *Journal of Experimental Psychology: Learning, Memory and Cognition, 14*, 240–247.

Jacoby, L. L., & Dallas, M. (1981). On the relationship between autobiographic memory and perceptual learning. *Journal of Experimental Psychology: General, 110*, 306–340.

Jacoby, L. L., Kelley, C. M., & Dywan, J. (1989). Memory and attributions. In H. L. Roediger, III & F. I .M. Craik (Eds.), *Varieties of memory and consciousness.* Hillsdale, NJ: Lawrence Erlbaum Associates.

Jacoby, L. L., Kelley, C. M., Brown J., & Jasechko J. (1989). Becoming famous overnight: Limits on the ability to avoid unconscious influences of the past. *Journal of Personality and Social Psychology, 56*, 326–338.

Keller, K. L. (1993). Conceptualizing, measuring and managing customer-based brand equity. *Journal of Marketing, 57*, 1–22.

Lynch, J. G., Marmorstein, H., & Weigold, M. F. (1988). Choices from sets including remembered brands: Use of recalled attributes and prior overall evaluations. *Journal of Consumer Research, 15*(3), 169–184.

Mandler, G., Nakamura Y., & Van Zandt, B. J. S. (1987). Nonspecific effects of exposure on stimuli that cannot be recognized. *Journal of Experimental Psychology: Learning, Memory and Cognition, 13*, 646–648.

Mantel, S. P., & Kardes, F. R. (1999). The role of direction of comparison, attribute based processing in consumer preference. *Journal of Consumer Research, 25*, 335–352.

Mitchell, A. A. (2002). *The effect of brand and attitude accessibility on memory based choice.* Unpublished manuscript, Rotman School of Management, University of Toronto, Toronto, ON, M5S 3E6.

Nedungadi, P. (1990). Recall and consumer consideration sets: Influencing choice without altering brand evaluations. *Journal of Consumer Research, 17*(4), 263–276.

Nedungadi, P., Mitchell A. A., & Berger, I. (1993). A framework for understanding the effects of advertising exposure on choice. In A. A. Mitchell (Ed.), *Advertising exposure, memory and choice.* Hillsdale, NJ: Lawrence Erlbaum Associates.

Ratneshwar, S., Pechmann, C., & Shocker, A. D. (1996). Goal-derived categories and the antecedents of across-category consideration. *Journal of Consumer Research, 23*, 240–250.

Roskos-Ewoldsen, D. R., & Fazio, R. H. (1992). On the orienting value of attitudes, attitude accessibility as a determinant of an object's attraction of visual attention. *Journal of Personality and Social Psychology, 63*, 198–211.

Sanbonmatsu, D. M., & Fazio, R. H. (1990). The role of attitudes in memory-based decision making. *Journal of Personality and Social Psychology, 59*, 614–622.

Schwarz, N., & Bless, H. (1992). Constructing reality and its alternatives: Assimilation and contrast effects in social judgment. In L. L. Martin, & A. Tessor (Eds.), *The construction of social judgments.* Hillsdale, NJ: Lawrence Erlbaum Associates.

Shapiro, S., MacInnis, D. J., & Heckler, S. E. (1997). The effects of incidental ad exposure on the formation of the consideration set. *Journal of Consumer Research, 24*(2), 94–104.

Stapel, D. A., Koomen, W., & van der Pligt, J. (1997). Categories of category accessibility: The impact of trait concept versus exemplar priming on person judgments. *Journal of Experimental Social Psychology, 33*, 47–76.

Yi, Y. (1990). The effects of contextual priming in print advertisement. *Journal of Consumer Research, 17*, 215–222.

Yi, Y. (1993). Contextual priming effects in print advertisement: The moderating role of prior knowledge. *Journal of Advertising, 22*(1), 1–10.

Wall Street Journal (2001, April 23). Ad Nauseam.

Witherspoon, D., & Allan L. G. (1985). The effects of prior presentation on temporal judgments in a perceptual identification task. *Memory and Cognition, 13*, 101–111.

Wyer, R. S., & Srull T. K. (1981). Category accessibility: Some theoretical and empirical issues concerning the processing of social stimulus information. In E. T. Higgins, C. P. Hermann, & M. P. Zanna (Eds.), *Social cognition: The Ontario symposium.* Vol.1, 161–198. Hillsdale, NJ: Lawrence Erlbaum Associates.

CHAPTER SIX

Factors Affecting Click-Through Rate

Jean-Louis Chandon
IAE Aix en Provence

Mohamed Saber Chtourou
EDHEC Business School

The top six United States' advertisers have been spending less than 1% of their budgets on Internet advertisements, according to Morgan Stanley (Business Week, 2001). Minimal spending on Web advertising may represent a shared feeling among advertisers that the "Web is still a developing medium, with no firmly established standards for either presenting advertising or measuring its effectiveness". Skepticism that the Internet is a viable advertising medium is probably underserved. The Internet audience has grown rapidly. According to the Netratings 75% of American households are connected to the Internet in 2004 (GreenSpan, 2004). (The Industry Standard, 2001). According to Nielsen NetRatings, Internet users spend about 10 hours per month connected from home and 29 hours from offices. This audience is switching from the other media. Internet advertising revenues in the United States in 2001 was more than 4 times the amount of outdoor advertising ($8.2 billion vs. $1.8 billion) and nearly equaled spending on cable television ($11.2 billion) (Gibson 2003). This chapter addresses difficulties in defining Internet advertising and measuring its effectiveness, issues likely faced by the other media when they first started.

WHAT IS ADVERTISING ON THE INTERNET?

Before discussing ways to improve Internet Advertising effectiveness, we will define our field of investigation. Many authors define Internet advertising to include both advertisements (e.g., banners of all forms and sizes that are displayed on editorial sites) and commercial Web sites (e.g., Rossiter & Bellman, 1999). Combining banners with Web sites is problematic because of four main differences between them:

1. The first difference is that their goals differ. Banner advertising is primarily a persuasive communication, while a Web site is that plus often a distribution channel and/or a means to gather information for a customer database. The Web site thus becomes a platform for direct marketing.

2. The most important distinction can be found in their mechanisms. For a Web site, exposure is typically initiated by the customer, while the banner is controlled by the advertiser. In the case of the Web site, the visitor decides whether to visit a site or not, what areas within the site to visit, and when to leave. In this case, attention is primarily focused on the site and the visitor is generally trying to fulfill a particular goal, such as searching for a dealer of a particular product or an instruction book). In the case of banner advertising, there is passive exposure (Hoffmann, Novak, & Chatterjee, 1998). The advertiser initiates the communication by placing the ad on a particular Web site (e.g., portal or search engine), chosen for its specific audience. Here, the advertiser decides what banner to show, the timing of the exposure (the period and not the precise moment as in television or radio), and possibly the exposure frequency by determining the maximum number of exposures before the ad is removed or changed. The consumer's attention is usually devoted to the content of the site hosting the ad but may be disrupted by the banner. Hence, catching a visitor's attention becomes crucial in the banner's persuasion process whereas it can be virtually assumed for the Web site.

3. Another point of difference is that the space allocated on screen to the banner as is a limited part of the entire site, which is obviously not true for the Web site. One implication is that banners are affected by other elements on the site. Most, if not all, of the other elements are not under the advertiser's control.

4. Finally, creating an Internet advertising campaign involves elements similar to the media planning associated with non-Internet advertising. Banner advertising may be scheduled based on seasonal or marketing changes. For example, travel advertising may increase before a holiday period or in conjunction with an increase in offline advertising. Although Web site content may change as well in response to environmental changes, the actual number of times it is visited is not controllable.

Based on the four above considerations, we conclude that only banners (as well as some new formats such as pop under and interstitial) are true advertisements.

They most closely share the characteristics of advertisements in other media (disruptive, attention catching, limited size, and controlled appearances).

WEB AD EFFECTIVENESS

Two alternative paradigms can be distinguished in order to study the effectiveness of Internet advertisements. The first paradigm argues that banner ads represent the company communication's strategy by increasing brand recall, attitude toward the ad, and attitude toward the brand. The second paradigm argues that the Internet is a direct-marketing tool. Thus, the banner is akin to a newspaper coupon and its effectiveness should be measured through the return rate. This latter view is consistent with the practice for Internet sites in general, that is to use click-through rates as the primary effectiveness measure. This second paradigm was used in the earlier empirical research Onnein Bonnefoy (1997). The ease of collecting click-through rates also contributed to its being widely used in academic research (e.g., Briggs & Hollis, 1997; Cho, 1999; Chtourou & Chandon, 2000, Drèze and Hussherr, 2001) and its popularity among practitioners. However, several companies (such as Diameter Research and Millward Brown, are proposing alternative measures of ad effectiveness (e.g., recall, attribution, brand image) collected through online questionnaires. The movement away from click-through rates appears to be growing. For example, the financial news Web site, Marketwatch.com, announced plans to drop click-through rates in its reports to marketing clients. Further, as Internet advertisers observe a huge decline in their click-through rates, they worry that this will discourage potential advertisers in this medium. We propose that the two approaches are complementary, and limiting effectiveness to only one of them results in several weaknesses. On one hand, restricting ad effectiveness to its capacity to generate immediate click throughs ignores its capabilities to communicate information. On the other hand, ignoring click-through rate overlooks a unique feature of the Internet as a new medium—interactivity and immediate response to the advertising stimulus.

The Click-Through Rate

The *click-through rate* is the number of clicks occurring on a banner related to the total number of displays. This indicator considers the banner ad's primary role as attracting the site visitor's attention and transporting the individual to the advertiser's site. It corresponds to the first objective of the Internet advertiser, which is to generate visitors to their sites. In addition, this indicator satisfies the information system background of the pioneer Web designers and their enthusiasm about the accountability of this new medium.

Later, the click-through rate was highly criticized (Briggs & Hollis, 1997). Click-through rates cannot measure all aspects of advertising effectiveness and do not encompass all the objectives an advertiser can assign to an Internet advertisement. Three limits to the usefulness of click-through rates are:

The Rate Is Not Comparable to Other Advertising Measures. Even if we consider that the action of clicking (the transfer from the editorial site to the advertiser site) as the ultimate objective, the way it is computed makes it not comparable with other media. For example, the direct-mail return rate is the number of items mailed back compared to the number distributed. This rate does not change if some people read the mailing more than once. Whereas, the click-through rate is computed not out of the number of persons reached, but out of the number of exposures (impressions). For example, if an Internet user goes to a page more than once in the same session, the number of exposures increases and the click-through rate goes down. This penalizes ads placed on frequently visited Web sites as most visitors will not have a need or want to repeatedly click on the same banner ad.

Clicking on a Banner Is Not Always a Useful Behavior? Because some visitors will click on a banner advertisement by mistake or without full understanding of where they will be taken, many click throughs are of little value to the advertiser. Although many authors support the idea of measuring the depth and width of the information-search by the number of clicks (Stewart & Pavlou, 2002), we have learned from focus groups[1] that a certain amount of the clicks on banners is due to error or arise without any particular interest or commitment to the brand. Assuming that the advertiser's goal is to use the ad to attract users interested in the advertiser's site (and acknowledging that the success depends somewhat on the site's qualities), a good banner should transfer to the site only useful traffic by indicating the right content of the site. To illustrate the financial effect, a report from the Web site Engage indicated that its conversion rate was greater when the visit resulted from a voluntary visit rather than a click (36% vs. 25%).

The Click-Through Rate Is an Immediate Effectiveness Measure That Ignores Several Stages of the Persuasion Process. Click throughs are limited as a measure of ad effectiveness because they measure only the immediate and direct response to the ad. Exposures to the banner may initiate cognitive and emotive processes that are ignored by the click-through rate. Ad testing in the traditional media considers intermediary effects, such as attention, learning, and changes in brand beliefs. Some Internet users may remember and later type in a site's address after seeing the ad rather than clicking on the banner because they want to finish their actual session. Engage indicates, through a tracking study, that 62% of the visitors came to its site at least 30 minutes after seeing the ad, including 28% who visit more than 7 days later. As is true for direct marketing, click throughs turn out not to be the best way to measure all of the ways an ad drives sales. A December

---

[1] Through focus groups: ongoing research to be published.

2000, study from the interactive ad agency, Avenue A, showed that only 20% of consumers who made a purchase at one popular travel site had clicked on a banner to get there. The other 80% saw the ad initially and then returned later to the travel site to make a purchase.

The Click-Through Rate Ignores Offline Effects.   Another issue is that some Internet users might spread positive word of mouth or even buy the product directly at a physical outlet without ever visiting the advertiser's site.

The above mentioned limits combined with the considerable decrease in click through rates suggest skepticism about its role as the sole measure of Internet ad effectiveness. This, in turn, stimulated the desire to find a better measure.

Click-Through Advantages.   Despite the noted weaknesses, the click-through rate possesses numerous advantages: It measures a voluntary action of prospects looking for supplementary information, if is relatively reliable and easy to collect because it is based on an automated collection, and it does not require an investigator or visitor's cooperation. These qualities make this indicator frequently used by advertising agencies. According to research on Iconocast subscribers, traditional click-through measures still rank ahead of cost per click (29%), cost of conversion (26%) and cost per lead (21%) in measuring online advertising effectiveness.

Measuring the click-through response to an advertisement is consistent with an important new capability the Internet offers marketers—accountability. It enables a "shift from a survey-based to a census-based method of assessing effectiveness" (Drèze & Zufryden, 2000). As accountability differentiates online advertising from the less exact forms of offline advertising, some warn that any movement away from this accountability will hurt Internet advertising in the long term.

Another advantage is that the Internet is an interactive medium. The user, target of the communication, can also be an actor in the process. The user can respond to the advertiser by forwarding the message or offering a counter message to others. With many Internet sales messages, the stimulus and the response occur in the same medium, often at the same time. This happens because the Internet allows one to integrate information seeking and commercial transaction. An Internet user can respond to a commercial, decide to buy the item, and then buy it in a few minutes. With this shortening of the decision-process, immediate reactions to the ad gain in importance. Thus, if publishers convince advertisers that the medium's major benefit is improving brand image, then they lose their major advantage (being both a communication medium and distribution channel) against more traditional media.

Attitudinal and Other Measures

The other side of the ad effectiveness measurement controversy revolves around attitudinal and other measures. Following the practice used in traditional advertising, researchers initially tried to demonstrate that banners are effective. Ad effectiveness is usually defined as changes in consumer beliefs and attitudes rather than behavior. This assumption was based on the argument that this is the traditional way of measuring the ad effectiveness for the other media and that there's no reason to have different effectiveness measures for the Internet. This was first proposed by Briggs and Hollis (1997) who found that exposure to a banner resulted in an increase in the different scores of advertising effectiveness they tested. Although these results were criticized by some authors (e.g., Lendrevie, 2000) for reasons such as that the difference between those exposed and those not exposed was based upon the users' declaration and not upon a strict control, they suggest that attitudinal effects are possible.

Eye tracking experiments demonstrate that Internet users tend to avoid seeing the ads when they become more experienced with the Internet (Drèze & Hussherr, 2003). "The size of the banner often being much smaller than advertisement in print medium, marketers have reservation on ability of banners to communicate brand image adequately" (Kompella, 2001, p. 67). Paradoxically, Drèze and Hussherr (2003) proved that there is no difference in term of recognition and image between the two different sizes they tested (234×60 pixels and 468×60 pixels). In another eye-tracking study, found that banner ads were actually seen 45% of the time—and the average fixation period was one second, which the author says is enough for the Web user to comprehend the brand message (DeVigal, 2000).

More recently, other studies seems to conclude to the effectiveness of the simple exposure to the ad. Kompella (2001) proved, using an experimental design, that exposed users had better memories and brand attitudes than nonexposed users. He distinguished within the users who were exposed to the ad, those who noticed the ad, and those who did not. Those who noticed the ad rated the brand more favorably. In addition, Bergkvitz, Fristrom, and Melander (2001) concluded that the exposure to an Internet ad may enhance the brand recognition and value, even if the campaign was exclusively performed on the Internet. He compared the brand ratings before and after a campaign. Moreover, Rapp (2001) performed a study on a charity brand and he demonstrated that the brand recognition and image were enhanced after exposure to the Internet banners. This study also demonstrated that the repetition enhanced the ad effectiveness (there was no wearout observed after eight exposures).

All of these studies, even if their methodologies can be criticized, tend to conclude that Internet ads can be effective and that their small size does not handicap effectiveness. More recently, the Interactive Advertising Bureau (IAB) announced the results of a study that compare the effectiveness of the new and larger format (e.g., Skyscrapers) to the standard banners format.[2] Brand awareness and brand image shows spectacular increases. Nevertheless, we should treat these results

---

[2]www.iab.net

carefully since they may be due more to the novelty than to the size or position of the new ad format.

Toward an Integrative Model of Internet Advertising Effectiveness

Continued discussion of the conflicting paradigms for measuring Internet effectiveness is not productive. The traditional models that describe the persuasion process—even if they show some divergence about the order and the measurement of each stage—agree on the fact that persuasion involves three stages: cognitive, affective, and conative (see Vakratsas and Ambler 1999 for details). The conative stage is related to the favorable action toward the brand. Classical studies tried to measure this aspect using intention to buy or brand consideration for a future buy. The main limit of such measures is the gap between intention and action. Click-through rates, despite their weaknesses, are valuable for advertising research since they measure a favorable action toward the brand, whether it is seeking further information or an interaction with the brand. This measure is particularly suited for products with high-information content or with a long buying process. These products require a comparison between the different brands. The typical availability and low cost of information on the Internet can enhance customers' self-confidence in their brand evaluation.

We conclude that the act of clicking is a part of the persuasion process and there is no need to oppose the click through to the traditional measurements of advertising effectiveness.

The Objective Matrix. We propose a practical approach for ad effectiveness measurement by relating ad effectiveness measures to the goals that an advertiser can pursue (see Table 6.1). We divide these goals on two axes: Space and Time.

Space: Will the desired consumer action occur online or offline?
Time: Will the final expected outcome occur in the long or short term? A short-term goal must be reached within (or nearby) the campaign duration, while a long-term goal may need more than one campaign to be reached.

TABLE 6.1
The Goals Matrix

Measures	Short Term	Long Term
Online goal	Click-through rate, Clicker/exposed rate, Visitors/exposed rate Cost per click, per action, conversion rate.	Brand awareness, brand image, site's visit consideration or recommendation, number of citation on forums.
Offline goal	Additional traffic to the point of purchase. Additional sales.	Traditional ad effectiveness measurement (e.g., brand awareness, attribution, ad recognition, brand image).

For these measures we assume that the number of unique visitors provided by an ad server's software is reliable, despite the problem associated to cookie identification. As brand awareness, brand attributions, brand image, etc. are well and so forth-known measures in traditional media research and they are not defined here.

Online Short-Term Campaign.   The click-through rate is only one among several measurements, even for short-term online objectives. Other measures proposed include:

- *Clickers/exposed rate:* This rate is similar to the click-through rate but is computed using unique clickers and unique visitors. It overcomes the click-through rate weakness of not being comparable with measures used for other media. In addition, it still measures the target audience directly transferred to the site.
- *Visitors/exposed rate:* Since the banner ad objective is to drive visitors, a useful measure is the number of unique visitors to the target site out of the number of users exposed to the ad. This considers only new visitors and assumes that they have come because they were affected by the ad. More sophisticated techniques identify whether the Internet users have or have not been exposed to the campaign. We can then calculate the ratio of the number of those who visited after being exposed to the ad out of the total number of people exposed to the ad.
- *Cost per click:* This rate measures advertising efficiency. This combines the quality of the ad with proper placement. Analysis can fix the creative aspect of the ad and compare different placements, or we can compare different ads with equivalent placements.
- *Conversion rate:* As the ultimate objective is to have individuals accomplish the final task, such as subscribing in a mailing list or participating in a game, this measure determines how many did this out of the total number of clickers.

Online Long-Term Campaign.   The final proposed measure tallies those who have been exposed to the banner ad and do not visit the site but engage in a desirable behavior, such as favorable word of mouth. For positive word of mouth, declarative measures can be completed by objective measures such as the number of citations in forums or newsletters. Counting these people seems an almost impossible task but solutions using search engines are being developed.

FACTORS AFFECTING THE CLICK-THROUGH RATE

In the second part of this chapter, we consider the performance of the banner Ads in terms of fulfilling short-term online goals. Among the many measures proposed, we concentrate on the click-through rate since it is still the standard measure of the industry and we have a sufficient database to analyze it. We present here our assumptions about the effect of several variables. Then, we present the results of a study conducted in collaboration with Wanadoo Regie, a large French ad agency.

How to Compare the Click-Through Rate (CTR)

It is important to conceptually define the click-through rate since it is a relatively new measurement. We use different analogies to derive a set of assumptions about the factors that can explain its variability. We have already noted that there is little agreement about what best to compare to CTR. This lack of comparability explains current skepticism about the viability of CTR. The first comparison analysts did was with the mailing return rates (less than 0.5% for CTR in average compared to 2% or 3% for the mailing). This comparison supposes that the Internet is a supplementary channel for direct marketing. We think that the mailing return rate can not be compared directly to the click-through rate. The mailing return rate is based on the number of prospects, whereas the click-through rate is based on a number of exposures, including persons exposed more than once. A prospect may need to read an advertisement 10 times before deciding to interact with the company (we have then 10 click-through exposures compared to one for the mailing return rate).

We prefer the comparison with impulsive buying.

Impulse Buying. Beatty and Ferrell (1998) define impulse buying as "A sudden and immediate buying without intention of preliminary purchase, neither of the specific product, nor the category of product" (p. 170). This behavior is a spontaneous act done without thinking that takes place after having a feeling of urgent desire. Purchases motivated by a sudden recollection (e.g., "I have no more sugar in the house") are not considered impulsive purchases. According to Bellenger, Robertson, and Hirschmann (1978), impulse buying represents between 27% and 62% of sales.

We see enough similarity in this impulse buying definition with clicking on a banner to allow us to make an analogy between them. One is that both are **unplanned** acts. If one planned to visit the target site, the connection would have been direct and not via the banner. The second is that both follow from the **perception of an urgent desire**. By clicking on a banner, the Internet user must immediately stop visiting the current site in order to move on to the advertiser's site. However there are some differences. The costs associated with a click are lower than those associated with impulsive buying. Furthermore, we cannot be sure that the Internet user who clicks on a banner does it with no advanced thought. Hence, this comparison only partly suggests the antecedent of click through are comparable to antecedent of impulse buying.

The Antecedents of the Impulsive Purchase. Beatty and Ferrell (1998) noticed that "it is surprising to see how few are the studies on the process and on the antecedents of the impulsive buying" (p. 169). They propose and validate a model of the process of impulse buying. Their research shows that positive affect is an important antecedent of an impulsive purchase, suggesting that the creative factors aimed at establishing a positive attitude will have a positive effect on impulsive acts. Clicking on a banner ad is consistent with this view.

Form Factors

Effect of Size. The effect of size on advertising effectiveness has been much studied in traditional media. This research shows that size improves memory. Since large banners occupy more of the screen, they are more likely to get attention, be read, and, therefore, be remembered. Studies on print advertising are consistent with this view (Naccarato & Neuendorf, 1998; Kelly & Hoell, 1991; Finn, 1988). However, results concerning the attitudinal effects of size are less clear. Size does not always have a positive influence on brand attitudes. For example, Homer (1995) showed that size has a reversed U-shape effect on attitude. The effect is positive until a certain level beyond which the advertisement is perceived as an act of manipulation. Internet studies that examine the size of banners disagree on its effect. Drèze and Hussherr (2003) and Chtourou and Chandon (2000) did not find any effects of the size on memory. In contrast, Cho (1999) showed that size explains the intention to click in situations of weak involvement.

Effect of Animation. Animation effects have not been discussed much in the traditional advertising literature because the Internet is the first medium providing animation capabilities. Professionals say that animated banners catch the eye better than nonanimated ones, and, thus, attract more attention. Nevertheless, technical considerations often limit creativity. Indeed, the current network bandwidth is insufficient to transmit real videos. Banners are limited to sending a succession of fixed images (technically called animated Gif). By postulating that clicking is a voluntary action resulting from a conscious response to an advertisement, it seems reasonable to predict that clicking will be improved if the stimulus is made more attractive.

Reviews of published Internet studies show that the effect of animation depends on the effectiveness measure adopted. Rae and Brennan (1998) found no significant effects of animation on recall. However, other authors found significant effects of animation on the click-through rate (Onnein-Bonnefoy, 1997) and the intention to click (Cho, 1999). Further, Chtourou and Chandon (2000), suggest that animation's effects depend upon ad size. For example, because the space available in the quarter-size banners (234 × 30 pixels) allows less animation, this size banner can easily become overcrowded.

Effect of Picture's Presence. The effect of including a picture in an advertisement has been much studied for traditional media albeit with inconsistent results. Finn (1988) found significant and positive relations between pictures and comprehension in 3 cases out of 5, and between pictures and learning in 8 cases out of 12. The greater learning is linked to the fact that graphic information generates more mental codes than verbal information (Childers & Houston, 1984; Unnava & Burnkant, 1991). Schweiger and Hruschka (1980) show, in a business to business context, that the number of calls from persons who see an advertisement increases when the proportion of the text relative to the image decreases. They show as well that the presence of photographs does not affect the number of calls. Armstrong's (1999) evaluation of advertisements (ESAP) integrates the illustrations and distinguishes photos from drawings. Singh, Lessig, Kim, Gupta, and Hocutt (2000) stipulate that the positive effect depends on the image's fit with the contents. Image can be considered as an integral part of the message or just a peripheral item.

Kisielius and Sternthal (1984) conclude that factors such as the images in the message become an inextricable element of the message itself and that evaluations depend on the fit between the advertising content and the image. Edell and Staelin (1983) show that individuals exposed to announcements with a framed image (that is, one with text connecting the image to the product) better remember and evaluate the product's attributes compared to individuals exposed to an unframed image. On the other hand, images can merely enhance the message's vividness (Fortin, 1997). This greater vividness should increase an ad's effectiveness in being processed and remembered. Moreover, according to the ELM model (Petty, Cacioppo, & Schumann, 1983), vividness should motivate favorable responses by those using the peripheral route, for example, those with a weak motivation to process. In an Internet study, Chtourou and Chandon (2000) find that the effects of the picture's presence on memory and the intention to act were not linear—that a picture's effect depended on the size of the banner.

Action Relative Mention. Several studies show that Internet specific variables, notably the mention "click here" as well as the presence of "trick banners" (e.g., www.bannertips.com) have a very large effect on the click-through rate (see Figures 6.1 and 6.2). These are considered to reflect craftiness more than creative content.

Trick banners include deceptive tactics such as inserting a simulation of the operating system, trying to persuade the user that the banner is a system message, and hoping that the user clicks on the cross in the upper right corner to remove it

FIG. 6.1 An example of a trick banner that suggest to push a button "search".

FIG. 6.2   An example of a trick banner that suggests to scroll down the menu.

and continue to work. The deception is that this click not only closes the message box but transports the user to the advertiser's site.

Some banners simulate the operating system but with less intrusiveness. They induce people to click on the banner thinking they can scroll a menu.

We propose that devices like "click here" and "trick banners" are particularly effective because clicking is an impulsive behavior. Although they may have a negative aspect in creating hostility, we can not determine their effect on the advertiser's image because our research is limited to the behavioral effect of clicking. These techniques represent a major source of irritation to Internet users and future research should explore the nonbehavioral effects because these methods are popular with advertisers and often recommended by advertising agencies.

Content Variables

Effect of Targeting the Banner.   One of the advantages of the Internet is that it enables very precise thematic targeting. Banner server software can display the banner closest to an appropriate keyword or subject matter selected by the Internet user. The result should be a close affinity between the subject matter of interest to the Internet users and the advertisements they are exposed to. One can reasonably assume that Internet users who consult a targeted page will be more involved in the page's content than the average Internet user. Internet users doing a thematic search or a keyword search should be more goal oriented and thus more attentive to the advertisement. These Internet users should be more inclined to seek additional information about the product. They should click more often than the not involved Internet users, like those exposed randomly to a banner displayed in general rotation or to a banner displayed in the home page of the site. This supposition has been generally validated by professionals and academic studies (Hussherr, 1999). In addition to reexamining this result, we look for interactions between involvement and the other variables related to advertising creation. Petty and Cacioppo's (1983) ELM model stipulates that since involved people are more goal oriented they should be less sensitive to the peripheral element of the message (e.g., images or animation). If true, the effects of animation and images will be more important in the case of nontargeted compared to targeted ads.

Effect of Mentioning the Price.   Mentioning the price in an advertisement is a common technique to promote an immediate decision. Theoretical justification for this method relies on the belief that mentioning the price increases sales by reducing a hurdle in the buying process. Also, knowing the price may make the product more acceptable. Thus, we suppose that mentioning the price encourages Internet users to request more information, enhancing the click-through rate. In addition, we propose that this effect should be stronger for persons already involved in the product category and who should already know the prices of such products.

Effect of Promotion.   The Internet is a good medium for promotions (e.g., games, events) because the user's response often occurs immediately in the same medium (i.e., there is no need to mail anything back to participate in the game). The minimal cost to participate, often nothing more than click on the banner, also should make these promotions effective devices to generate click throughs.

The goal of advertising tactics studied here, such as price mention and promotions is mainly a short-term (within the same campaign) stimulation on sales (Chandon, 1994). This suggests that they should enhance click-through rate since it is a short-term measure of Internet ad effectiveness. Clicking through a banner with price information is more likely to occur when customer are price sensitive, for example, they are in a buying situation or they have a chronic involvement with the product category. The latter is illustrated by a frequent traveler who is attentive to travel-related offers. On the other hand, promotions can be effective with everyone because it triggers the urge to act immediately (most promotions are time limited and oriented toward impulse buying). Thus, we expect a positive effect of mentioning price or promotion on the click-through rate or the intention to click. In addition, price/promotion mentions may interact with ad targeting. Visitors to targeted pages are mostly interested in the objective product features and therefore should be less sensitive to promotion or price information.

Effect of Mentioning the Brand Name.   Two other factors are identified. One is that including the brand name in the announcement should reassure Internet users and legitimize their information-search cost (connection time and cost). On the other hand, not mentioning the brand could stimulate their curiosity and motivate the seeking of additional information. Not mentioning the brand name is analogous to the technique of "teasing," often used to introduce new products. This is supposed to be beneficial for memory but may introduce the problem of false ad recognition (i.e., attributing the ad to another brand).

We complete the list of factors by considering the type of advertiser, click-only versus click-and-mortar companies. For advertisers that exclusively sell on the Internet, it is likely that their click-through rate will be superior because the Internet is the only medium to access their operation.

Our last consideration relates to the media plan, defined here as the number of impressions (displays is a better suited term). We expect a decrease in the click-through rate as the banner campaigns become intense. This reflects the effects of repeated exposures to the same individuals and advertising being directed to less and less targeted audiences (saturation effect).

METHODOLOGY

For our study, we closely examined all the advertising insertions of 77 customers of an Internet agency over the period running from April 1999 until April 2000. This yielded 1,690 insertions with 1,065 banners. The total responses for each was computed. From this exhaustive base, we filtered in several ways. For example, not executed orders were eliminated as well as orders used in technical attempts. We eliminated insertions that had less than 25 impressions and in-house ads (i.e., announcements were inserted by the agency for its own account). Our final sample included 1258 banner insertions representing many varied economic sectors.

Several aggregation levels can be chosen to study the click-through rate. The DART database contains all the insertions. An insertion corresponds to a banner placed in a specified page for a specified date and it is the most elementary level of analysis. For our analysis, we studied the click-through rate at the placement level (and not the banner one) since we tested the effect of the type of page.

To measure a variable's effect, we calculate variations in the click-through rate using a 4-point exposure scale and an intention to click (Yes/No). Each banner was seen by 173 respondents on average. All the banners tested were in the standard format (468×60 pixels), using the animated Gif technique (no Flash or HTML banners to avoid comparability problems). Table 6.1 provides the mean of each banner.

RESULTS

Preliminary Results

Average click-through rate (on the filtered sample) is 1.5%. Weighted average is 0.9%, which is very close to the total market average in France for the studied period. The shape of the distribution is quite asymmetric and concentrated round the low values, as shown in Fig. 6.3.

For methodological reasons, we used logarithm of the click-through rate as it is more reliable but still allows us to interpret the results.

Table 6.2 gives for each factor the strength and the direction of their effect on CTR (+ : the click-through rate is higher when the variable is present, − : the click-through rate is higher when the variable is absent. 0 no effect. * nonlinear effect).

The results support conclusions from previous empirical studies. The largest effect is obtained by the technique of trick banners. Their presence explains the

TABLE 6.2
Synthesis of the Results

Source	Effect
Trick banners	+ + +
Online	+ +
Click here	+ +
Size	+ +
Targeting	+
Brand name	−
Motion	+ +
Size*Motion	*
Motion*Target	0
Pictures	0
Pictures*Target	0
Pictures*Size	0
PROMO*Placement	*
Clear price*Placement	*
Number of impressions	−

* The effects are illustrated in Fig. 6.6 and Fig. 6.7.

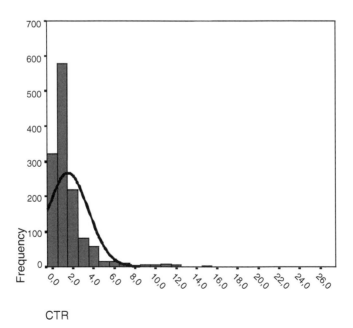

FIG. 6.3   Distribution of the click-through rate.

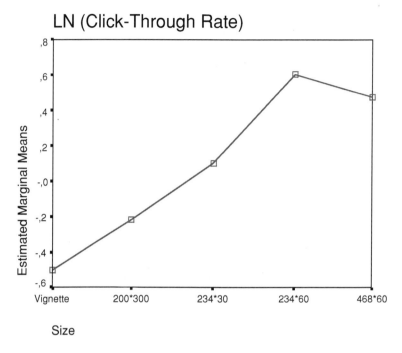

FIG. 6.4   Effect of different banner sizes on CTR.

largest part of the variation in click-through rates, and the effect is, as expected, positive. The second largest effect is the nature of the advertiser. Online advertisers, those who have no physical shops, have a higher click-through rate than sites associated with physical locations. The third significant factor is the mention click here. It has a positive effect on the click-through rate. Lastly, the saturation effect is significant but weak.

Effect of the Size

Overall, a banner's size has a significant and positive effect. If we plot the five sizes, the Fig. 6.4 shows a ceiling effect. The contrast analyses and Post Hoc tests indicate that there is no significant difference between the two bigger sizes: 234 × 60 pixels and 468 × 60 pixels.

These results reconcile those of Drèze Hussherr (2003), who showed that the size difference between the 468 × 60 pixels and 234 × 60 pixels banners has no significant effect on recall, and those of Chtourou and Chandon (2000), who showed that the difference between the sizes 468 × 60 pixels and 234 × 30 pixels has a significant effect on the intention to spread positive word of mouth.

Ln(CTR)

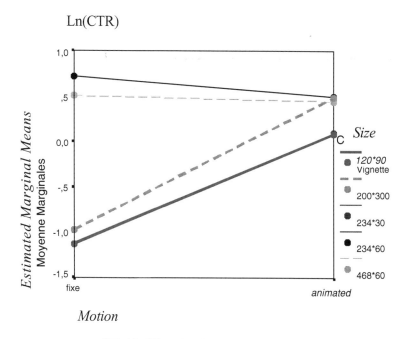

FIG. 6.5   Effect of motion for the different sizes.

Effect of the Animation

The advertisers studied the overwhelming use of animation. Only 91 insertions over the 1,258 studied are not animated. This choice turns out to be wise because animation improves the click-through rate in a significant way. However, the effect is weak (Eta^2 < 1%). The hypothesis of an interaction between animation and size is confirmed. The effect of animation is positive for small announcements (mainly 120 × 90 pixels) but the effect for the biggest banners (234 × 60 pixels and 468 × 60 pixels) is nonexistent (even negative).

The interaction between animation and targeting is not significant. The effect of animation is positive, no matter the page targeting. The fixed announcements always generate fewer clicks than animated banners.

Effect of the Presence of Images

The presence of images seems to have no effect on the click-through rate, whatever the size and place of the banner (i.e., the direct effect and the two interaction effects are not significant). This result is similar to the one obtained by Bhargava, Naveen, & Caron (1994). They show that there is no significant relation between the proportion of space occupied by an image and memory for outdoor advertising. On the surface, this suggests that the effect of images does not depend on the medium.

However, another explanation is that the analysis of images should consider their fit with the message. Images that are tangent to the product (low fit) probably do not benefit the message. Finally, it should be noted that the poor quality of the images (drawn representations rather than artistic photos), may have minimized their effectiveness for the ads studied.

Effect of Tricks and "Click Here"

As expected, tricks and "click here" mentions have major effects on the click-through rates. However, these effects probably decrease over time. Tricks may be particularly effective with inexperienced users who are unfamiliar with their system messages. Experienced users are likely to realize that the images are tricks and not be deceived by them. Chtourou & Guerin (2001) show that using tricks on banners significantly decreases intentions to click and attitudes toward the ad. This demonstrates that even for limited size samples, when people are aware of the real purpose of these ads, their reactions are unfavorable. Thus, these techniques are best used carefully so as not to deceive users.

Effect of the Targeting

As expected, the effect of targeting is positive. Insertions on targeted pages have a better click-through rate than those that are not targeted. This confirms results from prior research and reinforces the idea that clicking on a banner is guided by an information-search goal.

Effect of Mentioning the Price on the Banner

Mentioning the price on the banner seems to generally decrease the click-through rate. This decrease is particularly important in the case of targeted placements as shown in Fig. 6.6. This may be due to several elements. Prices mentioned on the banners can be too aggressive, to the point of becoming not credible. We have seen many ads with claims such as "a trip to Rome for 1 Franc" with a little footnote saying that this is the starting price of the auctions. Such claims decrease trust toward the advertiser and thus lower CTR. This is particularly likely for involved consumers, for example, persons likely to know true market prices. Another factor is that the price is often the final product characteristic motivating users to visit the advertiser's site. Including it directly inside the banner removes this motivation.

Effect of Promotion

We note that price information has an effect that depends on the technique used. For example, promotion has no significant linear effect but interacts with the placement (linked to involvement), as illustrated in Fig. 6.7. Here, we see that the promotion has a weak positive effect for individulas in the untargeted environments (noninvolved), but has a negative effect on persons in targeted environments (involved).

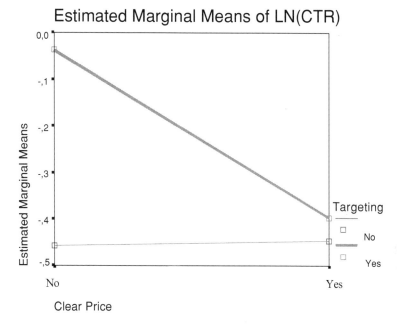

FIG. 6.6   Effect of price information on CTR according to type of placement.

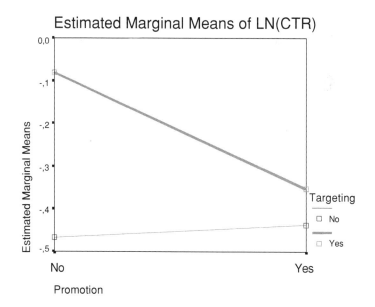

FIG. 6.7   Effect of promotion on CTR according to type of placement.

Since involved users are more knowledgeable about the product category, they should rely more on their opinion about the real value of the goods and be less sensitive to the pricing argument. The same reasoning applies to discount. It may be that discounts, which are common on the Internet, lack credibility. Such techniques are unproductive in targeted placements where visitors are familiar with the product or service and thus sensitive to the face validity of a claim.

However, it is important to note that in this study we do not distinguish among the different forms of promotion because of sample size constraints. We can guess that promotions based upon games have better effects than those that are not. Games add an entertainment component to the promotion that simple rebates do not. And that gives an extra reason for user to accept to interact with the advertiser. This is confirmed by another survey where such banners have higher intention to click and attitude toward the ad than banners without promotions. This argument is consistent with Fig. 6.6. Involved people (who use targeted placement) are more goal-oriented and thus less sensitive to the entertaining part of the ad.

Effect of the Presence of the Brand Name

As for the animation, the effect of brand name was difficult to study because of the few number of announcements not mentioning the brand (87). Nevertheless, the effect is negative. Advertisements that do not mention the brand have a better click-through rate than the ones that mention the brand. The explanation lies probably in the fact that, by not mentioning the brand, the advertiser stimulates the Internet users' curiosity and invites them to look for additional information by clicking on the banner.

CONCLUSIONS

The Internet is a new advertising medium to research advertising efficiency. The fact that browsing behavior is recorded automatically eases data collection. Despite some limits, click-through rates are an interesting and original measure of advertising effectiveness that can partly fit with an advertiser's goals. It can be viewed in two ways: an immediate impulsive response to the ad, or an action to get extra information. Our research should be considered quasi-experimental. Consequently, the sizes of the various cells of the design are not wellbalanced, which in turn limits testing of the treatments. However some recommendations can be drawn from our results. First, we can say that the techniques that capture attention—introducing more and more fluent motion, using bigger sizes—improve short-term effectiveness. Using pictures—at least on the banners—is not useful. Possibly, the availability of broadband connection and new advertising sizes will allow more creativity for designers and ultimately enhance the effect of images.

The effect of the trick banners raises some questions. On the one hand, they are most effective in influencing the click-through rate, even though they are no longer a novelty. This suggests several questions about the reasons for such effectiveness and the proper objectives for internet advertising campaigns. Is it not wise to increase clicks at all costs without worrying about consequences for the brand image of deceived users unsatisfied with their navigation experience to the advertiser's Web site? On the other hand, such results can encourage the developers of fully interactive banners, since people may be interested in interacting with the banner without being transferred to the brand's site.

Concerning ad banner content, our research shows that it should fit with the content of the site, stimulate clicks and transfer to the right page in the advertiser's site. Although the click is—at least partially—driven by an information-search goal, we found no evidence in favor of mentioning price. Price mentions appear to even discourage involved visitors. Using games and nonmonetary promotion techniques can also help advertisers to drive people to their site, especially for those that are not goal oriented or already involved in a searching task. Such techniques can invite "surfers"—those who are looking for fun and excitement on the Internet—to visit the Web site and establish relationship with the brand. Such visitors can recruit other users. For users more involved with the product category, we think that the ad should be related to the goal of their research. Advertisers should study banners individually and try to adapt their message to each target segment separately. This is feasible because the production costs for Internet ads are still quite low.

Other questions about measuring Internet advertising effectiveness remain unanswered. For example, how best to enhance long-term effectiveness of the ad on the Internet? Do consumers perceive ads differently when they are broadcasted on the Internet? How best to connect the "virtual world" with the "real world"? How to motivate people to act outside the Internet after seeing an Internet ad? Another question that can be raised is whether there is any relationship between click-through rates and other classical effectiveness measurements? Although this chapter demonstrated that click-through rates do not encompass all of the persuasion potential of an Internet advertisement, they appear useful for large-scale ad testing.

REFERENCES

Armstrong, J. S. (2000, January). ESAP Manual. *Advertising Principle*. Retrieved November 29, 2004, from http://morris.wharton.upenn.edu/advertising/evaluatng_ads.htm.

Beatty S. E., & Ferrell, M. E. (1998). Impulsive buying: Modeling its precursors. *Journal of Retailing, 74*(Summer), 169–191.

Bellenger, D. N., Robertson, D. H., & Hirschmann, E. C. (1978). Impulse buying varies by product. *Journal of Advertising Research, 18*(December), 15–18.

Bergkvitz, L., Fristrom, M., & Melander, J. (2001). *Measuring the brand effects of banner advertising campaigns.* Worldwide Online Measurement ESOMAR Athens 6-2001

Bhargava, M., Donthu, N., & Caron, R. (1994). Improving the effectiveness of outdoor advertising: lessons from a case study of 282 campaigns. *Journal of Advertising Research, 34*(March–April), 46–55.

Briggs, R., & Hollis, N. (1997). Advertising on the web is there response before click-through? *Journal of Advertising Research, 37*(March–April), 33–46.

Business Week "Online advertising it's just the beginning" July 12, 2001 http://www.businessweek.com/technology/content/jul2001/tc20010712_790.htm

Chandon, J. L., Chtourou, M. S., & Fortin, D. R. (2003). *An examination of the effects of ad configuration and exposure levels on behavioural responses to Web-based advertisements. Journal of Advertising Research, 43*(2), 217.

Chandon, P. (1994). "Dix ans de recherche sur la psychologie et le comportement des consommateurs face aux promotions" (Ten year's research on customers' psychology and behaviour towards' promotion) Recherche et Application en Marketing.

Childers, T. L., & Houston, M. J. (1984). Conditions for a picture-superiority effect on consumer memory. *Journal of Consumer Research, 11*(2), 643–654.

Cho, C. (1999). How advertising works on the WWW: Modified elaboration likelihood model. *Journal of Current Research in Advertising, 27*(1), 33–50.

Chtourou M. S., & Chandon, J. L. (2000). *Impact of motion, picture and size on recall and word of mouth for Internet banners.* Paper presented at the INFORMS Internet and Marketing Science Conference, University of Southern California, LOS Angeles.

Chtourou, M. S., Chandon, J. L., & Zollinger, M. (2001). Effect of price information and promotion on click-through rates for internet banners, *Acts of the international seminar of marketing research and consumer behavior.* Lalonde les maures.

Chtourou, M. S., & Guerin, F. (2001). *What makes people like and click on Internet banners.* Worldwide Online Measurement ESOMAR Athens 6-2001.

DeVigal, A. (2000). Putting the eyetrack study to good use. *PoynterOnline.* Retrieved November 29, 2004, from http://www.poynter.org/content/content_view.asp?id=38357.

Donthu, N., Cherian, J., & Bhargava, M. (1993). Factors influencing recall of outdoor advertising. *Journal of Advertising Research, 33*(May–June), 65–72.

Drèze, X., & Hussherr, F. X. (2003). *Internet advertising: Is anybody watching?* Publication: Journal of interactive marketing 2003 Vol. 17(4) pp. 8–23.

Drèze X., & Zufryden, F. (2000). Internet advertising: The medium is the difference. *Consumption, Markets & Culture.* 2000 Vol. 4(1) pp. 23–37.

Edell, J. A., & Staelin, R. (1983). The information processing of pictures in print advertisements. *Journal of Consumer Research, 10*(1), 45–62.

Finn, A. (1988). Print ad recognition scores—An information processing perspective. *Journal of Marketing Research, 25*(May), 168–178.

Fortin D., & Dholakia, R. (2000). *The impact of interactivity and vividness on involvement: An empirical test of the Hoffman-Novak Model.* Paper presented at the INFORMS Internet and Marketing Science Conference, University of Southern California, Los Angeles.

Gibson, O. (2003, October 14). Surfers switch off TV for PCs. *Guardian Unlimited.* Retrieved November 29, 2004, from http://www.guardian.co.uk/online/news/0,12597,1062675,00.html.

Hoffmann D. L., Novak, T. P., & Chatterjee, P. (1998). Modeling the clickstream: Implication for Web-based advertising efforts. Unpublished manuscript, Vanderbilt University, Nashuille.

Homer, P. M. (1995). Ad size as an indicator of perceived advertising costs and effort: The effects on memory and perceptions. *Journal of Advertising, 24*(Winter), 1–12.

Hussherr, F. X. (1999). *La publicité sur Internet: un modèle économique dépendant de l'efficacité publicitaire.* Unpublished doctoral dissertation, Ecole Nationale Supérieure des Télécommunications, Paris.

Infoseek (1996). "Determinants of click through rates: Some preliminary results" http://infoseek.com in Onnein-Bonnefoy, C. (1997). "Les bandeaux publicitaires sur Internet: mesures d'efficacité" (Internet banners: Effectiveness measures). Décision Marketing Vol. 11 (May–August) pp. 87–92.

Journal du net (2000). "12,8 millions de Français ont un comportement actif sur Internet" (12,8 millions French are active on the in termed). Journal du net November 17, 2000.

Kelly, K. J., & Hoel, R. F. (1991). The impact of size, color, and copy quantity on Yellow Pages advertising effectiveness. *Journal of Small Business Management, 29*(4), 64–72.

Kisielius, J., & Sternthal, B. (1984). "Detecting and Explaining Vividness Effects in Attitudinal Judgments." *Journal of Marketing Research, 21*(1), 54–64.

Kompella, K. (2001). *Evaluating the use of banner advertising in strengthening the brand relationship.* Worldwide Online Measurement ESOMAR Athens.

Lendrevie, J. (2000). "Internet est il doué pour la publicité? (did the internet have a gift for advertising). Revue Française du Marketing, Vol. 177–178, N=2–3, pp. 102–118.

Naccarato, J. L., & Neuendorf, K. A. (1998). Content analysis as a predictive methodology: Recall, readership, and evaluations of business-to-business print advertising. *Journal of Advertising Research, 38*(May–June), 19–33.

Onnein-Bonnefoy, C. (1997). Les bandeaux publicitaires sur Internet: Mesure d'efficacité. Décision Marketing Mai-Aout.

Petty, R., Cacioppo, J., & Schumann, D. (1983). Central and peripheral routes to advertising effectiveness: The moderating role of involvement. *Journal of Consumer Research, 10*(September), 135–146.

Rae, N., & Brennan, M. (1998). The relative effectiveness of sound and animation in Web banner advertisements. *Marketing Bulletin, 9*, 76–82.

Rapp, E. (2001). *Make a wish: A case study on the branding effects of frequency for online advertising.* Worldwide Online Measurement ESOMAR Athens.

Rossiter, J., & Bellman, S. (1999). A proposed model for exmlaining and measuring Web ad effectiveness. *Journal of Current Issues & Research in Advertising, 21*(Spring), 13–31.

Schweiger, G. C., & Hruschka, H. (1980). Analysis of Advertising Inquiries. *Journal of Advertising Research, 20*(5), 37–39.

Singh, S. N., Lessig, V. P., Kim, D., Gupta, R., & Hocutt, M. A. (2000). Does your ad have too many pictures? *Journal of Advertising Research, 40*(January–April), 11–27.

Stewart, D., & Pavlou, P. A. (2002). From consumer response to active consumer: Measuring the effectiveness of interactive media. *Journal of the Academy of Marketing Science, 30*(Fall), 376–396.

Strazzieri, A. (1994). Mesurer l'implication durable vis à vis d'un produit indépendemment du risque perçu. *Recherche et Applcations en Marketing, 9*, 73–91.

Unnava, H. R., & Burnkant, R. E. (1991). An imagery-processing view of the role of pictures in print advertisements. *Journal of Marketing Research, 28*(May), 226–231.

Vakratsas. D., & Ambler, T. (1999). How advertising works: What do we really know? *Journal of Marketing, 63*(January), 26–43.

CHAPTER SEVEN

Exploring Consumer Response to "Advergaming"

Michelle R. Nelson

School of Journalism & Mass Communication
University of Wisconsin–Madison

Octopi officials say advergames promote repeat traffic to Web sites and reinforce brands in compelling ways. Because users choose to register to be eligible for prizes, the games help marketers collect customer data. And because gamers may invite their friends to participate, the brand benefits from word of mouth, or what these days is called viral marketing.

—Goldstein (August 8, 2001)

Approximately 450 million people are online worldwide, about one third of these in the United States (Nielsen/Net Ratings, 2004)—they are surfers, chatters, shoppers, information seekers, game players, and more (Fallows, 2004). Many of these online consumer activities are investigated in other chapters within this book. This chapter focuses on the entertainment aspect of online consumer behavior, particularly gaming, and suggests ways that brands can be incorporated into entertainment content. The first part of the chapter provides an overview of gaming and then describes a taxonomy of brand usage in games, drawing on real-world examples and academic research to explore consumer response and brand effectiveness. The second part of the chapter presents results of primary research designed to investigate effectiveness of background ads in racing games. Areas for future research and ethical and public policy implications are also discussed.

THE RISE, REACH, AND REALITY OF GAMES

A national conference on computer and video games was held at Massachusetts Institute of Technology (MIT) in February 2000 to explore the state of an "emerging entertainment medium" (Wright, 2000). The consensus from participants, according to conference organizer and professor Henry Jenkins, was that games were at an important threshold economically, technologically, culturally, and aesthetically. Five years later, these predictions hold true. From an economic viewpoint, revenues in the U.S. game sector ($11.2 billion) were higher than Hollwood box-office revenue ($9.185 billion) for the third year in a row (Gaudiosi, 2004). Worldwide figures for video game spending were estimated at $22 billion in 2003, with projections at $55.6 billion by 2008 as compared to the world music industry at $33.7 billion (Christman, 2004). These figures reflect the growing popularity of games among consumers of all ages. According to the Entertainment Software Association, more than half of the U.S. population over the age of six plays video and computer games. Importantly, these people are males and females across demographic groups (34% are younger than 18 years, 46% are 18–50 years, and 17% are over 50 years).

Consumers play games for fun or, according to a media uses and gratifications approach, for entertainment purposes, including social escapism (Korgaonkar & Wolin, 1999), social interaction (Rutkowska & Carlton, 1994), and relaxation (Papacharissi & Rubin, 2000). Fun games, according to children ages 5–14, include those with a goal or challenge and an uncertain outcome, as well as those that engage curiosity and imagination (Malone, 1981). Girls (ages 10–13) said the best interactive games had good graphics, music, challenging game play, and the possibility of winning, while their older counterparts (ages 14–16) liked thinking, graphics, challenge, mystery, and strategy. Males (ages 10–13 years) liked action, violence, graphics, and speed, while the older males liked violence, action, difficulty, and challenge, and also winning (Gilmour, 1999). For a discussion of gender differences and motivational factors, see Cassell and Jenkins (1998).

Culturally, games have entered high, low, and popular culture and have sparked academic study (e.g., see www.game-culture.com). Games are also the subject and medium for art exhibits (Glaser, 2001), movies (e.g., *TombRaider, Final Fantasy*), exercise equipment (Austen, 2001), educational tools (e.g., Pillay, Brownlee, & Wilss, 1999), armed forces training (Naisbitt, 1999), and now advertisements (Bannan, 2002; Elkin, 2001; Gunn, 2001; Marriott, 2001). Technologically and aesthetically, games have vastly changed since *Spacewar*, the world's first computer game played with a typewriter and punch cards in the early 1960s. In the last four decades, games have changed formats (from arcade halls to television consoles to computers and handhelds), and technology has advanced game realism from black and white to color, from 2-D to 3-D graphics, and today, moving rapidly into virtual reality environments (Herz, 1997). In 1997 alone, the industry invested approximately $2 billion in research and development of new gaming technology

(Naisbitt, 1999). This research and development has gone into creating a more realistic, multisensory gaming environment, which has made this medium more immersive than any other.

This immersive environment may allow for much greater audience involvement than other media have offered to date (Vorderer, 2000). Instead of receiving information through a single sensory modality as in radio (auditory) or print (visual) or with these two senses combined (e.g., television), entertainment-seeking consumers are able to experience additional senses. For instance, haptic technology (touch) allows the consumer to feel the vibrations of a racing car in a game, and in the near future consumers may experience digital smells. Further, the active control aspect of gaming, along with a first-person perspective, also creates an interactive perspective (Grodal, 2000), which increases the vividness of the medium (Steuer, 1992).

Relevant for this book, online gaming as a consumer activity varies from 5-minute distractions to hours of leisure activity. Games can be played by oneself or with others in personal computer (PC) rooms or across the world. For example, Korea's multiplayer *Lineage: The Blood Pledge* is a role-playing game that boasts 2 million active accounts and as many as 180,000 simultaneous users from all over the world. Like other Internet activities, online gaming spans international boundaries, age, class, and gender. Indeed, game sites typically represent 8 of the top 10 entertainment sites on the Internet (Marriott, 2001). Gaming played over the Internet was born in the late 1980s and early 1990s as early adopters of email participated in turn-based, text-based adventure games followed by interaction in multiuser dungeons (MUD) (Osborne, 2000). As technology advanced through faster processors and modems, gaming companies developed visual 3-D graphics games such as *Doom* in the mid-1990s. Today, increases in bandwidth and processing speed are broadening the types of games offered and the appeal of online interactive gaming.

Although video/computer games have been around since the 1960s (Herz, 1997) and online multiplayer gaming since the late 1980s, the practice of *advergaming*, defined by Chen and Ringel (2001) as "the use of interactive gaming technology to deliver embedded advertising messages to consumers," or product placement in games has only recently emerged as a viable industry (Pope, 1994). Early examples of branded entertainment content include Domino's Pizza in *Avoid the Noid* (1989) and the 7-Up mascot in *Cool Spot* (1993). More recent brand-blurring is offered in the online arena where advertisers use games as a way to form brand relationships with consumers, create "sticky" sites (e.g., Lynch, 2000), and collect information about consumers at the same time (Marriott, 2001). Although automobiles are among the most frequently cited examples of successful advergaming (Lienert, 2004; Naughton, 2003), numerous branded Web sites are now targeting children. For instance, one of the most popular is neopets.com, a Web site targeted to children, which features adoptable furry creatures. This site boasts 11 million users, 39% under age 13 (Fonda, 2004), who are given points for watching advertising, among other tasks. These points can be used to purchase Oreo cookies or other branded products for their pets at the virtual stores.

Indeed, brands are infiltrating several genres of online and offline games in many different ways as advertisers consider advergaming a viable alternative to banner ads (Marriott, 2001; Vranica, 2001) or even to broadcast advertising (Grover, Lowry, Khermouch, Edwards, & Foust, 2004). The industry is changing from one of surrogate advertising to a standardized business practice. Costs for brand placements currently range from $25,000 to $700,000 depending on the prominence and level of interactivity (Moran, 2004), and analysts predict that commercial placements in games will become a $5-billion industry (Leeper, 2004). To further aid in the media buying and planning process, Nielsen has announced it will start gauging effectiveness of game brand placements (Gough, 2004).

Given the growth of the game industry and of the advergaming process, it is surprising how few research studies have investigated the practice. Therefore, the following questions will be addressed from managerial and theoretical perspectives:

- Where and how do brands fit into digital entertainment environments?
- How do consumers respond to brand placements in games?
- What factors might influence consumer response to advergaming messages?

HOW BRANDS FIT INTO GAMING ENVIRONMENTS

Introduction: The Business of Gaming

Video and PC games are produced by small teams (designers, producers, programmers, artists) or multimillion-dollar companies funded by publishers or console manufacturers. Typically, a video game is produced in 12 months to 2 years and costs, on average, $10 million (Nussenbaum, 2004). Game developers must sell their ideas through storyboards or demonstrations to game publishers who are responsible for marketing and distribution, which may cost an additional $10 million per game (Nussenbaum, 2004). In recent years, the growing economic opportunities within the game industry have also resulted in an increased number of development companies and more competition (Cole, 1999). Publishers are looking for the sure hit as well as the newest idea in an increasingly crowded industry. It is estimated that only 1 of 20 games developed actually make it to the retail shelf and that only 2 of 10 make a profit (Nussenbaum, 2004). Sure hits can include game sequels and the use of licensed names such as the National Basketball Association or National Football League or Hollywood movies. In addition to licensed names, there are several other ways that developers can include brand contacts within games, from passive background props to more active forms such as equipment and characters (see Table 7.1 for taxonomy).

Branded content may be introduced and negotiated through the use of a product placement company such as Jam International who acts as the go-between for

TABLE 7.1
Advergaming taxonomy: Identifying brand uses in games.

Brand Use	Proposed Brand Effectiveness	Examples
Sponsorship/Banner Ads	Brand awareness, reinforce brand image Enhance consumer involvement	NBA Live 2001 *FIFA 2001* *Kawasaki Jet Ski Racing* *Adidas Power Soccer*
Contests, gamelettes on Web sites	Increase stickiness of site, involve consumer	Pepsiworld's Aqua Flier (Sea-Doo Hydro Cross) Skittles Green Apple Madness Flavor Shoot Game Snickers Cyber Crunch Game
Background (visuals) ads and brand props (e.g., billboards, side-boards, clothing, accessories)	Brand recall Familiarity may enhance brand attitudes	Nokia phones in *X Files* Bass Angler Sportsman Society sign in *Bass Fishing* Seiko Scoreboard in *Gran Turismo2* Gummi LifeSavers in *Croc 2*
Background (auditory). Licensed music, brand sound effects, sports commentators	Increases game realism and consumer involvement, good method for cross selling	*Gran Turismo2* soundtrack (alternative) *Dance Dance Revolution* (dance variety) *Razor Freestyle Scooter* (punk, pop) *FIFA 2001* (British sports commentators)
Brands are major part of game play (equipment, tools)	Consumer can try products in virtual life, before buying products in real life. Build & reinforce brand loyalty	Auto brands (BMW) *Gran Turismo 2*, *Ford Racing* Cue sticks/carrying cases (Joss, Viking) in *Virtual Pool 3*
Characters are branded images (real or fictitious)	Brand liking/relationships. Aids in consumer identification with character/brand	Tiger Woods in *Cyber Tiger* Lara Croft in *Tomb Raider Michelle Kwan Figure Skating* Any professional player featured in NBA, FIFA, NHL, NFL games
Game players create their own ads/brands through customization	Increases brand involvement, loyalty	*Nascar Racing*–custom sponsors *FIFA 2001*–select sponsors *Dave Mirra Freestyle BMX*—attract sponsors with each game level completed

the advertiser and the game developer, or it may be coordinated directly through the game developer or publishing company. Currently, the game development community expresses ambivalence about the increasing use of brands appearing in games. Although financial rewards are welcome, critics have articulated concerns over loss of artistic freedom and increased commercialization (Nelson, Keum, & Yaros, 2004), echoing those within the film industry (e.g., Gupta & Gould, 1997; Vollmers & Mizerski, 1994). Although developers Eidos Interactive (creator of the *TombRaider Chronicles*) and Electronic Arts embrace product placements (Brown, 1999; Nussenbaum, 2004), other game creators are not positive at all. Ernest Adams

(1999), a freelance game designer for *Madden NFL Football*, blatantly speaks out on the topic in an online game industry publication:

> There's no question we could use the money. We'll make good use of the money. And we'll like the money and begin to need the money and eventually we'll become completely addicted to the money and unable to function without it. And when that day comes, your game design decisions will be subordinated to the question of how much breakfast cereal they will sell.

In the online gaming arena, there are a wide variety of business models and game forms (MacInnes, 2000). Many online games (e.g., Sony's *EverQuest*) charge a monthly subscription fee up to $10 per month (Non, 2001) and others are supported through advertisers. Advertiser support is based on sponsorship, on banner ads, and increasingly through custom product use in the game. The attraction of using online games for brand placement over PC or video games is due to lower production costs (and therefore, less risk), more flexibility, greater access to market information, and increased measurability. Compared to millions of dollars for computer and video games, online games cost advertisers $150,000 to $500,000 to create depending on the graphics (Vranica, 2001).

Although games can appear in multiple platforms, there is an increasing blurring across media as consoles connect to the Internet and games are offered across platforms; for example, *Tony Hawk's Pro Skater 3* skateboarding game is offered on six platforms including PlayStation 2, Xbox, GameBoy Advance, PC, PlayStation, and Game Boy Color. Advertisers are also including game advertising as part of a larger cross-promotional strategic communications effort. For example, during the Super Bowl, HotJobs.com released a video game version of its television ad where players guided a ball through a maze. More than 55,000 people played the game, and HotJobs.com collected 5,000 email addresses (Vranica, 2001). Steven Spielberg's film *AI* was first introduced through a subversive Web game (Clewley, 2001), which some players claimed was more entertaining than the film (discussion on www.slashdot.org).

From a consumer standpoint, several of the ways that brands appear in games are similar across gaming media (e.g., sponsorship, background props), although Web-based versions also can allow consumers to link directly to the advertisers' Web sites. Therefore, the following discussion of the taxonomy of advergaming presents an initial outline of methods for including brand images in games in general. Examples are organized from passive/incidental to interactive/integrated with game content and are drawn from all game platforms. Relevant theories and examples for exploring consumer response are presented.

Exploring an Advergaming Taxonomy

Sponsorship and Banner Ads in Portals, Gaming Networks, and Video Games. Advertisers can sponsor on- or offline games or use banner ads as methods to create brand awareness or enhance brand liking among game-playing consumers. In consumer research investigating interactive advertising, online sponsorship has been defined as "an indirect form of persuasion that allows companies to carry out marketing objectives by associating with key content" (Rogers, 2000, p.1). The positive association and feelings gained from game play should transfer to the sponsor's brand through classical conditioning methods (e.g., Gorn, 1982) and result in positive brand attitudes. Further, because sponsor identifications usually appear merely as a brand name and/or a slogan (Hansen & Scotwin, 1995), which can be interactive (Rogers, 2000), they take up less space and are less obtrusive than other Web forms (e.g., pop-ups), which may explain their higher credibility among Internet users. In online games, for example, consumers may realize that their game play is free because of the sponsorships, which would presumably offer positive carry-over benefits for advertisers. In addition, sponsorships have been found to work particularly well when the sponsor is somehow linked to the content. In games, this synergistic effect should occur, for example, when sporting leagues such as the National Football League license football games or with games such as *Adidas Power Soccer* or *Kawasaki Jet Ski Racing*.

In online environments, games are often regarded as content to attract and retain consumers. As such, several Internet portals such as Yahoo! and MSN have offered free matching services for online games. The games attract users who then view ads and are able to purchase the products featured. Apparently, an additional stickiness benefit results from the increased chatting that occurs on game sites. Merrill Lynch estimated about 50% of user time on game sites is spent chatting with others (exchanging tips, discussing tournaments, etc.). Under this method, brands may or may not be a part of the game itself, but the game increases the Web site's entertainment value and thus increases the stickiness factor. In these cases, usually, the ads and products are incidental to the gaming experience, although consumers can usually link directly to sponsors or advertisers' Web sites.

Top portals in January 2001 included MSN gaming in the United States, hangame.com in Korea, and ourgame.com in China (www.netvalue.com). The popularity of these Web sites is because "they're free, they appeal towards both men and women, and they're just plain addictive" (Horowitz, 2001). Importantly, these Web sites also attract large advertisers, including AT&T, Visa, and Hasbro (Horowitz, 2001). On a multiplayer game site, for example, banner ads are sold to potential advertisers wishing to reach the gaming community. Advertisers are promised brand awareness and click-through rates. According to copy written on the http://www.mpogd.com/ Web site, "On average you will see your ad refer one potential customer to your organization's site for every one hundred times it is displayed. At the current price, this breaks down to about 20 cents for each new potential customer."

What makes gaming sites and portals different from other Web sites is the amount of time players spend at these sites and their international reach. For example, Pogo (which claims four million active players worldwide) has held partnerships with Taco Bell, Real Networks, and the leading women's network, iVillage.com, because of its social appeal. According to its chief executive officer, people come to the Web site, enjoy themselves, and end up inviting their friends, which creates a community (Horowitz, 2001). The Web site also encourages players to remain at the Web site by offering incentives and prizes supported by the numerous advertisers. Consumers at the Pogo site play games for free but must view timed ads before game launches, and ads temporarily interrupt play after about 15 minutes (Horowitz, 2001).

There is no standard form of brand contacts for online games; however, many employ sponsorships and banner ads. Although various studies have examined the effectiveness of banner ads in interactive environments, the consumer motive is an important consideration for understanding effectiveness (Rogers & Thorson, 2000), and game-playing consumers who are online for entertainment or social purposes are likely to react differently than active information seekers or Web browsers investigated in previous research. Indeed, the recall, click through, and persuasion for banner ads and sponsorships in online games are areas to be researched.

Multisensory Background Ads and Brand Props Appearing in the Game. Although banner ads and sponsorships appearing on game sites or portals may enhance brand awareness, they are usually incidental to the game experience itself. Players must wait until the ad is finished before game play begins or they may choose to ignore the banner ads altogether. However, another method for brand placement is offered within the game content itself as background ads or product props, which are not controlled by the user but offer important contextual information and increase the realism of the mediated environment (Nelson, 2002). A form of unobtrusive brand inclusion, background brand placements are currently the most common form of branded image in video and PC games, occurring most frequently in the games that would be odd without them, including sports and racing games or those with cityscapes (e.g., *Crazy Taxi*).

Consumer research on product placement effectiveness in other media (such as film or television) has been conducted using recall, recognition, and attitudinal measures (e.g., Law & Braun, 2000; Russell 1998, 2002); for reviews, see DeLorme and Reid (1999) and McCarty (2004). Effectiveness studies use experiments, whereby consumers are exposed to the medium, then queried with explicit (memory) or implicit (brand evaluation) measures (Law & Braun-LaTour, 2004). Free and aided recall are the most common dependent measures (e.g., Babin & Carder, 1996; d'Astous & Seguin, 1999; Gupta & Lord, 1998) followed by recognition (Babin & Carder, 1996; d'Astous & Chartier, 2000; Law & Braun, 2000). These studies note that brand prominence, high plot connection, and multisensory visual/auditory sensory cues can lead to greater recall (see also Russell 1998, 2002). Given that increased brand awareness is one of the goals for product placement, then memory-based measures seem appropriate ways to test effectiveness, based on the premise that effectiveness measures should conform to the goals of the advertiser (e.g., Gregan-Paxton & Loken, 1997; Krishnan & Chakravarti, 1999; Stewart, 1989).

Several theories appropriate for understanding product placements have been advanced (e.g., Russell, 1998), such as the mere exposure effect (Zajonc, 1968), which proposes that familiarity breeds liking. In other words, an enhanced attitude toward an object results from repeated exposures to that object. For this theory, the fact that a baseball game player sees a new brand's logo on the side each time she or he is up to bat would be enough to facilitate positive feelings. It is unknown, however, whether repeated exposure to existing, familiar brands would enhance brand evaluations. The excitation transfer theory suggests that the positive arousal associated with the media consumption experience can be transferred to other concurrent available stimuli and cause viewers to evaluate those stimuli favorably (Zillman, 1971). In this case, the feel-good experience of game playing may transfer to the brands found within the game. Finally, the increased arousal may, however, lead to less efficient information processing, which may negatively impact recall (Mundorf, Zillman, & Drew, 1991), especially for peripheral stimuli such as brand placements (Bello, Pitts, & Etzel, 1983). For example, Pham (1992) found that viewers of a televised sports event experienced arousal that produced a negative effect on recognition of background advertising. Similarly, feelings of arousal induced by a computer game might negatively impact processing and recall of background ads.

How each of these theories operates in interactive gaming environments has not yet been tested. Games may offer a longer shelf life and a greater number of exposures to brands than other media would, suggesting a greater familiarity and liking. However, wearout effects for games and the brands within them are also possible, especially for games played an average of 30 hours or more (in total). Excitation transfer, which relies on measures of consumer arousal levels, may also offer unpredictable results for brands because of the varied emotions experienced during game play. Whereas in movies products are placed in scenes that remain the same for every viewing, games are typically structured to be a different experience every time the game is played. In addition, game players' emotions and arousal change throughout the game because of learning, curiosity, surprise, and suspense molded by game play (Grodal, 2000). Thus, the effects of emotions and arousal on brand recall and persuasion in a gaming context offer a challenging area for future exploration.

Background brands can be visual or auditory. One example of a visual brand cue is offered by Diesel, an international clothing company, that commissioned game developer Infogrammes for a number of games where characters sport Diesel wear or billboards show off the brand logos. Such games are mainly sports related (snowboarding, futuristic motorcycle racing, extreme sports), although one called *G Police II* allows players to blow up Diesel stores as part of a mission to kill evil corporations. Apparently, game producers offered to create more positive games where the brand came off as hero, but the company opted for the opposite effect instead (Ebenkamp, 1998).

Sound can also increase the realism of visual images (e.g., the skidding of car tires, the echo of gunfire, or the crack of the bat) and may enhance consumer processing (Atwood, 1989) and recall (Gupta & Lord, 1998). In a previous study using radio as the medium, sound effects were found to lead to an increased level of imagery processing (Miller & Marks, 1992), which may lead to greater emotional response and increased learning. In addition, sound bytes can be regarded as important trademarks and brand identifiers. Consider the Intel notes, for example.

In a gaming environment, auditory brands are offered through background music and through sportscasters' or licensed characters' voices. For example, the British football (soccer) game *FIFA 2002* uses well-known British sports commentators to enhance the verisimilitude to the real FIFA games. Cross-promotions are offered with music, which can be promoted and sold separately as soundtracks. For example, the *Gran Turismo2* soundtrack "Music at the Speed of Sound" features the Cardigans' song "My Favorite Game." Interestingly, in a free recall task, game players who played *Gran Turismo2* listed the musical group Garbage (whose song was also heard during the game) as a brand placed in the game (Nelson, 2002).

Additional sensory elements, such as smell, may also increase sensory realism, induce immersion, facilitate nostalgia (Mitchell, 1994), and enhance recall (Herz & Cupchik, 1992). Indeed, smells may operate like sounds, offering brand information and becoming cross-promotion brands themselves. For example, a Lara Croft (fictional character in the *TombRaider* game and movie) perfume created by France's Sodip is created for women who are dynamic, exotic, and independent (http://www.sodip.fr/eng/croft.htm). In the future, the aroma of Starbuck's coffee might be incorporated into a *Sim's* game or 76 petrol fumes into a Nascar racing game.

How all of these senses operate together should be investigated further to understand imagery processing (Gutman, 1988; Holbrook, 1981) and multisensory influence on brand recall and persuasion. Indeed, in other media environments, the use of single or multiple senses metaphorically (e.g., Nelson & Hitchon, 1999) or literally (e.g., Mitchell, Kahn, & Knasko, 1995) has enhanced the persuasion of ad messages; therefore, one might expect the literal inclusion of multiple senses to create a richer environment that would enhance brand messages. However, some media critics have suggested that multiple senses may actually impede processing (that is, "undo our capacity to think") (Postman, 1986) or create conflict among multiple sensory channels, which might interfere with message transmission (Gutman, 1988).

Character Identification and Product Use.   Past research in advertising has found that the use of celebrities can enhance message recall (Friedman & Friedman, 1979). In addition, celebrity spokespersons can improve the recognition of brand names (Petty, Cacioppo, & Schumann, 1983), create a positive attitude toward the brand (Kamins, Brand, Hoeke, & Moe, 1989), and aid in building brand personality (McCracken, 1989). In the product placement literature, it has been suggested that product use incorporated into the movie plot (plot placement) offers greater chance of brand recall (Russell, 1998), and that consumers regularly view themselves metaphorically as the characters in novels, plays, or movies (Hirschman, 1988). Consistent with Kelman's theory of social influence (Kelman, 1961), and an empathy dimension of viewing media (Fiske, 1992), these beneficial celebrity effects may depend on the receiver's identification with the spokesperson (Basil, 1996). Identification, compliance, and internationalization are processes of social influence (Kelman, 1961), of which identification is particularly relevant for celebrity endorsements. According to the theory of social influence, identification occurs when an individual takes on the behavior of another person (or group), primarily because the individual wishes to be like the person, and the behavior boosts his or her self-image.

When playing games, the player often becomes the celebrity character (e.g., Lara Croft, Barbie, Tiger Woods) that actively uses products, some of them branded, in the games. Turkle (1984) described this altered state as a second self. As part of this self, "you have to do more than identify with a character on the screen. You must act for it. Identification through action has a special kind of hold" (p. 83). Although the implied endorsements may operate similar to endorsements or product use in other media, the feeling of being in the game offered from the first-person perspective and player-controlled movements may increase identification between player and character. However, similar to other media, the characteristics of the brand or product should match the image conveyed by the celebrity (Kamins, 1990), so celebrity placements should be considered carefully. In addition, character likeability or traits may transfer to the brand through classical conditioning. For example, the bold moves of Lara Croft may create a "tough" brand image (like her perfume described earlier) or the glamour of Barbie may transfer to her products.

In sum, the observation that games use celebrities or characters in games become celebrities suggests that celebrity endorsement of brands in a game context may become an interesting area of future study. For example, how much do players identify with characters and how is that identification related to brand recall, attitudes, and use? Second, how might character likeability or character traits influence brands?

Use of the Branded Product. Whether the game player identifies with the character or even if there is no character provided, she or he is still operating from a first-person perspective. This allows the player to act out or imagine actions in virtuality. For example, players can select their own automobile brand and color to race in *Grand Turismo2*, choose their brand of poolstick in *Virtual Pool3*, or try out Sassaby Jane makeup in *McKenzie & Co*. When consumers select a branded product that becomes an instrumental part of the game, it is likely that their associations, emotions, and attitudes toward that brand will be formed, revised, or challenged during or after game play. Increasingly, in online, game console, and PC games consumers are able to select branded products rather than generic versions.

It is assumed that the active control aspect of interactivity leads to more effective advertising (Johnson, 2000; Lombard & Snyder-Duch, 2001), perhaps in part because it allows consumers to be actively involved in the persuasion process (Roehm & Haugtvedt, 1999). Product interactivity through online environments offers a particular type of interactivity where consumers can virtually try out or imagine owning products before they buy them. According to results of two experiments presented at the online consumer psychology conference (Schlosser & Kanfer, 2001), product interactivity (rather than passive information) on a Web site can lead to intentions to buy the product. In addition, the product-interactive site also created relatively stronger product attitudes than did the passive site. Schlosser and Kanfer pointed out that this finding is consistent with the research on attitudes (Fazio & Zanna, 1981) and consumer learning (see Hoch & Deighton, 1989), which claim that attitudes formed under direct experience are more predictive of behavioral intentions than attitudes formed from indirect experience.

Although the motives of the Web-surfing and game-playing consumer may differ, games offer a unique symmetry for entertainment and product trial. Indeed, simulation games that match consumers' real-life interests such as hunting and fishing simulations, *Nascar* racing, and sports showed an increase in sales in the late 1990s, possibly because of a greater number of casual gamers and increased home computer usage (Cole, 1999). These sales suggest a match between online and offline leisure pursuits, which may translate into virtual brand building and real-life brand purchasing.

In an exploratory experiment where consumers played a racing game (discussed in greater detail in part two of this chapter), all of the 20 game players except for 1 recalled the brand of the car they selected after game play (Nelson, 2002). The game, *Grand Turismo2*, offered more than 26 automobile brands available in multiple colors. Many different brands were selected among this university-aged population. Interestingly, however, the reasons listed for choosing a particular car were commonly the same: speed, aesthetics, handling, brand experience, and brand loyalty. For example, one player said, "Subaru rally car; I am loyal to Subaru. They sponsor cool outdoor events that I am involved with … it looked cool, nice, and blue." Another commented, "I drove the Mitsubishi Lancer Evo. I greatly enjoy auto racing, the Evo is possibly one of my favorite cars." One player even suggested, "I chose a VW because I have one in real life," and another, "When I can afford a Corvette, I think I'll get a red one like the one I drove." These findings demonstrate the apparent effectiveness for automobile brand placement in racing games when players select their own cars and suggest the possibility of carry-over effects into the real world (and vice versa).

Real-life marketing case studies also show positive results for interactive branded product use. Ford created a 5-minute online game, where players first viewed interior shots of the Ford Escape to select their desired color and then raced their Escape on a logo-filled racecourse on the moon. Viral marketing techniques were employed so that players could email the game to friends and "issue a challenge to beat their score" (Vranica, 2001, p. 11). The game attracted about 29,000 unique users to the site over 3 months, and it also allowed relationship building with consumers beyond the game. Approximately 12% of those users registered with the carmaker, while 55% gave permission for Ford to pitch them new products. The success of the game encouraged GM to create its own game to promote the eMotion brand. In this game, racers calibrated the online vehicles to perform better in different environments, such as high-altitude mountainous areas. Toyota has also showed increased brand awareness among game players after the brand appeared in the game *Adrenaline* on MSN Gaming Zone (Marriott, 2001), and Daimler Chrysler's Jeep 4 x 4 EVO adventure game contest combines sales promotion with gaming on its Jeep Web site.

The cases mentioned here focus on consumer selection of automobile brands in a racing game to demonstrate the use of branded products in games. However, the application to other game genres is also possible, particularly in sporting games where equipment may be selected, and even in role-playing games where products are closely tied to the storyline. For example, in the game *Darkened Skye,* "Skye will gain Skittles of various colors that can be found by killing monsters, solving puzzles, and searching. By combining different colors and amounts of Skittles, Skye can cast numerous spells. More powerful spells require more Skittles" (Padilla, 2001). In the popular *Sim's* role-playing game, the attainment of branded goods becomes an end (much like real life?). Herz (2001) noted how the Sims live in a consumer society where attaining more expensive stuff makes their lives more fulfilled. In sum, many opportunities exist for branded products to become major features of games across genres.

International or Localization of Brand Placements. Product placements in games offer a more targeted audience than do films or television and a greater ability to tailor content (Turcotte, 1995); this is particularly true for online games and entertainment sites where content providers can customize information to focus on specific known audiences in a timely manner (Stanley, 1999). These practices coincide with increasing personalization occurring in marketing because of new media technology. Such personalization or localization may increase consumer attention or involvement in the game. According to theories of selective perception and the notion of brand relevance studied in gauging traditional advertising effectiveness (e.g., Thorson & Zhao, 1997), these personalized brands will likely be attended to, recalled, liked, and perhaps purchased to a greater extent than national or nonrelevant brands.

Games already recognize the need to tailor content to consumers. According to a game developer, localizing is quite common in games today (Andersson, 1999). For example, manuals, interface languages, and sound effects are redesigned and adjusted to fit the country in which the product is sold (e.g., *FIFA 2004* offers team-specific chants). Cultural differences in game preferences and styles also raise the question of standardization or localization of content (much like the advertising debate). For example, in an attempt to attract Western game players, Japanese game developer Konami licensed ESPN for multiple sports. However, as noted by UK game reporter Simon Carless (2000), "The problem is that their sports games are actually still very Japanese-specific, especially baseball, which in all their best-selling Japanese incarnations is super-deformed (big-headed cartoon characters smacking the ball around)."

Add Your Favorite Brand! Consumer Customization of Branded Material. In addition to selecting one's color and brand of car, game players are provided with additional customization features, many of which promote the opportunity to display one's favorite sponsors and brands or offer rewards in the form of brands. For example, the instruction manual for *Nascar Racing3* offers the following under the personalization benefit: "Click on this button to repaint the car with your favorite sponsor: Spinner Rotors, Ichabod's Ice Tea, or whatever corporate image you'd like to flaunt as your sponsor."

These types of brand contacts suggest consumers are as actively involved, voluntarily, in branded images as they are in the game content so that everything becomes a form of communication and entertainment (Schmitt, 1999). For example, in *FIFA 2001* players can edit individual attributes and change the color and look of team uniforms, which now carry team crests and sponsors. *Links 2001* includes a course designer to create a golf course, and *Tony Hawk's Pro Skater 2* offers the chance to design a 3-D skateboard park and to make your own skater with or without a tattoo, cap, shoes, shirt, and pants. One game even uses sponsors as part of the game play:

> The career mode lets you start out as a rookie who has no sponsors, the worst bike, and only one track to practice on, and to top it off you have to compete in a tank top and denim shorts while other competitors are clad in sponsored clothing. By completing different objectives on each track, you unlock more tracks, and you also begin to receive attention from different sponsors, like Adidas. Your BMX freestylist reflects endorsements by wearing different articles of clothing from the company during a race. (*Dave Mirra Freestyle BMX*, 2001).

When queried about customization features, game players in a focus group showed mixed responses (Yoo, 2001). Although a 20-year-old woman indicated she personally was not interested in messing around with that stuff, she said she knew some guys who did. One gamer discussed his feelings about customization:

> I like that a lot. My roommate and I bought a football game for college football. So we would pick the, you know, Badgers and, some other Big Ten team that we knew, and then you could input the names. So if you know the roster of the football game, you can put in the names of the players you watched on the weekend and then the

whole process makes it very interactive. If you have a long season ahead of you, you want to come home and draft people, or play their next game. And, which just kind of makes you want to come back and play it.

The realism gained by adding real sports players' names or real sponsors enhances game play and perceived interactivity for game players. Indeed, the practice is moving beyond sports and into role-playing games where branded products are actively created or sought out. For example, in *The Sims* game players create a household of virtual characters who have personalities and needs, including consumer needs. The consumer needs can be fulfilled at the Mall of the Sims, an independent portal supported by advertising revenue and made up of virtual stores offering merchandise at Sims furniture showrooms, sporting-goods outlets, and clothing stores, all of which can be downloaded and inserted into a virtual Sims household (Herz, 2001). In addition, consumer good accumulation is regarded as a goal in the game *Sims Online*, which creates a place for characters to sell each other SimGoods and SimServices and allows players to bookmark retail objects, as explained by Herz (2001):

> For instance, if you see a cool chair at someone's house, you bookmark it. If you buy the chair, a commission flows back to the person from whom you bookmarked it, and the person from whom they bookmarked it, as well as the creator of that object. This motivates people to buy expensive stuff and throw parties. It also makes it economically attractive to buy one of every chair in the Sim universe and open a Chairs "R" Us showroom. Imagine a world where you could earn an Amazon-style affiliate commission for every product on your homepage—it makes retail into a massively multiplayer game.

The Mall of Sims Web site solicits advertisers for their virtual stores by explaining the consumer need for realism, which can be fulfilled through products: "Sims players strive to make their Sims' environments as **REAL** as possible. The connection between real-life items and 'Sims' items includes the ability to portray a brand name in the actual 'in-game' description of the items." Additional, futuristic Bladerunner type games such as *StarTopia* (which challenges the player to rebuild a once thriving network of space stations) may offer additional opportunities for brands. In *StarTopia*, capitalism is the theme, with accumulation of wealth as the goal:

> Set in the aftermath of an intergalactic war that scattered the remnants of civilization to the far corners of space, Your goal is to unite the denizens of nine distinct alien races under your corporate banner, creating a stable system of commerce and communication for the common good. And, yeah, you just might turn a tidy profit in the process. Of course, most galaxies tend toward Darwinian dynamics, so expect stiff competition from enterprising (and sometimes unscrupulous) individuals pursuing the same goals. Technology and goods can be bartered and traded with visiting starships, or amongst the players themselves. You can also trade directly with Arona Dall,

the porcine Zenoc merchant infamous for his amazing array of goods at ridiculous prices. (Barba, 2001)

In these games, consumers add the products, brands, and sponsors, which offer social meaning and realistic environments, and can be tightly linked to game play. Another form of gaming that utilizes brands is found in gamelettes or interactive sales promotions on corporate Web sites used to increase the site's stickiness and to collect consumer information. For example, the Mountain Dew site promoted its Code Red beverage by asking consumers to "Crack the Code" in a game that offered prizes for the top 100 players. The Skittles Web site offered a GreenApple Power game, which allowed consumers to "juice the limes." The cost of producing these games is minimal, although the effectiveness has not yet been researched.

CONSUMER RESPONSE TO ADVERGAMING: AN EXPLORATION

Although the previous discussion of advergaming or product placement practices offers several ways that marketers can and currently do insert brands into interactive game environments, almost no published academic research in this area exists (but see special issue on gaming in the *Journal of Interactive Advertising*). Results of an initial investigation of brand recall for background ads placed in racing games (Nelson, 2002) is presented next.

Method and Rationale

Across two exploratory studies, game players in Madison, Wisconsin, were asked to play a car racing game for approximately 15 minutes and then responded to the following measures: free recall of brands, telepresence (sense of being there; Kim & Biocca, 1997), and attitudes and thoughts toward product placements. The players ranged in age from 18 to 28 and were predominately males. The first study employed an existing Playstation console game, *Grand Turismo2,* which allowed players to select their automobile brand and contained numerous background billboard and guardrail ads for brands like motor oil, tires, and autos. The second game offered an experimental approach. A PC racing game demo was altered to contain a mixture of brands: local/national, typical/atypical for racing games, and familiar/unfamiliar, which appeared on billboards (Google, 76, Mad Dog Restaurant) and guard rails (Mad Radio, Musiconline.com, Exxon, Pepsi, Mobil). Dependent measures included free recall directly after game play and long-term recall when game players were recontacted after a 5-month delay. Because these were the first known studies to examine brand effectiveness in interactive game environments, it was exploratory in nature. The first study was conducted to discern if players would remember any brands. The second study sought to delve into various issues related to brand placement for short- and long-term recall.

Results and Discussion

Across two exploratory studies and game contexts, it was demonstrated that game players, even on playing a game for the first time and for only a limited amount of time, were readily able to recall about 30% of brands placed within games in the short-term and (in the second study) about 10% in the long-term. The results of the *Grand Turismo2* study showed that players enjoyed selecting their own cars and were able to recall the auto brands they selected when asked directly following game play. This suggests that when brands are a major part of game play, and consumers actively choose their brand, they are likely to recall that brand. Players also easily identified key reasons for selecting their cars, including relations to real-life cars (e.g., "I own a VW in real life"). In addition, players in general (all except one), were able to recall a number of brands within the games when asked directly after playing the game, including the background music being played.

The second study showed short- and long-term recall superiority for UW-Madison, Google, Mad-Dog, and Musiconline.com, while the other brands suffered. This suggests that when the brand is local or highly relevant to computer-savvy game players (like UW-Madison or Google) both short- and long-term recall are enhanced. This finding fits with past research on the importance of brand relevance for recall and attitudinal measures in gauging traditional advertising effectiveness (Thorson & Zhao, 1997). Recall superiority might also be related to the perceived novelty of certain brand placements in this type of media environment. Although this factor was not measured directly, the typical brands seen in racing games (e.g., motor oil) or the market leaders (e.g., Pepsi), which are currently advertised frequently, did not fare as well as the atypical or newer brands (e.g., Google, Musiconline.com). Novel or distinctive stimuli might be remembered more than other stimuli (Waddill & McDaniel, 1998).

A measure of telepresence ("experience of presence in an environment by means of a communication medium"; Steuer, 1992, p.76) based on a scale used by Kim and Biocca (1997) was also included as a possible factor or mediator for brand recall. Telepresence was made up of two factors: (1) *departure* (not being in the physical environment) and (2) *arrival* (being there, in the virtual environment). Although presence or telepresence has been considered in other interactive models of advertising (e.g., Rogers & Thorson, 2000) or in studies of e-commerce behaviors (e.g., Li, Daugherty, & Biocca, 2001), it has not been examined previously in a gaming context. The telepresence construct seems particularly suited to gaming as it scores high on the two dimensions related to this construct across which communication technologies can vary (Steuer, 1992), which are *vividness* ("the ability of a technology to produce a sensorially rich mediated environment," p. 80) and *interactivity* ("the extent to which users can participate in modifying the form and content of a mediated environment in real time," p. 84). As discussed previously, games offer a sensory-rich media environment and interactivity as the player controls the point of view, including visual input (e.g., selecting a car or dressing a character) or storyline (e.g., player decides what door to open, what bat to swing) (Grodal, 2000). Although such interactivity is likely to increase the sense of telepresence for the consumer, advertising researchers have claimed presence can lead to a variety of effects, including enjoyment and persuasion, which are the primary goals of advertising (Lombard & Snyder-Duch, 2001). Anecdotal evidence suggests the same. However, it could also be the case that brand placement recall might suffer if telepresence is too high because of cognitive capacity constraints.

Results of quadratic regression analyses revealed a significant relationship between the arrival factor of telepresence and free recall. Results show that a minimum amount of telepresence in the game environment seemed necessary for brand recall, but also that too much telepresence harmed brand recall. Perhaps if the players demonstrate a high level of telepresence (i.e., they are too into the game), the attention paid to nonessential game elements will suffer (see Fig. 7.1). These results are exploratory; they are based on a small number of players and on one game genre, yet they offer some insight into the psychological dimensions of consumer game players. Further research should examine this construct more closely in a variety of interactive game experiences.

Telepresence is thought to be a construct of flow, which is another psychological dimension that has been examined previously with relation to Web-surfing behaviors (e.g., Hoffman & Novak, 1996; Rettie, 2001; Vermeulen, 2001), and may be of interest to understanding game-playing experiences. Flow has been defined in many ways, but generally refers to a state or sensation of total involvement during an event, object, or activity (Csikszentmihalyi, 1990). Importantly, this sensation has been found to be pleasurable and encourages repetition (Trevino & Webster, 1992). Thus, consumer researchers have suggested the inclusion of flow opportunities on Web sites will help retain consumers and encourage them to return to the sites (Hoffman & Novak, 1996). Research on games suggests that gaming is an excellent flow opportunity for marketers. Indeed, game researchers Bryce and Rutter (2001) reported that the feeling many gamers have of being in the zone (i.e., totally engrossed, losing sense of time) is comparable to what athletes feel on the field. Using in-depth interviews of online game players, Moore, Mazvanceryl, and Rego (1996) found that players referred to the fun of game playing but also to factors of intense involvement and distorted notions of time and space. Many also mentioned the pleasure and adrenaline rush they received from playing games, similar to playing real-life sports. Flow may be related to arousal, which is relevant for understanding how the excitation transfer theory may operate in games. Future research might investigate the influence of flow or telepresence on consumer response to advergames.

Attitudes Toward Advergaming

Many of the advergaming methods described in this chapter are fairly unobtrusive or player-enacted activities, which suggests that advergaming practices may be less irritating than traditional advertising or more interruptive Web forms (e.g., pop-ups). Indeed, some consumers have indicated they are not opposed to brands used in this way. N-generation kids (ages 2–22) indicated "they don't mind unobtrusive ads such as the use of the Digital Equipment company logo on Alta Vista or the ads for Pepsi, Butterfinger, Mountain Dew, and Crunch along the racing track of the video game Jet Moto" (Tapscott, 1998, p. 199). Conversely, game players may resent the use of brands in their virtual environments as reflected in discussions on the Web blog Slashdot (www.slashdot.org,); see Nelson and colleagues (2004).

An initial test of game-playing consumers' attitudes toward advergaming was conducted (Nelson, 2002). Results of university-aged game players' attitudes toward background brands placed in racing games demonstrated generally positive attitudes and thoughts about the practice. To assess attitudes toward product placement, game players were asked, "How do you feel about product placements/advertising in games?" and they responded to three questions: Do you think it is ... deceptive, not deceptive; adds to the realism of the game, does not add to the realism of the game; and impairs/interrupts the game-playing experience; does not impair or interrupt the game-playing experience? The players who played *Gran Turismo2* and the racing demo PC game were all generally positive toward product placement. They did not consider the practice deceptive, nor did they think it impaired or interrupted the game-playing experience. In fact, players generally agreed with the statement that product placements could add to game realism.

However, responses to open-ended questions showed that players of the racing games thought product placements were good or bad depending on the game genre and how and where the brands appeared. The most commonly listed types of games considered well suited to product placements were sport games, racing games, and wrestling/fighting games. The key issue seemed to be how well the context of the game matched reality. In other words, if the setting was one where in real-life ads existed, then it was okay in a game, too. A few exemplar quotes are shown below:

> Sports or action games where characters you control are in the real world.
> Games where you use the products to accomplish the gamer's goal (e.g., board for snowboarding, car for car racing), not just random signs in an action, shoot-em-up.
> I find advertising in sports stadiums to be fairly unobtrusive and life like.
> Sports or games where the scenery has advertising in real life.
> Advertisements have to be looked on as what type of game it is; racing games are most acceptable. The ads are there and gone, don't have to think about them.

In addition, several gamers mentioned games where they felt product placement would *not* work:

> Games where ads could exist, such as a race track, but not in games where ads would be oddly placed, like in forests.

> A big flashing sign in *Medieval Times* would be a foul!
> Sports are OK—but it would be weird to see a Pepsi in Mario Brothers.
> I really can't imagine having an unrealistic brand, like a flying monkey person wearing Nikes or something of that nature.

A second published academic study combined surveys with a netnography (ethnography on the Internet; Kozinets, 2002) to investigate how game players felt about advergaming and other commercial practices (Nelson et al., 2004). Analysis of 805 postings on Slashdot (2002–2004) revealed active discussions and insight into gamers' beliefs about the effectiveness and appropriateness of marketers' tactics related to gaming. Players were fairly positive about real brands in games when they added realism to appropriate contexts, but others noted the entertainment value of including fake brands, which could act as "spoofs" on real brands. Those who were negative about product placements were also negative about other advertising practices. Although some players did not think they were influenced by product placements, others reported instances of learning about and then purchasing new brands. The most often cited example was when the beverage Red Bull appeared in a game called *Wipeout*. The survey of gamers empirically tested observations from the netnography. Positive relationships between attitudes toward advertising in general and attitudes toward product placement in games were noted, and each of these was positively related to perceived impact on purchasing behaviors. Attitudes toward product placements in games partially mediated the effect of attitudes toward advertising on respondents' perceived purchasing behaviors. Although these studies offer some insight into game players' evaluations of the practice in general, future research might investigate their attitudes toward the different types of advergaming found in Table 7.1 to discern positive or negative feelings.

Ethical Concerns and Public Policy Implications

Ethical concerns over brand placements in games are related to the nature of game content in general and to the notion of marketing to children. Video and computer games and commercial sites for violent computer games have raised concerns from parents, educators, and legislators (Simons, 1999; Tribe, 1999). The Entertainment Software Rating Board (an independent, self-regulatory entity) has rated over 7,000 game titles and also rates Web sites and online games to help parents decide what games are appropriate for children. However, several states have considered legislation to curtail minors' access to violent video or computer games (Anders, 1999), even though more than 20 years of research on effects of video/computer games has produced inconclusive results. Game playing has been linked to both positive and negative effects (Colwell & Payne, 2000).

A second issue deals with the apparent lack of regulation of hybrid messages such as brand placements in games (Balasubramanian, 1994) and the increased opportunity the practice offers for marketing to children (MacInnes, 2000). According to a report in *Business Week*, 55% of children's and teen's Web sites include games, many containing product-related offers (Neuborne, 2001). For example, FoxKids.com features a Sweet Tarts game, and Candystand.com contains a minigolf game with LifeSavers to mark the holes. In offline environments, Fox Interactive has begun accepting brands, including Nabisco Lifesavers in *Croc2*, which replace the "jelly jumps" with the brand's Gummi Savers (Kuchinskas, 1999). Cross promotions and licensing activities on gaming and corporate Web sites further blur the line between advertising and content.

Although advertising and content are supposed to be separate in U.S. broadcast media, Balasubramanian (1994) noted that hybrid messages, like product placements in all other media, are not subject to Federal Communication Commission regulations. Likewise in Britain where Cunningham (2000) asserted that "sponsorship and product placement within computer game software will probably increase since in Britain there is as yet no regulations of such practices" (p. 215). Lack of regulation may mean products not typically (legally) targeted to children gain access to this audience as in a scenario that Tapscott (1998) described "as the user of an online auto racing game speeds through the virtual desert, empty tequila bottles are only slightly buried in the sand so their labels remain recognizable" (p. 199). Thus far, only the tobacco industry is not allowed to place brands in games aimed at children, according to a 1998 regulation (Lavender, 1998). Media advocates urge that parents educate their children so that they can recognize the persuasive commercial intent as well as the entertainment value (Neuborne, 2001). Future research might seek to discern children's and parent's awareness of and attitudes toward such marketing practices.

CONCLUSION

Although consumers have played mediated games since the 1960s, only recently have advertisers noted the opportunity for brand placements, and this practice seems to be growing, in particular, for online games. Trends suggest that advergaming may offer a viable alternative to other forms of interactive advertising (Marriott, 2001) or broadcasting advertising (e.g., Grover et al., 2004), yet few academic studies exist on this topic. This chapter has brought the issue of consumer gaming and the opportunities the medium offers for marketers to the attention of researchers and practitioners in advertising and consumer behavior. An overview of the game industry as well as a taxonomy of brand placement methods is presented, including relevant real-world cases, related theories, and areas of research to investigate consumer response. In addition, results of exploratory studies gauging racing game players' recall of background brands are presented. These initial examinations offer some interesting results, including promise for enhanced recall when brands are used in the game (e.g., choice of racing cars), are relevant for the consumer, or novel brands for games. In addition, players' attitudes toward such product placements were fairly positive, indicating that at least in a racing game the ads actually added realism to the game-play experience. Future research might investigate the relative effectiveness of each of the methods offered in the taxonomy in Table 7.1 across demographic groups and products and seek to discern whether psychological states of telepresence or flow can help explain consumer response.

As technology advances and reaches across the digital divide, faster connections through broadband services are enhancing online game play and offering additional unique opportunities for marketers. Games will continue to become more immersive and realistic, even crossing boundaries with real life. Already technology exists so players can insert pictures of their own faces onto the game characters (Gardner, 2001). Games are also including the use of other media, including pagers and cell phones. One such scenario includes a player receiving pages during the day instructing him or her to log on to the game because the player's character is in danger. The ability to reach such highly involved consumers at any time on any medium poses an interesting opportunity for marketers.

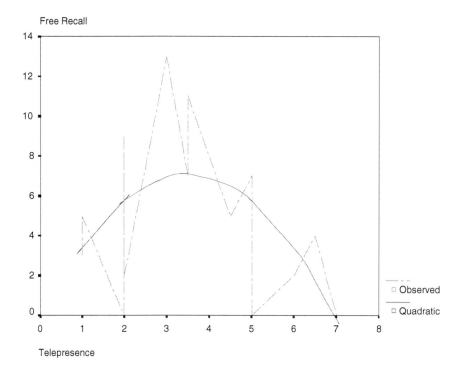

FIG. 7.1   Exploring the relationship between telepresence and brand recall.

REFERENCES

Adams, E. (1999). The slippery slope of advertising. *Gamasutra,* The designers' notebook. Retrieved May 28, 1999, from http://www.gamasutra.com/features/designers_notebook/19990528.htm.

Anders, K. (1999). Marketing and policy considerations for violent video games. *Journal of Public Policy & Marketing, 18*(2), 270–273.

Andersson, B. (1999). Investor insight. *GASource Business News,* Issue #7. Retrieved December 19, 1999, from http://www.ga-source.com/business/investor7.shtml.

Atwood, A. (1989). Extending imagery research to sounds: Is a sound also worth a thousand words? *Advances in Consumer Research, 16,* 587–594.

Austen, I. (2001, May 31). The latest fitness craze: Play more video games. *New York Times,* p. D3.

Babin, L. A., & Carder, S. T. (1996). Viewers' recognition of brands placed within a film. *International Journal of Advertising, 15,* 140–151.

Balasubramanian, S. K. (1994). Beyond advertising and publicity: Hybrid messages and public policy issues. *Journal of Advertising, 23*(4), 29–46.

Bannan, K. J. (2002, March 5). Companies try a new approach and a smaller screen for product placements: Video games. *New York Times,* p. C6.

Barba, R. (2001, February 28). Preview: *StarTopia,* Eidos Interactive. Retrieved August 8, 2001, from http://www.primagames.com.

Basil, M. D. (1996). Identification as a mediator of celebrity effects. *Journal of Broadcasting & Electronic Media, 40*(4), 478–496.

Bello, D. C., Pitts, R. W., & Etzel, M. J. (1983). The communication effects of controversial sexual content in television programs and commercials. *Journal of Advertising, 12*(3), 32–42.

Brown, J. (1999, March 22). Coming soon to computer games—advertising. *Salon.* Retrieved August 2001, from www.salonmag.com/21st/feature/1999/03/22feature.html.

Bryce, J., & Rutter, J. (2001). *In the game—in the flow: Presence in public computer gaming.* Poster presented at the Computer Games & Digital Textualities Conference, IT University of Copenhagen, March 2001.

Carless, S. (2000, July 27). Mecha Godzilla Tokyo report, back from the brink. Retrieved August 8, 2001, from http://www.gamasutra.com/newswire/mgt_report/20000727/index.htm.

Cassell, J., & Jenkins, H. (1998). *From Barbie to Mortal Kombat, gender and computer games.* Cambridge, MA: MIT Press.

Chen, J., & Ringel, M. (2001). Can advergaming be the future of interactive advertising? kpe Fast Forward white paper. Retrieved August 8, 2001, from http://www.kpe.com.

Christman, E. (2004, July 10). By 2006, music biz will be in shadow of videogames. *Billboard, 116* (28), 7.

Clewley, R. (2001, May 1). Robot sites a web of deception. Retrieved August 8, 2001, from http://www.wired.com/news/digiwood/0,1412,43422,00.html?tw=wn_story_related.

Cole, D. (1999, March). *Retail channels for interactive entertainment.* Paper presented at the GameXecutive Conference, San Jose, CA.

Colwell, J., & Payne, J. (2000). Negative correlates of computer game play in adolescents. *The British Journal of Psychology, 91*(3), 295–310.

Csikszentmihalyi, M. (1990). *Flow: The psychology of optimal experience.* New York: Harper Perennial.

Cunningham, H. (2000). Moral Kombat and computer game girls. In J. T. Caldwell (Ed.), *Electronic media and technoculture* (pp. 213–226). New Brunswick, NJ: Rutgers University Press.

Dave Mirra Freestyle BMX. Retrieved August 8, 2001, from http://www.gamespot.com/pc/sports/davemirrafreestylebmx/preview_2657334.html.

d'Astous, A., & Chartier, F. (2000). A Study of factors affecting consumer evaluations and memory of product placements in movies. *Journal of Current Issues and Research in Advertising, 22*(2), 31–40.

d'Astous, A., & Seguin, N. (1999). Consumer reactions to product placement strategies in television sponsorship. *European Journal of Marketing, 33*, 896–910.

DeLorme, D. E., & Reid, L. N. (1999). Moviegoers' experiences and interpretations of brands in films revisited. *Journal of Advertising, 28*(2), 71–94.

Ebenkamp, B. (1998). Diesel grabs exposure via video games. *Brandweek, 39*(31), 48.

Elkin, T. (2001, June 25). The fame game. *Advertising Age, 72*(26), 36.

Entertainment Software Association. (2004) Top Ten Industry Facts. Retrieved August 25, 2004, from http:// www. theesa.com/pressroom.html.

Fallows, D. (2004, August 11). The Internet and daily life. Pew Internet & American Life Project. Retrieved August 20, 2004, from http://www.pewinternet.org/.

Fazio, R. H., & Zanna, M. P. (1981). Direct experience and attitude-behavior consistency. In L. Berkowitz (Ed.), *Advances in experimental social psychology* (pp. 161–202). New York: Academic Press, Inc.

Fiske, J. (1992). *Television culture.* London: Methuen.

Fonda, D. (2004, June 28). Pitching it to kids. *Time, 163*(26), 52–55.

Friedman, H., & Friedman, L. (1979). Endorser effectiveness by product type. *Journal of Advertising Research, 19*, 63–71.

Game-Culture (2004). Thinking about games. Retrieved August 31, 2004, from http://www.game-culture. com/.

Gardner, L. (2001, July 9). Put your face in video games. Retrieved August 8, 2001, from http://www. cnet.com/*CNET News.com.*

Gaudiosi, J. (2004, February 8-14). Game software sales up in 2003. *Video Store Magazine, 26*(6),13–15.

Gillen, M. A. (1995). Ads begin to pop up in cd-rom games. *Billboard, 107*(12), 58.

Gilmour, H. (1999). What girls want: The intersections of leisure and power in female computer game play. In M. Kinder (Ed.), *Kids' media culture* (pp. 263–292). Durham, NC: Duke University Press.

Glaser, M. (2001, August 9). Museum raiders: As artists draw inspiration from video games, curators are starting to play along. *New York Times*, Circuits, p. D1.

Goldstein, A. (2001, August 8). Web firm's ads play to gamers. *The Dallas Morning News.* Retrieved August 8, 2001, from http://www.wordspy.com/words/advergame.asp.

Gorn, G. J. (1982). The effects of music in advertising on choice behavior: A classical conditioning approach. *Journal of Marketing, 46*, 94–101.

Gough, P. J. (2004, April 9). Nielsen, Activision unveil video game plan, size potential ad market. *Media Daily News.* Retrieved May 1, 2004, from http://www.mediapost.com.

Gregan-Paxton, J., & Loken, B. (1997). Understanding consumer memory for ads: A process view. In W. D. Wells (Ed.), *Measuring advertising effectiveness* (pp. 183–202). Mahwah, NJ: Lawrence Erlbaum Associates.

Grodal, T. (2000). Video games and the pleasures of control. In D. Zillmann & P. Vorderer (Eds.), *Media entertainment: The psychology of its appeal* (pp. 197–214). Mahwah, NJ: Lawrence Erlbaum Associates.

Grover, R., Lowry, T., Khermouch, G., Edwards, C., & Foust, D. (2004, February 2). Can Mad Ave. make zap proof ads? *Business Week*, 36–37.

Gunn, E. (2001, February 2). Product placement prize. *Advertising Age, 72*(7), 10.

Gupta, P. B., & Gould, S. J. (1997). Consumers' perceptions of ethics and acceptability of product placements in movies: Product category and individual differences. *Journal of Current Issues and Research in Advertising, 19*(1), 37–50.

Gupta, P. B., & Lord, K. R. (1998). Product placement in movies: The effect of prominence and mode on audience recall. *Journal of Current Issues and Research in Advertising, 20*(1), 47–59.

Gutman, E. (1988). The role of individual differences and multiple senses in consumer imagery processing: Theoretical perspectives. *Advances in Consumer Research, 15*, 191–196.

Hansen, F., & Scotwin, L. (1995). An experimental inquiry into sponsoring: What effects can be measured? *Marketing and Research Today, 23*(3), 173–181.

Herz, J. C. (1997). *Joystick nation.* New York: Little, Brown.

Herz, J. C. (2001, March 26). Learning from the Sims. *The Industry Standard.* Retrieved August 8, 2001, from http://thestandard.net/article/0,1902,22848,00.html.

Herz, R. S., & Cupchik, G. C. (1992). An experimental characterization of odor-evoked memories in humans, *Chemical Senses, 17,* 519–528.

Hirschman, E. C. (1988). The ideology of consumption: A structural-syntactical analysis of "Dallas" and "Dynasty." *Journal of Consumer Research, 15,* 344–359.

Hoch, S. J., & Deighton, J. (1989). Managing what consumers learn from experience. *Journal of Marketing, 53,* 1–20.

Hoffman, D. L., & Novak, T. P. (1996). Marketing in hypermedia computer-mediated environments: Conceptual foundations. *Journal of Marketing, 60,* 50–68.

Holbrook, M. (1981). The esthetic imperative in consumer research. In E. C. Hirschman & M. B. Holbrook (Eds.), *Symbolic consumer behavior* (pp. 36–37). Provo, UT: Association for Consumer Research.

Horowitz, J. (2001, August 9). O'er the land of the free and the home of the games, examining the browser-based, free online game phenomenon.*The Arenaline Vault.* Retrieved September 5, 2001, from http://www.avault.com/articles/getarticle.asp?name=landofree.

Johnson, B. (2000). It's just the future. *Advertising Age, 71*(16), 8.

Kamins, M. A. (1990). An investigation into the "matchup" hypothesis in celebrity advertising: When beauty may be only skin deep. *Journal of Advertising, 19,* 4–13.

Kamins, M. A., Brand, M. J., Hoeke, S. A., & Moe, J. C. (1989). Two-sided versus one-sided celebrity endorsements: The impact on advertising effectiveness and credibility. *Journal of Advertising,* 18, 4–10.

Kelman, H. C. (1961). Processes of opinion change. *Public Opinion Quarterly, 25,* 57–78.

Kim, T., & Biocca, F. (1997). Telepresence via television: Two dimensions of telepresence may have different connections to memory and persuasion. *Journal of Computer-Mediated Communication, 3*(2) Retrieved October 15, 2000, from http://www.ascusc.org/jcmc/vol3/issue2/kim.html.

Korgaonkar, P. K., & Wolin, L. D. (1999). A multivariate analysis of web usage. *Journal of Advertising Research,* 53–68.

Kozinets, R. V. (2002, February). The field behind the screen: Using netnography for marketing research in online communities. *Journal of Marketing Research, 39,* 61–72.

Krishnan, H. S., & Chakravarti, D. (1999). Memory measures for pretesting advertisements: An integrative conceptual framework and a diagnostic template. *Journal of Consumer Psychology 8*(1), 1–37.

Kuchinskas, S. (1999, May 10). What's in a game? *Brandweek, 40*(19), 52.

Lavender, J. E. (1998). Tobacco is a filthy weed and from the devil doth proceed: A study of the government's efforts to regulate smoking on the silver screen. *Hastings Communications and Entertainment Law Journal, 21*(1), 205–237.

Law, S., & Braun, K. A. (2000). I'll have what she's having: Gauging the impact of product placements on viewers. *Psychology and Marketing, 17*(12), 1059–1075.

Law, S., & Braun-LaTour, K. A. (2004). Product placements: How to measure their impact. In L. J. Shrum (Ed.), *The psychology of entertainment media* (pp. 63–78). Mahwah, NJ: Lawrence Erlbaum Associates.

Leeper, J. (2004, January 8). A place for product placement. Retrieved January 10, 2004, from http://www.gamespy.com/.

Li, H., Daugherty, T., & Biocca, F. (2001, May 17–19). *Characteristics of virtual experience in e-commerce: A protocol analysis.* Paper presented at the 20th annual advertising and consumer psychology conference, Online Consumer Psychology: Understanding and Influencing Consumer Behavior in the Virtual World, Seattle, WA.

Lienert, A. (2004, February 15). Video games open new path to market cars. Gamers are influencing new vehicle designs, advertisements. *The Detroit News.* Retrieved February 16, 2004, from http://www.detnews.com/2004/autosinsider/0402/15/b01-64356.htm.

Lombard, M., & Snyder-Duch, J. (2001). Interactive advertising and presence: A framework. *Journal of Interactive Advertising,* 1(2). Retrieved August 8, 2001, from ttp://jiad.org/vol11/no2/Lombard/.

Lynch, P. D. (2000, October 29). Mood and involvement get customer attention. Accenture, Research Note. Retrieved August 8, 2001, from http://www.accenture.com/.

MacInnes, I. (2000, June 5). Internet business models: New options for game developers. Retrieved August 8, 2001, from http://www.gamasutra.com/features/20000605/macinnes_0$_1$.htm.

McCarty, J. (2004). Product placement: The nature of the practice and potential avenues of inquiry. In L. J Shrum (Ed.), *The psychology of entertainment media* (pp. 45–61). Mahwah, NJ: Lawrence Erlbaum Associates.

McCracken, G. (1989). Who is the celebrity endorser? Cultural foundations of the endorsement process. *Journal of Consumer Research, 16,* 310–321.

Malone, T. W. (1981, December). What makes computer games fun. *Byte,* p. 266.

Marriott, M. (2001, August 30). Playing with consumers: Games to pitch products. *New York Times,* p. D1.

Miller, D. W., & Marks, L. J. (1992). Mental imagery and sound effects in radio commercials. *Journal of Advertising, 21*(4), 83–93.

Mitchell, D. J. (1994). For the smell of it all: Functions and effects of olfaction in consumer behavior. *Advances in Consumer Research, 21,* 330.

Mitchell, D. J., Kahn, B. E., & Knasko, S. C. (1995). There's something in the air: Effects of congruent or incongruent ambient odor on consumer decision making. *Journal of Consumer Research 22,* 229–238.

Moore, E. G., Mazvanceryl, S. K., & Rego, L. L. (1996). The Bolo game: Exploration of a high-tech virtual community. *Advances in Consumer Research, 23,* 167–171.

Moran, G. (2004, March). Get in the game. *Entrepreneur,* p. 24.

Multiplayer online games directory. Retrieved August 8, 2001, from http://www.mpogd.com/.

Mundorf, N., Zillman, D. and Drew, D. (1991). Effects of disturbing television on the acquisition of information from subsequently presented commercials. *Journal of Advertising, 20*(1), 46–53.

Naisbitt, J. (1999). *High tech high touch.* London: Nicholas Brealey Publishing.

Naughton, K. (2003, March 10). Pixels to pavement. *Newsweek,* pp. 46–47.

Nelson, M. R. (2002). Advertisers got game: Exploring effectiveness of brand placements in games. *Journal of Advertising Research, 42*(2), 80–92.

Nelson, M. R., & Hitchon, J. C. (1999). Loud tastes, colored fragrances, and scented sounds: How and when to mix the senses in persuasive communications. *Journalism and Mass Communication Quarterly, 76*(2), 354–372.

Nelson, M. R., Keum, H., & Yaros, R. (2004). Advertainment or adcreep? Game players' attitudes toward advertising and product placements in computer games. *Journal of Interactive Advertising,* 5(1), http:www.jiad.org/.

Neuborne, E. (2001, August 13). For kids on the web, it's an ad, ad, ad, ad world. *Business Week, 3745,* 108.

Nielsen Net Ratings. (2004, July). Global Internet index: Average usage. Retrieved August 31, 2004, from http://www.nielsen-netratings.com/news.jsp?section=dat_gi.

Non, S. G. (2001, July 5). Online gaming's room to run. Retrieved August 8, 2001, from http://www.cnet.com/.

Nussenbaum, E. (2004, August 22). Video game makers go Hollywood. Uh-Oh. *New York Times,* p. BU5.

Osborne, S. (2000, December 14). Online gaming: In a league of its own. Retrieved August 8, 2001, from http://www.zdnet.com/.

Padilla, R. P. (2001, August 1). Darkened Skye: Taste the rainbow with Simon & Schuster's Skittles-based action-adventure game. Retrieved August 8, 2001, from http://www.gamespy.com/.

Papacharissi, Z., & Rubin, A. (2000). Predictors of Internet use. *Journal of Broadcasting & Electronic Media, 44*(2), 175–196.

Petty, R. E., Cacioppo, J. T., & Schumann, D. (1983). Central and peripheral routes to advertising effectiveness: The moderating role of involvement. *Journal of Consumer Research, 10*, 135–146.

Pham, M. T. (1992). Effects of involvement, arousal and pleasure on the recognition of sponsorship stimuli. In J. F. Sherry Jr. & B. Sternthal (Eds.), *Advances in consumer research*, Vol. 19 (pp. 85–93). Provo, UT: Association for Consumer Research.

Pillay, H., Brownlee, J., & Wilss, L. (1999). Cognition and recreational computer games: Implications for educational technology. *Journal of Research on Computing in Education, 32*(1), 203–217.

Pope, K. (1994, December 5). Product placements creep into video games. *Wall Street Journal*—Eastern Edition, p. B1.

Postman, N. (1986). *Amusing ourselves to death: Public discourse in the age of show business*. New York: Viking Press.

Rettie, R. (2001, May 17–19). *A qualitative exploration of flow during Internet use*. Roundtable discussion paper presented at the 20th annual advertising and consumer psychology conference, Online Consumer Psychology: Understanding and Influencing Consumer Behavior in the Virtual World, Seattle, WA.

Roehm, H. A., & Haugtvedt, C. P. (1999). Understanding interactivity of cyberspace advertising. In D. W. Schumann & E. Thorson (Eds.), *Advertising and the World Wide Web* (pp. 27–39). Mahwah, NJ: Lawrence Erlbaum Associates.

Rogers, S. (2000). *Predicting sponsorship effects using the sponsorship knowledge inventory*. Unpublished doctoral dissertation, School of Journalism, University of Missouri, Columbia.

Rogers, S., & Thorson, E. (2000, fall). The interactive advertising model: How users perceive and process online ads. *Journal of Interactive Advertising, 1*(1). Retrieved August 8, 2001, from http://www.jiad.org/.

Russell, C. A. (1998). Toward a framework of product placement: Theoretical propositions. *Advances in Consumer Research, 25*, 357–362.

Russell, C. A. (2002, December). Investigating the effectiveness of product placements in television shows: The role of modality and plot connection congruence on brand memory and attitude. *Journal of Consumer Research, 24*(2), 33–41.

Rutkowska, J. C., & Carlton, T. (1994, March). *Computer games in 12–13 year olds' activities and social networks*. Paper presented at the British Psychological Society annual conference, Brighton, England.

Schlosser, A., & Kanfer, A. (2001, May 17–19). *Impact of product interactivity on searchers' and browsers' judgments: Implications for commercial web site effectiveness*. Paper presented at the 20th annual advertising and consumer psychology conference, Online Consumer Psychology: Understanding and Influencing Consumer Behavior in the Virtual World, Seattle, WA.

Schmitt, B. (1999). Experiential marketing. *Journal of Marketing Management, 15*, 53–67.

Simons, J. (1999, May 5). Gore to announce resources to protect kids from offensive Internet material. *Wall Street Journal*, p. B6.

Slashdot. News for nerd, stuff that matters. Retrieved January 1, 2004, from http://slashdot.org/.

Sodip, F. Lara Croft Tombraider. Retrieved August 31, 2004, from http://www.sodip.fr/eng/croft.htm.

Stanley, T. L. (1999, December 13). Behind Iwin's twin win. *Brandweek, 40*(47), 21–23.

Steuer, J. (1992). Defining virtual reality: Dimensions determining telepresence. *Journal of Communication, 42*(4), 73–93.

Stewart, D. (1989). Measures, methods, and models in advertising research. *Journal of Advertising Research, 29*, 54–60.

Tapscott, D. (1998). *Growing up digital: The rise of the net generation*. New York: McGraw-Hill.

Thorson, E., & Zhao, X. (1997). Television viewing behavior as an indicator of commercial effectiveness. In W. D. Wells (Ed.), *Measuring advertising effectiveness* (pp. 221–237). Mahwah, NJ: Lawrence Erlbaum Associates.

Trevino, L. K., & Webster, J. (1992). Flow in computer-mediated communication. *Communication Research, 19*(5), 539–573.

Tribe, L. H. (1999, April 28). The Internet vs. the First Amendment. *New York Times*, p. 29.

Turcotte, S. (1995). *Gimme a Bud! The feature film product placement industry.* Unpublished master's thesis, University of Texas, Austin.

Turkle, S. (1984). *The second self: Computers and the human spirit.* New York: Simon & Schuster.

Vermeulen, M. (2001, May 17–19). *E-learning activities and flow.* Roundtable discussion paper presented at the 20th annual advertising and consumer psychology conference, Online Consumer Psychology: Understanding and Influencing Consumer Behavior in the Virtual World, Seattle, WA.

Vollmers, S., & Mizerski, R. (1994). A review and investigation into the effectiveness of product placements in films. In K. W. King (Ed.), *Proceedings of the 1994 American advertising conference* (pp. 97–102). Athens, GA: American Academy of Advertising.

Vorderer, P. (2000). Interactive entertainment and beyond. In D. Zillmann & P. Vorderer (Eds.), *Media entertainment: The psychology of its appeal* (pp. 21–36). Mahwah, NJ: Lawrence Erlbaum Associates.

Vranica, S. (2001, July 26). GM is joining online video game wave. *Wall Street Journal*, p. B11.

Waddill, P. J., & McDaniel, M. A. (1998). Distinctiveness effects in recall: Differential processing or privileged retrieval? *Memory & Cognition, 26*, 108–120.

Wright, S. H. (2000, February 16). Conferees discuss computer games. Tech Talk. Retrieved August 8, 2001, from http://web.mit.edu/newsoffice/tt/2000/feb16/games.html.

Yoo, H. (2001). *Uses and gratifications of computer/video game players: Exploring cultural and gender differences in Korean and American gamers' playing patterns and motivations.* Unpublished master's thesis, University of Wisconsin, Madison.

Zajonc, R. B. (1968). Attitudinal effects of mere exposure. *Journal of Personality and Social Psychology Monograph Supplement, 9*, 1–27.

Zillman, D. (1971). Excitation transfer in communication-mediated aggressive behavior. *Journal of Experimental Social Psychology, 7*(4), 419–434.

CHAPTER EIGHT

Going Mobile: Marketing and Advertising on Wireless Networks Around the World

Robert J. Kent
University of Delaware

Patrick D. Lynch
Accenture Institute for Strategic Change

Srini S. Srinivasan
Drexel University

Consumers and companies are adopting technologies that combine the most important communication innovations since television: the mobile phone and networked computer. Current global projections state that more handsets than personal computers (PC) will be used in Internet access by 2006 (Accenture, 2001), and wireless networking may soon provide a limitless range of services for business, shopping, security, travel, health, entertainment, and convenience. But the advent of mobile networking presents high-stakes issues for telephone companies, device makers, system providers, software producers, media firms, and marketers. For example, telecommunication (telecom) firms will spend over $200 billion dollars, much of it borrowed, on spectrum licenses and network backbones for faster wireless networks (Wireless, 2000). Proceeds from the voice business will not cover these massive start-up costs, so other revenue streams must be explored (Mathieson, 2001). Falling prices for telecom securities and lower bids in the latest license auctions show that concern is growing over the amount of nonvoice income mobile networks can produce (Nakamoto, 2001).

Most analyses of income sources from mobile networks emphasizes the role that marketing and advertising can play (e.g., Wireless, 2000; Stroud, 2001). While these discussions focus on the services that technology will make possible (e.g., location-based ads), we consider arguably more tractable and important questions: What it is the current state of wireless networking and commerce in some major economies and leading markets? What makes wireless networking different from other marketing and advertising media? What are the barriers to mobile access and marketing? What marketing and advertising do consumers want on their wireless devices, an what marketing and ads will they accept? How can marketers move in to wireless communication without burning users out?

Because the answers to these questions are shaped by prevailing technologies, online experience, culture, common knowledge, general privacy and security concerns, we present findings of structured surveys and focus groups with thousands of mobile-network users in the United States, United Kingdom, Germany, Finland, and Japan. We also examine differences between mobile and wired networks. Finally, to help marketers understand mobile marketing and advertising, we offer some speculations about the future of wireless networks.

THE UNWIRED WORLD

Even a quick scan shows that the unwired world is different: While American firms lead in many areas of online networking, the largest mobile-communication operator is Vodaphone; the leading handset maker is Nokia; and the dominant system-network provider is Ericsson (Wireless, 2000). Countries including the United Kingdom, Italy, and Japan have mobile-phone penetration rates that are near twice the US level. Some excommunist states also have high rates of mobile phone use, in part because the devices provide an alternative to installation delays, high costs, and unreliable service in wired telephones.

Who Uses Wireless Networks?

Survey respondents were asked about their levels of experience in wired and wireless networking, and the real action was in access via mobile devices. Those from Japan and Finland report the highest rates of Internet access via personal digital assistants (PDA) at 86% and 71%, respectively. About one quarter of German and British respondents have wireless experience with their PDA, while only 15% of American users have mobile-network experience. Access by phone show even greater variance: A stunning 72% of Japanese poll respondents use their mobile phone to access the Internet, versus only 6% of the respondents from the United States and Finland, 10% for those from the United Kingdom, and 16% for German respondents.

The I-mode Phenomenon. Japan's towering rate of network access from mobile phones may be explained in part by the [i-mode] system's speed, graphics, and color displays (see Nakamoto, 2001). Devices also differ in Japan. For example, NEC and Panasonic, not Nokia and Motorola, lead in Japanese mobile-phone sales, and some phones in Japan display ten lines of text (Cane, 2001). Cultural factors, such as an interest in expanding the circle of friends, and lifestyle matters, such as long train commutes, may also be involved. The efficiency of the written Japanese for communication in a small-screen medium (fewer characters are required per concept versus written English, German, or Finnish) may also help to explain Japanese mobile-networking phenomenon.

Japanese focus group participants report that web-enabled phones are essential in professional and social life ("I didn't want to be left behind," "without one you are likely to be left out of parties and social events"), and for some users the devices replace watches, newspapers, and landline phones ("it's so convenient that it's a bother to go back to a landline," "I no longer need to spend money on magazines or newspapers; I can get all the information on my mobile"). Business users enjoy working from nonoffice locations ("I love the ocean; I now have the freedom to check stock prices and invest while I am at the beach"), saving time and adding value ("I use it to send digital-photo images; the client no longer has to come on site"), and having new technology ("it allows me to keep up with foreign clients who are more advanced in their use of email for business").

Barriers

Respondents from the various countries are concerned about the costs of mobile networking; German respondents are most concerned about this factor, while Americans show somewhat less concern. Difficulty reading from small screens is also an important issue across countries, with Japanese users the most concerned. Slow access speeds, difficulty of inputting information, and a limited selection of products/services are widely seen as drawbacks. Privacy concerns are greatest in Japan and the United States, while worries over system and service reliability are highest among users in the United Kingdom.

When asked about mobile networking via various devices, German and Japanese respondents expressed concern about the costs and difficulty of reading information from phones, while many respondents from the other countries saw no need for Internet access from a phone. PDA use is most popular with American, German, and British respondents, but many users from these counties cite "no need" as the biggest barrier to wireless networking over the devices.

What Users Do

Marked differences exist in activities over wireless networks. Sending and receiving email is popular across countries, and it is by far the most common activity for Japanese wireless-network users. Text messaging is popular in the three European countries, while news viewing is particularly common in Japan and the United States. British and American users seek more weather information, while more Japanese users access train schedules. Shopping and buying levels are low in all countries, while participants from Finland and Germany do the most mobile banking.

Buy on the Fly? Despite the myths about grandmothers in Finland charging parking meters with their mobile, few respondents have made a purchase over a wireless device: 5% in Finland, 6% in the United Kingdom, 7% in Japan, 9% in

Germany, and 12% in the United States. The poll and focus group responses show that mobile commerce is not common in Finland, but some users order screen savers or pay phone bills over their device, and increased mobile buying is expected. Interestingly, respondents from Finland report the lowest levels of shopping and buying online at 19% versus 77% for Germany, 67% in the United Kingdom, and 62% for US respondents.

Given the high rates of mobile network use in Japan, it is interesting that wireless-buying rates are lower for Japanese participants than those from the United States or Germany. Some Japanese focus group participants are reluctant to buy through a personal computer, and their concerns about data ownership and credit card security are amplified for mobile buying (as one respondent put it, "it's kind of creepy, who will own our personal data?"). Only 56% of Japanese users shop for and buy products online, the second-lowest figure across countries.

Wireless networkers in the United Kingdom are more familiar and experienced with online buying, but they are often unfamiliar with mobile buying options and concerned about security, service interruptions, and trust in vendors.

The mobile-buying rate is highest in the United States, a known laggard in wireless penetration and technology. The higher US-buying rate may be fueled by Americans greater use of credit cards and online shopping. Familiar sources and/or time-saving established accounts with Ebay, Amazon, and so forth, may also ease buying over mobile devices. Americans who use PDAs for mobile networking are more likely to have made a purchase than those using phones. This raises the possibility that the United States could become a mobile commerce leader if PDAs or handhelds (with bigger screens and better input devices) become its wireless-networking standard. In discussing mobile commerce, Americans tend to emphasize the technical limitations of their devices, for example, "it's too clunky and not big enough," "you need more than just a text description to buy a bikini," "I would definitely be into it if the screens were bigger or I had a T1."

Contact by Marketers

Wireless users have relatively little experience with promotional messages: only 15% to 25% of non-Japanese respondents get such messages, while 40% of Japanese users receive them. American and British users tend to find the promotional messages intrusive and annoying. German and Japanese users are more positive about messages from companies, but difficulty reading the messages is a major concern in Japan. Interestingly, respondents in all markets but Finland would rather be contacted by "name" portals such as Yahoo and Excite than by their phone companies or other name-brand firms.

Location Information: Your Place Data, or Mine?

Marketers and advertisers want to reach consumers at the place and time of decision making, so the concept of location-based messages has a very strong appeal.

Respondents were asked whether they would allow no companies, selected companies, or all companies to access to their location information. Very low levels of "all companies" responses were noted. Indeed, large numbers of American (63%), German (58%), Finnish (54%), and British (48%) respondents are not comfortable with any company having their location information. But only 38% of Japanese users feel this way, and only in Japan do most respondents (60%) feel comfortable with selected companies having access to their location. When asked what location-based information they want to receive, Japanese users mention restaurant, weather, local/community, and travel information. German and Japanese users are more positive about the idea of receiving a coupon as they walk by a favorite store, while users in Finland are the least positive.

MOBILE MARKETING

How Wireless Networking Is Different

Wireless networking presents marketers with a unique combination of media attributes:

Ubiquitous Access. Unlike the desktop computer with its big boxes and all those wires, wireless devices can always be with the consumer. In some ways, wireless networks may resemble a slower subset of the Internet (with enhancements such as global positioning systems[GPS]). However, mobility changes everything: the only place where it is safe to say that wireless devices will not be used is in the presence of a faster, more flexible networked personal computer. Because the times and places of use will be different, uses will often be new as well. Users will also access old uses at different times and from different places. What would you do on a network while waiting in the mall, at a football game during halftime, or on a long car ride (with someone else driving)?

Real-Time Location Data. Unlike any other medium, wireless devices will make real-time location-based services and messages possible. System utilities will be able to know user location (Harvey, 2001). If mobile-ad access were made easy and cheap, the prospect of reaching consumers known to be near their store, visiting their city, and so forth, would be hard for marketers to resist. But sellers will face new and important consumer privacy concerns and reactions in applying location information. These privacy concerns vary significantly between countries and cultures, with issues such as experience levels with wireless technology and general safety levels playing a role. One size will not fit all.

Multi-Purpose Devices. Unlike television, the electronic medium that marketers are most familiar with, wireless devices such as phones and PDAs have a wide range of uses, and they are often used for work. Interference across uses will be higher for wireless devices than networked PCs (e.g., multitasking is restricted by limited displays, data speeds, and information entry). Mobile advertising models will have to anticipate these differences, which will affect ad receptivity (Cane, 2001; Jackson, 2001).

Asymmetry of Input/Output Rates. Given the limitations of input devices (e.g., 12-key pads on phones, tiny qwerty keypads on two-way pagers), the degree of asymmetry between information input and output rates will be much greater in wireless than online networking. For example, a net-enabled phone might let a user read a 100-word email message in a few minutes, but entry of a 100-word reply would require a much longer (and less pleasant) period. Moreover, there is a tension between the current trends toward smaller devices and network access (Jackson 2001).

Limited Creative Power and Sensory Input. Marketers may be tempted to approach wireless networking with television and computing analogies in mind, but the common small, black and white, text-based displays may restrict message creative and worsen reactions to unwanted messages.

Metered Pricing for Information Packets/Time. Unlike television (and online networking for many users), wireless networking usually involves metered user charges for information packets or time of use. Messages from marketers may be seen as an unfair financial burden on users.

My System. Wireless networks are proprietary systems. Open systems such as television and radio send the same signal out to the widest possible audience, and consumers accept a high volume of mass-market ads as the cost of free service and programming. But most messages in wireless networks are specific to the user. People do not want others to have access to their conversations, mail, and data: the connection is often private, even intimate, with the person they are speaking to. Message and targeting practices developed for mass audiences are not optimal for a proprietary system.

Individual Ownership. Users feel a greater sense of ownership and control over their wireless devices. The devices are conspicuous, and some users even customize their phones, two-way pagers, and so forth, with fashion face plates, sounds, screen savers, and other such fitings. These actions suggest a desire for control over their systems, and perhaps a desire to keep their systems free of the sort of unwanted and intrusive marketing efforts that are experienced in related media (e.g., wired phones and email).

M-ADVERTISING REVISITED

The upside of advertising over wireless networks involves relationship building, frequent contact, attractive demographics, and the seductive prospect of reaching users at the time and place of decision making. But the downside and barriers of mobile advertising are vivid, too: The volume and nature of advertising must be controlled, intrusion and annoyance may be greater, and, since the user pays for the device and its use, tolerance of off-target advertising will be low. Inappropriate advertising messages may interfere with primary device uses including work tasks, and deleting them may be a chore. Perhaps most importantly, experience with persistent junk email and telemarketing has many users concerned about keeping control over marketing in their wireless networks.

So what would advertising on wireless networks look like?

Who Makes the Register Ring? The great frustration of many advertisers is that they can not precisely target their user base through traditional advertising in, for example, network television. If Saab accounts for 2% of car sales in the United States, a television (TV) show where even 5% of the audience owns a Saab is hard to find. But the customer most likely to buy a new Saab is the customer who already owns a Saab. He or she already likes the brand and wants to be associated with it. A marketer can't find a television or print audience of mostly Saab owners. But a sponsored service for Saab owners on wireless is a more-powerful presence in their life.

Many people think about advertising the wrong way: Ad effects are often greatest on consumers who already use the brand. Because ad exposure and information elaboration are selective processes, current customers are more likely to pay attention and respond. Ads must maintain interest and develop business by encouraging buyers to buy in a higher percent of occasions, to use more, or to use the brand in new situations. Exposure to your current user base keeps people coming back.

If this is true, many companies should rethink their mobile ad strategy. Coke does not want to pay for their ads to appear on the closed networks of the most loyal Pepsi buyers. And these Pepsi fans would not want a Coke ad on their network, anyhow.

Coke's first ad dollars should go to the customers who make the register ring. But the usual lifestyle and demographic data are too broad and ineffective to do this. Instead of targeting proxies such as adults 25–54 years old who own pets, or people who check off "I like travel" or "I like outdoor sports" in surveys, marketers need to know about the brand usage and interests of message recipients. The demographic and lifestyle data used to direct tens of billions of television ad dollars do not give this critical information. But brands can help marketers to connect with customers, and reach them with less waste.

Opt-In Receptivity. Mobile marketers might use an opt-in strategy based on brands (e.g., choose brands within categories, or just choose brands) to send advertising to mobile users. Such advertising should include category or even marketing exclusivity. Given the chance to choose the brands that can advertise on their device, consumers will tend to select brands that they use, or would like to use.

Receptivity is the key. While ad receptivity is sometimes enhanced in traditional media by using time properties (e.g., financial messages at tax time), the critical factor in wireless will be consumer opt-in for and control over messages. Functional interference must be avoided by using screen savers, and so forth, to display messages. User interfaces that do not require repeated entry of user ID or account numbers, and are not case sensitive may be required in marketing interactions. Over time, higher bandwidth, color, and better devices will reduce the time and hassles and increase the creative possibilities.

Call Off the Dogs.   Given the nature and uses of wireless networking, methods used to arrest attention in broadcast or print advertising (e.g., dogs, babies, sexy images, odd sounds, unusual scenes) should be used with great caution. With less advertising, different units (e.g., no breaks of five 30-second television ads), and more of a relationship, attention-borrowing devices will not be as important. Consumers should have an easy, simple, and effective mechanism to fire or switch advertisers so that marketers do not spend money to annoy potential buyers.

Do Not Just Count Clicks.   Marketers will have to avoid a natural tendency to think of wireless networks as just another interactive medium, or a new form of direct-response advertising. For example, message pricing models should be based on relationship building and continuity, and not just on precisely tracked response totals. Marketers who make costs per click too important in ad evaluation or space buying focus on only a small minority of the people exposed to their messages. Interactivity is important, but m-commerce shouldn't be treated as an interactive e/m-coupon.

While marketers should exploit the interactive potential of mobile networking, brand and relationship building must not be compromised (with, e.g., overly loud or price-focused messages) just to move the response needle from four to six percent. Brand managers should consider the communication effects on the greater audience: the 90% who will not be counted in the response totals. As in other media, the best mobile advertising will both build and sell the brand, and it will be evaluated on both scores.

Data Control and Location-Based Messages.   Data control will be more important than on the Internet. Since users will opt-in based on brand, firms can sponsor free ring tones, screen savers, or permitted location-based services (air time for a restaurant finder). These are the applications most used in Japan and Europe where wireless has taken off. The piece that has been missing is an advertising supported sponsorship that would generate revenue.

Marketers should be very cautious in deploying location-based messages. In fact, a failure on a system-wide basis to control the volume and nature of ads on wireless devices, particularly location-based ads, might kill the goose before an egg is laid. Given their time- and place-specific nature, junk location-based messages may prove to be more personally relevant, and therefore more distracting or annoying at lower volumes (imagine receiving any volume of messages along the lines of "You're Near a McDonald's Now!"). Marketers might argue that common technologies from automated teller machines (ATM) to the EZ-Pass record users' location information, but privacy perceptions will be an important mobile marketing reality.

Still, we believe that location-based marketing can be conducted with appropriate forms of permission and consumer control over data use and archives. Effective volume, source, and [opt-out] control will be critical. This is an important way that the central utility can add value to both advertisers and system users.

THE FUTURE OF MOBILE MARKETING

Today's small gray scale screens will give way to mobile devices that will support rich color video and sophisticated processors. Limited text based and graphic ads will give way to interactive screensavers, networked mobile games with airtime sponsored by advertisements. Location-based services provided by sponsors will also grow to include sponsored alerts for events, discounts, and promotions requested by the user.

Marketers may target users in specific segments like families, teens, business users, with an ad subsidy for devices, time, or information packets. For the user, this model allows lower costs, greater control of advertising on their system (e.g., ads put in nonwork time window), less advertising for the small-screen medium, more interesting and relevant messages, and reduced privacy concerns. For the provider, permission-based receptivity allows more advertising in a "user pays" medium, higher advertising rates can be charged, click-though rates will be increased, and opt-in ad acceptance and receptivity will help marketers cope with the medium's creative limitations.

In the near term, paid-content offerings will be those that deliver a tangible return on investment to consumers—helping consumers build their wealth, advance their careers, or improve their personal lives. Eventually, as broadband wireless penetration deepens, entertainment may emerge as the biggest opportunity for consumer-paid content. As one [wag] put it, the "killer app" in wireless devices may be "killing time" with communication, entertainment, and information (Nielsen, 2000).

REFERENCES

Accenture Institute for Strategic Change. (2001). *The future of wireless.*
Cane, A. (2001, March 13). Third generation mobile phones. *The Financial Times,* p. 24.
Fisher, A. (2000, December 6). Consumer frustration with WAP phones has been well-documented, but a new generation of services looks set to better meet their needs. *The Financial Times,* p. 4.
Harvey, F. (2001). *Preparing for lift-off.* Retrieved November 11, 2004, from www.ft.com/understanding3g/FT3MEA8UENC.html.

Jackson, T. (2001, January 16). Betamax of telephones: WAP phones are slow to access the internet and will be overtaken by competitors. *The Financial Times*, p. 14.

Mathieson, C. (2001, April 7). Mobile revenues will not cover 3G costs, says jupiter. *The London Times*, p. 7.

Nakamoto, M. (2001, April 25). DoCoMo to eat humble pie over its 3G services: Japanese mobile phone operator's president faces some embarrassing questions tomorrow. *The Financial Times*, p. 33.

Nielsen, J. (2000). *Alertbox: WAP field study findings*. Retrieved November 11, 2004, from http://www.useit.com/ alertbox/ 20001210.html

Stroud, J. (2001, June 3). Cell phone technology leaps into the future: New standard will bring a wide range of communication services. *St. Louis Post-Dispatch*, p. E1.

The wireless gamble. (2000, October 14). *The Economist*, 19–20.

III. CUSTOMIZATION

CHAPTER NINE

Online Product Customization: Factors Investigating the Product and Process

Janis J. Crow
Department of Marketing
Kansas State University

James Shanteau
Department of Psychology
Kansas State University

Consumers can customize a range of products. Examples of some of these products include shampoo (reflect.com), men's dress shirts (shirtcreations.com), engagement rings (bluenile.com), and furniture (smartfurniture.com). These are just a sampling. One Web portal (digichoice.com) boasts access to more than 2,000 customizable products. Swaminathan (2001) identified "a high degree of customization across almost all industry segments" (p. 125). Estimates indicate 5% of businesses currently customize products or services and expectations suggest that number will increase to 20% by the year 2010 (Solomon, 2003).

Although personalization and customization are synonymously used, there is a distinct difference (Newell, 2003). In personalization, a firm offers products and services by controlling what the consumer sees. Using consumer demographics or past purchasing behavior, a firm can personalize its products (Windham & Orton, 2000).

Customization, on the other hand, is radically different. The key difference between personalization and customization is who controls the outcome. When consumers select the features of a product to customize it, they have control over the process. For example, at bluenile.com consumers can customize an engagement ring by selecting the band, the mounting and the diamond. They also can select the diamond's cut, color, clarity, and carat as well as the mounting on different styles setting with different metals. Consumers make these selections to meet their own preferences and not ones imposed by the firm. For the firm, the market is the market of one (Peppers & Rogers, 1993).

The research described in this chapter focuses on customization. That is, we want to understand when the consumer controls the outcome. Our exploratory research examines factors that may influence a consumer when he or she customizes a product. We note that customization could occur for services such as selecting features of a vacation package as well as customizing products. However, for the purpose of this investigation we focus on product customization.

THE EVOLUTION OF CUSTOMIZED PRODUCTS

The evolution of customized products has changed how we think about creating and delivering customized goods. In preindustrial economies, the norm was to tailor everyday items such as tools and clothing to meet the unique needs of consumers. Craft societies made it possible for consumers to get what they needed. For example, a tailor or seamstress would make a clothing item to the exact specifications of an individual's size as well as the purpose for the garment. During this period, the producer created one-of-a-kind items in small quantities. Consumers received unique goods meeting their exact needs. Unfortunately, consumers had to wait a long time for their order.

In the early 1900s, the introduction of mass production systems provides more products produced for more consumers. In this system, the producer and consumer benefit by having more goods at a cheaper price. A producer created and sold products quickly. A consumer purchased less-expensive products without waiting. The only drawback was that there was a limited selection of products (Hounshell, 1984). A consumer could get a brand-new Ford automobile. Unfortunately, it was only available in black. Everything else the styling and accessories were identical. Strategies focusing on efficiencies in production result in an average product created to meet the majority of consumers' needs.

In the 1950s, mass production evolved into market segmentation. Smith (1956) identified that this strategy matches product production with marketing efforts. Market segmentation targets products to specific groups of consumers, permitting producers to create specialized products to meet the needs of consumers. In this system, producers anticipate the needs of the consumer. With market segmentation, a producer could get closer to meeting individual needs.

The downfall of the marketing-segmentation approach is the exponential growth of available products. Growth since the 1970s include over-the-counter painkillers from 17 to 141, running shoes from 5 to 285, and breakfast cereals from 160 to 340, for example (Reeves, 1998). Instead of selecting from a few brands of coffee, now a consumer selects from numerous product variations from the same brand (e.g., drip-blend, instant, flavored, etc.). The increase in product proliferation serves to meet the range of consumer needs (Kahn, 1998), while pleasing multiple market segments (Bardakci & Whitelock, 2003). However, even with a large assortment a consumer can select an alternative for a lack of an appropriate one (Whitelock & Pimblett, 1997). Pine, Peppers, and Rogers (1995) suggested that when a firm uses a marketing segmentation–type strategy, there is always a difference between company offerings and consumers desires.

In the era of mass production, a consumer could still have customized products. Unfortunately, the products were restricted to specialty products such as luxury boats or designer clothing. In addition, the consumer would have a long time to wait to receive his or her customized product. These one-of-a-kind products were costly for the producer and the consumer as well.

A new era was born in the late 1980s with the introduction of mass customization. Companies with information technologies and flexible work processes can customize products on a large scale (Gilmore & Pine, 1997). Firms can produce customized products in large quantities for a greater number of consumers. These technology-based systems can give every consumer a unique product (Yolovich, 1993).

The evolution of the Internet allowed for affordable products for consumers to customize (Siebel & House, 1999). In addition, in some cases delivery of a product is possible within 24 hours from placing the order. Motorola supplies cell phones the next day after the consumer places the order (Swaminathan, 2001). Mass customization has the potential to revitalize customization on a grand scale. It offers an affordable return to customization (Da Silveira, Borenstein, & Fogliatto, 2001). In fact, customization has come full circle in getting consumers the exact product that fits their needs.

Customization offers many benefits. Through customization, consumers can get what they want without having to search the shelves for a product that substitutes for what fits their needs. It also affords producers the ability to eliminate the guesswork in what consumers want. Producers have less inventory of finished goods and spend fewer dollars marketing variations of the same product.

The main component of customization is the involvement of consumers. Describing consumers' involvement has been with stages of producing the product (Lampel & Mintzberg, 1996) and the amount of participation by the consumer (Gilmore & Pine, 1997). Involving consumers in producing a product is on a continuum from establishing how to create the product (e.g., design) to having features altered to fit specific needs (e.g., modifications). As well, the involvement of the consumer can be with full or little involvement.

An important question deals with understanding this involvement as a consumer customizes a product in an online environment. Internet-based customization offers the consumer the benefits of product information and the convenience of shopping at home. The literature is beginning to identify consumers' behavior in an online environment. Some investigations have broadly identified consumer characteristics (Alba et al., 1997) or, more specifically, browsing behavior from clickstream data

(Bucklin & Siseiro, 2003), as well as models of behavior for online shopping (i.e., Wolfinbarger & Gilly, 2003).

More significantly, what is necessary is an understanding of the consumer in the customization process. We know little when a consumer customizes a product. A specific question is what factors influence customization. One factor is the number of attributes a consumer customizes. Another factor to consider is whether a consumer can customize products remotely in an online environment without the aid of a salesperson. As well, an understanding of individual differences of consumers is necessary in understanding consumers while customizing.

Consumers visiting Web sites offering customizable products find diverse methods to create products. For some sites, only one or two attributes are customizable. In others, many features are customizable. In addition, the process to customize products is different. Some Web sites display all the customizable features at once. Others present customizable product features sequentially. Many sites offer very little product information let alone how to customize the firm's product. Although consistency is not necessary, it is crucial to know how and what to present.

Much discussion has focused on adding customization to a manufacturing process (for a review, see Da Silveira, Borenstein, & Fogliatto, 2001) or even to a service organization (Bettencourt & Gwinner, 1996). Some investigations have made progress in understanding customization from the consumer's perspective. Specifically, investigations involving choice boards (Liechty, Ramaswamy, & Cohen, 2001) and algorithms (Chin & Porage, 2001) explore methodologies to assess consumers' preferences for customization. However, we know little when a consumer goes through the process of customizing a product. The fundamental element of customization is that the consumer controls the process. Yet we know very little of what influences a consumer when he or she is in control. As well, empirical studies have not investigated customization from the consumer's perspective. This chapter addresses the psychological factors that influence the customization process in an online environment. The following is an explanation of the factors under investigation. Next is the description of the empirical investigation.

BACKGROUND ON FACTORS INFLUENCING CUSTOMIZATION

The first question this research addresses is the number of attributes a consumer customizes. Some researchers suggest that too much variety could frustrate a consumer (Huffman & Kahn, 1998; Iyengar & Lepper, 2000; Schwartz, 2004). A perusal of Web sites offering customization found 8 to 10 customizable attributes. Is this too many or too few? Would too many attributes make it difficult to customize? Cognitive psychologists have long identified that the amount of information can limit what an individual can process (Miller, 1956; Simon, 1957). We would predict that the number of attributes to customize would influence the process as well as the product customized.

The second question addresses the presence of a default value. A default value is a recommendation or start value for the attribute. Kahn (1998) suggested that with too much variety consumers will use "simplistic decision rules" (p. 48). One-rule decision-making concepts suggest that people rely on simple heuristics (Gigerenzer, 2000) or default values (Tversky & Shafir, 1992). Tversky and Shafir found that people relied on defaults as the number of gambles increased. Given that, if the number of attributes increased, would consumers rely on default values? A default value can provide a suggestion to a remote consumer who is customizing a product. Would consumers find the process less difficult with default values? Based on previous research, we predict that consumers would rely on default values, especially in online environment (Reips, 2002). Specifically, consumers would find the process less difficult to customize products with default values. However, given that a consumer could choose any attribute level while customizing, we would predict participants would be less likely to purchase a product with a default value.

The premise of customization is that an individual can get a product designed exactly to fit his or her needs. As such, individual needs are central. Thus, it is likely that individual difference variables will influence the customization process. For example, does the amount of experience that an individual has with a product influence the process? Does familiarity with the Internet make a difference? Does gender or the education of a consumer influence the customization process?

Alba and Hutchinson (1987) proposed that the more familiar a decision maker is with a domain, the more information he or she draws from prior knowledge. Thus, one could suggest a frequent buyer might find it easier to customize product features. Coupey, Irwin, and Payne (1998) proposed that "in a familiar product category, choice is likely to be an easily performed task; even if a consumer does not have a preferred brand, he or she is likely to know which attributes are most important" (p. 461). It is possible that familiarity with a product would aid in customizing that product. We predict experience will make the process of customizing products less difficult and that those with experience would be more likely to purchase a customizable product.

As expectations for Internet-based customization continue to grow, it would make sense to investigate consumers' experience with the Internet. Hoffman, Novak, and Peralta (1999) argued that the more experience one acquires online, less significant are the functional barriers to shop online. If experience using the Internet can remove barriers to ordering, then potentially this experience can facilitate customizing items online. We predict Internet experience will aid decision making by making the process less difficult to customize products and those individuals will be more likely to purchase a customizable product.

Online shopping is a similar remote shopping experience as using mail-order catalogs. Windham and Orton (2000) revealed motivations were similar for those shopping online and from mail-order catalogs. The question to address is whether these experiences (using mail-order catalogs and shopping online) influences customization. We would expect that individuals with remote shopping experience would find customizing products less difficult and would be more likely to purchase customizable products.

In summary, the factors proposed to influence customization are the number of attributes and the presence a default value. We predict that as the number of attributes increase, the process will become more difficult and individuals will be less likely to purchase their customizable product. However, we predict an opposite result with the presence of default values. When presenting an attribute with a default value, individuals will find the process less difficult as well as will be less likely to purchase the customizable product. Experiences with the product, Internet, and online and mail-order shopping experience are considered. We predict that individuals with these types of experiences will find the process less difficult and be more likely to purchase a customizable product. The individual difference variables of gender and education may also influence customization. We do not make predictions as to the direction of the individual differences, rather we expect differences.

TESTING OF FACTORS

The factors tested are the number of attributes, the presence of a default or starting value, and individual difference variables of experience, gender, and education. To determine the influence of the number of attributes, participants customized products with a high number of attributes as well as with a low number of attributes. Participants customized 12 attributes in the high condition. This exceeds the number of attributes on most product customization Web sites. Participants customized four attributes in the low attribute condition.

Half of the products participants customized displayed default values and the other half did not. A default value is a starting point for an individual to customize product attributes. For example, the color "red" was the default value for the color of shoes, as shown in Fig. 9.1. A participant could choose the predefined default level or select another from a drop-down box. In the nondefault mode, the attribute level presented was "Select one." The default values were arbitrarily predetermined and randomly placed in the list. The attribute list was consistent for each product and condition. The attribute chosen for the default condition was identical for each repeated measure.

The testing of the factors was conducted on an interactive Web site created for this investigation (Crow, Shanteau & Casey, 2003). Participants customized products modeled after existing electronic commerce Web sites. The program included securing informed consent, presenting trial pages for practice stimuli, and disclosing debriefing procedures. The goal of the Web-based program was to simulate an experience of customizing a product. For the main portion of the study, the program presented multiple-page stimuli with repeated measures. Each Web page was a unique product for participants to customize. This allows participants

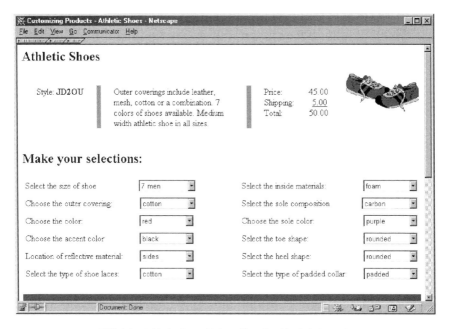

FIG. 9.1   Athletic shoes, high attribute level in default mode.

to focus on the immediate task. We were able to randomly display stimuli in the attempt to reduce order effects.

All product displays had similar layout and design. Figure 9.1 shows a typical display for athletic shoes. The format had minimal graphics in order to not infer with the purpose of the study. The figure shows a graphic illustration of the product along with information about the product. Product information included a description of its features. Wording was slightly different to make the individual products appear unique. Pretests confirmed participants were not aware of the product information differences. Crow (in press) described the extensive pretesting as well as the preliminary studies leading up to examining factors.

Listservs of college students working at the library and graduate students from the college of business at a Midwest university received an email announcement requesting volunteers to evaluate Web sites offering customized products. In the email message, participants received the Web address and a password to activate the study. At the Web site, participants received instructions on how to complete the study. They were encouraged to customize product features to suit their needs. As an incentive, participants completing the study received a coupon for a discounted pizza. The reasoning for using a pizza coupon was to authenticate the process. One of the products participants customized was a pizza. If a participant customizes a pizza knowing that in the end he or she could purchase his or her own pizza, the coupon adds a sense of realism to the task. So that participants did not customize a particular type or style of pizza, they did not find out the brand of pizza until they received their coupon. Once at the Web site, participants read the informed consent form and instructions, then they customized sample pages of greeting cards. After completing the practice trials, participants customized a randomized order of products on individual Web pages.

Each Web page was a different product for participants to customize. The products were a medium-size pizza, a personal digital assistant (or PDA), and athletic shoes. We identified a number of criteria for selecting the products participants customized. Products were pretested to ensure they met the required criteria. The first criterion was that the products were ones purchased by our subject pool. Thus, we were directly assessing consumer's opinions. Second, the products were from different product categories. In this case, the product categories were food, electronic products, and clothing. This allows us to test factors for multiple products.

The third criterion for choosing products was whether the product is currently customizable. We were interested in understanding whether there is a difference if a product is currently customizable or one that could conceivably be customizable. For instance, when a consumer selects the toppings of a pizza, he or she is in essence customizing a pizza. Product categories of clothing and electronic products are typically customizable. However, presently PDAs are not customizable. At the time of the study, athletic shoes were not customizable. Now a consumer can customize a pair of Nike athletic shoes. Thus, for the products chosen participants are or could conceivably think of them as customizable.

Purchase frequency and price was the final set of criteria. College students purchase pizza frequently and it is inexpensive. As determined by a pretest, this group of consumers purchases athletic shoes but not as frequently as pizza. In addition, shoes are typically a medium-priced item for a college student. Finally, PDAs are the least purchased items and the most expensive of this set. These criteria factors permit us to test purchase frequency and the price to see its impact on the factors investigated.

Many studies have found that consumers identify price with quality (Monroe, 1976; Alba, Broniarczyk, Shimp, & Urbany, 1994; Schindler, 1994; Chang & Wildt, 1996). We determined that price was an important element to include, because leaving it out may lead participants to infer a lower quality product. Product prices as shown in Fig. 9.1 were the mean price of retail, mail-order, and online catalog prices. Pizza was $12.00. Athletic shoes were $45.00. PDAs were $250.00. To appear as if each product was different, prices fluctuated 1% to 2%. Pretests found that there were no perceived differences in the quality associated with the price of the product. Thus, the diversity of these products offers the ability to tap into the broad range factors influencing customization.

We did not show product brand names, rather we referred to them as model numbers. Because consumers use brand names as a heuristic cue (Maheswaran, Mackie & Chaiken, 1994), to avoid this participants received instructions indicating that the withholding of brand names was for confidentiality reasons. In addition, we used the term PDA instead of the commonly known brand name, Palm Pilot. Apparently, this tactic was believable as some participants after completing the study wanted to know the brand names of the products.

Our exploratory study was interested in understanding the effect of each factor on the product itself as well as the process of customization. Do some factors influence the product and not the process or vice versa? To determine these effects after customizing each product, participants answered two questions. For the effects on the product, participants answered the question "Now that you have made the selections, how likely are you to purchase this item?" Participants rated the likelihood to purchase from 0, not likely to purchase, to 100, likely to purchase. To determine the effect on the process of customization, participants answered the question "Rate the degree of difficulty in completing this order." Participants rated the degree of difficulty from 0, not difficult, to 100, very difficult. For both questions, participants were encouraged to use the full range of the scale. Overall, the mean and standard error for the likely to purchase were $M = 39.50$, $SE = 1.12$ and $M = 11.97$, $SE = .64$ for difficulty to customize.

Participants customized 24 product variations using a repeated measures design. After customizing all of the products, participants answered questions relating to the frequency of their product usage and Internet and shopping experiences. Also collected was demographic information such as age, gender, and education. Finally, after the participants were thanked for their cooperation, they received debriefing instructions.

RESULTS

A repeated-measures factorial design with $3 \times 2 \times 2$ (product $\times$ default values $\times$ attributes) within and $2 \times 2 \times 2 \times 2 \times 2 \times 2$ (product experience, Internet experience, mail-order experience, online shopping experience, gender, & education) between factors investigated product customization as well as the process of customization. Thirty-one participants, 20 female and 11 male, completed the study. The median age was 22. Eight (28%) graduate students and 23 (74%) undergraduate students participated in the study. A median split grouped participants into those with experience and those without experience. The median split for pizza and shoes was on how frequently a participant purchased the item and for PDAs it was on those who had and those who had not purchased a PDA.

The examinations of the factors using an analysis of variance (ANOVA) were for all products combined as well as on the individual products themselves. For simplicity, we will report only the main effects for all of the products combined. Tables 9.1 and 9.2 summarize the main effects by describing the F statistic, mean square error, partial omega square, and power. A partial omega square (ω^2) describes the variance accounted for as well as the size of the effect (Cohen, 1977). The power statistic identifies the sensitivity of the test, or more specifically, it

TABLE 9.1
Summary of Factors Influencing Product Customization by the
Likelihood to Purchase

Factor	Mean	SE	F	MSE	ω^2	Power
Attribute						
Low (4)	35.91	2.22				
High (12)	43.09	2.25	10.33	930.54	0.20	0.89
Mail-Order Experience						
Experience	36.67	2.84				
Without	42.93	3.54	7.75	932.22	0.11	0.79
Online Shopping Experience						
Experience	37.57	2.62				
Without	44.21	4.25	7.25	932.85	0.10	0.77
Education						
Undergraduate	37.01	2.58				
Graduate	46.66	4.35	14.34	924.10	0.12	0.97

$\omega^2 =$ partial omega squared, $p < 0.05$.

TABLE 9.2
Summary of Factors Influencing Product Customization by the
Difficulty to Customize

Factor	Mean	SE	F	MSE	ω^2	Power
Default						
Default	10.63	1.06				
Nondefault	13.31	1.21	4.92	270.54	0.07	0.60
Attribute						
Low (4)	6.46	0.74				
High (12)	17.49	1.53	83.64	270.54	0.15	1.00
Internet Experience						
Experience	13.30	1.65				
Without	10.73	1.55	4.06	301.70	0.08	0.52
Online Shopping Experience						
Experience	11.00	1.32				
Without	14.35	2.17	5.71	301.30	0.10	0.66
Gender						
Male	8.89	1.53				
Female	13.67	1.53	13.04	298.11	0.12	0.95

$\omega^2 =$ partial omega squared, $p < 0.05$.

refers to the probability of making a correct decision when the null hypothesis is false (Keppel, 1991).

In Table 9.1, we find the factors that influence the likelihood to purchase a customizable product. As this table shows, there was a significant difference for a high number of attributes ($M = 43.09$) versus a low number of attributes ($M = 35.91$), $F(1, 30) = 10.33$, $\omega^2 = .20$, power $= .89$. Other significant factors were for persons *without* mail-order shopping experience ($M = 42.93$ vs. $M = 36.67$), $F(1, 184) = 7.75$, $\omega^2 = .11$, power $= .79$; *without* online shopping experience ($M = 44.21$ vs. $M = 37.57$), $F(1, 184) = 7.25$, $\omega^2 = .10$, power $= .77$; and graduate education ($M = 46.66$ vs. $M = 37.01$), $F(1,184) = 14.34$, $\omega^2 = .12$, power $= .97$. There was no effect on the likelihood to purchase on the presence of default values, Internet experience, or gender.

Table 9.2 lists the factors that influence the difficulty to customize. There was a significant difference for the default ($M = 13.31$) versus nondefault ($M = 10.63$), $F(1, 30) = 4.29$, $\omega^2 = .07$, power $= .60$. In addition, significant results indicate effects for a high number ($M = 17.49$) versus a low number of attributes ($M = 6.46$), $F(1, 30) = 83.64$, $\omega^2 = .15$, power $= 1.00$. Individual difference variables that were significant include persons *with* Internet experience ($M = 13.30$ vs. $M = 10.73$), $F(1, 184) = 4.06$, $\omega^2 = .08$, power $= .52$; without online shopping experience ($M = 14.35$ vs. $M = 11.00$), $F(1, 184) = 5.71$, $\omega^2 = .10$, power $= .66$; and female participants ($M = 13.67$ vs. $M = 8.89$), $F(1, 184) = 13.04$, $\omega^2 = .12$, power $= .95$. There was not a significant difference for mail-order experience or education on the difficulty to customize.

Although focus of this study investigates the influence of factors on customization, a byproduct of these results is an understanding of what products an individual would likely to customize. In the ranking of "likely to purchase," pizza had the highest mean ($M = 54.56$, SE $= 2.07$), followed by PDAs ($M = 33.22$, SE $= 1.77$), and then athletic shoes ($M = 30.71$, SE $= 1.62$). The ranking for "difficulty to customize" found PDAs were the most difficult ($M = 13.79$, SE $= 1.23$), athletic shoes were less difficult ($M = 13.46$, SE $= 1.17$), and finally the least difficult was pizza ($M = 8.66$, SE $= .86$).

Participants could make comments after customizing a product. The following is a sampling of typical comments. One participant expressed frustration when completing an order in the nondefault mode by saying, "I don't like the having 'select one' [option] staring at me." Another participant liked the high number of attributes commenting, "More choices are better." Finally, one participant took the value of customizing pizza one step further. She commented, "Come on, with all the options don't I get to pick the cute delivery boy, too."

FACTORS INFLUENCING CUSTOMIZATION

This chapter addresses the factors that influences customization. All factors empirically tested predict how consumers will customize products. The direction of some of the results were not as predicted. However, they were indicators of factors influencing the customization process and product customized. The number of attributes is an indicator for the likelihood to purchase and the difficulty to customize. Contrary to others, variety or in this case the number of attributes does not deter individuals from selecting from a larger set (Huffman & Kahn, 1998;

Iyengar & Lepper, 2000). In fact, for all product types individuals rated the likelihood to purchase higher with a greater number of attributes. Thus, these results suggest individuals are more likely to buy a product that offers more attributes to customize.

Unfortunately, with a high number of attributes, persons found the process more difficult. This opposing position of "liking" (e.g., wanting to purchase) and "not liking" (e.g., finding it more difficult) makes for an intriguing dilemma. On one hand, individuals prefer to customize with a higher number of attributes; however, at the same time it is more difficult. The use of default values may partly addresses this paradox. Results indicate default values are a factor in making the process less difficult. Because these values provide a suggestion or starting point, this makes it easier to customize a product.

Contrary to our expectations, product-related experience was not a factor for influencing customizing a product. Previous expertise research indicates prior knowledge aids a decision maker (Alba & Hutchinson, 1987). As well, familiarity of product category makes the task of selecting a product easier (Coupey, Irwin, & Payne, 1998). In addition, an individual with experience is capable of handling complex sets of information (Shanteau, 1999). Our results suggest product experience is not a good predictor for customization. Further research is necessary to understand why experience in the offline world does not translate to an online world.

Results for remote shopping experiences were contrary to our expectations. We anticipated persons with experience either using mail-order catalogs or shopping online would be more likely to purchase products. Results reveal persons *without* experience were more likely to purchase products they customized. Interestingly, remote shopping experiences did not make the same predictions for the process of customization. Although mail-order shopping experience was not a factor, on the other hand, as expected, persons without online shopping experience found the process more difficult. Thus, persons without remote shopping experiences are a predictor to buying products and will have less difficulty customizing a product.

As well, we assumed persons with experience using the Internet would be more likely to purchase customizable products and find the process less difficult. Again, contrary to our expectations this was not the result. Internet experience was not a predictor in whether an individual would purchase a customizable product. However, persons with experience indicated the process was more difficult.

An explanation of these results from experience may be because of an individual's need to experiment. When given the opportunity to try something different, customization offers a platform for such experiment. The customization process may provide a learning experience for the individual. Just as when someone reads product literature or seeks advice from a salesperson, the act of customization may provide similar learning experiences.

Part of this experimentation is an understanding of how the customizable attributes "fit" a consumer's own needs. Huffman and Kahn (1998) suggested customization requires that the consumer "know what the attributes are, his/her preferences within those attributes and which attributes are more or less important" (p. 491). It is through the process of customization that consumers identify what is appropriate for their own needs. Our own results suggest this is what may be happening. In a follow-up question, participants indicated if they would purchase a PDA in the future. Interestingly, we found 68% of non-PDA users would purchase one. We conclude participants use the process of customization to examine their preferences through trial and error.

An alternative explanation could be that individuals with experience using the Internet and shopping online are apprehensive of the experience. For example, for those who had a delayed shipment or did not get the product they ordered, they may not want to customize products online. We did not ask participants about the type of experience they had using the Internet or shopping online. It is possible they had bad experiences and thus these individuals would not consider customizing online. Whether the explanations are consumers' need to experiment or that they are apprehensive, it is safe to say we need a better understanding of consumers in this online environment.

The individual difference variables of education and gender have interesting results. As our results indicate, graduate students are more likely to purchase customizable products. Support for our findings indicate a relationship to education and the purchase of mass customized goods (Goldstein & Freiden, 2004). It may be that graduate students better understand their preferences more so than undergraduates do. It is also possible that graduate students perhaps see that in the future they would have the money spend on these products. For gender, our results suggest females find the process of customization more difficult. Results for gender did not predict the likelihood to purchase. In general, we conclude gender is a factor for the process of customizing products. Future research is necessary to understand individual difference variables when and where they influence customization.

The discussion up to this point has been on the overall, combined product results. For this, we collapsed the experience variable over all products. When we separate out experience by each product, we find a unique result. For only one product, pizza, there is a significant effect related to product experience. However, quite the opposite than what we would expect. Persons *without* pizza experience are more likely to purchase customizable pizza than those *with* experience ($M = 62.75$ vs. $M = 49.39$, $F(1, 246) = 10.29$, $\omega^2 = .20$, power $= .89$). Again, we conclude customization allows consumers to experiment by trying out their preferences. There was no effect for the difficulty to customize.

In summary, factors influencing the customizable product are the number of attributes, mail-order experience, online shopping experience, and graduate students. Factors that influence the process of customization include the number of attributes, the presence of default values, Internet experience, online shopping experience, and gender.

IMPLICATIONS AND DIRECTIONS

This research makes major contributions in understanding how individuals customize products. First, participants customized products on a Web site that simulates the shopping experience. These participants were actual consumers of the products they typically purchased. Second, the project produced significant results. These results identify factors that influence the customization process as well as customized product. Finally, this research establishes that individuals can customize products in an online environment, even common everyday items. As well, these products are from diverse product categories (food, clothing, and electronics) with different pricing levels. Finally, individuals can customize products in an online environment whether the products are currently customizable or could potentially be customizable.

It is essential to understand the process by which consumers customize products. The consequences are high, given the dramatic failure rate of online providers. It is imperative that we understand this process. Aside from the economic impact, increased usage of the Internet alone will lead to a higher degree of customization (Swaminathan, 2001). In addition, consumers' expectations will continue to escalate with continued enhancements of technological capabilities (Rust & Lemon, 2001).

Although this research has identified factors of customization, a fuller description of how a consumer makes a choice is vital. Tradition choice models cannot explain how a consumer creates a product through customization. These models assume consumers react to information (Solomon, 2003). A step in the right direction is identifying how consumers control information (Ariely, 2000). An elaboration of how controlling information influences a product or the process of customization is necessary. As well, current methodologies of investigating choice (e.g., choice boards) restrict our understanding of the options consumers create (Crow, Shanteau & Casey, 2003).

It might be tempting for a firm to consider personalization rather than customization. That is, offering personalized products without involving consumers. The methodologies of collaborative filtering or data-mining techniques identify hidden patterns in information to build consumer profiles. Rust and Lemon (2001) rightfully acknowledged that the use of past consumer purchase patterns may cause problems. These methodologies may create a personal customer profile built on wrong assumptions, for instance, buying a gift. We suggest an overt, rather than covert, method of understanding consumers is more viable. This study demonstrates it is possible to collect consumers' preferences of products they customize. It is vital that the consumer is involved in the identification of what is important (e.g., attributes and attribute levels). The consumer becomes an active participant defining articulated and unarticulated needs (Wind & Rangaswamy, 2001).

Customization has the potential to offer many benefits to the consumer, the producer, and society. Customized products offer the consumer the benefits of products that fit their needs. No longer will a consumer have to search for a product that may come close. In addition, once a consumer has customized his or her product, the process builds in a repeat purchase. That is, the consumer as well as the producer know what he or she wants. Producers of customizable products will have a competitive advantage over producers who do not customize. They can create products for a specialized niche markets—the market of one (Peppers, Rogers, & Dorf, 1999). With efficiencies of manufacturing and information technology, producers can create cheaper products more quickly. Thus, they are more profitable. For society, customizable products will mean consumers will not wastefully purchase and dispose of products that do not fit their needs. We will become a society that produces only what we need and consume. Benefits to the consumer, producer, and society are all dependent on understanding the consumer and the factors that influence the customization process. This research is a step in the right direction.

REFERENCES

Alba, J. W., Broniarczyk, S. M., Shimp, T. A., & Urbany, J. E. (1994). The influence of prior beliefs, frequency cues, and magnitude cues on consumers' perceptions of comparative price data. *Journal of Consumer Research, 21*(2), 219–235.

Alba, J. W., & Hutchinson, J. W. (1987). Dimensions of consumer expertise. *Journal of Consumer Research, 13*(2), 411–454.

Alba, J. W., Lynch, J., Weitz, B., Janiszewski, C., Lutz, R., Sawyer, A., & Wood S. (1997). Interactive home shopping: Consumer, retailer, and manufacturer incentives to participate in electronic marketplaces. *Journal of Marketing, 61*(3), 38–53.

Ariely, D. (2000). Controlling the information flow: Effects on consumers' decision making and preferences. *Journal of Consumer Research, 27*, 233–248.

Bardakei, A., & Whitelock, J. (2003). Mass-customization in marketing: the consumer perspective. *Journal of Consumer Marketing, 20*(5), 463–479.

Bettencourt, L. A., & Gwinner, K. (1996). Customization of the service experience: The role of the frontline employee. *International Journal of Service Industry Management, 7*(2), 3–20.

Bucklin, R., & Siseiro, C. (2003). A model of Web site browsing behavior estimated on clickstream data. *Journal of Marketing Research, 40*(3), 249–268.

Chang, T. Z., & Wildt, A. R. (1996). Impact of product information on the use of price as a quality cue. *Psychology and Marketing, 13*(1), 55–75.

Chin, D., & Porage, A. (2001). Acquiring user preferences for product customization. In M. Bauer, P. J. Gmytrasiewicz, & J. Vassileva (Eds.), *Proceedings of the 8th International Conference User Modeling 2001*, 2109. Berlin: Springer-Verlag.

Cohen, J. (1977). *Statistical power analysis for the behavioral sciences.* New York: Academic Press.

Coupey, E., Irwin, J. R., & Payne, J. W. (1998). Product category familiarity and preference construction. *Journal of Consumer Research, 24*(4), 459–468.

Crow, J. J. (in press). Factors influencing product customization. *International Journal of Internet Marketing and Advertising.*

Crow, J. J., Shanteau, J., & Casey, J. D. (2003). Using the Internet to investigate consumer choice spaces. *Behavior Research Methods, Instruments, and Computers, 35*(2), 259–262.

Da Silveira, G., Borenstein, D., & Fogliatto, F. S. (2001). Mass customization: Literature review and research directions. *International Journal of Production Economics, 72*, 1–13.

Gigerenzer, G. (2000). *Adaptive thinking: Rationality in the real world.* New York: Oxford University Press.

Gilmore, J. H., & Pine, B. J. (1997). The four faces of mass customization. *Harvard Business Review, 75*(1), 9–11.

Goldstein, R. E., & Freiden, J. B. (2004). Have it your way: Consumer attitudes toward personalized marketing. *Marketing Intelligence & Planning, 22*(2), 228–239.

Hoffman, D. L., Novak, T. P., & Peralta, M. (1999). Building consumer trust online. *Communications of the ACM, 42*(4), 80–85.

Hounshell, D. A. (1984). *From the American systems to mass production 1800–1933: The development of manufacturing technology in the United States.* Baltimore, MD: Johns Hopkins University Press.

Huffman, C., & Kahn, B. E. (1998). Variety for sale: Mass customization or mass confusion? *Journal of Retailing, 74*(4), 491–513.

Iyengar, S. S., & Lepper, M. R. (2000). When choice is demotivating: Can one desire too much of a good thing? *Journal of Personality and Social Psychology, 79*(6), 995–1006.

Kahn, B. E. (1998). Dynamic relationships with customers: High-variety strategies, *Journal of the Academy of Marketing Science, 26*(1), 45–53.

Keppel, G. (1991). *Design and analysis: A researcher's handbook.* Upper Saddle River, NJ: Prentice-Hall.

Lampel, J., & Mintzberg, H. (1996). Customizing customization. *Sloan Management Review, 38*(1), 21–31.

Liechty, J., Ramaswamy, V., & Cohen, S. H. (2001). Choice menus for mass customization: An experimental approach for analyzing customer demand with an application to a Web-based information service. *Journal of Marketing Research, 38*(2), 183–196.

Maheswaran, D., Mackie, D. M., & Chaiken, S. (1994). Brand name as a heuristic cue: The effects of task importance and expectancy confirmation on consumer judgments. *Journal of Consumer Psychology, 1*(4), 317–336.

Miller, G. A. (1956). The magical number seven, plus or minus two: Some limits on our capacity for processing information. *Psychological Review, 63*, 81–97.

Monroe, K. B. (1976). The influence of price differences and brand familiarity on brand preferences. *Journal of Consumer Psychology, 3*, 42–49.

Newell, F. (2003). *Why CRM doesn't work: How to win by letting customers manage the relationship.* Princeton, NJ: Bloomberg Press.

Peppers, D., & Rogers, M. (1993). *The one-to-one future: Building relationships one customer at a time.* New York: Currency/Doubleday.

Peppers, D., Rogers, M., & Dorf, B. (1999). Is our company ready for one-to-one marketing? *Harvard Business Review, 77*(1), 151–160.

Pine, B. J., Peppers, D., & Rogers, M. (1995, March–April). Do you want to keep your customers forever? *Harvard Business Review*, pp. 103–115.

Reeves, M. (1998). *The right stuff: America's move to mass customization (1998 Annual Report)* Dallas: Federal Reserve Bank.

Reips, U.-D. (2002). Internet-based psychological experimenting: Five does and five don'ts. *Social Science Computer Review, 20*(3), 241–249.

Rust, R. T., & Lemon, K. N. (2001). E-service and the consumer. *International Journal of Electronic Commerce, 5*(3), 85–101.

Schindler, R. M. (1994). How to advertise price. In E. M. Clark & T. C. Brock (Eds.), *Attention, attitude, and affect in response to advertising* (pp. 251–269). Hillsdale, NJ: Laurence Erlbaum Associates.

Schwartz, B. (2004). *The paradox of choice: Why more is less.* New York: Ecco.

Shanteau, J. (1999). Decision making by experts: The GNAHM effect. In J. Shanteau, B. A. Mellers, & D. A. Schum (Eds.), *Decision science and technology: Reflections on the contributions of Ward Edwards* (pp. 105–130). Boston: Kluwer Academic Publishers.

Siebel, T. M., & House, P. (1999). *Cyber rules, strategies for excelling at e-business*. New York: Currency/Doubleday.

Simon, H. A. (1957). *Administrative behavior: A study of decision-making processes in administrative organizations*, 2nd ed. New York: The Free Press.

Smith, W. (1956). Product differentiation and market segmentation as alternative marketing strategies. *Journal of Marketing, 21*, 3–8.

Solomon, M. R. (2003). *Conquering consumerspace: Marketing strategies for a branded world*. New York: AMACOM.

Swaminathan, J. (2001). Enabling customization using standardized operations. *California Management Review, 43*(3), 125–135.

Tversky, A., & Shafir, E. (1992). Choice under conflict: The dynamics of deferred decision. *Psychological Science, 3*(6), 358–361.

Whitelock, J., & Pimblett, C. (1997). The standardisation debate in international marketing. *Journal of Global Marketing, 10*(3), 45–66.

Wind, J., & Rangaswamy, A. (2001). Customerization: The next revolution in mass customization. *Journal of Interactive Marketing, 26*(1), 13–32.

Windham, L., & Orton, K. (2000). *The soul of the new consumer: The attitudes, behaviors, and preferences of e-consumers*. New York: Allworth Press.

Wolfinbarger, M., & Gilly, M. (2003). eTailQ: Dimensionalizing, measuring and predicting etail quality. *Journal of Retailing, 79*, 183–198.

Yolovich, B. G. (1993, November). Mass-customization sparks sea change, *Business Marketing*, p. 43.

CHAPTER TEN

Marketing to Individual Consumers Online: The Influence of Perceived Control

John Godek
J. Frank Yates
University of Michigan

Prior to the widespread retail use of electronic media such as the Internet in the mid- to late-1990s, one of the primary methods firms used to meet the needs of consumers was to divide the overall heterogeneous market into smaller, homogeneous segments, with the goal being more precise satisfaction of individual wants and needs (Smith, 1956). Such efforts resulted in an increase in the availability of products that match consumers' preferences, but at the cost of offering large, high-variety assortments (Baumol & Ide, 1956). This type of strategy ultimately led to the creation of large "category-killer" stores such as Best Buy and Circuit City where dozens of product variants are displayed in order to appeal to a wider range of consumers than possible at much smaller stores that carry more narrow assortments of products. Although such a strategy makes it more likely that retailers will carry products that consumers desire, sorting through such large assortments is extremely effortful for consumers, to the point where the size of the assortment can create dissatisfaction with the process and can decrease the likelihood that the consumer will actually select a product consistent with his or her preferences (Huffman & Kahn, 1998; Keller & Staelin, 1987). In order to better facilitate a match between consumers' preferences and firms' product offerings without increasing the burden on the consumer, companies have recently begun using new media to implement collaborative strategies with individuals (Kahn, 1998; Prahalad & Ramaswamy, 2000; Sheth, Sisodia, & Sharma, 2000), facilitated in large part by the interactive nature of the Internet, which makes two-way, real-time communication between firms and consumers economically practical (Hoffman & Novak, 1996). Consistent with this capability, seven of the top ten Internet retail sites tailor some part of their product offerings to the preferences of individual consumers, altogether grossing nearly $4 billion in 2000 (National Retail Foundation, 2000).

This use of new technology to market to individual consumers allows firms to engage in marketing activities not previously feasible. Although merchants have helped consumers sort through alternatives for centuries, and skilled artisans have made build-to-order products available long before mass production was commonplace, the advent of interactive communications, flexible manufacturing, and just-in-time delivery systems has made it economical for many companies to offer different products to individual consumers on an unprecedented scale. These new technologies enable firms to employ individualized efforts that enhance both the likelihood of purchase as well as consumers' postpurchase satisfaction by providing products that match consumers' preferences as closely as possible. In the course of attempting to achieve such matches, however, the product selection process has been transformed in such a way as to influence consumers' decision processes. Instead of passively viewing the product offerings that a firm has to offer and deciding which ones they like best as might have been done in the past, consumers now play an active role in determining what products are offered to them for consideration. Although these changes in consumer-firm interactions are designed to enhance the likelihood that consumers obtain products that match their preferences, they also have other unforeseen, and perhaps negative, implications for consumers' decision processes. In particular, we expect that consumers' perceptions of control will be affected by the differences in how products are offered, and that these differences will in turn influence consumers' evaluations of chosen products. In this chapter we investigate the role that perceived control plays in two strategies that firms may employ in order to meet the needs of individual consumers, *personalization* and *customization,* and compare it to what occurs when consumers make a selection from an *assortment* of available alternatives, as that was commonly the case prior to the changes enabled by new media. In the next section we shall discuss each of these methods by which consumers can select products in more detail.

PRODUCT SELECTION PROTOCOLS

Each of the strategies employed by firms for offering products requires consumers to follow a script of activities in order to facilitate the choice process. Thus, we refer to the different ways that consumers identify and choose alternatives as *product selection protocols.* There are several different types of product selection protocols as well as various combinations of these types. In this chapter we focus on three that are commonly employed by firms: *assortment, personalization,* and *customization.* Each of these product selection protocols differs from the other two in several ways that are relevant to consumers' decision processes. We shall discuss the protocols in terms of their *provisions* (the particular benefits that the selection protocols provide to consumers), their *demands* (the costs that the selection protocols cause consumers to incur), and their *constraints* (the limitations that the selection protocols impose upon consumers). Based on differences between protocols, we identify the *defining characteristics* of the protocols (what, in particular, conceptually distinguishes one type of protocol from others). We next discuss the effects of these characteristics on consumers' perceptions of control, and then two studies designed to determine some of the control-related outcomes that we expect.

Assortment

Assortment refers to a product selection protocol in which consumers are offered an array of alternatives from which to choose. The aim of this protocol is to provide consumers with alternatives of sufficient variety such that they will find one that is suitable for purchase. These alternatives usually represent all of the unique product offerings that the firm has available in a particular product category and are typically organized in some fashion. In order to meet the heterogeneous needs of many individual consumers, firms may offer very large assortments of products, as might be the case of a car dealership that offers multiple makes and models. As the number of different attributes and attribute levels of the product increases, so does the number of alternatives that are displayed in an all-inclusive assortment. In addition to organizing the alternatives in the assortment (say, by brand, model, or other feature), firms also may provide indicators for consumers that show where particular types of products can be located. These may take the form of a store directory, signage around different sets of alternatives, or other displays that are designed to aid consumers in determining where different products are located within the array. In an online environment, retailers using an assortment strategy might display or describe all of their offerings together on the same page, or possibly have a listing of alternatives on a page with links to other pages where the alternatives are described in further detail. Figure 10.1 is an example of how Dell Computers displays an assortment of their products online.

Provisions.   Assortments provide an array of whole alternatives for the consumer to consider, rather than piecemeal sets of individual features. The display may be structured in different ways (e.g., by brand or by quality tier). In addition, the display of alternatives may or may not be exhaustive in terms of the firm's product offerings. It also might be argued that assortments provide an implicit recommendation from the firm in terms of the quality of the alternatives, based on the notion that if the firm offers a particular alternative, then there must be some market segment to which it appeals (Prelec, Wernerfelt, & Zettelmeyer, 1997).

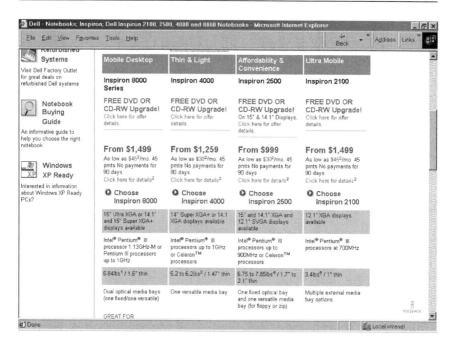

FIG. 10.1   Example of how Dell Computers offers products using the assortment
protocol. © 2004 Dell Inc. All Rights Reserved. Used with permission.

Demands.   Assortments require the consumer to identify which of the alternatives (if any) are viable for meeting his or her wants and needs. Once viable
alternatives have been identified, the consumer must analyze them in order to determine which one to select. Since the firm controls what alternatives are displayed,
as well as their order, it is possible that both the identification and analysis of alternatives may be skewed by the firm's actions. The cognitive effort required by
the consumer to both identify and select viable alternatives dramatically increases
as the number and complexity of alternatives increases.

Constraints.   Consumers' choices are limited to the alternatives presented in
the assortment. In addition, consumers normally have no control over the way or
the order in which information is presented.

Defining Characteristic.   The defining characteristic of an assortment is that it
displays the alternatives that the firm has to offer as an array of complete products
from which the consumer may select a product. This array is typically structured
in such a way as to facilitate identification of those alternatives that the consumer
wishes to consider.

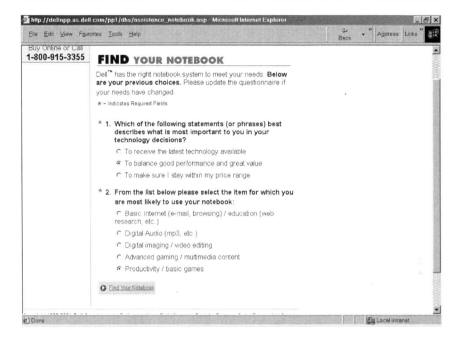

FIG. 10.2 Example of how Dell Computers elicits consumers' preferences for product benefits in order to make a recommendation. © 2004 Dell Inc. All Rights Reserved. Used with permission.

Personalization

Rather than simply letting consumers find their own way though the firm's offerings, some firms employ a mechanism whose task is to help consumers ascertain which products from among the firm's offerings best meet any particular consumer's personal preferences. This mechanism may take the form of a salesperson in a store, or perhaps that of a search and recommendation tool on a firm's Web-site. Both act as agents for the firm, and thus, although they aid the consumer in locating a product to purchase they also may be biased in that they have the firm's, and not the consumer's, best interests at heart. This process, whereby an agent attempts to understand the individual consumer's preferences with respect to a particular domain or product category and then presents the consumer with recommended alternatives, is referred to as personalization (Häubl & Trifts, 2000). Figure 10.2 shows how Dell Computers elicits consumer preferences.

Figure 10.3 shows what a recommendation from Dell Computers might look like.

Using the personalization protocol, the consumer is provided with a set of recommendations from the agent as to which product(s) should fit the consumer's preferences best. This recommendation may come in the form of a rank-ordered list of all the alternatives that the firm sells, or perhaps just a relevant subset (as

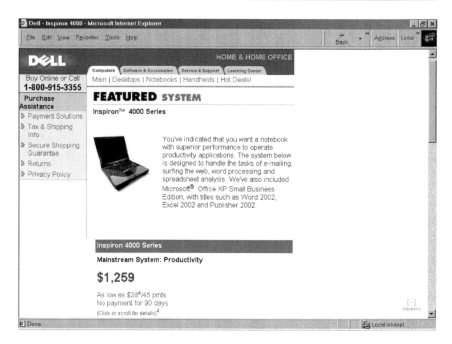

FIG. 10.3   Example of a personalized recommendation made by Dell Computers
to a consumer. © 2004 Dell Inc. All Rights Reserved. Used with permission.

determined by the agent) of the firm's offerings. Similar to the process that occurs with an assortment, the consumer using the personalization protocol then
screens alternatives in order to determine which ones are viable for meeting his
or her wants and needs. If the agent performs well, then the most highly recommended items should be those that best fit the consumer's preferences. The
number of recommended alternatives that the consumer considers, though, will
be highly dependent upon both the number of items recommended, as well as his
or her perceptions of the agent's ability to match products with the consumer's
preferences. If the agent is very accurate but the consumer is hesitant to rely on
the recommendations, then more alternatives are considered. If the consumer relies heavily upon the agent's recommendation, then the consumer may consider
few alternatives, regardless of the agent's accuracy at determining the consumer's
preferences. Thus, the consumer's perceptions of the agent's ability to accurately
determine consumer preferences is important, as is the consumer's reliance on the
agent's recommendations.

Provisions.   Personalization provides consumers with a recommendation regarding the suitability of one or more products for the consumer. In addition,

personalization usually provides some implied or explicit rationale for the recommendation to the consumer.

Demands. Similar to assortment, personalization requires consumers to identify which of the presented alternatives should be considered for selection. If consumers positively receive the recommendations, then fewer alternatives are considered as compared to an assortment, thus making this task less effortful for the consumer. In addition to the tasks of identifying and analyzing alternatives, the consumer must also analyze the recommendation and/or the rationale underlying that suggestion.

Constraints. With personalization, choice may be limited to only those alternatives provided in a recommendation. In addition, it may be difficult for consumers to appraise the motivation and performance of the agent.

Defining Characteristic. The defining characteristic of personalization is that it provides the consumer with a recommendation of one or more products. This recommendation is based upon the understanding that the agent has of the consumer's preferences, and is usually accompanied (either explicitly or implicitly) by the rationale that was used in determining the recommendations.

Customization

Customization is a product selection protocol whereby firms use flexible and responsive manufacturing systems to create products to meet the needs of individual consumers (Pine, 1993). An example of how a consumer might select a customized computer from Dell is shown in Fig. 10.4

In contrast to assortment and personalization, consumers using the customization protocol construe the selection task in a slightly different manner. Rather than review alternatives presented by the firm to determine potential candidates for selection, as is done in assortment and personalization, consumers themselves specify which features they prefer to have in a product, in essence creating their exact ideals rather than attempting to find existing products that are merely close to their ideals.

Provisions. Customization provides an invitation to consumers to specify the products they desire. As such, customization provides consumers with information regarding individual attributes rather than each product as a whole.

Demands. In order for consumers to choose via customization, they must first specify the features of at least one alternative. In order to select appropriate features, consumers must have sufficient knowledge of how product benefits derive from product attributes.

FIG. 10.4   Example of how Dell Computers offers products using the customization protocol. © 2004 Dell Inc. All Rights Reserved. Used with permission.

Constraints.   Customization may not provide a representation of a whole product, thus altering how consumers conceptualize their choices. In addition, only the selected alternatives are presented to consumers; forgone alternatives are not.

Defining Characteristic.   The defining characteristic of customization is that it enables consumers to specify some or all of the features that are to be included in the products to be selected.

Although several of the distinctions between product selection protocols are expected to influence the decision-making processes of consumers, in this chapter we focus on the influence that product selection protocols have on consumers' perceptions of control. In particular, the ability to specify some or all of the attributes to be included in the product, as well as the number of alternatives that consumers perceive they have to choose from, are expected to influence consumers' perceptions of control, which in turn may effect their evaluations of chosen products.

SELECTION PROTOCOLS AND PERCEIVED CONTROL

Although each of these protocols may provide consumers with the same range of alternatives from which to choose, they allow consumers to arrive at their selections by employing different types and amounts of attribute specification. With assortment, consumers indirectly specify the attributes to be included in the products they select by choosing from among the prespecified alternatives that are presented to them. With personalization, consumers again select among the prespecified options explicitly offered. In addition, however, consumers may also be asked to provide information about their preferences, in essence specifying some of the criteria to be used in the recommendations that the firm will provide. With customization, consumers are able to directly specify some or all of the attributes to be included in the products that they consider for selection. These differences in specifiability have significant implications for consumers' decision processes, in particular on consumers' perceptions of control while choosing an alternative.

Perceived Control

The degree to which consumers can directly specify the particular attributes to be included in a selected product influences their perceptions of control over the products they choose. This is based on the notion that specification gives consumers the opportunity to dictate to firms precisely what they wish to have in the products they purchase, while lack of specification requires consumers to rely on firms to determine the alternatives from which consumers will choose. While both leave consumers free to choose which alternatives they think best fit their preferences, the ability to specify attributes also influences consumers' perceptions of control, which has additional implications.

Control has been conceptualized as having three components (Averill, 1973): *behavioral control,* the "availability of a response, which may directly influence or modify the objective characteristics of an event" (pp. 286–287); *cognitive control,* the cognitive reinterpretation of the event in order to adapt to the outcomes; and *decisional control,* the opportunity to choose among courses of action (p. 287). A higher level of specifiability should lead consumers to perceive a greater amount of behavioral control as their ability to affect the outcome of the process (i.e., attributes of the selected product) is much more apparent. To the extent that specifiability affects the salience of available alternatives, it may also negatively affect perceived decisional control if consumers feel that their choices have been somehow limited (Brehm, 1966). Through cognitive control, consumers can experience the impression of high levels of control through the reinterpretation of situations where behavioral or decisional control is objectively low.

Differences in decisional control have been shown to affect consumers' evaluations of the purchase process, but not the purchased product, when it becomes clear to them that some potential alternatives are not available for selection, as might be the case when particular products are sold out (Fitzsimons, 2000). Increases in cognitive control have been shown to lead decision makers to more positively evaluate outcomes, independent of any actual difference in behavioral or decisional control (Thompson, 1981). Behavioral control has been viewed as a basic motivator of human behavior, with people having a general desire for mastery over their environment (White, 1959). A relevant outcome of increased perceptions of behavioral control in a product selection task is that when consumers perceive that they have more control over a selected product, they are also more likely to engage in dissonance reduction activities such as bolstering of chosen alternatives or denigrating of forgone alternatives, as they have no one else to blame if they perceive that they have made poor choices (Janis & Mann, 1977). Such bolstering should result in higher evaluations of selected products when consumers perceive they have greater behavioral control.

Conditions also exist, however, where consumers do not wish to exert behavioral control, as when consumers think that others would be better able to identify the product that best fits the consumers' preferences. In such cases consumers might wish to relinquish to someone else control for selecting a product (Hollander & Rassuli, 1999). Even though they do not exercise direct control over the selection decision, such consumers may still perceive that they have control to the extent that they feel they have a competent agent working on their behalf. This results from a reinterpretation of the situation as one where a superior has delegated authority to a subordinate. By altering the cognitive representation in this way, consumers are still susceptible to evaluative biases that might be associated with perceptions of greater behavioral control, even though they may actually exert less behavioral control.

The Effects of Protocols on Evaluations

Assortment, personalization, and customization provide consumers with different levels of specification, which in turn has important implications for how consumers value the products they select. Assortment provides consumers with little opportunity to directly specify the attributes to be included in a selected product, but it does make salient the range of options that are available to choose from. This lack of specifiability suggests that consumers may perceive little behavioral control over the alternative selected, while the salience of a wide range of options may lead consumers to perceive they have considerable decisional control. With personalization, consumers again are unable to directly specify the attributes to be included in the products they select. However, if their preferences are directly elicited, they may perceive that they have some input to the specification of the alternatives that are offered, and thus perceive greater behavioral control than when choosing via assortment. Because the number of alternatives made salient via personalization is less than that of assortment, consumers should also perceive less decisional control with personalization than assortment. Consumers choosing an alternative via customization should perceive that they have greater behavioral control than consumers choosing via assortment or personalization as customization allows for direct specification of the attributes to be included in the product selected. However, perhaps because only the specified attribute is made salient, consumers may perceive that they have less decisional control than via the other two product selection protocols. Thus, consumers selecting via assortment should perceive little behavioral control but considerable decision control, while for consumers selecting via customization, these should be reversed. With personalization, consumers should perceive a moderate level of each.

To the extent that product selection protocols affect consumers' perceptions of control, they should also affect consumers' evaluations of chosen products. Assortments may lead to higher evaluations if consumers perceive they have greater decisional control. The effects of customization on evaluations should influence evaluations if consumers perceive that they have greater behavioral control due to the ability to specify the attributes to be included in a product. Personalization, which affords only minimal assortment and attribute specifiability, should only moderately influence evaluations as it does not affect decisional and behavioral control to the same extent as assortment and customization.

Conditions may exist, however, where consumers do not desire behavioral control, and thus the ability to specify attributes does not lead to higher evaluations of a chosen product. For example, consumers may perceive that a firm or agent has greater information resources or product knowledge than they themselves, and thus would choose to relinquish behavioral control (Hollander & Rassuli, 1999). When this occurs, consumers may cognitively reinterpret the situation as one where a capable party is selecting a suitable alternative on their behalf. As such, they may actually perceive themselves as having more control when selecting a product via personalization than customization, and thus evaluate products selected via personalization accordingly higher.

In summary, product selection protocols that provide consumers with the opportunity to specify attributes, such as customization and to a lesser extent personalization, where consumers' preferences are directly elicited, should lead to perceptions of greater behavioral control as well as higher evaluations of subsequently selected products. This effect, however, may not hold in conditions in which the consumer feels less competent than the agent or firm in selecting a suitable alternative. Under these conditions, consumers may prefer to relinquish behavioral control, and thus will evaluate products selected via personalization more highly than similar products selected via customization or assortment.

METHOD

In order to test some of our predictions concerning product selection protocols, we conducted two laboratory studies. In each of these studies, participants completed a simulated online shopping experience, where we controlled for several factors in order to determine the effects of the protocol on the participants' responses.

General Procedures for Both Studies

Participants completed both studies in small groups of 5 to 10, seated in front of individual computer terminals that were separated by partitions. Participants used a specific Web browser (Internet Explorer 5.0) to proceed to a Web address where they were then randomly forwarded to one of the experimental treatment conditions. Participants were then presented with a cover story in which a national company was conducting marketing research about a product of interest to college students in their area. After the cover story, each participant was asked to select a product using the product selection mode indicated in the condition. After making their selections, participants completed an online questionnaire containing the dependent measures, were debriefed, and dismissed. More specific descriptions of the two studies are discussed next.

STUDY ONE

The purpose of this study was to determine the effects of customization on perceptions of control as well as evaluations. This study used four conditions, with two conditions where the customization protocol was used, and two conditions where the assortment protocol was used. In addition, we also had two conditions where a large choice set was offered to participants, and two conditions where a small choice set was offered to participants. Thus, we used a two (Product Selection Protocol—Customization vs. Assortment) by two (Choice Set Size—Large vs. Small) between participants design. We choose to manipulate choice set size in addition to product selection protocol as we expected to see a difference in terms of participants' perception of assortment between the large and small choice set assortments, but no such difference between the two for customization (this perception was confirmed through earlier pretests). Per Averill (1973), we expected that this in turn would induce a difference in decisional control, while the difference in specifiability between the customization and assortment conditions would induce a difference in behavioral control. In this way, we would be able to determine both the individual and compounded effects of these two types of control on product evaluations. As part of a course requirement, each of 136 undergraduate marketing students was randomly assigned to one of the four conditions.

Stimuli

After reading the cover story, participants were asked to engage in a product selection task that entailed selecting upgrades to a base computer system offered by a company. Participants in the customization condition were shown the base computer system and the various types of upgrades from which they could choose (there were six different attributes to choose from, and participants in the small choice set condition could select one, while participants in the large choice condition could select two). Participants in the assortment condition were shown the base system along with all of the possible unique alternatives, six for the small choice set condition and fifteen for the large choice set condition. Thus, in both conditions participants had the same alternatives to choose from, but the means

TABLE 10.1
Means (Standard Deviations) of Dependent Variables by Selection
Protocol: Study 1

Perception/Judgment	Customization	Assortment
Perceived control	3.67 (1.43)	4.25* (1.53)
Perceived assortment	4.01 (1.56)	4.31 (1.53)
Product evaluation	4.00 (1.30)	4.46* (1.05)

$^*p < 0.05$.

through which they indicated this was either selection of a preconfigured system, or specification of the upgrades to be included in the system.

Dependent Measures

A range of perceptual and evaluative measures was employed. Multi-item, seven-point semantic differential measures were used to assess perceived control, perceived assortment, and product evaluations. The items for perceived control were similar to those used by Thompson (1981). The items for perceived assortment incorporated both a cognitive component related to the count of items available and an affective component related to the fit of products to consumer needs as suggested by prior research (Broniarczyk, Hoyer, & McAlister, 1998). Product evaluations assessed the participant's subjective valuation of the product selected. Items for each scale were averaged to provide overall indices for each. Confirmatory factor analysis indicated that a three-factor model was most appropriate, with items loading high on the predicted factors and no significant cross-loadings. Cronbach's α for each of the scales was between 0.79 and 0.88, indicating good reliability of the scales.

Results

The main effects for product selection protocol are summarized in Table 10.1. We conducted analyses of variance on the dependent measures to determine if there were significant main effects or interactions for the manipulations in the four conditions. As shown in Table 10.1, there was a significant main effect for product selection protocol such that participants perceived that they had more control in the assortment condition (mean = 4.25 versus 3.67). There were no significant main effects of selection protocol on perceived assortment. For evaluations, there was a main effect in line with the control results, such that participants who selected via assortment had higher evaluations than those selecting via customization (mean = 4.46 versus 4.00).

There were no main effects for choice set size. However, there was one significant interaction between product selection protocol and choice set size, with participants perceiving more assortment in the assortment-large set condition than in the customization-large set condition, but there was no difference between the participants in the two small choice set conditions.

Discussion

This study provided an empirical test of whether or not the ability to specify attributes via customization does indeed lead to perceptions of higher control as well as subsequently higher evaluations. Our results show that, at least in this instance, the opposite is true. In order to reconcile these findings with our predictions, we examined the cognitive responses that were also collected in conjunction with the dependent measures. These suggested that, although there was no significant difference in perceived assortment between the two customization and assortment conditions (mean = 4.01 versus 4.31), many participants in the customization condition felt that they were provided with too few upgrades to choose from relative to what was available in the real world at computer sites such as Dell Computers. In the current study, participants were allowed to select either one (small choice set) or two (large choice set) upgrades from a listing of six that were available. Computer sites that offer customization, on the other hand, offer consumers as many as 20 different attributes that can be upgraded. When such sites offer an assortment to consumers, however, they typically only display three to five different configurations. Our manipulation of assortment afforded participants either 6 (small choice set) or 15 (large choice set) alternatives to choose from. Thus, it appears that the current manipulation of customization may offer considerably less decisional control than what participants expected, while the assortment conditions offered at least as much as they expected should be offered. Even so, it appears that perceived control does indeed play a prominent role in how these protocols influence evaluations, although the role of specification and behavioral control afforded by customization control was still not clear.

STUDY TWO

We conducted a second study in order to determine the effects that the specification of attributes would have on perceived control and evaluations in a choice task that was more consistent with participants' expectations. The purpose of this study was to determine the role of perceived control in customization independent of any effects on perceived assortment that might not agree with participants' expectations. As such, we pretested manipulations in order to create ones in which participants perceived that they had equal levels of assortment. To do so, we had participants engage in identical choice tasks, but framed one to make them believe they were directly customizing the product, and thus had more control, and framed the other such that participants thought that they were providing information to the firm in order to receive a personalized recommendation, and thus had less behavioral control. In this way, we were able to manipulate the choice task such that it affected only perceptions of control, and not perceptions of assortment, and this was confirmed via several pretests.

Besides affecting participants' perceptions of control, the effects of these selection protocol manipulations also may interact with participants' perceptions of the firm implementing the protocol due to the recommendation being made in the personalization condition. In particular, we would expect that in instances where the consumer felt that the firm could facilitate a better decision, he or she would be willing to relinquish control, and thus evaluate products selected via personalization higher. Similarly, we would expect that the same consumer, if he or she thought he or she could better identify the products that matched his or her preferences than the firm, would evaluate products selected via customization higher. As such, we included a second manipulation of product category, where for one product participants perceived (as confirmed by pretest) that the firm could do a much better job at identifying products that matched their preferences (air travel), and for the other product participants felt that they themselves could better identify the product that matched their preferences (pizza). Thus, Study Two was a two (Selection Protocol) by two (Perceived Matching Ability) between participants design, with 87 undergraduate marketing students participating for partial course credit.

Stimuli

After reading the cover story, participants were asked to complete a product selection task that was identical across the selection protocol conditions except for how it was framed. In the customization condition, participants were asked to indicate which attributes they wanted to include in a product they designed, while participants in the personalization condition were asked for input that they were led to believe would be used by the firm to locate the existing product that best matched their preferences (this manipulation was confirmed by pretest to yield the desired perceptions). The product category manipulation substituted air travel arrangements for pizza, depending on condition, with appropriate attributes used for the manipulation.

Dependent Measures

The measures of perceived assortment and evaluations used in Study One were again applied. In addition, we also developed and pretested a measure of perceived firm facilitation and used confirmatory factor analysis to validate the scale (Cronbach's $\alpha = 0.82$). All items in Study Two used nine-point semantic differential scales.

TABLE 10.2

Means (Standard Deviations) of Dependent Variables by Selection Protocol and
Product Category: Study 2

	Customization		Personalization	
Perception/Judgment	Pizza	Air Travel	Pizza	Air Travel
Product evaluation	7.16 (2.09)	6.39 (1.43)	7.00 (1.65)	7.68 (1.26)
Perceived control	6.61 (1.75)	5.29 (2.20)	5.36 (1.90)	5.76 (1.58)
Decision facilitation	5.03 (2.32)	4.44 (1.77)	4.10 (1.84)	5.08 (2.13)

Note. Scores were the average of multiple-item, 9-point scales, with higher scores indicating higher
levels. The interaction between selection protocol and product category was significant for evaluation
and control, $p < 0.05$. The interaction between selection protocol and product category for decision
facilitation was marginally significant, $p < 0.08$.

Results

The means of the dependent measures for all four conditions are summarized in
Table 10.2. There were no significant main effects for selection protocol or product
category. However, the interactive effect of the two was significant for evaluations
and perceived control, and the interaction of the two approached statistical significance for perceived decision facilitation (i.e., $p < 0.08$).

As we predicted, when participants selected products via the customization protocol, they evaluated such products more highly when they belonged to a category
where the participants felt capable of identifying the products that matched their
preferences (pizza in this case). However, when participants selected products via
the personalization protocol, they evaluated such products more highly when they
belonged to a category where they felt the firm was more capable of identifying
the products that matched their preferences (air travel in this instance). In addition,
participants perceived that they had more control when they customized products
belonging to a category in which they felt they could identify the best matches with
their preferences, while there was no such difference when they selected products
via personalization. Finally, participants perceived that the firm facilitated the decision to a greater degree when participants customized products in which they
felt they could identify the best matches with their preferences, while participants
selecting via personalization felt the firm facilitated decisions to a greater degree
for products they perceived the firm was better at matching to preferences.

GENERAL DISCUSSION AND IMPLICATIONS

The goal of firms' individual level marketing efforts is to enable consumers to
select products that match their preferences better than might occur when products are selected from an assortment. While strategies such as customization and

personalization may actually yield such results, they also frame the decision task in a different way, which then affects consumers' decision processes. In this chapter we outlined these two strategies and contrasted them with each other as well as with a strategy previously employed by firms in the past, assortment. One of the key distinctions between these product selection protocols is how they affect consumers' perceptions of control. Although customization should enhance consumers' perceptions of control through the ability to specify attributes to be included in a product, it also may negatively affect consumers' perceptions of assortment. This in turn has been shown to negatively affect store choice (Broniarczyk et al., 1998), as well as lead to negative reactions by consumers who feel that their selection has been limited as suggested by both prior research (Brehm, 1966) and the results from Study One.

Even in instances where consumers perceive that they have considerable assortment to choose from, our results from Study Two suggest that they also must believe that they can accurately identify the products that best match their preferences in order for the additional control afforded by customization to have a positive effect on evaluations. When products are very complex or the number of alternatives appears to be too large to process (as might appear to be the case with air travel arrangements), consumers may instead defer the task of identifying a matching product to a firm, presumably because the firm has more advanced means of searching and screening alternatives than might be available to the consumer. Thus, in such instances, the consumer willingly gives up some measure of control in the decision process yet still evaluates the selected product highly.

The findings of these two studies suggest that although perceived control plays a prominent role in how consumers respond to firms' individual level marketing efforts, these responses are contingent upon other context-specific and consumer-specific factors. Product category, as well as consumers' experience and expertise within the product category, undoubtedly plays an important role in whether or not consumers benefit from customization. If consumers do not know which attributes lead to which benefits, then they have nothing upon which to base their attribute selections (West, Brown, & Hoch, 1996). Similarly, consumers may have a notion of which attributes relate to which benefits, yet be poorly calibrated in their preferences for those benefits (Alba & Hutchinson, 2000). In either instance, consumers do not benefit from the additional control afforded by customization, and might be better off choosing via personalization, even if they do not think this is the case. In addition, factors that influence the degree to which consumers are willing to rely on the recommendations of firms, such as trust in the firm as well as perceived firm manufacturing competency, affect consumers' confidence in the recommendations that they receive via personalization, further compounding the effects on product evaluations.

In addition to their implications for consumers' evaluations of chosen products, the different product selection protocols may also affect what consumers actually choose, and this effect should be taken into account as it would be expected that consumers who choose poorly should also evaluate what they choose less highly than consumers who choose well. Differences in choice can come about due to a couple of different reasons.

Prior research has shown that how information is presented to consumers significantly affects how it is processed, and in particular affects which aspects of the information consumers consider (Bettman & Kakkar, 1977). Assortment, personalization, and customization each present information on alternatives in a different way. Assortment presents consumers with an array of whole alternatives that represent all of the firm's product offerings in a particular product category. Personalization presents consumers with whole alternatives in a ranked order, ostensibly based upon the preferences of the consumer as determined by the firm. In addition, personalization may only include a subset of the alternatives offered by the firm. Customization presents consumers with the specifiable attributes of the product. Thus, in order for consumers to view whole alternatives via customization, they must first specify the features to be included in the product. One effect of these differences in information presentation is that alternatives vary in terms of their salience under each of these product selection protocols, which in turn has been shown to affect what consumers consider and choose (Nedungadi, 1990).

Another distinction between these product selection protocols that could affect choice is the nature of the recommendations that consumers receive via each procedure. With assortment, although no explicit recommendation is made to the consumer, consumers may infer an implicit recommendation. This can occur as consumers, theorizing that firms would not offer products that no consumer would be interested in purchasing, infer that each of the products offered by a firm in their assortment is suitable for some consumer (Prelec et al., 1997). With personalization, consumers receive an explicit recommendation from the firm as to which products the firm thinks the consumer should purchase. With customization, the firm makes no direct recommendation. Because personalization makes an explicit recommendation to consumers, it also establishes a reference point from which comparisons are made during the consideration process, while assortment and customization do not. Recommended items become the focus of comparison, and as such are more favorably viewed during the comparison process than non-recommended items, thus increasing the likelihood that a recommended item will eventually be selected (Dhar & Simonson, 1992). This setting of a reference point in turn should enhance the likelihood of a recommended alternative being chosen. Researchers report results supporting this prediction, where merely including an attribute in a consumer recommendation increases the likelihood that an alternative with that attribute is selected, even if the attribute is irrelevant to the consumer (Häubl & Murray, 2001).

As firms shift their strategies more toward marketing to individuals rather than segments, it becomes increasingly important to understand the effects that these individual level efforts have on consumers' decision processes. In this chapter we have explored how the distinctions between several possible strategies that firms might follow, as well as the mechanisms through which they might influence evaluation independent of an effect on choice. In the future, researchers should seek to understand how these strategies may also influence choice, and then take this into account as they examine the effects on evaluations. Clearly this is a research area of great importance to both marketers and marketing scholars.

REFERENCES

Alba, J. W., & Hutchinson, J. W. (2000). Knowledge calibration: What consumers know and what they think they know. *Journal of Consumer Research, 27*(2), 123–156.

Averill, J. R. (1973). Personal control over aversive stimuli and its relationship to stress. *Psychological Bulletin, 80*(4), 286–303.

Baumol, W. J., & Ide, E. A. (1956). Variety in retailing. *Management Science, 3*(1), 93–101.

Bettman, J. R., & Kakkar, P. (1977). Effects of information presentation format on consumer information acquisition strategies. *Journal of Consumer Research, 3*(1), 233–240.

Brehm, J. W. (1966). *A theory of psychological reactance*. New York: Academic Press.

Broniarczyk, S.M., Hoyer, W. D., & McAlister, L. (1998). Consumers' perceptions of the assortment offered in a grocery category: The impact of item reduction. *Journal of Marketing Research, 35*(2), 166–176.

Dhar, R., & Simonson, I. (1992). The effect of the focus of comparison on consumer preferences. *Journal of Marketing Research, 29*(4), 430–440.

Fitzsimons, G. J. (2000). Consumer response to stock-outs. *Journal of Consumer Research, 27*(2), 249–266.

Häubl, G., & Murray, K. B. (2003). Preference construction and persistence in digital marketplaces: The role of electronic recommendation agents. *Journal of Consumer Psychology, 13*, 75–91.

Häubl, G., & Trifts, V. (2000). Consumer decision making in online shopping environments: The effects of interactive decision aids. *Marketing Science, 19*(1), 21–31.

Hoffman, D. L., & Novak, T. P. (1996). Marketing in hypermedia computer-mediated environments: Conceptual foundations. *Journal of Marketing, 60*(1), 50–68.

Hollander, S., & Rassuli, K. M. (1999). Shopping with other people's money: The marketing management implications of surrogate-mediated consumer decision making. *Journal of Marketing, 63*(2), 102–118.

Huffman, C., & Kahn, B. E. (1998). Variety for sale: Mass customization or mass confusion? *Journal of Retailing, 74*(4), 491–513.

Janis, I., & Mann, L. (1977). *Decision making*. New York: Free Press.

Kahn, B. E. (1998). Dynamic relationships with customers: High-variety strategies. *Journal of the Academy of Marketing Science, 26*(1), 45–53.

Keller, K. L., & Staelin, R. (1987). Effects of quality and quantity of information on decision effectiveness. *Journal of Consumer Research, 14*(2), 200–213.

National Retail Federation (2000). *Top 100 Internet retailers*. Washington, DC: NRF Enterprises, Inc.

Nedungadi, P. (1990). Recall and consumer consideration sets: Influencing choice without altering brand evaluations. *Journal of Consumer Research, 17*(3), 263–276.

Pine, B. J. (1993). *Mass customization: The new frontier in business competition*. Boston: Harvard Business School Press.

Prahalad, C. K., & Ramaswamy, V. (2000). Co-opting customer competence. *Harvard Business Review, 78*(1), 79–87.

Prelec, D., Wernerfelt, B., & Zettelmeyer, F. (1997). The role of inference in context effects: Inferring what you want from what is available. *Journal of Consumer Research, 24*(1), 118–125.

Sheth, J. N., Sisodia, R. S., & Sharma, A. (2000). The antecedents and consequences of consumer-centric marketing. *Journal of the Academy of Marketing Science, 28*(1), 55–66.

Smith, W. R. (1956). Product differentiation and market segmentation as alternative marketing strategies. *Journal of Marketing, 21*(1), 3–8.

Thompson, S. C. (1981). Will it hurt less if I can control it? A complex answer to a simple question. *Psychological Bulletin, 90*(1), 89–101.

West, P. M., Brown, C. L., & Hoch, S. J. (1996). Consumption vocabulary and preference formation. *Journal of Consumer Research, 23*(2), 120–135.

White, R. W. (1959). Motivation reconsidered: The concept of competence. *Psychological Review, 66*(5), 297–333.

CHAPTER ELEVEN

Smoother Surfing Across Cultures: Bilinguals on the Web

David Luna
Baruch College

Laura A. Peracchio
University of Wisconsin–Milwaukee

María D. de Juan
Universidad de Alicante

Consumers all over the world can access the Internet, making it a unique medium with global reach. Although a Web site may be hosted in the United States, consumers everywhere can surf that site. Despite the worldwide reach of the Internet, most Web sites are offered only in English (Fox, 2000). This was not much of an issue in 1996 when 80% of web users' first language was English. Today, less than half of web users' first language is English. In two years, projections indicate that only one third of web users will speak English as their first language (Crockett, 2000).

Despite the presence of bilingual consumers on the Internet, very little attention has been devoted to how web users react to sites that are presented in their first versus their second language. This language issue is possibly one of the most important topics in cross-cultural e-commerce. Yet, little is known about whether our current ideas about persuasion are applicable to second language processing of web-based messages (Luna & Peracchio, 2001). Even less is known about the factors that influence bilingual consumers' attitudes toward second language Web sites and the products they feature.

Consequently, in this chapter we explore several language and culture-related issues that are of importance in cross-cultural e-marketing. We begin by discussing the role of language in determining Web site effectiveness across cultures. For example, suppose that a consumer in Spain is looking for a camera retailer on the Web. She visits her favorite search engine, and the first link that appears on the results of her search sends her to the English-language site of a camera e-tailer based in Germany. Or consider the case of a Korean consumer looking for information on the latest music CD by French singer Manu Chao. This time, his search engine sends him to the review in *Rolling Stone* magazine. How will these consumers react to the sites in English? Will they retreat to the familiar world of sites in their own language? Will they try to understand what the sites in English are telling them? How will they form their attitudes toward the sites and toward the products featured in them?

Next, we discuss how other cultural factors may influence the effectiveness of a Web site in multicultural markets. For example, suppose that our Spanish consumer is looking for a camera in the English-language site of the German e-tailer. Would she react more favorably if the graphics or the text included in the site were familiar to her culture? In other words, would she evaluate more positively a foreign site if it contained endorsements by Spanish actors versus German actors? Considering that Spaniards tend to be very family oriented (and not likely to own house cats), would she be able to relate more to the site if it showed how to use a specific camera in family gatherings instead of focusing on taking pictures of a favorite pet cat?

Finally, we outline the relevance of attitudinal measures of Web site effective-ness in a cross-cultural setting. We will develop a model tying attitudes toward a Web site with the achievement of an optimal navigation experience, which we will show can lead to more "sticky" sites—sites that make people stay longer, want to come back, and purchase products. For instance, will our Spanish consumer want to go back to a site that is in accord with her cultural values and symbols? Will she feel more comfortable purchasing her camera from such a site?

LANGUAGE AND ATTITUDES TOWARD THE SITE

Language Processing

The demographics and social characteristics of international web users are such that they tend to be highly educated, innovators, and of medium-to-high social standing and income. Thus, a large number of consumers targeted through the Web at the international level have a working knowledge of English (Fox, 2000; Ryan, 1999). However, most of them are more fluent in their native language, so navigating through English-language sites is likely to be somewhat challenging. Thus, second language sites may present bilingual consumers with a task that requires increased processing effort relative to first language sites. In addition to language, other factors may impact the effort involved in Web site processing. For instance, site design factors, such as the consistency of site graphics with text, may influence the effort involved in processing a Web site. Previous research seems to suggest that if language and site design factors impact the difficulty of web-site processing, they might also impact persuasion (Peracchio & Meyers-Levy, 1997).

To understand the circumstances in which second language processing on the Web may influence persuasion, it is useful to examine psycholinguistic models that describe how individuals process and store language. A recent and widely accepted model of bilingual concept representation is the Revised Hierarchical Model or RHM (Dufour & Kroll, 1995; Kroll and de Groot, 1997). This model builds on previous findings (Durgunoglu & Roediger, 1987; Snodgrass, 1984) suggesting that there exist two levels of representation in the bilingual's mind: the lexical (word) level and the conceptual (meaning) level. At the lexical level, each language is presumed to be stored separately. However, at the conceptual level, there is a unitary system in which words in each language access a common semantic representation or meaning. Thus, according to Dufour and Kroll (1995), bilingual individuals possess a "hierarchical arrangement of words and concepts, with a separation at the lexical level but with connections to a semantic system that is shared across languages (p. 166)."

The connections between words in different languages made at the lexical level are referred to as word associations or *lexical links*, while the connections in memory between lexical representations in either language and the meanings they represent are referred to as *conceptual links*. The model specifies stronger conceptual links between the lexical representations in an individual's first language and their corresponding semantic representations in memory (concepts) than between second language lexical representations and their corresponding concepts. Conceptual links to the individual's second language are weaker than first language links because it is only after individuals have achieved a high level of proficiency in their second language that they rely less on their first language to gain access to meaning. Thus, the strength of conceptual links are a function of the second language proficiency of the individual in question. However, even after the individual has become fluent in both languages there is a residual asymmetry in conceptual links (Dufour & Kroll, 1995; Kroll & de Groot, 1997). Because of this asymmetry, the RHM would suggest that processing a second language message at the semantic level is more cognitively effortful and less likely to succeed than processing a first language message.

Empirical testing of the RHM supports the proposition that semantic processing of second language stimuli is likely to be more difficult than the processing of equivalent first language stimuli. This effect has been explained by suggesting that first language stimuli have more direct access to concepts than second language stimuli due to the asymmetry in the strength of first language and second language conceptual links. At the same time, research in psycholinguistics testing the RHM has found that the accessibility to concepts of a second language lexical stimulus (e.g., a written word) may be facilitated by manipulating other elements of the stimulus, such as whether it is accompanied by a consistent picture.

For example, La Heij, Hooglander, Kerling, and Van Der Velden (1996) found that translation of written stimuli from second language to first language was facilitated in the form of shorter latencies by the presentation of related pictures, while unrelated pictures resulted in higher latencies. Thus, pictures seem to aid or hamper language processing, depending on their level of relatedness to the textual stimulus. La Heij et al. (1996) imply that pictures may moderate the language effects predicted by the RHM. That is, the weaker second language conceptual links may be strengthened by a pictorial cue, which facilitates activation of the concept represented by the second language word.

Confirming this reasoning, Luna and Peracchio (2001) showed that pictures that are consistent or related to the copy of a second language ad enhanced recall by bilingual consumers. Hence, a second language ad could be as memorable as a first language ad if nonverbal cues were provided to facilitate message processing. Preliminary findings from this research also indicated that first and second language messages seem to have an impact on persuasion. Second language ads appear to benefit from high levels of picture-copy consistency resulting in increased product evaluations. By contrast, first language ads exhibited a trend toward lower product evaluations as ad consistency increased. These preliminary attitudinal findings would seem to suggest that language does have an impact on persuasion for bilingual consumers.

In this chapter, we extend the domain of the RHM to the persuasive impact of international Web sites. Our extension of this model builds on the initial findings of Luna and Peracchio (2001) in predicting that first language sites will generally be more easily processed than second language sites. This processing asymmetry may, however, be moderated by the presence or absence of consistent site graphics. The first two studies we describe examine the effect of this graphic consistency on evaluative responses. The third study examines another type of consistency, cultural consistency, as a potential moderator of language effects on site effectiveness. Therefore, we build upon the recall findings of previous research and extend them to evaluative responses, an important gauge of Web site effectiveness. We believe that language and consistency impact a site visitors' attitudes. In particular, we will examine product evaluations and attitude toward the site.

Attitude Toward the Site and Attitude Toward the Ad

The concept of attitude toward the ad (A_{ad}) has been extensively studied in the marketing literature. MacKenzie and Lutz (1989) define it as "a predisposition to respond in a favorable or unfavorable manner to a particular advertising stimulus during a particular exposure occasion" (p. 49). A_{ad} has been found to mediate the influence of advertising and brand attitudes, or A_b (Homer, 1990; MacKenzie, Lutz, & Belch, 1986). Mitchell (1986) offers evidence that A_{ad} and A_b are indeed separate concepts and examines the process through which verbal and visual components of ads affect both attitudinal concepts. That study found that both picture and copy manipulations could affect A_{ad}.

In an interactive medium like the Web, a similar concept to attitude toward the ad, A_{site}, should be expected to have an important effect (Chen & Wells, 1999).

In order to have a sticky site, one that retains visitors for longer durations and motivates them to return to it, visitors must have a positive attitude toward a site, A_{site}. Popular, consumer-oriented e-commerce sites frequently belong to cyber-mediaries, or e-tailers. These Internet marketers normally carry different brands, so in this chapter A_b is denominated $A_{products}$, or consumers' general evaluation of all the products available at a particular Web site. Therefore, in this chapter we focus on the effect of the language and site design factors (i.e., consistency) on individual's attitude toward the site (A_{site}) and product evaluations ($A_{products}$).

The extant literature seems to indicate that Web site design elements may affect both A_{site} and $A_{products}$. Resource matching views of ad processing (Peracchio & Meyers-Levy, 1997) suggest that the optimal level of processing occurs at the midpoint between too much processing and too little. If there is an opportunity for extensive processing, where resources far exceed the task requirements, consumers tend to generate counterarguments or a high number of negative thoughts for the ad. If there is not a sufficient opportunity for processing, such as when the resources required to process a message are higher than the resources available for the task, attitudes also suffer. Therefore, if first language sites, which are more likely to be processed successfully than second language sites, are accompanied by high consistency graphics, they may provide an opportunity for extensive processing, which can result in diminished attitudes. On the other hand, second language sites are not as likely to be processed semantically. Therefore, high consistency graphics may assist bilinguals in processing second language sites resulting in more successful processing. This idea would seem to apply to both A_{site} and $A_{products}$.

In sites containing low consistency graphics, pictures will not facilitate seman-tic processing, so site visitors may not be able to use the pictures to encode the site content, thus reducing the opportunities for extensive processing in general. While visitors to low consistency first language sites may still engage in semantic processing of the site content because of the relative easiness of processing first language stimuli, visitors to low consistency second language sites will not be pro-vided enough opportunity for processing, since both the language and the pictures do not facilitate visitors' elaborative processing.

In summary, language effects on attitude toward the site may be moderated by the level of consistency between the graphics and the verbal content of the Web site. Attitudes toward the products ($A_{products}$) featured in the site should follow a similar pattern to A_{site}. To test this reasoning, we conducted two empirical studies. One was conducted in Spain and the other in the United States (Southern California), with respondents who were fairly proficient Spanish-English bilinguals.

Research Studies and Key Findings

For the studies we created the Web site of a fictitious camera retailer. It was modeled on typical camera retailing sites. The site consisted of 61 pages, which contained a total of 50 pictures/graphics including a home page and the following sections: What do you need? (an interactive quiz directing visitors to the cameras they might be most interested in); New Products (a total of 12 cameras in four sections: manual, automatic, compact, and digital); Used Products (a long list of a variety of used cameras and photographic equipment); About Us (pages describing the company and its management, personnel, and history); Testimonials (pages containing comments from past customers); Photo Contest (a page encouraging visitors to send their pictures to enter a contest); Contact Us and Order pages; and an internal search engine.

The experiments took place in computer rooms equipped with PCs. Participants were asked to sit at their computers individually and key into their web browser the Internet address where they would begin the experiment. This address instructed them to fill out the first questionnaire in the language of their choice (English or Spanish). Once participants completed the first questionnaire, they were directed automatically to the home page of the experimental Web site to which they were assigned, where they began browsing the site. Respondents were randomly assigned to one of the four Web sites: (1) Spanish language and consistent graphics, (2) Spanish language and inconsistent graphics (3) English language and consistent graphics, and (4) English language and inconsistent graphics. After they were finished browsing at their leisure, they were instructed to click on and fill out the final questionnaire in the language of their choice.

The first questionnaire contained items regarding their language use and other demographic measures. The final questionnaire included the dependent measures. These consisted of five 7-point scales to measure attitude toward the site (the site was boring/exciting, not interesting/interesting, not appealing/appealing, mediocre/exceptional, not fun/fun) and five 7-point scales to measure product evaluations (the products were boring/exciting, not worthwhile/worthwhile, not appealing/appealing, overall inferior/superior, common/unique). Higher scores represented higher evaluations. Additionally, participants were asked to type all thoughts that occurred to them.

The results were analyzed as a language by graphic consistency experimental design. The moderating effect of language and graphic consistency on attitude toward the site follows the anticipated pattern in both studies. Figure 11.1 presents the results for the Spain study. The results reveal a significant two-way interaction of language and graphic consistency on A_{site}. A closer inspection of the interaction reveals that in the high consistency condition the second language site results in more positive attitudes than the first language site. However, in the low graphic consistency condition the reverse effect is found: the first language site results in more positive attitudes than the second language site.

Attitudes toward the products featured in the site ($A_{products}$) were also examined in both studies. Analysis of this measure showed a two-way interaction of language by graphic consistency for the two studies. The results of this measure suggest the superiority of second language over first language under high graphic consistency. However, in the low graphic consistency condition there was no significant

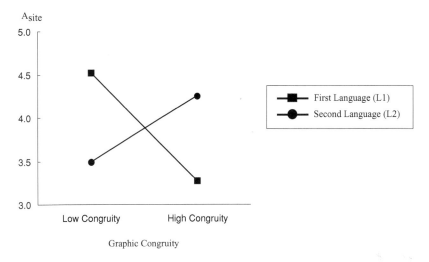

FIG. 11.1   Study 1: Two-way interaction on attitude toward the site.

difference between first language and second language. A possible reason for this measure's failure to support our expectations could be related to the nature of the products and brands offered on the Web site. All products on the site were actual products representing real brands. In this more effortful and demanding low consistency condition, bilinguals in both language conditions may have relied on their general positive attitudes toward these products rather than processing the site's product information in a detailed manner.

Overall, in these empirical studies we explore the effect of two site design elements, language and graphic consistency, on the effectiveness of cross-cultural Web sites targeting bilingual consumers. The results suggest that the level of graphic consistency can moderate language effects on attitudes toward cross-cultural Web sites. Thus, our findings are consistent with previous research on advertising recall (Luna & Peracchio, 2001). Countering marketers' intuitions, first language sites do not always deliver superior persuasion effects relative to second language sites, particularly when the sites' graphics support their verbal content. Indeed, in such high consistency conditions, second language sites may be even more persuasive than sites in the visitors' local language. For low consistency sites, however, we find mixed results. Attitude toward the site confirmed our expectations indicating that first language sites were more persuasive than second language sites under low consistency conditions, but attitude toward the products featured in the site did not support our predictions.

While this section addresses the issue of graphic consistency in Web site navigation and its effect on attitudinal responses, the next section explores the role of cultural consistency on the same type of responses. Hence, we seek to establish a parallel between cultural and graphic consistency. If we found similar effects for both manipulations of consistency, we could argue that culture can affect ad responses through cognitive processes.

CULTURE AND ATTITUDES TOWARD THE SITE

The impact of culture on consumer behavior is evident through the observation of particular manifestations of culture such as values, symbols, rituals, and heroes (Luna & Gupta, 2001). Values play a central role, as they are centrally held beliefs that guide human actions and tend to be culture specific (Rokeach, 1968). Symbols are a broad category of processes and objects that carry a meaning that is unique to a particular group of people (Geertz, 1973). Language can be considered a symbol in that it expresses certain values and concepts through arbitrary signs. Rituals are a "a social action devoted to the manipulation of the cultural meaning for purposes of collective and individual communication and categorization. Ritual is an opportunity to affirm, evoke, assign, or revise the conventional symbols and meanings of the cultural order" (McCracken, 1988, p. 84). Lastly, heroes are "persons, alive or dead, real or imaginary, who possess characteristics which are highly prized in a culture, and who thus serve as models for behavior" (Hofstede, 1997, p. 8)

Could we make our Web sites more international user-friendly by adapting them to the visitors' cultural manifestations, values, symbols, rituals, and heroes? What is the relationship between nonlanguage cultural manifestations and language? Could the two types of manifestations interact with respect to attitudinal responses? These are questions that we attempt to address in this section. For that purpose, we designed a study that manipulated the cultural consistency of an experimental Web site to evaluate whether this factor moderates language effects on Web site effectiveness.

We achieved three levels of cultural consistency: high (cultural manifestations expressed both through the site's text and graphics were consistent with visitors' culture); moderate (either the text or the graphics were culturally consistent with visitors' culture); and low (neither the text nor the graphics were consistent with the visitors' culture). The design of the study explored these three levels of cultural consistency and first versus second language. Consistent with the findings of the studies described in the previous section, we expect that in the high consistency condition there should be a superiority of second language over first language because consistency facilitates processing of the site's second language content to an optimal point. Also similar to the findings in the previous section, we expect that low consistency will lead to a language superiority of first language over second language with respect to attitudes.

In the moderate conditions, however, we expect that first language sites should be superior to second language sites. This is because the processing of first language sites is enhanced to an optimal point by a moderate level of consistency making the site neither too unchallenging nor too difficult. However, as described by the RHM, conceptual processing of second language stimuli is less likely than first language processing, so a moderate consistency level may not be enough to facilitate second language processing. Indeed, lack of total consistency may represent a hurdle for effective processing in a second language, thus we expect a superiority of first language over second language in moderate consistency conditions.

Research Study and Key Findings

To test the effect of culture on Web site attitudes, we developed an experimental Web site different from the one used in the studies described in the previous section. It was a fictitious camera retailer's site, which included 20 pages and 17 different pictures. The site had several sections, all accessible from a menu embedded in every page of the site. The sections were Home, Our Cameras (including two pages, a benefits page and a specifications page, for each of the five featured cameras), Testimonials, Our Cameras and You (depicting situations in which the cameras could be used), a contact form for bilinguals to email the company, and a search engine.

This study was conducted in Spain with Spanish-English bilinguals. Cultural consistency was explored through changing the site's content. Two factors were manipulated, text and picture. Thus, the text was either Spanish- or American-specific in nature. The picture was neutral, Spanish-specific or American-specific. The resulting consistency conditions were as follows: Spanish text/Spanish picture (high consistency); Spanish text/neutral picture and American text/ neutral picture (moderate consistency) and American text/American picture (low consistency).

The two levels of cultural consistency of the text were achieved by using values, heroes, and symbols that were typical and specific of each culture (Spain versus United States). For example, the Spanish-specific text of the Web site included a page in which the value of extended-family orientation was emphasized, while its US-specific equivalent focused on fraternization with roommates. A symbol included in the Spanish-specific site was a paella, while its US-specific equivalent mentioned a barbecue. A hero mentioned in the Testimonials section of the Spanish-specific site was Penélope Cruz (the study was conducted prior to her recent American success), while the US-specific equivalent was Helen Hunt. A ritual included in the Spanish-specific site was the feast to three kings, while the US-specific site described a Thanksgiving dinner. The text of each of the pages in the site was developed through focus groups in Spain and the United States. Care was taken that the structure, length, and descriptive and narrative content of the text was equivalent across cultural versions.

The procedure, measures, and respondents were similar to the studies in the previous section. Respondents included 142 bilinguals in Spain. The results were analyzed as a language by cultural consistency experimental design. Our analysis of the attitudinal data revealed that for A_{site}, the two-way interaction of language by cultural consistency was not significant. However, we observed a marginally significant main effect of cultural consistency on A_{site}. High consistency sites resulted in lower site evaluations than moderate and low consistency sites. The lack of the predicted language effects on this measure is perhaps due to the simpler design of the site and the more prominent place that the products sold by our fictitious camera e-tailer occupied in the design of the site for this study.

For $A_{products}$, however, the two-way interaction of language by cultural consistency was significant. Similar to our graphic consistency findings, in the high cultural consistency condition second language sites resulted in higher product evaluations than first language sites. On the other hand, in the moderate consistency condition there was a superiority of first language sites over second language sites. Replicating the product evaluation findings of the graphic consistency studies, in the low consistency condition there was no difference between first language and second language sites. Hence, for both of our conceptualizations of consistency (graphic and cultural), low consistency seems to dampen evaluations even in respondents' first language.

The results of this study provide evidence for the moderating role of cultural consistency on language processing. Similarly to graphic consistency, high cultural consistency results in enhanced $A_{products}$ for second language versus first language individuals. Consistency, therefore, regardless of how it is operationalized, can lead to enhanced persuasion in second language conditions. It is reasonable to conclude, then, that cultural factors impact site responses through cognitive processes (i.e., schema consistency). However, while the studies in the previous section found that graphic consistency moderates language effects on A_{site} and $A_{products}$, this study did not find a significant interaction of language and consistency for A_{site}. This result should be kept in mind and suggests that factors not included in this study may have an impact on site evaluations such as the relative complexity and sophistication of the site.

The results of this study are also consistent with previous research on the impact of language on advertising recall (Luna & Peracchio, 2001). That research suggests that second language processing does not benefit from moderate levels of consistency. While first language processing is enhanced by moderate consistency, second language requires a higher level of consistency before it can reap benefits.

To this point, we have shown that a Web site's content can affect site and product evaluations. However, we have not yet related these constructs to the Web site navigation experience. In the next section we use data from the three studies described in this research to examine the relationship between site content and visitors' optimal navigation experience, or flow (Hoffman & Novak, 1996). We examine whether the experience of flow has any impact on the stickiness of the site. In other words, do site content and design affect international consumers' ability to engage in flow? If so, why does flow matter? And, finally, do positive attitudes lead to flow?

SITE CONTENT, ATTITUDES, AND FLOW

Computer-mediated environments like the World Wide Web have a unique characteristic: interactivity. In such an environment, individuals may reach a state in which their attention is focused solely on the universe contained within the boundaries of their network navigation experience. This state is frequently evidenced by users' comments like "I forgot where I was," or "I completely lost track of time." Such state has been labeled *flow* in previous research (e.g., Csikszentmihalyi & LeFevre, 1989). Recently, Hoffman and Novak (1996) defined flow in the context of web navigation as "the state occurring during network navigation, which is (1) characterized by a seamless sequence of responses facilitated by machine interactivity, (2) intrinsically enjoyable, (3) accompanied by a loss of self-consciousness, and (4) self-reinforcing" (p. 57).

An e-commerce site's capacity to induce a state of flow in their visitors is an important attribute. Prior research exploring flow in the general context of web navigation has found that some of the key consequences of flow for individuals are increased learning, exploratory and participatory behaviors, positive subjective experiences, and a perceived sense of control over their interactions in a computer-mediated environment. In this research we focus on two potential consequences of flow that have been previously unexplored: intentions to revisit the site and intentions to purchase from the site. These two constructs are important to marketers and add increased relevance to the flow construct.

Antecedents of flow examined by previous literature include: the challenges that a Web site presents for its visitors and whether those challenges present a good fit with their skills; interactivity of the site, and the focused attention of the visitors (Hoffman & Novak, 1996; Novak, Hoffman, & Yung, 2000). This research also examines flow in a multicultural context. An antecedent of flow not examined by previous research is site content, perhaps because most other studies of flow have been concerned with individuals' navigation of the Internet in general instead of specific Web sites. When examining specific Web sites, it is likely that site content will have an effect on the flow experience. In this research we examine whether site content, for example the language of the site, influences flow directly or if visitors' attitudes mediate that relationship. In particular, attitude towards the site may mediate the effect of site content. As our research suggests thus far, site content impacts attitude toward the site. A positive attitude towards a Web site may predispose visitors to respond in other positive ways to a Web site, facilitating the flow experience.

We will test this proposition adapting the path analysis method (Cohen & Cohen, 1983; Deshpande & Stayman, 1994). In addition to testing the mediational effect of attitude toward the site (A_{site}) on flow, we will also examine whether A_{site} influences $A_{products}$, as suggested by previous advertising research.

Key Findings

Table 11.1 shows the results of our analysis. Table 11.2 includes the scale we adapted from Novak, Hoffman and Yung (2000) to measure the flow construct. For each of our three multicultural studies, we performed three analysis of covariance. The first analysis consisted of modeling A_{site} as a function of site content. The results of this analysis have been described in previous sections of this paper. The second analysis modeled $A_{products}$ as a function of site content and A_{site}. As can be observed, A_{site} had a direct relationship with $A_{products}$, replicating previous research studies. Most significantly, however, is the third analysis, in which we modeled flow as a function of ad content, A_{site} and $A_{product}$. As can be observed, when we add A_{site} and $A_{product}$ as covariates, ad content does not significantly affect flow. Further, $A_{products}$ does not consistently have a significant effect on flow, while A_{site} does across the three studies. We can conclude, therefore, that A_{site} mediates the effect of ad content on flow for multicultural Web sites. Indirectly and with some caution, we can say that $A_{products}$ also mediates that relationship for multicultural Web sites.

Thus far, we have examined the impact of ad content on flow, suggesting that A_{site} mediates that effect. In other words, design decisions for our Web site such as the language we choose or the graphics we use may lead consumers to have more positive attitudes toward our site. In turn, if they have more positive attitudes toward our site, they will be more likely to achieve an optimal navigation experience or flow. But then, what are the implications of engaging in flow? Why should marketers be concerned about helping consumers achieve flow? In the next section we develop a formal model of flow, including some antecedents and consequences relevant for e-marketers. Our goal is to build a model that can be applied to single Web sites rather than to multisite web navigation and to incorporate a cross-cultural dimension. We will test and validate this model utilizing data from the three research studies described in this chapter.

A MODEL OF FLOW FOR SPECIFIC WEB SITES

The model of flow we present in this section does not attempt to be all inclusive. In other words, we do not attempt to tackle all the potential antecedents of flow as previous research has successfully done in the context of web navigation in general (Novak, Hoffman, & Yung, 2000). Rather, we focus upon a subset of these antecedents, with the goal of showing the mediational effect of A_{site} and some of the marketing consequences of flow in a multicultural context. Thus, our model of flow incorporates some of the constructs examined by the existing literature and includes

TABLE 11.1
Path Analysis Results

	Study 1 – Spain			Study 1 – USA			Study 2 – Spain		
	A_{site}	$A_{products}$	Flow	A_{site}	$A_{products}$	Flow	A_{site}	$A_{products}$	Flow
Language × Consistency	$F = 12.25$, $p < .001$	$F < 1$	$F = 1.11$, $p = .30$	$F = 14.08$, $p < .001$	$F = 1.94$, $p = .17$	$F < 1$	$F < 1$	$F = 3.37$, $p < .05$	$F = 2.06$, $p = .11$
A_{Site}		$F = 19.53$, $p < .001$	$F = 12.33$, $p < .001$		$F = 24.82$, $p < .001$	$F = 3.77$, $p < .05$		$F = 22.14$, $p < .001$	$F = 15.70$, $p < .001$
$A_{Product}$			$F = 1.33$, $p = .25$			$F = 5.24$, $p < .05$			$F = 6.16$, $p < .01$

TABLE 11.2

Variables Used in Study and Their Reliabilities

Variable (α)	Code	Scale
A_{site} (.92)	A1	1. Boring/Exciting
	A2	2. Not appealing/Appealing
	A3	3. Mediocre/Exceptional
	A4	4. Not fun/Fun
Challenge (.87)	C1	1. Visiting the Tandem site challenged me.
	C2	2. Visiting the Tandem site challenged me to perform to the best of my ability.
	C3	3. Visiting the Tandem site provided a good test of my skills.
Flow (.94)		The word "flow" is used to describe a state of mind sometimes experienced by people who are deeply involved in some activity. One example of flow is the case where a professional athlete is playing exceptionally well and achieves a state of mind where nothing else matters but the game, he is completely and totally immersed in it. The experience is not exclusive to athletics—many people report this state of mind when playing games, engaging in hobbies, or working.
		Activities that lead to flow completely captivate a person for some period of time. When in flow, time may seem to stand still and nothing else seems to matter. Flow may not last for a long time on any particular occasion, but it may come and go over time. Flow has been described as an intrinsically enjoyable experience.
		When you were visiting Tandem Camera's Web site:
	F1	1. Do you think you experienced flow?
	F2	2. Of the time you spent visiting the site, how much time were you in flow?
	F3	3. How intense do you think your flow experience was?
	F4	4. Most of the time you felt you were in flow.
Focused attention (.75)	FA1	1. When visiting the Tandem site, you were aware of distractions.
	FA2	2. When visiting the Tandem site, you thought about other things.
Interactivity (.90)	I1	1. The Tandem site gave you the option to find different types of information about cameras.
	I2	2. The Tandem site provided enough camera choices based on what your needs are.
	I3	3. You were able to find all the information you needed about the cameras in which you were interested on the Tandem site.
Purchase intent (.90)	PI1	1. I would buy a camera from Tandem if I needed one.
	PI2	2. In the future, I will consider buying from Tandem when I need a camera.
Revisit intent (.87)	RI1	1. Next time I need a camera, I will visit the Tandem site.
	RI2	2. I will visit Tandem's site in the future if I need to look for information on cameras.

others previously unexplored in the context of web-site navigation. In particular, flow is modeled as a function of consumers' perceptions of two site characteristics, interactivity and challenge, and two psychological constructs, focused attention and attitude toward the site. A_{site} is expected to mediate the effect of the other three variables on flow. In turn, flow is expected to result in higher intentions to purchase products from the site and to revisit the site. This model will be tested with the three independent samples of the studies described in this chapter—two European samples and one US sample, to examine its validity. Hence, we will validate our model cross-culturally with different populations and on different stimuli/Web sites.

A_{site}, Flow and Web Site Effectiveness

We include in our model three potential antecedents of A_{site}: focused attention, challenge, and interactivity. Following MacInnis and Jaworski's (1989) cognitive framework of ad processing, we hypothesize that focused attention may be an antecedent of A_{site}. Attention is defined as the general distribution of mental activity to the tasks being performed by the individual (Moates & Schumacher, 1980). Attention can be allocated in various degrees to the site, or primary task, or to secondary tasks such as unrelated thoughts or social interaction. The relationship between A_{site} and focused attention is such that if visitors do not dedicate enough undivided attention to the site, they may not process the site's information to a point in which they can form attitudes toward the site (MacInnis & Jaworski, 1989). Therefore, focused attention can be considered an antecedent of A_{site}.

Similarly, the level of challenge provided by a Web site can impact attitude toward the site. Web sites, like advertisements, that are not challenging enough may lead to boredom (Anand & Sternthal, 1990). Therefore, we should expect that if a Web site offers enough challenge to interest visitors, more positive attitudes toward the site might result. The last antecedent of A_{site} investigated in this research is interactivity. We define interactivity as the visitors' perception that the site offers effective and customized methods to search and retrieve information from the site. In other words, the degree to which the Web site aids in consumers' process of selective exposure. Interactivity engages consumers in elaboration, which increases their perception that the site's information is needs-relevant. This perception in turn increases the likelihood of processing and attitude formation (MacInnis & Jaworski, 1989).

Table 11.2 contains the 7-point scales we used to measure our model's constructs: intention to revisit the site, intention to purchase from the site, flow, A_{site}, the challenge presented by the site, interactivity, and focused attention.

Our scale of flow, focused attention, and challenge were adapted from Novak, Hoffman, and Yung (2000). The original scales had been applied in that study to web navigation in general, and we adapted them to reflect responses to a specific Web site. Table 11.2 also includes the reliabilities (Cronbach's α) for each of the scales. The scales were available on line in either Spanish or English and participants were able to choose which version they wished to complete by clicking on the appropriate link. The questionnaires' original English-language scale was translated to Spanish using the back-translation method (Hui & Triandis, 1985).

Key Findings

We developed our model based on data from three samples and using two Web sites. Sample 1 was Spanish and navigated through Website A. Sample 2 was from the United States and navigated through Website A. Sample 3 was Spanish and navigated through Website B. The model was estimated with sample 1 and validated across cultures and across Websites with samples 2 and 3. Figure 11.2 includes our model depicting our hypothesized paths and their parameter estimates for sample 1.

We found that the model fits the data well. All the parameter estimates relevant to the hypotheses were statistically significant, lending support to our expectations. Three additional significant paths were found: those going from interactivity to purchase intent and revisit intent, and a path from attention to flow.

To validate our model, we analyzed data from the other two samples. Sample 2 was analyzed to validate our model across cultures with a different population and the same Web site as our original model estimation. Participants in sample 2 were Hispanics in Southern California. For this sample, we utilized the same Web site as with the estimation sample. Sample 3 was analyzed in an attempt to replicate the results of the first sample with the same population and a different Web site. Thus, data from sample 3 was collected 6 months later with a similar group of respondents. While the brand name and the product category were the same as in sample 1, the content was completely different. The site was also simpler in design, containing 20 pages. There were different versions of this site, which varied by

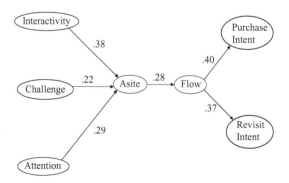

FIG. 11.2   A model of flow for single Web sites.

language and cultural consistency of the content. Identical scales to the estimation sample were provided.

The methodology used to validate our model was adapted from Byrne (1998), Durvasula , Andrews, Lysonski, and Netemeye (1993), and Jöreskog and Sörbom (1996). The results of our validation procedure were encouraging. We found that factor and covariance structures were not significantly different across the three samples, and that the structural parameters were also not significantly different from sample to sample. Interested readers are directed to the specific results detailed in Luna and Peracchio (2001b). Therefore, we can conclude that our model is robust across Web sites and populations. We validated the model cross-culturally with two populations and two Web sites, and the results yielded similar fit and structure characteristics. Our hypothesized model was expanded with three additional parameters, underscoring the importance of perceived interactivity in e-commerce sites. Perceived interactivity of a Web site directly influences common measures of marketing effectiveness such as consumers' intentions to revisit and purchase from a Web site. Also, a direct path from focused attention to flow is consistent with the findings of prior research that links the two constructs (Novak, Hoffman, & Yung, 2000).

Our study also highlights the important role of attitude toward the site. We find that A_{site} mediates a great deal of the influence of interactivity, challenge, and focused attention on flow. This finding is of particular relevance considering that prior research on flow in e-commerce had not explored this effect. It is also significant that we found flow to mediate the effect of A_{site} on intentions variables. Altogether, the successful integration of flow with more traditional measures of marketing effectiveness in one single model may constitute an important step forward in our understanding of the flow construct and its influence on consumer behavior.

Lastly, our findings suggest the applicability of our model of flow across cultures. This result will add to the growing corpus of studies that find that many structural models of consumer behavior indeed apply to different cultures (e.g., Durvasula et al., 1993; Lee & Green, 1991). Perhaps if marketers designed their marketing communications materials carefully enough so they could be easily processed by individuals from different cultures, similar responses could be expected across cultures. While this would be a very appealing hypothesis, much research remains to be done in its exploration.

CONCLUSION

In this chapter, we suggest that consistency facilitates second language processing. Two types of consistency are examined, picture-text consistency and cultural consistency. In our empirical studies we find that both types of consistency moderate language effects on attitudinal variables. Further, our multicultural empirical studies show that consistency, a site design factor, can influence consumers' attainment of an optimal navigation experience, or flow. However, this effect is mediated by their attitude toward the site. We then model flow as a function of several antecedent variables, including A_{site}, and find that A_{site} mediates most of the effect of site content and psychological antecedents on flow. At the same time, the flow experience can lead to higher intentions to revisit and purchase products from a site.

What does this mean for consumers and marketers? Let us return to our Spanish consumer looking for a camera in the English-language site of a German e-tailer, we could say that if the site's graphics support the verbal content and express similar meanings, the consumer's attitudes toward the site will be even more positive than if the site were in Spanish. Additionally, her attitudes toward the products will be improved if some culturally-Spanish content is incorporated into the Web site. Finally, if her attitude is positive while visiting the site, she is more likely to have an optimal navigation experience, which will lead to her intention to revisit the site and to purchase a camera there.

For marketers, these findings could result in increased effectiveness and potential savings when they engage in multicultural e-marketing. Increased effectiveness is derived from the targeting possibilities facilitated by server tools that can identify the domain to which a visitor belongs. If the domain belongs to a Spanish Internet service provider, marketers could serve certain culture-specific content that would not be available to visitors from a German domain. With currently available technology, this procedure could be made completely transparent to the end user. Potential savings are derived from the finding that if marketers design their Web sites to include graphics that "make sense," that support the verbal content and can be used to decode it, translation to the site visitors' first language may not be necessary. We must be cautious regarding this last point, however, because as Internet use becomes more widespread around the world, we may begin encountering users who do not speak English with a sufficient level of fluency.

In conclusion, our empirical exploration helps shed light on how consumers process information online. Our results are particularly significant because we build into our model a cross-cultural dimension, which is very important for a global medium like the Internet.

ACKNOWLEDGMENTS

This research was supported by a grant from the *Marketing Science Institute* to fund the study of bilingual consumers' web-based information processing.

REFERENCES

Anand, P., & Sternthal, B. (1990). Ease of message processing as a moderator of repetition effects in advertising. *Journal of Marketing Research, 27*(August), 345–353.

Byrne, B. M. (1998). *Structural equation modeling with Lisrel, Prelis, and Simplis.* Mahwah, NJ: Lawrence Erlbaum Associates.

Celestino, M . (1999, February). Electronic commerce. *World Trade,* 76–79.

Chen, Q., & Wells, W. (1999). Attitude toward the site. *Journal of Advertising Research, 39* (September–October), 27–37.

Cohen, J., & Cohen, P. (1983). *Applied multiple regression/correlation analysis for the behavioral sciences.* Hillsdale, NJ: Lawrence Erlbaum Associates.

Crockett, R. O. (2000, December 11). Surfing in Tongues. *Business Week,* 18.

Csikszentmihalyi, M., & LeFevre, J. (1989). Optimal experience in work and leisure. *Journal of Personality and Social Psychology, 56*(5), 815–822.

Deshpande, R., & Stayman, D. (1994). A tale of two cities: Distinctiveness theory and advertising effectiveness. *Journal of Marketing Research, 31*(February), 57–64.

Dufour, R., & Kroll, J. (1995). Matching words to concepts in two languages: A test of the concept mediation model of bilingual representation. *Memory and Cognition, 23*(March), 166–180.

Durgunoglu, A., & Roediger, H. L. (1987). Test differences in accessing bilingual memory. *Journal of Memory and Language, 26*(August), 377–391.

Durvasula, S., Andrews, J. C., Lysonski, S., & Netemeyer, R. G. (1993). Assessing the cross-national applicability of consumer behavior models: A model of attitude toward advertising in general, *Journal of Consumer Research, 19*(March), 626–636.

Fox, J. (2000, September 18). The triumph of English. *Fortune,* 209–212.

Geertz, C. (1973). *The interpretation of cultures.* New York: Basic Books.

Hoffman, D., & Novak, T. (1996). Marketing in hypermedia computer-mediated environments: Conceptual foundations. *Journal of Marketing, 60*(July), 50–68.

Hofstede, G. (1997). *Cultures and organizations: Software of the mind.* New York: McGraw-Hill.

Homer, P. M. (1990). The mediating role of attitude toward the ad: Some additional evidence. *Journal of Marketing Research, 27*(February), 78–86.

Hui, C. H., & Triandis, H. C. (1985). Measurement in cross-cultural psychology: A review and comparison of strategies. *Journal of Cross-Cultural Psychology, 16*(2), 131–152.

Jöreskog, K., & Sörbom, D. (1996). Lisrel 8: Users' reference guide. Chicago: Scientific Software International.

Kroll, J. F., & de Groot, A. (1997). Lexical and conceptual memory in the bilingual: Mapping form to meaning in two languages. In A. de Groot & J. F. Kroll (eds), *Tutorials in bilingualism: Psycholinguistic perspectives* (pp. 169–199). Mahwah, NJ: Lawrence Erlbaum Associates.

La Heij, W., Hooglander, A., Kerling, R., & Van Der Velden, E. (1996). Nonverbal context effects in forward and backward word translation: Evidence for concept mediation. *Journal of Memory and Language, 35*(October), 648–665.

Lee, C., & Green, R. T. (1991). Cross-cultural examination of the Fishbein behavioral intentions model. *Journal of International Business Studies, 22*(2), 289–305.

Luna, D., & Gupta, S. (2001). An integrative framework for cross-cultural consumer behavior. *International Marketing Review, 18*(1), 45–69.

Luna, D., & Peracchio, L. A. (2001). Moderators of language effects in advertising to bilinguals: A psycholinguistic approach. *Journal of Consumer Research, 28*(September), 284–295.

Luna, D., & Peracchio, L. A. (2001b). *Cross-cultural web site effectiveness: Antecedents and consequences of flow.* Unpublished manuscript.

MacInnis, D. J., & Jaworski, B. J. (1989). Information processing from advertisements: Toward an integrative framework. *Journal of Marketing, 53*(October), 1–23.

MacKenzie, S. B., & Lutz, R. J. (1989). An empirical examination of the structural antecedents of attitude toward the ad in an advertising pretesting context. *Journal of Marketing, 53*(April), 48–65.

MacKenzie, S. B., Lutz, R. J., & Belch, G. E. (1986). The role of attitude toward the ad as a mediator of advertising effectiveness: A test of competing explanations. *Journal of Marketing Research, 23*(May), 130–143.

McCracken, G. (1988). *Culture and consumption: New approaches to the symbolic character of consumer goods and activities*. Bloomington: Indiana University Press.

Mitchell, A. (1986). The effect of verbal and visual components of advertisements on brand attitudes and attitude toward the advertisement. *Journal of Consumer Research, 13*(June), 12–24.

Moates, D. R., & Schumacher G. M. (1980). *An introduction to cognitive psychology*. Belmont, CA: Wadsworth.

Novak, T. D., Hoffman, D., & Yung, Yiu-Fai (2000). Measuring the customer experience in online environments: A structural modeling approach. *Marketing Science, 19*(1), 22–42.

Peracchio, L. A., & Meyers-Levy, J. (1997). Evaluating persuasion-enhancing techniques from a resource-matching perspective. *Journal of Consumer Research, 24*(September), 178–191.

Rokeach, M. (1968). *Beliefs, attitudes and values: A theory of organization and change*. San Francisco, CA: Jossey-Bass.

Ryan, J. (1999, June 3). In Spanish and Portuguese, Web growth spurt. *The New York Times*, pp. D1–D8.

Snodgrass, J. G. (1984). Concepts and their surface representations. *Journal of Verbal Learning and Verbal Behavior, 23*(February), 3–22.

CHAPTER TWELVE

Processes of Preference Construction in Agent-Assisted Online Shopping

Kyle B. Murray
University of Western Ontario

Gerald Häubl
University of Alberta

PERSONALIZATION AND THE OPPORTUNITY TO INFLUENCE

Thanks to Moore's Law,[1] marketers now have the ability to remember and respond to the tastes and preferences of individual consumers. Advances in technology, and techniques for database marketing, have created the opportunity for retailers to resurrect business practices over 100-years-old. At that time, the local shop owner was able to develop individual relationships with each customer, providing personalized service and product recommendations. Peppers and Rogers (1993) explain it this way:

> We are facing a paradigm shift of epic proportions—from the industrial era to the Information Age. As a result, we are witnessing a meltdown of the mass-marketing paradigm that has governed business competition throughout the twentieth century. The new paradigm is one to one (1 : 1)—mandated by cheaper and faster data management, interactive media, and increasing capabilities for mass customization. (p. xiii)

While the idea of one to one marketing is no longer revolutionary, the effective implementation of such systems in an online retail setting is still in its infancy. The leaders in the field, such as Amazon.com and ActiveDecisions.com, continue

---

[1] Moore's law states that computing power doubles approximately every 18 months.

to experiment with their approach and refine their techniques, yet their execution remains awkward and is often rudimentary. For example, Amazon.com found itself in hot water over the apparent personalization of prices across different segments of consumers. According to *USA Today* (2000), "Amazon has faced allegations—which it denies—that the varying prices were based on customer data it obtained via software interactions with shoppers as they visited its site. Because of the consumer outcry, Amazon ended up refunding 6,896 customers an average of $3". While such dynamic pricing has been common place among airline passengers for years, customers buying DVDs at Amazon were not willing to accept different prices (whether they were randomly chosen, as Amazon claims, or based on knowledge about the individual shoppers as some customers have claimed).

In addition, some early anecdotal evidence and academic research have suggested that the personalized recommendations of firms such as Active Decisions may not be meeting customers needs (Fitzsimons & Lehmann, 2001). Therefore, it appears that while the potential benefit of personalization on the Internet is substantial, effectively implementing such a system remains an elusive goal. Although the science and practice of influence have been thoroughly researched and refined for interactions between humans (e.g., Cialdini, 2001)—for example, between a shopper and a retail salesperson—little is known about the ability of an electronic device, such as a computer, to influence a human. In the quest to play a more active role in their customers' decision processes, e-tailers have turned to personalizing individual shopping experiences, without a detailed understanding of what the underlying processes of influence may be when the interaction is between a human and a computer. This chapter reviews some well established theories from marketing and psychology that we believe can contribute to a solid foundation for the personalization of the shopping experience and provide Internet merchants with the conceptual keys to take a more active role in online consumers' decision-making processes. In particular, we focus on some of the early evidence regarding the personalization of product recommendations by interactive computer-mediated decision aids.

CONSUMER RATIONALITY AND THE STABILITY OF PREFERENCES

The Standard Economic Model

Given that we are interested in how consumers make decisions in environments that can be personalized at the individual level, a brief review of contemporary perspectives on consumer decision making is in order. Traditional economic analyses of preference and consumer choice are based on a formal axiomatic approach. According to McFadden (1999) "the *standard model* in economics is that consumers behave *as if* information is processed to form perceptions and beliefs using strict Bayesian statistical principles (*perception-rationality*), preferences are primitive, consistent and immutable (*preference-rationality*), and the cognitive process is simply preference maximization, given market constraints (*process-rationality*)" (p. 75). The economic perspective is primarily concerned with connecting the inputs of the decision process to the ultimate decision. This approach has contributed a great deal to the development of models that aim to predict consumer choice. However, the past 25 years of research into consumer judgment and decision making have found evidence that the standard assumptions about preference, perception, and process rationality almost never hold. While most human behavior is to some degree rational, there is overwhelming evidence against the assumptions of rationality as the basis of any broadly applicable model of consumer decision making. In the following section we briefly review two approaches[2] to understanding consumer choice that have led the way in the accumulation of evidence against the standard economic theory.

The Perceptual Framework

One approach, the perceptual framework, is most closely associated with the work of Tversky and Kahneman (e.g., Tversky & Kahneman, 1974, 1981; Kahneman & Tversky, 1979; Tversky & Simonson, 1993), and is built upon a large body of research, which demonstrates that consumers' preferences are sensitive to the way in which a choice is presented. In their 1981 article, *The Framing of Decisions and the Psychology of Choice*, Tversky and Kahneman summarized their findings as follows: "The psychological principles that govern the perception of decision problems and the evaluation of probabilities and outcomes produce predictable shifts of preference when the same problem is framed in different ways" (p. 453). In essence, they found in study after study that the choices people made were not based so much on the objective merits of the choice alternatives under investigation as on the subjective context in which the problem was set. This evidence is in direct contrast to the assumption that preferences are consistent and immutable (preference-rationality).

The Effort/Accuracy Framework

Another approach to the study of consumer decision making takes a cost-benefit perspective and views the decision making process as a trade-off between the accuracy of the decision and the effort required to make the decision. This approach to understanding choice, epitomized by Payne, Bettman, and Johnson (1993) is based on the idea that consumers have a number of different strategies available to them that they can use to make any particular choice. Which strategy is ultimately chosen depends "on some compromise between the desire to make an accurate decision and the desire to minimize cognitive effort. Since the accuracy and effort

---

[2]See Bettman, Luce, and Payne (1998) or Payne (1982) for a more complete review of these two approaches.

characteristics generally differ across strategies for a given decision environment and across environments for a given strategy, strategy usage will vary depending on the properties of the decision task" (Bettman, Luce, and Payne, 1998, p. 192). The evidence from this stream of research contradicts the assumption that value maximization is the only strategy used by decision makers (i.e., process-rationality), and the assumption that consumers form beliefs and preferences using strict Bayesian statistical principles (i.e., perception-rationality).

Constructive Consumer Choice Processes

Recently, Bettman, Luce and Payne (1998)[3] have argued that these two streams of research can be tied together under a more general heading of constructive preferences. They propose a framework, which recognizes that individuals' information-processing capacity is limited (e.g., Bettman, 1979) and that most decisions are consistent with the notion of bounded rationality in that decision makers seek to attain some satisfactory, although not necessarily maximal, level of achievement (Simon, 1955). As a result of these constraints, individuals typically do not have well-defined preferences that are stable over time and invariant to the context in which decisions are made (Bettman, Luce, & Payne, 1998). Instead, decision makers tend to construct their preferences on the spot when they are prompted either to express an evaluative judgment or to make a decision (Payne, Bettman, & Johnson, 1993).

THE POTENTIAL FOR INFLUENCE IN ELECTRONIC ENVIRONMENTS

The theory of constructive preferences views choice as a function of the task, the decision maker, and the environment in which the decision is made. Because the task environment plays an important role in consumers' construction of preference, digital environments, such as those found on the World Wide Web, which are interactive (rather than static) and personalizable at the individual level (rather than standardized), have the potential to influence consumer preferences and, ultimately, purchase decisions in a significant way (Johnson, Lohse, & Mandel, 2004).

Recent research has highlighted the role of one particular type of online personalization tool in the construction of consumer preference (Häubl & Murray, 2003): a recommendation agent. We conceptualize an electronic recommendation agent as a software tool that attempts to understand a human decision maker's multiattribute preference with respect to a particular domain or product category based on a learning (or calibration) phase during which the human reveals subjective preference information to the agent, and makes recommendations in the

---

[3]The reader is directed to the original paper for more detail on the constructive preferences theory of consumer decision making.

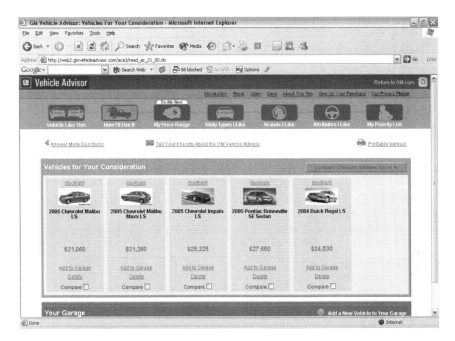

FIG. 12.1   GM's vehicle advisor screen shot. © 2003 General Motors Corporation.
All Rights Reserved.

form of a sorted list of alternatives to the human based on its understanding of that individual's preference structure (see also Häubl & Trifts, 2000).

One real-world example of this type of recommendation agent is General Motor's Vehicle Advisor (http://web2.gmvehicleadvisor.com), which plays the role of a virtual salesperson by asking the shopper questions about his or her preferences for different automobile attributes. For example, if you were in the market for a new vehicle, the vehicle advisor may ask you what body types you like, how much you care about acceleration, how important fuel economy is, and how much you are willing to spend. After answering these questions, you are presented with a list of product recommendations that has been personalized for you based on your responses (Figure 12.1).

The ability of this type of recommendation agent to effectively assist consumers in their decision-making process has recently come under investigation. In general, researchers have found that a recommendation agent can be a very effective decision aid, which allows consumers to make better decisions with less effort than decisions made by consumers without access to an agent (Häubl & Trifts, 2000). This is an important benefit to consumers who have traditionally been forced to make a trade-off between the quality of their choice and the amount of effort they devote to making a decision. However, for the recommendation agent to effectively improve decision quality while simultaneously reducing the consumer's effort, the

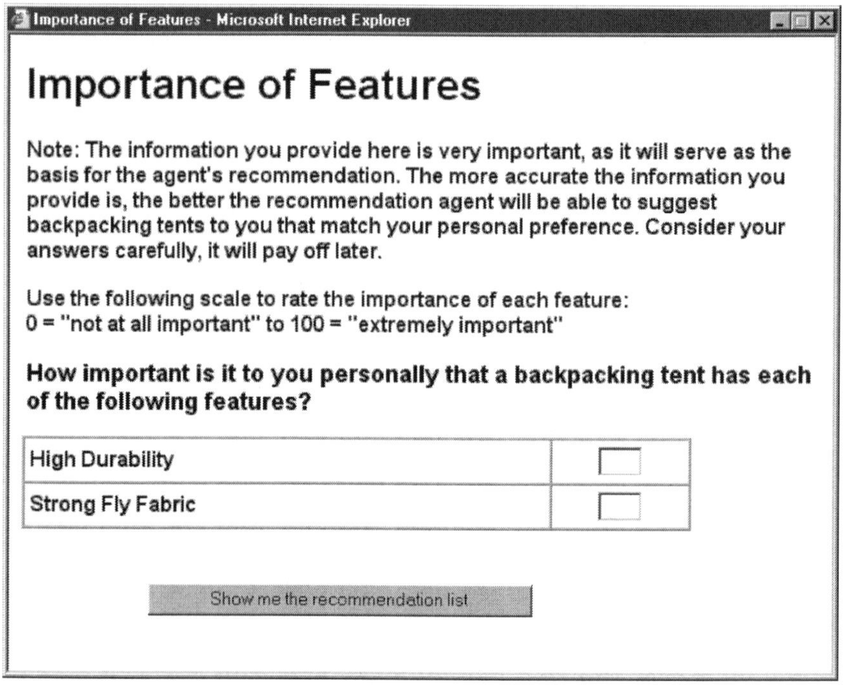

FIG. 12.2   Elicitation of preference information.

human must rely upon the machine to screen the universe of products (i.e., the marketplace) and return a personalized recommendation. Clearly, this requires that the human place some trust in the operation of the recommendation agent. As a result, the consumer can become vulnerable to being influenced by such agent.

We recently examined this possibility in a laboratory study that used an online store in which participants were invited to shop for a backpacking tent (Häubl & Murray, 2003). All participants used a recommendation agent, which asked the shoppers to specify their preferences for particular tent attributes. However, unlike the recommendation agent in Häubl and Trifts (2000), this agent was very selective in terms of the information it elicited from different shoppers.[4] In particular, shoppers were separated into two groups. One group was asked how important weight and warranty is to them when choosing a tent. The other group was asked how important durability and fly fabric is to them when choosing a tent (see Fig. 12.2).

_____

[4]Recommendation agent's of the type used in Häubl and Murray (2003) and Häubl and Trifts (2000) elicit consumer preferences for particular attributes that are relevant to the recommendation being made. The recommendation agent then develops a model, typically a multiattribute preference model, based, for example, on a weighted additive evaluation rule (Payne, Bettman, & Johnson, 1993), which it uses to develop its recommendation.

Therefore, the recommendation agent in this experiment was highly selective: each group was asked about only two attributes, and the agent did not attempt to elicit any further preference information. The recommendation agent then searched the product space based only on this selective preference information and provided the shopper with a list of tents that was rank-ordered based on the attribute preferences the shopper had reported. As a result, although all products were available to the shopper for viewing, their presentation order was based only on the preference information for two attributes.

The recommendation agent was made selective because, almost inevitably, real-world attribute-based recommendation agents are selective in the sense that only a subset of all the relevant product attributes can be used in their calibration and, thus, in the algorithm used to generate the recommendations. This is apparent in the implementation of many commercial recommendation systems for online shopping (see, e.g., Active Decisions' Guide or GM's Vehicle Advisor). The reasons for such selectivity in recommendation agents include: the very large number of attributes that exist in many product categories; the substantial amount of data about, or interaction with, a consumer that would be required to develop an accurate understanding of the consumer's subjective preference in a high-dimensional attribute space; an inclination to use only those attributes that are common to most or all available products; and a tendency to include only attributes that are quantitative in nature (i.e., the levels of which can be represented numerically). Apart from these reasons, the selective inclusion of attributes in a recommendation agent may also be driven by strategic objectives (e.g., to de-emphasize specific attributes) on the part of whoever controls the design of the agent.

We found that the attributes that were included in the recommendation agent became more important in the shoppers' decision-making process than those attributes that were excluded from the agent. Therefore, as seen in Fig. 12.3, the

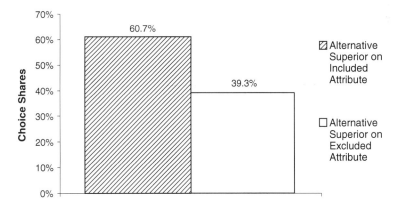

FIG. 12.3 Attribute inclusion in the agent and choice shares in the agent-assisted shopping task.

TABLE 12.1
Effect of Perceived Rationale for Attribute Inclusion on Amount
of Information Search

Perceived Rationale for Attribute Inclusion in Recommendation Agent	Mean Amount of Time Spent Searching (in seconds)	Mean Number of Alternatives Searched
Strong		
(Attributes were selected because they are important.)	62.71	7.75
Neutral		
(Attributes were selected arbitrarily.)	81.91	9.00
Weak		
(Attributes were selected because they are unimportant.)	83.60	9.64

majority of subjects chose products that were superior on attributes included in the recommendation agent. This *inclusion effect* was especially strong when subjects were forced to make trade-offs between attributes in choosing a tent, – that is, when buying a more durable tent means that the tent is heavier or when buying a lighter tent means that the tent is less durable.[5] When trade-offs were necessary, we found that the vast majority of shoppers chose the tent that was superior on the attributes that were included in the recommendation agent. However, this effect was not ubiquitous. We did not find any effect when subjects shopped in a marketplace that did not require trade-offs between attributes, that is, when buying a more durable tent meant that the tent was also lighter[6] (see Fig. 12.3). Moreover, we found that the amount of effort, in terms of the number of alternatives searched and the time spent searching through the marketplace, that consumers exerted during the decision process was influenced by the rationale we provided for the selectivity of the agent[7] (see Table 12.1). These results clearly indicate that the preferences of human decision makers can be influenced in a systematic and predictable manner by an electronic recommendation agent.

---

[5]With regards to the experimental design, subjects who shopped in such a marketplace were choosing among tents whose primary attributes (weight and durability) were negatively correlated in terms of utility. This marketplace closely resembles real-world marketplaces wherein trade-offs between attributes (for example, price and quality) must normally be made.

[6]A marketplace wherein the primary attributes (weight and durability) were positively correlated in terms of utility.

[7]The *perceived rationale for attribute inclusion* (the reason provided to participants as to why the recommendation agent was selective) was manipulated at three levels. Subjects were informed that the attributes included in the recommendation agent were selected (1) because of their high importance to a relevant group of consumers who participated in a recent study ("strong" rationale), (2) randomly from the set of pertinent attributes ("neutral" rationale), or (3) because, although they have been considered to be of low importance by other consumers who participated in a recent study, they should be given some attention in the decision process ("weak" rationale). This manipulation was embedded (as one sentence) in the task instructions that participants were asked to read at the beginning of the experiment. For greater detail on the method, procedure, and results of this study, see Häubl and Murray (2003).

Consumer Susceptibility to Influence

Given the potential influence of a recommendation agent on consumers' choice processes, one may wonder why a consumer would be willing to provide personal preference information to such an agent. Earlier we suggested one of the reasons, which is apparent from the results of Häubl and Trifts (2000): by using a recommendation agent, consumers can make a better decision with less effort. As a result, the consumer is able to circumvent the usual effort/accuracy trade-off when they rely on the recommendations provided by an agent.

A second reason that consumers may use a recommendation agent even though it can affect their choice process stems from consumers' own beliefs about the strength of their preferences and about the ability of an electronic tool to influence them. Research in this area recognizes that consumers, and human decision makers in general, tend to be overconfident about what they know and their ability to make appropriate choices (Alba & Hutchinson, 2000). Of particular relevance to our discussion here is the tendency for people to be overconfident or overly optimistic about their abilities when the outcome is potentially desirable but difficult to forecast (Pulford & Colman, 1996)—the desirability bias. This applies to consumers and their relationship with agents insofar as they may be overly optimistic about their ability to counteract any influence that an electronic recommendation system may have on their behavior. Alba and Hutchinson (2000) explain this general tendency as follows:

> Some biases are too subtle to be corrected by even the most vigilant decision maker. Other biases achieve a level of awareness that may prompt efforts to take corrective action. Wilson and Brekke (1994) reviewed various aspects of "mental contamination" and provide some preliminary evidence that people overestimate their ability to avoid it. We speculate, based in part on the evidence reviewed above, that it would be unsurprising to find overconfidence is one's immunity to the biasing influences in life. Indeed, embedded throughout Nisbett and Wilson's (1977) critique of verbal reports is informal evidence that people hold confident but erroneous beliefs about the determinants of their own decisions. (p. 137)

Consumers may not be aware of the influence that a recommendation agent can have on their decision making; however, even if they are, evidence exists to suggest that they may be overly optimistic about their ability to correct for this bias and to avoid mental contamination in their decision making. Therefore, it is reasonable to believe that consumers will rely on recommendation agents to assist them in their shopping even though such assistance requires that the consumer trust and rely upon the agent. This trust and reliance on the recommendation agent is analogous to a traditional shopper's reliance on a salesperson. The shopper may know that recommendations are partial, yet believe that she or he is capable of correcting for this bias in their decision making. Therefore, consumers may be willing to rely upon biased recommendations, hoping to reduce their effort while improving the quality of their decisions.

Given the potential for electronic decision aids to influence consumers' decision-making processes, their preferences, and ultimately their choice of products, it is important for us to better understand the processes by which online shoppers may be influenced. In the next section, we discuss three mechanisms for preference construction in digital marketplaces and in particular examine the potential of each of these mechanisms to operate when an online shopper uses a recommendation agent.

PROCESSES OF PREFERENCE CONSTRUCTION IN PERSONALIZED DIGITAL SHOPPING ENVIRONMENTS

In this chapter we consider three mechanisms that can play an important part in preference construction when online shoppers rely on a recommendation agent to personalize their shopping environment: priming, format driven processing, and inferences based on conversational logic. While other mechanisms may also be at work in situations that allow for a personalized presentation of product information, these three mechanisms have been selected because they have strong theoretical foundations and because early research into online consumer behavior has recognized their importance (Häubl & Murray, 2003). These mechanisms range in the level of consumer consciousness at which they operate from the unaware (priming) to conscious cognitive processes (inference based on conversational logic). Although a combination of these mechanisms may play a part in consumers' preference construction in electronic environments, different processes are likely to play a predominant role in different situations.

Priming

One mechanism for influencing consumer preference formation in online environments is through the use of associative feature-based priming. This form of priming implies a spreading activation mechanism that renders one or more cognitive concepts more easily accessible in memory (see, e.g., McNamara, 1994; Srull & Wyer, 1979). In turn, this enhanced accessibility may lead to an increase in the likelihood that the primed concept (e.g., a category, decision rule, or feature) is used by an individual, as long as the concept is relevant to the cognitive task at hand and no other competing concept is chronically more accessible (see Herr, 1989).

In a consumer decision-making context, exposure to a prime that is associated with a particular product category-relevant feature or attribute may lead a consumer to attach greater weight to this attribute when evaluating available products or making a purchase decision. For example, priming certain product attributes prior to exposure to an advertisement may increase the salience of these attributes in consumers' minds and, by affecting the manner in which ambiguous advertising information is processed, influence product evaluations (see Yi, 1990). Similar feature-based priming is also evident in recent work by Mandel and Johnson (2002), which demonstrates the possibility of influencing individuals' preferences by merely altering the background of a web page that subjects view prior to completing a product choice task. These researchers systematically varied the background of an introductory web page, with different types of backgrounds intended to prime different product attributes, and showed that the weight of an attribute in preferential choice was enhanced as a result of the priming manipulation. For example, in one experiment Mandel and Johnson invited participants to shop for a sofa in a simulated online store. They then primed the participants using either a background with clouds, which pretests indicated was a prime for comfort, or a background with pennies, which pretests indicated was a prime for price. They found that those who had pennies in the background preferred cheaper, less comfortable sofas as compared to those who were primed on comfort.

In general, the effectiveness of a prime depends on subjects being unaware of the priming effect (Higgins, Bargh, & Lombardi, 1985). Because prime-related increases in construct activation and accessibility are temporary (Wyer & Srull, 1981), one would expect any preference construction effects based on feature priming to be confined to situations in which the exposure to the prime occurs. The long-term effect on consumer preferences is likely to be minimal. In other words, because the priming effect simply increases accessibility and does not involve a change in the internal representation of preference for the primed attributes, the effect of priming a particular attribute or set of attributes in a choice task should not persist beyond the initial context of the prime. However, the preference constructed as a result of the influence of the prime may persist if the preference itself is reflected upon and therefore becomes deeply encoded. For example, in our sofa buying scenario, it may be the case that the buyer is unaware of the impact of the pennies' prime. Nevertheless, the prime activates the concept of price, which leads to thoughts about the importance of price, which in turn results in a preference for cheaper sofas that may endure long after exposure to the initial prime. Having purchased a cheaper sofa results in a preference for cheaper sofas, because price is subsequently considered an important feature by which sofas should be compared (Carpenter & Nakamoto, 1989).

This type of feature-based priming—where a given attribute is primed by exposure to a stimulus associated with that feature immediately before an evaluation or choice task—may explain the predicted preference construction effect due to the inclusion of an attribute in a recommendation agent. In the process of interacting with (i.e., calibrating) such an agent, consumers may be primed on those attributes that are considered by this decision aid. As a result, the inclusion of a set of attributes in a recommendation agent during an online shopping trip may enhance their salience in consumers' minds and, therefore, increase the importance of these attributes in a purchase decision made during this shopping trip.

Format of Information Presentation

A substantial amount of research effort has been devoted to studying the effects of the format of information presentation on how individuals acquire and process information. The results of this body of work suggest that the manner in which information is presented tends to have a substantial impact on human information processing and decision making (Bettman & Kakkar, 1977; Jarvenpaa, 1989, 1990; MacGregor & Slovic, 1986). The notion that the format of information presentation may influence decision making is formalized in Slovic's (1972) *principle of concreteness*. The latter suggests that human decision makers tend to use only that information that is explicitly displayed in a stimulus environment and process this information only in the form in which it is presented. This principle is based on the argument that, in order to reduce the cognitive costs associated with the integration of information, decision makers will discount, or even ignore, any information that has to be stored in memory, inferred from the display, or transformed (see Payne, Bettman, & Johnson, 1993).

An important property of the information presentation format created by a recommendation agent is that decision makers are provided with a rank-ordered list of products. The findings of a classic study by Russo (1977) suggest that information displays that are in the form of a list in which the available alternatives are sorted by a particular attribute (unit price, in his case) make it easier for individuals to process that attribute and increase the latter's importance in decision making. Similarly, a selective recommendation agent's list format[8] may render the included attributes relatively more processable, since it is these attributes that determine the order in which alternatives are displayed.[9] In turn, this enhanced processability may lead to an increase in the relative weight that consumers attach to the included attributes when making a purchase decision. Thus, the mere inclusion of an attribute in a recommendation agent may affect consumer preferences via the format in which information about available products is presented.

However, such an effect on consumer preferences cannot be expected to hold under all circumstances. In particular, individuals do tend to depart from the particular type of processing that is encouraged by the format of information presentation if the cost of the potential inaccuracy (e.g., of making an inferior choice) that may

---

[8] In general, recommendation agents make their recommendations in the form of a list, ranked in descending order with the most attractive products (based on the preference information provided by the shopper) at the top of the list.

[9] It is worth noting, however, that a recommendation agent does not merely provide a list of products that are sorted by a single attribute, but rather a list that is *personalized* in that products are rank-ordered by their likely attractiveness to the consumer based on the agent's understanding of the consumer's preference with respect to (a subspace of) the multiattribute product space.

result from such processing is significant (see Coupey, 1994). Consumers will use the information in the format in which it is provided when doing so results in acceptable decision quality, but not when this would lead to a vastly inferior decision outcome. This suggests that, if the inclusion effect were a result of the format of information presentation, it would depend critically upon the level of decision quality that may be achieved by considering only the attributes that are included in the recommendation agent relative to the quality of a decision that is based on all attributes.

Similar to, but distinct from, the format driven processing mechanism is the notion recently articulated by Kivetz and Simonson (2000) that, in their decision making, consumers give more weight to attributes that are common between options. In other words, when information is selectively presented or when complete information about each product is unavailable, buyers will tend to compare the alternatives on the basis of the information (or attributes) that are common between the alternatives. Moreover, the authors demonstrated that consumers tend to interpret the information that is not common between alternatives (i.e., the missing information) in a way that supports the choice they made based on the common information. This is interesting because it suggests that when presenting products in side-by-side comparisons, an online store can influence consumer choice by controlling what information is common across products and what information is unavailable. Although not directly applicable to the recommendation agent example from Häubl and Murray (2003), these findings do provide further evidence that the format in which information is presented can have a considerable effect on consumer judgment and decision making.

Inferences Based on Conversational Logic

A third possible mechanism by which a recommendation agent may influence consumer preferences is based on the notion that the inclusion of an attribute in the agent may be *informative* with respect to the *importance* of that attribute. Consumers might assume that the particular attributes that are used in the calibration of a recommendation agent have been included because they are relevant and important aspects of the alternatives in the product category of interest. In line with the theory of conversational logic, which suggests that exchanges of information are generally guided by a cooperative principle (Grice, 1975; Levinson, 1983), consumers likely to believe that the electronic agent has been designed so as to be a meaningful tool that is capable of assisting them in their decision making. This is also consistent with the finding by Wernerfelt (1996) that, in most circumstances, it is in a firm's best interest not to mislead its customers, but rather to help them make purchase decisions that, given their subjective preference, are optimal for them. Since the providers of recommendation agents (e.g., online retailers) can be expected to be well-informed with respect to the nature of preferences in the population (e.g., which attributes are, on average, the most important ones), this expertise should be reflected in the choice of attributes that are included in such tools. Therefore, the composition of the set of included attributes may carry information about the relative importance of the different attributes in the marketplace.

Since consumers tend to have preferences that are less than well-defined (see Bettman, Luce, & Payne, 1998), they may revise or refine these preferences on the basis of what they learn about other consumers' preferences. Through the set of attributes that it is based on, a recommendation agent may convey information about attribute importance in the population of relevant consumers. Individuals may use this information regarding others' preferences to make inferences about their own preferences and, consequently, revise their beliefs as to how important different attributes are to them personally. That is, the selective inclusion of certain attributes in a recommendation agent—and thereby, the exclusion of other attributes—may cause consumers to alter the internal representation of their preference such that the subjective importance of the included attributes is increased relative to that of the excluded attributes. The information value of the inclusion of attributes in an electronic agent and its effect on preferences is, therefore, a potential explanation of the inclusion effect found by Häubl and Murray (2003). This mechanism is similar in spirit to the one documented by Prelec, Wernerfelt, and Zettelmeyer (1997), who found that consumers tend to view the characteristics of the set of available alternatives as carrying some information about the distribution of tastes in the population of consumers and, in turn, use this information as a basis for making inferences about their own preferences. The difference is that, in the present context, it is the inclusion of attributes in a recommendation agent, rather than the composition of the set of available alternatives, that is deemed to convey information about others' preferences.

The Three Mechanisms and the Inclusion Effect

While the format driven processing and the priming mechanisms may well have played a role in the inclusion effect found by Häubl and Murray (2003), these two mechanisms are unable to provide an adequate explanation as to why the effect fails to appear in the marketplace where no attribute trade-offs are required (i.e., the marketplace with positive interattribute correlations, see Fig. 12.4).

In contrast, the mechanism based on the information value of attribute inclusion predicts that this preference construction effect will be more pronounced when the correlation between included and excluded attributes is negative than when this correlation is positive. In a decision environment in which interattribute correlations are positive, consumers may quickly realize that any attribute can be used as a basis for their decisions without sacrificing accuracy, because an alternative that is favorable on one attribute tends to also be favorable on other attributes. However, in a marketplace characterized by negative interattribute correlations, a more attractive level of one attribute tends to be associated with a less attractive level of another attribute and, therefore, purchase decisions require trade-offs among

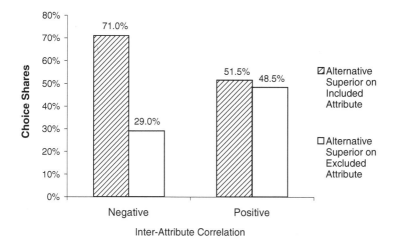

FIG. 12.4 Inclusion effect: Moderating role of inter-attribute correlation.

attributes. In such an environment, which may be characterized as a highly efficient market, the relative importance that is attached to different attributes tends to be highly consequential with respect to the decision outcome—even very small changes in relative attribute importance may affect which of a set of alternatives is chosen. Therefore, if the inclusion effect were due to a revision or refinement of subjective importance weights based on the information value of attribute inclusion, we would expect this type of preference construction effect to be stronger when the correlation between included and excluded attributes is negative rather than positive.

Does Preference Construction in Digital Marketplaces Persist?

Given the evidence that preferences can be constructed during online shopping with the assistance of a recommendation agent, it is interesting to consider whether or not such preferences will persist into situations where the agent is no longer present. In the experiment described earlier (Häubl & Murray, 2003), we investigated this possibility by asking participants to make choices between pairs of tents after they had completed their shopping trip. We found that the constructed preferences did persist into decision making situations where the agent is not present and does not make any recommendations. In choices made without agent assistance, we found that consumers whose preferences were initially affected by the selectivity of the recommendation agent had a 48% greater preference for those attributes that had been included in the agent during an earlier agent-assisted shopping trip than for those that had not been included.

Recent work by Muthukrishnan and Kardes (2001), examining persistent preferences for attributes, provides support and context for our findings. In particular, their research has demonstrated that in "choice contexts that create very little preference uncertainty, the initial preference for the focal attribute offers a tentative causal theory that links the attributes of the chosen brand with the key benefits of the product" (p. 101). We know from the work of Häubl and Trifts (2000) that an external (and objective) recommendation from an agent can increase consumers' confidence in (i.e., reduce their uncertainty about) the choice they have made. In the case of a selective recommendation agent, the focal attributes are those that the agent asks the consumer for preference information about, which results in a constructed preference for those attributes (Häubl & Murray, 2003). Therefore, it is likely that when a recommendation agent leads a consumer to believe a particular attribute (or set of attributes) is important—whether that belief is driven by priming, the format of presentation of the information, or an inference based on conversational logic—the preference for that attribute will persist beyond the initial decision making context to subsequent choices within the same product category. This notion of persistent preferences based on preference construction in an earlier choice environment is also supported by the literature on pioneering and the first-mover advantage (e.g., Carpenter & Nakamoto, 1989; Carpenter, Glazer, & Nakamoto, 1994).

Preference Construction and Online Shopping

Over 30 years of research in consumer behavior and decision making taught us that, in many instances, consumer preferences are constructed as opposed to the traditional economic assumption that preferences are consistent and immutable. As a result, consumers are highly sensitive, even vulnerable, to the properties of the task environment. In this chapter we discussed three cognitive processes that can influence consumer choice: priming, format driven processing, and inferences based on conversational logic. Although we used the example of recommendation agents, and discussed their ability to influence consumers' preferences and consumers' choices, these same processes are likely to apply much more broadly in digital shopping environments. Because consumers are limited in their ability to process information, and because they are weighing required effort against decision accuracy, a personalized choice environment that reduces effort while improving accuracy is very attractive. However, relying on an electronic tool to personalize a digital environment may make the consumer vulnerable to influence within that environment.

Based on the research discussed in this chapter, it is apparent that some important differences do exist between shopping in a traditional retail format and shopping in electronic environments. In particular, we focused on the potential of a vendor to influence consumers' choice processes by exerting control over the decision environment to an extent that would be impossible in a traditional store. For example, GM's Vehicle Advisor is able to sort and present all of its vehicles, across numerous brands and models, without the limitations inherent to any one dealer's inventory, based on the information provided by the shopper. Moreover, it is able to do this for each individual shopper, whether there is one person at the site or thousands of people are receiving advice simultaneously. Clearly, it is worth the effort to better understand the processes that affect consumer choice in electronic environments, because the ability to personalize the shopping environment, and thereby influence the shopper, has the potential to be a significant source of competitive advantage for online retailers.

ACKNOWLEDGMENT

The authors gratefully acknowledge the support provided by the Social Sciences and Humanities Research Council of Canada (SSHRC grant 410-99-067 & 538-2002-1013), the University of Alberta, the Institute for Online Consumer Studies (www.iocs.org), and Allaire Corporation. This research also benefited from a Canada Research Chair in Behavioral Science, the R. K. Banister Professorship in Electronic Commerce, a Petro-Canada Young Innovator Award and a Nova Corporation Faculty Fellowship, awarded to Gerald Häubl, as well as from the Pool Ph.D. Endowment Fellowment Fellowship, the University of Alberta School of Business Ph.D. Fellowship, and the Province of Alberta Graduate Fellowship awarded to Kyle Murray. Correspondence should be addressed to the first author at the Richard Ivey School of Business, University of Western Ontario, 1151 Richmond St. N., London, Ontario, Canada, N6A 3K7. Email: kmurray@ivey.uwo.ca

REFERENCES

Alba, J. W., & Hutchinson, W. (2000). Knowledge calibration: What consumer know and what they think they know. *Journal of Consumer Research, 27*(September), 123–156.

Bettman, J. R. (1979). *An information processing theory of consumer choice.* Reading, MA: Addison-Wesley.

Bettman, J. R., & Kakkar, P. (1977). Effects of information presentation format on consumer information acquisition strategies. *Journal of Consumer Research, 3*(March), 233–240.

Bettman, J. R., Luce, M. F., & Payne, J. W. (1998). Constructive consumer choice processes. *Journal of Consumer Research, 25*(December), 187–217.

Carpenter, G. S., Glazer, R., & Nakamoto, K. (1994). Meaningful brands from meaningless differentiation: The dependence on irrelevant attributes. *Journal of Marketing Research, XXXI*(August), 339–350.

Carpenter, G. S., & Nakamoto, K. (1989). Consumer preference formation and pioneering advantage. *Journal of Marketing Research, XXVI*(August), 285–298.

Cialdini, R. B. (2001). *Influence: Science and practice (4th ed.).* Needham Heights, MA: Allyn & Bacon.

Coupey, E. (1994). Restructuring: Constructive processing of information displays in consumer choice. *Journal of Consumer Research, 21*(June), 83–99.

Fitzsimons, G., & Lehmann, D. (2004). Reacting to recommendations: When unsolicited advice yields contrary responses. *Marketing Science, 23*(1), 82–94.

Grice, H. P. (1975). Logic and Conversation. In P. Cole & J. L. Morgan (Eds.), *Syntax and semantics, 3: Speech acts* (pp. 41–58). New York, NY: Academic Press.

Häubl, G., & Murray, K. B. (2003). Preference construction and persistence in digital marketplaces: The role of electronic recommendation agents. *Journal of Consumer Psychology, 13*(1), 75–91.

Häubl, G., & Trifts, V. (2000). Consumer decision making in online shopping environments: The effects of interactive decision aids. *Marketing Science, 19*(1), 4–21.

Herr, P. M. (1989). Priming price: Prior knowledge and context effects. *Journal of Consumer Research, 16*, 67–75.

Higgins, E. T., Bargh, J. S., & Lombardi, W. (1985). The nature of priming effects on categorization. *Journal of Experimental Pyschology: Learning, Memory and Cognition, 11*, 59–69.

Jarvenpaa, S. L. (1989). The effect of task demands and graphical format on information processing strategies. *Management Science, 35*(March), 285–303.

Jarvenpaa, S. L. (1990). Graphic displays in decision making—the visual salience effect. *Journal of Behavioral Decision Making, 3*, 247–262.

Johnson, E. J., Lohse, G. L., & Mandel, N. (2004). Designing marketplaces of the artificial: Four approaches to understanding consumer behavior in electronic environments. Unpublished manuscript, Columbia University, New York.

Kahneman, D., & Tversky, A. (1979). Prospect theory: An analysis of decision under risk. *Econometrica, 47*(2), 263–291.

Kivetz, R., & Simonson, I. (2000). The effects of incomplete information on consumer choice. *Journal of Marketing Research, XXXVII*(November), 427–448.

Levinson, S. C. (1983). *Pragmatics.* Cambridge, UK: Cambridge University Press.

MacGregor, D., & Slovic, P. (1986). Graphical representation of judgmental information. *Human Computer Interaction, 2*, 179–200.

Mandel, N., & Johnson, E. J. (2002). When Web pages influence choice: Effects of visual primes on experts and novices. *Journal of Consumer Research, 29*(2), 235–245.

McFadden, D. (1999). Rationality for economists? *Journal of Risk and Uncertainty, 19*(1), 73–105.

McNamara, T. P. (1994). Theories of priming II: Types of primes. *Journal of Experimental Psychology: Learning, Memory, and Cognition, 20*(3), 507–520.

Muthukrishnan, A. V., & Kardes, F. R. (2001). Persistent preferences for product attributes: The effects of the initial choice context and uninformative experience. *Journal of Consumer Research, 28*(1), 89–104.

Nisbett, R. E., & Wilson, T. D. (1977). The halo effect: Evidence for unconscious alteration of judgments. *Journal of Personality and Social Psychology, 35*(April), 250–256.

Payne, J. W. (1982). Contingent decision behavior. *Psychological Bulletin, 92*(September), 382–402.

Payne, J. W., Bettman, J. R., & Johnson, E. J. (1993). *The adaptive decision maker.* New York, NY: Cambridge University Press.

Peppers, D., & Rogers, M. (1993). *The one to one future: Building relationships one customer at a time.* New York, NY: Doubleday.

Prelec, D., Wernerfelt, B., & Zettelmeyer, F. (1997). The role of inference in context effects: Inferring what you want from what is available. *Journal of Consumer Research, 24, 1*(June), 118–125.

Pulford, B. D., & Colman, A. M. (1996). Overconfidence, base rates, and outcome positivity/negativity of predicted outcomes. *British Journal of Psychology, 87*(August), 431–445.

Russo, J. E. (1977). The value of unit price information. *Journal of Marketing Research, 14, 2*(May), 193–201.

Simon, H. A. (1955). A behavioral model of rational choice. *Quarterly Journal of Economics, 69*(Feb), 99–118.

Slovic, P. (1972). From Shakespeare to Simon: Speculations—and some evidence—about man's ability to process information. *Oregon Research Institute Bulletin, 12*(2).

Srull, T. K., & Wyer, R. S. (1979). The role of category accessibility in the interpretation of information about persons: Some determinants and implications. *Journal of Personality and Social Psychology, 37*, 1660–1672.

Tversky, A., & Kahneman, D. (1974). Judgment under uncertainty: Heuristics and biases. *Science, 185, 27*(September), 1124–1131.

Tversky, A., & Kahneman, D. (1981). The framing of decisions and the psychology of choice. *Science, 211, 30*(January), 453–458.

Tversky, A., & Simonson, I. (1993). Context-dependent preferences. *Management Science, 39*(10), 1179–1189.

USA Today (2000, September 29). *Amazon may spell end for dynamic pricing.* Retrieved August 15, 2000, from: http://www.usatoday.com/life/cyber/tech/cti595.htm

Wernerfelt, B. (1996). Efficient Marketing Communication: Helping the Customer Learn. *Journal of Marketing Research, 33*(May), 239–246.

Wilson, T. D., & Brekke, N. (1994). Mental contamination and mental correction: Unwanted influences on judgments and evaluations. *Psychological Bulletin, 116*(July), 117–142.

Wyer, R. S., & Srull, T. K. (1981). Category accessibility: Some theoretical and empirical issues concerning the processing of social stimulus information. In E. T. Higgens et al. (Eds.), Hillsdale, NJ: Lawrence Erlbaum Associates.

Yi, Y. (1990). The effects of contextual priming in print advertisements. *Journal of Consumer Research, 17*, 215–222.

IV. SITE DESIGN

CHAPTER THIRTEEN

Effects of Visual Consistency on Site Identity and Product Attitude

Richard C. Omanson
User Centric, Inc.

June A. Cline
Wayne State University

Christie L. Nordhielm
University of Michigan

INTRODUCTION

As use and acceptance of the Web grows, companies have expanded their online presence. As Web channels have expanded to include multiple product families, two contrasting approaches to presenting products have emerged. One approach focuses on differences in the target market of products (cf., Eccleshare, Forsyth, Gollmer, Haldar, Kirillova, & Ortega, in press) and varies the presentation across product families. A contrasting approach focuses on making navigation easy (cf., Lynch & Horton, 1999; Nielsen, 2000) and adopts a single presentation style.

Consider the experience of Joe who is shopping for stereo systems for his apartment and car. He goes to Sony's Web site (hereinafter referred to as site) (www.sony.com) to look for both products. When he goes to the home audio section to look for a stereo, he sees a blue and white page with clean navigation and product photos (see Fig. 13.1).

After making his selection, Joe navigates to the car stereo section. Here he is taken to red and white section with an irreverent attitude and scattered navigational controls (see Fig. 13.2). Except for the Sony name, these two sections look like sites from different companies.

Contrast Joe's experience with that of Jennifer who is shopping for the same two products at Panasonic's site (www.panasonic.com). Jennifer goes to Panasonic's home audio section and finds a silver and blue page with photos of individual

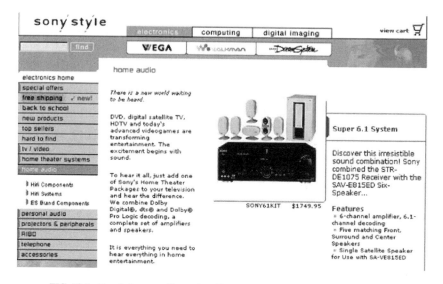

FIG. 13.1 Sony's home audio section. From www.sony.com, November 1, 2001. Copyright 2001 by Sony Electronics, Inc. Used with permission.

FIG. 13.2 Sony's car stereo section. From www.sony.com, November 1, 2001. Copyright 2001 by Sony Electronics, Inc. Used with permission.

FIG. 13.3   Panasonic's home audio section. From www.panasonic.com, September 11, 2001. Copyright 2001 by Matsushita Electric Corporation of America. Reprinted with permission.

products and side-bar navigation (see Fig. 13.3). After making her selection, she goes to the car stereo section. The color scheme, layout, navigation, and font are similar to that used in the home audio section. There is no doubt that Jennifer is on the same site (see Fig. 13.4).

A striking difference between the product presentation strategies adopted by Sony and Panasonic is their visual consistency. Panasonic maintains visual

FIG. 13.4   Panasonic's car stereo section. From www.panasonic.com, September 11, 2001. Copyright 2001 by Matsushita Electric Corporation of America. Reprinted with permission.

consistency in its presentation of different products while Sony does not. The research presented in this chapter examines some effects that the visual consistency of product presentation has on customers' perceptions of Web sites and products. In regards to site perceptions, the first experiment examines aspects of visual consistency that affect site identity (i.e., knowing the site to which one has gone). In regards to product perceptions, the second experiment examines the joint effect of visual consistency and repetition (how many pages are viewed) on product attitudes. Considered together, these experiments have implications for customer relationships and brand strategy.

SITE IDENTITY

Background

The relation between visual consistency and site identity is complex because visual consistency is not a unitary construct. Visual consistency varies along multiple dimensions or features such as logo, page layout, background, and color scheme. Conceivably, individual features of sites could be used to make site identity judgments in a number of ways. The notion considered here is that multiple features are considered in site identity judgments, but that some features, notably the logo, are given more weight than other features.

The notion that some features are more relevant to site identity has intuitive appeal. For example, the authors conducted a pilot study with 18 web-site designers attending the 2000 Digital Edge Convention sponsored by Greenfield Online. Using a 4-point scale (not important, somewhat important, important, very important), the designers were asked to rate the importance of seven features (logo, font, page layout, color palette, page title, background, and navigation scheme) in establishing site identity in various situations. When a site is first created, 78% said the logo was very important; when two sites are combined, 94% gave it the highest rating. In contrast, the dimension with the next highest rating, navigational scheme was given the highest rating by 67% of the designers in both situations. Thus, the designers rated multiple features as important to site identity, but considered the logo the most important.

Omanson, Cline, Kilpatrick, and Dunkerton (1998) provided empirical evidence that users weight the logo more than other features in making site identity judgments. These authors investigated what features of web pages are used while making site identity judgments. Nineteen participants viewed a series of 42 web pages taken from 17 Web sites. After each page, the participants were asked to rate on a 5-point scale whether they were at the same or different site. For each judgment, they were also asked which aspects of the site influenced their judgment. The participants' written descriptions were categorized revealing nine features of web pages, which are summarized in Table 13.1.

TABLE 13.1
Features of Web Pages Used in Site Identity Judgments

Dimension	Definition	Type
Topic	The subject matter of the web page.	Within page: semantic
Heading	Title at the top of the page.	Within page: semantic
Logo	Company symbol and tag line.	Within page: visual
Background	Background color or pattern of the page.	Within page: visual
Layout	Organization of the page's text and graphics.	Within page: visual
Navigation	Graphical or text links to the major sections of the site that are grouped together along the left, right, top, or bottom of the page.	Within page: visual
Graphics	Style of graphics used in pictures, banners, and illustrations.	Within page: visual
Typestyle	Font style used and its characteristics such as size, color, and emphasis.	Within page: visual
Link label	Correspondence between a link label and the target page.	Between pages: semantic

To see if some of these features are relied upon more than others, Omanson et al. (1998) then showed 24 of the web pages to a second group of 168 participants. For each page, participants rated on a 5-point scale if they were on the same or different site. For each judgment, they also checked which of the eight within-site features they used to make the judgment. Regression analyses were done separately for participants with previous and no previous Web experience and for within and between site judgments. Users with previous Web experience relied on multiple dimensions to make site identity judgments. Only the logo, however, accounted for an appreciable amount of variance (>.20 compared to <.06 for the other dimensions).

The Omanson et al. (1998) study suggests that users consider multiple features of web pages when making site identity judgments, and that of those features, logo is relied on most. Building on these previous results, the relative importance of logo versus the remaining visual features was examined. To do so, changes in logo were varied independently from changes in other visual features (e.g., those comprising the overall "look and feel"). Specifically, we examined how site identity judgments were affected when going to a different site (site transitions) was marked by (i.e., were in sync with) changes in either logo or look and feel.

The notion that people consider multiple features, but give more weight to logo, when they note site identity suggests the following predictions:

1. Site identity judgments will be equally accurate when site transitions are marked only by changes in logo as when they are marked by changes in the entire look and feel.
2. Site identity judgments will be most accurate when site transitions are marked by changes in both logo and look and feel.

TABLE 13.2
Relation of Site Transitions to Experimental Conditions

	Transitions marked by (in sync with) changes in logo	Transitions not marked by (out of sync with) changes in logo
Transitions marked by (in sync with) changes in look and feel	Condition 1	Condition 3
Transitions not marked by (out of sync with) changes in look and feel	Condition 2	Condition 4

Method

Procedure.   The study had four conditions, each with its own set of materials. Each set consisted of 17 web pages taken from four different sites. Two elements, logo and look and feel were manipulated in varying degrees (see Table 13.2).

As shown in Table 13.2, transitions to new sites were marked by changes in both logo and look and feel in Condition 1, by changes in look and feel in Condition 2, by changes in logo in Condition 3, and were not marked by changes in either logo or look and feel in Condition 4.

Each set of web pages was shown to 20 different graduate and undergraduate students at two large Midwestern universities. For each page, students indicated if they were on the same or a different site from the previous page. Identity judgments were scored in terms of their correspondence to site transitions. Scores could vary from 0 to 16, depending on how many judgments corresponded to the site transition cues.

Results

A 2×2 factorial analysis of variance (ANOVA) was used to determine if there was a difference in the number of correct responses to the site identification task by logo and look and feel. The two levels of logo were in or out of sync. The same two levels were used for look and feel. The results revealed a significant difference for both logos, $F(1, 76) = 32.04$, $p. < .001$, and look and feel, $F(1, 76) = 16.76$, $p. < .001$. Performance was better when either of these dimensions were in sync with site transitions. These results are shown in Fig. 13.5.

To further examine the significant results for the two main effects, three nonorthogonal comparisons using t tests were made. As shown in Fig. 13.5, users were more accurate when site transitions were marked by changes in both the look and feel and logo ($M = 14.6$) than when they were marked by either just logo, ($M = 12.5$, $t = 2.2$, $p = .031$), or by just look and feel ($M = 11.4$, $t = 3.28$, $p = .002$). There was not a significant difference in accuracy between transitions marked by only the logo versus by only the look and feel ($t = 1.09$, $p = .277$).

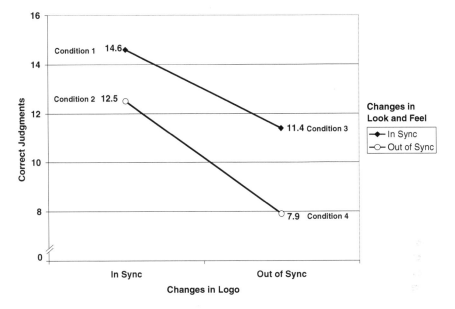

FIG. 13.5   Effect of logo and look and feel on site identity judgments.

Discussion

The results of this experiment supported the notion that people consider multiple features, but give more weight to the logo, when they make site identity judgments. The results supported the prediction that judgments will be most accurate when transitions were marked by changes in both logo and look and feel as well as the prediction that site identity judgments will be equally accurate when transitions by marked by changes in either just the logo or just the look and feel. Although changes in logo were as effective as changes in the entire look and feel in signaling site transitions, users did not rely on the logo to the exclusion of all other cues. In fact, in the Conditions 3 and 4, where logo was out of sync with site transitions, users tended to ignore the logo altogether.

PRODUCT ATTITUDES

Background

The second impact of visual consistency considered here is its effect on customers' attitude toward products. An interesting result of Web shopping on pages with the same look and feel is that customers are repeatedly exposed to the same visual features. Conversely, changes in the look and feel across pages will result in a different pattern of repetition. A rich literature on repetition effects in advertising can therefore inform our theoration in this area.

Advertising Repetition Effects. The predominant finding in advertising repetition studies is that their positive effect on product attitude wears out with repeated viewing (e.g., Calder & Sternthal, 1980; Craig, Sternthal & Leavitt, 1976; McCullough & Ostrom, 1974; Schumann, Petty, & Clemons, 1990). When people first see ads, they feel more positive about and are more willing to buy, the advertised products. After a few exposures, however, people get tired of the ads, and after that point, the more they see the ads, the less they like the products.

The underlying mechanism of the ad repetition effect involves the conscious processing described by a two-factor theory. Initial repetitions generate familiarity (positive habituation), resulting in positive thoughts so that the number of positive thoughts increases during initial presentations. Later repetitions generate tedium resulting in negative thoughts so that the number of negative thoughts increases. How well products are liked is hypothesized to be the net of both positive and negative thoughts. Therefore, liking will increase initially as the number of positive thoughts increases with additional exposure, then decline as the influence of negative thoughts exceeds that of positive thoughts (Batra & Ray, 1986; Cacioppo & Petty, 1979).

An exception to the wearout effect of ads was reported by Nordhielm (in press-a, in press-b). Nordhielm noted that ads are composed of visual features (similar to those discussed in Omanson et al., 1998). Repeated exposure to specific features of an ad has a positive effect on product attitude that does not wear out. In one experiment, female participants were shown either 8 or 80 pictures of jewelry. Each picture had the same horizontal or vertical background. Following these exposures, participants were shown an additional picture of jewelry displayed on the same background and asked to rate their attitude toward and willingness to buy the final piece of jewelry. Participants who were exposed to 80 pictures had higher liking and intent to purchase ratings than those who were exposed to only 8 pictures.

To explain these results, Nordhielm proposed a dual-process model in which features of an ad are processed either perceptually or conceptually. Perceptual processing involves encoding of surface features of stimuli, whereas conceptual process involves evaluation of the semantic content (Jacoby & Dallas, 1981). According to the dual process model, the benefit on affect of repeated exposure to features that are processed conceptually wears as described by the two-factor theory. In contrast, the benefit on affect of repeated exposure to perceptually processed features does not wear out and is described by a perceptual fluency/misattribution (PF/M) model (Bornstein & D'Agostino, 1994; Jacoby, Toth, Lindsay, & Debner, 1992; Mandler, Nakamura, & Van Zandt, 1987). Perceptual fluency is defined as the ease with which people perceive, encode, and process stimulus information. According to the PF/M model, the perceptual fluency of a stimulus can be heightened by factors such as prior exposure. While people often experience increases in their perceptual fluency following stimulus exposure, they generally lack insight into the true cause of such experiences. In these instances, they misattribute the cause of their perceptual fluency to any variable (such as liking) that happens to be salient at that moment.

Repeated exposure to a feature that is perceptually processed increases the ease with which the feature is perceptually processed on subsequent trials (i.e., it increases perceptual fluency, Mandler et al., 1987). Thus, after viewing different ads for a product that uses the same background, users are more apt to say they like the product because they misattribute the increase in perceptual fluency.

Web Page Repetition Effects. Extending Nordhielm's work to the Web, we predict that repeated exposure to visual features that are perceptually processed will enhance customers' attitude toward products (product attitudes). Just as Nordhielm found that background features were perceptually processed, we hypothesize that the features constituting a page's look and feel (i.e., color, graphical style, layout, and navigation, Omanson et al., 1998) likewise will be perceptually processed. Specifically, we predict that repeated exposure to the same look and feel will result in more positive attitude toward products. A second prediction concerns the location of the pages with the same look an feel, the positive effects of repeated exposure will not be limited to the section in which the product is displayed.

There are two lines of reasoning to support this second prediction. First, since the mechanism behind the hypothesized repeated exposure effect is nonconscious perceptual processing, the conceptual context in which the exposure occurs should not have an effect. Second, changing the look and feel across sections may result in the visual features to be conceptually rather than perceptually processed. This is because the addition of new perceptual objects captures attention (e.g., Atchley, Kramer, & Hillstrom, 2000; Watson & Humphreys, 1995).

To test these predictions, participants were shown pages from a Web site in which the number exposures to the same look and feel and whether they occurred in either the same or different sections of the site was varied.

Method

Procedure. The study had four conditions, each with its own set of materials. Each set of materials consisted of web pages taken from three sections (Kitchenware, Closet and Bath, and Dinnerware) of a retail Web site. Two of the sets (high repetition) had nine pages per section while the remaining two (low repetition) had three. Also, in two of the sets (consistency between) the look and feel of the sections was the same, while in the remaining two (consistency within) the look and feel of the sections was different. In addition, the two low repetition sets also had 18- filler pages from a Web site depicting desktop photos of scenery so that both the low and high repetition set contained 27 web pages (see Table 13.3).

Each set was shown to 22 graduate and undergraduate students at a large-urban university on a PC (for a total of 88 participants). After viewing the

TABLE 13.3
Relation of Repetition to Experimental Conditions

	Nine pages per section (High repetition)	Three pages per section (Low repetition)
Sections look the same (Consistency between)	Condition 1	Condition 3
Sections look different (Consistency within)	Condition 2	Condition 4

pages, the participants were asked a series of demographic questions. Then they were asked to rate the last three products on five 9-point bipolar affect scales (appealing/unappealing; high quality/low quality; pleasing/not pleasing; desirable/undesirable; satisfying/unsatisfying) and on two 9-point buying scales (willing to try/not willing to try; would buy/would not buy).

Results

A 2 × 2 factorial multivariate analysis of variance (MANOVA) was used to determine if there were differences in the like and buy responses between section. The two levels of repetition were high and low. The two levels of visual consistency were between and within sections.

The results of the multivariate analysis of variance provided no evidence of statistically significant differences for the two main effects, repetition and visual consistency. The interaction effect between repetition and visual consistency was not statistically significant.

PRODUCT ATTITUDE: DELAYED TESTING

Background

The fact that repeated repetition to the same look and feel had no statistically significant effect on product attitude was surprising. One possible reason for the lack of significance may be related to the time of testing. In similar work on perceptual priming, the effects of exposure persisted, and in some cases, grew stronger, over time (Sloman, Gordon, Ohta, Law, & Tulving, 1988). The reason for growing stronger over time seems to be due to factors in the immediate situation (e.g., product preference, recency effects) that mask the effect. When testing occurs after these factors fade from short-term memory, the effects of mere exposure emerge. To see if the effect of repeated exposure to the same look and feel increased after more time elapsed, the participants rated the products a second time, approximately 2 to 4 weeks after the initial exposure.

TABLE 13.4
Number of Respondents in Each Condition

Condition	N
1 - High repetition – Sections look the same	8
2 - High repetition – Sections look the same	11
3 - Low repetition – Sections look different	11
4 - Low repetition – Sections look different	14

Method

Procedure.   The product-rating questionnaire used during immediate testing was sent to all the participants via email; who were asked to rate the products again. Half of the participants ($N = 44$) returned the questionnaire. The number of questionnaires returned in each condition is presented in Table 13.4.

Design.   The design of the delayed testing product attitude experiment was the same as that used in immediate testing, namely a 2×2 between subjects design. The first independent variable, repetition, was the number of web pages (high = 9, low = 3) in each of the three sections (Kitchenware, Closet and Bath, Dinnerware). The second independent variable, visual consistency, was whether the look and feel of the three sections were the same or different. Since only half of the participants returned their questionnaires, the seven rating scales were summed to yield a single product attitude score for each participant.

Results.   A 2×2 factorial univariate analysis of variance was used to determine if there were differences in the overall product attitude responses, using two independent variables: repetition and visual consistency. Scores for the high repetition conditions ($M = 6.2$, $SD = .25$) were significantly higher than scores in the low repetition conditions ($M = 5.7$, $SD = .22$) $F(1, 43) = 6.32$, $p = .016$. Although there was a difference between the high and low visual consistency conditions, the effect was not statistically significant. These results are shown in Fig. 13.6.

To further examine the significant results for the repetition main effect, a nonorthogonal comparison using a t test was developed comparing the high repetition/within section visual consistency with low repetition/between section visual consistency. A statistically significant difference was obtained, $t(76) = 2.2$, $p = .031$.

Discussion

There are two conclusions that can be drawn from the delayed testing. First, testing 2 to 4 weeks later supported the prediction that repeated exposure to the same look and feel will result in more positive attitude toward products. Participants who

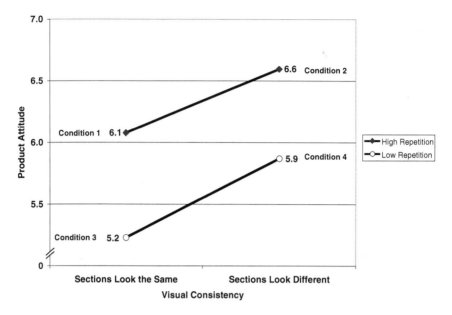

FIG. 13.6   Effect of repetition and visual consistency on product attitude.

were exposed to many rather than few exposures of the look and feel had a more positive attitude toward the target products.

Second, the prediction that increasing the exposures to pages in different sections that had the same look and feel will result in more liking was not supported. Increasing the exposures to pages with the same look and feel did not enhance product attitude if the exposures occurred in sections different from those containing target product. This localization of the repetition effect was particularly evident in the planned comparison. Both Conditions 2 and 3 had nine repetitions of the target products' look and feel. In Condition 3, the repetitions were evenly distributed across all three sections. In Condition 2, the repetitions occurred in only the target section. The result of this comparison indicated that receiving nine exposures to the look and feel had a greater positive impact on product attitude when if occurred within a section than between sections.

GENERAL DISCUSSION

Effects of Presentation Style

The results of these two experiments have several implications for Web channel design. One set of implications concerns the effects of varying the presentation style of products. The first experiment demonstrated that varying the look and feel of a site can mislead users into thinking they have left the site when in fact they have just gone to a different section (site identity confusion). Site identity confusion can disrupt the development of loyalty and good customer relationships; a positive experience on a site won't enhance loyalty if it is attributed to the wrong company. This is of particular concern for manufacturing companies who have adopted a distinct branding (as opposed to umbrella branding) strategy. Single-product branding presents each brand or product family to its target market with a unique presentation and selling proposition to meet the expectations of the different market segments (cf., Eccleshare et al., in press). For example, a packaged goods company such as Procter & Gamble (P&G) manufacturers a wide variety of products under distinct brand names and product positioning strategies. In the brick-and-mortar world where these products are distributed in separate sections of a supermarket, this strategy is unproblematic. A consumer visiting the P&G Web site, however, may experience confusion as they move from brand to brand within the Web site. In contrast, the strong umbrella identity of a company such as BMW (Bauarian Motor Works) will be further enhanced in an online environment. As companies increasingly utilize the Internet to communicate with consumers, the strategic issue of the relative benefits of umbrella versus distinct branding strategies must be considered for this specific arena.

The most effective way to avoid site identity confusion is to present products throughout the site in the same manner. If for branding reasons, it is important to vary presentation of products, the results of the first experiment also suggest that placing the logo on every page will reduce site identity confusion. The amount of change in the look and feel, however, needs to be modest or a transition to a new site still will be falsely signaled. In other words, even when logo is held constant, there still is a need to provide enough continuity to prevent different sections from looking like different sites.

While the first experiment suggests that site identity confusion is an important concern, differences in look and feel do not appear to have a negative impact on product liking as long as there is consistency within each section. Whether or not other sections of the site had the same look and feel neither enhanced nor diminished this effect. This differential impact of look and feel on site identity confusion versus product liking warrants further investigation. Intuitively it makes sense that confusion about site identity would lead to negative affect toward specific products, yet this result was not observed here. In addition, future research on the effects of visual consistency on site identity confusion should focus on understanding how many changes can occur before a site transition is signaled, and how signaling interacts with site activity, content, and design.

Effects of Repetition

A second set of implications concern the effects repetition. The main aspect of product presentation that affected product attitudes was repetition. The more pages people saw (within a section that looked the same) the better people liked the product. It is important to distinguish the concept of within site repetition studied here with the concept of stickiness that has been considered important for site performance in the past. Several years ago, designers were encouraged to create sticky sites that kept users on a site (e.g., Davenport, 2000). Critics (e.g., Sherwin & Avila, 2001) point out that stickiness is ineffective in boosting sales because features like chat and games that promote stickiness do not promote sales. The repetition effect observed in this work differs from stickiness in that it is the result of seeing many pages that present products in the same manner rather than the amount of time spent anywhere on site.

As previously discussed, the study of the influence of repetition on liking has a rich research heritage in both the consumer behavior and cognitive psychology literature. The online environment is unique with respect to this research because it provides a context where the total number of distinct exposures to an image over the course of a particular site visit can be extremely high. Given this distinctive aspect of the online milieu, further exploration of the influence of repetition in this specific environment is clearly warranted. In particular, research into the impact of extremely high exposure frequency as well as further exploration of the influence of exposure duration on online attitudes would provide valuable information.

Effects of Time

A final set of implications concerns the effect of time. The second experiment showed that repeated exposure to the same look and feel affected product attitudes only after the person had been away from the site. The finding that the amount of interaction people had with products on the Web site affected long-term attitudes toward the products has implications for cross-channel merchandising. This finding implies that attitudes formed from viewing products on the Web may influence purchases made later in the store. More research is needed in this area to understand the nature of cross-channel shopping and what influences the buying decision.

ACKNOWLEDGMENTS

This research was supported in part with funding from the Kraft Corporation. The authors would like to thank the following people who contributed their time and expertise to this research: Dr. Sally Large, Dr. Bill White, and Dr. Donald Marcotte for making their classes available for testing; Bob Domenz and Sidney Raynal for collecting and summarizing data at the 2000 Digital Edge Convention; Stuart Stoddard for writing the web page display program and for assisting in testing sessions; Ian Watts and Roberta Lai for constructing testing materials; Sara Omanson and Hannah Roberts for assisting in the testing sessions; and Karen Keenan for providing editorial comments.

REFERENCES

Atchley, P., Kramer, A. F., & Hillstrom, A. P. (2000). *Journal of Experimental Psychology: Human Perception and Performance. 26*(2), 594–606.

Batra, R., & Ray, M. (1986). Situational effects of advertising repetition: The moderating influence of motivation, ability and opportunity to respond. *Journal of Consumer Research, 12*, 432–445.

Bornstein, R. F., & D'Agostino, P. R. (1994). The attribution and discounting of perceptual fluency: Preliminary tests of a perceptual fluency/attributional model of the mere exposure effect. *Social Congnition, 12 (Summer)*, 103–128.

Cacioppo, J. T., & Petty, R. E. (1979). Effect of message repetition and position on cognition response, recall, and persuasion. *Journal of Personality and Social Psychology, 37*, 97–109.

Calder, B., & Sternthal, B. (1980). Television commercial wearout: An information processing view. *Journal of Marketing Research, 17*, 173–186.

Craig, C. S., Sternthal, B., & Leavitt, C. (1976). Advertising wearout: An experimental analysis. *Journal of Marketing Research, 13*, 365–372.

Davenport, T. H. (2000, February 1). Sticky business. *CIO Magazine*. Retrieved April 24, 2002, from http://www.cio.com/archive/020100/davenport.html

Eccleshare, W., Forsyth, J., Gollmer, J., Haldar, S., Kirillova, S., & Ortega, M. (in press). Different audiences exhibit different behavior and have different expectancies: Understanding the e-consumer: A behavioral approach to e-market segmentation. In C. P. Haugtvedt, K. Machleit, & R. Yalch (Eds.), *Online consumer psychology: Understanding and influencing consumer behavior in the virtual world*. Hillsdale, NJ: Lawrence Erlbaum Associates.

Jacoby, L. L., & Dallas, M. (1981). On the relationship between autobiographical memory and perceptual learning. *Journal of Experimental Psychology: General 110*, 306–340.

Jacoby, L. L., Toth, J. P., Lindsay, D. S., & Debner, J. A. (1992). Lectures for a layperson: Methods for revealing unconscious processes. In R. F. Bornstein & T. S. Pittman (Eds.), *Perception without awareness: Cognitive, clinical and social perspectives*. New York: Guilford.

Mandler, G., Nakamura, Y., & Van Zandt, B. J. S. (1987). Nonspecific effects of exposure on stimuli that cannot be recognized. *Journal of Experimental Psychology: Learning Memory and Cognition, 13*, 646–648.

McCullough, J. L., & Ostrom, T. M. (1974). Repetition of highly similar messages and attitude change. *Journal of Applied Psychology, 59*, 395–397.

Nielsen, J. (2000). *Designing Web usability: The practice of simplicity*. Indianapolis, IN: New Riders.

Nordhielm, C. L. (2002). The influence of level of processing on advertising repetition effects. *Journal of Consumer Research, 29*, 371–382.

Nordhielm, C. L. (2003). A dual-process model of advertising repetition effects. In R. Batra & L. Ray (Eds.), *Persuasive imagery: A consumer response perspective*. Mahwah, NJ: Lawrence Erlbaum Associates.

Omanson, R. C., Cline, J. A., Kilpatrick, C. E., & Dunkerton, M. C. (1998, October). Dimensions affecting web site identity. Paper presented at the meeting of the Human Factors and Ergonomics Society, Chicago, IL.

Schumann, D., Petty, R., & Clemons, D. S. (1990). Predicting the effectiveness of different strategies of advertising variation: A test of the repetition-variation hypotheses. *Journal of Consumer Research, 17*, 192–202.

Sherwin, G., & Avila, E. (March, 2001). The fall of the cult of stickiness. *ClickZ Network*. Retrieved November 16, 2004, from http://www.clickz.com/experts/archives/ebiz/ecom_comm/article.php/839661.

Sloman, S. A., Gordon, C. A. G., Ohta, N., Law, J., & Tulving, E. (1988). Forgetting in primed fragment completion. *Journal of Experimental Psychology: Learning, Memory, and Cognition, 14*, 223–239.

Watson, D. G., & Humphreys, G. W. (1995). Attention capture by contour onsets and offsets: No special role for onsets. *Perception and Psychophysics, 57*(5), 583–597.

CHAPTER FOURTEEN

Gendered Information Processing: Implications for Web Site Design

Elizabeth Purinton
Marist College

Deborah E. Rosen
University of Rhode Island

In an era of such books as *Men Are From Mars: Women Are From Venus* (Gray, 1992) and *You Just Don't Understand: Women and Men in Conversation* (Tannen, 1990), it is no surprise that there is a wealth of theory and supporting research on the differences in how males and females process information. This chapter examines those differences and then goes on to explore how those differences will play out in the Web environment. The purpose of this chapter is to:

1. Describe gendered differences in information processing.
2. Present cognitive landscape theory as a way of understanding Web sites.
3. Present some ways males and females will process Web sites differently and some research in this field.
4. Offer examples of Web site elements that illustrate elements of effective Web site design.
5. Suggest what Web site designers should keep in mind.

The first step in understanding this link between information processing, sex differences, and Web site design is to examine gender differences in information processing.

INFORMATION PROCESSING AND GENDER

Information processing refers to how stimuli are received, interpreted, stored, and retrieved. Understanding this process is important to many disciplines including communication, cognitive psychology, marketing, and advertising.

How individuals process information will be greatly influenced by personal factors such as motivation, attitude, knowledge, culture, social class, and education. One of these factors is gender. Why gender affects information processing may be because of biological (sex differences) or social factors (gender differences) and possible origins of those differences are discussed later in this section. Although in lay terms *sex* and *gender* are synonymous, the two terms are different. Sex is biologically determined and considered "dichotomous" whereas gender incorporates gender identity, sex roles, and socially learned behaviors and expectations.

A vast number of studies, undertaken in a wide variety of fields including social psychology, anthropological psychology, and biology, have looked at gender differences. Although differences have been found in spatial ability, memory, and making judgments, the most dramatic difference between males and females is in their information-processing strategies. Males and females use different strategies in processing information, including use of different types of information and different levels of elaboration, resulting in different judgments.

Males and females, when faced with the same information, will use different amounts of it when they form judgments. These differences have often been explored using the Selectivity Model (Meyers-Levy, 1988; Meyers-Levy & Maheswaran, 1991; Meyers-Levy & Sternthal, 1991). This states that males typically employ a single cue or a few cues that lead to a single inference. That is, men will rely on a subset of highly available cues to form a judgment (Darley & Smith, 1995).

This combination of different use of information and different levels of processing can be summed up by saying that males are "selective processors" and more likely to use *heuristic processing* in place of more detailed processing. That is, they will use simplified processing or educated guesses so that they are able to base their conclusions on less information. These heuristics, which substitute for more detailed processing, are focused on the goal of efficiency.

Females, on the other hand, are "comprehensive processors" and will attempt to assimilate all available cues (Tanaka, Panter, & Winborne, 1988). Females are more likely to make use of all available information (Meyers-Levy, 1988; Meyers-Levy & Sternthal, 1991). This results in deeper processing of all information given whereas men are more apt to draw inferences (Meyers-Levy & Sternthal, 1991). Then, they will draw logical conclusions from the available information and "fill in" the missing parts (Stern, 1993) in order to form judgments and make sense of confusing or cluttered visual stimuli such as a Web site. This has further implications for preferences in the organization of material, use of graphics and pictures, and differentiation of a Web site.

When forming opinions, women's judgments reflect greater consideration of message cues than do men's judgments. Women evoke more description and more associative, imagery-laced interpretation when faced with nonverbal stimuli (Wood, 1966; Nowaczyk, 1982). Furthermore, women seem to be more able to readily access the thoughts that led to their judgments (Stern, 1993).

Although there is ample evidence to demonstrate that sex differences exist, the next question is: Are there factors that will mitigate these differences? Two of those factors discussed here are time allowed for processing and gender-orientation of the stimuli.

Some of the studies regarding sex differences have found time to be an issue. Sex differences are evident when the subjects are given time to process the information, but when time is greatly limited, sex differences disappear (DePaulo & Rosenthal, 1979; Meyers-Levy & Sternthal, 1991). These findings suggest that, when under a time pressure to process information, males and females both use heuristics to come to a judgment as quickly as possible (Meyers-Levy & Sternthal, 1991). It is only when sufficient time is allowed, such as in unhurried Web surfing, that males and females use different strategies.

Another factor manipulated in some studies was gender schema. That is, when males and females are exposed to gender-specific stimuli, they may react differently. Previously, the theory was that women will engage in greater elaboration of female-specific stimuli[1] and males will engage in greater elaboration of male-specific stimuli. Presenting males with masculine items or females with feminine items is considered "congruous." In one study, women engaged in greater elaboration of visual stimuli whether the content was male (incongruous), female (congruous), or nongender specific (Krugman, 1966).

Many studies of gendered information processing have been done in cognitive and anthropological psychology and in biology. Another area of this research is marketing. Current marketing research on gendered information processing has been done in product judgment (Meyers-Levy, 1988; Meyers-Levy & Sternthal, 1991), product information evaluation and advertising (Darley & Smith, 1995). Figure 14.1 provides a summary of the studies presented here.

As Web activity requires information processing, it is logical to expect these differences to persist and possibly be useful in Web design.

Potential Origins of Gendered Information Processing

There are several, often interwoven, explanations for these gender differences. Often, researchers outside the fields of biology or psychology profess to unknown causes or will cite several potential origins but are unwilling or unable to discern which is at work. Most will leave the topic untouched.

---

[1]Female-specific objects used in studies included such pictures as grooming appliances, children, a feminine hat, and a unicorn. Male-specific objects included tools, sports equipment, a cowboy hat, and a necktie. Nongender- specific objects included an umbrella, a clock, a key, and animals.

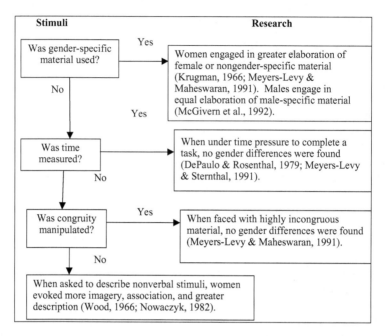

FIG. 14.1 A Summary of Research on Gender Differences in Information Processing.

Theories originate from two disciplines: social psychology (gender) and biology (sex). Social psychological explanations tend to coalesce around two concepts, division of labor and sex roles. These are discussed first. Biological foundations are centered in sex hormones and in brain structure.

Division of labor and sex roles are two highly related concepts that have been theorized to result in different information-processing strategies. The theory that division of labor results in different cognitive skills is rooted in the concept that, as gatherers (rather than hunters), women have greater spatial ability[2] than males. Studies measuring this had conflicting results (Silverman & Eals, 1992, 1994, found females to have greater spatial ability; Nyborg, 1983, found males to have greater spatial ability). Division of labor, in turn, is one of the origins of sex roles.

Male and female sex roles are considered "agentic" and "communal," respectively. That is, males are more concerned with themselves and females with others (Bem, 1981; Meyers-Levy, 1988). Originally, this communal aspect came from women's submissive and subordinate role in society. Hall (1984) theorized that this subordinate/submissive role and a greater dependence on others has motivated

---

[2]Spatial ability is the ability to imagine the position and relationship of imaginary objects. For example, subjects might imagine what an irregularly shaped object would look like if it were rotated in space.

women to greater need to understand "subtle interpersonal cues." This means that greater message elaboration may have originally been socially driven rather than biological.

Further credible explanations for these differences can also be found in biology. Descriptions differ in whether they are rooted in differences in sex hormones or in brain structure, as a result of sex hormones. No solution is given here, merely an overview of the current perspectives.

There are two points in a person's life when sex hormones have a great effect. The first is before birth, the second at puberty. Although it is easy to think of the strong influence of hormones at puberty, at least one group of researchers (Moir & Jessel, 1991) found significant differences in memory capabilities of males and females that were present in both adults and children.

The second perspective is that male and female brains process information differently because of structural differences brought on by sex hormones before birth. This results in greater specialization of men's brains than women's (Moir & Jessel, 1991). Whereas men use one side or another on a problem, women use both. The more feminine the brain (as measured by levels of female hormones) the more diffuse the functions (Hutt, 1972). Furthermore, the hemispheres are organized differently in men and women. Language function in men is in the front and back areas of the left hemisphere whereas in women, these areas are more focused and concentrated in the front (research by Doreen Kimura of Canada, reported in Moir and Jessel, 1994). This means that males and females may perceive the same information differently.

Given different information-processing strategies, does this result in different preferences in Web site design? Site design clearly requires information processing. Hence, it is logical to explore whether these sex differences affect information processing on the Web and how they might impact Web site preferences.

INFORMATION PROCESSING AND THE WEB ENVIRONMENT

Rather than assuming that processing a Web page is like processing any visual stimulus, the Web environment needs to be examined. This section explores relevant theory from cognitive psychology as well as some recent research.

One way of improving our understanding of how consumers process Web sites is to examine cognitive landscape theory and the work of Kaplan and Kaplan and their co-authers (e.g., R. Kaplan, 1973; S. Kaplan, 1973; Kaplan & Kaplan, 1982; Kaplan, Kaplan, & Ryan, 1998) in particular. The Preference Matrix (Kaplan & Kaplan, 1982, 1998) provides a means of sorting out the many site design options (page layout, use of graphics, color, text versus images, etc.) for effectively building a Web landscape.

Cognitive Landscapes

Kaplan and Kaplan (1982) view environments as providing information in many ways—through signs, icons, with or without words. Their studies deal with physical landscape architecture and how to apply cognitive psychology to this area. Further, through their research, they have found that informational needs influence preferences for certain landscapes.

In many ways, designing effective Web content is very similar to designing a physical landscape. Computer interaction is intensely cognitive, involving perceptions and preferences. Interactivity implies not only perceiving the Web landscape but also entering into it and "experiencing" the space. People both want to make sense of and get involved in their landscapes.

Rachel Kaplan and Stephen Kaplan's research, now spanning several decades, stems from the belief that experts do not view the world the way the general public does. The perceptions and preferences of experts, because of their experiences and training, are different from those of the general public. Their research examined physical environments in an attempt to come up with designs that appeal to the users and not the experts designing the landscapes.

Kaplan and Kaplan's research is also predicated on the love-hate relationship that people have with information. We are inundated with information from a wide variety of sources. Some of this information is important, some of it is trivial. In the case of Web design, many developers have lamented that they just started piling on the elements and once they put things in, they were afraid to take things off (Hamilton, 1999). The targets of this information blitzkreig are left with the onerous task of sorting through all of it. Although the seemingly endless capacity of the Web makes it tempting to add more detail, Web designers sometimes forget that information overload is detrimental to both understanding and the ability to keep a viewer's attention.

One way in which humans cope with processing information is through the use of cognitive maps. Using a cognitive or mental map provides us with a means of sorting and storing information from our environment.

Having a cognitive map, however, is not enough. Humans must be motivated to use and extend these maps. One way to encourage this is to provide them with environments that enable them to take advantage of their cognitive maps (S. Kaplan, 1973). Kaplan and Kaplan's research found two critical factors that play a role in motivating the use of cognitive maps: making sense and exploration. Consequently, if designs facilitate making sense and exploration, people will feel more comfortable in a landscape. When people are more comfortable, they are more likely to spend time in an environment, exploring it further by drawing on the information stored in their cognitive maps.

Based on the research of psychologists, architects, and planners, Kaplan and Kaplan (1982) developed a preference framework (Table 14.1) to describe how people satisfy their needs of making sense and exploring in an uncertain world. These desires parallel the needs of Internet users who come to the Web for many reasons (information, to perform transactions, for entertainment, and in some cases, to develop relationships with retailers), which requires making sense of and getting involved in the Web landscape. Making sense (understanding) and exploring (involvement) represent the two basic informational needs. Web users need to be

TABLE 14.1
Preference Matrix

	Understanding	Exploration
Two dimensional	Coherence	Complexity
Three dimensional	Legibility	Mystery

Source: Kaplan, Kaplan & Ryan, 1998, p.13.

able to navigate Web sites, which requires understanding the site content well enough to know how to proceed. One's involvement level will determine whether one wants to proceed.

These needs are further categorized by a time dimension that focuses on immediate versus longer term possibilities that can occur quickly but sequentially. Individuals have preferences for environments that will enable them to meet these needs in the future. What Kaplan, Kaplan and Ryan (1998) term "two-dimensional" time means a focus on immediate surroundings and represents a direct perception of the elements in a scene. In the case of immediate exploration, a relevant question would be, "Does the current Web page provide enough content and variety (complexity) for the Web surfer to be satisfied?" Their three-dimensional time frame refers to future need fulfillment. Humans, as cognitive animals, can quickly calculate the future possibilities of present choices. In future exploration of the Web, a relevant question would be, "Does the current page and the preceding paged explored (if any) lead the surfer to feel there is enough promise of future satisfaction to go on?"

The Preference Framework and The Internet

The Preference Matrix (Table 14.1) makes sound theoretical sense in the context of an information approach to human functioning and is applicable to the Internet as computer interactivity is a highly cognitive, information-laden environment. Each of the elements of this framework can be associated to elements of the Web landscape.

Coherence refers to the degree to which the environmental landscape hangs together. As such, coherence relies on redundancy of elements and textures. This repeat of elements, textures, and structural factors sets the surfer's expectation of how the Web site will be laid out regardless of what page he or she is on and allows one to predict from one portion of a scene to another. In exploring a coherent Web site, a visitor would feel that the page, individually, and the Web site, as a whole, make sense and are well-organized. An example would be the coordinated colors in L.L. Bean's Web site (http://llbean.com). All of the colors in the menubars and the products highlighted give an "outdoorsy" feel, utilizing shades of blue, green, and brown, and this is repeated throughout their Web site.

Legibility is defined by distinctiveness. By possessing a memorable component, a scene facilitates finding one's way. On the Web, this is similar to having a site map to make navigation of the Web site easier or having a distinctive graphic or icon that makes way-finding much more straightforward. The first-time site visitor would feel he or she could navigate the site without any previous experience with it. For example, on L.L. Bean's Web site, the menubar remains positioned at the bottom of the screen no matter to what page one moves. It is relatively easy to see how these first two dimensions can be related to Web site design through elements such as a distinctive icons or including a "return to home page" option on every page.

Complexity refers to the richness of the elements in a setting. A complex Web site would contain a lot of different elements. For example, FTD's Web site (http://ftd.com) contains color photos of floral arrangements, product selection suggestions, short articles, as well as a left-hand menubar for navigation.

Mystery is used in landscape design whereby a curved path is far more enticing than a straight one. Mystery enhances one's desire to explore a space by conveying the feeling that much more can be found if one keeps on going. Mystery may be the one element of Kaplan and Kaplan's (1982) framework that is not relevant to the Web. Consumers, though purchasing online in ever-increasing numbers, actually turn to the Web more for information than purchase. According to a recent study by the Strategis Group (1999), Web use for research is four times greater than Web use for purchasing. The promise of appropriate information rather than intrigue is far more important in explaining Web site preferences. If the information is clear, interesting, and distinctive, one will want to go on. With the Web's ever-present threat of information overload, there is rarely a question of whether the information desired is present but rather how much effort it will take to excavate it. Effort spent on intrigue would, therefore, not be an important consideration for a Web surfer.

Making Web sites "user friendly" requires making them easy to use and understand. By tapping into the cognitive maps individuals employ to make sense of their world, a Web developer can use coherence, complexity, and legibility to build sites users return to over and over again. The Preference Matrix provides a useful way to begin to develop an understanding of how to select appropriate Web content elements.

One of the constant themes of site development guides is that the site must be designed to fit the audience. Many sites have multiple segments to which they cater. We already know that males and females process information differently; does this lead to different preferences? How much flexibility must be built into Web site content to satisfy the increasing diversity of users? The goal of this chapter is to examine differing preferences depending on the sex of the audience.

SEX DIFFERENCES IN WEB SITE PREFERENCE

Combining substantial evidence of differences in information-processing strategies employed by different sexes with what can be learned from cognitive landscape theory, it can be surmised that different Web site designs and combinations of elements will appeal to different sexes. For example, because men make greater use of highly available cues, then they would prefer more graphics. Women, on the other hand, would be more sensitive to more logical, unambiguous layouts so that all information can be assimilated. Therefore, the following hypothesis should be tested.

H1: Men and women will exhibit differences in overall preferences for Web site design.

More specifically, differences in elaboration that facilitate males and females making sense of Web sites will be seen. For instance, women make more use of subtle cues (Meyers-Levy, 1988; Darley & Smith, 1995) and do more elaborative processing (Meyers-Levy & Sternthal, 1991). Men are more likely to be detached readers requiring more validation of source credibility (Stern, 1993). This means women may "read into" the information given more than will men. Hence, scores on coherence will be higher for women because they will find it easier to make sense of the information provided. Thus, within this study, the following hypothesis should be tested.

H1a: Women will rate sites higher on coherence than will men.

The ability to make sense of the Web site information will further allow women to ascertain subtle differences among sites. In Kaplan and Kaplan's (1982) terms, this would mean a greater level of legibility in this site. (Legibility is distinctiveness, a perceived identity and identifiable elements that facilitate navigation.) Further, their greater propensity for elaborative processing means that they are thinking more about the sites, which implies they are more likely to compare sites they have seen. Hence, within this study, women will perceive sites are higher on legibility than men leading to the following hypothesis test.

H1b: Women will rate sites higher on legibility than will men.

Differences will also be seen in exploration preferences. Because men rely on the information given rather than "filling in" with their minds, they are also relying on the visual elements more heavily than women. Men were more likely to be detached readers requiring more validation of source credibility (Stern, 1993) and, hence, more complexity. Darley and Smith (1995) confirmed that men tend to use heuristics processing to form attitudes and make judgments. Hence, within this study, the following hypothesis should be tested.

H1c: Men will rate sites with low complexity scores lower in preference than will women.

On the basis of the preceding discussion, a research study was undertaken to test these hypotheses.

THE STUDY

Purpose of the Study

This empirical study was designed to ascertain whether significant differences exist in preferences of males and females. To this end, a survey measuring Kaplan and Kaplan's (1982) preference factors was administered to a sample of college students as they browsed 10 pre-selected Web sites. A list of the Web sites used can be found in the Appendix.

Measurement and Instrument Development

Each of the dimensions of Kaplan and Kaplan's (1982) Preference Matrix was measured using multiple items, operationalized as a 5-point rating scale where 1 = Strongly Agree and 5 = Strongly Disagree. These items were developed from the work of Kaplan, Kaplan and Ryan (1982, 1998), previous Web site surveys, and open-ended questionnaires in which the respondents (drawn from a student population with the same demographic characteristics as those used in the study presented later) described elements of their Web navigation behavior. Subjects were also asked to assess each site on its overall impression.

An initial draft of the questionnaire was pretested and some questions were modified to correct ambiguities. The revised version of the questionnaire was used in this study.

During factor analysis of the scale items, coherence, complexity, and legibility emerged as separate factors. Mystery did not. This can be seen in Table 14.2. These dimensions exhibit high reliability with coefficient alphas of .86, .84, and .76, respectively. Validity was assessed using focus groups and debriefing sessions.

Data Collection. Subjects in the study were 211 undergraduate students at two Northeastern institutions of higher education. The group was comprised of an equal number of males and females with an age range of 18–25.

One hundred and four males and 105 females completed the survey. As each subject responded to 10 Web sites, this resulted in 1,040 and 1,050 male and female responses, respectively. This represents a near 50/50 split and equal cell sizes for analysis. The males and females in this study were both used to shopping at a mall but substantial differences emerged in catalog and Internet shopping habits. For instance, nearly half of the females purchased from a catalog two to six times per year whereas only one third of the males did. On the other hand, males were more likely to purchase from the Web.

TABLE 14.2
Web Site Preference Factors

	Coherence	Complexity	Legibility
Has logically organized information	.832		
Makes sense	.824		
Is easy to navigate once you get past the home page	.710		
Is well written	.699		
Has enough content to be interesting to repeat visitors	.691		
Caused me to want to learn more	.594		
Easy to get back to the home page from deep within	.460		
Uses many visual images		.814	
Graphics and pictures fit with content		.793	
Uses different types of visual images		.763	
Unlike other sites I have visited			.873
Has created a distinct identity			.832
Has memorable elements			.569
Coefficient alpha	*.8671*	*.8376*	*.7647*
Variance explained	*45.8%*	*12.5%*	*7.72%*

In contrast to their Web-purchasing behavior, where 49% of the students never purchased online, their Web research behavior indicates greater familiarity with the Web. 1% of the respondents never use the Web for research and over 82% use the Web for research on a weekly basis. Consequently, the subjects were generally conversant in navigation on the Web but not necessarily heavy purchasers. This pattern of Internet behavior is representative of user trends at the time of the study (Strategis Group, 1999).

The students were asked to evaluate 10 Web sites while thinking of the site as a whole. The sites selected represent the broad spectrum of sites that Web surfers might visit. Research sites as well as retail sites were selected. The e-retailers and information sites were selected from a variety of categories that this population might patronize. As actual Web sites were chosen for this study, the subjects' familiarity with the sites as well as familiarity with the brands were also assessed as a part of background data-collection efforts.

Data collection took place in a controlled setting. The students were instructed to wander through each site as if they were searching for information using their regular surfing behavior. Because time pressure may mitigate sex differences (DePaulo & Rosenthal, 1979; Meyers-Levy & Sternthal, 1991), students had as much time as they needed to complete the tasks. They were instructed not to complete the evaluation of the site until after they had navigated through the home page and at least three subpages of the site. Evaluation sheets for the sites were distributed in a random order to avoid an order effect. Students were supervised to minimize any discussion and to make sure Web sties, navigational software, and hardware were functioning. To test the hypotheses, the students were asked to evaluate coherence, complexity, legibility, and overall impression.

After data collection, students were debriefed as part of this exploratory study to gain further insight. At this time, subjects were shown Web pages that were exemplars of high and low coherence, legibility, and complexity and were solicited for their opinions of what led to disparities of ratings. Overall exaltations of Web sites in general were discussed.

Hypotheses Tests

Analysis of covariance was performed to test whether differences in Web site preferences exist between different sexes. Familiarity with the Web site was used as a covariate to ensure that familiarity with, and hence preference for, a given Web site or brand name was not responsible for any differences. H1, which states that males and females will have different preferences, was supported by the following tests. H1a states that females will rate sites higher on coherence (Factor 1). The dependent variable was coherence, the degree to which the Web site hangs together. H1a was confirmed at $p < .05$ ($F = 39.985$, $df = 2038$). Females showed a higher average score for coherence (females $X = 8.96^3$, males $X = 9.65$).

H1b, which states females exhibit higher scores on legibility than will males, was supported at $p < .05$ ($F = 5.112$, $df = 2050$). Here, the dependent variable was legibility, or distinctive identity. Females had a higher average score for legibility than males (females $X = 6.1088^4$, males $X = 6.3135$).

To test H1c, which states that in sites with low ratings of complexity, males will rate these sites lower than will females, the four Web sites with the lowest ratings in complexity, or richness of elements, were examined. Four sites were chosen because of a natural break in the ratings. This hypothesis was significant but in the wrong direction at $\alpha = .05$ ($F = 5.488$, $df = 819$). Males exhibited higher preference for sites with low complexity than females (males $X = 2.70$, females $X = 2.75$).

All research hypotheses were tested at $\alpha = .05$ level.

Discussion

This study supports the existing literature that states males and females process information differently and further demonstrates that those differences extend to the Internet. In this study, women demonstrated a greater ability to make sense and find their way in a Web environment.

To further explore these differences, a regression was performed using males' and females' factor scores as independent variables and overall impression as the dependent variable. The resulting regression equations highlight sex differences in preferences. Greater weight was placed on coherence when females were rating overall impression of each site whereas males weighted complexity and legibility

---

[3]Lower scores indicate higher preference.
[4]Lower scores indicate higher preference.

more heavily. The following regression equations show the relative weight of each factor in overall impression:

$$\text{Females' overall impression} = .606 \text{ coherence} + .215 \text{ complexity}$$
$$+ .104 \text{ legibility}$$
$$\text{Males' overall impression} = .538 \text{ coherence} + .225 \text{ complexity}$$
$$+ .167 \text{ legibility}$$

As was confirmed in H1a, females rated sites higher on coherence. This is because they are better able to make sense of the information they are seeing. As can be seen in the regression equations for females, coherence was also more important in their overall impression of each site. This reflects women's ability to make sense of a Web environment by reading into information further. Aliza Sherman, president of Cybergrrl, Inc., a publisher of three women-oriented Web sites, believes women are interested in simplicity more than anything else (Strout, 2000).

Web sites will need to present information in a clearly coherent manner. The evidence from the regression equations gives further evidence to the idea that coherence has the potential to drive overall impression. Although females are better able to make sense of the presented material, coherence is preferred by both sexes and necessary for males. As males do not read into information as extensively as females, Web site designers have to take this into account and provide more cues for the male audience. The strong desire for coherence by both males and females makes this strong advice for all Web site designers. Importantly, these cues need to be presented in a logical manner for information processing.

There were comments from both sexes regarding coherence. They wanted Web sites that were "easy to use," "easy to navigate," and "easy to search." Figure 14.2 shows an example of legibility in a Web page. Notice how there is little text but there are links to categories of information. In this way, an interested Web surfer can quickly understand what this site is about and feel comfortable in the ability to navigate through the site without ever having visited it before.

One the other hand, an illegible Web page, like the one in Fig. 14.3, is cluttered with extraneous, often little-related information, and too few hints as to where to find the desired information.

That females rated sites higher on legibility also has implications for marketing to males. The ability to understand the Web site well enough to discern differences between the Web sites represents the marketing concept of differentiation, and male customers would require greater effort or greater levels of legibility to ensure a distinct identity for the Web site. Care must be taken to distinguish one site from another for men. The challenge is to create a Web site that is distinctly unlike other sites yet is coherent. For example, the new Web site may use a completely different format to be unique but result in being different enough to be confusing.

Females, in particular, appreciated sites that were "easy to navigate . . . groups products by category and type within category," had "ease of obtaining this

FIG. 14.2   A Coherent Web Page.

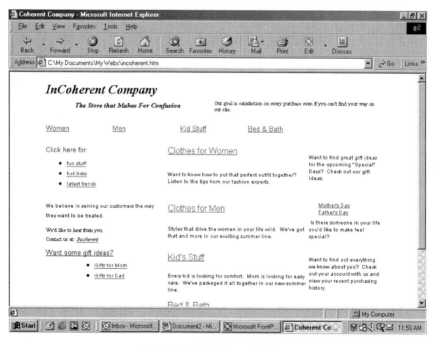

FIG. 14.3   An Incoherent Web Page.

FIG. 14.4   A Legible Web Page.

information through their site maps," and had "paths [that] are clear." An example of a legible Web page is show in Figure 14.4.

The hypothesis that stated that males will dislike sites with low complexity even more than females was not supported, but the overall analysis provides some enlightenment as to how males use complexity, and legibility when processing Web sites. With minor exceptions (rei, nordstrom's, peapod) males and females ranked the sites similarly. The significant differences appeared in how much emphasis each sex places on coherence, complexity, and legibility. That is, there are differences in how males and females use information to form preferences.

The different regression equations for males and females means that males rated the sites they prefer higher on legibility and complexity than females. Thus, they were making different connections from the information than were females. It further means that females relied less heavily on legibility and complexity and males relied more heavily on them to form overall impressions.

Additional Insight From the Debriefing Session

Elaboration of the research hypotheses was gained during the debriefing sessions following each data-collection occasion. Males were concerned with the coherence of Web pages, desiring fewer extras and more concise format. They mentioned they "would like to see sites less 'cluttered,' " "like sites because they are simple and don't try to accomplish too much," and preferred "no-frills" sites as opposed to those whose "screens are cluttered with banner ads, multiple options for advanced searches . . . " Further, they enjoyed taking "advantage of 'no-frills' links for advanced users." The implication is that once a user has experience, he or she is more concerned with obtaining information and is not impressed with "the bells and whistles."

Though evidence thus far does not strongly confirm that sex differences in information processing exist on the Web, even this limited study indicates that thought needs to be given to the presentation of information, particularly in providing enough clarification for male visitors. Web site designers need to be certain that their design is easily understood without the users "filling in" missing information in order to make sense of the site. The greater ability of female users to grasp the content of the site allows marketers to concentrate more on understanding and filling the needs of their female customers without as much concern for improving coherence. The same imperative holds that the site design still must be clearly worded, uncrowded, and thoughtfully formatted.

Another issue that came to light during the debriefing sessions was the females' desire for what might be termed *relationship elements* within sites. There seemed to be a greater desire on the part of females for interaction and personalization. Some of their comments included, "The site allowed me to sign up for emails that I am interested in [by topic] . . . offers chat rooms to communicate with other women . . . " They appreciated when a "site can recognize what type of purchases I make and send an occasional email when a favorite author or musician is offering a new book or CD." Also, "I wish that sites that I frequently make purchases with could recognize what types of purchases I have made and send me emails with similar offers." Males seem more interested in getting to their objective, whether it be shopping, seeking information, or the like quickly and not being slowed down by what they consider to be "frills." Exploring whether females are more motivated by relationship issues such as personalization, interaction with other Web users, or with the Web sites themselves would be a logical extension of this stream of research.

Limitations

Although almost all of the research hypotheses were confirmed, prudence must be used in interpretation of the results. Limitations of this sample prevent generalization of results to the entire population. Two limitations were the makeup of the sample and the data-collection instrument.

This study has limited external validity because of the subjects utilized. Though not heavy Web purchasers, these students do surf the Web on a frequent basis. They demonstrate a Web pattern similar to that identified in a recent study of Internet use trends (Strategis Group, 1999). Future studies, however, need to verify that this pattern of preferences holds in other populations.

CONCLUSIONS AND FUTURE RESEARCH

The goal of this chapter was to examine whether gendered information processing extended to the Web environment. There are many reasons for gender differences in preferences, two of which (different levels of elaboration and use of different types of information) were examined in this study.

This examination of gender differences in information processing combined with an empirical study of sex differences in Web site preferences has highlighted both differences and similarities between genders. The similarities found were that both males and females agree on the need for simplicity of design and a legible format that allows ease of navigation.

Sex differences in preferences were also apparent. As predicted, women were found to attain a greater sense of clarity and comprehension from the same information resulting in greater overall impression. Women were also better able to discern subtle differences among sites that led to differentiation. That is, men required more information to form preferences among sites, a requisite in any marketing channel but perhaps more imperative among competing e-retail sites.

The contributions of this study have practical implications and highlight areas for future research.

Practical Implications

A study by Forrester Research (1995) states that the average cost of developing the content of a Web site is $267,000 (Dreze & Zufryden, 1997) and these costs have not diminished over time. Considering the size of this investment, it is amazing how little empirical research has been done regarding Web surfers and their differences in preferences.

Everyone, like the subjects of the described study, wants Web sites that are easy to use, easy to search, and easy to navigate. Making Web sites "user friendly," however, requires making them easy to understand. The Preference Matrix provides insight into selection and placement of appropriate Web content elements to accomplish this goal. A Web developer can use coherence, complexity, and legibility to build sites users return to over and over again as these appear to facilitate how individuals make sense of their world. For example, if individuals are more interested in simplicity (coherence), then cluttering the homepage with information is ill-advised.

Because message characteristics, such as cue incongruity, can increase the degree of attention and elaboration they prompt (Wright, 1979), careful consideration of site features is warranted. For example, one eye-catching feature or one element that seems unusual (incongruous) can encourage Web surfers to pay more attention to a page. But our study demonstrates that an overabundance of such cues leaves an impression of a cluttered site, which can lead to a sense of confusion and frustration.

Examining gender differences in information processing on the Web extends previous work to this new media. Two recent trends, however, provide very practical reasons for exploring gender differences. One recent trend is the proliferation of women-only sites such as oxygen.com and ivillage.com. Second, there are currently 33.6 million women online (Cyber Dialogue, 2000). Females now account for nearly half of all Internet users (Strout, 2000) in spite of women having been late to adopt the Internet compared to men. The changing nature of the Web environment thus lends itself to an examination of possible gender preferences on the Web.

Within the women-only sites lies a great variety of styles. Some (i.e., www.ivillage.com) resemble popular mass-marketed sites (i.e., www.amazon. com),using the fast-becoming-standard three-column format, an (over) abundance of text, and minimal use of graphics. Others (i.e., www.oxygen.com and www.cybergrrl.com) are utilizing animation, more color, and greater use of categories. Obviously, there is not a proven standard that demonstrates better acceptance by the target audience. Although these sites offer chat rooms and, libraries of topics of supposed interest to the visitors, resulting in a more targeted, hence more relationship-oriented impression, which features best promote a relationship atmosphere have not yet been identified. Consequently, future research should determine which format and elements of site design do a better job of meeting the female audience's information-processing needs.

Information needs that vary based on gender include a more coherent format and better differentiation for male markets and more emphasis on intimacy, both from a perspective of privacy and personalization for female markets. It should not be necessary, however, to create different Web sites for each gender but rather to take more care in the design of one Web site to ensure that both gender's needs are met.

Future Research

There are many future directions that this research should take. Aside from continuing to test gender differences with other, nonstudent populations, there are many other variables that might provide insight into effective Web site design. Other variables worth investigation include level of expertise and motivation and possibly traditional segmentation variables such as age and geography. Expertise may influence Web site preference because experts will have more highly developed cognitive structures that allow more effective problem structuring and problem solving (Chi, Feltovich, & Glaser, 1981; Alba & Hutchinson, 1987). This means that they may have different levels of ability in making sense of the Web site information and may have different judgments of the coherence and ease of navigation of any site (Brucks, 1985). Recall, though, that McGivern and colleagues (1997) found experience not significant whereas gender persevered.

Testing for differences among motivations should also yield worthwhile information. Web surfers use the Web for a variety of purposes including research (information motivation), purchase (economic motivation), and enjoyment (social motivation). These purposes may change ratings scores.

The Web as an information media is obviously here to stay. How to best use this communication vehicle is just starting to be explored. Interestingly, online companies have a wealth of data at their disposal to examine information-processing preferences. Yet theoretical foundations for how to go about making use of this data is woefully absent. Many factors can play a role in effective Web design. This chapter explored what role gender might play in providing online organizations with guidance in developing effective Web site designs. Although the findings on gender differences to date are not dramatic, they do point to the value of providing visitors with Web site designs that make them comfortable in the Web landscape. In doing so, the site's designer will foster *stickiness* by promoting both understanding of the site's offering and a motivation to explore the site further.

APPENDIX: Sites Used

Company Name	Overall Impression	Males	Females
Banana Republic	1.9000	2.020 (1st)	1.762 (2nd)
The Gap	1.9279	2.091 (3rd)	1.733 (1st)
Net Grocer	2.3619	2.430	2.267
Macy's	2.2000	2.276 (4th)	2.070
L.L. Bean	1.9904	2.050 (2nd)	1.939 (3rd)
Nordstrom's	2.2255	2.381	2.030 (4th)
REI	2.3575	2.330	2.366
Peapod	2.7067	2.850	2.525
Wall Street City	2.8986	2.844	2.931
Market Guide	2.9712	2.792	3.130

Note: Lower score indicates higher preference.

REFERENCES

Alba, J. W., & Hutchinson, J. W. (1987). Dimensions of consumer expertise. *Journal of Consumer Research, 13*(4), 411–455.

Bem, S. L. (1981). Gender Schema Theory: A Cognitive Account of Sex Typing. *Psychological Review, 88*(July), 354–364.

Biersdorfer, J. D. (1999, February 28). Click here for less confusion. *New York Times Magazine.*

Brucks, M. (1985). The effect of products class knowledge on information search behavior. *Journal of Consumer Research, 12*(1), 1–17.

Chi, M. T. H., Feltovich, P. J., & Glaser, R. (1981). Categorization and representation of physics problem by experts and novices. *Cognitive Science, 5,* 121–152.

Crowell, A. (1997). Age brings capabilities, not limitations. *Research Horizons.*

Cyber Dialogue. (2000). Cyber dialogue finds women reluctant to shop online due to security concerns. Retrieved February 4, 2000, from http://www.cyberdialogue.com/pre/releases/ecomwomen_security.html.

Darley, W. K., & Smith, R. E. (1995, Spring). Gender differences in information processing strategies: An empirical test of the selectivity model in advertising response. *Journal of Advertising, 24,* 41–56.

DePaulo, B. M., & Rosenthal, R. (1979). Sex differences in accommodation in nonverbal communication. In R. Rosenthal (Ed.), *Skill in nonverbal communication*. Cambridge, MA: Oelgeschlager, Gunn and Hain. 137–159

Dreze, X., & Zufryden, F. (1997, March–April). Testing web site design and promotional content. *Journal of Advertising Research*, pp. 77–91.

Forrester Research. (1995). People and technology strategies. Retrived August 13, 2000, from http://www.forrester.com.

Fram, E. H., & Grady, D. B. (1997). Internet shoppers: Is there a surfer gender gap? *Direct Marketing, 59*(9), 46–55.

Gray, J. (1992). *Men are from mars, women are from venus: A practical guide for improving communication and getting what you want in your relationships*. New York: HarperCollins.

Hall, J. A. (1984). *Nonverbal sex differences: Communication accuracy and expressive style*. Baltimore: Johns Hopkins University Press.

Hamilton, J. (1999, September 27). Clearing up web-site clutter. *BusinessWeek e.biz*, pp. EB88–EB90.

Hutt, C. (1975). *Males and Females*. Harmondsworth UK: Penguin Books.

Kaplan, R. (1973). Predictors of environmental preference: Designers and clients. In W. F. E. Preiser (Ed.), *Environmental design research*, Vol. 1 (pp. 265–274). Stroudsburg, PA: Dowden, Hutchinson and Ross.

Kaplan, R., & Kaplan, S. (1982). *Cognition and environment: Functioning in an uncertain world*. New York: Praeger.

Kaplan, R., Kaplan, S., & Ryan, R. L. (1998). *With people in mind*. Washington, D.C.: Island Press.

Kaplan, S. (1973). Cognitive maps, human needs and the designed environment. In W. F. E. Preiser (Ed.), *Environmental design research*, Vol. 1 (pp. 274–283). Stroudsburg, PA: Dowden, Hutchinson and Ross.

Krugman, H. E. (1966, Winter). The measurement of advertising involvement. *Public Opinion Quarterly, 30*, 583–596.

McCarthy, J. E., & Perrault Jr., W. D. (1990). *Basic marketing: A managerial approach* (10th Ed.), Boston: Irwin.

Meyers-Levy, J. (1988, March). The influence of sex roles on judgment. *Journal of Consumer Research, 14*, 522–530.

Levy, J., & Heller, W. (1992). Gender differences in human neuropsychological function. In *Handbook of behavioral neurobiology, Vol. 11: Sexual differentiation*. New York: Plenum.

Meyers-Levy, J., & Maheswaran, D. (1991, June). Exploring differences in males and females' processing strategies. *Journal of Consumer Research*, 63–70.

Meyers-Levy, J., & Sternthal, B. (1991, February). Gender differences in the use of message cues and judgments. *Journal of marketing Research, 28*, 84–96.

Moir, A., & Jessel, D. (1991). *Brain sex: The real difference between men and women*. New York: Dell Publications.

Nowaczyk, R. (1982, July–September), Sex-related differences in the color lexicon. *Language and Speech, 25*, 257–265.

Reinisch, J. M., Rosenblum, L. A., Rubin, D. B., & Fini Schulsinger, M. (1991). Sex differences emerge during the first year of life. *Journal of Psychology and Human Sexuality, 4*(2), 19–36.

Rosen, D. E., & Purinton, E. (1999). *Web site design: Mapping the cognitive landscape*. Paper presented at the Conference on Telecommunications and Information Markets, Providence, Rhode Island, September 1999.

Silverman, I., & Eals, M. (1992). Sex differences in spatial abilities: Evolutionary theory and data. In J. H. Barkow, L. Cosmides, & J. Tooby (Eds.), *The adapted mind: Evolutionary psychology and the generation of culture*. New York: Oxford University Press. 352–378.

Silverman, I., & Eals, M. (1994). The hunter-gatherer theory of spatial sex differences: Proximate factors mediating the female advantage in recall of object arrays. *Ethology and Sociobiology, 15*(2), 95–105.

The Strategis Group. (1999, November 15). Internet use trends: Mid-year 1999. Retrieved August 13, 2004 from http://www.cyberatlas.com.

Stern, B. B. (1993). Feminist literary criticism and the deconstruction of ads: A postmodern view of advertising and consumer responses. *Journal of Consumer Research, 19,* 556–565.

Strout, E. (2000). Tough customers. *Sales and Marketing Management, 152*(1), 63–69.

Tanaka, J. S. A., Panter, T., & Winborne, W. C. (1988, January). Dimensions of the need for cognition: Subscales and gender difference. *Multivariate Behavioral Research, 23,* 35–50.

Tannen, D. (1990). *You just don't understand: Women and men in conversation.* New York: Morrow.

Tracy, B. (1997, April). How to get serious shoppers to visit your virtual salesroom. *Advertising Age, 68,* M-6.

Wood, M. M. (1966, April–August). The influence of sex and knowledge of communication effectiveness of spontaneous speech. *Word, 22,* 112–37.

Wright, P. (1979, December). Concrete action plans in TV messages to increase reading of drug warnings. *Journal of Consumer Research, 6,* 256–269.

CHAPTER FIFTEEN

The Effect of Site Design and Interattribute Correlations on Interactive Web-Based Decisions

Barbara Fasolo
Gary H. McClelland
Katharine A. Lange
University of Colorado at Boulder

Nearly 100 million Americans go online to gather information and to decide what products to buy online or offline, and 67 million buy products online (Pew Internet & American Life Project, 2003). A number of "decision-facilitating Web sites," such as www.activebuyersguide.com, have appeared on the Internet to help consumers formulate judgments and to make choices for a wide array of product categories. Decision sites contain the information necessary for consumers to make a good decision; this information is typically organized as a list of products (or *options*), described along a number of features (or *attributes*) that qualify these products. But rather than just present information, decision sites guide consumers through an interactive process that allows them to reduce the number of options to a manageable size (*winnowing*), and to compare a few surviving options side by side (*comparison*). Although side-by-side comparison is the feature most frequently used by consumers (Morrison, Pirolli, & Card, 2001), our focus is the interactive features for winnowing. Helping consumers winnow the choice set is increasingly important because of the larger databases of product information available on the Web. For example, suppose you need a new cell phone plan. If you visit the local phone store, you might find about 10 plans that are available for your area. If you go online, at www.point.com, you will likely find that there more than 100 plans for you to choose among. Searching for information on the Web has suddenly increased the options set by at least an order of magnitude, making winnowing features particularly necessary and useful.

Along with the number of products, the Web increases the number of attributes that describe any list of products consumers might want to consider. Although *Consumer Reports* tables usually contain at most 7 or 8 different attributes, decision sites may present more than 40 distinct attributes for users to consider. Processing dozens of attributes is not much easier than processing dozens of options, so the winnowing of attributes may be just as important as the winnowing of options. However, to date few sites provide users with any decision tools for winnowing attributes.

In this chapter we investigate how consumers use and evaluate interactive features for option winnowing and describe how consumers' information processes, actual choices, and ultimate satisfaction are affected both by decision site design and by the kinds of attribute information that these sites display.

DECISION SITE DESIGN

The ways decision sites are currently designed for winnowing will likely look familiar to experts in decision making and decision analysis. Decision sites are nothing but Web-based decision support systems that facilitate a given "choice heuristic." As in the work of Payne, Bettman, and Johnson (1993), such heuristics imply specific strategies for acquiring information, stopping information search, and making a decision. These strategies are either "compensatory" or "noncompensatory." Choice strategies are compensatory when in the course of the choice process trade-offs among conflicting attributes are made. Usually compensatory strategies are consistent with a systematic search, by option. They are called compensatory because a bad value on one attribute can be compensated for by a good value on another attribute. Choice strategies are noncompensatory when a choice is reached avoiding trade-offs among conflicting attributes. Usually they are consistent with a selective search by attribute. They are called noncompensatory because a bad value on one attribute is sufficient to eliminate the option; there is then no opportunity for the bad value on that attribute to be compensated by other good attributes the option might have.

The same distinction emerges in the designs of the most common decision sites available today: They are designed to make users process choice information either in a compensatory or a noncompensatory fashion. There are sites that help users consider all attributes at the same time and make trade-offs among them in ways that are consistent with the precepts of multiattribute choice theory (Keeney & Raiffa, 1976)—these are what we refer to as compensatory sites. Figure 15.1 shows an example for a digital camera choice. Users are encouraged to make a trade-off between price and ease of download for two hypothetical cameras. On the other hand, there are sites that make users consider one attribute at a time or set attribute cutoffs, or ranges—these are what we refer to as noncompensatory sites. Figure 15.2 shows an example for a cell phone plan choice. Users are encouraged to

Assuming all other features are the same, which product do you prefer?

click ⓘ for definition

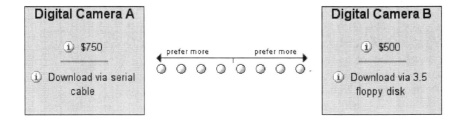

FIG. 15.1   Snapshot of a compensatory decision site (www.activebuyersguide.com).

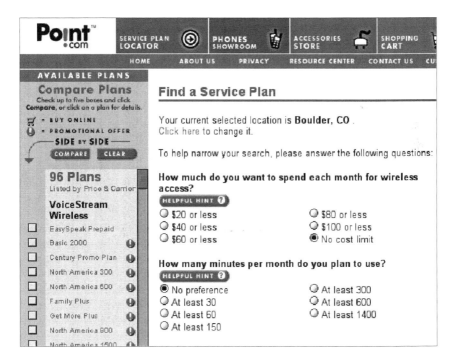

FIG. 15.2   Snapshot of a noncompensatory decision site (once available at http://www.point.com).

narrow the overall number of plans available for choice (96) by setting a threshold along each attribute (monthly cost, monthly minutes, etc.). Overall, compensatory sites tend to focus the attention of users on options' values, noncompensatory sites on attributes' values. For a more detailed overview on available decision sites from a decision-analytic perspective, we refer to Edwards and Fasolo (2000).

In this chapter we are interested in the effects of using a compensatory or a noncompensatory decision site on consumers' decision process and outcome. Our research intent is to understand when it is good to use a compensatory or a noncompensatory decision site.

Research conducted by decision process researchers in the 1970s and 1980s (e.g., Payne et al., 1993; Russo & Dosher, 1983) showed that compensatory, option-based strategies are generally associated with more thorough and accurate choices than noncompensatory, attribute-based ones. This suggests the possibility that compensatory decision sites might assist or improve decision making on the Web more than noncompensatory aids.

However, such increased accuracy comes at the cost of more effort, and decision researchers have also showed that when faced with the trade-off between effort and accuracy, decision makers generally prefer less effortful, noncompensatory information search processes instead of more accurate compensatory ones (e.g., Payne et al., 1993; Rieskamp & Hoffrage, 1999). With regard to "effort," it is important to draw the distinction between "arithmetic" and "psychological" effort. Although the arithmetic effort of making trade-offs among conflicting attributes may be significantly reduced by Web sites that do the processing for the decision maker (see the chapter "Rationality Unbounded: The Internet and Its Effects on Consumer Decision Making" in this volume), the psychological effort of facing trade-offs might still remain. This preference for noncompensatory, attribute-based processing was in fact also established in studies of consumer decision making on the Web (Fasolo, McClelland, & Lange, submitted) and suggests the alternate possibility that compensatory decision sites conflict with the users' preferred processing behavior, hence might hinder decision making on the Web.

However, the issue of "preferred choice style" is not so clear-cut: On average, it is true that people prefer to process information by attribute, but individual-level data reveal that search processes vary substantially across individuals: across decision makers (some might feel comfortable making trade-offs, others might want to avoid them, Shiloh, Koren, & Zakay, 2001); across choice tasks (some tasks might be more important than others, such as when the decision maker is accountable for the decision, Rieskamp & Hoffrage, 1999); even across stages of the same choice problem (in the initial stage, options get reduced in a noncompensatory way, in the final stage options are compared in a compensatory fashion).

Let's take a hypothetical consumer choice problem. Imagine that someone has to buy one from the set of five products displayed in Fig. 15.3. The products (O1–O5)

	O1	O2	O3	O4	O5
A1	++	+	+	+	0
A2	+	0	-	−	+
A3	+	+	++	-	+
A4	0	0	− −	+	++
A5	++	0	0	+	0
	All				

FIG. 15.3   Positive interattribute correlation and choice strategies.[1]

are described along five different attributes (A1–A5). On the matrix, products differ in their attributes values, from excellent $(++)$ to very bad $(--)$. The buyer can process this attribute information in two alternate ways: compensatory and noncompensatory. If information were processed with the compensatory additive rule (summing all the plusses and minuses one option at a time), the buyer would likely choose the product that is best overall (01, with the highest sum of plusses and minuses equal to 6). If the buyer processes the information in a noncompensatory fashion (like Elimination by Aspects, Tversky, 1972), the buyer would examine the information by attribute and eliminate all options that do not meet his or her attribute thresholds. A threshold of "0" on all attributes would eliminate O5 along attribute A1 and would eliminate O2, O3, and O4 along attribute A2, leaving again O1 to buy. The way information is processed, whether in a compensatory or a noncompensatory fashion, does not make a difference on the final choice.

Let's now suppose that the product needs to be chosen from the set of five displayed in Fig. 15.4: Using the compensatory additive rule, now O5 would be chosen (again, with the highest sum of plusses equal to 6). Using the noncompensatory Elimination-by-Aspects rule (with the same threshold of 0), O5 would be instead eliminated along A1; 01, 02 and 04 would be eliminated along A2, leaving only O3 to be chosen. This time, processing information in a compensatory or a noncompensatory fashion made a difference in the final choice. Why?

---

[1]From the large repertoire of choice strategies studied in decision making (e.g., Payne et al., 1993), we refer to only five: (a) Lexicographic: A choice is made on the most important attribute; (b) Satisficing: A choice is made when the first "good enough" option is found; (c) Elimination by Aspect: A choice is made after eliminating the options that do not satisfy minimal criteria on the important attributes; (d) Tally: A choice is made when the option with the highest number of satisfactory attributes is found; (e) Weighted Additive: A choice is made after weighting all attributes in order of importance, adding up all weighted value, and selecting the option with the highest expected value. For a detailed description of these choice rules and heuristics, we refer to the chapter "Rationality Unbounded: The Internet and Its Effect on Consumer Decision Making" in this volume.

	O1	O2	O3	O4	O5
A1	++	+	+	+	0
A2	–	0	+	–	++
A3	–	+	++	+	++
A4	–	0	– –	+	++
A5	–	0	0	+	0
	Lexicographic	Satisficing	Elimination by Aspect	Tally	Weighted Additive

FIG. 15.4   Negative interattribute correlation and choice strategies.

INTERATTRIBUTE CORRELATION

The answer lies in the way attributes were related to each other in the two matrices. In Fig. 15.3, the average correlation among the choice attributes was just slightly positive and equal to +0.5. In Fig. 15.4, the average interattribute correlation was just slightly negative (–0.05). The average interattribute correlation was obtained computing the average correlation among all possible pairs of attributes A1–A5, after having translated "++" into a value of 2, "+" into a value of 1, "–" into –1, and "– –" into –2.

When the choice is characterized by negative interattribute correlations, using different strategies is more likely to yield to different choice outcomes than when the choice is characterized by positive interattribute correlations. This has important implications for Web-based decision making: Site design might not only affect the process (compensatory or not) by which users choose, but also the final choice made, especially if interattribute correlations are negative.

And how frequent are negative interattribute correlations? Unfortunately, negative interattribute correlations are more the norm than the exception in consumer decision making. They are the norm because of consumers' preferences. Think of the relationship between price and quality: Consumers generally want low price and high quality—negatively related. Importantly, they are the norm also because of the way efficient markets operate. Different manufacturers try to provide products in a given price range. To keep the price in that range, they have to give up some desirable features. Even the same manufacturer might have different models in the same price range, each with some desirable and less desirable attribute levels. This naturally induces negative correlations. Consider the case of the choice between two equally expensive digital cameras (Fig. 15.1): One is large and bulky, but images can be downloaded via serial cable, the other is small and handy, but images can be downloaded via 3.5 floppy disks. In front of this choice, most people hesitate because neither camera is good on both attributes—size and ease of download are negatively interrelated at this particular price level.

In fact, negative interattribute correlations are important to consider not only because they affect the choice outcome, but also because they affect the decision makers' confidence in, and satisfaction with, the choice made: In the presence of negatively related attributes, consumers rate the decision to be more difficult, and to be less confident and less satisfied with their choices than in the presence of positively related attributes (Fasolo et al., submitted). A likely psychological explanation goes as follows: With positive interattribute correlations, options can easily be judged overall as good or bad. With negative interattribute correlations, options can only be judged in their overall value if the conflicting attributes are considered simultaneously. In the example earlier, to form an overall impression of the two cameras, one needs to consider how small a camera needs to be in order to compensate for the pain of carrying around, and maybe losing, a floppy disk containing personal pictures. Trade-offs and compensations like these are difficult to make—one reason why more negative evaluations of the process accompany negative interattribute correlations.

Finally, besides affecting consumers' perceptions and final choices, negative interattribute correlations also affect the way users search for information (Bettman, Johnson, Luce and Payne, 1993; Fasolo et al., submitted). As we stated earlier, on average people tend to process information in a noncompensatory fashion, looking at information by attribute instead of forming an overall evaluation of each option. With negative interattribute correlations, however, users tend to process information in a more option-based manner (i.e., tend to process multiple attributes for the same option before moving to the next option)—a strategy generally associated with compensatory processes. When attributes are positively related, users processed information more by attribute—a strategy generally associated with noncompensatory processes.

Interattribute correlations are an important factor to consider when evaluating how good a given decision site is. When choice attributes are positively related, noncompensatory tools can be expected to better assist decision makers than compensatory tools can, because users have a stronger tendency to process in a noncompensatory fashion with positive interattribute correlations. But will the noncompensatory tool be a better aid with positive than with negative correlations? The issue is not so clear-cut, because, with positive correlations, an option that is good on one attribute is also good on other attributes—so setting a threshold on more than one attribute will not reduce the options set easily. On the other hand, when the correlation is negative, setting a threshold on more than one attribute will reduce the option set quickly (but the best option overall might be excluded). Users will likely have to interact with the noncompensatory tool for a longer time with positive than with negative correlations. This implies that positive interattribute correlation might cause a noncompensatory tool to be more appealing than a compensatory one from a decision process perspective, but less so from a mere usability perspective.

Based on the finding that in the presence of negative interattribute correlations, users' natural response is to confront trade-offs processing information by option (Fasolo et al., submitted), we expect that users find decision processing easier with positive rather than with negative correlations, and that compensatory aids make decision processing easier and more effective, especially in the presence of negative interattribute correlations.

WEB-BASED CHOICE STUDY

To investigate whether interattribute correlations (positive or negative) and site design (compensatory or noncompensatory) affect how users make choices on consumer decision sites, we devised the following Web-based choice study (currently available at http://psych.colorado.edu/~mcclella/webratenpebapn.html).

Choice Task

Participants (60 undergraduates of the University of Colorado at Boulder) were given the task to choose among digital cameras with the assistance of a decision site. Each decision site was preceded by several introductory training pages showing (by means of inactive screen images) the function of each site feature (the buy-it button, the compare button, the attribute description, the option description, etc.). Participants were encouraged to read all instructions, to use all site features, and to take as much time as they wished to acquire information before their recommendation. Each participant had to make four distinct choices, using four different decision sites. Each decision site offered a choice of 40 fictitious digital cameras described along seven attributes (Delay Between Shots, Image Capacity, LCD Display, Light Sensitivity, Zoom, Resolution, and Weight). Forty different camera names were used each time, to prevent participants from using information learnt on a previous site. For each attribute (e.g., Delay Between Shots), participants were provided with (a) a short and comprehensible description (e.g., "The amount of time, in seconds, it takes the camera to process and store an image when shooting in normal mode, at the camera's maximum resolution setting. This feature is also known as lag time."); (b) the direction of preference (e.g., "The less Delay, the better."); (c) the range of the attribute (e.g., "1–20" secs); and (d) the levels of the attribute (e.g., "1-2-5-7-20 secs"). Users could also click on the name of a single camera to see all its attributes at once.

To ensure that all participants were making choices from the same basis (and to make it plausible for us to compare their decision-processing behavior), the participants' task was to choose from each decision site which camera they would recommend to a friend. A memo displayed the friend's needs (e.g., "She plans on trying to make posters and other enlargements from the pictures.") and preferences for each attribute (e.g., "She prefers higher resolution.").

After each choice, a short questionnaire asked participants how satisfied they were with their choices, how confident they were that the choices met their preferences, and how difficult they found the choice tasks. Participants were also asked how easy the decision site was to use and how satisfied they were with how it assisted decisions.

Site Design

The design for the compensatory decision site was developed after perusing several decision sites that we had previously collected and analyzed (e.g., www.activebuyersguide, and others that are no longer available online, such as www.personalogic.com). The typical design of these sites includes several pages of preference elicitation, followed by a page with the list of products, ranked in order of decreasing weighted added value (for a more extensive description, see Edwards and Fasolo, 2000). We simplified this design to a more compact, two-screens-long, compensatory site, which we called "RATE," because it presents overall options ratings: On the first screen (Fig. 15.5), participants specified the relative importance weights for the seven attributes; on the second screen (Fig. 15.6), participants saw the list of 40 cameras, ranked from highest to lowest "fit" scores. These scores were computed by multiplying the importance weights times the attribute values and summing them to obtain an overall fit score for each camera.

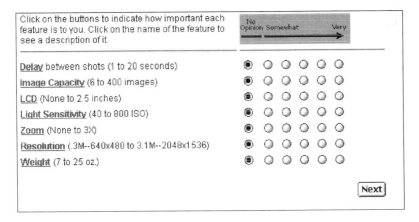

FIG. 15.5   Experimental compensatory decision site (RATE)—attribute weights editing.

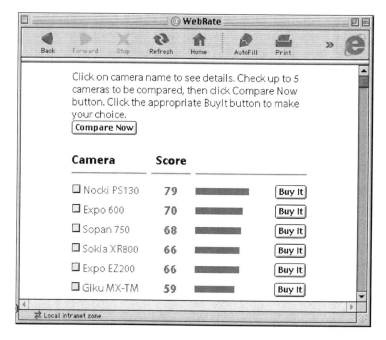

FIG. 15.6   Experimental compensatory decision site (RATE)—overall "fit" scores.

The design for the noncompensatory decision site was inspired by an earlier version of www.point.com (Fig. 15.2), a third-party Web site that facilitates choices of cell phone plans, according to an Elimination-by-Aspects strategy. As in www.point.com, also in our experimental site participants specified the minimum acceptable level on the attributes and could see how the list of options contracted or expanded as thresholds were set on each attribute (Fig. 15.7).

Both site designs allowed participants to specify up to five cameras to be compared side by side. The final choice could be made at any point by clicking on a "buy it" button displayed beside the cameras' brands. The order of presentation of the site design was counterbalanced: One group of participants saw the two noncompensatory sites first, the other group saw the compensatory sites first.

The experimental Web site was implemented in Javascript and run on Macintosh computers using Internet Explorer 5.1. Decision site design (compensatory and noncompensatory) and correlation (positive and negative) were varied in a 2 × 2 within-subjects design. Interattribute correlation was varied such that on two decision sites the seven attributes were positively related (average pairwise correlation = +0.5), and on the other two they were negatively related (average pairwise correlation = −0.14). In summary, there were four decision sites the users used to make four different recommendations to a friend. Participants saw these four sites either in this order: (a) noncompensatory and positive correlation

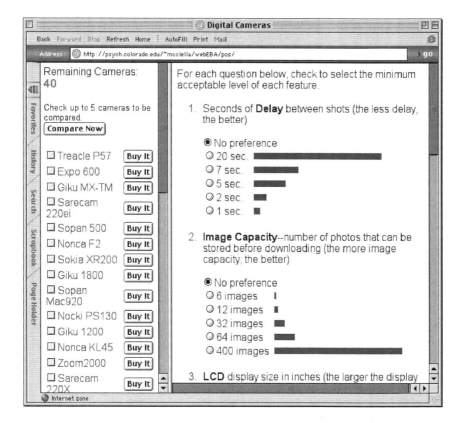

FIG. 15.7   Experimental noncompensatory decision site (EBA).

(EBAPos), (b) noncompensatory and negative correlation (EBANeg), (c) compensatory and negative correlation (RateNeg), and (d) compensatory and positive correlation (RatePos); or in this order: (a) RatePos, (b) RateNeg, (c) EBANeg, and (d) EBAPos.

Analysis and Measurement

Analyses were conducted on the participants' clicks on the four decision sites, on the quality of their choices, and on the questionnaire responses.

Clicks.   Clicks were of interest because they indicate where the users' action, attention, and effort were concentrated during the interactive choice task. They are a conventional measure of users' behavior in Internet research. Three categories of clicks were of interest: (a) total clicks: The total number of clicks is simply all the clicks that a user made on the decision site before making the final choice; (b) option clicks: The overall number of option clicks is the sum of the times users clicked on an option name (either for inclusion in the comparison table, or for consideration of its details); and (c) attribute clicks: The overall number of attribute clicks is the sum of the times users clicked on an attribute (either by expressing an importance weight on the compensatory site, or by setting a threshold in the noncompensatory site).

Choice Quality. On the compensatory site choice quality was recorded under the form of the rank order corresponding to the camera chosen (where a rank of 1 means that the camera with the highest expected value was chosen, 2 means that the camera with the second highest expected value was chosen, and so on). On the noncompensatory site, participants' actual choices were recorded under the form of the type of camera that they confirmed they would recommend to their friend. Because the friends' preferences were presented to each participant, it was possible to identify objectively which camera best met his or her preferences. On the noncompensatory site, choice quality was therefore measured as the match between the choice actually made by each subject and the objective "best."

Self-Reported Measures. All questionnaire responses (satisfaction with choice made, satisfaction with decision site used, confidence in choice made, ease of choice made, and ease of use of decision site utilized) were rated on 5-point scales, ranging from "very satisfied" (confident, easy) to "very unsatisfied" (unconfident, difficult).

Results

Total Clicks. The correlation manipulation had a significant impact on the overall number of clicks: Users produced fewer clicks when the attributes were positively related than when they were negatively related ($F(1, 59) = 39.45$, $p < 0.01$).[2] The site design manipulation also had a significant effect: Users clicked more on the noncompensatory decision site than on the compensatory one ($F(1, 59) = 7.07$, $p < 0.01$). This was more true when the correlation was negative ($F(1, 59) = 18.12$, $p < 0.01$). Order of presentation did not have any effect: Total clicks did not depend on which decision site was used first. Figure 15.8 represents these results.

Option Clicks. The site design manipulation had a significant impact on option clicks: Users clicked more on options when the site was designed for the

---

[2]The analyses reported in this section are from a two-way repeated-measures ANOVA conducted as a series of planned contrasts for main effects, interactions, and simple effects. This use of planned contrasts is recommended by Rosenthal and Rosnow (1985), Judd and McClelland (1989), Abelson (1995), and Rosenthal, Rosnow, and Rubin (2000), among others. By so doing, results can be presented in terms of substantive comparisons instead of in terms of statistical abstractions. More importantly, in the case of repeated-measures, one-degree-of-freedom contrasts avoid the troublesome and seldom satisfied sphericity assumption required in the usual repeated-measures ANOVA (see Chapter 14 of Judd and McClelland, 1989).

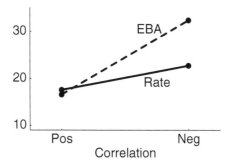

FIG. 15.8   Total clicks, by site design and interattribute correlation.

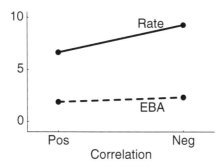

FIG. 15.9   Option clicks, by site design and interattribute correlation.

compensatory option-based strategy than for the noncompensatory attribute-based strategy ($F(1,59) = 38.61$, $p < 0.01$). The effect of the correlation manipulation was marginally significant ($F(1,59) = 3.46$, $p = 0.067$) but only on the compensatory site. When using the compensatory site, users clicked more on options in the negative than in the positive correlation condition. Order of presentation did not have any effect. Figure 15.9 presents these results.

Attribute Clicks.   Interattribute correlation again affected users' attention on attributes (Fig. 15.10). When using the noncompensatory elimination-by-aspect site, users clicked to set and revise attribute thresholds more when the correlation was negative than when it was positive ($F(1,59) = 79.21$, $p = 0.0001$). When using the compensatory weighted additive site, users clicked to set and revise attribute weights more when the correlation was negative than when it was positive ($F(1,59) = 7.05$, $p < 0.01$). Overall, users clicked more on attributes on the noncompensatory site than on compensatory one. Again, order of presentation did not have any effect.

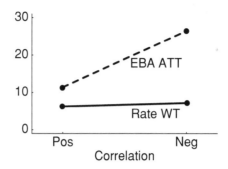

FIG. 15.10   Attribute clicks, by site design and interattribute correlation.

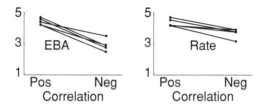

FIG. 15.11   Self-report ratings (satisfaction, confidence, difficulty of choice and satisfaction with decision site) by site design and interattribute correlation.

Self-Reported Measures.   Interattribute correlation and site design affected all self-reported measures in the same way: Perceptions were more negative with negative interattribute correlations than with positive correlations and with the noncompensatory decision site than with the compensatory one. This pattern of results is displayed in Fig. 15.11. The experience with the noncompensatory site was particularly negative when the correlation was negative. Order of presentation of the decision sites had an effect on this interaction: It was generally more painful for participants to choose with the noncompensatory tool in the presence of negative correlations when the noncompensatory tool was encountered first. Figure 15.12 represents the typical pattern of results for the measure "satisfaction with choice made": Users were less satisfied with the choice made when the attributes were negatively related than when they were positively related ($F(1,59) = 151.3$, $p < 0.01$) and when the decision site was compensatory rather than noncompensatory ($F(1,59) = 42.25$, $p < 0.01$). Users felt less satisfied with the choice made especially when they used the noncompensatory decision site with choice attributes that were negatively related ($F(1,59) = 40.05$, $p < 0.01$) and when they used the noncompensatory site before the compensatory one ($F(1,59) = 7.52, p < 0.01$).

Decision Outcomes.   On the compensatory site, 60% of the choices corresponded to the camera that appeared with the highest expected value. Of these

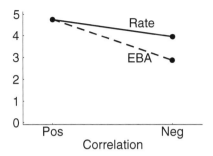

FIG. 15.12 Satisfaction with choice made: site design × correlation interaction.

choices, 71% occurred when the correlation was positive and 29% when the correlations was negative. On the noncompensatory site, only half of the choices corresponded to the "objective best." Of these choices, 89% occurred when the correlation was positive, and 11% when the correlations was negative.

Discussion

As expected, site design shaped users' choice behavior and specifically their focus on attributes rather than options. When the site was designed for the compensatory weighted additive, users focused more on options, individually or on side-by-side tables. When the site was designed for the noncompensatory Elimination-by-Aspect strategy, users focused more on attributes, setting and revising thresholds, even if it was still possible for participants to click on options' descriptions and compare them side by side.

Interattribute correlation also affected choice behavior on decision sites: When correlation was negative, users clicked more than when the correlation was positive. This result is consistent with our previous findings (Fasolo et al., submitted), using a different task, showing that negative correlation is perceived and dealt with even if it requires more effort and time.

Another important result concerned the interaction between interattribute correlation and site design, showing that negative correlation affected users' behavior differently on the two sites. On the noncompensatory site, the negative correlation made users revise attribute thresholds more, thus increasing attribute clicks. On the compensatory site, the negative correlation made users select more options for further consideration, thus increasing option clicks. This result provides further evidence that site design affects the way users behave and, in this case, how they deal with negative interattribute correlations.

Like users' behavior, their psychological perception of the task was also affected by site design and interattribute correlation. More positive perceptions were associated with the compensatory site than with the noncompensatory site and with choices characterized by positive rather than negative interattribute correlations. In general, the real difference between the two designs emerged when attributes were negatively related. In this case, the noncompensatory site was particularly disliked, considered of difficult use, and of little decision help, especially when encountered before the compensatory one and by users with less Web experience.

Last, according to the measures of decision quality used, it seemed that the compensatory site enabled choices that were more consistent with the rational principles of the weighted-additive rule and more robust to negative interattribute correlations. Measures of decision quality need to be refined and improved in order to better capture and compare across sites the quality of the choice made on these sites.

CONCLUSIONS

These results offer some important insights into the dynamics of Web-based decision making and some indication of ways in which it could be improved. Our study indicates that with positive correlations, decisions are easy to make, and compensatory and noncompensatory sites are equally good in assisting them. The story is very different when attributes are negatively correlated. In this case, users find it more difficult to decide, and compensatory sites like RATE are more helpful than noncompensatory ones, like EBA. This result will probably please those decision theorists and analysts who believe decision makers need to be assisted in the "normative" way, such as by the normative rules of Multi-Attribute Utility Theory (Keeney and Raiffa, 1976).

Drawing from these results, and some experience with decision analysis tools, we conclude this chapter with suggestions for how to build better decision sites. First, a helpful decision site should be simple to use. Compensatory sites like the RATE we used in our experiment were at least as simple to use as the noncompensatory EBA site. Real compensatory sites on the World Wide Web are instead usually more cumbersome than noncompensatory ones.

Second, a helpful decision site should be robust; that is, it should always lead to the best possible choice for the user, regardless of how related the attributes are. Noncompensatory sites typically lack this capacity, and our experiment shows that this is perceived and disliked by users.

Third, it should elicit and make good use of decision makers' preferences. Noncompensatory sites usually skip the preference elicitation stage, while compensatory ones devote screens and screens to it. Focusing on consumer's preferences seems important for the user to make a good informed choice.

Last, it should be transparent. Users should be able to understand how their choices are affected by any selection or button click they make at any point. This is trickier to achieve with compensatory sites, because they rest on multiattribute computations that are typically cumbersome and lengthy. Our current research program is trying to find ways to combine all four conditions in a plausible and usable decision site, by means of simulation and experimental data.

DIRECTION FOR FUTURE RESEARCH

In this section we include a few directions for future research suggested by our findings. The first direction is suggested by the finding that on the site designed for the noncompensatory Elimination-by-Aspect strategy, users focused more on attributes, setting and revising thresholds, even if it was still possible for participants to click on options' descriptions and compare them side by side. This result might be because of the specific size of the window allowing for options comparison (small in our experiment and on most Web sites) as opposed to attributes thresholds (large). Future research might explore whether different allocation of window space between options and attributes can influence and possibly shift search processes from compensatory to noncompensatory (and vice versa).

A second direction concerns the issue of the visibility to the users of trade-offs among conflicting attributes. It is possible that users had a more positive perception of the compensatory site, not because of its normative superiority, but because it concealed from users the impact of negative interattribute correlations. On the noncompensatory site, users could see online how the options set was affected by setting an attribute threshold after another. With the presence of negative correlations, the options set was soon emptied, and, as we expected, this made participants dissatisfied and uncomfortable. On the compensatory site instead, all computations are out of the users' sight and out of the users' mind. The higher transparency and feedback offered by the noncompensatory site, coupled with its focus on attributes, made the impact of negative correlations more direct and troubling for users, whereas the less-transparent compensatory site made users oblivious of the impact of negative correlation on the relative standing of options along each attribute.

The issue of transparency is important. Although we have no precise data to support it, we are under the impression that real World Wide Web compensatory sites are having rougher and shorter lives than noncompensatory sites. This would be hard to explain if compensatory sites were more adequate decision aids than noncompensatory sites. We have anecdotal evidence that transparency and length might be a reason for the lack of success of compensatory ones. Real compensatory decision sites are usually longer than the two-screen version we used in our experiment. The process of preference elicitation is often a dozen of pages long, with no feedback whatsoever as to how these data are used for the final recommendations. More research is needed to understand the way users can be confronted with trade-offs in a way that is transparent and yet not threatening or cumbersome. The creation of visual tools that incorporate sensitivity analyses and exploit the exciting interactivity of the Internet is one research possibility that we encourage.

REFERENCES

Abelson, R. P. (1995). *Statistics as principled argument*. Hillsdale, NJ: Lawrence Erlbaum Associates.

Bettman, J. R., Johnson, E. J., Luce, M. F., & Payne, J. W. (1993). Correlation, conflict and choice. *Journal of Experimental Psychology: Learning, Memory and Cognition, 19*, 931–951.

Edwards, W., & Fasolo, B. (2001). Decision technology. *Annual Review of Psychology, 52*, 581–606.

Fasolo, B., McClelland, G. H., & Lange, K. A. (submitted). Interattribute correlations influence whether decision processing strategies are attribute-based or option-based.

Häubl, G., & Trifts, V. (2000). Consumer decision making in online shopping environment: The effects of interactive decision aids. *Marketing Science, 19*(1), 4–21.

Judd, C. M., & McClelland, G. H. (1989). *Data analysis: A model comparison approach*. San Diego: Harcourt Brace.

Keeney, R. L., & Raiffa, H. (1976). Decisions with multiple objectives. New York: Wiley.

Morrison, J., Pirolli, P. L., & Card, S. K. (2001, March 31–April 5). A taxonomic analysis of what World Wide Web activities significantly impact people's decision and actions. *CHI 2001 Extended Abstracts*, Seattle, WA.

Payne, J. W., Bettman, J. R., & Johnson, E. J. (1993). *The adaptive decision maker*. Cambridge, UK: Cambridge University Press.

Pew Internet & American Life Project (2003). America's online pursuits: The changing picture of who's online and what they do. Retrieved September 10, 2004, from http://www.pewinternet.org/pdfs/PIP_Online_Pursuits_Final.PDF

Rieskamp, J., & Hoffrage, U. (1999). When do people use simple heuristics and how can we tell? In G. Gigerenzer, P. M. Todd, & the ABC Research Group (Eds.), *Simple heuristics that make us smart* (pp. 141–167). New York: Oxford University Press.

Roehm, H. A., & Haugtvedt, C. P. (1999). Understanding interactivity of cyberspace advertising. In D. W. Schumann & E. Thorson (Eds.), *Advertising and the world wide web* (pp. 27–39). Mahwah, NJ: Lawrence Erlbaum Associates.

Rosenthal, R., & Rosnow, R. L. (1985). *Contrast analysis: Focused comparisons in the analysis of variance*. New York: Cambridge University Press.

Rosenthal, R., Rosnow, R. L., & Rubin, D. B. (2000). *Contrasts and effect sizes in behavioral research: A correlational approach*. New York: Cambridge University Press.

Russo, J. E., & Dosher, B. A. (1983). Strategies for multi-attribute binary choice. *Journal of Experimental Psychology: Learning, Memory, & Cognition, 9*(4), 676–696.

Shiloh, S., Koren, S., & Zakay, D. (2001). Individual differences in compensatory decision-making style and need for closure as correlates of subjective decision complexity and difficulty. *Personality and Individual Differences, 30*, 699–710.

Tversky, A. (1972). Elimination by aspects: A theory of choice. *Psychological Review, 79*(4), 281–299.

V. DECISION MAKING

Is the Internet Empowering Consumers to Make Better Decisions, or Strengthening Marketers' Potential to Persuade?

Paul Henry

The University of Sydney

No one would deny that rapidly advancing technology in media and information delivery—from cable, wireless, and Internet developments to enhanced data storage and the ability to integrate and share information across massive user networks—is destined to have its effects on consumer behavior. Consumers increasingly use the Internet to search for information and evaluate product alternatives before purchasing. Many commentators claim that information access will empower consumers with enhanced decision-making capabilities. This has been stimulated by the belief that if a more complete range of information is made available to consumers they will take the time to sift through the material to arrive at a more thought-through, considered decision. But will they? This chapter explores the issue of whether the Internet puts consumers in the "driving seat," or whether delivery of this promise will be impeded by fundamental limitations of the human condition.

Will new media such as the Internet fundamentally change the way consumers collect and use information to make purchase decisions? Will it be that new "rules" apply? Although others have proposed a vision of consumer empowerment, my view is that it will largely remain just that—a vision. This is because the marketing communicators behind these developments will, as always, employ the same toolbox of fundamental persuasive techniques that have been reapplied with each successive media innovation. Granted these techniques will require some reinterpretation for the Internet, but the fundamentals remain the same. My central proposition is that the same basic communication rules that have been successfully employed in traditional offline media also hold true in the online space. Principles of human decision making that underpin the universality of these communication rules (regardless of media channel) will be reviewed. Despite the impact of innovation on media alternatives, we must realize that we are faced with human characteristics that remain constant over time. These characteristics hold tangible limits for any new media technology, both now and in the future. They are the products of long evolutionary development. Each of the characteristics to be discussed is well established. However, the implications for developing effective communications on the Internet are still very much underappreciated by both practitioners and academics.

HUMAN NATURE CAN ILLUMINATE KEY QUESTIONS

This exploration illuminates several key questions central to the future of the Internet. First, to what extent will access to information lead to better consumer decision-making capability? Many observers appear to automatically equate more information with better decisions. Although there is no doubt that access to information has been dramatically expanded as a result of the Web, I argue later that we should be very guarded in equating this with better consumer decisions.

Second, to what extent will consumers change their basic search and decision strategies? There is ample evidence that more and more consumers are using the Internet as an additional search option across a range of need areas. However, the pattern that I am often seeing is reflected in survey findings whereby a high proportion have tried the Internet as a search option, but a low proportion have found this option to be among the most useful source alternatives. The other highly debatable issue to be explored lies in whether consumers are employing new decision strategies that take advantage of the broader range of available information. I argue that decision strategies have not and will not change. Some say that development of so-called recommendation agents hold the potential to change consumer decision strategies, but I also detail reasons to remain skeptical of this proposal.

Third, how much information is too much? A source of continual surprise for individuals involved in developing advertising messages is just how little information it takes to confuse a consumer. I have viewed too many advertising research studies for main media commercials composed of supposedly simple messages where it turned out that the subjects did not comprehend the message as intended. The point is that if it is challenging to successfully communicate short television messages—even when subjects are encouraged to pay attention—then it stands to reason that the more information-loaded messaging generally attempted on the Internet faces even greater hurdles.

Fourth, are we likely to see a new breed of empowered consumers? Predictions of a trend toward "empowered" consumers flow from the growth of information availability. You can imagine that if I am indicating skepticism about enhanced decision capability, search patterns, and new decision strategies, and see potential for confusion, then I would also be skeptical about the extent of consumer empowerment. An additional reason for such skepticism lies in examination of literacy standards in the United States. Yes, there are ways to simplify information presentation, but there is no getting away from the fact that the literacy levels of a large proportion of Americans will limit their capability to absorb and comprehend. This evidence is examined later.

WE ARE ALREADY OVERLOADED WITH INFORMATION

For most purchase decisions, consumers are already overloaded with information. The volume of information will only increase. The key issue is that we have already passed the point at which we are able to use all the available information for most major decisions. As decision complexity increases, we tend actually to use less of the available information. This suggests a paradox in that less information can hold greater utility than more—so long as it consists of the right bits. Information technology that makes available too much information confuses rather than clarifies. This in itself is not surprising, but the point is just how little information a consumer actually uses when making a decision. Cialdini (2001) highlighted the efficiency of "single-feature" responding, noting that rather than delving deeply we tend to revert to a focus on just a single portion of available information.

The greatest challenge for any new information delivery system is not the technology itself, but rather determining which bits of information the consumer can effectively use. Currently, we are more adept at developing the technology than at advancing our understanding of information presentation—typically, because technological development precedes consideration of user-friendly information content, presentation, and delivery issues. This approach parallels a "product orientation" in marketing, long associated with high-risk outcomes. Evaluation of a new information technology should focus on how users will consume the information, a "marketing orientation" long associated with more rewarding outcomes. However, it is too often the vague allure of the technology for its own sake that drives the development process. The challenge of understanding just how consumers use information in specific circumstances represents the most significant hurdle to successful technological implementation.

This is not to deny that a minority of consumers have become more educated. However, basic human strategies for decision making have not changed. For example, across a range of research projects in the online health care arena I have observed that patients hold limited understanding about their disease condition and treatments, even among regular Internet health-information seekers. Despite extensive health information available on the Internet, even fundamental issues about disease conditions are often not well comprehended. Information seekers are quickly confronted with such an array of information that they often feel less certainty than before they started. Research with doctors has turned up similar findings. Even these professional experts tend toward cursory evaluation of new medical information and form subjective impressions based on limited information. Doctors are just as time pressed as patients (if not more so) and face a continual flood of medical news that they feel obligated to sort through and keep up with.

Online health presents an interesting case, because this represents one of the largest online search activities. Many consumers are putting considerable time into this search activity. The high-involvement nature of one's health suggests this should be a category where individuals invest high levels of attention and effort in examining the information. Proprietary research has found consumers to be often frustrated in sifting through the mountain of health information. There are also issues in evaluating the credibility of particular sources. Consumers often leave their search with the same level of unresolved uncertainty that stimulated the search in the first place. Although the initial reaction is "WOW, there is so much good stuff," consumers often still end up having to take health decisions based on some global impression or gut-feel—a consumer case of the blinding power of data.

Brewer and Chapman (2001) found at best minimal difference in disease knowledge between those disease sufferers (MS and HIV) who searched the Internet for information and those who did not. Similar lack of difference in disease knowledge has been observed in proprietary research for health conditions such as asthma. The big issue in the online health arena is why the promise of empowering consumers with information that should allow them to take better control of their health remains unfulfilled. Is it because of weaknesses in early Internet technology that will be overcome in time, or is it because of the inherent complexity of health messaging? Could it be that inherent complexity of health topics will force the bulk of consumers to continue to rely (and prefer) on expert advice?

A MIX OF CONSTRAINING FACTORS

How does the mind select from the flood of encountered stimuli and then process and interpret? Despite changing conditions of information explosion, the squeeze on time availability and the expansion of available choice, basic principles endure. Figure 16.1 centers on how we select and use information. Arrayed around the inner circle are four conflicting pressures that are at work whenever a consumer "decides." The first three are well documented: the so-called information explosion that engulfs us; the expansion of choice in terms of media alternatives, product variations, services, and lifestyle activities; and increased time pressure. Time constraint conflicts with expanded information availability and also with greater choice. It is telling that the term "information" rather than "knowledge" explosion is typically employed. Information is just raw material for good decisions. It can only be harnessed when analysis, interpretation, and integration

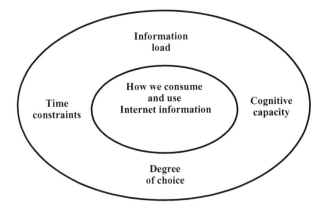

FIG. 16.1 Constraining factors in consumer decision making.

transform the information into useful knowledge. The fourth issue—limits to human processing—constitutes an enduring characteristic of mental life.

LIMITS TO HUMAN INFORMATION PROCESSING

The limit to human information processing is the major constraint faced by consumers. It is the one constant of the four pressures identified earlier. Conscious attention at any moment is extremely limited as a result of the distinctive roles of working memory and long-term memory. Working memory is the mind's information gateway. Conscious stimuli arriving through the senses are processed in working memory. They are then either "deleted" or moved to storage in long-term memory. Whereas the capacity of long-term memory is potentially enormous, working memory is extremely limited. The general finding is that working memory can hold between five and nine pieces of information, including information drawn from the senses and from long-term memory (Miller, 1956).

Take a simple example: Someone blurts out a telephone number (7 to 10 numbers long—right at the threshold of what is and is not easily remembered)—and you start to dial it. Three punches into the task, someone else asks who you are calling. You reply with the individual's name. But what happens? Bringing that name into working memory invariably displaces part of the phone number and you are unable to complete this otherwise simple task. It is impossible to pay conscious attention to the bulk of stimuli to which we are exposed. The human strategy is to be highly selective.

Often when thinking through a problem, working memory is almost entirely taken up with stimuli drawn from long-term memory. This further reduces attention to external information. Take another example: multiplying 862×87 in your head. To succeed at this task, you certainly cannot be thinking of anything else. You hold the numbers in working memory, and draw "rules for multiplication" from long-term memory. This fills working memory to the brim. Now imagine a product-selection situation in which you seek to evaluate three product alternatives across three separate attributes, each of which has three levels—a 27-piece information space to manipulate mentally. Quite clearly we don't examine every combination when we make decisions. In fact, the limits to human processing make this prohibitive.

Think about it. Three product alternatives evaluated on three attributes does not seem to be that complex of a decision to make. However, what about the much greater number of alternatives and potential attributes that require consideration when making a financial planning decision or a car purchase or deciding the best course of treatment when diagnosed with a chronic health condition? These limits to human processing raise a real question as to how (or if) consumers will use expanded information access. It is not at all clear how people in the future will handle this better. Some commentators revert to a fallback position in claiming that consumers will benefit in cases where they just want to search for the best price. For commodity products where there is little tangible difference, then price comparison is fine. However, the claims of consumer empowerment usually imply more than just search for the lowest price. Others claim that the empowering nature of the Internet lies in ability to obtain recommendations. Again, this is fine. However, there is nothing new in consumers basing their choices on recommendations. We already have access to a great range of recommendation sources—friend's opinion, professional experts, media news, consumer reports, or observing others using products that satisfy.

LIMITED TIME, EXPANDED INFORMATION, AND CHOICE

We are living in a world where we often have to pack more activities into less time— we are busier than ever. The phrase "juggling time" has entered the popular lexicon. This has contributed to the perception that modern life is associated with greater stress. The dominant view is that heightened stress derived from juggling limited time will be a continuing trend. We are now even reading about the pressures felt by time-poor children. Another complication comes into play with the observation that affluence and modern life presents us with a continuing expansion of personal choice. Consumers have a greater range of products and services to select from. The fact that these new product options are often more complex in terms of their construction, or sophistication, adds to the difficulty of the alternative evaluation task. Consumers also have a greater range of media and content options, together with an increase in recreation and entertainment alternatives.

At face value, most individuals claim to welcome the greater range of choices. However, a contradiction becomes evident when consumers must actually take additional time to make these choices. Although choice appears to be empowering, supposedly giving consumers a sense of control, choice also places responsibility back on the individual to gather information, evaluate alternatives, and select. This takes time and judgment and generates the same sort of doubt and uncertainty that was produced by the deregulation of public utilities, health insurance, and financial services. In a marketplace where the range of health insurance options suddenly expands, it is difficult and daunting to make the new choices—even though customers may have complained bitterly about the old service and the lack of alternatives. Though consumers may not have liked the old system, they were at least spared the burden to choose. A great paradox lies in a world of greater choice, yet heightened sense of powerlessness.

Godek and Yates (2001) uncovered these same basic conflicts when examining the effects of online product customization. They found that greater range of choice may not be preferred, because the customer often does not feel confident in his or her ability to decide—less choice can actually be better under conditions of uncertainty. The idea that customization is more appropriate when the customer knows what he or she wants (i.e., there is low uncertainty) seems to be an anomalous fit with the proposition that the Internet empowers consumers. Surely sense of empowerment is more related to sources that aid decision making under conditions where uncertainty prevails. Situations where you are most uncertain about a decision are the times when you really need a helping hand. The proposition that too much choice may not be good for us is routed in the idea that although people claim to want options, in practice, the comfort of what is known and familiar usually holds greatest appeal. The knowledge that we are part of a socially supportive community gives comfort that we can fall back on the opinion of those whom we trust. We don't want to add to the anxiety of an already stressed life.

Information explosion is one of the most talked about conditions of the new economy. Niche cable television covers specific topic areas in previously unheard-of depth, while the Internet provides access to exponentially growing content sources. The information explosion holds conflicting implications for consumers. On the positive side, information potentially empowers an individual to make more informed choices, to increase participation in community decision making, and to enhance control of one's destiny. However, realization of these potential benefits depends on consumer's motivation and the availability of tools and skills to sift through, integrate, and form judgments. This presents a substantial problem, given the constraining forces discussed earlier. Consumers confronted with increased information must devote more effort to use it effectively. In many instances, the difficulty is compounded by alternative Internet sources presenting information that is either incompatible or outright conflicting. The Internet, at least at this stage, is not like the offline world where we have come to know which sources are most reliable.

Will this uncertainty in identifying the most credible online sources change? Yes, quite possibility, but the way this will happen is when particular sites take on the role of trusted brands—just like offline brands. The trouble with this scenario is that it seems to defeat the appeal of the online world in terms of much touted fluidity and breadth of source options. If we end up relying on just one or two sites to help us make decisions for each category, then what is the conceptual difference to current offline decision practices? Where is the real empowerment? It may be that a trusted site does actually give us a more complete range of information. However, the question remains as to whether consumers are able to process the more extensive information contained on the preferred site.

HOW WE REALLY MAKE DECISIONS

Difficulty in delivering information that communicates effectively can be felt in such apparently straightforward tasks as nutrition labeling, fair-balance copy in prescription-drug advertising, environmental and recycling education, and similar public-awareness programs (e.g., Petruccelli, 1996; Hae-Kyong, Ellinger, Hadjimarcou, & Traichal, 2000). The learning is that to be understood information must arrive in short, simple units rather than elaborated explanation. We typically make do by resorting to short-cuts. We seek to satisfy rather than to optimize. If a choice appears sufficient to satisfy a felt need, we invest no further in search and evaluation. The simplest short-cut is habitual repurchase. The persistence of habitual consumer purchase has been demonstrated in the work of Ehrenberg (see Ehrenberg & Uncles, 1996), in which strong stability of market share over time has been observed across many product categories. Will it be that over time consumers will settle into a similar habitual pattern when using the Internet? They will form a small set of preferred site locations in each category and simply revisit when the category need arises. This habitual process is already instilled into the book category, where there is one dominant player, a distant number two, and companies such as Borders Books that have found the number-three position to be an untenable business proposition. Similar limited preference sets are evolving for other categories as consumers fall into habitual patterns. This is usually led by the first entrant who successfully services a need area.

Another well-documented short-cut is to select the brand that is most well known. In studies where category users are asked to name brands within that category, it consistently turns out that the brand mentioned first is the category leader (Klenosky & Rethans, 1988). A well-recognized brand is safe. One fundamental that many of the failed dot coms did recognize is that they needed to get their brand name to the top of their consumer's evoked set. What they often did not appreciate was the amount of time and money involved in achieving this goal. Reliance on a well-recognized brand name as prime selection criterion holds true not just in low-involvement products but also in the most complex business-to-business purchases, such as corporate software systems. A study of high-priced whitegoods found that purchase selections were often based on limited information searches that included just one information source, one store visit, and consideration of a single brand (Wilkie & Dickson, 1985). Involvement theory suggests that these products should attract considerable information search and evaluation as a result of high cost, long period of product use, and infrequent purchase. But this has not been found to be the case. Evidence in fact points the opposite way. Consumers tend to simplify the decision process when faced with increasingly complex tasks (Bettman, Luce, & Payne, 1998). Under complex conditions, they are more likely to fall back on favoring the option that is judged superior on the most prominent attribute. The idea that the uncertainty derived from greater information complexity often results in an increased likelihood of the consumer resorting back to simple (limited processing) short-cuts holds profound implications regarding the potential for consumer empowerment via the online channel.

Other short-cuts are common too. Price can indicate quality; so can an expert's advice (Hoyer, 1984). Consumers do of course make use of more rational choice criteria. However, even for products with multiple attribute characteristics (such as automobiles), selection is typically based on no more than a couple of product attributes (Bettman, 1979). For example, we may first narrow the product alternates to a manageable few based on company reputation. Then we establish a minimum acceptable level for several key choice criteria and accept an alternative only if every criterion exceeds the cutoff. This is not to say that consumers follow a single rule or strategy when choosing from among alternatives. The point is that because consumers possess insufficient cognitive bandwidth to integrate multiple beliefs about many alternatives, they are forced to narrow to a limited portion of available information. Historically, the opinion of others has often carried significant weight in important decisions. Often consumers value the opinion of friends who are experienced. In other categories the main influence comes from experts, such as doctors in the medical area, or financial advisors in the money arena.

One approach to mimic the power of opinion comes from sites that claim expertise in a particular category—medical and finance are two such areas. Sites claiming objectivity and independence endeavor to set themselves up as advanced forms of decision short-cuts. Some do this by providing comparative information. Others claim to search for the best price. The development of interactive decision aids (or recommendation agents) has been touted as the way forward for consumer empowerment. These tools attempt to mimic a multiattribute decision approach in that a consumer can select and weight a listed set of product attributes. The tool then compiles a product comparison matrix based on the consumer's stated attribute importance. For example, in a bicycle selection the consumer could review dozens of bicycle alternatives (drawn from diverse suppliers) based on the weighted attributes they had selected.

This approach does hold some appeal and proponents of the Internet's potential to empower often use such examples. The claim is that these recommendation agents will lead to more "optimal" decisions. However, there are a number of issues that cast doubt on such optimistic claims. If we rely on these tools to make decisions, then is this not just the normal human strategy of falling back on expert advice? Clearly, the use of these tools requires a thing called "trust"—the same kind of trust that we place in a human advisor or a brand. The second issue lies in the level of human concern for making so-called optimal decisions. It seems that consumers make a great many choices in their lives—generally with minimal effort and information—yet we seem to regret a tiny proportion of them. Consumers may not follow strategies that even approach strict rationality yet they appear to get on with their lives just fine. Short-cuts have utility. We persist with them because they tend to work (Gigerenzer & Goldstein, 1996).

CAPABILITY VARIES ACROSS INDIVIDUALS

Another constraint that impedes consumer usage of information lies in differing abilities to process the information. I am talking about the distribution of functional literacy skills across the U.S. population. The National Adult Literacy Survey (Kirsch, Jungeblut, Jenkins, & Kolstad, 1993) defined literacy ability in terms of using printed and written information to function in society, to achieve one's goals, and to develop one's knowledge and potential. The survey attempted to measure a broad range of information-processing skills. The analysis broke the population into five levels of information-processing skill. More than 50% of the U.S. adult population fell into the bottom two functional literacy levels in which individuals exhibit difficulty integrating several facts from a longer document. Fewer than 20% of the U. S. adult population fell into the top two literacy levels in which they were found comfortable in integrating and synthesizing information from long text. Ability to integrate and synthesize would seem to be a prerequisite for any individual confronted with a range of information. Access is only empowering if one has these prerequisite skills. Limitations in the ability to draw logical inferences and think critically will constrain the value of additional information. The top 20% of the population have a clear advantage in harnessing the Internet. Examination of child literacy performance indicates that there is little evidence of any change trend. Child literacy levels remain flat in every grade (Federal Interagency Forum, 1999). The only exception is for a small group at the very top literacy level where an upward trend is evident.

Although functional literacy levels have remained at best flat over the last 20 years, the amount and the complexity of available information has continued to increase. This indicates a widening gap between the amount of information available and our ability to process it—our capability to use is lagging behind our access. As noted earlier, one of the most popular online search activities is for health information, yet the quality of the outcomes are questionable. Consumers go online to understand their conditions, make better informed decisions, and participate in their own care—to be empowered. Berland and colleagues (2001) examined the reading grade level of Internet health information for disease states including breast cancer, depression, obesity, and asthma. They concluded that high reading levels are required to comprehend the information. One potential area to aid limited comprehension lies in the use of visual, rather than text-format presentation—particularly the use of rich media involving moving pictures. Although I tend to agree with this possibility, I would also caution the potential for visual techniques to enhance persuasive manipulation on the part of marketing communicators. One only has to look at the visual power of television commercials for which persuasive techniques have been significantly refined since that mediums inception.

IS TECHNOLOGY TAKING US ON A CYCLE?

The discussion thus far has highlighted processing limitations together with basic environmental conflicts that consumers face. I have suggested that increased time pressure, expanded access to information, greater range of choice, together with cognitive limitations force consumers to be highly selective in their information usage. Confusion is likely to set in when the information is not "prepackaged" for easy consumption. One may then argue that the enabler of consumer empowerment will be just such easily digestible prepackaged information. The basic counterpoint is that as soon as information is dumbed-down into a simpler form, then what really happens is that the Internet source becomes a surrogate expert. If the Internet does not contribute additional understanding, then where is the difference from reliance on an offline expert?

Figure 16.2 depicts this line of argument in terms of a cycle. In the "old" off-line world, consumers often employed the short-cut of reliance on a perceived expert (doctor, experienced friend, observation, or salesperson). Over time, various types of online information sources have evolved. However, we are now at the point where confusion stemming from information clutter is more common. Consequently, I predict that consumers will tend to fall back on Internet applications

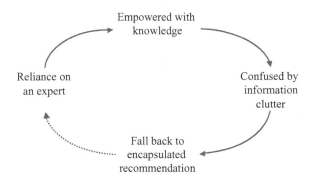

FIG. 16.2   Is technology taking us on a cycle?

that really constitute expert recommendation—trusted branded sites, independent intermediary sites, or the recommendation agents. If this approximates reality, then the Internet will indeed change consumer search in terms of sources employed, but it will not change the basic decision strategies, nor will it lead to substantial knowledge enhancement. The same issues of source credibility arise both online and offline. How do we know that a recommendation agent is performing accurately or inclusively? The bulk of consumers simply won't understand how these tools work in the first place. They must take them on trust—much like the kind of trust when we buy an insurance policy. How do we know that the recommendation agent is unbiased? Unscrupulous operators appear to take advantage of consumers in other media when the consumer lacks objective knowledge. The same risks exist online.

Lewis (2001) highlighted the potential for online deception in the arena of expert advice when relating the example of the 15-year-old boy who started dispensing legal advice on the AskMe.com site. This was a site where individuals could post questions about a range of topics and any other users could reply. Individuals attracted to reply were typically experts in the area (in this case legal) who were interested in promoting their businesses. The site incorporated a user-based rating system whereby recipients were able to rate the quality of the responses and a responder ranking was calculated. This 15-year-old eventually reached the number-one ranking out of about 150 participating experts—legal practitioners. First of all, this says much about the ambiguity of legal advice, but the point is that deceptions can and do succeed.

This example illustrates the potential for online deception where individuals seeking advice have limited points of reference as to source credibility. The consumer must make a trust judgment. The freewheeling open-access characteristic of the Internet is touted as the foundation of its empowering qualities. However, the characteristic of openness can also serve as a double-edged sword in that it can also drive questionable credibility.

ADAPTING OLD LESSONS FOR NEW MEDIA

So, how much information is too much when developing messaging in the online environment? Put simply, for each discrete communication, anything more than a single compact idea is too much. This most obviously applies to one-way communication. Marketers have long understood that a key to successful media advertising is to focus the message on the repetition of a single compelling idea, conveyed as a user benefit. A product or service often has a great many attributes and features. Consequently, the hardest challenge in developing messaging lies in the decision to leave information out. Time limitation makes this a necessity in the standard 30-second television commercial. However, few marketers have translated or extended focused messaging into new information technology forms where time and space limitations would not appear to be constraining. A marketer can of course pack seemingly limitless information in an Internet site. But, too few marketers tightly distill the messaging focus prior to site development. The same communication rules also apply—in appropriate ways—to newer, interactive (one-to-one) media and information technologies.

One might assume that interactive technology promises to negate (or at least alter) this single-idea rule. The promise of interactive is more than repetitive one-way messages; it rests on the potential to realize meaningful two-way communications. Yet the single-idea rule remains vitally important. In such cases the single idea may require adaptation with each discrete communication—depending on the consumer's decision stage. Attention to the single-idea rule will become even more critical as interactive practice develops. This will be because of heightened potential for confusion resulting from mismanagement of the multiple messages that are involved.

Best learnings for interactive implementation can be gained from the masters of two-way communication—successful salespeople. They understand messaging focus in the context of sequential delivery. This understanding rests on two elements: ability to classify customers into motivational types and the insight that each specific type of customer moves through a reasonably consistent decision sequence. They know that a specific focused message at each stage is optimal for moving each customer type to the next decision stage. Examination of successful salespersons has identified that even they (at least implicitly) operate off a finite number of sales "scripts." The sophisticated application of these scripts by successful salespeople supports the proposition that useful customer segments and identifiable decision stages are indeed evident for most any category.

A hypothetical example: New buyers in a category may first want to learn about which brands are most reputable; then they may focus on identification of key product attributes; followed by comparison of brand alternatives based on these attributes; finally the selection focus may fall on price and after-sales service. Armed with this knowledge a salesperson knows not to talk price at the stage where the customer is trying to learn which are the main brands. They know that talking about additional attributes (particularly unimportant ones) when the customer is focused on comparing alternatives will result in confusion. Their expertise allows them to tailor a focused message based on decision stage. The most successful salespeople better understand and leverage this knowledge (Weitz & Sujan, 1985).

TOWARD IMPLEMENTATION

Realizing the potential of focused messaging in a natural sequence is founded on developing a thorough understanding of customers' decision processes. This includes involvement with the category, identification of current information-search patterns, alternative evaluation criteria, and duration of the decision process. Simply knowing the extent of the process can be enlightening. Pinpointing the key evaluative criteria that consumers employ guides what information to eliminate. Identifying the single most important source of customer uncertainty also reveals opportunity.

Simple techniques can be employed to develop these decision insights. For example, one approach is to select a sample of prospects and offer them the opportunity to question a knowledgeable category expert. The subject's sequence of questions and reactions to the expert's answers will provide insight. Another approach is to ask subjects to recall the last time they identified a category need and then have them track back through the sequence of events and thoughts that led to purchase. A third approach—triadic sorting—isolates defining product characteristics by having subjects consider sets of three product alternatives, then select the one they think is most different from the other two. The reasons they give for this selection help identify the primary criteria for distinguishing among alternatives. A range of more sophisticated quantitative techniques is also available. However, regardless of methodological complexity, the research should result in a time line that lays out in a sequential manner just what consumers typically believe and do from the point of need identification through product purchase, and across purchase cycles.

Equipped with this foundation, marketers can identify the most useful role for the Internet at each stage of the decision process. It is important to settle on roles that are realistic. For example, a site designed for one global packaged-goods marketer had brand credibility as its objective—an indirect influence on final purchase. The driving insight was that the Target enters the category with scant product knowledge. Consequently, the purchase decision relies on brand trust. On the other hand, Internet domain-name registrars use their sites to expedite the sale. A key insight is that the registrars' customers are among the most comfortable of Internet users. Consequently, the purchase transaction conveniently fits with current usage patterns.

The importance of clearly specifying the role of selected technology tools often appears obvious only in retrospect. Note the belated realization emerging in the arena of financial and investment advice via the Internet. We witnessed an initial rush by financial players to move online, with many believing that consumers would shift their search and transaction activity to the Internet. This resulted in some of today's most sophisticated information delivery and transacting sites. However, not all activity moved to the Web. A combination of Web and physical presence is required. For example, one major online broker plans to open a chain of investor centers; others are moving to partner with office-based financial companies. In short, many financial industry players have had to refine the appropriate role for Internet applications within their consumers' overall decision processes.

CUSTOMER-CENTRIC BENCHMARKING: THE EXPERT PROXY

There are many metrics that help evaluate the worth of an interactive program. Examples include sales/ROI growth and comparison with industry standards. However, the following may be the ultimate question if a consumer perspective is adopted: How close does the interactive program come to replacing the informative supremacy of an expert consultant? Some may say that this is too unrealistic a qualifying test for a remote technology today. However, consumers make the comparison, whether or not we want them to. If they can get immediate, custom answers by talking to a perceived expert, then the Web site can at best be a bridge to that level of service and at worst a frustrating barrier that threatens the relationship it seeks to build. The notion of a "Live, Adaptable Expert" provides the ideal against which consumers judge new technology. It may not be immediately attainable, but realistic evaluation of the gap provides a useful sense of worth from the perspective that counts most—the customer's.

REFERENCES

Berland, G., Elliott, M., Morales, L., Algazy, J., Kravitz, R., Broder, M., Kanouse, D., Munoz, J., Puyol, J., Lara, M., Watknis, K., Yang, H., & McGlynn, E. (2001). Health information on the internet: Accessibility, quality, and readability in English and Spanish. *The Journal of the American Medical Association, 285*(20), 2612–2621.

Bettman, J. (1979). *An information processing theory of consumer choice.* Reading, MA: Addison-Wesley.

Bettman, J., Luce, M., & Payne, J. (1998, December). Constructive consumer choice processes. *Journal of Consumer Research, 25*, 187–217.

Brewer, N., & Chapman, G. (2001). *Consumer's of health information on the internet: Impact on knowledge, attitudes and behavior.* Presented at the 20th annual Advertising and Consumer Psychology Conference: On-line consumer psychology: Understanding and influencing consumer behavior in the virtual world. Seattle, Washington.

Cialdini, R. (2001). *Influence: Science and practice.* Boston: Allyn & Bacon.

Ehrenberg, A., & Uncles, M. (1996). *Dirichlet-type markets: A review.* Working Paper Series, South Bank University Business School.

Federal Interagency Forum on Child and Family Statistics (FIFCFS). (1999). *America's children: Key national indicators of well-being.* Washington, DC: U.S. Government Printing Office.

Gigerenzer, G., & Goldstein, D. (1996). Reasoning the fast and frugal way: Models of bounded rationality. *Psychological Review, 103*, 650–666.

Godek, J., & Yates, F. (2001). *Evaluation of customized products: The effects of assortment and control.* Presented at the 20th annual Advertising and Consumer Psychology Conference: Online consumer psychology: Understanding and influencing consumer behavior in the virtual world. Seattle, Washington.

Hae-Kyong, B., Ellinger, A., Hadjimarcou, J., & Traichal, P. (2000). Consumer concern, knowledge, beliefs, and attitudes towards renewable energy. *Psychology & Marketing, 17*(6), 449–468.

Hoyer, W. (1984, December). An examination of consumer decision making for a common repeat purchase product. *Journal of Consumer Research*, 822–829.

Kirsch, I., Jungeblut, A., Jenkins, L., & Kolstad, A. (1993). *Adult literacy in America.* Washington, DC: National Center for Education Statistics, U.S. Department of Education.

Klenosky, D., & Rethans, A. (1988). The formation of consumer choice sets. In M. Houston (Ed.), *Advances in consumer research*, Vol. 15. Provo, UT: Association of Consumer Research.

Lewis, M. (2001, July 15). Attack of the masked cyberdudes! *The New York Times Magazine*, 12–13.

Miller, G. (1956). The magic number seven, plus or minus two: Some limits on our capacity for processing information. *Psychological Review, 63*, 81–97.

Petruccelli, P. (1996, Spring). Consumers and marketing implications of information provision: The case of the Nutrition and Labeling Education Act of 1990. *Journal of Public Policy, 15*, 148–150.

Weitz, B., & Sujan, M. (1985). Knowledge, motivation, and adaptive behavior: A framework for improving selling effectiveness. *MSI Research Report*, No. 85–100. Cambridge, MA: Marketing Science Institute.

Wilkie, W., & Dickson, P. (1985). Shopping for appliances: Consumers' strategies and patterns of information search. *MSI Research Report*, No. 85–108. Cambridge, MA: Marketing Science Institute.

CHAPTER SEVENTEEN

Rationality Unbounded: The Internet and Its Effect on Consumer Decision Making

Saurabh Mishra and Richard W. Olshavsky

Indiana University, Bloomington

We are in the midst of an information revolution. The Internet and the advancement in digital technology have brought about this revolution. The new technology is changing the way we receive and process information. This has widespread consequences for the field of marketing. Specifically, this new information explosion will drastically affect the way consumers will behave. Research in marketing is still grappling with this new development. Though some papers (Deighton, 1997; Peterson, Balasubramaniam, & Bronnenberg, 1997) investigated the implications of the Internet on consumer decision making, this research is still at a very early stage. One possible reason for this can be the dynamic nature of these innovations. Nobody is sure how the new technology will evolve over time and so it is difficult to predict or analyze any substantial changes in the consumer decision-making process. Based on the latest developments in the technology this chapter attempts to bridge the gap in the research. Specifically, this chapter focuses on how the new technology is evolving toward a more intelligent and consumer-friendly scheme. One example of new technology helping consumers is the availability of Web sites that help consumers conduct online digital auctions and thus facilitate consumer-to-consumer and consumer-to-manufacturer marketplace interactions (see the chapter "Consumer Behavior in Online Auctions: An Exploratory Study" *in this volume* for more details on how such auction Web sites are making it easier for consumers to acquire and dispose goods). The chapter then discusses the impact of this change on the rationality of consumers. In other words, the chapter attempts to point out how the new technology is helping consumers move toward a more optimal decision-making process.

There have been two dominant views in the literature regarding consumer behavior. One view emerges from the neoclassical economics literature and assumes perfect rationality on the part of consumers while they engage in making decisions regarding their consumption baskets. The other view that predominates the thinking in psychology and marketing literature is the one of "bounded rationality" (Simon, 1955). According to this view, consumers are inhibited by their basic cognitive capabilities (for example, limited short-term memory, slow rates of processing, availability and accessibility of information in the long-term memory) to be perfectly rational. Instead of being perfectly rational, consumers form their decisions using less effortful, but less accurate heuristics. These heuristics are constructed based on a benefit-cost or an accuracy-effort trade-off (Bettman, 1979; Payne, Bettman, & Johnson, 1993). This accuracy-effort trade-off view assumes that consumers in decision situations will "adapt" and will try to form a trade-off between the cognitive effort they have to expend in making decisions and the accuracy of their decisions. Consumers in this framework are assumed to form satisficing decisions (Simon, 1956) rather than optimal ones.

The outline of the chapter is as follows. First, the chapter discusses the assumptions of theories based on perfect rationality and contrasts them with the assumptions of theories based on bounded rationality. Second, the latest developments in the field of information technology are pointed out. Third, the effects of developments in information technology on consumer information-processing constraints are considered. Fourth, a few guidelines for the future development of Web-based services are provided. Lastly, future research directions are presented.

RATIONALITY AND SATISFICING

In the neoclassical economics literature there are various versions of what perfect rationality means. Initial theories started with very strict assumptions but later developments in research moved on to relax them. The earlier theories described perfect rationality as people having perfect knowledge about their possibility sets, including knowledge about the relationships between the strategies available to people and the outcomes associated with these strategies. Also transitivity of preferences was assumed (Tisdell, 1996). This assumption implies that if a person prefers A over B and prefers B over C then he or she will prefer A over C; further, such a scheme of preferences exists for all the alternatives available to the consumer. Later theories like expected utility theory (von Neumann & Morgenstern, 1953) and other works showed that people could be rational in their decisions even if the perfect knowledge assumption is relaxed. Also research showed that if people choose the optimal alternative it doesn't matter if the preferences for the other options in the possibility set are transitive or not (Tisdell, 1996). The basic idea behind the new relaxed assumptions was that people choose an option that maximizes their utility. To reach this optimal choice, it is not important that people have complete information on all the other options and thus have a transitive set of preferences across all the possible options. If these people are presented with a mechanism that introduces to them a set of alternatives for which the decision makers have a higher utility compared to all the other possible alternatives they do not need to have clearly defined preferences for these inferior options as these preferences do not influence the rational choice of selecting the best alternative. We later see how the latest developments in technology help consumers make their optimal choice without needing them to consider all possible alternatives.

Taking the earlier-mentioned view of rationality, Simon (1955, 1956) argued that as individuals are bounded in their rationality, "satisficing" rather than optimizing is the rule in decision making. He based his assertion on the following assumptions:

1. Individuals have limited knowledge.
2. Information is costly to collect and store.
3. Economic behavior requires a trial-and-error search process.

Based on these constraints individuals are prepared to settle for satisfactory outcomes rather than continuing the search for an optimal one.

Based on the idea of bounded rationality, theories were developed showing how consumers use less-accurate heuristics as opposed to choosing the optimal choice rules (Payne et al., 1993). The choice of heuristics in these models depends on an accuracy-effort trade-off that the consumers face. That is, the theories assume that the meta goals for consumers while involved in a decision-making process are to minimize their cognitive effort and to maximize the accuracy of their judgment. The effort and accuracy involved with a decision are shown to be affected by the "task" effects and the "context" effects that consumers encounter. In these theories the task effects are factors associated with the general structural characteristics of the decision problem; these include time pressure, number of alternatives and attributes that consumers have to consider, and the response modes that consumers face. The context effects relate to the factors that are dependent on particular values of the objects in a consumer's consideration set, such as similarity of alternatives. While considering these task and context effects the theories assume that in the actual world consumers will be faced with time constraints, high task complexity, various response modes, and close similarities between alternatives.

Starting with the premise that consumers make a trade-off between effort and accuracy researchers have outlined a set of various decision strategies that consumers might use while making decisions. Some of the common strategies that are discussed in the literature are the weighted additive rule (WADD), the lexicographic heuristic (LEX), the elimination-by-aspects heuristic (EBA), and the equal weight rule (EQW) (Payne et al., 1993, Ch. 2). A more detailed description of these rules and heuristics is provided later. While following the WADD rule consumers form scores on alternatives by adding the weighted values (the weighted values are a function of the utility that consumers obtain from a particular attribute) of each attribute that the product possesses and then choosing the product that has the highest score (score represents the utility that the consumers get from each alternative and so the alternative with the highest score will mean that the alternative provides the maximum utility to the consumers). For the EQW rule, consumers still form scores on alternatives by adding the weighted values of each attribute that the product possesses and choosing the product that has the highest score; the only way in which EQW differs from WADD rule is that in this case the weights for the different attributes are taken to be equal and fixed and are not varied as in the WADD rule. This makes the EQW rule less effortful than the WADD rule. The EBA and LEX heuristics are even less effortful than the EQW rule. While following the EBA heuristic, individuals form a cutoff for the most important attribute and eliminate the products that do not meet the cutoff from their consideration set. If individuals are still left with more than one product, they form a cutoff for the next important attribute and follow the same process of eliminating the products that do not meet the cutoff from their consideration set. They continue with this process till they are left with just one product, which is their final choice. The LEX heuristic is one of the least effortful. Following the LEX heuristic, consumers determine the most important attribute and then examine the values for all alternatives on that attribute. The values of the alternatives on attributes are determined by the amount of that attribute possessed by the alternative. For example, while considering the purchase of a camcorder the consumer will put a value of the attribute picture quality for alternative A by comparing the picture quality of A with what he or she desires. So if A comes very close to what the consumer desires on picture quality, he or she will give it a 4 or 5 on a scale of 6. The alternative with the best value on the most important attribute is selected. If two alternatives have tied values, consumers decide on the next most important attribute and follow this process till the tie is broken.

The strategies mentioned here differ in terms of the effort required by consumers and the accuracy of the decision consumers can achieve following them. Marketing and psychology researchers have long grappled with the issue of how to measure the effort required by the consumers in following these different strategies. In their book *The Adaptive Decision Maker*, Payne and colleagues (1993, Ch. 3) showed that the process of measuring effort through the elementary information process (EIPs) as proposed by Huber (1980) and Johnson (1979) is a very robust technique. They have outlined how this technique can be used to measure the effort required in making a decision both when the consumers follow the WADD rule and the EBA rule with an example in Chapter 3 of their book. We use a similar example as theirs to show how much effort is required while a consumer follows the two strategies of WADD and EBA for a scenario where the consumer is faced with a three-alternative, three-attribute decision problem. In our example the consumer

TABLE 17.1

Set of EIPs Used

READ	Read an alternative's value on an attribute into short-term memory (STM)
COMPARE	Compare two alternatives on an attribute and/or total scores
ADD	Add the products in STM
PRODUCT	Attribute Weight * Attribute Value (multiply)
ELIMINATE	Remove an alternative or attribute from consideration
CHOOSE	Announce preferred alternative and stop process

Adapted from Payne et al. (1993) Chapter 3, Table 3.1.

TABLE 17.2

Example of a Three-Alternative, Three-Attribute Decision
Problem While Following the WADD Rule

	Attributes		
	Picture Quality	Versatility	Convenience
Weights	6	4	2
Alternative A	4	7	4
Alternative B	2	7	2
Alternative C	4	6	3

is considering purchase of a camcorder. He or she has the option of choosing from three different brands—A, B, or C—that differ on three different attributes—picture quality, versatility, and convenience. In a later section we show how with the help of the processing capabilities of computers and the World Wide Web, a consumer's effort gets lowered while following either WADD or EBA decision strategies. The set of EIPs that we use to show how the method works are listed in Table 17.1.

We first consider the case where the consumer follows the WADD rule to make a decision. The details of the weights for the three attributes and the values of the three attributes for the different alternatives are shown in Table 17.2.

The consumer first READS the values of the three attributes for alternative A and READS the weights for the three attributes (six READS). He or she then multiplies the corresponding attribute weights to the attribute values; this means he or she computes three PRODUCTS. Following this, the consumer ADDS the three PRODUCTS he or she gets (two ADDS). This helps the consumer to get at the final score for alternative A, which is 60. Therefore the total number of EIPs the consumer uses to arrive at this score is six READS, three PRODUCTS, and two ADDS. The consumer then follows this process for alternatives B and C. The final scores for B and C are 44 and 54. The consumer then COMPARES (two COMPARISONS) the scores for the three alternatives. Because A has the highest

TABLE 17.3
Example of a Three-Alternative, Three-Attribute Decision
Problem While Following the EBA Rule

| | Attributes | | |
	Picture Quality	Versatility	Convenience
Weights	6	4	2
Cutoffs	3	7	4
Alternative A	4	7	4
Alternative B	2	7	2
Alternative C	4	6	3

score, he or she CHOOSES A (one CHOOSE). The total number of EIPs used by the consumer in reaching this decision is 18 READS, 9 PRODUCTS, 6 ADDS, 2 COMPARISONS, and 1 CHOOSE. This means a total of 36 EIPs. (Note we are here considering the simple case where all the EIPs are given equal weights while calculating the total effort.)

In comparison to this, let's consider the case when faced with the similar scenario: The consumer now uses the EBA heuristic rather than the WADD rule. The values that he or she will use to come to a decision in this case are shown in Table 17.3. Notice that the only way in which Table 17.3 differs from Table 17.2 is that it has the various cutoff values that the consumer will use for eliminating the various alternatives. While following the EBA rule, the consumer first READS the weights for the three attributes (three READS). The consumer then COMPARES these three weights to arrive at the attribute he or she would first use to ELIMINATE alternatives. In our example the consumer would need three READS and two COMPARISONS. Because picture quality has the highest weight, the consumer would use it. He or she would then READ the value of picture quality for the cutoff, and the three alternatives (four READS). Following this, the consumer will COMPARE these four values and eliminate all the values that do not meet the cutoff. This would mean four READS, three COMPARISONS, and one ELIMINATION. Following these steps, alternative B would be eliminated. Because the consumer is still left with two alternatives, he or she would then choose the next attribute. Following the same procedure as earlier, the consumer would use versatility as the attribute on which to base the decision and will choose A as his or her final choice. The whole process would require 12 READS, 8 COMPARISONS, 2 ELIMINATIONS, and 1 CHOOSE, for a total of 23 EIPs.

Another factor that the consumer has to consider is accuracy. The WADD rule is considered to be the normative rule and is assumed to arrive at the most optimal outcome (Payne et al., 1993). While evaluating the other possible strategies, the accuracy of these strategies is measured relative to the WADD rule. Because,

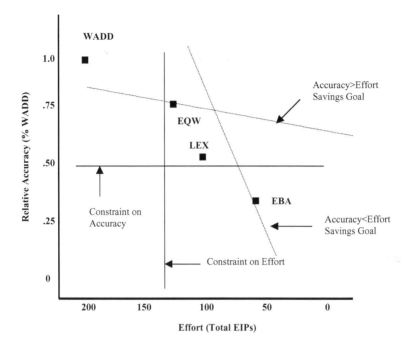

FIG. 17.1   Selection of strategies with different constraints on goals of effort and accuracy.

even for the simple case mentioned earlier, we could see that the WADD rule is more effortful than EBA, the present theories suggest that in the real world where consumers are faced with a very large number of alternatives and attributes, it is almost impossible for them to follow the WADD rule. Researchers have shown that when faced with task and context effects, consumers move from rules like the WADD rule, which are compensatory (where consumers can trade off loss in utility because of absence of a particular attribute in a product with the utility they derive from another attribute of the product), and use alternative-based processing (where consumers make decisions after considering all the alternatives) to heuristics like the EBA, which are noncompensatory (where consumers are not able to make these trade-offs) and attribute based (where consumers do not consider too many alternatives but base their decision on a particular set of attributes of a product) (Payne et al., 1993, Ch. 2.; Olshavsky, 1979). Such a shift implies that consumers move away from making a rational choice.

In Fig. 17.1 we see how the constraints on accuracy and effort do not permit the consumer to approach the WADD rule. We have drawn two lines representing two different preference functions a consumer can possess. One line (preference function) represents the case where the consumer values the accuracy goal more than the effort goal; the other line represents the case where the consumer values the effort goal more. We see based on the preference function of consumers regarding the relative priority of accuracy and effort (as measured by the slope of the preference function) how a consumer will use either the EQW strategy or the EBA strategy. For the case (Accuracy>Effort Savings Goal) the consumer chooses the EQW strategy; for the second case (Accuracy<Effort Savings Goal), the EBA strategy is chosen (Payne et al., 1993, Ch. 3, Fig. 3.3c).

INFORMATION TECHNOLOGY: WHERE DO WE STAND?

The past few years have seen an information revolution. The triggering factors for this revolution have been the advancement in digital technology and the growing use of personal computers. Connected to the World Wide Web people can now access unprecedented amounts of information sitting in their homes with the help of their personal computers or standing in a retail outlet with the help of wireless devices. As people are becoming more and more used to this new technology and as the interfaces are becoming more and more user-friendly it is not difficult to see that the way consumers are making their decisions is changing. The new technology can act as a powerful tool in the hands of the consumers through which they can overcome the traditional constraints they face while making decisions (Olshavsky, 1983). To assess and predict these changes it is very important for us to see where this new technology is heading.

The technology available in the form of personal computers and the various developments in software are changing at a very fast pace. Personal computers are becoming smaller and more accessible. Consumers can now access enormous amount of information from possibly anywhere. The use of this new technology is making the concept of a "consumer," as seen today in the marketing literature, obsolete. It is becoming increasingly important to conceptualize a consumer as a man-machine alliance, comprised of the consumer, the personal computer, the World Wide Web, and the supporting infrastructure. We can call this alliance "consumer-computer system." We define the consumer-computer system as an alliance between man and machine in which the two interact to make decisions. Because each system has different capabilities in handling the new technology and because each person derives a different use out of the new technology, it is becoming imperative to study these systems rather than study individuals or households.

The consumer-computer system includes the use of the World Wide Web. Connectivity to the World Wide Web is becoming faster and better. The advancement in cellular and related technology (e.g., wireless, broadband) means that people will soon be able to access the enormous database of information present on the World Wide Web from nearly any place, at any time. Additionally, new tools on the World Wide Web are emerging that assist consumers in the decision-making

TABLE 17.4
Sample Search Results for Camcorders From the Internet

Model Names (5)	Sharp VL-AH30U Photo (2)	Samsung SCL 550 Photo (3)	Sony CCD-TR416 (1)	Model Names
Key facts				*Key facts*
List price	$450.00	$450.00	$449.00	List price
Today's price	$399.67	$449.99		Today's price
Product review	Review		Review	Product review
Available online	Stores & pricing	Stores & pricing		Available online
General features				*General features*
Format (4)	Hi-8 (1)	Hi-8 (1)	Hi-8 (1)	Format
Built-in auto light (3)	Yes (1)	No (0)	Yes (1)	Built-in auto light
LCD screen monitor (5)	Yes (1)	Yes (1)	No (0)	LCD screen monitor
Image stabilization (3)	No (0)	Yes (1)	Yes (1)	Image stabilization
Snapshot (3)	No (0)	Yes (1)	No (0)	Snapshot
Remote (2)	Yes (1)	No (0)	Yes (1)	Remote
Optical zoom (4)	16 (1)	22 (3)	18 (2)	Optical zoom
Digital zoom (0)	No data	440	180	Digital zoom
Computer editing capable (3)	No (0)	No (0)	Yes (1)	Computer editing capable
Battery type (2)	Nickel Metal Hydride (NiMH) (1)	Li-Ion (2) Battery	Lithium (3) Ion	Battery type
Weight (lbs.)	1.52	Info. Not Available	1.7	Weight (lbs.)
	Remove	Remove	Remove	

processes. One such tool that has been around for some time now is the search engine. Consumers can access information on any topic using these search engines (also refer to the chapter "The Effect of Site Design and Interattribute Correlations on Interactive Web-Based Decisions" where the authors investigate the use of these search engines). We have provided the results of one such search in Table 17.4. The table provides side-by-side comparisons of three camcorders on different attributes.

One of the possible drawbacks of using search engines is that they can give too much information for each search. This would mean that consumers using this as an information source can be cognitively strained to make an optimal decision. In their article, Hoque and Lohse (1999) showed that while using search engines consumers may consider only the first few options that the screens show, making it far from what rational behavior will require them to do. This means that the design and effectiveness of the specific search engine(s) must also be included in defining the system.

Another technology is rapidly evolving, that of search robots. These robots come into action each time a consumer logs on to the Web. They maintain a record of the consumer's evaluative criteria and automatically search the World Wide Web for appropriate options, often at the lowest prices. Moreover, they interact with the consumer each time the consumer accesses them. They use this interaction and tracking of consumers' movements on the World Wide Web to suggest relevant options when the consumer searches for some information. This means that when consumers get information through these search robots they get a smaller number of alternatives that have to be considered. Moreover, because search robots suggest only relevant options to the consumer this implies that the consumers will end up making more rational decisions even if they consider only these few alternatives. Yet another development is the large number of "calculators" that are available on the Web; these enable consumers to perform inherently complex decisions (for example, buying versus leasing a car, refinancing a mortgage and saving for retirement) in a simple manner.

In the next section, we see how, with the use of these technologies, some of the constraints on rationality are being relaxed.

RATIONALITY "UNBOUNDED"

Earlier we described the specific assumptions that Simon (1955, 1956) made while formulating the idea of "bounded" rationality. The first two constraints he pointed out were the inability of decision makers to collect and store large amounts of information and their low knowledge level. In the last section we saw how consumers are becoming "systems." Computers are developing as tools that people can use to *store* large amounts of data. And the latest advancements in cellular and Internet technology are making it possible for consumers to *access* this database from any place in the world at any time (just in time). This makes Simon's (1955, 1956) assumption regarding the cost for consumers to collect and store large amounts of data irrelevant for these new consumer systems.

In the previous section we further saw how new tools such as search engines and robots can immensely enhance the knowledge level of consumers without adding substantial cognitive efforts for them. We further show, using the example cited earlier in the chapter, how the effort that consumers would require in terms of the number of EIPs needed to process information is getting reduced. Therefore, we see how two of Simon's assumptions on which he based his theory of bounded rationality are becoming obsolete at least for some consumers, in some choices. Later we show how the third assumption is also becoming obsolete. All of this implies that rationality is not as bounded now as when Simon proposed his theory (prior even to the advent of the electronic calculator).

We have seen earlier that the accuracy-effort trade-off–based theories assume that it is impossible or very difficult for consumers to adopt the WADD rule. Because these theories consider WADD to be highly representative of a rational rule this means that consumers are restricted from making a rational choice. This assertion is based on the task and context complexities that consumers face and the effort required to execute the large number of EIPs that consumers need to overcome these complexities. In this chapter we argue that the constraints imposed by task and context complexities are reduced with the new technology. So, the WADD rule is becoming a possibility for consumers.

Some of the task effects that are considered in the literature are time pressure, the large number of alternatives, and the large number of attributes that are to be considered for each decision for the decision to qualify as a rational one.

Research on the effects of time pressure predicts that when consumers have less time for making a decision they will use simplifying heuristics as they will have no other choice (Simon, 1981). In this situation a strategy such as the WADD may exceed the information-processing capacity of most consumers no matter how motivated they are to make an accurate decision (Payne et al., 1993, Ch. 2). Also it has been shown that under time pressure individuals only access a limited amount of information (Keinan, 1987) and they shift to noncompensatory strategies such as the LEX heuristic (Zakay, 1985). This implies a less-optimal decision. Assuming that consumers have strictly increasing preferences for accuracy, we can assert that consumers will shift toward more efficient rules such as the WADD given that they have the opportunity and mechanisms to do so in the time pressure that they face. This is possible with consumer-computer systems. In today's world the speed with which consumers can access information with the help of the Internet and process it with the help of their personal computers is very high. Also shopping online is rapidly evolving. Virtual stores eliminate the necessity of going to brick and mortar stores and thus considerable time is saved. The consumers can then spend this time more efficiently in evaluating the alternatives. This means that with the use of these new technologies consumers can overcome the constraint of time to a great extent. This will allow them to execute the WADD rule without any major burden on their time.

With regards to the multitude of alternatives and attributes it has been shown experimentally that when consumers are faced with lots of alternatives with numerous attributes, the consumers prefer noncompensatory strategies (Tversky, 1972). Also, Braunstein and Payne (1973) and Olshavsky (1979) showed that as the number of alternatives increases consumers use more attribute-based processing than alternative-based processing. This clearly marks a shift from the WADD rule that requires both alternative-based and compensatory processing to less-accurate heuristics. The robustness of these shifts has been proved by the observation that these shifts to less-accurate decision heuristics are even made by expert consumers, who have better cognitive capabilities than average consumers (Gaeth & Shanteau, 1984). We have seen how rapidly new technologies such as search robots are becoming available; these robots form a preference structure that is similar to the consumer's preference structure. So when consumers request information, the search robots evaluate a large number of alternatives and attributes for the consumers and present them with only those that match the consumer's preference structure. This means that consumer systems face fewer alternatives. That is, the constraint imposed by the task complexity is greatly reduced without lowering the quality of the decision. We have discussed earlier that a decision can be perfectly rational even if the consumers have not accessed all the information themselves, (Tisdell, 1996). So we can conclude that with this technology consumers can make a more rational decision than they could till now.

Among the context effects, similarity of alternatives has been considered as a feature that inhibits consumers to make a rational choice. It has been shown (Briggs, Bedard, Gorber, & Linsmerei, 1985) that as the similarity among alternatives increases, consumers need more and more information before they can make an optimal decision. Without more information, the theories predict that consumers would not be able to make a rational choice. We have shown earlier, using the camcorder example (Table 17.4), how consumers can get information in a side-by-side comparison format on various attributes for three different brands of camcorders using a search engine. We now show with a simple example how, with the help of the higher processing capacity of personal computers, consumers can overcome this processing requirement.

Earlier in the chapter we discussed an example of how the effort consumers expend while making a decision is calculated using EIPs. We had calculated the various EIPs that consumers used while reaching a decision when faced with a three-alternative, three-attribute decision problem. For the WADD rule we had seen that consumers used 18 READS, 9 PRODUCTS, 6 ADDS, 2 COMPARISONS, and 1 CHOOSE to arrive at a decision. For the EBA heuristic, on the other hand, the consumer used 12 READS, 8 COMPARISONS, 2 ELIMINATIONS, and 1 CHOOSE. The consumer can now perform all the ADDS, COMPARISONS, PRODUCTS, and ELIMINATIONS EIPs using the computer. Software is available today (for example, Excel) that the consumers can use to put the information in matrix format. (For an exposition of this assertion, see the Appendix where we have provided an Excel sheet that utilizes the information available from Table 17.4.) Also it should be noted that the example in the Appendix is only an exposition of the idea. Today there are decision sites available that automatically do the WADD computation for users, thereby mitigating the need to retype values in an Excel sheet (for example, www.activebuyersguide.com) and thus reducing the efforts required from consumers even further.

Using the simple options available in such software, the consumer can perform thousands of ADDS, COMPARISONS, PRODUCTS, and ELIMINATIONS automatically. The consumer is then left with only performing the READ and the CHOOSE process. In our example this will mean that for the WADD rule a consumer has to perform 18 READS and 1 CHOOSE, a total of 19 EIPs. For the EBA heuristic the total effort expended by a consumer will be 12 READS and 1 CHOOSE, totaling to 13 EIPs. Therefore, we see that the difference in effort required with WADD as compared to the effort required with EBA is greatly reduced with the help of the new technology. If we agree that the EBA heuristic was available to consumers if they do not use the new technology (a total of 23 EIPs), then it is clear that with the help of this new technology the WADD rule is now available to the consumers (a total of 19 EIPs, which is fewer than 23 EIPs). Because WADD is more accurate, the consumers should strictly prefer it if it is available. Therefore, in reaching a decision consumers are likely to follow the WADD rule and arrive at a more rational decision.

According to the present discussion, we can see that the scenario represented by Fig. 17.1 gets transformed into one represented by Fig. 17.2. That is, when we reduce the effort required by consumers as seen in Fig. 17.2, we find that optimal

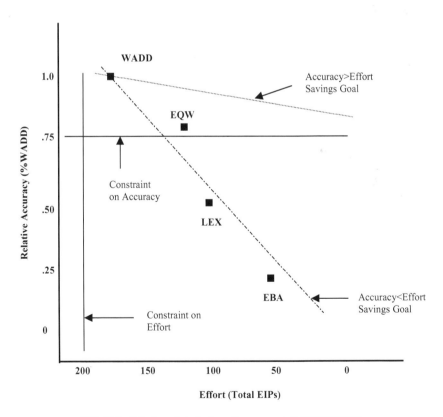

FIG. 17.2   Selection of strategies with consumer-computer systems.

rules like the WADD rule, which were not executable by the consumers in the earlier scenario, are now possible. This relaxation in effort is shown to be because of the additional power made available to the consumers from the use of computers. Additionally, the figure shows that consumers will increase the levels of accuracy they desire from their decisions. This is shown in the increase of the accuracy goal in Fig. 17.2. Figure 17.2 thus represents the trend toward more optimal decision making. We argue in this chapter that because consumers have increasing preferences for accuracy they would now include the WADD rule. Because optimal rules like the WADD are both available and preferred by consumers, it follows that consumers will choose these rules or search engines/robots that use these rules (For example, www.activebuyersguide.com) as opposed to any other less-accurate rules or heuristics.

Although it may be difficult for most consumers to delegate the WADD rule to their computers, online retailers are already providing evaluations of the brands they carry, in the form of recommendations. Consumers can use these evaluations directly or as proxies to establish the appropriate weights they would like to attach to the different attributes in their decision process (Rosen & Olshavsky, 1987). Today there are Web sites available that follow the WADD rule and elicit user's preferences/weights. The availability of these Web sites further reduces the effort required from consumers.

Does this earlier discussion imply that consumer systems are already making rational decisions or are there any other constraints that are inhibiting them from being rational? We see that though there have been rapid developments in technology, a lot is still desired before consumers can make optimal choices. In the next section, a few guidelines for the future development of computer software technology are presented.

FUTURE DIRECTIONS FOR INTERNET TECHNOLOGY

As we have seen, the latest developments in the Internet and computer technology have started relaxing the constraints that consumers face while making some decisions. But can we say that these developments are sufficient for optimal decision making. The answer to this question is: It depends. Some systems can already do it and for many others it will be possible very soon. Consumer behavior research can provide useful insights for these important developments. This chapter initiates this process by illustrating one example, thus showing the path that later researchers can follow.

It has also been demonstrated that consumers often restructure the information provided to them so that it is easier for them to compare alternatives and attributes. Coupey (1994) showed that consumers form matrix-like structures while evaluating information and this step makes consumer decisions more accurate while reducing the effort burden. *Consumer Reports* magazine also follows this matrix approach in their reporting format. It is to be noted that this option is already available for consumers getting information on the Internet from most online retailers or search engines (see Table 17.4). Because computer screens are made of rows and columns, it is not hard to develop software that can provide the desired information to the consumers in a matrix format. This development alone should improve the efficiency of consumers and help them move toward a more optimal decision, as they will be able to tap the information advantage provided by the World Wide Web to the fullest. In addition, as stated earlier, retailers frequently provide their "recommendations" for the best brands. This helps to reduce the trial-and-error search process that Simon (1955, 1956) considered as his third assumption while describing bounded rationality. One counterargument is that *Consumer Reports* has already been providing recommendations to consumers. Though this is true the Internet as an information resource has many advantages over these reports.[1]

It is not only research in marketing that can be used for guiding future development of Internet tools. Research in other fields such as statistics or mathematics can also be used to make computers more useful for consumers. In a recent article in *Scientific American*, Swets, Dawes, and Monahan (2000) showed that new statistical techniques have been developed that help in determining accurate cutoffs for important decisions that involve a range of options. These new techniques are already being used in medicine and other areas to form cutoffs on the basis of which doctors are determining whether a patient is ill or not. These statistical models can be used in search robots to form cutoffs on various attributes based on their interaction with consumers. This will help improve the efficiency of robots in limiting the information they provide to the consumers, thus making it easier for consumers to make intelligent decisions and to eventually automate the entire choice process. In the future we also expect these robots to evolve to enable consumers to "customize" the robot's basic search procedure (for example, some people might like the robots to search only on price, others might have two or more non price-related criteria) and thereby further increase consumer's accuracy in achieving utility maximizing decisions. Following the earlier-mentioned steps to improve the options available to consumers for decision making will help to improve the chances that consumers prefer the World Wide Web as an information source to any other brick-and-mortar options (when the desired information is available online). Thus, a lot needs to be done before rationality is totally "unbounded" but already some of the constraints that were assumed by theorists a few decades ago are rapidly disappearing.

---

[1] Although it is generally recognized that Consumers Union (CU) provides valuable information concerning products/services based on objective tests, the information from CU is not readily available. A consumer must obtain the information either by subscription to *Consumer Reports* (CR) (approximately 5 million households out of 105 million households) or by visiting a library. Access to the CU Web site is currently limited to subscribers. In order to access the desired information, subscribers to *CR* magazine must store past reports (something that many subscribers may not do).

LIMITATIONS AND FURTHER RESEARCH

The underlying theme of this chapter has been the change brought about by the information revolution in consumer decision making. We expect consumers to resort to technological aids whenever "accuracy" is very important and/or "effort" involved in making a decision is very high. For example, the need for accuracy of the decision and the amount of effort required to reach the decision will be high for risky products or services (such as stock purchases and major surgery) and for expensive products or services (such as automobiles, life insurance, mortgages). As more and more consumers are starting to use computers and the World Wide Web in their daily lives, it is becoming imperative for researchers in marketing to incorporate this change into their studies. The idea of replacing consumers with consumer-computer systems as the basic unit of analysis as proposed in this chapter is something not dealt with in any studies in marketing so far. Issues concerning the behavior of these consumer-computer systems should now be the focus of consumer research. This chapter has attempted to highlight how much of the past research on consumer decision making is rapidly becoming obsolete or irrelevant. A lot needs to be done. A typical example can be the irrelevance of theories that model consumer behavior based on the storage or retrieval limitations of long-term memory of consumers. It is easy to see how the limits of long-term memory can be overcome by relying on the large memory of today's computers and the ease of accessing and then reaccessing updated information from the World Wide Web. Further, we believe that the very concept of "the adaptive decision maker" should be broadened to include adaptations not only in the evaluation strategies, but also in the evaluative criteria, the consideration set, and the image of alternatives within these considerations sets. That is, all four components of a consumer's "choice space" are impacted by the use of the Internet (Olshavsky & Kumar, 1999). With respect to marketing management implications we expect that all aspects of marketing strategy and all four elements of the marketing mix (product, price, place, and promotion) are greatly impacted. For example, to be included in a consumer's consideration set, firms will have to know what consumer's cutoffs on price are and adjust their prices accordingly. (Note that Chrysler already had to do this on their minivans [White, 2001].) Also advertising effectiveness may change dramatically because a consumer's image or knowledge of alternatives will be obtained directly from the company's Web site and from other Internet sites (beyond the control of the company).

This chapter also highlights how a synergy between research in marketing and other fields such as statistics, mathematics, and artificial intelligence is needed to provide guidelines for the companies that wish to operate successfully on the Internet. Empirical testing of the assertions made in this chapter provides another avenue for future inquiry. One such attempt has been made in the chapter "The Effect of Site Design and Interattribute Correlations on Interactive Web-Based Decisions" in this volume. In this chapter, the authors empirically show that users are more appreciative of WADD–like search engines than EBA-like search engines when it is more rational to use WADD. Also they provide evidence that more EIPs (operationalized as the number of clicks while working on the Internet) are needed to execute the EBA than the WADD. Finally, even more profound developments brought about by the Internet such as "file sharing" among consumers (e.g., Napster), 3-D visualization, virtual environments, and product simulations not only change our conception of consumer capabilities but also provide major changes in the *structure, content,* and *delivery systems* of entire industries (e.g., publishing, entertainment, education).

APPENDIX: Camcorder Comparison

Weights	Features	Sharp	Scores	Samsung	Scores	Sony	Scores
5	Model names	2	10	3	15	1	5
4	Format	1	4	1	4	1	4
3	Built in auto light	1	3	0	0	1	3
5	LCD screen monitor	1	5	1	5	0	0
3	Image stabilization	0	0	1	3	1	3
3	Snapshot	0	0	1	3	0	0
2	Remote	1	2	0	0	1	2
4	Optical zoom	1	4	3	12	2	8
0	Digital zoom	0	0	1	0	2	0
3	Computer editing capable	0	0	0	0	1	3
2	Battery type	1	2	2	4	3	6
	Total Score		30		46		34

AUTHOR NOTE

Saurabh Mishra is a doctoral student in the Department of Marketing, Kelley School of Business, Indiana University, Bloomington, Indiana (samishra@indiana.edu). Dr. Richard W. Olshavsky is professor of marketing, Kelley School of Business, Indiana University, Bloomington, Indiana (olshavsk@indiana.edu).

REFERENCES

Bettman, J. R. (1979). *An information processing theory of consumer choice.* Reading, MA: Addison-Wesley.

Braunstein, M. L., & Payne, J. W. (1973). Risky choice: An examination of information acquisition behavior. *Memory and Cognition, 6,* 554–561.

Briggs, S. F., Bedard, J. C., Gorber, B. G., & Linsmerei, T. J. (1985). The effects of task size and similarity on the decision behavior of bank loan officers. *Management Science, 31,* 970–987.

Coupey, E. (1994, June). Restructuring: Constructive processing of information displays in consumer choice. *Journal of Consumer Research, 21*, 83–99.

Deighton, J. (1997). Commentary on exploring the implications of the internet for consumer marketing. *Journal of the Academy of Marketing Science, 25*(4), 347–351.

Gaeth, G. J., & Shanteau, J. (1984). Reducing the influence of irrelevant information on experienced decision makers. *Organizational Behavior and Human Performance, 33*, 263–282.

Hoque, Abeer Y., & Lohse, G. L. (1999, August). An information search cost perspective for designing interfaces for electronic commerce. *Journal of Marketing Research, 36*, 387–394.

Huber, O. (1980). The influence of some task variables on cognitive operations in an information-processing decision model. *Acta Psychologica, 45*, 187–196.

Johnson, E. J. (1979). *Deciding how to decide: The effort of making a decision.* Unpublished manuscript, University of Chicago.

Keinan, G. (1987). Decision making under stress: Scanning of alternatives under controllable and uncontrollable threats. *Journal of Personality and Social Psychology, 52*, 639–644.

Olshavsky, R. W. (1979). Task complexity and contingent processing in decision making: A replication and extension. *Organizational Behavior and Human Performance, 24*, 300–316.

Olshavsky, R. W. (1983). A theoretical perspective for predicting the impact of personal computers on marketing. In Donald F. Mulvihill (Ed.), *The impact of personal home computers on marketing* (pp. 39–47). Muncie, IN: Bureau of Business Research, Ball State University, American Marketing Association Workshop.

Olshavsky, R. W., & Kumar, A. (1999). Adaptive decision making: Toward an integrated explanation. *Proceedings of the 1999 Annual Conference of the Society of Consumer Psychology*, 176–180.

Payne, W. J., Bettman, J. R., & Johnson, E. J. (1993). *The adaptive decision maker.* New York: Cambridge University Press.

Peterson, R. A., Balasubramaniam, S., & Bronnenberg, B. J. (1997). Exploring the implications of the Internet for consumer marketing. *Journal of the Academy of Marketing Science, 25*(4), 329–346.

Rosen, D. L., & Olshavsky, R. W. (1987). A protocol analysis of brand choice strategies involving recommendations. *Journal of Consumer Research, 14*, 440–444.

Simon, H. A. (1955). A behavioral model of rational choice. *Quarterly Journal of Economics, 79*, 99–118.

Simon, H. A. (1956). Rational choice and the structure of the environment. *Psychological Review, 74*, 29–39.

Simon, H. A. (1981). *The sciences of the artificial.* Cambridge, MA: MIT Press.

Swets, J. A., Dawes, R. M., & Monahan, J. (2000, October). Better decisions through science. *Scientific American*, 82–87.

Tisdell, C. (1996). *Bounded rationality and economic evolution: A contribution to decision making, economics and management.* UK: Brookfield, VT, Edward Elgar Publishing Limited.

Tversky, A. (1972). Elimination by aspects: A theory of choice. *Psychological Review, 79*, 281–299.

Von Neumann, J., & Morgenstern, O. (1953). *Theory of games and economic behavior.* Princeton: Princeton University Press.

White, J. B. (2001, August 31). Chrysler cuts some vehicle prices as honda Offers "special" packages. *The Wall Street Journal* p. B.6.

Zakay, D. (1985). Post-decisional confidence and conflict experienced in a choice process. *Acta Psychologica, 58*, 75–80.

CHAPTER EIGHTEEN

Consumer Relationships with an e-Brand: Implications for e-Brand Extensions

JongWon Park
Hyun-Jung Lee
Korea University

Hyung-Il Lee
Kookmim University

BACKGROUND

The number of Internet users is rocketing, along with the number of online or Internet site brands (hereafter, e-brands) on the Web.[1] Although the Internet made its commercial debut only a few years ago, by 1999 there were already more than 800 million pages of content on the Web. This is largely attributed to low entry barriers on the Internet whereby creation of a new Internet site brand is relatively inexpensive. Because of extreme difficulty in attracting consumers to a particular site, however, much of the focus of Web marketing has been directed toward acquiring consumers. Furthermore, it is difficult to keep customers once they are "acquired" for there are many factors that determine if online experiences enhance the brand relationship (see the chapter "Effects of Visual Consistency on Site Identity and Product Attitude," this volume). Therefore, it is not surprising to observe that many of the recent publications in this field heavily stress the need for building a strong relationship with your customers (e.g., Carpenter, 2000; Hagel & Singer, 1999; Newell, 2000). However, does it really matter in a strategic sense (i.e., in increasing revenue or market share, etc.) to build and maintain a strong consumer-brand relationship in an online setting? Although the consumer-brand relationship displays an intuitive sense and has been advocated recently by

---

[1] This chapter considers only "pure-play" or online-only companies such as Amazon and e-Bay.

some academic researchers (e.g., Fournier, 1998), empirical evidence supporting the strategic importance of the consumer-brand relationship is rather scarce (e.g., Fournier, 2000; Park & Kim, 2001). Further, to the best of our knowledge, no empirical evidence has been reported under the context of e-brands. The present research intendes to fill this gap.

In addressing the issue of concern, we evaluated the role of consumer-brand relationships within the context of introducing new extensions of an e-brand.[2] Specifically, we investigated whether or not a strong consumer-brand relationship of an e-brand helps to obtain consumers' acceptance of new extensions of that brand. This is an important issue because dot-com companies are actively seeking ways to broaden their business scope both vertically and horizontally (e.g., Amazon.com, Yahoo.com, eBay.com, etc.), that is, making brand extensions aggressively, under the assumption that that's the way to go (see Afuah & Tucci, 1999). On the other hand, the brand extension literature suggests that extensions, unless carefully selected and managed, are likely to fail in the market, sometimes even causing a fatal damage to the parent brand as well. Thus, those factors elevating the probability that consumers respond to the extensions of an e-brand favorably would be of great strategic importance. In this regard, a strong relationship between an e-brand and consumers would be proven as strategically important, if it demonstrates the capacity to increase that probability.

The remaining part of this chapter is organized as follows. First, what is known about brand extensions and interpersonal relationships is presented. Then, a study to examine the viability of presented hypotheses is derived regarding the effects of consumer-brand relationships on the success of extensions of the brand is described. Finally, the future of e-brand strategy is projected, together with suggestions for further exploration.

THEORETICAL CONSIDERATION

Consumer-Brand Relationship

Can a brand have a relationship with a consumer as people do with each other? The answer is affirmative. For example, brands can be perceived as a "partner" if they were celebrities or famous historical figures that relate to one's own self. This often has to do with various strategies by marketers to imbue a brand with personality traits such as anthropomorphization (e.g., California Raisins), personification (e.g., Jolly Green Giant), and the creation of user imagery (e.g., Charlie girl). Brand-person associations of a more personal nature are also common. A

---

[2]A common practice of many companies is to broaden their product offering. When this is done without creating a separate brand, the existing brand is "extended" to cover these new products. The quality of the consumer-brand relationship becomes evident when it is stretched to accommodate a brand extension.

brand of cologne that the ex-husband always used or brands originally received as gifts can become strongly associated with the past significant others. Thus, they may evoke the person's spirit reliably with each use. In fact, recent research by Fournier (1994, 1998) documents compelling evidences for the existence of consumer-brand relationships and further proposes a relationship-quality framework in consumer-brand contexts. According to the framework, consumer and brand actions determine the brand relationship quality. This relationship quality is then assumed to be associated with the intermediate process of developing and maintaining the relationship as well as with ultimate consequences such as relationship stability and satisfaction.

One of the critical conditions for relationship formation and development is interaction between two partners (e.g., Anderson & Weitz, 1992; Bersheid & Reis, 1998). In the consumer-brand relationship context, a consumer and a brand constitute the two partners. Fournier (1998) documented several cases in the traditional offline setting that provided examples of active interactions between consumers and brands. We expect such consumer-brand interactions to be much more likely in the online setting. This is because of the interactive potential of the Internet. Unlike the media such as magazines or television, the Internet facilitates two-way communication between actors.[3] This new medium possesses what Blattberg and Deighton (1991) termed interactivity: It has the facility for individuals and organizations to communicate directly with one another regardless of distance or time. Therefore, it is reasonable to suppose that strong consumer-brand relationships are likely to be more common in the online setting than in the offline setting. As such, marketers might be able to develop such a relationship more actively and perhaps more easily for e-brands than for traditional offline brands.

The research issue of concern here is how such a relationship works. Specifically, how will the strength or quality of consumer-brand relationships influence the degree to which consumers would accept extensions of e-brands? To elaborate on this issue, we now turn to the literature on brand extensions as well as the literature on interpersonal relationships.

Factors Affecting Success of Brand Extensions

A number of factors have been proposed to influence consumers' acceptance of extensions, including brand characteristics, extension characteristics, strategic characteristics, and firm characteristics. Much focus has been on how extension judgments might be shaped by overall attitudes toward and/or specific associations with the original brand that consumers currently hold (e.g., MacInnis & Nakamoto, 1991), congruity or similarity between the extension and the original

---

[3]We are not saying that the Internet is the most interactive of all. The Web is more interactive than most advertising channels. However, it is less interactive than many sales channels such as stores and catalogs.

brand category (e.g., Aaker & Keller, 1990; Park, Milberg & Lawson, 1991), and the interaction between these two (Aaker & Keller, 1990; Keller & Aaker, 1992). Strong evidence has been found for these determinants of evaluations of extensions.

There is ample empirical evidence that strong brands benefit extensions more than weak brands. For example, Smith and Park (1992) argued that stronger brands might have a greater ability to reduce perceived risk than weaker ones. Further, they showed a positive and significant relationship between brand strength and the brand extension's market share. In addition, it has been experimentally demonstrated that the perceived quality of a parent brand is likely to be transferred to its extensions. In this experimental research, brand strength is often conceptualized in terms of consumers' attitudes or judgments of quality associated with the brand (Aaker & Keller, 1990; Smith & Park, 1992). Another important conclusion in the literature is that the similarity between an extension and the original brand category moderates the transfer of attitude or affect. Substantial evidence has implicated category similarity in brand extension evaluations (Aaker & Keller, 1990; Boush & Loken, 1991; Keller & Aaker, 1992).

Perhaps the most useful conceptual framework that can be used to account for these results might be the dual-processing formulations of person-impression formation postulated by social cognition researchers (e.g., Brewer, 1988; Fiske, 1982; Fiske & Pavelchak, 1986). These formulations are based on the distinction between the category-based and piecemeal processing (for a recent review, see Fiske, Lin, & Neuberg, 1999; Fiske & Neuberg, 1990). Briefly, on being exposed to an evaluation object, perceivers first attempt to categorize that object on the basis of salient cues. These cues can take the form of physical characteristics, such as skin color or body shape, or a verbally transmitted categorical label such as race or gender. On receiving additional features or individuating information, perceivers may engage in a confirmatory categorization process to preserve the initial categorization, but this additional process is largely dependent on the level of personal relevance of the evaluation object for the perceivers. Whether or not the initial categorization is maintained is a function of the degree of congruence between the features of the stimulus object and the features of the category prototype (e.g., Loken & Ward, 1990). If the categorization is successful, the evaluation of the object is likely to be based on the affect associated with the category. If the categorization is not successful, however, subtyping or piecemeal integration of various features may serve as basis for forming an evaluation (e.g., Bodenhausen & Wyer, 1985).

Similar category-based processes have been observed in the context of forming product judgments (e.g., Meyers-Levy & Tybout, 1989; Rao & Monroe, 1988; Sujan, 1985; Sujan & Dekleva, 1987). For example, frozen microwave entrees fit the consumers' previous category of TV dinners; automobiles are often grouped by categories such as sports cars, family cars, and subcompacts. It has also been shown that a brand name can serve as a category label and thus lead to a category-based evaluation (e.g., Chaiken & Maheswaran, 1994; Hong & Wyer, 1989; Maheswaran, Mackie, & Chaiken, 1992). That is, consumers may simply base their judgment of a particular product on the general attitude associated with the brand, such as "Kraft food products are superior" or "Betty Crocker makes good baking products." In line with these findings, the evaluations of an extension that are contingent on its similarity to the original brand category have been conceptualized as a category-based processing phenomenon (e.g., Boush & Loken, 1991; Meyers-Levy, Louie, & Curren, 1994; Milberg, Park, & McCarthy, 1997). That is, the level of congruity with a previously defined category (i.e., brand) is viewed as varied by the similarity between the original brand and its extension. Therefore, when a brand extension is perceived as similar to the original brand and thus identified as belonging to the brand category, the affect or perceived quality associated with that category is likely to be transferred to that extension. Consider how often a major soft drink manufacturer will introduce a new beverage (e.g., Diet Coke with Lemon) that is an immediate success because of the similarity to the original high brand equity product (Coke).

More recently, research has shown that brand extensions can be well accepted by consumers in the market even when the product-level similarity is low. This is likely to be the case when the extension's brand concept is consistent with that of the parent brand or when the extension effectively utilizes the strong specific associations of the original brand. For example, Park and colleagues (1991) reported that perceptions of the extension's fit depended not only on product-level similarity, such as features or attributes, but also on the consistency of the extension with a parent brand's concept. Broniarczyk and Alba (1994) found that a brand's specific association (flavor, durability, economy, etc.) made a substantial contribution to the evaluation of brand extensions and that such influence was greater when that association was "relevant" in the extension category than when it was not. Although different in more specific aspects, the earlier-mentioned studies strongly suggest that similarity or fit between a parent brand and its extension moderates the effects of brand associations such as brand affect, brand concept, and specific features. Finally, people experiencing a positive mood tended to accept an incongruent extension quite well, and sometimes even better than a quite similar extension (Barone, Miniard, & Romeo, 2000). However, all of these effects are likely to operate only when the extension's incongruity is relatively moderate. When it is rather extreme, an extension is doomed to fail. In this chapter, however, we propose that an extension in a very dissimilar category can be successful if the parent brand has already developed a strong relationship with consumers. This proposition is explained next.

Interpersonal Relationships

Research on interpersonal relationships has attempted to identify key determinants of the stability of close relationships as well as the processes underlying them (see

Berscheid & Reis, 1998, for a review). One conclusion from this literature is that a relationship, once developed, tends to stabilize at a particular level of intimacy or closeness. According to the investment model of close relationships (Rusbult, 1983), individuals become increasingly dependent on their relationships to the degree that (a) satisfaction level is high, (b) quality of alternatives is poor, and (c) investment size is high. As a result, they become increasingly "committed" to the relationships. Here, commitment represents long-term orientations toward the relationships, including psychological attachment and intent to persist in the relationship, thus including cognitive, affective, and behavioral components. It has been demonstrated that commitment is the critical determinant of relationship stability.

The investment model further suggests that once a relationship reaches a satisfactory level, it is likely to be maintained at that level. The literature provides compelling empirical evidences supporting that commitment reliably promotes persistence in a relationship (for a review, see Rusbult & Van Lange, 1996). Commitment also promotes so-called prorelationship behaviors. Specifically, commitment encourages willingness to sacrifice or tendencies to forego desired activities for the good of the relationship (Van Lange et al. 1997). Further, it promotes accommodative behaviors or tendencies to accommodate rather than retaliate when a partner engages in a potentially destructive behavior. Thus, although a partner's destructive behavior may seem harmful or unjustifiable, the person in a satisfying relationship may exhibit a high level of affect and submission and react constructively. For example, Rusbult, Verelter, Whitney, Slonk, & Lipkus (1991) found that students who were more satisfied with their relationships exhibited greater accommodation such as loyalty (e.g., "I give my partner the benefit of the doubt and forget about it") than did those in less-satisfying relationships.

These commitment processes are largely motivational. However, commitment also influences cognitive processes and thus creates cognitive biases such as positive illusion or tendencies toward excessively favorable evaluations of one's partner or relationship. According to this cognitive perspective, interpersonal interactions and ongoing relationships result from cognitive processes around self-partner schemas. This schema has been posited and empirically demonstrated to often guide the individual's behavior in social interactions and in the development and *maintenance* of relationships (e.g., Baldwin, 1992; Berscheid & Reis, 1998; Bradbury & Fincham, 1990). Specifically, schemas about the self-partner relationship (also called "relational schema") often lead to top-down processes in new instances, thus creating interpretation biases, as well as attributions that cast the partner's behavior in a positive or negative light depending on the quality of the relationship. For example, Murray, Holmes, and Griffin (1996) showed that individuals' impressions of their partners were more a mirror of their self-images and ideals than a reflection of their partners' self-reported attributes. These impressions were more positive than their partners' self-reports, reflecting positive illusion.

Implications

Will consumers exhibit the sort of commitment processes described earlier when they have a relationship with a brand? The research on interpersonal relationships along with the Fournier's (1998) consumer-brand relationship framework discussed earlier seems to provide an implication for this question. That is, an extension into a dissimilar or incongruent category may be metaphorically viewed as a brand's "deviant" behavior and perhaps as an unjustifiable act, or at best a surprise. However, if consumers have established good relationships with this brand and thus feel strongly committed to their relationships, they might exhibit so-called prorelationship behaviors to a great extent. For example, they may interpret the dissimilar (i.e., incongruent) extension in light of the existing relationship schema, which is positive in nature. Thus, they might perceive that extension as an "adventurous" act rather than as a "reckless" act (see Higgins, Rholes, & Jones, 1977; Park et al., 2001). Or they may see the possibility that the extension can be a success rather than a failure via positive illusion processes. These cognitive processes are likely to lead to a more favorable judgment of the extension's quality, which in turn would increase the purchase intention of the extension. On the other hand, consumers in a good relationship with that brand may just as well accommodate the dissimilar extension as it is, or at any rate, be willing to try it for the sake of the relationship. As a consequence, they might be willing to at least try that extension, even when their impressions of the extension's quality may not be favorable.

Based on the earlier discussion, we hypothesized that consumer-brand relationships would play an important role in potential extensions of an e-brand. Specifically, the relationship quality was expected to enhance the favorableness of the perceived quality as well as the purchase intention of brand extensions through both cognitive and motivational processes noted earlier. In addition, these effects were expected to be above and beyond the effects that might be produced by a traditional measure of brand strength, perceived brand quality. The following study tested these expectations.

METHOD

Subjects and Design

A total of 123 undergraduate students participated in the study as part of the course requirement. These students were randomly assigned to either similar or dissimilar extension category conditions. Within each category similarity condition, the students evaluated online product extensions as well as offline extensions of an Internet site brand. Thus, the study involved a 2 (extension category similarity: similar/dissimilar) by 2 (extension mode: offline/online) mixed design with the second factor being a within-subject variable. This is further explained later.

Focal Internet Site Brand and Extension Categories

Characteristics of the Focal e-Brand.   A popular Internet game site brand was used as the focal parent brand in the present study. It was currently the market leader in terms of the size of membership among the major online game sites. This choice was made based on three considerations. First, the site category must be relevant for the population from which the subjects were drawn. Second, the site must be well known to the subjects so that at least some of them exhibit a strong relationship with that site. Third, it should not have already extended to other categories extensively. A pretest suggested that the game site chosen met these criteria.

Four Potential Extension Categories.   The similarity of extensions to the parent brand category (Internet game site) was manipulated by considering both whether or not the extension category was game related (extension category similarity) and whether the extension was an online product or an offline product (extension mode). For this manipulation, a large pool of game-relevant as well as game-irrelevant product categories was initially prepared. It included both online and offline product categories. Then, a pretest was conducted with this pool, and based on its results eight product categories (two per each of extension category similarity [similar/dissimilar] by extension mode [online/offline] combinations) were selected as the final extension categories to be evaluated in the study. Table 18.1 shows these categories.

After this, two versions of questionnaires were constructed for the manipulation of extension category similarity. One version contained the measures to assess the successfulness of two online and two offline extensions, all of which were "similar" category extensions. The other version questioned about the four "dissimilar" category extensions (two per each extension mode). The contents of the questionnaire are explained in more detail later.

Procedure

On arrival in classrooms, the participants were seated and randomly given a folder containing a version of the questionnaire for either similar category extensions or

TABLE 18.1
Extension Categories

	Similarity of Extension Category	
Extension Mode	*Similar*	*Dissimilar*
Online	Game review site	Internet bookstore
	Game league site	Joint-purchasing site
Offline	Joy stick	Hand-bag
	Electronic dance-game machine	Educational videotape

dissimilar category extensions. The experimenter introduced the study as a part of a survey regarding college students' perceptions of various e-brands. Participants were told that (a) they would soon be shown a number of Web screens about a particular Internet game site through a beam projector and (b) they would then be asked to complete a series of questions regarding the site as well as other related questions.

Then, the experimenter turned on the beam projector and showed a total of 24 Web pages of the focal Internet game site with an interval of approximately 30 seconds. This was to refresh the memory associations the subjects might have of that focal e-brand. After this, the participants were asked to open the folder provided, pull out the questionnaire, and fill it out according to the instructions. It was emphasized that there were no right or wrong answers in this survey, thereby stressing the need for direct and honest responses to the survey.

Measures

The questionnaires consisted of three parts. The first part examined the participants' perceptions of the quality about the focal e-brand (parent brand). The second part examined their judgments about four extensions (two online and two offline extensions) of that e-brand. The third part measured the relationship quality that participants might have with that e-brand. These measures are explained in the following sections.

Assessment of Quality of The Focal e-Brand. The perceived brand quality of the focal e-brand was measured by two 7-point semantic differential scales: ("1"—bad, "7"—good) and ("1"—poor quality, "7"—good quality). These scales are most frequently employed in the previous brand extension research to measure the strength of perceived quality of the focal brand (e.g., Aaker & Keller, 1990; Smith & Park, 1992). Because the two scale items were highly correlated, they were averaged into a composite-brand quality index of the focal e-brand for later analyses (hereafter, BQ, Cronbach $\alpha = .89$).

Assessment of Brand Extensions. The effectiveness of brand extensions was assessed in terms of participants' perceived quality and purchase intention of the extensions. Respondents first indicated their quality judgments about an extension on two 7-point scales: ("1"—bad, "7"—good) and ("1"—poor quality, "7"—good quality). These two items were highly correlated, thus were averaged into a composite quality index of the extension for later analyses (hereafter, QUAL, Cronbach $\alpha = .90$). Next was the assessment of their purchase intention of that extension. Respondents were instructed to assume that they were about to make a purchase decision in that given product category. Then, they were asked to indicate the likelihood with which they would seriously consider the focal brand's extension if it was available in the market ("1"—very unlikely, "7"—very likely). This purchase intention will be denoted by PI, hereafter. All of these items were then repeated for the remaining three extensions in each condition of extension category similarity. In administering them, however, the order of online versus offline extensions to be evaluated was counterbalanced across subjects to eliminate possible order effects. Because this order did not have any appreciable impact on the results, we do not discuss it any further.

Note that there was a replication within each of extension category similarity (similar/dissimilar) by extension mode (online/offline) combinations. For example, the "similar online" extension condition included an Internet game review site as well as an Internet game league site to be evaluated (see Table 18.1). Because we were not interested in the replication factor per se (i.e., differences between the game review site and the game league site), we simply used the average perceived quality of the two replication extensions as well as the average purchase intention of the two for later analyses.

Perceived Similarity of Extensions. After the effectiveness of all four extensions was assessed, subjects were asked to indicate the overall similarity of each extension to the original brand category along a 7-point scale ("1"—very dissimilar, "7"—very similar). This served as a manipulation check measure for the overall extension similarity.

Brand Relationship Quality Measures. A set of self-report rating scales was carefully constructed to measure the consumer-brand relationship quality of the focal e-brand. This was based on the existing literature and several pretest results. Research on the relationship quality distinguishes between different components of perceived relationship quality. In fact, many researchers have developed scales that purport to measure distinct components of perceived relationship quality (e.g., Fletcher, Simpson, & Thomas, 2000; Fournier, 1994). A review of the empirical and theoretical literature revealed seven dimensions that were commonly claimed to represent the distinct components. They were: commitment, trust, self-connection, intimacy, love/passion, nostalgic connection, and partner quality. These dimensions have their origins in different theoretical perspectives. For example, commitment is a principal determinant of the relationship stability in Investment Model (Rusbult, 1983). Trust lies at the theoretical core of both Attachment Theory (Bowlby, 1969) and Erikson's (1968) model of psychosocial development. Passion has theoretical origins in various models of love (e.g., Sternberg, 1986). Partner quality is a core component in Fournier's (1998) consumer-brand relationship framework.

These seven components (or dimensions) were used as a basis for initially generating a large number of Likert-type scale items that purported to tap the multifaceted nature of the relationship quality construct. Then, a couple of pilot tests were run to reduce and to refine the items, resulting in a total of 39 items.

TABLE 18.2

Relationship Quality Measures and Final Factor Solution*

Factor	Item	Factor Loadings
Commitment ($\alpha = 92$)	I will stay with this game site through good times and bad.	.890
	I am willing to make sacrifices to keep using this game site.	.857
	I keep this game site in mind all the time.	.827
	I have made a commitment to this game site.	.773
	I feel something amiss when I stop using this game site.	.676
	This game site plays an important role in my daily life.	.653
Trust ($\alpha = 88$)	This game site is reliable and dependable.	.796
	I have a lot of respect for this game site.	.791
	I feel safe and secure when I use this game site.	.739
	This game site adds a sense of stability to my life.	.643
Self-connection ($\alpha = 87$)	This game site and I have a lot in common.	.864
	This game site's image and my self-image are similar in many ways.	.810
	I feel this game site is a part of me.	.645
Intimacy ($\alpha = 87$)	I know a lot about this game site.	.909
	I feel as though I really understand this game site.	.895
	I know things about this game site that many people just don't know.	.692
Brand partner quality ($\alpha = 86$)	This game site treats me like a valuable customer.	.784
	This game site shows continuing interest in me.	.778
	This game site takes good care of me.	.603
Love & passion ($\alpha = 70$)	No other game site can replace this game site.	.784
	I would be very upset if I couldn't access this game site when I wanted to.	.737
	I feel a powerful attraction toward this game site.	.687
Nostalgic connection ($\alpha = 64$)	This game site reminds me of what I was like at a previous stage of my life.	.747
	This game site reminds me of someone important in my life.	.703
	This game site reminds me of things I've done or places I've been.	.696

Note: Until this final factor solution was obtained, the items with low loading scores or those high cross-loading on two or more factors were dropped.

This set of items was then used to measure the relationship quality of our focal site brand in the study (see Table 18.2). Not surprisingly, these items well overlap the items used in previous studies (e.g., Fournier, 1994).

Composite Index of Relationship Quality (RQ). Participants in the study indicated the degree to which they agreed or disagreed on each of the 39 items along the 7-point scale ("1"—absolutely disagree, "7"—absolutely agree). These responses were then factorized with a VARIMAX rotation, resulting in an initial solution of seven factors with eigenvalues greater than 1. Items with low loading scores and those high cross-loading on two or more factors were then dropped. Several repetitions of this procedure finally obtained 25 items loading greater than .6 on their primary factor (see Table 18.2). This final factor solution accounted for 77.1% of the total variance of the data.

As apparent in the table, the seven factors well represented the seven components of perceived relationship quality described earlier. The final 25 items were broken down by factors as follows: 6 items for commitment, 4 items for trust, 3 items for self-connection, 3 items for intimacy, 3 items for brand partner, 3 items for love/passion, and 3 items for nostalgic connection. After this, a composite index for each of the seven components (dimensions) was calculated by averaging only those items classified to the corresponding factor. Reliability scores indicated that all seven component indices were highly reliable (Cronbach α's ranging from .64 to .92, see Table 18.2). Finally, these seven component scores were summed to create an ultimate index of the overall consumer-brand RQ of the focal e-brand for later analyses.

RESULTS

Manipulation Check

The extension similarity was manipulated by whether or not an extension was related to the focal brand's original category (extension category similarity) and whether it was an online or offline extension (extension mode). To verify the successfulness of this manipulation, participants were asked to indicate how similar/dissimilar each extension was to the original brand category. A two-way ANOVA on these responses indicated that the manipulation was successful. First, the predicted main effect for extension category similarity indicated that extensions were perceived as more similar to the original brand category when they were game related (3.95) than when they were not (2.71), $F(1\ 116) = 45\ 6\ p < 001$. Second, the main effect for the extension mode was also significant, $F(1\ 116) = 31\ 6$, $p < 001$. As expected, online extensions were perceived as more similar to the original brand category than offline extensions (3.56 vs. 2.85). Finally, the interaction effect emerged significantly, $F(1\ 116) = 5\ 66, p < 005$. It suggested that the difference in perceived similarity of similar versus dissimilar category extensions was more pronounced when they were online extensions (4.48 vs. 2.86) than when they were offline extensions (3.41 vs. 2.43), although the difference was statistically significant both in the former condition ($F = 48\ 1\ p < 001$) and in the latter condition ($F = 17\ 5\ p < 001$). In summary, the extension similarity was successfully manipulated as intended.

Extension Judgments

Consistent with the previous research, we expected that an extension would be judged more favorably when it was a similar extension than when it was not. Independent of this, however, we further expected that the extension would be judged more favorably when the existing relationship quality with the focal e-brand was strong than when it was weak. To test these expectations, we first divided the participants into relatively strong versus weak relationship quality groups based on their overall relationship quality scores. The median score was used as a basis for this split, and five subjects with that score were eliminated to enlarge the contrast between the two groups. This procedure assigned 58 subjects into the strong RQ group and 60 subjects into the weak RQ group (their respective means were 21.3 vs. 11.5), $F(1\ 116) = 274\ 1\ p < 001$. Then, our hypotheses were assessed by analyzing participants' perceived quality (QUAL) and purchase intentions (PI) of extensions as a function of this "dichotomized" relationship quality variable as well as extension category similarity (similar/dissimilar) and extension mode (online/offline). The results for QUAL and PI are reported separately in the next sections.

Perceived Quality of Extensions (QUAL). The upper half of Table 18.3 shows the mean values of the perceived quality of extensions as a function of extension category similarity, extension mode, and relationship quality. Several effects are noticeable. First, the quality of an extension was judged more favorably when it was a similar category extension than when it was a dissimilar one (4.12 vs. 3.23), $F(1\ 114) = 35\ 4\ p < 001$. This nicely replicates the previous findings in the literature (e.g., Aaker & Keller, 1990). Second, the quality was also judged more favorably when it was an online extension than when it was an offline one (4.00 vs. 3.28), $F(1\ 114) = 45\ 2\ p < 001$. This is consistent with the manipulation check result that online extensions were perceived as more similar to the original brand category than offline extensions. Furthermore, an interaction of extension similarity and extension mode emerged significantly, $F(1\ 114) = 8\ 5\ p < 005$. This interaction suggested that the relative favorableness of the similar category extensions over the dissimilar ones was more pronounced when they were online extensions (4.73 vs. 3.44) than when they were offline extensions (3.63 vs. 3.01). This in fact was consistent with the results of similarity manipulation check, which showed that the extension category similarity manipulation was more pronounced under online extensions than under offline extensions. Finally and most importantly, the extension was judged more favorably by those participants currently having a relatively strong relationship with the focal e-brand (3.90 vs. 3.39), $F(1\ 114) = 10\ 5\ p < 005$. This was not contingent either on whether it was an online extension (4.29 vs. 3.71) or an offline extension (3.51 vs. 3.06), $F < 1$, or on whether it was a similar category extension (4.38 vs. 4.00) or a dissimilar one (3.56 vs. 2.89), $F < 1$. These results clearly support the prediction that an e-brand

TABLE 18.3

Mean Extension Judgments As a Function of Extension Category Similarity,
Extension Mode, and Relationship Quality

Dependent Measures	Online Extension		Offline Extension	
	Similar Category	Dissimilar Category	Similar Category	Dissimilar Category
(1) Perceived Quality (QUAL):				
Low RQ Group	4.56	3.02	3.44	2.75
High RQ Group	4.91	3.85	3.85	3.26
(2) Purchase Intention (PI):				
Low RQ Group	4.44	2.24	2.69	1.76
High RQ Group	4.65	3.53	3.10	2.75

can benefit from having a good relationship with the customers in introducing its
extensions.

Purchase Intention (PI). The lower half of Table 18.3 shows the mean values
of the purchase intentions of extensions as a function of extension category similarity, extension mode, and relationship quality. The three-way mixed ANOVA
produced three main effects. First, as expected, PI was higher when the extension was a similar category extension than when it was a dissimilar one (3.71
vs. 2.58), $F(1\ 114) = 35\ 1\ p < 001$. This parallels the extension category similarity effect observed in the QUAL data. Second, PI was also higher when it
was an online extension than when it was an offline extension (3.61 vs. 2.53),
$F(1\ 114) = 83\ 1\ p < 001$. This also parallels the pattern of the QUAL data. Finally and importantly, PI was higher when the participants were currently having
a relatively strong relationship with the focal e-brand than when they were not
(3.44 vs. 2.70), $F(1\ 114) = 13\ 9\ p < 001$. This confirms our hypothesis and
also parallels the pattern of the QUAL data.

Besides the three main effects, the predicted interaction of extension category similarity and relationship quality emerged significantly, $F(1\ 114) = 4\ 6$,
$p < 05$. This interaction suggested that the effect of relationship quality on the
purchase intention was more pronounced when it was a dissimilar category extension (3.13 vs. 2.00) than when it was a similar one (3.85 vs. 3.56). In fact,
simple effect tests indicated that the former difference was statistically significant
($p < 001$), whereas the latter difference was not ($p > 10$). The fact that the three-
way interaction was not significant ($F = 1$) suggested that the observed two-way
interaction was true regardless of the extension mode.

Finally, the interaction of extension category mode and extension similarity also
emerged significantly, $F(1\ 114) = 16\ 5\ p < 001$. This suggested that the effect
of extension category similarity was more pronounced under online extensions

(4.54 vs. 2.90) than under offline extensions (2.89 vs. 2.26). This parallels the same kind of interaction observed in the QUAL data.

Causal Path Analyses. The ANOVA results indicated that as predicted, the quality and purchase intention judgments of extensions were more favorable when the participants had a relatively strong relationship with the focal e-brand than when they did not. In addition, the effects of RQ on purchase intentions were more pronounced under dissimilar category extension conditions than under similar category extension conditions. These results are largely consistent with the hypothesized influence of the consumer-brand relationship quality on the successfulness of brand extensions.

On the other hand, there is one crucial question that needs to be addressed. That is, were the relationship quality effects observed above and beyond the effects that the perceived quality of the focal brand (BQ) might have had on extensions? More generally, does the relationship quality measure, RQ, add to our ability to explain and predict consumers' acceptance of brand extensions over what is already provided in the more traditional and much simpler attitudinal measure of brand quality? This question is of vital importance because it bears on the issue of the discriminant and predictive validity of the relationship quality construct. That is, if RQ does not have such incremental value vis-à-vis BQ, then the former construct suffers from a lack of discriminant validity, or at best it is less parsimonious in the predictive power, compared to the traditional construct, brand quality. A path analysis approach was employed in order to address this important issue.

In the causal path model tested here, both consumer-brand relationship quality and perceived brand quality were simultaneously included as exogenous variables, with the perceived quality of brand extensions (QUAL) and the purchase PI as endogenous variables. Further, RQ and BQ were allowed to correlate with each other (see Figure 18.1). According to our hypothesis, RQ should affect QUAL and PI at least to some extent, even if the effects because of BQ were modeled simultaneously. That is, BQ was expected to influence QUAL, which in turn would influence PI (RQ -> QUAL -> PI). By contrast, RQ was expected to directly influence PI (RQ -> PI) and in addition, indirectly influence PI by first affecting QUAL (RQ -> QUAL -> PI). Moreover, we further expected that these RQ effects would be more pronounced under dissimilar category extensions than under similar category extensions, as suggested by the significant interaction of RQ and extension category similarity in the previous ANOVA analyses. Therefore, the hypothetical causal path model in Fig. 18.1 was tested in the similar versus dissimilar extension category conditions separately. Figure 18.1 summarizes results from these analyses.

The validity of the path model was assessed using LISREL 8 (Joreskog & Sorbom, 1993) in each of the similarity conditions. Four conventional model-fit indicators were used: the chi-square statistics, the goodness-of-fit index (GFI), the root mean square residual (RMR), and normed fit index (NFI). In Fig. 18.1, it was apparent that the model fit the data fairly well in both similar and dissimilar

(1) Similar category extensions

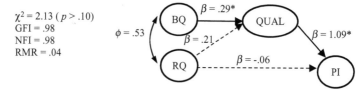

$\chi^2 = 2.13 \ (p > .10)$
GFI = .98
NFI = .98
RMR = .04

(2) Dissimilar category extensions

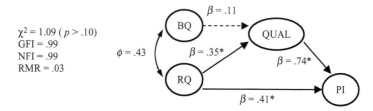

$\chi^2 = 1.09 \ (p > .10)$
GFI = .99
NFI = .99
RMR = .03

FIG. 18.1 Results from path analyses as a function of similarity.

Note: $^*p < 05$; BQ: Original brand quality; RQ: Brand relationship quality;
PI: Purchase intention of extensions; QUAL: Perceived quality of extensions.

extension cases and slightly better in the latter case. GFI, NFI, and RMR indices indicated a very good fit of the model regardless of similarity levels. Also, χ^2 statistics supported the model in both cases. Therefore, these results indicated that the causal path model well accounted for the data both in the similar extension and in the dissimilar extension conditions.

Next, beta coefficients for causal paths were estimated. The statistics in Fig. 18.1 strongly suggested that BQ and RQ had different roles in brand extensions, depending on the similarity level. Specifically, the effect of BQ on QUAL was significant in the similar extension condition ($\beta = 29$), $t = 2\ 38$ $p < 05$, while it was not in the dissimilar extension condition ($\beta = 11$), $t = 1\ 14$ $p > 10$. These in fact are consistent with the previous ANOVA results and replicate the past findings in the literature that the affect or evaluation associated with the parent brand is transferred to the extension only when it is similar to the parent brand category. Different results emerged for the effect of RQ. Specifically, RQ had no significant effect either on QUAL ($\beta = 21$, $t = 1\ 32$, $p > 10$) or on PI ($\beta = -06$, $t = -49$, $p > 10$) when the extension was a similar category extension. In the dissimilar category extension conditions, however, RQ exerted a significant influence on QUAL ($\beta = 35$, $t = 2\ 60$, $p < 05$) as well as a significant direct effect on PI ($\beta = 41$, $t = 3\ 42$, $p < 05$). These results are also consistent with the previous ANOVA results and strongly indicate that as expected, the relationship quality effect was much more pronounced under dissimilar extensions than under similar extensions.

Altogether, the results strongly indicated that the relationship quality of the focal e-brand had a significant impact on acceptance of potential extensions of that brand, and that it was above and beyond the effects because of the traditional measure, BQ, at least under dissimilar category extensions. Further, the consumer-brand relationship construct was found to have both discriminant validity and nomological validity.

DISCUSSION

The strategic importance of the relationship quality of an e-brand was examined within the context of introducing potential extensions of that brand. The brand extension literature has suggested that extensions of an e-brand are likely to be successful only when consumers perceive the focal e-brand as strong in quality and the extensions as similar to the original brand category. On the other hand, the relationship literature suggests that a strong consumer-brand relationship may enhance consumers' acceptance of such dissimilar extensions via perhaps both cognitive and motivational processes around the partner relationship. This possibility was supported in the present study.

Overall, the ANOVA analyses indicated that the perceived relationship quality of the focal e-brand significantly influenced quality judgments about the extensions and the purchase intentions. This effect was not contingent on whether the extension was an online or an offline product. Further, the causal path analyses confirmed this effect in the dissimilar category extension conditions, even when the effects because of the original brand quality were statistically controlled. Specifically, the relationship quality of the focal e-brand significantly influenced subjects' purchase intentions of the dissimilar category extensions via initially affecting their judgments of the quality of those extensions. This result seems to reflect cognitive biases caused by the relationship schema in memory during the judgment formation. In addition, the relationship quality further influenced the purchase intentions directly. This direct effect seems to reflect a sort of prorelationship behavior that was motivationally driven for the good of the relationship. These results in combination were supportive of our expectation that the relationship quality effect would be more pronounced in the dissimilar category extension conditions than in the similar category extension conditions.

It is intriguing that according to the causal path analyses, the effect of the relationship quality on extension quality judgments increased as the extensions became dissimilar, whereas the effect of the original brand quality decreased. In fact, consistent with the previous findings in the literature (e.g., Aaker and Keller 1990), the effect of perceived quality of the focal e-brand on evaluations of the extension was limited to the situation in which there was congruence between the extension and the original brand category. By contrast, the effect of the relationship quality on extension quality judgments was insignificant in the former conditions but was very strong in the latter conditions. One possibility is that people may be motivated to bolster the efficacy of their partner's act (i.e., the brand extension), but will do so only when they feel it is necessary (i.e., only when the extension is a dissimilar one). In such case, the extent to which the bolstering occurs is likely to be a function of the strength of the relationship quality. Another possibility is that cognitive biases because of the activation of the relationship schema are subject to the ambiguity of the target object (e.g., Herr, Sherman, & Fazio, 1983; Stapel, Koomen, & Van Der Plight, 1997). Thus, when an extension is similar to the original brand category, the quality implication of that extension might be clear. Thus, there might be no room for consumers' relationship schema to operate in determining the extension's quality. On the other hand, the implication of a dissimilar extension may not be straightforward, thus permitting cognitive biases to take place.

This research makes several contributions to the current literature. On the one hand, it contributes to the brand relationship research by providing concrete evidence for the strategic importance of consumer-brand relationships in the online setting. On the other hand, it increases our understanding of the brand extension phenomenon by providing a circumstance in which very dissimilar extensions might be successful in the market. Managerial implications of this research seem straightforward. Brand managers are better off when they manage their e-brands from the perspective of relationships with consumers, not just on the basis of consumers' cognitive evaluations of the brands. In addition, our results suggest that online extensions of an e-brand tend to be perceived as more similar to the original brand category than offline extensions of the same brand. As a result, the online extensions are more likely to be accepted by consumers relative to the offline extensions, although both extensions are quite similar to the original brand category. Therefore, online companies may have to restrict their extensions to the online setting unless they have built a strong relationship with their customers, although integration with offline businesses is often strongly advocated in practice.

A couple of future research directions are noted. First, the explanations we provided concerning the pattern of the relationship quality effects observed in this study are rather speculative in nature. More precise mechanisms need to be outlined and tested empirically in the future. Second, the present research did not address the methods on how to develop and strengthen a relationship with brand. Undoubtedly, future research addressing these issues would be of great importance for many years to come.

ACKNOWLEDGMENTS

We would like to thank Professor Robert S. Wyer at University of Illinois and members of the Korea University B.E.S.T. Marketing Group for their helpful comments on earlier versions of this chapter. A special note of thanks is given to Kyeong-Heui

Kim at University of Minnesota for assistance in data analysis and interpretation of results.

REFERENCES

Aaker, D. A., & Keller, K. L. (1990, January). Consumer evaluations of brand extensions. *Journal of Marketing, 54*, 27–41.

Afuah, A., & Tucci, C. L. (1999). *Internet business models and strategies.* Boston, MA: McGraw-Hill.

Anderson, E., & Weitz, B. (1992). The use of pledges to build and sustain commitment in distribution channels. *Journal of Marketing Research, 29*(1), 18–34.

Baldwin, M. W. (1992). Relational schemas and the processing of social information. *Psychological Bulletin, 112*(3), 461–484.

Barone, M. J., Miniard, P. W., & Romeo, J. B. (2000, March). The influence of positive mood on brand extension evaluations. *Journal of Consumer Research, 26*, 386–400.

Berscheid, E. (1985). Interpersonal attraction. In G. L. & E. Aronson, (Eds.), *Handbook of social psychology* (3rd ed., pp. 79–129). New York: Random House.

Berscheid, E. (1994). Interpersonal relationships. *Annual Review of Psychology, 45*, 79–129.

Berscheid, E., & Reis, H. T. (1998). Attraction and close relationships. In D. T. Gilbert, S. T. Fiske, & G. Lindzey (Eds.), *The handbook of social psychology* (4th ed., pp. 193–281). Boston, MA: McGraw-Hill.

Blattberg, R. C., & Deighton, J. (1999). Interactive marketing: Exploring the age of addressability. *Sloan Management Review, 33*(1), 5–14.

Bodenhausen, G., & Wyer, R. S. (1985). Effects of stereotypes in decision and information-processing strategies. *Journal of Personality and Social Psychology, 48*(2), 267–282.

Boush, D. M., & Loken, B. (1991, February). A process-tracing study of brand extension evaluation. *Journal of Marketing Research, 28*, 16–28.

Bowlby, J. (1969). *Attachment and loss: Attachment (Vol. 1).* New York: Basic Books.

Bradbury, T. N., & Fincham, F. D. (1990). Attributions in marriage: Review and critique. *Psychological Bulletin, 107*(1), 3–33.

Brewer, M. (1988). A dual process model of impression formation. In T. K. Srull & R. S. Wyler (Eds.), *Advances in social cognition* (Vol. 1, pp. 1–36) Hillsdale, NJ: Lawrence Erlbaum Associates.

Broniarczyk, S. M., & Alba, J. W. (1994, May). The importance of the brand in brand extension. *Journal of Marketing Research, 31*, 214–228.

Carpenter, P. (2000). *eBrands.* Boston, MA: Harvard Business School Press.

Chaiken, S., & Maheswaran, D. (1994). Heuristic processing can bias systematic processing: Effects of source credibility, argument ambiguity, and task importance in attribute judgment. *Journal of Personality and Social Psychology, 66*(3), 460–473.

Erickson, E. (1968). *Identity: Youth and crisis.* New York: Norton.

Fiske, S. T. (1982). Schema-triggered affect: Applications to social perception. In M. S. Clark and S. T. Fiske (Eds.), *Affect and cognition: The 17th annual Carnegie symposium on cognition* (pp. 55–78). Hillsdale, NJ: Lawrence Erlbaum Associates.

Fisk, S. T., Lin, M., & Neuberg, S. L. (1999). The continuum model: Ten years later. In S. Chaiken & Y. Trope (Eds.), *Dual-process theories in social psychology* (pp. 231–254). New York: Guilford.

Fisk, S. T., & Neuberg, S. L. (1990). A continuum of impression formation, from category-based to individuating processes: Influences of information and motivation on attention and interpretation. In M. P. Zanna (Ed.), *Advances in experimental social psychology* (Vol. 23, pp. 1–74).

Fisk, S. T., & Pavelchak, M. A. (1986). Category-based versus piecemeal-based affective responses: Developments in schema-triggered affect. In Richard M. Sorrentino, Edward Tory Higgins et al. (Eds.), *Handbook of motivation and cognition: Foundations of social behavior* (pp. 167–203). New York: Guilford.

Fletcher, G. J. O., Simpson, J. A., & Thomas, G. (2000). The measurement of perceived relationship quality components: A confirmatory factor analytic approach. *Personality and Social Psychology Bulletin, 26*(3), 340–354.

Fournier, S. (1994). *A consumer-brand relationship framework for strategic brand management*. Unpublished doctoral dissertation, University of Florida.

Fournier, S. (1998, March). Consumers and their brands: Developing relationship theory in consumer research. *Journal of Consumer Research, 34*, 343–373.

Fournier, S. (2000). *Dimensioning brand relationships using brand relationship quality*. Paper presented at the 2000 ACR conference, Salt Lake City, Utah.

Hagel, J., & Singer, M. (1999). *Net worth*. Boston, MA: Harvard Business School Press.

Herr, P. M., Sherman, S. J., & Fazio, R. H. (1983, July). On the consequences of priming: Assimilation and contrast effects. *Journal of Experimental Social Psychology, 19*, 323–340.

Higgins, E. T., Rholes, W. S., & Jones, C. R. (1977, March). Category accessibility and impression formation. *Journal of Experimental Social Psychology, 13*, 141–154.

Hong, S.-T., & Wyer, R. S. (1989, September). Effects of country-of-origin and product-attribute information on product evaluation: An information processing perspective. *Journal of Consumer Research, 16*, 175–187.

Joreskog, K. G., & Sorbom, D. (1993). *Structural equation modeling with the SIMPLIS command language*. Hillsdale, NJ: Lawrence Erlbaum Associates.

Keller, K. L., & Aaker, D. A. (1992, February). The effects of sequential introduction of brand extensions. *Journal of Marketing Research, 29*, 35–50.

Loken, B., & Ward, J. (1990, September). Alternative approaches to understanding the determinants of typicality. *Journal of Consumer Research, 17*, 111–126.

Maheswaran, D., Mackie, D. M., & Chaiken, S. (1992). Brand name as a heuristic cue: The effects of task importance and expectancy confirmation on consumer judgments. *Journal of Consumer Psychology, 1*(4), 317–336.

Meyers-Levy, J., Louie, T. A., & Curren, M. T. (1994, February). How does the congruity of brand names affect evaluations of brand name extensions? *Journal of Applied Psychology, 79*, 46–53.

Meyers-Levy, J., & Tybout, A. M. (1989, June). Schema congruity as a basis for product evaluation. *Journal of Consumer Research, 16*, 39–54.

Milberg, S. J., Park, C. W., & McCarthy, M. S. (1997). Managing negative feedback effects associated with brand extensions: The impact of alternative branding strategies. *Journal of Consumer Psychology, 6*(2), 119–140.

Murray, S. L., Holmes, J. G., & Griffin, D. W. (1996). The benefits of positive illusions: Idealization and the construction of satisfaction in close relationships. *Journal of Personality and Social Psychology, 70*(1), 79–98.

Newell, F. (2000). *Loyalty.com*. New York: McGraw-Hill.

Park, C. W., Milberg, S., & Lawson, R. (1991, September). Evaluation of brand extensions: The role of product feature similarity and brand concept consistency. *Journal of Consumer Research, 18*, 185–193.

Park, J.-W., & Kim, K.-H. (2001). Effects of relationships with a brand on brand extensions: Some exploratory findings. *Advances in Consumer Research, 28*, 179–185.

Park, J.-W., Yoon, S.-O. Kim, K.-H., & Wyer Jr., R. S. (2001). Effects of priming a bipolar attribute concept on dimension versus concept-specific activation of semantic memory. *Journal of Personality and Social Psychology, 81*(3), 524–539.

Peracchio, L. A., & Tybout, A. M. (1996, December). The moderating role of prior knowledge in schema-based product evaluation. *Journal of Consumer Research, 23*, 177–192.

Rao, A., & Monroe, K. B. (1988, September). The moderating effect of prior knowledge on cue utilization in product evaluations. *Journal of Consumer Research, 15*, 253–264.

Rusbult, C. E. (1983). A longitudinal test of the investment model: The development and deterioration of satisfaction and commitment in heterosexual involvement. *Journal of Personality and Social Psychology, 45*, 101–117.

Rusbult, C. E., Johnson, D. J., & Morrow, G. D. (1986). Impact of couple of patterns of problem solving on distress and nondistress in dating relationships. *Journal of Personality and Social Psychology, 50*, 744–753.

Rusbult, C. E., & Van Lange, P. A. M. (1996). Interdependence processes. In E. T. Higgins & A. Kruglanski (eds.), *Social psychology: Handbook of basic principles* (pp. 564–596). New York: Guilford.

Rusbult, C. E., Verette, J., Whitney, G. A., Slovik, L. F., & Lipkus, I. (1991). Accommodation processes in close relationships: Theory and preliminary empirical evidence. *Journal of Personality and Social Psychology, 60*(1), 53–78.

Smith, D. C., & Park, C. W. (1992, August). The effects of brand extensions on market share and advertising efficiency. *Journal of Marketing Research, 29*, 296–313.

Stapel, D. A., Koomen, W., & Van Der Plight, J. (1997). Categories of category accessibility: The impact of trait concept versus exemplar priming on person Judgments. *Journal of Experimental Social Psychology, 33*, 47–76.

Sternberg, R. J. (1986). A triangular theory of love. *Psychological Review, 93*, 119–135.

Sujan, M. (1985, June). Consumer knowledge: Effect on evaluation processes mediating consumer judgments. *Journal of Consumer Research, 12*, 31–46.

Sujan, M., & Dekleva, C. (1987). Product categorization and inference making: Some implications for comparative advertising. *Journal of Consumer Research, 14*, 372–378.

Van Lange, P. A. M., Rusbult, C. E., Drigotas, S. M., Arriaga, X. B., Witcher, B. S., & Cox, C. L. (1997). Willingness to sacrifice in close relationships. *Journal of Personality and Social Psychology, 72*, 1373–1395.

Wieselquist, J., Rusbult, C. E. Foster, C. A., & Agnew, C. R. (1999). Commitment, pro-relationship behavior, and trust in close relationships. *Journal of Personality and Social Psychology, 77*(5), 942–966.

CHAPTER NINETEEN

Finding the Best Ways to Combine Online and Offline Shopping Features

Aron M. Levin
Northern Kentucky University

Irwin P. Levin
University of Iowa

C. Edward Heath
Xavier University

OVERVIEW

It's 2:00 AM Tuesday morning and you suddenly realize that your brother's birthday is 3 days from now. Of course you have no gift and a very busy schedule that fills the rest of the week. So you turn on your computer and begin to search for the perfect gift. The light from the screen illuminates the room and opens your search to a myriad of possibilities. To narrow your search you could visit AOL or Yahoo! Shopping and follow the numerous categories and listings until you find what your brother absolutely needs. If you know what you are looking for, a search engine like Google can lead you in a matter of seconds to find a large number of sites, brands, and products. A price comparison site such as pricegrabber.com presents a list of possible products and various features and then lists Web retailers that carry your selection ranked by price. Finally, a visit directly to a Web retailer or manufacturer's Web site can help you find products from a brand name that you are loyal to and trust.

Suppose that have narrowed your possible present selections to a DVD player or a leather jacket. You love how easy it is to search and compare online, plus it is 2:00 AM and you can shop in your pajamas. However, online shopping makes you wonder. If you purchase online, will your brother receive his present in time? Would he be able to return or exchange the product with little hassle? In addition, you would like to be able to see the jacket, feel its material, and try it on. You wonder how helpful a service person could be in helping you pick the best model or the latest style.

In this chapter, we start with the idea that the relative advantages and disadvantages of shopping online and offline will play out differently for different classes of products, at least in the mind of the consumer. We provide initial results of a survey that assesses consumer preferences for online and offline sources at different stages of the shopping experience for different categories of products. These results are used to suggest when it would appear to be useful for online firms to have an offline presence and when it would be useful for offline firms to have an online presence.

This then leads to the second main idea of this chapter. Alliances between online and offline brands may represent a particularly useful strategy for utilizing the complementary advantages of online and offline sources for different products. We then present the results of a second study in which evaluations of online and offline brands are compared for independent brands and brands that enter online-offline alliances. We conclude by suggesting when such strategic alliances may be particularly beneficial.

BACKGROUND

Within the wake of online shopping's exponential growth, many advantages and some perceived disadvantages of shopping online as compared to shopping offline at traditional brick-and-mortar stores have become apparent. Among the advantages are rapid and extensive display of information and ease of comparison between the attributes of different brands. The conference on "Online Consumer Psychology" referred to many such advantages of online shopping. For example, Mishra and Olshavsky (2001) pointed out that Internet technology will allow consumers to make more rational decisions by providing more complete information for narrowing down the number of choice options.

Lack of personal service, inability to inspect or handle the product, and concern about delivery and exchange processes including giving out credit card numbers over the Internet have been realized as perceived disadvantages. The relative salience of such favorable and unfavorable features when comparing online and offline shopping options undoubtedly varies across products, consumers, and situations. In particular, conference presentations by Fang (2001) and by Lynch, Kent, and Srinivasan (2001) distinguish between "high-touch" and "low-touch" products in this regard. Fang (2001) concluded that the Web is neither sufficiently mature nor effective as a shopping channel for products demanding high touch and feel. Thus, buying clothes online was perceived to be inferior to buying clothes from a traditional store on a number of dimensions.

This chapter expands on this theme by comparing consumer perceptions of shopping online versus shopping offline for different products at different stages of the shopping experience. Furthermore, we explore the idea that the ability to touch or feel the product is but one of a number of features that drive the decision of whether to use online or offline sources at each of the various stages. We believe that consumer needs for online and offline services vary predictably across products that emphasize different features such as large selection, personal service, and speedy delivery, as well as the ability to see, touch, or try the product. We explore these possibilities in this chapter, emphasizing the potential complementarity of online and offline services.

If features favoring online shopping and features favoring offline shopping can be seen as complementary for at least some products, then we can address the following issue: How might marketers and managers take advantage of the potential complementarity of online and offline shopping features? For click-and-mortar stores, those comprised of both an offline and online presence, taking advantage of these features can be accomplished relatively easily. For example, Barnes and Noble, the book retailer, allows customers to purchase online and return the product to their physical stores if not satisfied. Similarly, Best Buy, the electronics superstore, permits customers to search, purchase, and pay online and pick the merchandise up from their closest Best Buy location.

Nevertheless, not every company possesses the resources for providing both online and offline services. For these companies, other possibilities exist to integrate their resources. However, the integration of features is less simplistic for the combination of online with offline companies. One method for these firms to capitalize on this complementarily between online and offline companies is to form strategic brand alliances. The effect of combining two or more distinct brand names in a single marketing strategy is a growing area of research. Work by Levin, Davis and Levin (1996), Rao and Ruekert (1994), and Shocker, Srivastava, and Ruekert (1994) suggests that brand alliances will continue to increase in popularity into the future. Consumers tend to believe that when high-quality brands enter alliances, they will protect their reputations by only aligning with other high-quality brands, thus providing an alliance that is built on mutual strengths.

It should be possible for online and offline companies to form alliances that maximize the benefits of online shopping and minimize consumer concerns by providing backup offline services. Examples of existing alliances that attempt to do this are Amazon.com/Toys-R-Us and Drugstore.com/CVS Pharmacy, and a proposed Amazon.com/Wal-Mart alliance is in the works.

These alliances form for a number of important reasons. First, research has suggested that consumers place more trust in well-established offline brands than they do in lesser-known Internet brands. By teaming up with a branded offline company, an online company can enhance its credibility and trust for online consumers. Conversely, brick-and-mortar companies with little experience with the online consumer can take advantage of the primary expertise of the offline company—the ability to interface and form relationships with their customers—and extend this expertise to online consumers. In addition, an online company can utilize one of these alliances to take advantage of an offline company's existing distribution system instead of having to develop a network of its own in a tight and extremely competitive marketplace.

In this chapter we focus on issues concerning the potential complementarity of online and offline shopping features by addressing the following questions:

1. For what types of products is shopping online preferred to shopping offline?
2. What specific features of shopping online and shopping offline are seen as most desirable for different types of products?
3. What steps in searching for and purchasing a product are seen as better done online and what steps are seen as better done offline, for different products?
4. For what types of products might alliances between online brands and offline brands be most beneficial?
5. How are brand perceptions influenced by such alliances?

SURVEY OF CONSUMER PREFERENCES

In order to provide preliminary answers to some of these questions, we conducted a multipart survey. The survey was administered to a sample of 40 undergraduate marketing students in the summer 2001. Products were chosen to be appropriate to this group: airline tickets, books, CDs, clothing, computer software, electronic products, health and grooming products, and sporting goods.

For each of the eight types of products, respondents were asked to consider the following steps in the shopping process: search for options, compare options, and make a purchase. For each step for each product the respondents were asked to indicate whether they would prefer to complete that step online or offline. The following conclusions can be drawn from the results of the survey (see Table 19.1).

For about half the product categories, online methods are preferred over offline for the search and compare steps. Offline is greatly preferred over online for the final purchase step for most product categories. Thus, in many circumstances, consumers would prefer to log onto the Internet to look at their possible choices, compare those choices on their various features, but prefer to make the final purchase at a retail location.

TABLE 19.1
Online/Offline Shopping Preferences at Each Step for Each Product
(data are % who prefer online)

	Airline Tickets	Books	CDs	Clothing	Computer Software	Electronic Products	Health & Grooming	Sporting Goods
Search	92.5	50	55	22.5	80	50	12.5	30
Compare	95	47.5	37.5	15	77.5	52.5	12.5	20
Purchase	52.5	12.5	12.5	5	42.5	12.5	2.5	5

Different preference patterns emerged across products and these seemed to fall into several clusters. For clothing, health and grooming products, and sporting goods, respondents preferred using offline sources for every step in the shopping process, especially the final purchase step. When respondents considered the purchase of both airline tickets and computer software, there was a strong preference for searching for and comparing options online, but there was about equal preference for purchasing online or offline. Books, CDs, and electronic products elicited a slightly different response. There was about equal preference for online and offline search-and-compare processes, but there was strong preference for offline purchasing.

On the whole, then, it appears that there is general agreement about the relative advantages and disadvantages of online and offline features but that the importance of these features varies over products. Additional evidence for classifying products into different clusters such as these and for suggesting ways in which the complementarity of online and offline features can be used to best advantage for different products is presented later.

The previous section details how consumers prefer to use either online or offline sources depending on where they are in the purchasing process. The next section discusses the comparative strengths and weaknesses of online and offline sources in regards to numerous attributes. In this part of the survey, respondents were asked to rate the extent to which they think shopping online or shopping offline is better on each of a number of features. The features investigated include shopping enjoyment, quickness of shopping, selection, price, tactile investigation of the product, personal service, speed of delivery, and product exchange. Ratings were on a 10-point scale where low numbers represent preference for shopping offline and high numbers represent preference for shopping online.

The results, summarized in Table 19.2, suggest that consumers see online shopping sources as better for shopping quickly and having a large number of selections. Consumers believe that it is quicker to shop online than it is to visit a physical

TABLE 19.2
Mean Ratings of Extent to Which Online or Offline is Better for Each Attribute
(Data are on a scale of 1 to 10 where 1 = "Shopping offline is much better" and
10 = "Shopping online is much better.")

Enjoy shopping:	2.88	
Shop quickly:	8.23	Offline better: see-touch-handle, personal service, enjoy shopping, no-hassle exchange, speedy delivery
Large selection:	7.35	
Best price:	6.35	Online better: shop quickly, large selection, best price
See-touch-handle:	1.25	
Personal service:	2.25	
Speedy delivery:	4.00	
No-hassle exchange:	3.05	

TABLE 19.3
Mean Attribute Importance Ratings (1–10 scale) for Each Product

	Enjoy Shopping	Shop Quickly	Large Selection	Best Price	See-Touch-Handle	Personal Service	Speedy Delivery	No-Hassle Exchange
Airline Tickets	3.70	7.23	7.10	9.05	2.23	6.10	7.05	7.63
Books	6.00	5.05	8.30	7.68	7.30	6.33	7.63	8.05
CDs	5.78	5.58	8.93	9.03	6.25	5.70	7.83	7.98
Clothing	7.25	5.60	8.50	8.15	8.60	7.40	7.23	8.98
Computer Software	4.18	6.60	7.40	8.55	4.43	7.43	7.00	8.33
Electronic Products	5.40	5.60	8.28	8.78	8.15	7.40	7.18	8.43
Health & Grooming	4.30	6.43	7.30	7.63	7.30	6.35	6.83	7.18
Sporting Goods	5.70	5.33	8.18	8.63	7.73	6.80	6.93	8.40

retailer and that they have access to more products with a greater number of features online. In addition, online shopping was perceived to be the source for the best prices. Considering that most online retailers use an aggressive low-price strategy to draw customers to their Web sites to shop, this result is not especially surprising.

Offline shopping sources rated higher for enjoying the shopping experience, being able to see-touch-handle the product, personal service, no-hassle exchange, and receiving speedy delivery. This emphasizes the importance of the physical aspects of the shopping experience and the strengths of offline retailers in providing these services. The finding concerning enjoyment of the shopping experience is consistent with other conclusions from the "Online Consumer Psychology" conference. Jones and Vallaster (2001) raised the question of whether the Internet is an effective tool in creating emotions. Villegas and Stout (2001) concluded that emotionally, online shopping is somewhere between reading an ad and doing offline shopping. The present results support the idea that online shopping falls short of offline shopping in creating an enjoyable experience.

Having established that, for at least most of the attributes, there was clear preference for one method over the other; we now turn to the issue of which of these attributes is considered more important for different products.

In the next part of the survey, respondents rated the importance of each feature for each of the different product categories. From the results, summarized in Table 19.3, a number of conclusions can be drawn.

For every product category presented, price, selection, speedy delivery, and no-hassle exchange were rated as being important. Regardless of the product type, consumers saw low prices, a large varied selection, fast delivery, and the right to exchange or return the product as being very important to the shopping experience. The ability to see-touch-handle the product is especially important for clothing, electronic products, sporting goods, books, and health and grooming products. Personal service is especially important for clothing, computer software, and sporting goods. Having a large number of selections is especially important for clothing, books, electronic products, and sporting goods. Enjoying the shopping experience is more important for clothing than for any other product category.

It is clear from these results that consumers have different service expectations depending on the product for which they are shopping. In addition, it is apparent that neither online nor offline sources are able to adequately provide the consumer with every attribute that they find important in the purchasing process. For example, the products clothing, books, electronic products, and sporting goods emphasize both attributes that favor online methods and attributes that favor offline methods.

We use the combination of findings to summarize the similarities and differences between the different products and to infer what benefits are provided by online and offline services for each product category. We then propose how alliances between online and offline brands might serve complementary functions for different product categories and we describe an experiment to test these propositions.

Summary of Product Categories

The previous analyses have clearly demonstrated that each product category is unique in relation to consumers' purchase behaviors. For each product category, the most relevant features for differentiating the benefits of online and offline services are described. Then "clusters" of products with similar features are defined and introduced.

Airline ticket purchases can be characterized by a strong preference for searching and comparing options online and an even split for preferring to make the final purchase online or offline. Being able to see-touch-handle the product is not deemed particularly important, nor is the enjoyment of the shopping experience. The initial success of Priceline.com and growth of Orbitz.com can be attributed to the desire of consumers to search for fares and find the best price possible before making a purchase either online or by visiting the local travel agent.

Book purchases appear to call for offline purchasing, whereas participants were split in preferring to search and compare options online or offline. The ability to personally inspect the product is an important reason for purchasing offline. The perceived larger selection of options online makes online search and comparing options attractive to some consumers. Obviously, Amazon.com has been an e-commerce success story paving the way for other retailers online. In this category, online retailers have the advantage of offering an enormous selection without needing to physically stock or display each title on a shelf. Considering the success of Amazon.com and Barnes and Noble.com, it is surprising that consumers prefer to purchase offline. However, it is likely that the relative low cost of the product in comparison to shipping charges as well as the ability to browse the books before the final purchase may drive consumers to their local bookstores for books that they have found at the Amazon.com Web site.

CD purchases are preferred to be completed offline, whereas there is mixed preference for searching and comparing online or offline. The desire for speedy delivery and personally inspecting the product are important features favoring offline purchasing. A larger number of selections available online makes this the preferred search method for many consumers. CD buyers, like book purchasers, prefer the instant gratification that buying offline provides. However, online retailers like CDnow.com and Amazon.com can list and cross-list millions of titles complete with track information and song samples.

Clothing purchases are characterized by offline preferences at each step, especially the final purchase step. The ability to see-touch-handle the product, personal service, and shopping enjoyment are attractive offline features for clothes shopping. These preferences are evidenced by the absence of significant online retailers in this product category. The exceptions, Land's End, The Gap, Eddie Bauer, and Victoria's Secret rely on strong brand associations, customer-friendly return policies, and offline associates to be competitive in the category.

Computer software purchases are seen as benefiting from the greater selection provided by online services but also for some consumers the personal service provided offline. Thus, search and comparison of options is preferred online but participants were about evenly split between online/offline preferences for final purchase. Although offline retailers like Best Buy carry numerous software titles, their selection is dwarfed by online retailers' inventory.

Electronic products show a strong preference for purchasing offline but mixed preferences for searching and comparing online or offline. The importance of having a larger number of selections is the reason why some consumers prefer to search and compare on the Internet. However, almost all consumers appear to weigh the opportunity to see, touch, and handle the product as a key reason for purchasing offline. The actual sale of electronic products online has proven to be difficult for companies. Amazon.com, buy.com, Best Buy.com, and even Sony have seen mediocre sales at best. The offline retailer allows the consumer to experience the product before purchasing it and taking it home immediately. Online sources have been extremely popular for information about products and as a tool to compare the features of products utilized before a physical visit to an offline retailer.

Health and grooming products appear to elicit preference for brick-and-mortar shopping at each step of the process because of the see-touch-handle feature of offline shopping. Consumers probably also believe that large selections are available offline as well as online for this particular product class, thus negating the usual advantage of searching online. The world's largest offline retailer, Wal-Mart, does not carry health or grooming products in their online store. High relative shipping costs, frequency and volume of purchases, and channel arrangements have all contributed to the absence of online retailers in this product category.

Sporting goods also elicit offline preferences at each step, especially the final purchase step. Again, the see-touch-handle and personal service features of traditional brick-and-mortar stores tend to predominate. For some consumers, however, greater selection makes online search and comparison attractive. Though heavily promoted, Fogdog.com and MVP.com have failed in their attempt to sell sporting goods online because of the features described earlier.

Though each product category is unique in their feature preferences, the following product categorizations can be made. For high-touch products—clothing, sporting goods, and health and grooming products—traditional brick-and-mortar shopping methods are preferred because of the special importance of being able to personally handle and inspect the product before purchasing. Low-touch products—airline tickets and computer software—are products that generally require fewer offline services; however, some consumers desire personal service at the final purchasing step. Books, CDs, and electronic products appear to be mixed in that hands-on experiences are apparently sought after by some consumers but not others during the initial steps, but almost all consumers prefer making the final purchase offline at traditional stores.

COMPLEMENTARY SERVICES PROVIDED BY ONLINE/OFFLINE BRAND ALLIANCES

We started this chapter by saying that new online services provide some advantages and some disadvantages when compared to traditional brick-and-mortar offline services. Some features are clearly better provided by online services, some by offline services, and some are perceived differently by different consumers. In addition, features favoring online sources and features favoring offline sources are weighted differently for different products. As a consequence of this, consumers prefer to utilize online and offline services at different steps in the shopping process and for different product types.

For example, Table 19.1 shows that for each product, preferences for online methods decrease across successive shopping stages, especially between the search-and-compare stages and the final purchase stage. Clearly, online firms need an offline presence if they want to capture the sale. Of course, this is more important for some products than for others, as indicated by the varying online purchase preferences. Five percent or less of consumers preferred shopping online for clothing, sporting goods, and health/grooming products versus about 50% for airline tickets and computer software. This discrepancy represents a clear-and-present danger for online firms. On the other hand, if consumers' experience with online shopping leads to the development of more trust and less aversion to closing the sale online, then offline firms need to be aware of the perceived advantages of online shopping for products like books, CDs, and electronics products, which have traditionally been shopped for at brick-and-mortar stores. This indicates that offline firms in these product categories need to cultivate an online presence.

Forming online/offline brand alliances is one potentially useful way that an offline firm can cultivate an online presence. In addition, these alliances suggest a way to complement desirable online and offline features. Interestingly, the existing click-and-mortar stores we identified earlier sell products that fit into the "mixed" category where consumers are approximately evenly divided between those who prefer to complete these steps online or offline, but almost all prefer purchasing offline. It seems that Best Buy, a leading supplier of electronic products, has the optimal strategy for this situation. The existence of Best Buy.com satisfies the customer's desire for features best performed online, searching and comparison, then eases concern about delivery of online purchase by allowing merchandise to be picked up from the nearest store. Our research supports the establishment of such click-and-mortar combinations for the category of products that includes books, electronic products, and CDs. However, there is a potential danger associated with this strategy. A particular brand name may be associated with high-quality online services or high-quality offline services, but probably not both. The combination of a respected online brand and a respected offline brand may be received better than a brand of one type that expands into an entirely new area.

The formation of alliances between online and offline brands has the potential of complementing the advantages of both types of brands by allowing consumers to use both brands at different stages of the shopping experience within the same alliance. However, it should be clear from what has been presented earlier in this chapter that such alliances must strategically take into account consumers' perceptions and preferences in different product categories. Some product categories might especially benefit from such alliances and, within those alliances, one brand might profit more than the other.

Before we discuss alliances in different product categories, we want to make some general comments. Some consumers might not be comfortable with online shopping or be distrustful of giving out personal information such as credit card number and thus may not see any benefit in having their favorite stores aligned with dot.com brands. In addition, some consumers might have strong loyalty to their traditional shopping outlet and thus be swayed to make their final purchase there even if they engage in online search to form their selection. Distrust in online exchange and refund processes might deter some consumers from making final purchases online. One pattern seen for some products is to search and compare online, but purchase offline. This pattern is clearly disadvantageous to e-commerce. For such products, alliances may provide attractive ways of combining online searches with offline purchases without sacrificing the image of either brand.

For high-touch products like clothing, sporting goods, and health and grooming products, where the ability to inspect or try on the product is paramount, online brands should especially be helped by alliances with offline brands that provide the requisite hands-on experience at traditional stores. For mixed products like books, CDs, computer software, and electronic products, where attributes that favor online brands and attributes that favor offline brands are comparable in importance, both brands should be helped by the alliance.

The next section describes a study designed to see how consumers react to hypothetical online/offline brand alliances for different products.

CONSUMER REACTIONS TO ONLINE/OFFLINE BRAND ALLIANCES

In response to the potential complementarity of online and offline brand features, strategic alliances of this type have begun to be formed by companies like
Amazon.com and Wal-Mart. Consumer experience with such alliances is, however, limited at this point in time, so our controlled experiment asked for reactions
to hypothetical alliances.

Although brand alliances between online and offline companies are relatively
rare, there has been considerable research with other types of brand alliances that
shows that there is transfer of affect between brands that are strategically aligned
through marketing strategies such as cobranding, dual-branding, and brand extensions. Research and theory development by Boush and Loken (1991), Keller and
Aaker (1992), Levin and Levin (2000), Prelec, Wernerfelt, and Zettelmeyer (1997),
and Rao and Ruekert (1994) suggest that one brand's equity can be transferred to
other products with which it is strategically linked. In other words, a brand's good
reputation can enhance the image of an alliance that includes that brand.

Of particular relevance to the present investigation of alliances between online
and offline brands, Levin and Levin (2000) developed a model and empirical test
of the role of brand alliances in the assimilation of product evaluations. They
showed that when two brands described by different attributes and qualities are
strategically linked, consumers are apt to assume that the two brands share common
levels of overall quality. For example, in cobranding of two restaurants where one
restaurant is known to have good service and the other's service reputation is
unknown, the consumer tends to infer that the unknown restaurant also has good
service. In the case of an alliance between an online and an offline brand, each
brand possesses different key attributes. Thus, the likelihood of assimilation effects
in both directions appears to be great.

The present experiment addresses this untested proposition and asks the following questions about online-offline brand alliances:

1. Are assimilation effects similar to those found by Levin and Levin (2000)
   found for online-offline brand alliances? That is, are the evaluations of one
   brand affected by the known qualities of the other brand?
2. Does the potential complementarity of online and offline brand attributes
   lead to an overall perceived advantage of such alliances?
3. Do evaluations of online/offline brand alliances differ across product categories in a manner consistent with our earlier survey of product differences
   in perceptions of online and offline services?

To investigate these questions, a study was conducted in the spring 2001. Subjects (126 students in undergraduate marketing classes) were assigned to either
the experimental condition ($N = 70$) or the control condition ($N = 56$). In the experimental (alliance) condition, brands within a category were presented in pairs,

where each pair was described as a hypothetical alliance between an online brand and an offline brand. The cover story mentioned an actual alliance of this type. In the control (nonalliance) condition, brands were described individually with no mention of alliances. The same fictitious brand names and attribute descriptions were presented in each condition. This allowed us to compare evaluations of the same brand when it was or wasn't part of an alliance.

Subjects in the experimental group judged 12 different alliances, each consisting of an online brand paired with an offline brand within one of three product categories: Books, sporting goods, and CDs. Subjects in the control group judged the same 12 online brands and 12 offline brands.

To test the reactions to alliances between strong and weak partners, ratings regarding select attributes specific to either the online or the offline brand were manipulated by assigning fictitious ratings that were said to have come from an independent consumer magazine. Attributes about the online brand—ease of navigation, selection, and return policy—were assigned a rating of either moderate or positive. The offline brand attributes—store atmosphere, convenience of location, and employee helpfulness—were also assigned a rating of either moderate or positive.

A 7-point scale with the ends labeled Very Good and Very Bad was used to rate individual brands. In the experimental group, subjects were asked to rate each brand "based on how well you think it will perform after the alliance has been formed." (In the experimental group subjects were also asked to rate the overall alliance between the two brands, but these ratings are not of primary concern for this chapter.)

Results

Table 19.4 presents the mean response to each individual brand as a function of whether or not it is part of an alliance and the type of alliance. The difference score (Diff) column shows the extent to which that brand's ratings were higher (+) or lower (−) in the alliance (Exp) condition than in the nonalliance (Cont) condition. A positive difference score thus represents a gain for a brand when it is described as part of an alliance compared to when it is described as a separate entity. Although there were some differences (to be discussed shortly) between product categories, several trends can be observed across categories: (a) Ratings are, on average, higher in the alliance condition than in the nonalliance condition. (b) In alliances between a brand with moderately favorable attributes and a brand with positive attributes, ratings are increased for the moderate brand and decreased for the positive brand. This represents the assimilation effect predicted by the Levin and Levin (2000) model and it holds for both online and offline brands. In order to track this in Table 19.4, note that in each product category an alliance between a positive online brand and a moderate offline brand led to a negative difference score for the online brand and a positive difference score for the offline brand

TABLE 19.4
Ratings of Individual Brands (1–7 scale)

Type of Brand	Type of Alliance (online-offline)	Mean Rating		
		Exp	Cont	Diff
Books				
online	pos-pos	5.14	5.70	−0.56*
offline	pos-pos	5.33	5.79	−0.46*
online	pos-mod	4.90	5.55	−0.65*
offline	pos-mod	4.29	3.34	+0.95*
online	mod-pos	4.13	3.50	+0.63*
offline	mod-pos	5.03	5.43	−0.40*
online	mod-mod	3.54	3.18	+0.36*
offline	mod-mod	3.64	3.16	+0.48*
Sports				
online	pos-pos	5.53	5.39	+0.14
offline	pos-pos	5.56	5.57	−0.01
online	pos-mod	5.04	5.54	−0.50*
offline	pos-mod	4.23	3.27	+0.95*
online	mod-pos	4.09	3.25	+0.84*
offline	mod-pos	5.33	6.04	−0.71*
online	mod-mod	3.74	3.32	+0.42*
offline	mod-mod	3.81	3.43	+0.38*
CDs				
online	pos-pos	5.53	5.73	−0.20
offline	pos-pos	5.24	5.11	+0.13
online	pos-mod	5.24	6.14	−0.90*
offline	pos-mod	4.17	3.32	+0.85*
online	mod-pos	4.19	3.38	+0.81*
offline	mod-pos	5.21	5.96	−0.75*
online	mod-mod	3.87	3.43	+0.44*
offline	mod-mod	3.79	3.27	+0.52*

*= Statistically significant at the .05 level.
+= The first term in the pair represents the quality of the online brand and the second term in the pair represents the quality of the offline brand.

and conversely for an alliance between a moderate online brand and a positive offline brand. (c) In alliances between two brands each with moderately favorable attributes, ratings for both brands are increased in the alliance condition compared to the nonalliance condition. This holds for each of the three product categories. This is probably the most important finding as it represents an effect above and beyond the assimilation effect and reveals the residual influence of forming an alliance. It attests to the perceived complementarity of online and offline features where both types of brands benefited from the alliance.

It can be seen that the relative magnitude of difference scores differs across product categories. The average difference score is higher for offline brands than for online brands in the categories of books and CDs, meaning that alliances in these categories helped the offline brands more than the online brands. Recall that in our survey having a large number of selections was important for Books and for CDs and that this feature favored online search-and-compare steps to complement a final offline purchase. By contrast, the average difference score is higher for online brands than for offline brands in the sporting goods category, meaning that alliances in this category helped the online brands more than the offline brands. Recall that for sporting goods, consumers preferred to utilize offline sources for all of the steps in the shopping process. The reliability of this different pattern for different products was confirmed by a significant interaction between online-offline brand, experimental/control condition, and category.

CONCLUSIONS

The most general finding of the experiment on online-offline brand alliances is that, like other types of brand alliances, there is transfer of affect between brands. Specifically, the assimilation effects predicted by the Levin and Levin (2000) model were found when the two brands in an alliance differed in attribute-level favorability. Evaluations of the brand with the less-favorable attributes in the pair were raised in comparison to evaluations of the same brand in the control (nonalliance) condition. Conversely, evaluations of the brand with the more favorable attributes were lowered. Thus, any brand, whether it is an online or an offline brand, should be cautious in forming an alliance with a brand of lesser quality that could bring down its image (see also Rao, Qu, & Ruekert, 1999). However, there appeared to be a unique feature of online-offline brand alliances. In addition to the assimilation effect, there was also an elevation of the ratings of each brand in an alliance between two brands with moderately favorable attribute levels. This could be because of the perceived complementarity between the benefits of the features of the online and offline brands. This makes online-offline brand alliances an especially promising strategy that is worthy of further consideration.

Our survey data led to suggestions of how different products might benefit from alliances between online and offline brands. However, continued consumer exposure to online shopping may reduce concern for online purchasing and change the current picture. Continuous surveying of the perceived advantages and disadvantages of online shopping features should be a priority for marketers. The controlled experiment provides more evidence that the benefits to each brand in an alliance between an online and offline brand depend on the product category. In particular, online brands benefited more from alliances with offline brands for sporting goods than for books or CDs. Recall that sporting goods, compared to the other products in the experiment, can be considered as high-touch products requiring personal inspection and handling. Thus, having a brick-and-mortar component may be seen as particularly beneficial for sporting goods.

Other work in this series (for example, Fang, Lynch, and so on) made the distinction between high-touch and low-touch products and suggest that the latter type of product might be quite compatible with online marketing while the former type would be more compatible with offline marketing. For some consumers, however, even high-touch products benefit from increased selections and speed associated with online search. A new suggestion based on the current results is that online marketing of high-touch products could be aided by forming an alliance with an offline company. At a more general level, many types of products appear to benefit from consumers taking advantage of the complementary desirable features of online and offline shopping.

There are, of course, other strategies beyond brand alliances that can capitalize on the perceived advantages while overcoming the perceived disadvantages of online or offline shopping. For example, in this volume Nelson ("Exploring Consumer Response to Advergaming") describes "advergaming" as a promising new marketing strategy in which products are placed in, or even play a critical role in, cyber games. As she describes them, these games can take on realistic properties approaching virtual reality. This may be especially beneficial for products we identify here as requiring high touch and for which shopping online has been seen as less enjoyable than shopping offline. The ability to approximate the feel or touch of a product while immersed in an enjoyable game may help the consumer overcome his or her reluctance to be influenced by the Internet for products like clothing, health and grooming items, and sporting goods.

Nevertheless, our survey showed that for the same product categories, different consumers showed preferences for different shopping patterns. For some products (airline tickets, computer software), there was near unanimity in preference to searching for and comparing options online but an approximately even split between those preferring to make the final purchase online or offline. For other products (books, CDs, electronic products), there was near unanimity in preference to purchasing offline but an approximately even split between those preferring to search and compare online or offline. These different consumers might well represent different segments of the population who would respond differently to brand alliances. For those who prefer online service for some steps and offline service for other steps, alliances between online and offline brands would be more valuable than for those who prefer to stay with one mode throughout. For those who prefer to mixed modes, alliances with a highly valued brand name for each mode would be particularly attractive. Future research can capitalize on these individual differences by identifying the personal characteristics of these different market segments.

In summary, our major message is that some features of the shopping experience are seen to be better online and some are seen to be better offline. Furthermore, these features play different roles for the different steps that comprise the shopping experience. For example, large selections and quick access to information are perceived to be desirable features of online shopping while the ability to see-touch-handle the product and personal service are perceived to be desirable features of offline shopping. These features take on different importance for different products. Thus, we observed a cluster of low-touch products including airline tickets and computer software where the overwhelming preference was for online search and comparison of options, with mixed preference for actually purchasing the product online or offline. By contrast, we observed a cluster of high-touch products like clothing, sporting goods, and health and grooming products where even the search and comparison processes, but especially the final purchase phase, favored offline shopping. For other products like books, CDs, and electronic products, a trade-off between desirable online and offline features appeared to govern the search-and-compare phases but, again, the ability to personally inspect the product and receive personal service led to strong preference for purchasing the product at traditional stores.

Our research suggests that product managers can strategically align online and offline brands to complement the features of either type of brand by itself. Evaluation of the alliances and the transfer of feelings between components differ for different product categories. For example, high-touch products like clothing and sporting goods have traditionally been purchased offline so that online brands can particularly benefit by providing an offline link. Other products like airline tickets have been on the forefront for Internet search services and thus alliances may particularly benefit offline brands that can add an online component. We expect that the future will see the establishment of more online-offline brand alliances, as well as new click-and-mortar stores. We hope that these new strategic developments are backed by solid research, which tracks changes in consumer perceptions of online and offline services. More research like the present is needed for product managers to determine which features of online shopping and offline shopping are seen as especially important for their particular product and at what stage of the shopping experience these features come into play for different segments of the market. Creating strategic alliances that capitalize on the complementarity of online and offline services is one way to put such research to good use.

REFERENCES

Boush, D. M., & Loken, B. (1991). A process tracing study of brand extension evaluations. *Journal of Marketing Research, 28,* 16–28.

Fang, W. (2001). *Buying clothes from online and physical store for different reasons? An integrative perspective.* Paper presented at Online consumer psychology: Understanding and influencing consumer behavior in the virtual world, 20th annual Advertising and Consumer Psychology Conference, Seattle, WA, May 2001.

Jones, M., & Vallaster, C. (2001). Branding on the internet: A virtual competitor to conventional media? Paper presented at Online consumer psychology: Understanding and influencing consumer behavior in the virtual world, 20th annual Advertising and Consumer Psychology Conference, Seattle, WA, May 2001.

Keller, K. L., & Aaker, D. A. (1992). The effects of sequential introduction of brand extensions. *Journal of Marketing Research, 39*, 35–50.

Levin, I. P., & Levin, A. M. (2000). Modeling the role of brand alliances in the assimilation of product evaluations. *Journal of Consumer Psychology, 9*, 43–52.

Levin, A. M., Davis, J. C., Levin, I. P. (1996). Theoretical and empirical linkages between consumers' responses to different branding strategies. In K. Corfman & J. Lynch (Eds.), *Advance in Consumer Research*, Vol 23 (pp. 296–300). Valdosta, GA: Association for Consumer Research.

Lynch, P., Kent, R., & Srinivasan, S. (2001). The global internet shopper: Effects of trust, affect, and site quality in shopping tasks for low- and high-touch products in twelve countries. Paper presented at Online consumer psychology: Understanding and influencing consumer behavior in the virtual world, 20th annual Advertising and Consumer Psychology Conference, Seattle, WA, May 2001.

Mishra, S., & Olshavsky, R. (2001). Rationality "unbounded": The internet and its effect on consumer decision making. Paper presented at Online consumer psychology: Understanding and influencing consumer behavior in the virtual World, 20th annual Advertising and Consumer Psychology Conference, Seattle, WA, May 2001.

Prelec, D., Wernerfelt, B., & Zettelmeyer, F. (1997). The role of inference in context effects: Inferring what you want from what is available. *Journal of Consumer Research, 24*, 118–125.

Rao, A. R., Qu, L., & Ruekert, R. W. (1999). Signaling unobservable quality through a brand ally. *Journal of Marketing Research, 36*, 258–268.

Rao, A. R., & Ruekert, R. W. (1994, Fall). Brand alliances as signals of product quality. *Sloan Management Review, 36*, 87–97.

Shocker, T., Srivastava, S., Ruekert, P. (1994). Challenges and opportunities facing brand management: An introduction to the special issue. *Journal of Marketing Research, 2*(31), 149–158.

Villegas, J., & Stout, P. (2001). Measurement and the role of emotions while browsing on the web. Paper presented at Online consumer psychology: Understanding and influencing consumer behavior in the virtual world, 20th annual Advertising and Consumer Psychology Conference, Seattle, WA, May 2001.

CHAPTER TWENTY

Consumer Behavior in Online Auctions: An Exploratory Study

Eugene Sivadas
Barbara Stern
Rutgers, The State University of New Jersey

Raj Mehta
University of Cincinnati

Melanie Jones
Loyola University

The purpose of this chapter is to examine consumer responses to online auctions, using eBay as the data source for the number and dollar value of bids on selected products and for the influence of seller ratings (word of mouth, WOM) on these bids. Its focus on factors that influence bidding behavior aims at contributing not only to the research stream, but also to enhancing managerial understanding of online auctions so that sites can continue to grow apace. In this regard, auction sites—not even a decade old—have already assumed importance as a new and profitable form of retailing that enables consumers to engage directly in purchase activity rather than going through other channels of distribution. That is, consumer-to-consumer auction sites (C2C), much like the earliest marketing exchanges, enable individuals to act as vendors and purchasers. Yet despite American consumers' reputed dislike of haggling and a concomitant tendency to treat list prices as sacred (*Economist*, 2000; Coy & Moore, 2000), the number of bidders and site profits keep growing. Sharp increases in consumer purchases have already occurred and are predicted to continue: in 1999 consumers spent $3.3 billion (Business Week, 1999); in 2004 consumer spending on one site, eBay, alone is expected to exceed $20 billion (Hof, 2004). Overall spending is well in excess of the fivefold increase from 1999 to 2004 that was anticipated by Wilcox (2000). As the average price per item rises, so do profits (Riley, 1989; Wilcox, 2000), fueled by the affluence of bidders, about half of whom are college educated and earning over $50,000 annually (Crockett, 1999).

Of the 142 dedicated Internet auction firms-those whose only business is auctions (Lucking Reiley, 2000), eBay is by far the largest, with over 332.3 million new listings in Quarter 2 of the year 2004, and 48 million active users and over $8 billion worth of merchandize traded in the second quarter of 2004 alone (ebay.com). On any given day, eBay has about 12 million listings (Hof, 2004). Thus, the site has grown exponentially since Bradley and Porters' (2000) article which indicated that eBay received approximately 800,000 bids per day. In the 5-year period from eBays inception in 1995, it had received approximately 186 million bids for more than 50 million items. The rise in the number of auction participants coupled with growing sales volume and high profits has fueled the adoption of auctioning by over 200 firms whose primary business is not auctions (Hanson, 2000). For example, PNC Bank Corporation in Pittsburgh occasionally uses consumer bids to set interest rates on select certificates of deposits; John Deere auctions off used farm equipment (Dalton, 1999); and retailers such as JC Penney use auctions to dispose of excess inventory (Kemp, 2001).

However, even though cyberauctions have become vast retail bazaars (Pitta, 1999) with billions of dollars changing hands annually, the research literature on online consumer bidder behavior (Riley, 1989) is rather scanty. Wilcox's work (2000) is a notable exception; he examined the way that nonprofessional bidders behave in the market for lower-stake items where consumers are buyers and sellers of items and consumption experiences moderate behavior. We propose extending his research to address three questions of interest to consumer behavior researchers: (a) What product characteristics influence consumer bids? (b) How do consumers respond to dynamic pricing? and (c) How do seller ratings influence bids? In light of Wilcox's description of consumers as nonprofessional bidders, let us first summarize the ways that traditional (offline) business-to-consumer auctions (B2C) and professional ones differ from online C2C purchase situations.

TRADITIONAL OFFLINE AUCTIONS

Differences from traditional offline auctions flow from the adaptation of the purchase mechanism to the computer-mediated environment (CME) (Hoffman & Novak, 1996) and the new role of consumers in an anonymous situation where there is no face-to-face contact. Prior to the 1990s, traditional auctions took place at sites where bidders had to be physically present, and the primary items offered were relatively unique and valuable—real estate, estate jewelry, or artworks (Hanson, 2000; Wilcox, 2000). Selling lower cost items in this venue is relatively impractical, for high transaction costs, labor-intensive paperwork, and the requirement that bidders/items be in the same place make such sales unprofitable. Further, the requirement that bidders be present may intimidate those who are not comfortable in so public and social a milieu. It was not until online auctions emerged that the following constraints of traditional auctions were overcome:

1. Bidders need not be physically present at a brick-and-mortar site.
2. Bidders need not be physically present online, for automated bids can be entered electronically.
3. Bidders need not make on-the-spot decisions, because online auctions can run for days or weeks.
4. Bidders have access to a nearly limitless variety of items at any price rather than to the limited variety offered at any one physical site.
5. Bidders can find items easily via powerful search engines (Lucking-Reiley, 2000; Mishra & Olshavsky, 2002).

On eBay, for example, auctions run for up to 10 days; participants compete electronically via automated bids; and bidders have search engines at their disposal so that they can find whatever they want quickly (Lucking-Reiley, 2000; Mishra & Olshavsky, 2005). A vast array of items are sold in categories such as antiques and art, books, computers, coins and stamps, collectibles, dolls, hardware supplies, real estate, sports, and so forth. Subcategories are even more specific, with sports, for example, further divided into autographs, memorabilia, sporting goods, and trading cards. Items in all categories may cost as little as a dollar and may be new, used, "as-is," refurbished, or sold for parts. The most popular product types once were collectibles, which include almost every antique and nonantique item that consumers value, and accounted for 60% of items on eBay (Lucking-Reiley, 2000). Today eBay motors is the dominant category in terms of dollar volume. Even though researchers and practitioners point out that not all products are appropriate for the online world (Li & Gery, 2000), consumers seem willing to bid on just about anything at any price, including things that Kirk Loevner, president of Internet Shopping Network, calls "bizarre" items such as preowned nose-hair trimmers (Pitta, 1999, p. 61). The diversity of items, lower transaction costs, and impersonal interactions have increased the number of bidders by attracting consumers who, for one or another reason, never participated in traditional auctions.

PROFESSIONAL AUCTIONS

Even more dramatic differences than those in online versus offline C2C environments are those apparent in B2B high-stake auctions with professional bidders versus C2C low-stake ones with nonprofessional bidders. In professional auctions for bonds, electricity, communication licenses, and so forth, billions of dollars change hands, and bidders are "sufficiently financially motivated to fully understand the game" (Wilcox, 2000, p. 365). Further, no matter how educated C2C bidders may be, they are typically nonprofessionals who lack the sophistication and trained response repertoire of professionals. Yet most prior research on professional auctions does not take bidding behavior into account, for it draws from the economics and marketing literature rather than from the social sciences. Topics of interest

(Milgrom, 1989) include bidder collusion, product valuation, and pricing, with the following issues among the most well-researched ones:

1. Subjective or "private" product value, in which items have no single objective value, versus objective or "common" value, in which items have an objective value based on resale or expected returns. Each bidder for private-value items such as a Barbie collectible or a gown worn by Princess Diana sets a personal price based on what the unique item is worth to the bidder. That is, there is no commonly accepted market value, for value is in the mind of the individual bidder. In contrast, each bidder for a common-value item such as a computer or branded product is aware that the item is not unique, that it has an accepted market value, and that this value is the same for all bidders.

2. The "winner's curse" (Greenleaf, Rao, & Sinha, 1993; Rothkopf, 1991; Wilcox, 2000), a phenomenon in which bidders overpay because they overestimate the true value of an item. This occurs when items have a commonly accepted fair value, but bidders do not know it with certainty. In this situation, bidders who win, overpay to get the item; they must outbid all others, but in so doing, they inevitably pay more than the item is worth because the winning bid is more than what the ostensible losers will pay.

3. Pricing mechanisms, which include the following: seller strategies for maximizing revenue and for motivating participation by bidders who place the "highest true value" (Hanson, 2000) on items; bidder and seller strategies in auctions where multiple identical items are offered (Swinkels 2001); the impact of price guarantees on bidding; and implications of allowing winners to withdraw bids (Greenleaf et al., 1993; Rothkopf, 1991; Wilcox, 2000).

In summary online consumer bidders are likely to differ from both professionals and participants in offline auctions, and prior research must be revisited to ascertain the effects of the virtual environment on behavior.

eBAY

To determine the effects of the online auction environment on consumer behavior, our study takes eBay as an exemplar, for it is the pioneering online auction site whose mechanisms were developed to suit the purchase situation. To begin, it is solely a listing-agent site for sellers, offering no merchandise from the site itself. Sellers must register to list an item and must provide the following details about the sale item: product category, description, and picture (if seller wants one); duration of sale period; seller location; and starting (minimum) price plus reserve price (the lowest price seller will accept). For an extra charge, sellers have the opportunity to add options such as prominent placement on the eBay site and graphics designed to make the seller products stand out. Sellers set their own prices, and the seller reserve price is not disclosed to bidders. eBay's profits come from the seller listing fee (30 cents to $4.80, depending on the desired opening bid); additional advertising fees for extras such as $39.95 for a listing to appear on eBay's product category home page; and a percentage of the final sale price, which depends on the closing value of the item.

Sellers on eBay can select from four auction formats:

1. Adult-only, in which listings of erotic materials are made available only to adults who have registered for this site. That is, the listings do not appear on the general eBay site, lest they be accessed by minors or consumers who would be offended by the items.

2. Dutch auctions, in which sellers list multiple identical items and specify the quantity available and the minimum bid. Bidders must specify the quantity they want, and the minimum price is the least they can bid. When the auction ends, the highest bidder has the first opportunity to buy, and then the next-highest, and so forth. However, because the seller priority is to sell all of the items above the minimum price, the highest bid that is not for all items will not prevail. Rather, all buyers end up paying the lowest accepted bid price. For example, let us say that a seller will accept a minimum bid of $15 each for 100 golf shirts and receives bids ranging from $15 to $25, but the winning bid for the full quantity is only $18. All bidders—including the one who offered $25—then pay $18.

3. Private auctions, in which only the seller knows who bought the item because the bidders' email addresses are kept secret.

4. A combination of English and second-priced sealed bid auctions, in which sellers specify a reserve price (the minimum price they will accept) that is not made known to bidders, and each bidder submits a maximum bid that is not made known to other bidders (Wilcox, 2000). For example, let us say a seller starts an auction for an item with a hidden reserve price of $10, and bidder 1 opens by specifying a maximum bid of $20. eBay then lists the highest outstanding bid as $11 ($10 seller reserve plus $1), and bidder 2 follows with a maximum bid of $15, which is below the $20 that bidder 1 offered. Now eBay adjusts the highest outstanding bid to $16 ($15 plus $1). If a third bidder specifies a maximum bid of $30, she or he becomes the highest bidder, but the eBay price for the highest outstanding bid is only $21 ($20—bidder 1's bid, which is the second highest + $1 = $21).

STUDY HYPOTHESES

Shopping Versus Specialty Products

Although there are only a limited number of standardized auction formats, there is no standardized system across sites for classifying products (Lucking-Reiley, 2000). Hence, the current study adapts Murphy and Enis's (1986) product-classification scheme, itself based on Copeland's (1924), as the theoretical grounding for a context-relevant 2×2 typology. The original typology classifies all consumer goods into three types—convenience, shopping, and specialty—differentiated by consumers' reasons for buying, need for information, and shopping and purchase behaviors. However, we include only shopping and specialty goods, for convenience goods such as newspapers or gum are not suitable. Figure 20.1 shows the typological axes: shopping versus specialty products and objective versus subjective reference prices (see Mazumdar & Papatla, 2000; Milgrom, 1989).

Shopping goods include products such as automobiles, clothing, furniture, insurance, and educational services for which consumers engage in an extensive search process and brand evaluation. They are willing to expend effort to find products and compare brands (Murphy & Enis, 1986) in terms of price, quality, style, and suitability (Kotler, 2000), for they perceive high risk and moderate to high purchase uncertainty (Li & Gery, 2000) and often turn to online sites for brand information.

In contrast, specialty products include paintings by well-known artists, expensive cars, jewelry, watches, and vintage wines for which consumers engage in a limited search process and do not compare brands. Buyers tend to be brand loyal, unwilling to accept alternative items, and well-informed about the item (Li & Gery, 2000). Consumers perceive "unique characteristics" in specialty goods (Kotler, 2000), and the more expensive ones are often sold by traditional brick-and-mortar auction houses capable of serving customers who demand a high-quality sales atmosphere and after-sales services (Li & Gery, 2000). In many cases, consumers want not only to see the items in person, but also to be seen seeing them, with some auctions such as those for the Duchess of Windsor's jewels or Jacqueline Onassis' possessions serving as elite social events. Here, consumers are not motivated by the desire for convenience or information, and the online environment does not provide the satisfactions they seek. Thus, we hypothesize that more bidders will vie for shopping than for specialty goods.

H1: Shopping goods will attract a larger number of bidders than will specialty ones.

	Shopping	Specialty
Objectively Priced	Computers	RoLex Watches
Subjectively Priced	Furniture	Fine Paintings

FIG. 20.1   Product-Price Typology.

Objectively and Subjectively Priced Products

A related distinction is that of objectively versus subjectively priced products based on consumer perceptions of a reference price (Kalyanaram & Winer, 1995; Mazumdar & Papatla, 1995, 2000). Objectively priced products are shopping items such as computers that have commonly accepted value expressed by an objective reference price such as the manufacturers' list price, but whose price is open to negotiation. Consumers decide what they should pay by accessing memories of what they paid in the past or by turning to external information sources such as advertisements or point-of-purchase displays (Mazumdar & Papatla, 2000). In contrast, subjectively priced products are specialty items such as art masterpieces that are so unique that prices are determined by whatever buyers will pay.

The objective/subjective basis for the formation of a reference price is subject to debate. Some researchers claim that consumers remember prices from previous purchases and use their memory to decide how much the item is worth (Kalayanaram & Little, 1994). This situation applies to shopping goods with commonly accepted value, and consumers are said to find it easier to form reference prices when products have easily comparable attributes and/or engender brand loyalty. In contrast, some researchers claim that consumers adjust reference prices to the current purchase situation and use a personal value system to decide how much the item is worth to them (Hardie, Johnson, & Fader, 1993). This situation applies to specialty goods with private value, and consumers are said to find it more difficult to form reference prices when products are of uncertain value and fluctuate greatly. Thus, consumers are less likely to bid, for they are concerned about overpaying and fear the winner's curse. Thus, we hypothesize that more bidders are likely to compete for objectively priced products (Wilcox, 2000) than for subjectively priced ones.

H2: Objectively priced products will attract a larger number of bidders than will subjectively priced ones.

Word of Mouth (WOM)

In addition to product type and reference prices, WOM is a major influence on consumer decision making (Bansal & Voyer, 2000; Brown & Reingen, 1987; Duhan, Johnson, Wilcox, & Harrell, 1997), for consumers view it as an unbiased information source (Arndt, 1968; Bansal & Voyer, 2000). Although WOM is difficult to measure directly, it can be measured by proxy via eBay's seller rating system. Here, successful bidders rate sellers by characterizing the purchase experience as positive, negative, or neutral, and potential bidders can use the ratings to make purchase decisions. This is the way for online bidders to get information about sellers, but it is viewed as weak-tie WOM because consumers have no personal ties to the informants and sellers. In contrast, offline WOM is viewed as strong tie because consumers know their informants as friends, relatives, neighbors, and colleagues. Kotler (2000, p. 560), for example, claimed that WOM in the form of "loyal, satisfied customers that brag about doing business with you is the dream of every business owner." We hypothesize that in the absence of other information sources, as is the case on eBay, consumers are more likely to bid on items whose sellers have favorable ratings.

H3: Items with more favorable seller ratings (WOM) will attract a higher number of bidders than those with less favorable ratings.

METHOD

Data Collection

Even though sellers must register to offer items and buyers must register to make purchases, anyone can log on and gain access to seller information. This made it possible for the authors to collect real-time data and in this way avoid the unreal experimental setting where lack of meaningful economic incentives and artificially short bidding rounds diminish verisimilitude (Wilcox, 2000). In the current study, unobtrusive data collection on eBay's site (www.eBay.com) took place over a 30-day period during which the researchers observed listed purchase activity and monitored 100 randomly selected items in each product category: Rolex watches (objectively priced specialty goods), fine art paintings (subjectively priced specialty goods), notebook computers (objectively priced shopping goods), and living room furniture (subjectively priced shopping goods). Both Rolex watches and notebook computers are branded manufactured goods with manufacturers' suggested retail prices as objective reference points, whereas paintings and preowned furniture lack such reference points and can only be subjectively priced. In selecting these products, we followed prior research on categorizations of watches and paintings as specialty products and furniture and computers as shopping products (see Copeland 1923, 1924; Murphy & Enis, 1986; Li & Gery, 2000).

The Rolex sample was taken from 267 watches, with starting bids ranging from $50 to $7,250 and the fine art sample from approximately 575 items, with starting bids from $200 to $20,000. The living room furniture sample was taken from approximately 284 items—primarily couches and sofas—with starting bids ranging from $40 to $2,543. The notebook computer sample was taken from approximately 200 items, with starting bids ranging from $10 to $2,254. Small-value items in all categories such as throw pillows in the furniture sample and batteries in the notebook sample were excluded. The following information was collected and recorded.

1. Starting bid
2. Competing bids

3. Final bid
4. Seller reserve or minimum acceptable price
5. Reserve price met/not met by bidders
6. Seller ratings
7. Bidder email addresses
8. Seller email address
9. Total number of bids
10. Number of days auction lasted
11. Item description

FINDINGS

Table 20.1 presents the data summary for the four products that were examined. A one-way ANOVA shows significant differences in the number of bids across the four products (F = 36.87, p = .000), with the mean number of bids higher for computers and Rolexes and lower for paintings and sofas. Many subjectively priced items did not generate even a single bid, with 67% of the paintings and 39% of the sofas attracting no interest at all.

Next, we compare shopping with specialty products and objectively priced products with subjectively priced ones. An independent samples t test comparing product types indicates that shopping products (mean = 9.50) attract a significantly greater number of bids (t = 3.86, p = .000) than specialty items (mean = 5.85), even though shopping items were listed for shorter durations (mean = 8.05 days) than specialty ones (mean = 8.87 days), t = 3.57, p = .000. An independent samples t-test comparing pricing types indicates that objectively priced products (mean = 11.66) generate a significantly greater number of bids (t = 9.10, p = .000) than subjectively priced ones (mean = 3.69), even though objectively priced items were listed for fewer days (7.79) than subjectively priced ones (9.13), t = −6.07, p = .000. A further indication of consumer preference for this type of item relates

TABLE 20.1
Comparison of Bidder Response

	Paintings n = 100	Sofas n = 100	Computers n = 100	Rolexes n = 100
Mean # of bids	1.69	5.69	13.31	10.01
Range of number of bidders	0-20	0-32	0-41	0-47
Mean duration of bids in days	9.29	8.98	7.13	8.45
Mean price of winning bid	$347.32	$287.38	$692.74	$1410.51
% items with zero bids	67%	38%	14%	21%
% items with no reserve price set	10%	19%	42%	11%
% items where reserve was met	37%	21%	25.5%	15.7%

to the acceptance of seller reserve prices, listed for 318 (79.5%) of the 400 items. The reserve price was met for 25% of objectively priced products, but only 8.8% of subjectively priced products ($X^2 = 15.54$, p = .000). Similarly, it was met for 25.2% of the shopping goods, but only for 9.5% of the specialty items ($X^2 = 14.06$, p = .000). Thus, both H1 and H2 are supported, with consumers more inclined to bid on objectively priced shopping products.

To test H3, a regression analysis was run in which the number of bids was the dependent variable and the seller rating the independent one. Even though the relationship was positive (r = .081), it was not significant (p = .107). To determine whether product category was a moderator of the relationship, we conceptualized "a basic moderator effect . . . as an interaction between a focal independent variable and a factor that specifies the appropriate conditions for its operation" (Baron & Kenny, 1986, p. 1174). Baron and Kenny pointed out that a moderator hypothesis is supported if the interaction is found to be significant, regardless of a possible significant relationship between main effects for the predictor variable and moderator. Following their reasoning, we found a significant moderator relationship of product type and seller rating on the number of bids (F = 2.6, p = .005). When product type was included in the model, the main effect relationship between seller rating and number of bids became significant (F = 6.424, p = .000). Our model explains 26% of the variation in the data (adjusted $R^2 = .263$), and H3 is supported. This seems to confirm that a positive relation between sellers' WOM ratings and the number of bids they receive is moderated by product category. Thus, an objectively priced good being sold by a seller with a high WOM rating is likely to get a greater number of bids than a subjectively priced item sold by a seller with a similar WOM rating. Thus, we find support for all three hypotheses, with objectively priced shopping goods attracting the highest number of bids and WOM influencing consumer bidding behavior.

LIMITATIONS

Even though the study used observational data to overcome the biases inherent in self-reports, the limitation of observational methods is that they do not provide insight into the driving forces of motives, attitudes, and intentions that underlie behavior (Malhotra, 1996). Despite findings that support the study's hypotheses, we did not gather information about why consumers are reluctant to bid on subjectively priced items or specialty goods. Further, although the use of 4 product categories can be defended as both representative and theoretically grounded, it obviously excludes the other 4,000 categories that may or may not influence bidding. In this vein, the sample size of 100 products in each cell may be satisfactory in exploratory research, but should not be taken as the optimal size for larger studies that can yield more generalizable results.

DISCUSSION

If we regard the limitations not as a threat but as an opportunity to move ahead, the robust findings suggest the need for future research on topics such as consumer attitudes to negotiated prices and perceptions of risk. To begin, the supposed consumer aversion to negotiated prices must be reexamined, for it is no longer clear that this is valid. Managers of auction sites can benefit from the development of decision-making models and optimal dynamic price-setting strategies, as can managers of the growing number of firms that use dynamic pricing to sell goods online. There is some urgency for research in this area as well, for the Internet has been identified as a locus of "perfect markets"—those in which buyers and sellers negotiate the optimal price. The argument that objectively priced products mimic perfect market models has also led to the suggestion that auctionlike pricing may eventually replace sticker prices on a wide variety of goods (*Business Week*, 1999). Insofar as many firms are jumping on the auction bandwagon, researchers and managers alike need to learn more about consumer bidding behavior.

One of the most obvious gaps in knowledge is a lack of scientific evidence about consumer perception of risk in C2C auctions, where WOM may be the only source of information (Bradley & Porter, 2000; Massad & Tucker, 2000). Controversial research claims have been made about the importance of perceived risk, and so much public attention has been directed to instances of fraud that a growing number of bidders are concerned about whether an item is really what it is represented to be and whether they are paying in advance for something they will never receive. Consumer fears have been fueled by publicity about instances of fraud (Herschlag & Zwick, 2002), most recently (Squatriglia, 2001) the selling of fake art "masterpieces" for as much as $135,000. Here, bad publicity drives out good data, for the fact is that the fraud rate on eBay is low—fewer than 0.1% (Roth, 2000), or 30 fraudulent transactions out of every million (Holland, 1999). Still, consumers are afraid of a purchase situation in which "you mail off a check to the individual who is selling—and pray that you don't get stiffed. In most cases, buyers pay the freight, too" (Pitta, 1999, p. 2). In this environment, it is the seller who controls product and price information, and WOM is the sole source of buyer feedback.

Nonetheless, some researchers claim that "information synergies present in online auctioneering . . . are unparalleled in the history of marketplaces" (Cox, 1999, p. 321). From this perspective, online auctions are said to offer unprecedented access not only to information about the seller business practices via WOM but also to information about previous sales of comparables (Cox, 1999, p. 319). Hence, online auctions are viewed as less risky than traditional ones, and perceived risk is said to be moderated by the consumer's ready access to information that will reduce purchase uncertainty. However, an alternative view is presented by Mishra and Olshavsky (2005), who claimed that more available information helps to lower the bounds on consumer rationality. Future research must be directed at adapting general consumer behavior research models of perceived risk (Dowling & Staelin, 1994; Oglethorpe & Monroe, 1994) to development of a context-appropriate model and measurement instruments. This is but one of many areas for future inquiry that can both borrow from traditional consumer research and give back to the field. The study of online bidding behavior can also extend to topics such as gender differences, satisfaction, postpurchase dissonance, and auction addiction, for at the end of the day, very little is known about the way that consumers respond to the new retailing environment.

REFERENCES

Arndt, J. (1968). Selective process in word-of-mouth. *Journal of Advertising Research, 8*, 19–22.
Bansal, H. S., & Voyer, P. A. (2000). Word-of-mouth processes within a services purchase decision context. *Journal of Service Research, 3*(2), 166–177.
Baron, R. M., & Kenny, D. A. (1986, December). The moderator mediator variable distinction in social psychological research: Conceptual, strategic, and statistical considerations. *Journal of Personality and Social Psychology*, SI, 1173–1182.
Bradley, S. P., & Porter, K. A. (2000). eBay, Inc. *Journal of Interactive Marketing, 14*(4), 73–97. (Also published as HBS Case 700-007).
Brown, J. J., & Reingen, P. (1987, December). Social ties and word-of-mouth referral behavior. *Journal of Consumer Research, 14*, 350–362.
Business Week, (1999, April 12) Going Going Gone.
Copeland, M. T. (1923, April). The relation of consumers' buying habits to marketing methods. *Harvard Business Review, 1*, 282–289.
Copeland, M. T. (1924). *Principles of merchandizing.* Chicago: A.W. Shaw.
Cox, J. C. (with Samuel H. Dinkin and Vernon I. Smith). (1999, March). The winner's curse and public information in common value auctions: comment. *American Economic Review, 89*, 319–324.
Coy, P., & Moore P. L. (2000, November 20). A revolution in pricing? Not quite. *Business Week.*
Crockett, R. O. (1999, December 13). Going, Going . . . Richer. *Business Week.*
Dalton, G. (1999, October 4). Going, Going, Gone. *Information Week*, 45–50.
Dowling, G. R., & Staelin R. (1994). A model of perceived risk and intended risk-handling activity. *Journal of Consumer Research, 21*(1), 119–134.
Duhan, D. Johnson, S. D., Wilcox J. B. & Harrell G. D. (1997). Influences on consumer use of word-of-mouth recommendation sources. *Journal of the Academy of Marketing Science, 25*(4), 283–295.
Ebay.com (August 30, 2004)
The Economist. (2000, February 26). Survey: E-commerce: In the great web bazaar, S40–44.
The Forrester Brief. (2001, February 22). ebay well set to dominate global auction market.
Greenleaf, E., Rao, A. G., & Sinha A. R. (1993). Guarantees in auctions: The auction house as negotiator and managerial decision maker. *Management Science, 39*(9), 1130–1145.
Hanson, W. (2000). *Principles of internet marketing.* Cincinnati, OH: Southwestern College Publishing.
Hardie, B., Johnson E., & Fader, P. S. (1993, Fall). Modeling loss aversion and reference dependence effects on brand choice. *Marketing Science, 12*, 378–394.
Herschlag, M., & Zwick, R. (2002). Internet auctions—popular and professional literature review. *Quarterly Journal of Electronic Commerce, 1*(2), 161–186.
Hof, Robert D., The eBay Economy, *Business Week*, 8/18/2003-8/25/2003, 124–128.
Hoffman, D. L., & Novak, T. P. (1996). Marketing in hypermedia computer-mediated environments: Conceptual foundations. *Journal of Marketing, 60*(3), 50–68.
Holland, K. (1999, January 25). eBay cracks down on fraud. *Business Week*, 49.

Kalyanaram, G., & Little, J. D. C. (1994, December). An empirical analysis of latitude of price acceptance in consumer packaged goods. *Journal of Consumer Research, 21,* 408–418.

Kalyanaram, G., & Winer, R. S. (1995). Empirical generalizations from reference price research. *Marketing Science, 14*(3), 161–169.

Kemp, T. (2001, August 6). Retailers auction surplus online—Merchants are turning to eBay and others to sell unsold, returned items. *Information Week,* 12–13.

Kotler, P. (2000). *Marketing management: Millenium edition.* Upper Saddle River, NJ: Prentice-Hall.

Li, Z. G., & Gery N. (2000, November–December). E-tailing—For all products. *Business Horizons,* 49–54.

Lucking-Reiley, D. (2000, September). Auctions on the internet: What's being auctioned, and how? *The Journal of Industrial Economics, XLVIII* 227–252.

Malhotra, N. K. (1996). *Marketing research: An applied orientation* (2nd ed.). Upper Saddle River, NJ: Prentice-Hall.

Massad, V. J., & Tucker, J. M. (2000, Summer). Comparing bidding and pricing between in-person and online auctions. *Journal of Product & Brand Management, 9,* 325–332.

Mazumdar, T., & Papatla, P. (1995). Loyalty differences in the use of internal and external reference prices. *Marketing Letters, 6*(2), 111–122.

Mazumdar, T., & Papatla, P. (2000, May). An investigation of reference price segments. *Journal of Marketing Research, XXXVII* 246–258.

Milgrom, P., (1989). Auctions and bidding: A primer. *Journal of Economic Perspectives, 3*(3), 3–22.

Mishra, S., & Olshavsky R. W. (2005). The internet and its effects on consumer decision making. In C. Haugvedt, K. Machleit, and R. Yalch (Eds.). *Online consumer psychology: Understanding and influencing consumer behavior in the virtual world.* Mahwah, NJ: Lawrence Erlbaum Associates.

Murphy, P. E., & Enis, B. M. (1986). Classifying products strategically. *Journal of Marketing, 50*(3), 24–42.

Oglethorpe, J. E., & Monroe, K. B. (1994). Determinants of perceived health and safety risks of selected hazardous product activities. *Journal of Consumer Affairs, 28*(2), 326–346.

Pitta, J. (1999). Competitive Shopping. In A. C. Ekin (Ed.), *Perspectives: Marketing on the internet* (pp. 61–62). St. Paul, MN: Coursewise.

Riley, J. (1989). Expected revenue from open and sealed bid auctions. *Journal of Economic Perspectives, 3*(3), 41–50.

Roth, D. (2000). Fraud's booming in online auctions, but help is here. *Fortune, 141*(11), 276.

Rothkopf, M. (1991). On auctions with withdrawable winning bids. *Marketing Science, 10*(1), 40–57.

Squatriglia, C. (2001, March 9). 3 indicted in ebay art sales scam/they're accused of faking a Diebenkorn, inflating bids at auctions. *The San Francisco Chronicle,* A1.

Swinkels, J. M. (2001). The Efficiency of large private value auctions. *Econometrica, 69*(1), 37–68.

Wilcox, R. T. (2000). Experts and Amateurs: The role of experience in internet auctions. *Marketing Letters, 11*(4), 363–374.

CHAPTER TWENTY ONE

The Impact of Internet Use on Health Cognitions and Health Behavior

Noel T. Brewer

University of North Carolina

The chapter reviews the findings of four studies that examined the relation of Internet use to health knowledge, attitudes and behavior. Several trends were observed. First, health knowledge was generally greater among Internet searchers than non-searchers. However, the searchers tended to be overconfident (i.e., they thought that they knew more than they actually did). Second, health-related intentions and behaviors were related to past Internet use. Past Internet searching on club drugs was related to stronger intentions to use the drugs in the future. Searching by chronically ill patients on their illnesses (HIV or multiple sclerosis) was related to greater physician utilization. Third, the effects of experimentally controlled Internet searching were relatively large but restricted to knowledge and attitudes. Cross-sectional findings were stronger than experimental findings with regards to behavioral variables. Finally, these relations to Internet searching tended to be present only among people new to the topic of search.

Obtaining health-related information on the Internet has become a commonplace and even daily activity for many people. Over 50 million Americans have used the Internet to search for health information and 5 million of them are surfing the Web for health information on any given day (Fox et al., 2000). The widespread accessing of health information by consumers may amount to a massive public health intervention the effects of which are largely unknown. Despite its potential importance, very few studies have assessed the impact on consumers of health-related Internet use. This chapter presents four studies that address this gap in the literature by examining empirically the effects of Internet searching on health-related cognitions and behavior. For a more detailed treatment of the studies, see Brewer (2003 and under review).

A MODIFIED SELF-REGULATION MODEL

The studies presented in this chapter are loosely based on Leventhal's self-regulation (SR) model (Leventhal, Meyer, & Nerenz, 1980; Leventhal, Nerenz, & Steele, 1984). The original model contains several components not explicitly tested here, including the role of affect and physical symptoms. The studies focus instead on the SR model's conceptualization of illness cognitions and health behavior as well as the role of new health-related information.

The relation between psychological factors and health behaviors has been modeled by numerous theories that can be broadly categorized (for a review, see Horne & Weinman, 1998) as social cognitive models such as the health belief model (Rosenstock, 1974), stage models such as the precaution adoption process model (Weinstein, 1988), and the hybrid SR model. Among the many models that explain health beliefs and behavior, the SR model stands out for elaborating the complex ways that people think about health and illness. The SR model is commonly used to better understand chronically ill patients' health behaviors (e.g., Brewer, Chapman, Brownlee, & Leventhal, 2002; Meyer, Leventhal, & Gutmann, 1985). However, it is easily applied to behaviors that prevent illness such as abstaining from drug use (Brewer, 2003) and hypertension screening (Zimmerman, Safer, Leventhal, & Baumann, 1986).

Key components of the SR model are shown in Fig. 21.1: health cognitions, affective states, and health behavior. A component representing new health-related information is explicitly drawn to highlight its role in the model. For a more detailed diagram of the SR model, see Diefenbach and Leventhal (1996).

For a given disease, people have distinct beliefs that Leventhal calls illness cognitions. I will use in this chapter a broader term, *health cognitions*, that encompasses beliefs about staying healthy as well as and beliefs about particular illnesses. Health cognitions are organized into five discrete attributes (Leventhal et al., 1984). The first attribute, *identity* or *symptoms*, includes both the person's label for the health state as well as its symptoms. The second attribute, *consequences*, addresses the potential and expected repercussions of the health state. The third attribute, *timeline*, addresses the temporal course of the health state, whether it is acute or chronic, stable or cyclical. The fourth attribute, *cause*, addresses the perceived covariation of the health state with antecedent events. The fifth attribute, *controllability* or *cure*, addresses the severity of the health state and the extent to which it can be remedied.

Operating in parallel with the cognitive component is an affective component of the SR model. Participants have an emotion-based response to symptoms they

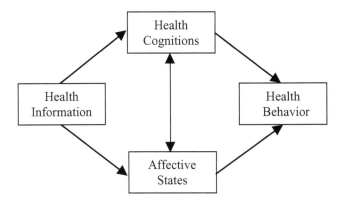

FIG. 21.1 Modified self-regulation model. The original model by Leventhal et al. (1984) separates health behavior into coping and appraisal stages and includes feedback loops between all stages.

believe to be caused by their illness and to new health information. Affect can include anxiety, anger, relief, and happiness. The health cognition and affect components, in turn, motivate health behaviors such as compliance with medical regimens (Brewer et al., 2002; Meyer et al., 1985) and recovery from illness (Petrie, Weinman, Sharpe, & Buckley, 1996).

Many of the pathways of the SR model, including those that lead to health behaviors, flow in multiple directions. For example, a person who feels anxious about breast cancer may see her doctor for breast cancer screening, a move "forward" along the pathway connecting affect and behavior. Engaging in the screening behavior may also reduce her anxiety, a move "backward" along the same pathway. The elaboration of bidirectional pathways is necessary for the generality of the model but is more intricate than is needed for the present discussion.

In addition to the explicit components of the SR model that are described earlier, there is an implied component, *external stimuli*, that can impact health cognitions and affect. (Of course, some internal stimuli such as symptoms and rumination on symptoms can also prompt health behaviors as well as initiating a search for new health information.) One example of an external stimulus is a fear appeal designed to increase a health behavior (e.g., Leventhal, Watts, & Pagano, 1967). Although the SR model is formulated for the more general case of "stimuli," I consider a particular stimulus: Internet-based health information.

An examination of Fig. 21.1 yields insights into ways that Internet use can impact users. Internet-based health information could *directly* alter health cognitions, affective states, or both. Furthermore, health behaviors can be altered *indirectly* by first altering affect or cognition. The next two sections consider these insights and present several hypotheses about the impact of health-related Internet use.

CHANGES IN HEALTH COGNITIONS

Changes in health cognitions could take the form of altered knowledge about
a health state. Such changes should reflect whether the stimulus information is
accurate or inaccurate. In other words, we should observe an increase in accurate
knowledge when people are exposed to accurate information that is new to them.
(An alternate account is that some searchers may conduct self-serving searches
to find information to support a viewpoint they want to believe or remain highly
skeptical of new information that does not fit their existing beliefs. This account
is not tested in the studies presented here.)

Most studies of health-related information presented on the Internet report that
it contains largely accurate information. The most authoritative study to date of
the accuracy of Internet health information is by Berland and colleagues (2001).
In their study, a team of 34 physicians examined the content of 25 of the most
frequently visited Web sites (and subsidiary Web pages) that contained information
on breast cancer, childhood asthma, depression, and obesity. They reported that
the Web pages were highly accurate. The percentage of English language Web
pages that contained mostly or completely accurate information ranged, according
to topic, from 97% to 100%. However, the number of Web pages offering more
than minimal coverage on a topic was low, ranging from 40% to 67%.

Berland and colleagues' (2001) findings are supported by other reports. A study
by Sandvik (1999) found that Internet information on female urinary incontinence
was largely accurate and would be helpful to patients. A similar study by Galimberti
and Jain (2000) reported that Internet-based information on hysterectomy was reasonably accurate and noted only a few cases of misleading information. Latthe,
Latthe, and Khan (2000) reported that information on menorrhagia (i.e., abnormally heavy menstrual flow) was frequently incomplete although the study did not
assess informational accuracy.

Various researchers and government officials have warned that the Internet contains substantial inaccurate information (Silberg, Lundberg, & Musacchio, 1997).
For example, the Federal Trade Commission (FTC) warns that the Web has substantial inaccurate information about treatments for diseases such as AIDS and
cancer (FTC, 2000). A search of 1,200 Web sites by FTC agents identified numerous spurious cures for HIV infection, cancer, and diabetes being peddled. With
the exception of the FTC's claim, little of the editorializing has been backed by
empirical research.

A small group of empirical studies have found substantial inaccurate health-
related information on the Internet. Davison (1997) reported that just under half
of 76 sites provided dietary information inconsistent with Canadian governmen-
tal standards for good nutrition. Whereas health organizations generally provided
little misinformation (1.3%), many private vendors provided a great deal of inaccurate information (57.1%). Pandolfini, Impicciatore, and Bonati (2000) reported
that Web sites with information on managing cough in children were typically

incomplete and that just under half of 19 sites contained more incorrect than correct information.

In summary, much of the health information available on the Internet can be considered accurate. Many Web sites have incomplete information, a problem that may be remedied by people reading multiple sites. A relatively small number of Web sites (or ones that are infrequently visited) have incorrect information. Among the studies finding substantial inaccuracy, there were few common threads other than that personal Web sites tended to be more likely to contain inaccurate information. It may be that inaccurate knowledge may accumulate in Internet users, but a more likely scenario is that readers will learn accurate information that is confirmed on multiple sites.

The studies reviewed here do not directly assess the impact of Internet-based health information on people who surf the World Wide Web. What effect, if any, widespread use of the Internet is having on the accuracy of people's health beliefs and on their behavior is little understood. Gustafson and colleagues have shown that placing computers in the homes of patients with HIV and breast cancer yielded a variety of positive outcomes including improved psychological functioning, decreased doctor visits, and greater participation in health care (Gustafson et al., 1999; Gustafson et al., 2000). However, the elaborate interventions reported by Gustafson, in which the computers were equipped with special educational and decision-making software, are substantially different than the experience of the typical Internet user. It is more common that Internet users encounter a wide variety of unregulated sources in a relatively unstructured format.

Support for the hypothesis that Internet use increases health knowledge is offered by Kalichman, Bentotseh, Weinhardt, Austin, and Luke (2002). In a cross-sectional survey of 147 patients with HIV, they found that Internet use correlated with more accurate knowledge about HIV treatment. (Surprisingly, Internet-using patients were also at higher risk for transmitting HIV to other people.) Based on the study by Kalichman and colleagues and reviews of health information on the Internet, it is reasonable to hypothesize that Internet use should generally be associated with higher levels of health knowledge in the domain searched.

H1: Increased Internet use will be associated with more accurate health knowledge.

Regardless of their actual knowledge, people have perceptions about their knowledge, a measure called *confidence*. When people experience a change in their knowledge, they should also experience a change in what they perceive their level of knowledge to be. However, past research has shown that, as people make more judgments in a given domain, their confidence increases (Dawson et al., 1993; Einhorn & Hogarth, 1978; Oskamp, 1962) even though their knowledge has not similarly increased. The mere act of searching (whether or not anything substantial was learned) may increase people's confidence about their level of knowledge.

H2: Increased Internet use will be associated with more confidence about health knowledge.

Information is better encoded and subsequently recalled more accurately when it has been processed deeply. Depth of informational processing is encouraged by such techniques as organizing information (Bower, Clark, Lesgold, & Winzenz, 1969) and elaborating on its meaning (Stein & Bransford, 1979). An interesting quality of health information presented on the Internet is that, although there is a great variety of information available, it is not presented in a way designed to facilitate recall. Typically, a Web page will contain one or more essays on a health topic that may be informative but difficult to translate into memorable facts. Reading information from multiple sites may further discourage deep processing of the health information.

A person may read a great deal on a topic and learn something, but I expect that what they learn may be difficult to remember. The exposure to so much information that is poorly organized and presumably poorly encoded should cause people's perceived knowledge to exceed their actual knowledge.

H3: Gains in confidence caused by searching will outpace the gains in knowledge.

The role of the Internet in altering health-related affect is not explored explicitly in the present studies. I focus instead on changes in health intentions and behavior. People who actively search the Internet may encounter new information about a health behavior or about a disease, triggering new beliefs about their own health or a reappraisal of their health-related habits. For example, Kalichman and colleagues (2001) found that although Internet-using HIV patients knew more about their disease, they were also more likely to be at risk for transmitting HIV to others. Thus, Internet-related improvements in knowledge are not necessarily linked to better health behaviors.

The studies presented in this chapter consider two types of health behavior: drug use by college students and physician utilization by chronically ill patients. Refraining from drug use is interesting as it represents a type of primary prevention (avoiding a health risk) and is a contrast to physician utilization by the chronically ill that represents a type of tertiary prevention (caring for an illness). In the case of drug use, college students who encounter drug information on the Internet may learn more about the drugs. At the same time, searching could also familiarize readers with the transient benefits of drug use and students could walk away from their search with elevated drug use-intentions.

For patients, the Internet may occasionally substitute for physician services. Some technical questions about a chronic illness could be handled adequately by searching the Internet and thus reduce calls to a physician. At the same time, new information that is encountered could prompt a patient to request a new treatment, or at least to visit the physician's office for a consultation on the topic. Given the examples of drug use and physician utilization, it should be apparent that it is not possible to make a general directional claim about how Internet use should affect health behavior. However, it is reasonable to expect that searchers will show differences in health behavior related to their topic of search.

H4: Internet searching will be associated with changes in health-related intentions and behavior.

Past research has shown differences between cross-sectional survey studies and laboratory-based experiments. For example, studies testing the theory of planned behavior (and the related theory of reasoned action) (Ajzen, 1991; Fisbein & Azjen, 1975) showed the strongest support for the theory when experimental methods were used (Liska, 1984). The most common way of assessing Internet accuracy has been to use experimental methods, a necessary approach that may limit generalizability and exaggerate the strength of the findings. The present studies allow for a comparison of cross-sectional and experimental findings related to Internet use.

H5: Internet searching will have a stronger effect when experimentally manipulated than when it is cross-sectionally measured.

This chapter reviews four studies that test the hypotheses introduced earlier. (Study 3 tests all the hypotheses except the hypothesis relating to health behavior, H4.) The final hypothesis relating to generalizability of experimental Internet findings is tested within Study 1, and by comparing Study 2 to Studies 3 and 4.

STUDY 1: STUDENTS AND CLUB DRUGS

As there is so little previous work examining how Internet use affects people's knowledge and behavior, I conducted a simple laboratory experiment that explored the effects of searching for club drug information on the Internet. *Club drug* is a loosely defined term referring to drugs that are most frequently used by college students and teens in environments such as dance clubs and raves. Club drugs include ecstasy (methylenedioxymethamphetamine, also called MDMA), speed (methamphetamine), LSD (lysergic acid diethylamide), GHB (gamma-hydroxybutyrate), rohypnol, and ketamine. The adverse effects of the drugs vary, but they include cognitive impairment, depression, addiction, and overdose (Ropero-Miller & Goldberger, 1998). Club drug use has risen in popularity to such an extent that the National Institute on Drug Abuse (NIDA, 1999) has sponsored a national initiative to combat their use.

Club drug information on the Internet may pose a substantial public health problem. Increased knowledge about club drugs' negative effects would not be a cause for concern, but an increase in permissive attitudes toward their use would be. A population of high concern is college students who typically use both the Internet and club drugs at a higher rate than other groups. Furthermore, college students in New Jersey have been identified by the Community Epidemiology Work Group (CEWG, 2000) as having notably high use of the club drug ecstasy, making them a compelling group to study.

Method

New Jersey college students ($N = 117$) were randomly assigned to search the Internet for 40 minutes on club drugs or a control topic, in spring 2000. Details of the study are available in Brewer (Under review). Previous drug use was common among participants with the majority having at least once used marijuana (53%) and many having used ecstasy (26%) or other drugs. A composite measure of drug use was created where a person was labeled as having "past drug use" if they had ever used marijuana, ecstacy, cocaine, GHB, ketamine, LSD, methamphetamine, or rohypnol.

Experimental condition participants were instructed to: "Imagine that a very close friend has started using club drugs. They just tried speed and ecstasy and have suggested that you should also try these drugs. They have asked you to look online to find out more information about club drugs because you have access to a computer. Be sure you learn something new about each of these things: speed (or methamphetamine), ecstasy (or MDMA), and club drug." Participants in the control condition searched on a topic unrelated to drug use.

After participants had finished browsing the Internet, they completed a survey that assessed their drug knowledge, attitudes, and intentions. A posttest-only design was used in Studies 1 and 2 to eliminate pretest sensitization that could have substantially altered participants' searching habits (Cook & Campbell, 1979). Had a pretest been used, participants may have been biased toward searching on the topics assessed in the survey, undermining substantially the ecological validity of the experiment.

The knowledge questions in the posttest survey asked about speed and ecstasy (24 on each topic) and were structured using the health cognitions portion of Leventhal's SR model (Leventhal et al., 1984). In other words, the knowledge questions asked about people's beliefs about the symptoms, cause consequences, timeline, and remedy for being intoxicated as a result of having taken ecstasy and speed. Answers to the knowledge questions were scored for accuracy based on information provided by NIDA on their Web sites. A composite accuracy score for ecstasy knowledge and another for speed knowledge were created for each participant. Participants' confidence in the accuracy of their ecstasy knowledge was assessed using a single question that asked what percentage of the knowledge questions on ecstasy participants felt they had answered correctly.

To simplify discussing the many findings in this chapter, I summarize various statistical analyses using a measure of effect size, r. The reader may be more familiar with r in its squared form as R^2, the percentage of variance explained by an effect. The effect size, r, is more formally called a semipartial correlation and is calculated by taking the sums of squares for an effect, dividing it by the total sums of squares for the model, and then taking the square root. (In cases where the original analysis concerned a dependent dichotomous variable, I report a standardized beta (β) from the equation predicting the odds ratio.) Note that these measures summarize various analyses that include t tests, ANOVAs, MANCOVAs, and multiple logistic regressions.

Does Internet Searching Affect Searchers?

Internet searchers showed a boost in knowledge, as shown in Fig. 21.2. Among nondrug users, experimental searchers showed higher knowledge about ecstasy than nonsearchers ($r = .43$, $p < .001$), whereas among drug users there was no difference between search conditions ($r = .01$, $n.s.$). Experimental searchers also knew more than nonsearchers about speed ($r = .39$, $p < .001$). The statistical models testing these relations covaried past drug use, past Internet searching for club drug information, demographic variables, and, as appropriate, knowledge and confidence. The differences for ecstasy and speed knowledge may be a function of the students' relative familiarity with the drugs. Almost a third had previously used ecstasy (and the drug was widely prevalent on the campus) whereas speed was rarely used. Put another way, students who had any experience with drugs had learned all they needed about ecstasy (but not speed) from their peers and had little use for the information they found.

Confidence about ecstasy knowledge was also boosted by Web searching ($r = .25$, $p < .001$). Confidence about speed knowledge was not assessed. One would

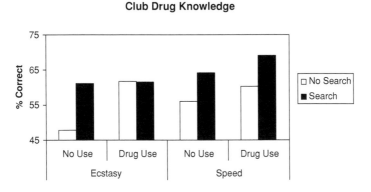

FIG. 21.2 Relation of Internet use to knowledge in Study 1.

hope that knowledge and confidence would move in tandem, but ecstasy knowledge and confidence were uncorrelated ($r = .04$, *n.s.*). A closer examination of the relation between ecstasy knowledge and confidence (after Kruger & Dunning, 1999) showed that those lowest in knowledge gave confidence ratings that were substantially above their actual knowledge (i.e., overconfident). In contrast, those high in knowledge were relatively well calibrated (correlation of knowledge and calibration-in-the-large, $r = -.47$, $p < .001$). It appears that those with lower knowledge were unaware of this fact.

Changes in attitudes showed a similar pattern to changes in knowledge. Searchers were more likely to agree that using club drugs would help them fit in at a party and to talk to people they did not know ($r = .18$, $p < .05$). Ratings of the usefulness of club drugs (that they would be fun, safe, mood enhancing, and have few side effects) also differed. Among nondrug users, searchers showed higher usefulness ratings than nonsearchers ($r = .38$, $p < .005$), whereas among drug users there was no difference between conditions ($r = .04$, *n.s.*). The differences in knowledge and attitudes did not result in stronger intentions to use drugs in the future.

Taken together, the knowledge and attitude findings suggest that nondrug users, that is, people who are relative novices to the topic of search, may be most strongly affected by their search.

Do Lab Experiments Mirror the Real World?

In addition to an experiment, one could examine the effects of Internet searching correlationally. Many participants (76%) had previously searched for club drug information on the Internet before they arrived for the experiment. Thus, one could compare those who had never searched for club drug information before the experiment to those who had (see Table 21.1).

The dissociation between the experimental and correlational findings is striking. The lab experiment generally showed large differences in knowledge and confidence (as shown in Table 21.1) accompanied by differences in attitudes. The correlational findings suggest minimal differences in knowledge, a small difference in confidence, few differences in attitudes, but a notable difference in intentions to use club drugs in the future.

Surprisingly, "previous searchers" did not know any more about ecstasy or speed than their "no-previous-search" counterparts. Confidence about ecstasy knowledge was modestly higher among the previous searchers ($r = .19$, $p < .05$). Less surprising is the finding that the benefits of drug use were rated higher by previous searchers than by nonsearchers ($r = .16$, $p < .05$). The finding has numerous explanations including that those with higher value for the drugs at the start were more likely to search.

Of most interest is that previous searching was related to stronger intention to use drugs in the future. The relation held even after covarying out knowledge

TABLE 21.1

Relation of Internet Searching to Knowledge and Confidence

	Knowledge	Confidence
	r	r
EXPERIMENTAL STUDIES		
Study 1, Students searched on club drugs	.39*[1]	—
Students searched on club drugs	.25**[2]	.25**[3]
Study 2, Students searched on MS	.24*	.64**
Students searched on HIV	.10	.44**
CROSS-SECTIONAL STUDIES		
Study 1, Students searched on club drugs	.01 [1]	—
Students searched on club drugs	.02 [2]	.19*[3]
Study 3, MS patients searched on MS	.23*	.14
Study 4, HIV patients searched on HIV	.08	.02

Note: Positive correlations indicate that Internet searching was associated with higher levels of knowledge or confidence. Knowledge and confidence measures are for the topic on which the participant searched (e.g., MS or HIV). The students searched the Internet under controlled lab conditions whereas the patients were asked about ever having searched on the topic in the past. Correlations are semipartial correlations from a multiple regressions that controlled for knowledge and confidence. For example, a regression predicting MS knowledge would covary MS confidence, HIV knowledge, and HIV confidence.

[1] Knowledge about speed.

[2] Knowledge about ecstasy (before covarying past drug use).

[3] Confidence about ecstasy.

$*p < .05, **p < .001$

and attitudes about club drugs, suggesting that searching may have some enduring link to intentions ($r = .24$, $p < .001$). As a correlational finding, the causal link between intention and searching remains ambiguous. Searching may elevate drug-use intentions, but it is also possible that elevated intentions lead to searching.

The relation between Internet searching and drug-use intentions should be mediated by knowledge if the SR model presented in Fig. 21.1 holds true. The test for mediation requires that the relation between searching and intentions disappear *after* covarying out the effects of knowledge (Baron & Kenny, 1986). This was not the case in the present study. It is of course possible that unmeasured affective variables would successfully mediate that relation (although the various attitude measures failed to do so). Another possibility is that there is a direct relation of Internet searching to intentions.

One explanation for the divergent findings between experimental and correlational measures is that the health information from the Internet was poorly encoded in the first place. Over time, the knowledge gained may quickly fade in the absence of rehearsal. The changes in attitudes appear to be more enduring, perhaps because attitudes are less well organized in memory than knowledge.

An unmeasured component, affective reactions, may also explain the difference between the experimental and correlational findings. Searching may cause changes in knowledge and attitudes, while at the same time increasing the positive affective response toward the drugs. Over time the knowledge fades and the attitudes weaken, but could be durably recorded by being translated into increased drug use intentions.

The distinction between correlation and experimentation in Study 1 is confounded with the passage of time. The experimental manipulation is by its nature the more recent. The effects of searching may have faded by the time they were assessed in the cross-sectional study. An experimental design that follows participants over time (and more directly measures affect) would help to clarify the relation of Internet use and drug-use intentions and behavior. This remedy was not pursued in the present studies and remains a topic for future research.

STUDY 2: STUDENTS AND MS/HIV

The second study examined more closely how Internet use affects knowledge. The knowledge and attitude findings in Study 1 suggest a modification to H1.

H1a: Internet searching will be most powerful in altering knowledge when the topic searched is little known to the searcher.

The revised hypothesis has implications for the design and results of Study 2. College students have received a great deal of education about HIV infection but commonly know little about multiple sclerosis (MS). It stands to reason that their HIV knowledge should be little affected by searching whereas their MS knowledge should show a large improvement.

Changing the search topic to HIV infection and MS offers several other benefits. The change links research with students to research with HIV and MS patients that I report later in this chapter as Studies 3 and 4. Furthermore, HIV infection and MS are the two most prevalent diseases affecting in people in their 20s to 40s. This same age cohort is also the group most likely to be using the Internet and thus most likely to be impacted by it.

Method

Study 2 used an experimental design very similar to that of the previous one. Students were randomly assigned to search the Internet for 40 minutes on HIV infection or on MS. Study participants were psychology undergraduates ($N = 92$) recruited in spring 2000. Details of the study (as well as Studies 3 and 4) are available in Brewer (under review).

Participants were asked to imagine that "a member of their family or a very close friend [has multiple sclerosis/is infected with HIV]." The instructions went on to say that the friend or relative had just been diagnosed with this disease and had asked the participant to search the Internet for information about it. Participants were supplied with the following suggested search terms: [multiple sclerosis/human immunodeficiency virus], [MS/HIV], and [MS disease/HIV disease].

After completing their search, participants answered a brief survey about their knowledge of HIV *and* MS (28 questions on each topic) as well as their confidence that their answers to the knowledge questions were correct (a single question on each topic). The knowledge questions were structured using the health cognitions portion of Leventhal's self-regulation model (Leventhal et al., 1984). Participants' responses were scored for accuracy using information from the National Institutes of Health Web sites and condensed into two knowledge accuracy scores, one each for HIV infection and MS.

The two search conditions served as controls for one another in statistical comparisons reported later. Effects on HIV knowledge and confidence reflect differences between the group that searched on HIV infection and the other that did not (i.e., the MS searchers). Similarly, effects on MS knowledge and confidence reflect differences between MS searchers and nonsearchers.

How Does Internet Searching Affect Knowledge and Confidence?

Internet searching again affected knowledge. When students searched on an unfamiliar topic, namely MS, they showed substantially higher knowledge ($r = .24$, $p < .05$). However, when students searched on a more familiar topic, namely HIV infection, they showed no differences in knowledge ($r = .10, n.s.$). This pattern of differences in knowledge mirrors the findings of Study 1, in which knowledge of an unfamiliar drug were substantially higher for all users whereas knowledge of a familiar drug was higher only for nondrug users.

Of even greater interest is that students believed that they had learned quite a bit more than they actually had. Although MS searchers showed higher MS knowledge, they showed even higher confidence ($r = .64$, $p < .001$). HIV searchers showed a similar pattern. Although they had the same level of HIV knowledge, they showed significantly higher confidence ($r = .44$, $p < .001$). In both cases, elevated knowledge was eclipsed by the perception (i.e., confidence) that they knew even more.

Knowledge and confidence about HIV were correlated ($r = .20$, $p < .05$) , while knowledge and confidence about MS were unrelated ($r = .04, n.s.$). The same pattern of differences in knowledge and confidence found in Study 1 was found in Study 2: Those lowest in knowledge gave ratings well above their actual knowledge (correlation of MS knowledge and MS calibration, $r = -.46$, $p < .001$; correlation of HIV knowledge and HIV calibration, $r = -.40$, $p < .001$). Those with lower knowledge were again largely unaware of this fact.

STUDIES 3 AND 4: MS AND HIV-POSITIVE PATIENTS

A natural question to ask is whether the changes in knowledge and confidence found among the student searchers would also be found among patients with the diseases. A related question is whether the patient searchers would show changes in health behavior that correlated with having searched on the Internet. Two additional studies addressed these questions among samples of patients with MS and HIV infection.

Method

Two cross-sectional survey studies examined Internet use among MS and HIV-positive patients. MS patients (N = 83) were recruited from physicians' offices, support groups, and MS Society events in the New Jersey area in fall 2000. At the same time, patients with HIV (N = 111) were recruited at the dining facility of the Gay Men's Health Crisis in New York City.

The MS participants' survey assessed MS knowledge using the same MS knowledge and confidence questions used in Study 2. Participants were also asked about their knowledge and confidence about a subset of the HIV infection items. A separate group of questions assessed how often they saw or called their primary care physician and their diseases specialist. The HIV participants' survey was identical except that it asked about the full complement of HIV questions and a smaller subset of the MS questions.

Participants also answered questions about involvement with their medical care and whether information gathering led to changes to their care. Involvement with care was assessed with a single item asking how involved in their medical care participants prefered to be. Participants responded using a 5-point scale labeled from "Keep decisions in my own hands" to "Leave decisions in my doctor's hands." Five questions assessed the extent to which research patients conducted research before visiting their physician causes them to inquire about changing their disease treatment. The five items were averaged to create a scale (Cronbach's $\alpha = .91$).

What Predicts Internet Use Among Patients?

The question of what predicts disease-specific Internet use can be examined here because, unlike the previous studies, patients assigned themselves to "search conditions." The data suggest two helpful distinctions among Internet search habits. The first distinction is whether patients have or have not searched the Internet for information on their disease. Those who have searched can be further categorized as light searchers (i.e., searched between one and five times) and heavy searchers (i.e., searched more than five times).

Among MS patients, 28% never used the Internet to search on their disease, 30% were light users, and 42% heavy users. Among Internet using MS patients, time since first Internet use (for any purpose) was a median of 3 years with a median weekly use of 1.5 hours per week. Among HIV patients, 56% never used the Internet to search on their disease, 36% were light users, 8% heavy users. For Internet using HIV patients, time since first Internet use (for any purpose) was a median of 2 years with a median weekly use of 3.5 hours per week.

Using pooled data from the two studies, greater Internet use was predicted in bivariate analyses by younger age, higher level of education, female gender, MS diagnosis (i.e., MS patients used the Internet more than HIV patients), and a lower research score. A multivariate logistic analysis showed that only younger age ($\beta = .31$, $p < .005$) and higher level of education ($\beta = .26$, $p < .01$) remained significant predictors. MS diagnosis was marginally related ($\beta = .38$, $p < .07$).

Internet use frequency (light versus heavy) was predicted in bivariate analyses by the same six variables. A multivariate logistic analysis showed that only MS diagnosis ($\beta = .82$, $p < .01$) remained a significant predictor. Disease severity was marginally related ($\beta = .26$, $p = .056$).

Do Experimental Findings Replicate With Patients?

As in the study of club drugs presented earlier in this chapter, there was a limited correspondence between what was found in correlational research and what was found in the lab. A comparison of the knowledge and confidence findings is shown in Table 21.1. The difference in confidence in Studies 3 and 4 was quite a bit smaller than what was seen in the experimental manipulations shown in Study 2.

Among MS patients, Internet use predicted MS knowledge ($r = .23$, $p < .05$) but not confidence. The MS patients showed no correlation between their MS knowledge and confidence ($r = .06$, $n.s.$). Among HIV patients, neither knowledge nor confidence was related to Internet searching, although HIV knowledge and confidence were modestly correlated with one another ($r = .18$, $p < .05$). Additional analyses with both populations again showed the interesting pattern that people with the lowest knowledge were least aware of this fact. Among MS patients, the MS knowledge and calibration were strongly negatively correlated ($r = -.50$, $p < .001$) and the same was true of HIV knowledge and calibration among HIV patients ($r = -.58$, $p < .001$).

There are several potential explanations for the difference between experimental and correlational findings. First, the experimental and correlational studies used slightly different operational definitions of Internet searching. In Studies 3 and 4, patients were asked how often they had searched the Internet for information on their illness. An indication of frequency does not reveal the "dose" of searching. A person who searched one time may have been at it for 10 hours while another who reported searching ten times may have only searched for 5 minutes at a go. In contrast, the students in Study 2 searched for exactly 40 minutes on one disease or another. The patients and students may have received different doses of searching.

Another explanation lies in the time elapsed between Internet use and survey completion. In Study 2, a trivial period of time elapsed between searching and reporting knowledge and confidence. In Studies 3 and 4, the length of time between searching and reporting of knowledge and confidence was not measured and could have been quite variable. The impact of Internet use may have waned as time passed, becoming heavily diluted by the time the patients completed the surveys.

A third explanation is that Internet searching in patients is strongly affected by unmeasured variables such as barriers or social support. Participants without a computer or access to one cannot use the Internet. Similarly, patients with an extensive support network of friends, fellow patients, and caregivers (including physicians) may have less need for Internet-based information on their illness.

A final explanation, the one I think is most interesting and likely to account for much of the observed difference, is that the reading grade level of Internet-based information is quite high. A study of 25 health Internet sites found that all sites required a high school or higher reading level (Berland et al., 2001). The experimental participants, being college students, clearly possessed the requisite reading skills. In the correlational studies, many of the patients had not been to college and even those who had been to college had probably done so many years before. Cognitive impairments associated with HIV infection and MS, a factor not assessed in Studies 3 and 4, may also play a role in limiting the information learned (and perceived as having been learned) on the sites.

Does Internet Use Predict Health Behaviors?

Internet users showed clear and consistent differences in physician utilization. There was a distinctive U-shaped distribution in the relation between Internet use and physician utilization as shown in Fig. 21.3. Although users and nonusers did not significantly differ, light and heavy users showed reliable differences. Both office visits and phone calls were higher among heavy than among light users ($rs = .17$, $ps < .02$). Calls to physicians were also predicted by greater involvement in own medical care ($r = .26$, $p < .001$) and a higher research score ($r = .17$, $p < .02$). Office visits were also predicted by greater involvement in own medical care ($r = .23$, $p < .001$).

The greater physician utilization among heavy searchers remains after covarying changes in knowledge, involvement with care, propensity to request changes in medical care as a result of personal research, and demographic characteristics. The differences in physician utilization between light and heavy searchers suggest that this is an important distinction to be made in future research.

The SR model strongly predicts changes in physician utilization should be mediated by knowledge, a condition that was not found in Studies 3 and 4. It remains a possibility that unmeasured affective variables would successfully mediate the relation.

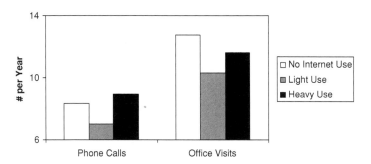

FIG. 21.3   Physician utilization among HIV and MS patients in Studies 3 and 4. DV = number of phone calls and office visits to the patients' specialist and primary care physician in the last year.

DISCUSSION

The four studies reviewed here show that Internet use is related to differences in health-related knowledge, confidence, intentions, and behavior. Internet searchers generally showed slightly greater knowledge but yet still greater perceived knowledge and often only among people new to the topic of search. Internet searchers also showed differences in health intentions and behaviors. Before discussing the findings, I first comment on several limitations of the present research.

Limitations

One goal of the present studies was to examine the effects of Internet searching on accuracy and confidence. It is not possible to examine the two unless questions relating to health cognitions have normatively accurate (and inaccurate) answers. The more common approach is to measure patients' qualitative beliefs about their own illness (e.g., the Illness Perception Questionnaire, Weinman, Petrier, Moss-Morris, & Horne, 1996) rather than factual questions about the disease. However, the "beliefs" approach all but eliminates the possibility of examining accuracy and confidence because many qualitative health beliefs may not be wrong in any normative sense. The operationalization of health cognitions as knowledge may limit the comparisons of the present findings to other studies that have used the SR model. It is also possible that Internet use has substantial and different effects on patients' illness cognitions when assessed using more traditional methods.

A second limitation is that the findings in the present studies may be limited in their generalizability to other populations, naturalistic conditions, and times. The samples used in the studies were all convenience samples. The HIV and MS patients may not be widely representative of other patients with the diseases. The relative artificiality of the lab experiments may also limit their applicability to more naturalistic situations where people may search for less time or, perhaps, more diligently. Finally, the Internet is a rapidly changing medium. These studies were all conducted in 2000. The content and nature of the sites searched may be quite different today than they were when the studies were first conducted.

Knowledge and Confidence

Internet use showed a small relation to higher knowledge and a moderate to large relation to higher confidence. The findings generally support the first three hypotheses about the effects of Internet use. Internet use was related to greater knowledge (H1) and changes in confidence (H2). Elevations in knowledge were outpaced by greater confidence in most of the studies (H3).

Even more interesting is that participants who had lower levels of knowledge appeared to have little insight into this fact. Correlations between knowledge and confidence were small to nil. However, a large and reliable finding was revealed once people with the lowest knowledge were looked at separately from those with higher knowledge. Those with low knowledge, whether patients or students, regularly showed the largest overestimation of their knowledge. Kruger and Dunning (1999) reported similar findings and suggested that those with minimal knowledge also lack the metacognitive capacity to realize how little they know. Studies 3 and 4 are an interesting replication of Kruger and Dunning's findings in two clinical populations.

The present study found no support for the concern that searching for health information on the Internet increases inaccurate beliefs. On the contrary, searching appears to increase accurate knowledge. One reason that we did not find greater inaccuracy may lie in what I call the "Anna Karenina" effect. The novel's famous first line states that all happy families are alike but that unhappy families are all unhappy in their own way. It may be that inaccuracies caused by Web searching are unique to each searcher, but that accurate information gleaned is largely the same. My standardized, closed-ended survey may have undercounted inaccuracies that are infrequent for any one searcher but are present in some form for all searchers.

Intention and Behavior

Intentions and behavior showed relations to Internet use when cross-sectionally assessed, findings that generally supported H4. First, intentions to use club drugs were higher among Internet users (those who searched prior to coming to the experiment). Second, physician utilization was higher among heavy Internet users than light users. Contrary to one of my predictions, patients did not appear to substitute Internet use for calling their physicians. The opposite pattern held such that Internet users both called and visited their physicians more often.

The SR model suggests that health behaviors are motivated by health cognitions and affect. In the present studies, health cognitions did not mediate the relation of Internet use to health behavior. It may be that an unmeasured variable such as affect could mediate the relations found. It is also possible that there is a direct relation between the two. Whatever the theoretical explanation, there remains the intriguing finding that Internet use is related to some health intentions and behavior.

Novice Users

There was a trend in the first two studies among people who were relatively inexperienced on the topic of search to be more affected by the search. Students who had never used drugs learned more about ecstasy and had stronger changes in attitudes than those who had previously used drugs. Similarly, students' knowledge and confidence about MS, a presumably unfamiliar disease, were more strongly affected than their knowledge and beliefs about HIV, a disease they have heard a great deal about. These results, if applied to patients, suggest that patients who are newly diagnosed are most susceptible to the effects of searching.

Comparing Experimental and Correlational Findings

The present studies suggest that cross-sectional and experimental studies of Internet use will yield different conclusions. The effects found in the experimental studies were relatively large but restricted to knowledge and attitudes. The cross-sectional findings were stronger than experimental findings with regards to behavioral variables such as drug-use intentions and physician utilization. These variables are the most interesting as they suggest that Internet searching on health-related topics may have an enduring impact on users. Future research is needed to better understand the apparent paradox in the cross-sectional and experimental findings. A prospective study of Internet use among patients (preferably an inception sample of those newly diagnosed with a disease) is a logical next step in this line of research.

This chapter opened with the comment that Internet use may represent a large-scale public health intervention. The four studies presented here suggest that Internet use affects some users and may contribute to various patient health behaviors. Although it is premature to claim that the Internet is a powerful force in changing the knowledge, attitudes, and behavior of health information consumers, ample evidence suggests that Internet use is an important factor in understanding these variables.

REFERENCES

Ajzen, I. (1991). The theory of planned behavior. *Organizational Behavior and Planned Decision Processes, 50,* 179–211.

Baron, R. M., & Kenny, D. A. (1986). The moderator-mediator variable distinction in social psychological research: Conceptual, strategic, and statistical considerations. *Journal of Personality and Social Psychology, 51,* 1173–1182.

Berland, G. K., Elliott, M. N., Morales, L. S., Algazy, J. I., Kravitz, R. L., Broder, M.S., Kanouse, D. E., Muñoz, J. A., Puyol, J.-A., Lara, M., Watkins, K. E., Yang, H. S., & McGlynn, I. (2001). Health information on the Internet: Accessibility, quality, and readability in English and Spanish. *Journal of the American Medical Association (JAMA)*, 285, 2612–2621.

Bower, G. H., Clark, M. C., Lesgold, A. M., & Winzenz, D. (1969). Hierarchical retrieval schemes in recall of categorized word lists. *Journal of Verbal Learning and Verbal Behavior, 8*, 323–343.

Brewer, N. T. (2003). The relation of Internet searching to club drug knowledge, and attitudes. *Psychology & Health*, 18, 387–401.

Brewer, N. T. (under review) Antecedents and implications of patients' confidence about illness.

Brewer, N. T., Chapman, G. B., Brownlee, S., & Leventhal, E. (2002). Cholesterol, adherence, and illness cognition. *British Journal of Health Psychology, 7*, 433–447.

Community Epidemiology Work Group (CEWG), NIH, NIDA. (2000). Epidemiologic trends in drug abuse: Advance report, June 2000. Retrieved September 18, 2002, from http://www.nida.nih.gov/CEWG/AdvancedRep/6_20ADV/0600adv.html.

Cook, T. D., & Campbell, D. T. (1979). *Quasi-experimentation: Design and analysis for field settings*. Boston: Houghton Mifflin.

Dawson, N. V. (2000). Physician judgments under uncertainty. In G. B. Chapman & F. A. Sonnenberg (Eds.), *Decision making in health care: Theory, psychology, and applications* (pp. 211–252). New York: Cambridge University Press.

Dawson, N. V., Connors, A. F., Speroff, T., Kemka, A., Shaw, P. S., & Arkes, H. R. (1993). Hemodynamic assessment in managing the critically Ill: Is physician confidence waranted? *Medical Decision Making, 13*, 258–266.

Davison, K. (1997). The quality of dietary information on the world wide web. *Clinical Performance and Quality Health Care, 5*, 64–66.

Diefenbach, M. A., & Leventhal, H. (1996). The common-sense model of illness representation: Theoretical and practical considerations. *Journal of Social Distress and the Homeless, 5*, 11–38.

Einhorn, H. J., & Hogarth, R. M. (1978). Confidence in judgment: Persistence of the illusion of validity. *Psychological Review, 85*, 395–416.

Federal Trade Commission (2001). Consumer alert: Virtual "treatments" can be real world deceptions. Retrieved October 26, 2004, from www.ftc.gov/bcp/conline/pubs/alerts/mrclalrt.pdf

Fishbein, M., & Ajzen, I. (1975). *Belief, attitude, intention, and behavior: An introduction to theory and research*. Reading, MA: Addison-Wesley.

Fox, S., Ranie, L., Horrigan, J., Lenhart, A., Spooner, T., Burke, M., Lewis, O., & Carter, C. (2000). The online health care revolution: How the web helps Americans take better care of themselves. Washington, DC: Pew Internet & American Life Project. Retrieved October 1, 2001, from http://www.pewinternet.org/reports/pdfs/PIP_Health_Report.pdf

Galimberti, A., & Jain, S. (2000). Gynaecology and the net: Evaluation of the information on hysterectomy contained in health-related web sites. *Journal of Obstetrics and Gynaecology, 20*, 297–299.

Gustafson, D. H., Hawkins, R., Boberg, E., Pingree, S., Serlin, R. E., Graziano, F., & Chan, C. L. (1999). Impact of a patient-centered, computer-based health information/support system. *American Journal of Preventive Medicine, 16*, 1–9.

Gustafson, D. H., Hawkins, R., Pingree, S., McTavish, F., Arora, N. K., Mendenhall, J., Cella, D. F., Serlin, R. C., Apantaku, F. M., Stewart, J., & Salner, A. (2000). Effect of computer support on younger women with breast cancer. *Journal of General Internal Medicine, 16*, 435–445.

Horne, R., & Weinman, J. (1998). Predicting treatment adherence: An overview of theoretical models. In L. B. Meyers & K. Midence (Eds.), *Adherence to treatment in medical conditions*. Amsterdam: Harwood Academic Publishers. p. 285–310

Impicciatore, P., Pandolfini, C., Casella, N., & Bonati, M. (1997). Reliability of health information for the public on the world wide web: Systematic survey of advice on managing fever in children at home. *British Medical Journal (BMJ), 314*, 1875–1879.

Kalichman, S. C., Bentotsch, E. G., Weinhardt, L. S., Austin, J., & Luke, W. (2002). Internet use among people living with HIV/AIDS: Association of health information, health behaviors, and health status. *AIDS Education and Prevention, 14,* 51–61.

Kruger, J., & Dunning, D. (1999). Unskilled and unaware of it: How difficulties in recognizing one's own incompetence lead to inflated self-assessments. *Journal of Personality and Social Psychology, 77,* 1121–1134.

Latthe, P. M., Latthe, M., & Khan, S. (2000). Quality of medical information about menorrhagia on the worldwide web. *British Journal of Obstetrics and Gynaecology, 107,* 39–43.

Leventhal, H., Meyer, D., & Nerenz, D. (1980). The common sense representation of illness danger. In S. Rachman (Ed.), *Medical psychology* (Vol. 2, pp. 7–30). New York: Pergamon.

Leventhal, H., Nerenz, D., & Steele, D. (1984). Illness representations and coping with health threats. In A. Baum & J. Singer (Eds.), *A handbook of psychology and health* (Vol. 4, pp. 219–252). Hillsdale, NJ: Lawrence Erlbuam Associates.

Leventhal, H., Watts, J. C., & Pagano, F. (1967). Effects of fear and instructions on how to cope with danger. *Journal of Personality and Social Psychology, 6,* 313–321.

Liska, A. E. (1984). A critical examination of the causal structure of the Fishbein/Ajzen attitude-behavior model. *Social Psychology Quarterly, 47,* 61–74.

Meyer, D., Leventhal, H., & Gutmann, M. (1985). Common-sense models of illness: The example of hypertension. *Health Psychology, 4,* 115–135.

National Institute on Drug Abuse (NIDA). (1999, December). *Community drug alert bulletin*, Washington, DC: National Institute on Drug Abuse.

Oskamp, S. (1962). The relationship of clinical experience and training methods to several criteria of clinical prediction. *Psychological Monographs: General and Applied, 76,* 1–27.

Pandolfini, C., Impicciatore, P., & Bonati, M. (2000). Parents on the web: Risks for quality management of cough in children. *Pediatrics, 105,* e1.

Petrie, K. J., Weinman, J., Sharpe, N., & Buckley, J. (1996). Predicting return to work and functioning following myocardial infarction: The role of patient's view of their illness. *British Medical Journal, 312,* 1191–1194.

Ropero-Miller, J. D., & Goldberger, B. A. (1998). Recreational drugs: Current trends in the '90's. *Clinics of Laboratory Medicine, 18,* 727–746.

Rosenstock, I. (1974). The health belief model and preventive behavior. *Health Education Monographs, 2,* 354–386.

Sandvik, H. (1999). Health information and interaction on the Internet: A survey of female urinary incontinence. *BMJ, 319,* 29–32.

Silberg, W. M , Lundberg, D. G., & Musacchio, R. A. (1997). Assessing, controlling, and assuring the quality of medical information on the Internet: Caveat lector et viewor-let the readers and viewer beware. *Journal of the American Medical Association (JAMA), 277,* 1244–1245.

Stein, B. S., & Bransford, J. D. (1979). Constraints on effective elaboration: Effects of precision and subject generation. *Journal of Verbal Learning and Verbal Behavior, 18,* 769–777.

Weinman, J., Petrie, K. J., Moss-Morris, R., & Horne, R. (1996). The illness perception questionnaire: A new method for assessing the cognitive representation of illness. *Psychology and Health, 11,* 431–445.

Weinstein, N. D. (1988). The precaution adoption process. *Health Psychology, 7,* 355–386.

Zimmerman, R. S., Safer, M. A., Leventhal, H., & Baumann, L. J. (1986). The effects of health information in a worksite hypertension screening program. *Health Education Quarterly, 13,* 261–280.

VI. RESEARCH TOOLS AND APPROACHES

Experiential Ecommerce: A Summary of Research Investigating the Impact of Virtual Experience on Consumer Learning

Terry Daugherty
University of Texas at Austin

Hairong Li
Michigan State University

Frank Biocca
Michigan State University

Consumers learn about products from the experience of interacting with people, objects, and the environment. However, an experience is more than simply the passive reception of external sensations or subjective mental interpretations of a situation. Rather, an experience is the result of an ongoing transaction that gains in quality, intensity, meaning, and value, integrating both psychological and emotional conditions (Mathur, 1971). These conditions are ultimately accomplished via the generation of thoughts and/or sensations brought together creating the experience (Hirschman, 1984). A product purchase is in many ways not the purchase of a physical good itself but of an experience that the product affords (Pine II & Gilmore, 1998). Thus, the role of consumer learning about a product prior to the purchase is mainly to assess what *consumption experience* the product can offer and how well it can meet the expectations of the anticipated experience (Hoch & Deighton, 1989).

Research has documented that consumers learn about products through indirect experience, such as advertising, and via direct experience, such as product trial (Deighton, 1984; Hoch & Ha, 1986; Hoch & Deighton, 1989; Kempf & Smith, 1998; Smith & Swinyard, 1982, 1983). However, it has been speculated that certain media may limit the effect of advertising (Chaudhuri & Buck, 1995) and a more powerful medium for communicating the details and experiences of a product, such as the Internet, could have a stronger impact on consumer learning (Li, Daugherty & Biocca, 2003). Three-dimensional (3-D), multiuser online environments constitute a new revolution of interactivity by creating compelling virtual experiences (Li, Daugherty & Biocca, 2001). McLuhan and McLuhan (1988) suggested that within any medium there is a connection between the human mind, the technology, and the environment that serves to immerse users. It is the interactive nature of the Internet that immerses consumers and offers the greatest potential to marketers because of the ability to offer user-controlled product interactive experiences (Schlosser & Kanfer, 2001). Because most products are 3-D objects that are experienced with the senses, the use of dynamic 3-D visualization in ecommerce is increasing as companies seek to give users a virtual experience with products. The implications are that a 3-D virtual product experience is a simulation of a real or physical product experience and can be construed to be located between direct experience and indirect experience within the spectrum of consumer learning (Daugherty, 2001; Li et al., 2001).

To fully understand the impact of a virtual experience and the use of 3-D product visualization in consumer learning, the unique and distinctive characteristics that distinguish a virtual experience from indirect and direct experience must be empirically explored. The implications of such findings could potentially provide marketers with a better understanding of consumer psychological processes and behavior online as well as improve the effectiveness of ecommerce sites. Therefore, in the proceeding sections we summarize existing literature, present key findings of several studies designed to characterize a virtual experience, and conclude with implications involving this emerging area of research.

DEFINING VIRTUAL EXPERIENCE

The Internet has the ability to serve as a more powerful medium than traditional media in the sense that consumers are able to interact with products in 3-D multimedia environments, thus simulating a new form of experience—*virtual experience* (Li et al., 2001, 2003). The conceptualization of a virtual experience has emerged because technological developments indicate a movement toward more multisensory interactions incorporating high quality visuals, stereo sound, and imagery (Soukup, 2000). Information and graphics can now be presented in a mediated 3-D environment in which consumers can interact with images, animation, video, and audio messages. Klein (1998) suggested the greatest value of a virtual experience is that it allows consumers to assess product performance prior to purchase, essentially turning experience goods into search goods. The consumer value of interactive media is that information is now more accessible, less costly, and more customizable. By transforming experience attributes into search attributes, a virtual experience could be perceived as being equivalent to a direct experience and thus reduce perceived risk prior to purchase (Klein, 1998). The premise is that experience goods have traditionally been suited for product trial and search goods for advertising with the best medium remaining the one that communicates the type of product information that is the most congruent (Wright & Lynch, 1995).

Product affordances refer to the ability of a product to provide visual clues that indicate the function of an object. For instance, consumers learn about the shapes, texture, and perceived functions of a product by moving their bodies or the product to visually inspect it from different angles. There are various affordances common to product inspection in conventional stores that come from the ability of the senses and motor systems to interact with products. This type of information and interaction can be simulated vividly within a 3-D environment, where consumers can freely examine, zoom-in or zoom-out, and rotate a product based on *virtual product affordances* (Li, Daugherty & Biocca, 2002).

The examination of how consumers interact with products in 3-D visualization also suggests several basic *interface features*. These properties are what help generate the necessary affordances to establish a virtual experience with a product in an online environment. In essence, virtual experiences utilizing 3-D product visualization incorporate interfaces based on visual, tactile, and behavioral simulations. Furthermore, each of these interfaces encompass different types of properties with visual translation, rotation, contextualization, and stereopsis in visual simulation; touch and manipulation in tactile simulation; and animation, customization, spatial navigation, and social simulation in behavior simulation (see Table 22.1). Common in human-computer interaction literature, the success in designing effective interfaces stems from creating appropriate affordances a user expects in new multisensory computer-mediated environments (Karat, Karat, & Ukelson, 2000). Previous communication research has addressed the role of certain interfaces in the cognitive process. For instance, Reeves and Nass (1996) noted that larger images likely are more arousing, better remembered, and better liked than small images. This finding implies the potential impact of zooming-in for inspection of 3-D visual products. Hoffman and Novak's (1996) elaboration of the flow theory indicated that the cognitive impact of seamless sequence of responses, facilitated by interactivity with the computer and self-reinforcement, lends support for the effect of the navigating interfaces. These studies and others (Biocca, 1997, Lombard & Dittion, 1997; Steuer, 1992) have justified the potential impact of interfaces in 3-D visualization in ecommerce.

What is the purpose of adding affordances to interfaces and simulations of product interaction? Presence is the experience established in a represented environment by means of a communication medium (Steuer, 1992). All media and telecommunication systems generate a sense of being in another place by bringing the experience and objects closer to us, allowing us to indirectly meet and experience other objects, other people, and the experiences of others. A medium functions the best when it delivers not only information but also a mediated experience. Thus, it is reasonable to expect that visual, tactile, and behavioral simulations in 3-D visualizations are likely to create a sense of presence, which in turn, can enhance richer consumption experiences online.

TABLE 22.1
Interface Features in 3-D Product Simulations

Domain/Interface	Description
Visual Simulation	
Visual Translation	Motor immersion and control via the mouse allows the product to be moved in 3-D. This changes the sensory properties of the product, most typically to increase or decrease the size of a product. For instance, a wristwatch can be zoomed in to appear larger than its actual size for visual inspection of its details.
Rotation	Unlike 2-D representation, motor control via the mouse allows the user to rotate the product or environment to view from any angle. For instance, a laptop computer can be viewed from the front, back, side, and with the screen open or the docking adapter attached.
Contextualization	The placement of a product in the context to simulate how the product can be consumed. For instance, a set of furniture is in an elegant room or trucks are on a rugged mountain road. It is much easier to contextualize a product in 3-D environments than in physical environments. Contextualization is related to customization (see later).
Stereopsis	The addition of stereopsis via 3-D glasses (i.e., a different viewpoint is presented to each eye) provides increased sensory information and fidelity, making information about the depth and shape of products and their settings more vivid and realistic.
Tactile Simulation	
Touch and Manipulation	Motor control and force feedback allows the consumer to feel haptic forces (i.e., weight, inertia, resistance) when manipulating a product to feel product properties such as the texture of a product, the smoothness, edges or softness of a product with the mouse or other devices.
Behavioral Simulation	
Animation	Products sensory features are tied to their behaviors: They move in certain predicable ways. For instance, car doors open on hinges when pulled. In virtual environments behaviors can simulate direct experience or be enhanced or fantastic. In addition, animations trigger prescribed feature descriptions or product behaviors (i.e., demonstration) on some user action such as approaching the object in a 3-D space or moving a mouse cursor over it.
Customization	The ability to allow the shopper to modify the form or content of a product. For instance, using a computer mouse, a consumer may change the colors of a bed sheet and comforter to see how well both match.
Spatial Navigation	People movethrough environments. Products are demonstrated in a commercial "space" such as a virtual mall to allow users to "window shop" by strolling through a 3-D or other simulation of physical shopping behavior.
Social Simulation	People interact with products with other people. Using either agents or avatars for a shopper to interact with salespeople in virtual environments.

STUDY I

Because the literature suggests that several characteristics of a virtual experience in computer-mediated environments exist, the purpose of the first study was to explore what constitutes a virtual experience. Specifically, we sought to discover how consumers form product knowledge, if consumers perceive a sense of presence, and how consumers treat product affordances in a virtual experience.

Research Design

The research was conducted in a laboratory setting with 30 undergraduate students at a major Midwestern university examining four 3-D products (bedding material, laptop computer, ring, and watch) from the Metastream Web site (see Fig. 22.1). The products constituted a "theoretical" sample selected on the basis of their

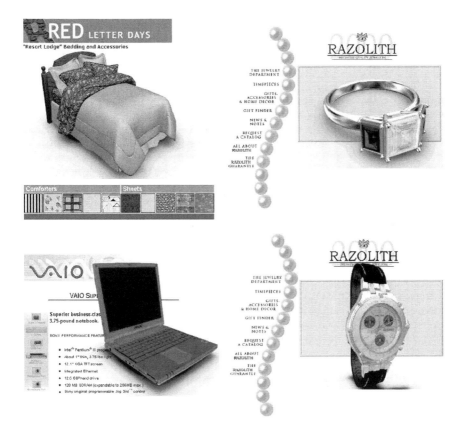

FIG. 22.1   Interactive 3-D test products. *Note:* Courtesy of Metastream, which has since been acquired by Viewpoint Corporation.

apparent design interfaces applicable to create a virtual experience (moveable, rotate, zoom, animation or customization). Furthermore, because the purpose of the study was to explore consumer experiences, the qualitative technique referred to as protocol analysis (Gould, 1999) was used for the message-evoking thoughts it inspires in consumers (Wright, 1980).

Participants were instructed to examine the products individually, taking as much time as needed to verbalize what they "think and/or feel." In addition, each participant was informed to continuously verbalize his or her thoughts and feelings as he or she examined each product. Concurrent verbalization was utilized in order to minimize memory loss because four separate products were evaluated and the entire session could last as long as 30 minutes (Wright, 1980). If participants were silent for more than 10 seconds, they were prompted: "Please tell me what you are thinking or feeling." The verbal reports for each product averaged 5 minutes and were ended by the researcher if the session extended beyond 8 minutes per product. Each session was videotaped for analysis and on completion participants were given a questionnaire to record their evaluation (the visual and survey data were not analyzed for this study).

Data Analysis

The verbal protocol tapes were transcribed and analyzed using a qualitative data analysis software program (N5 2000) in accordance with established content analytic procedures (Riffe, Lacy, & Fico, 1998). First, the content of each subject's verbal report was divided into "units of thought" (Gardial et al., 1994; Rook, 1987). A unit of thought is defined in this study as a smallest set of words that are meaningful out of its context. Hence, a coder is able to interpret the meaning of the statement, without reading the text before and after the statement. If it were further divided, a unit of thought would become meaningless. As a result, a total of 993 units of thought were identified from the transcribed data.

The second step involved coding each unit of thought into one or more of 13 categories. Coding categories were derived a priori as well as from emergent themes interpreted inductively, with the intent to characterize a virtual experience (see Table 22.2). Two coders independently analyzed 14% (142 out of 993) of the units of thought, which resulted in only 12 intercoder disagreements. Thus, an acceptable overall reliability of 92% was achieved, with a Scott's Pi accounting for chance agreement of .90 (Riffe et al., 1998). In addition, individual category reliabilities ranged between 80 to 100%.

Results

The results provide distinctly identifiable responses common to direct and indirect product experience as well as uniquely specific virtual experience characteristics. Exerts from the verbalizations are presented verbatim in this section, with gender and product references in parentheses. The percentage of participants who

TABLE 22.2

Categories. Definitions and Intercoder Reliability

Category	Definition	Agreement
1. Involvement—self	Perceived relevance of the product or product attributes to oneself.	95%
2. Involvement—third person	Perceived relevance of the product or product attributes to others.	100%
3. Product attribute attention	Attention to specific product attributes such as brand name, color, size, etc.	88%
4. Product attribute evaluation	Comment, either positive or negative, on the product or product attributes.	94%
5. Product attribute association	Connecting a product or product attributes to other objects to make sense of it.	100%
6. Questioning about product attributes	Uncertainty about a produce attribute (but no desire or intent to figure it out).	87%
7. Information seeking	Desire or intent to seek more information about product attributes.	100%
8. Purchase intention	Expressed intent to either purchase or not purchase a product.	100%
9. Presence—physical	Feeling as if he or she's with a physical product or perception of no difference between a physical and a virtual product.	100%
10. Presence—natural	Describing the virtual representation of a product as natural, real, or believable.	100%
11. Enjoyment with virtual product inspection	Feeling of pleasure or enjoyment of interacting with a virtual product.	80%
12. Expectation of richer virtual experience	Desire for more design features such as more customizable items, more brands, or colors to choose from.	100%
13. Affordances	Recognizing the lacking of tactile affordances.	100%

indicated a given category of psychological activity is reported as descriptive information. Because a small nonprobability sample was employed, the findings of this study are not intended to generalize to a larger population but to discover and theorize aspects of a virtual experience.

Involvement—Self

In order for any consumer to perceive and evaluate a product actively, it must hold some form of personal relevance. Krugman (1965) referred to this as a type of involvement. With 93% of the participants indicating personal engagement, examining a product within a virtual experience actually initiates this involvement:

> I'm not a big fan of watches with a leather band just because my experience with them is that they usually always deteriorate like after a year so. Then you have always got to replace it. (male, watch)

> I like blue so these look fine with me, but I think there are too many squares. I don't
> like that. For me, a ring should be more like a circle so I don't like that really much.
> (female, ring)

The ability to personally relate to a virtual product suggests that a certain level of
cognitive processing is involved during a virtual experience, which is more than
simply interest or curiosity.

Involvement—Third Person

In addition, 60% of the participants referenced the potential importance of the
product to someone else:

> It seems like something that people would want to buy, I guess just by the colors and
> the way the sheets go with the comforter. (female, bedding)
> It's like it might be for someone who is really into sports or something because it has
> a lot of different measurements on here. (male, watch)

Similarly, participants seemed to perceive the product realistically enough in a
virtual experience to evaluate the potential benefit for another individual.

Product Attribute Attention

During the evaluation, participants were consistently paying close attention to the
virtual product, with 100% making at least one reference to a specific attribute:

> Looks like probably a leather band, which is a little more comfortable than a metal
> band. (male, watch)
> I don't like the quilt, yuck, it looks like it's a nice quilt and everything but these
> colors they offer here are pretty horrible. (female, bedding)

Although each participant was instructed to express his or her thoughts about the
product, at no time were the participants instructed how or what to evaluate. The
close attention to detail and specifics is likely to be a result of examining a 3-D
product, suggesting that the virtual experience can generate active thoughts about
product attributes.

Product Attribute Evaluation

Evaluations are common measures to articulate attitudes, opinions, and feelings
about an object. When consumers find a product more pleasing, the potential is
greater for a positive transfer effect resulting in a behavioral response (Batra & Ray,
1985; Fazio, Powell, & Williams, 1989; Mackenzie & Lutz, 1989). While examining the four products, all 30 subjects made some type of spontaneous evaluation
reference, either positive or negative, regarding a specific product attribute:

> I like laptops and I'd like to have one so I always check the features out. I like the screen it looks big and there isn't much border around it, which is nice. (male, laptop)
>
> That looks like it is a nice leather band. Looks like it would probably be durable. Overall, I like the design of the watch. (female, watch)

The importance is not whether the participants made a positive or negative comment about a product but the fact that they were actively engaged in evaluating specific product attributes much the same way they would if asked to evaluate actual products.

Product Attribute Association

The act of associating products or specific attributes with other items signifies a mental connection between one's thoughts and previous experiences. Forty percent of the participants related the virtual products they examined to other objects:

> It's pretty thick; it looks like the thickness of a couple of notebooks put together which is nice. (female, laptop)

In many instances, mental imagery was used to associate the product or attribute to a remembered sensation or concrete object:

> That right there would match up to something you would throw on in the fall because it looks like the leaves on the comforter and the bed skirt. (male, bedding)

Questioning About Product Attributes

A common element within any type of active processing during product evaluation is the discovery of questions or missing information. Likewise, 80% of the participants indicated some form of uncertainty about a product attribute:

> I don't know what kind of a cut that is but it kind of stands out at you. (male, ring)
>
> I can't tell if this is like a full size bed or a twin bed. I'm not sure if that is oak or what but I like the color of it. (female, bedding)

The significance of these comments resides in the similarities between examining a virtual product and inspecting a physical product.

Information Seeking

A logical extension of raising questions about a product when actively processing information is indicating the desire to seek out answers. Indeed, 43% of the participants demonstrated this desire:

> I'm not sure if this is stainless steel or what. I'd like to know more about the materials that it's made of. (female, watch)
>
> It looks pretty nice but I'm not really sure what kind of stones these are. I'd probably want more information about that. I think that might prompt me to go to the store. (male, ring)

Although information seeking is also common when examining physical products, perhaps this area is where a virtual experience represents a relative advantage over direct experience. For instance, a virtual experience is able to easily call attention to certain product features, frame messages effectively, and offer a wide breadth of information not easily available by direct experience.

Purchase Intention

Purchase intention is one of the most common characteristics measured in advertising and marketing effectiveness research and is used to anticipate a behavioral response (Beerli & Santana, 1999). Here is how some participants indicated their intention to either buy or not to buy something:

> I think it gives you time in other countries possibly. I would buy it. I feel good about it so I would think about buying it. It depends on how much it costs. I would buy it. (male, watch)
>
> I don't know if it's anything I would buy but it kind of looks like a women's ring. Just for the simple fact it's kind of small and the band is kind of narrow. (male, ring)

Over half (57%) of the participants reported some type of purchase intention—either to buy or not to buy—when examining the products even though they were never questioned about purchasing. This implies the participants were engaged in active processing and evaluating the product within the virtual experience.

Presence—Physical

The sensation of physical presence is perhaps one of the most difficult characteristics of virtual experience to establish. It is because the feeling of "being there" with a product indicates a state of consciousness that the consumer normally perceives in the physical environment (Kim & Biocca, 1997). In this study, only 23% of the participants indicated this type of sensation and they did so exclusively when examining the laptop computer. In fact, a feeling of physical presence with the product seemed to be tied to the specific action of pressing the power button:

> I like that it just comes straight on like that, you don't have to go through the whole process of it warming itself up when you turn the computer on. (male, laptop)
>
> You can do that? Oh wow, actual resolution. (female, laptop)

It seems that participants ignored the difference in screen resolution between an actual and a virtual laptop. The perception of screen resolution suggests that physical presence is able to offer a unique virtual experience. Perhaps the perception of exerting control over a product combined with animation simulating a consequence, such as the computer powering on, certainly increases physical presence.

Presence—Natural

The feeling that a mediated environment, or in this instance a product presented in a mediated environment, looks more real has also been identified as a component of presence (Lessiter, Freeman, Keogh, & Davidoff, 2000). Thirty seven percent of the participants indicated this type of experience:

> Just because you get a sense of it, I mean you really get the look or feel of something before you actually buy it. (male, watch)

An increased perception of reality or naturalness, induced by a virtual experience, places the consumer at the store or with a product, potentially impacting evaluation:

> I think it makes it more real. When you go in a store and look at a watch or something you're going to do the same thing. I just think making it interactive just makes it more real like your actually at the store. (male, 3-D products)

Enjoyment With Virtual Product Inspection

Holbrook and Hirschman (1982) contended that products should incorporate enjoyment and fun into what they call an "experiential view" of consumption. This view supports a multisensory psychophysical perspective and could be represented within a virtual experience:

> It's definitely very interesting. I've personally never seen anything like this, you can actually rotate the product around and the coloring especially you can change stuff. I'd definitely like to see more stuff like that on the Internet instead of just seeing a flat 2-D object. (male, 3-D products)

With all participants indicating some type of enjoyment when interacting with the products, a virtual experience could potentially impact attitude and behavior:

> That's pretty neat because it gives you the impression that it can be yours and it puts more personality into the ring. They can actually do that to a ring if they buy it here and interact with it more. That's definitely a nice thing to have the interaction. (male, ring)

Expectation of Richer Virtual Experience

Research has indicated that a negative shopping experience occurs when expectations are not achieved (Machleit & Eroglu, 2000). Considering 37% of the participants reported a desire for additional interactive features, a negative virtual shopping experience could reflect the same results:

> I like the way it's pretty realistic. I think it would be a little more fun if you could do some other things once it was on. (female, laptop)
>
> It would be nicer if it had all the things that were on the laptop, you know the things that popped up as you went through the product. If I could somehow undo the watch so you could see it and lay it out and everything. (female, watch)

By incorporating all relevant interactive features for a specific type of product, advertisers and marketers may be able to minimize any negative feelings resulting from unmet expectations in virtual environments.

Affordances

A difference between virtual affordances and physical affordances is the tactile simulation. Although a 3-D product is able to simulate many aspects of a physical product, consumers who prefer the tactile affordances of a product may perceive a hindrance within a virtual experience. In fact, 63% of the participants explicitly referred to this limitation:

> In this kind of product the important thing is the softness of the bed so I want to feel texture. I want to go to the store so I can touch the bed so I can get the feeling and after that I will maybe decide to buy. (male, bedding)

The perception created by a virtual experience exceeds indirect product experience by providing virtual affordances that tend to promote consumer learning. Although additional affordances are sought, a virtual experience can still reinforce a response:

> I think the thing with rings is you have to see them on your finger to get a good idea. I think this is a good head start because you at least turn it around and see it from different angles. (female, ring)

Discussion

This protocol analysis generated vivid evidence on what consumers think and feel when they "virtually" experience products. We see from the evidence a number of characteristics of a virtual experience in ecommerce. One characteristic is what we call *active process*ing, which includes: product attribute attention, attribute evaluation, attribute association, attribute questioning, and information seeking.

These activities demonstrate that consumers are active learners when examining virtual products.

The active process of virtual experience is often accompanied and heightened by three other characteristics: presence, involvement, and enjoyment. We see *presence* as the perceptual base of a virtual experience because 3-D simulations of products and shopping environments render mental images that are traditionally created by consumers in conventional stores. As observed in this study, at a low level of presence, the participants feel that simulations appear "real" or "realistic," signifying a conceptual awareness of the simulation. At a high level of presence, virtual product attributes and physical product attributes are perceived equally and participants treat the virtual product just as they would a physical product.

Another characteristic of a virtual experience is *involvement*. We observed spontaneous comments indicating a participant's perception of the relevance of a product or product attribute to themselves or other individuals when examining the 3-D products. *Enjoyment* of a virtual experience per se represents a characteristic of this new kind of consumer experience, which may stem from the newness of this type of interaction and when virtual affordances exceed physical affordance. When consumers shop for a wedding ring in the store, they do not expect to see what the engraving will look like on the inner side of a ring. However, when some participants experienced the customization ability and interface in this study, they were pleasantly surprised. The findings of the study also indicate that participants have different physical affordances for different products.

These identified characteristics of a virtual experience help us define it and anchor its position on the spectrum of consumer experience. We come to conclude that virtual experience consists of vivid, involving, active, and affective psychological states occurring in an individual interacting with 3-D computer simulations (Li et al., 2001).

COMPARING INDIRECT, VIRTUAL, AND DIRECT EXPERIENCE IN CONSUMER LEARNING

Researchers have delineated two main types of experience associated with consumer learning of products or services: indirect experience and direct experience (Deighton, 1984; Hoch & Deighton, 1989; Hoch & Ha, 1986; Kempf & Smith, 1998; Smith & Swinyard, 1982, 1983, 1988; Wright & Lynch, 1995). Although indirect experience can occur from various sources (i.e., word of mouth, *Consumer Reports*, etc.), the most prevalent form explored in consumer learning is advertising. This form of experience can lend several advantages for both consumers and advertisers. First, advertising is a mediated experience where messages are framed to emphasize the most important product information. Second, advertising exposure can stimulate consumer awareness for unknown products. Third, exposure enables consumers to evaluate important information across multiple brands in a short amount of time. Of course, advertising is a biased form of communication that is often perceived as less credible than direct experience (Hoch & Ha, 1989). Direct experience is an unmediated interaction between a consumer and a brand in full sensory capacity and occurs from product sampling, trial, or purchase (Gibson, 1966). This multisensory interaction also leads to several consumer and advertiser advantages associated with direct experience. First, evidence in direct experience is self-generated and the most trustworthy for a consumer. Second, a consumer may manage the way a product is experienced by controlling the focus and pace of an inspection to maximize informational input. Third, direct experience promotes better memory because information is more vivid and concrete (Hoch & Ha, 1989). Fourth, this form of learning is more likely to influence behavior because of internal attributions and motivation (Smith & Swinyard, 1982). However, strong implications for both indirect and direct forms of experiences have been reported under certain circumstances.

As the notion of virtual experience evolves, vivid and imagery-based associations are more likely to generate richer experiences and enjoy advantages of both direct and indirect experience. Like traditional advertising, 3-D product visualization enables consumers to form prior hypotheses by framing information presented. However, different from traditional forms of advertising, dynamic 3-D visualization of products is able to offer user control over the inspection of a product, even from inside-out for certain types of products. This is an important advantage because high information control in ecommerce environments has been found to improve consumer decision quality and knowledge (Ariely, 2000). In fact, this type of control positions a virtual experience similarly to direct experience because consumers are able to inspect 3-D products from different perspectives at their own pace. This level of control is not simply a representation of an actual product but rather a simulation of the consumption experience. The result is a stronger impact for experience attributes compared to advertising and greater impact for search attributes relative to product trial. Nevertheless, a major disadvantage associated with virtual experience is the limited sensory input compared to direct experience. At present, consumers are not able to touch, smell, or taste a product on the computer even though these actions will soon be likely with the invention of the "force-feedback" technology (Grossman, 2000).

STUDY 2

Although we speculate that a virtual experience is perceived as richer than indirect experience and closer to direct experience because of interactivity, vividness, personal relevance, enjoyment, and a sense of presence stimulated when examining 3-D interactive products, there is no empirical research that supports or refutes this proposition. Therefore, the purpose of the second study is to compare the similarities and differences between direct, indirect, and virtual experience as derived from product trial, traditional advertising, and 3-D product visualization.

Research Design

A total of 90 undergraduate students enrolled at a major Midwestern university participated in a laboratory experiment with product knowledge, brand attitude, and purchase intention serving as the criteria for measuring the impact of indirect, virtual, and direct experience on consumer learning. A digital video camcorder (Panasonic) was selected from a pretest ($n = 76$) as the test product and measured for preference against four additional leading manufacturers (Sony, JVC, Canon, and Sharp). It was important for the presentation of the product to be as identical as possible throughout all of the stimulus materials, with the only differences stemming from the inherent features of each experience.

The 3-D product Web site, representing the virtual experience, provided the ability to rotate and control product movement from all angles, allowed users to zoom-in and out for detailed inspection, used animation to simulate movement of the LCD display, and identified each component as the mouse moved over the product (see Fig. 22.2). For the indirect experience, a professionally produced two-page full spread four-color print advertisement identical in layout and content as the Web site was constructed. Finally, the direct experience allowed the full sensory inspection of the digital video camcorder. However, in order to remain consistent across stimuli, the physical product was presented along with the exact information as each of the previous experiences using the magazine ad (minus the product image) as a point-of-purchase display. Because the purpose of the study was to isolate

FIG. 22.2   3-D product Web site representing the virtual experience stimulus.

each experience, the message content served as a control with the information held constant across each experience. The Panasonic logo, slogan, and graphic image of the product were placed in identical locations throughout the stimuli.

Participants were instructed that the purpose of the study was to record their evaluation of the product and to thoroughly examine the materials in order to determine how they think and feel about the product. Furthermore, in order to minimize overexposure of one type of experience yet provide enough duration not to hinder the inherent advantages associated with direct and virtual experiences, examination times were restricted to 5 minutes. Finally, participants were told that on completion of their examination they would be asked to complete a survey to record their evaluation.

Results

The results show significant main effects for product knowledge, $F(2,89) = 17.09$, $p < .01$, $\eta^2 = .28$, brand attitude, $F(2,89) = 3.90$, $p < .05$, $\eta^2 = .08$, and purchase intention, $F(2,89) = 8.69$, $p < .01$, $\eta^2 = .17$, suggesting the dependent measures were affected differently across the treatment conditions (see Fig. 22.3).

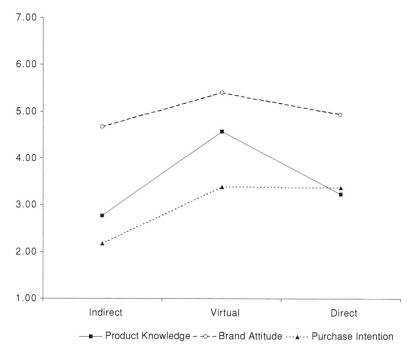

FIG. 22.3   Product knowledge, brand attitude, and purchase intention across experiences.

TABLE 22.3
Comparisons Between Experiences

	Indirect	Virtual	Direct	F	p <
Product Knowledge					
	2.78	–	3.23	2.01	.16
	–	4.57	3.23	21.0	.00
	2.78	4.57	–	27.63	.00
Brand Attitude					
	4.68	–	4.94	.94	.37
	–	5.40	4.94	3.75	.06
	4.68	5.40	–	6.79	.01
Purchase Intention					
	2.18	–	3.38	13.15	.01
	–	3.39	3.38	.003	.96
	2.18	3.39	–	12.21	.00

Surprisingly, participants indicated the highest level for product knowledge ($M = 4.57$, $SD = 1.21$), brand attitude ($M = 5.40$, $SD = .96$), and purchase intention ($M = 3.39$, $SD = 1.31$) when evaluating the product through a virtual experience.

The findings presented in Table 22.3 show that participants indeed reported greater product knowledge and more favorable brand attitudes after evaluating the test product from a direct experience than an indirect experience. Furthermore, a significant difference was detected for purchase intention with participants indicating they were more likely to purchase the test product following a direct experience rather than an indirect experience.

Based on the proposition that a virtual experience will function more closely as a direct experience, there should be no reported differences for product knowledge, brand attitude, or purchase intention between a virtual and direct consumer evaluation experience. In contrast, a significant difference was detected for product knowledge with participants indicating they felt more knowledgeable from the virtual experience than the direct experience. Although there were no significant differences detected between brand attitude and purchase intention for a virtual and direct experience, the reported evaluation scores were higher for a virtual experience than a direct experience. Finally, the findings verify that product knowledge, brand attitude, and purchase intention were indeed significantly higher following a virtual experience product evaluation versus the indirect experience.

Discussion

Internet advertising in the form of 3-D product visualization has the ability to moderate the advantages of indirect and direct experience by producing virtual product experiences that simulate product trial while maintaining the marketer control of a mediated environment. The result is that consumers are more likely to perceive the examination of products in a virtual experience as being richer than indirect experience and closer to direct experience because message framing is combined with interactivity and the visual simulation of user control. The findings of this study largely support this proposition. For instance, participants reported significantly higher levels of product knowledge, brand attitude, and purchase intention after evaluating the Web site incorporating 3-D product visualization compared to the magazine advertisement. This suggests a virtual experience enhanced by consumer learning, as measured from these constructs, over the indirect experience. In turn, a virtual experience was expected to emulate the effects of a direct product experience with no significant differences between the two evaluations. Although no significant differences between direct and virtual experiences were detected for brand attitude and purchase intention, surprisingly participants indicated more product knowledge after evaluating the test product in the virtual experience rather than the direct experience. A possible explanation stems from one of the unique advantages of presenting informational cues in a virtual experience. For example, as participants examined the 3-D test product, an informational cue providing the name of the component would display as the computer mouse moved over specific areas on the product. This interactive method of presenting and framing information is a feature of a virtual experience not possible with direct experience.

This study represents a single laboratory experiment into a new and unexplored area. Therefore, in order to fully understand the impact of virtual experience via 3-D product visualization, further research is needed exploring the key characteristics that impact ecommerce.

CHARACTERISTICS OF VIRTUAL EXPERIENCE

In considering the results from the first two studies, we feel that consumers undergo psychological processing when examining 3-D visual products in a virtual experience because of several characteristics associated with a virtual experience, such as interactive enjoyment, presence, and virtual affordances.

Interactivity

Interactivity is a multidimensional construct that can refer to numerous methods in which users of a medium can influence the form or content of a mediated environment (Ariely, 2000; Haubl & Trifts, 2000; Heeter, 2000). In computer-mediated environments, interactivity has been described as both the ability to communicate with people (person interactivity) and access information (machine interactivity) (Hoffman & Novak, 1996). Although interpersonal communication is an important advantage of the Internet compared to traditional media (i.e., email, chatrooms, etc.), interface design and the manner in which information is accessed are most applicable in 3-D product visualization. In fact, Haubl and Trifts (2000) found that interactive design aids in ecommerce environments have a substantial influence on consumer decision making.

Vividness

Vividness refers to the clarity and ability of an image to produce a sensory rich mediated experience and is generally thought to be more persuasive. However, research in this area has not produced consistent findings. For instance, Vriens, Loosschilder, Rosbergen, and Wittink (1998) designed a study to test the effects of verbal product representations versus vivid computer realistic images and found that pictorial representations improved understanding of design attributes. However, they emphasized that a higher degree of realism is possible with 3-D-rendered products that would probably result in stronger impact. Dahan and Srinivasan (2000) set out to test this proposition in order to identify a low-cost alternative for new product testing. Using a portable bicycle pump as the product category, actual physical products were measured against static and animated Web representations to predict overall market share. Surprisingly, the static and animated Web representations produced nearly accurate market share rankings compared to direct product experience.

It is the interactive and vivid nature of 3-D product visualization that stimulates sensory experiences in consumers by evoking memories, past feelings, and previous sensations, which results in the generation of mental imagery. The implication is that imagery processing is likely to have a positive impact on learning, encourage product evaluation, affect behavior, and provide sensory and emotional experiences that can substitute for consumption (MacInnis & Price, 1987). Thus, the more interactive and vivid a 3-D product experience, the richer mental imagery generated causing a heightened sense of presence.

Presence

The combination of vividness, interactivity, and sensory stimuli combine to create a sense of presence in virtual experience (Li et al., 2001). Presence, also known as telepresence, is the experience of "being there" in the virtual environment. This perceived sense is generated from sensory input, mental processes, and past experiences assimilated together in a current state (Gibson, 1966). Steuer (1992) described presence as the extent to which one feels present in a mediated environment. Although presence is the design goal of virtual reality, few media theorists would argue that the sense of presence is suddenly emerging with the debut of virtual reality, which consists of both immersive and nonimmersive 3-D visualization (Biocca, Kim, & Levy, 1995). According to Biocca (1997), "When we experience our everyday sense of presence in the physical world, we automatically generate a mental model of an external space from patterns of energy on the sensory organs.

In virtual environments, patterns of energy that stimulate the structure to those experienced in the physical environment are used to activate the same automatic perceptual processes that generate our stable perception of the physical world" (p. 5.3). The result is presence can be generated in a shopper when she or he is interacting with either a virtual product or a virtual environment.

By manipulating the sensory saturation of a consumer's visual perception, Kim and Biocca (1997) were able to detect significant differences in confidence levels regarding brand preference. More specifically, the sense of presence resulted in a stronger experience with subjects becoming more confident in their attitudes toward the product information presented. Kim and Biocca (1997) concluded that the virtual experience created by presence simulated a direct experience resulting in increased persuasion. This finding supports previous research that indicates the sense of presence created in a mediated environment will cause a user to believe the experience occurred firsthand, resulting in the same effect as direct experience (Lombard, 1995).

STUDY 3

The purpose of this study was to investigate the impact of visual sensory immersion (low, moderate, and high) on presence and traditional advertising effectiveness measures when interacting with 3-D products in an online environment (Biocca, Daugherty, Li & Chae, 2001).

Research Design

The experiment was conducted in a laboratory setting with 72 undergraduates from a major Midwestern university accessing a computer displaying a test product. Visual sensory immersion was manipulated by alternating the degree of interactivity and viewing angle as outlined by Kim and Biocca (1997). A 2-D flat noninteractive product displayed on a standard 17″ desktop monitor represented the low visual sensory immersive condition. Although the moderate visual sensory immersive condition display was also a standard 17″ desktop monitor, an interactive 3-D product was used to increase the visual acuity through the ability to rotate, move, and zoom-in or zoom-out for visual inspection. The viewing angles for both the low and moderate visual immersive conditions were 36.2 degrees. In contrast, the high visual sensory immersive condition included a 3-D interactive product displayed on a large video projection screen (120″ diagonal) at a viewing angle of 82.8 degrees. The formula for defining the viewing angles in this study are based on established research (Lombard, 1995).

A Web page was constructed using a suitable test product (AIWA®) Headphones) positioned in the center with information, such as brand name,

FIG. 22.4   Web site stimulus for study 4.

price, weight, and performance specifications, listed at the bottom (see Fig. 22.4). Participants were instructed that the purpose of the study was to record their evaluation of the product and to thoroughly examine the Web site in order to determine how they think and feel about the headphones. After examination (times ranged between 5 to 15 minutes), participants were immediately asked to complete a questionnaire with presence, product knowledge, brand attitude, and purchase intention serving as the dependent variables.

Results

The results show significant main effects for three classifications of presence across visual sensory immersion (Physical $F(2, 69) = 41.46$, p < .01, Engagement $F(2, 69) = 27.59$, p < .01, and Naturalness $F(2, 69) = 11.47$, p < .01. However, the effect of presence was primarily induced by the difference between the low and moderate visual immersive conditions (see Table 22.4).

Furthermore, a significant positive relationship was detected between presence and participants' reported brand attitude, product knowledge, and purchase

TABLE 22.4
Comparisons of Visual Sensory Immersion and Dimensions of Presence

Presence	Low	Moderate	High	T-Value	df	p <
Physical	1.71	3.08	–	8.64	46	.01
	1.71	–	3.05	7.54	46	.01
	–	3.08	3.05	.19	46	.85
Engagement	2.21	3.07	–	5.28	46	.01
	2.21	–	3.34	7.03	46	.01
	–	3.07	3.34	1.78	46	.08
Naturalness	2.66	3.47	–	3.78	46	.01
	2.66	–	3.63	4.41	46	.01
	–	3.47	3.63	.79	46	.43

Note: Low is a static 2-D product displayed on a standard 17″ monitor (n = 24), Moderate is an interactive 3-D product displayed on a standard 17″ monitor (n = 24), High is an interactive 3-D product displayed using a 120″ video projection screen (n = 24).

TABLE 22.5
Comparisons of Visual Sensory Immersion and Advertising Effectiveness

Effectiveness Measure	Low	Moderate	High	T-Value	df	p <
Brand Attitude	4.74	5.02	–	.94	46	.35
	4.74	–	5.61	3.36	46	.01
	–	5.02	5.61	2.20	46	.05
Product Knowledge	2.92	4.11	–	3.26	46	.01
	2.92	–	4.46	3.59	46	.01
	–	4.11	4.46	1.00	46	.32
Purchase Intention	1.96	3.50	–	3.84	46	.01
	1.96	–	4.20	5.48	46	.01
	–	3.50	4.20	1.74	46	.08

Note: Low is a static 2-D product displayed on a standard 17″ monitor (n = 24), Moderate is an interactive 3-D product displayed on a standard 17″ monitor (n = 24), High is an interactive 3-D product displayed using a 120″ video projection screen (n = 24).

intention. The results show significant main effects for brand attitude, $F(2, 69) = 4.90, p < .05$, product knowledge, $F(2, 69) = 9.03, p < .01$, and purchase intention, $F(2, 69) = 14.92, p < .01$, across three levels of visual sensory immersion. Although the significant differences again appear to be driven by the low versus moderate condition, an effect on brand attitude was also seen for the high visual sensory immersive condition (see Table 22.5). Nevertheless, the unexpected findings regarding the lack of difference between the moderate and high visual sensory immersive environments warrants further research.

STUDY 4

The purpose of the fourth study was to validate the results of the low versus moderate visual immersive conditions testing two different products (Biocca et al., 2001).

Research Design

The experiment was conducted in a laboratory setting with 93 undergraduates from a major Midwestern university accessing a computer containing a Web site displaying either a hooded pull-over jacket (n = 41) or a watch (n = 52). Furthermore, the low and moderate conditions were manipulated identically as in Study 3.

Consistent with previous studies, participants were instructed that the purpose of the research was to record their evaluation of the assigned product and to thoroughly examine the Web site in order to determine how they think and feel about either the jacket or watch. Immediately following their evaluation (times ranged between 5 to 15 minutes), participants were asked to complete a questionnaire with presence, product knowledge, brand attitude, and purchase intention serving as the dependent variables.

Results

The results show significant differences across three dimensions of presence for low versus moderate visual sensory immersion (see Table 22.6). Furthermore, a positive relationship was again identified between presence and the reported brand attitude, product knowledge, and purchase intention for the jacket with marginal support for the watch (see Table 22.7). Finally, the results also confirm significant differences for brand attitude, product knowledge, and purchase intention across low and moderate visual sensory immersion (see Table 22.8).

TABLE 22.6
Reported Degree of Presence Across Visual Sensory Immersive Conditions

Product	Presence	Low	Moderate	T-Value	df	p<
Jacket	Physical	1.84	2.81	4.78	40	.01
	Engagement	2.25	2.94	2.80	40	.01
	Naturalness	2.46	3.24	3.55	40	.01
Watch	Physical	1.66	2.44	4.47	51	.01
	Engagement	1.91	2.56	3.73	51	.01
	Naturalness	2.66	3.30	3.21	51	.01

Note: Low is a static 2-D product displayed on a standard 17″ monitor (jacket n = 21; watch n = 26), Moderate is an interactive 3-D product displayed on a standard 17″ monitor (jacket n = 20; watch n = 26).

TABLE 22.7
Relationship Between Advertising Effectiveness Measures and Presence

Product	Presence	Brand Attitude	Product Knowledge	Purchase Intention
Jacket	Physical	.66**	.57**	.67**
	Engagement	.63**	.44**	.76**
	Naturalness	.57**	.47**	.59**
Watch	Physical	.24	.29*	.47**
	Engagement	.31*	.16	.51**
	Naturalness	−.03	.13	.21

*p < .05, **p < .01

TABLE 22.8
Advertising Effectiveness Across Visual Sensory Immersive Conditions

Product	Effectiveness Measure	Low	Moderate	T-Value	df	p <
Jacket	Brand Attitude	4.55	5.42	2.46	40	.05
	Product Knowledge	2.98	4.62	3.48	40	.01
	Purchase Intention	2.76	3.65	1.77	40	.08
Watch	Brand Attitude	4.26	5.25	2.92	51	.01
	Product Knowledge	3.88	4.73	2.10	51	.05
	Purchase Intention	2.31	3.27	2.05	51	.05

Note: Low is a static 2-D product displayed on a standard 17″ monitor (jacket n = 21; watch n = 26), Moderate is an interactive 3-D product displayed on a standard 17″ monitor (jacket n = 20; watch n = 26).

Discussion

The verified relationship between presence and traditional advertising effectiveness measures, such as product knowledge, brand attitude, and purchase intention, is an important step in understanding the important characteristics of a virtual experience. Furthermore, the confirmation that examining products online utilizing interactive 3-D visualization increases presence over static 2-D images demonstrates the potential affect a virtual experience can have on consumer learning (Biocca et al., 2001; Li et al., 2002).

Affordances

Consumers inspect products in the conventional store following norms. When they select a computer, they may turn it on to see the color of the monitor screen or launch a program; however, they normally do not request to open the case to see what is inside. When consumers select chairs, they are likely to sit on them but less likely to stand on them. This type of expected interaction between consumers and products is referred to as *affordances* (Schuemie & Van der Mast, 1999). The affordances of any product represent the perceptual cues that influence how consumers expect to interact during direct experience. As Norman (1998) explained, when we assess our immediate environment, we are aware of some of the affordances each object offers. For instance, chairs are to sit on, doors to open or close, and lights to illuminate. An affordance is not a property of an object as much as it is a relationship between an object and the organism that is acting on the object. Heeter (2000) further noted, "In the design of experiences, real affordances are not nearly so important as perceived ones; it is perceived affordances that tell the user what actions can be performed on an object and, to some extent, how to do them."

There are various affordances common to product inspection in conventional stores that come from the ability of the senses and motor systems to interact with products. Visual inspection is probably the most common affordance as consumers learn about the shape, texture, and perceived functions of a product through examination. This type of interaction, and the information it yields, can be simulated vividly in a 3-D environment where consumers can examine, zoom-in or zoom-out, and rotate a product. As a result, the visual affordances associated with a virtual experience enhance a consumer's ability to acquire knowledge, form attitudes, and influence behavior relative to traditional static Internet advertising.

Another type of affordance is the tactile or haptic ability to interact with a product (Burdea, 1996; Durlach & Mavor, 1994). Human hands are able to gain additional information by feeling the warm/cold, soft/hard, smooth/rough, and light/heavy properties of surfaces and textures that compose products. For certain products that come in touch with skin, such as bed linens and clothes, consumers frequently try to touch them in order to feel the material. Although tactile sensations remain limited in a virtual experience, the act of physically manipulating a product is easily simulated in a 3-D environment, enabling consumers to control the direction and axis of rotation using a mouse, joystick, or glove-type interface. This type of virtual product simulation emulates the direct tactile and haptic interaction. However, tactile simulation remains inherently limited in a virtual experience because of the lack of physical sensory input. Consequently, consumer learning dependent on tactile stimulation beyond simple manipulation when examining a product is restricted in a virtual experience.

Many product functions such as levers, buttons, and handles suggest behavioral types of affordances associated with products. For instance, a consumer may want to press the power key in order to turn on a Palm Pilot to see the screen or examine how to write an address entry using a stylus. To a certain degree, these behavioral interactions between consumers and products can be simulated in a virtual experience. In fact, the utilization of animation, customization, and spatial navigation within virtual environments is able to facilitate a virtual experience when examining a 3-D interactive product.

The key issue of a virtual experience is the difference between affordances a consumer is likely to seek in physical environments (*physical affordances*) and affordances that a virtual environment can provide (*virtual affordances*) (Li et al., 2003). Consumers have different affordances for different products as well as different affordances for the same product, and it is these differences that exist among consumers that 3-D visual ecommerce sites need to take into account. Specifically, if visual inspection is the determining cue, consumer learning should be enhanced over indirect experience by examining 3-D virtual products. If tactile experience is the primary evaluation criterion, such as the case with the bedding material, the effectiveness of virtual simulations is limited. Yet when behavioral simulations are salient for inspection, virtual experience may offer a unique opportunity for marketers to simulate action through animation and customization.

STUDY 5

The purpose of this study was to test the impact of three kinds of virtual product affordances—visual, tactile, and behavioral—featured in 3-D product visualization and static 2-D graphic ecommerce sites (Li et al., 2003).

Research Design

Given the exploratory nature of the study, the first step was to select suitable test products representing each of the aforementioned affordances. Hence, three individual products (wristwatch, bedding material, and laptop computer) from a 3-D rendering service site (www.viewpoint.com) were identified as fitting test objects because each incorporated the desired design interfaces (rotate, zoom, animation, or customization) and affordances relevant to the consumption experience. In order to confirm the affordances associated with each product, a pretest utilizing a convenience sample of 33 undergraduates at a major Midwestern university was conducted. The results indicated affordances associated with visual inspection ($M = 10.63$) are more important when examining a wristwatch than tactile ($M = 7.69$) or behavioral ($M = 8.57$), $F(1, 33) = 21.17$, $p < .01$ (see Table 22.9). In contrast, when examining bedding material, subjects indicated affordances associated with tactile examination ($M = 10.42$) are more important than visual ($M = 9.63$) or behavioral ($M = 7.21$), $F(1, 33) = 22.22$, $p < .01$. Finally, behavioral ($M = 10.57$) affordances were indicated as more important when examining a laptop than visual ($M = 8.69$) or tactile ($M = 7.36$), $F(1, 33) = 36.97$, $p < .01$.

Following the pretest, a laboratory experiment was conducted with 73 undergraduates from a major Midwestern university each examining three products (wristwatch, bedding material, and laptop) in either the 3-D product visualization condition (n = 36) or the static 2-D graphic condition (n = 37). As in previously reported studies, participants were instructed to thoroughly evaluate each product to determine how they think and/or feel about products. On completion, participants

TABLE 22.9
Pretest to Identify Affordances Sought for Each Product

	Visual		Tactile		Behavioral			
	Mean	(St. dev)	Mean	(St. dev)	Mean	(St. dev)	F	p
Wristwatch	**10.63**	(.92)	7.69	(2.49)	8.57	(2.55)	21.17	.01
Bedding	9.63	(1.49)	**10.42**	(.93)	7.21	(2.97)	22.22	.01
Laptop	8.69	(1.97)	7.36	(2.86)	**10.57**	(.79)	36.97	.01

Note: An 11-point Likert-type scale (not important at all/extremely important) was used asking participants to rate how important visual, tactile, and behavioral inspection is when evaluating a wristwatch, bedding material, and laptop computer.

TABLE 22.10
Advertising Effectiveness for High Visual Affordances: Wristwatch

	3-D visualization		2-D Graphics				
	Mean	(St. dev)	Mean	(St. dev)	t	df	p
Product Knowledge	4.17	(1.76)	3.14	(1.55)	2.66	71	.01
Brand Attitude	5.14	(.97)	4.63	(1.20)	1.96	71	.053
Decision Quality	4.93	(1.16)	3.97	(1.53)	3.01	71	.01

were asked to complete a questionnaire designed to record their reported product knowledge, brand attitude, and quality of their decision if they were forced to make a purchase decision at this time.

Results

The results testing the visual affordances indicated that product knowledge and decision quality were both evaluated significantly higher when examining the interactive 3-D wristwatch. However, the difference for brand attitude was not significant compared to the 2-D product even though the direction is in line with the expected outcome (see Table 22.10).

The testing of the tactile affordances involving the bedding material shows no significant differences for the reported effectiveness measures between interactive 3-D and static 2-D products (see Table 22.11). This indicates that when tactile affordances are the most important for the consumption experience, such as the case with the bedding material, 3-D product visualization presents no advantage over static 2-D representations of products.

Finally, the testing of the behavioral affordances associated with the laptop computer reveal that the reported product knowledge decision quality were significantly greater from examining the 3-D interactive product compared to the static

TABLE 22.11
Advertising Effectiveness for High Tactile Affordances: Bedding Material

	3-D visualization		2-D Graphics				
	Mean	(St. dev)	Mean	(St. dev)	t	df	p
Product Knowledge	3.83	(1.52)	3.81	(1.78)	.05	71	.95
Brand Attitude	5.18	(1.40)	4.76	(1.28)	1.35	71	.18
Decision Quality	4.69	(1.39)	4.43	(1.55)	.76	71	.45

TABLE 22.12
Advertising Effectiveness for High Behavioral Affordances: Laptop Computer

	3-D visualization		2-D Graphics				
	Mean	(St. dev)	Mean	(St. dev)	t	df	p
Product Knowledge	4.08	(1.99)	2.96	(1.58)	2.71	71	.01
Brand Attitude	5.71	(1.04)	5.35	(.97)	1.53	71	.13
Decision Quality	4.63	(1.57)	3.87	(1.76)	1.95	71	.05

2-D version (see Table 22.12). However, no significant differences were found for brand attitude, although directionally consistent.

Discussion

Rather than claiming consumer learning is always superior when examining interactive 3-D visualizations compared to static 2-D graphics, this study explores the conditions under which 3-D visualization outperforms 2-D graphics. The results indicate that product knowledge and decision quality were both significantly higher from exposure to an interactive 3-D product than a static 2-D product. This suggests when the goal is to increase awareness and facilitate the decision process, marketers could be better served by stimulating a virtual experience than relying solely on indirect experience.

When tactile affordances are the most relevant to the consumption experience, a virtual experience is unable to influence consumer learning over indirect experience. This finding reinforces the notion that touching and feeling certain products, such as bedding material, likely prompts the consumer to seek direct experience maintaining a distinct sensory advantage over indirect and virtual experience. Furthermore, this implies that marketers would gain little from using either virtual or indirect types of experiences to facilitate consumer learning.

In turn, when behavioral affordances are the most relevant to the consumption experience, the results offer inconclusive support for enhanced consumer learning. For example, product knowledge was significantly elevated after exposure to an interactive 3-D product compared to a static 2-D product, as well as marginal support for decision quality. Yet brand attitude was not affected by a virtual experience. Although the results were not significantly different than the indirect experience, the scores were in the hypothesized direction. Two possible explanations could be that participants may have established prior attitudes toward the product, and that the behavioral affordance manipulation was somewhat weak for the laptop. For instance, the opening and closing of the lid, the removal of the battery, and the powering on of the computer were used as behavioral simulations. Perhaps a more relevant simulated behavior should have been using the keyboard to type or launch an application. Regardless, the fact that product knowledge was consistently heightened in a virtual experience for both a visual and behavioral driven product is important because it represents one of the initial steps in consumer learning (Li et al., 2003).

IMPLICATIONS AND FUTURE RESEARCH ON VIRTUAL EXPERIENCE

The purpose of this chapter was to summarize our existing research on virtual experience and 3-D product visualization to develop a foundation for future investigation and theory construction in an area we call *experiential ecommerce*. The study of experiential ecommerce has both industry and theoretical implications involving consumer perception and behavior with the goal of improving consumer learning and decision making in ecommerce environments. The development of computer technology and expansion of the Internet has resulted in a promising but challenging mass medium. Marketers have the ability to deliver highly targeted persuasive messages, strengthen customer relationships, and ultimately generate sales 24 hours a day (Tedesco, 1999). Although the Internet has demonstrated a high capacity for disseminating information about products and services, it has fallen short of expectations when consumers want to "experience" a product. However, the use of dynamic 3-D visualization in ecommerce is increasing with the potential to serve a unique role in consumer learning as companies seek to provide consumers with a virtual product experience. Thus, the understanding of the complexities and intricacies involved in creating a virtual experience is important as the Internet continues to evolve.

By creating compelling online virtual experiences with products, marketers could potentially increase the value of product information presented, engage consumers in an active shopping experience, increase the number of unique and repeat traffic visitors for a site, and ultimately establish an online competitive advantage. Furthermore, the potential benefits of message framing and product customization a virtual experience provides could enhance how consumers learn by saving time and eliminating unnecessary information. Fundamentally, the findings presented in the chapter have established a virtual experience as an alternative consumer experience previously unexplored in consumer learning research. The data suggest that this new type of experience resembles more closely a direct product experience than a traditional indirect experience. The underlying reason is that virtual experiences allow for vicarious learning because consumers are actively engaged in the inspection and control of a 3-D product rather than a passive observer common to more traditional forms of advertising. Theoretically, the increased visual sensory immersion and perceived control simulates the same sensory input expected when evaluating a physical product. Consumers are able to experience psychological states because the medium creates a sense of interactivity and enjoyment resulting in increased learning, altered behaviors, and a perceived sense of control (Hoffman & Novak, 1996). We see presence as the perceptual base of a virtual experience because 3-D simulations of products and shopping environments render mental images that are traditionally created by consumers interacting with physical products. This characteristic provides the sensation and feeling of "being there" with a product. At a low level of presence, the participants feel that simulations appear "real" or "realistic," signifying a conceptual awareness of the simulation. At a high level of presence, virtual product attributes and physical product attributes are perceived equally and participants treat the virtual product just as they would a physical product. This is obviously the mode that will greatly facilitate consumer learning and thus, the goal for any design of virtual products in ecommerce.

The ability to establish a virtual experience is not beyond the capabilities of ecommerce environments and technological conditions are almost ripe for advertisers and marketers to take advantage of this unique experience. The findings presented in this chapter represent initial attempts to conceptualize experiential ecommerce. As a result, additional paths of research may lead to important findings in this new area. To fully understand the impact of utilizing 3-D products in consumer learning, more theoretical research is needed designed to explore the unique and distinctive characteristics that separate virtual experience from other types of experiences. In addition, research designed to explore the impact of message content appeals, low-involvement products, and alternative types of sensory immersion (auditory) are essential to fully understand the potential impact a virtual experience offers marketers. Furthermore, research investigating the impact of product contextualization, informational cues, and consumer characteristics is needed as virtual product experiences continue to evolve. Research investigating these areas is not only essential to our understanding of this new challenging experience, but also significant for e-commerce practice. With advanced knowledge of virtual experience, marketers and advertisers can design more effective e-commerce environments to enhance consumer learning by highlighting relevant messages and eliminating trivial information.

Because advertisers are capable of exerting influence over the consumer learning process (Hoch & Deighton, 1989), a simulated virtual experience may extend product familiarity, affect motivation, and decrease product ambiguity, leading to elevated levels of arousal, enhanced shopping enjoyment, and heightened brand preference. Therefore, a virtual experience will become an increasingly important issue as more ecommerce sites move to the next generation of interfaces that present products using interactive 3-D visualization. The promise of experiential ecommerce is that a compelling online experience should facilitate and enhance consumer learning (Novak, Hoffman, & Yung, 2000). As a result, this new type of experience offers marketers, as well as consumers, numerous opportunities to communicate product knowledge, strengthen brand attitudes, and explore purchase decisions compared to traditional types of advertising and product trial.

REFERENCES

Ariely, D. (2000). Controlling the information flow: Effects on consumers' decision making and preferences. *Journal of Consumer Research, 27*(2), 233–249.

Batra, R., & Ray, M. L. (1985). How advertising works at contact. In L. F. Alwitt & A. Mitchell (Eds.), *Psychological processes and advertising effects* (pp. 13–43). Hillsdale, NJ: Lawrence Erlbaum Associates.

Beerli, A., & Santana, J. D. M. (1999). Design and validation of an instrument for measuring advertising effectiveness in the printed media. *Journal of Current Issues and Research in Advertising, 21*(2), 11–30.

Biocca, F. (1997). Cyborg's dilemma: Progressive embodiment in virtual environments. *Journal of Computer Mediated-Communication, 3*(2). Retrieved September 15, 2004, from http://jcmc.huji.ac.il/vol3/issue2/biocca2.html.

Biocca, F., Daugherty, T., Li, H., & Chae, Z. (2001). Effect of visual sensory immersion on presence, product knowledge, attitude toward the product and purchase intention. In F. Biocca (Ed.), *Experiential Ecommerce Conference Proceedings*, CD-ROM.

Biocca, F., Kim, T., & Levy, M. (1995). The vision of virtual reality. In F. Biocca & M. Levy (Eds.), *Communication in the age of virtual reality*, 1–25. Hillsdale, NJ: Lawrence Erlbaum Press.

Burdea, G. (1996). *Force and touch feedback for virtual reality.* New York: Wiley.

Chaudhuri, A., & Buck, R. (1995). Media differences in rational and emotional responses to advertising. *Journal of Broadcasting & Electronic Media, 39*(1), 109–125.

Dahan, E., & Srinivasan, V. (2000). The predictive power of internet-based product concept testing using visual depiction and animation. *Journal of Product Innovation Management, 17*(2), 99–109.

Daugherty, T. (2001). Consumer learning and 3-D ecommerce: The effects of sequential exposure of a virtual experience relative to indirect and direct product experience on product knowledge, brand attitude and purchase intention (Doctoral dissertation, Michigan State University, 2001). *Dissertation Abstracts International, 62*(7), 101.

Deighton, J. (1984, December). The interaction of advertising and evidence. *Journal of Consumer Research, 11*, 763–770.

Durlach, N., & Mavor, A. (1994). *Virtual reality: Scientific and technological challenges.* Washington, DC: National Research Council.

Fazio, R. H., Powell, M. C., & Williams, C. J. (1989, December). The role of attitude accessibility in the attitude-to-behavior process. *Journal of Consumer Research 16*, 280–288.

Gardial, S., Fisher, D., Clemons, S., Woodruff, R. B., Schumann, D. W., & Burns, M. J. (1994, March). Comparing consumers' recall of prepurchase and postpurchase product evaluation experiences. *Journal of Consumer Research, 20*, 548–560.

Gibson, J. J. (1966). *The senses considered as perceptual systems.* Boston: Houghton Mifflin.

Gould, S. J. (1999). Protocol and cognitive response analysis. In P. E. Earl & S. Kemp (Eds.), *The Elgar companion to consumer research and economic psychology*, 468–472. Northampton, MA: Cheltenham.

Grossman, L. (2000, September 18). Your technology. *Time*, 93.

Haubl, G., & Trifts, V. (2000). Consumer decision making in online shopping environmnets: The effects of interactive decision aids. *Marketing Science, 19*(1), 4–21.

Heeter, C. (2000). Interactivity in the context of designed experience. *Journal of Interactive Advertising, 1*(1), Retrieved September 15, 2004 from http://www.jiad.org/vol1/no1/heeter/index.html

Hirschman, E. C. (1984). Experience seeking: A subjectivist perspective of consumption. *Journal of Business Research, 12*, 115–136.

Hoch, S. J., & Deighton, J. (1989, April). Managing what consumers learn from experience. *Journal of Marketing, 53*, 1–20.

Hoch, S. J., & Y.-W. Ha. (1986, September). Consumer learning: Advertising and the ambiguity of product experience. *Journal of Consumer Research, 13*, 221–233.

Hoffman, D. L., & Novak, T. P. (1996, July). Marketing in Hypermedia Computer-Based Environments: Conceptual Foundations. *Journal of Marketing, 60*, 50–68.

Holbrook, M. B., & Hirschman, E. C. (1982, September). The experiential aspects of consumption: Consumer fantasies, feelings, and fun. *Journal of Consumer Research, 9*, 132–140.

Karat, J., Karat, C. M., & Ukelson, J. (2000). Affordances, motivations, and the design of user interfaces: Creating tools that enable rather than restrict add value to the product and loyalty from the customer. *Communications of the ACM, 43*(8), 49–51.

Kempf, D. S., & Smith, R. E. (1998, August). Consumer processing of product trial and the influence of prior Advertising: A structural modeling approach. *Journal of Marketing Research, 35*, 325–338.

Kim, T., & Biocca, F. (1997). Telepresence via television: Two dimensions of telepresence may have different connections to memory and persuasion. *Journal of Computer Mediated Communication, 3*(2). Retrieved September 15, 2001, from http://www.ascusc.org/jcmc/vol3/issue2/kim.html.

Klein, L. R. (1998). Evaluating the potential of interactive media through a different lens: Search versus experience goods. *Journal of Business Research, 41*, 195–203.

Krugman, H. E. (1965, Fall). The impact of television advertising: Learning without involvement. *Public Opinion Quarterly, 29*, 349–356.

Lessiter, J., Freeman, J., Keogh, E., & Davidoff, J. (2000). *Development of a new cross-media presence questionnaire: The ITC-sense of presence inventory*. Paper presented at *Presence*, 3rd International Workshop on Presence, Technical University of Delft, Delft, Netherlands, March 27–28.

Li, H., Daugherty, T., & Biocca, F. (2001). Characteristics of virtual experience in e-commerce: A protocol analysis. *Journal of Interactive Marketing, 15*(3), 13–30.

Li, H., Daugherty, T., & Biocca, F. (2002). Impact of 3-D advertising on product knowledge, brand attitude, and purchase intention: The mediating role of presence. *Journal of Advertising, 31*(3), 43–58.

Li, H., Daugherty, T., & Biocca, F. (2003). The role of virtual experience in consumer learning. *Journal of Consumer Psychology, 13*(4), 395–405.

Lombard, M. (1995). Direct response to people on the screen: Television and personal space. *Communication Research, 22*(3), 228–324.

Lombard, M., & Ditton, T. (1997). At the heart of it all: The concept of presence. *Journal of Computer-Mediated Communication, 3*(2). Retrieved September 15, 2001, from http://www.ascusc.org/jcmc/vol3/issue2/lombard.html.

Machleit, K. A., & Eroglu, S. A. (2000). Describing and measuring emotional response to shopping experience. *Journal of Business Research, 49*, 101–111.

MacInnis, D. J., & Price, L. L. (1987, March). The role of imagery in information processing: Review and extensions. *Journal of Consumer Research, 13*, 473–491.

MacKenzie, S. B., & Lutz, R. J. (1989, April). An empirical examination of the structural antecedents of attitude toward the ad in an advertising pretesting context. *Journal of Marketing, 53*, 48–65.

Mathur, D. C. (1971). *Naturalistic philosophies of experience*. St. Louis, MO: Warren H. Green, Inc.

McLuhan, M., & McLuhan, E. (1988). *Laws of media: The new science*. Toronto: University of Toronto Press.

Norman, D. (1998). *The invisible computer: Why good products can fail, the personal computer is so complex and information appliances are the solution.* Cambridge, MA: MIT Press.

Novak, T. P., Hoffman, D. L., & Yung, Y. F. (2000). Measuring the customer experience in online environments: A structural modeling approach. *Marketing Science, 19*(1), 22–42.

Pine II, B. J., & Gilmore, J. H. (1998). Welcome to the experience economy. *Harvard Business Review, 76*(4), 97–105.

Reeves, B., & Nass, C. (1996). *The media equation.* Palo Alto, CA: CSLI Publications.

Riffe, D., Lacy, S., & Fico, F. G. (1998). *Analyzing media messages: Using quantitative content analysis in research.* Mahwah, NJ: Lawrence Erlbaum Associates.

Rook, D. W. (1987, September). The buying impulse. *Journal of Consumer Research, 14*, 189–199.

Schlosser, A. E., & Kanfer, A. (2001). *Impact of product interactivity on searchers' and browsers' judgments: Implications for commercial web site effectiveness.* Paper presented at the *Society for Consumer Psychology Winter Conference*, Scottsdale, AZ, February 15–17.

Schuemie, M. J., & Van Der Mast, C. (1999). Presence: Interacting in VR? Paper presented at the *Twentieth Workshop on Language Technology*. Retrieved January 1, 2000, from http://is.twi.tudelft.nl/~schuemie/interactions.pdf.

Smith, R. E., & Swinyard, W. R. (1982, Winter). Information response models: An integrated approach. *Journal of Marketing, 46*, 81–93.

Smith, R. E., & Swinyard, W. R. (1983, August). Attitude-behavior consistency: The impact of product trial versus advertising. *Journal of Consumer Research, 20*, 257–267.

Smith, R. E., & Swinyard, W. R. (1988). Cognitive response to advertising and trial: Belief strength, belief confidence and product curiosity. *Journal of Advertising, 17*(3), 3–14.

Soukup, C. (2000). Building a theory of multi-media CMC. *New Media & Society, 2*(4), 407–425.

Steuer, J. (1992). Defining virtual reality: Dimensions determining telepresence. *Journal of Communication, 42*(4), 73–93.

Tedesco, R. (1999). Internet. *Broadcasting & Cable, 129*(1), 50.

Viewpoint. (2001). Just 1K short of reality. Retrieved September 15, 2001, from http://www.viewpoint.com

Vriens, M., Loosschilder, G., Rosbergen, E., & Wittink, D. (1998). Verbal versus realistic pictorial representations in conjoint analysis with design attributes. *Journal of Product Innovation Management, 15*(5), 455–467.

Wright, P. (1980, September). Message-evoked thoughts: Persuasion research using thought verbalizations. *Journal of Consumer Research, 7*, 151–175.

Wright, A. A., & Lynch Jr., J. G. (1995, March). Communication effects of advertising versus direct experience when both search and experience attributes are present. *Journal of Consumer Research, 21*, 708–718.

CHAPTER TWENTY THREE

Web-Based Consumer Research

Basil G. Englis
Berry College

Michael R. Solomon
Auburn University

Paula Danskin
Berry College

Exciting developments in interactive Internet technologies are transforming the way marketers and consumers speak to one another. The Web as a research medium has the potential to revolutionize consumer research for academic and industry researchers. The purpose of this chapter is to outline how the World Wide Web is fundamentally changing how researchers and respondents interact and to describe several Web-based technologies for data collection and presentation of research findings/data online. Although our approach emphasizes the use of rich visual materials, the Web also is increasingly well suited to the use of other media content. One of the primary advantages of online research methods is that they permit research participants to provide rapid-response feedback to research stimuli.

By November 2000, there were 407.1 million Internet users worldwide, with the majority of users residing in the United States and western European countries (http://www.nua.ie/surveys/how_many_ptonline/). Access to the Internet is expected to grow among all populations and thus the Internet is rapidly becoming an appealing medium to conduct research for academic and commercial purposes (Schillewaert, Langerak, & Duhamel, 1998; Stanton, 1998; Weible & Wallace, 1998). A number of studies (e.g., Schuldt & Totten, 1994; Yun & Trumbo, 2000) and commentaries (e.g., Landis, 1995; Rosen & Petty, 1995) have called for more research using the Internet as a medium and for examination of validity and reliability issues surrounding different Internet methods. Indeed, Kuhnert and McCauley (1996) noted that, " . . . the organizational survey, which in the past was primarily a paper and pencil device, is now and perhaps forever changed by advancing technology" (p. 233). Our purpose in this chapter is to provide a brief review of current Internet research methods and some associated validity and reliability issues, provide some details regarding the Web-based research methodology we have developed, describe alternative applications of its core functionalities, explore the capability of the Internet to serve as a results presentation and analysis medium, and speculate about exciting ramifications for consumer research and marketing practice.

THE MIGRATION OF THE "TRADITIONAL" OFFLINE METHOD TO THE INTERNET

State of the Art

Conversion from mail, telephone, or direct interviewing survey techniques to the Internet is a natural step in the evolution of electronically mediated consumer research methods. Since the 1970s we have seen the development of numerous research applications using local computer systems to mediate the data collection effort, such as computer-assisted telephone interviewing systems or computer-based laboratory control systems. These computer-mediated methodologies have been prevalent in academic research settings as well as industry research settings. Indeed, computer-assisted interviewing systems are the current state of practice among marketing research practitioners (e.g., Bethlehem, 2000). One of the central distinctions between traditional offline computer-mediated research and Internet-mediated methods is the ability to administer the research study "at a distance." That is, the data, stimuli, researchers, and respondents can each reside in widely different physical locations and be brought together in the virtual space of the Internet.

The transition to Internet-mediated research methods has several compelling advantages. In contrast to offline methods, response time can be minimized because of automation of response protocols. It is easier to modify the research instrument or to create multiple experimental versions of it, and the survey or experiment can be conducted around the clock. The researcher has the capability of reaching a larger and more diverse subject population, and it is possible that responses will be more veridical due to the anonymity afforded by the Internet. Because data collection is automated and coding errors all but eliminated, data costs per respondent can be considerably lower than with traditional research methods (see Englis & Solomon 2000).

Thus, researchers are beginning to identify specific areas in which Internet methods provide advantages. For example, Yun and Trumbo (2000) and Stanton (1998) listed several advantages as well as potential problems concerned with conducting research online through email, Web-based surveys, and so on. Among the benefits cited are lowered costs, improved response rates, the ability to have mixed-media research protocols and multiple respondent contacts, quality of response data, and response speed and geographic reach. Web-based surveys can also introduce a level of graphical sophistication that surpasses paper surveys. For example, questionnaires can be presented in color with interactive or cinematic images (Yun & Trumbo, 2000). Finally, a Web-based survey can provide results dynamically as often as a researcher requires (by the day, by the hour, etc.) (Schmitt, 1997).

On the other hand, widespread adoption of online formats for research purposes has been hampered by some troubling issues. Chief among these has been concern over sampling bias, because the universe of Web users has been skewed toward upscale, well-educated male technophiles (Stanton, 1998). Another problem is the inherent uncertainty about the real identity of the respondents at the other end of the modem connection (though this concern plagues phone and mail surveys as well). Web-based questionnaire forms may also act to limit the freedom of respondents to introduce information that is beyond the scope of the survey or to respond in a manner that is different than designed (e.g., restriction to a yes/no format rather than an open-ended format). A related issue is the unwillingness of respondents to provide sensitive information over what they perceive to be insecure lines. Although targeted emails have been used to recruit subjects who can respond anonymously, privacy concerns linger among consumers (Kuhnert & McCauley, 1996; Reips, 1997).

Despite these concerns, some research firms and many academics are embracing the use of Internet research methods. For example, the Wharton Virtual Test Market (www.fourps.wharton.upenn.edu/~wvtm/naomi/WWW_homepage/start1.htm) and Georgia Tech's Graphics, Visualization, and Usability Center (GVU) periodically conduct surveys regarding attitudes toward Web usage (Kehoe & Pitkow, 1996). More recently, Hoffman and Novak (1996) announced a major new online research initiative called "e-Lab," to be sponsored by academic and industry support (Schwartz, 2001). Major research firms including NPD and Greenfield regularly conduct online panels and surveys. Since 1996, the Harris poll has been conducted as an online research effort under the newly formed company Harris Interactive, and many other firms are likely to follow in this path.

A typical strategy currently used in online research efforts is to use an electronic mailing list to reach participants in a special-interest discussion group, who then respond to an online questionnaire related to this interest (Greguras & Stanton, 1996). Although empirical validation is in its early stages, few systematic differences in response patterns between such online and in vivo sampling and survey methods have been reported. For example, in one study where an identical questionnaire was administered in both paper and Web formats, similar covariance structures were obtained for each version (Stanton, 1998). Similar studies comparing online and offline research formats have been conducted by market research firms such as Total Research, Inc., Harris Interactive, and others. The general conclusion is that little if any differences arise between these formats, and that in the United States few differences emerge between online and offline sampling methods.

Despite the steady advances of online data-collection efforts, the most common Web-based research resembles standard paper-and-pencil measures that have simply been scanned into a computer system and converted to html file format, with response buttons, pull-down lists, or text input fields substituted for traditional hard copy paper-and-pencil scales. This reproduction of the traditional instrument is adequate for many research applications, but certainly not for all. More importantly, these conventional formats do not take full advantage of the Web's capabilities to present multimedia stimuli to large numbers of users simultaneously, nor do they take advantage of the ability to provide logical branching among procedures as a function of the behavior of the respondent. A few academic projects are pushing the envelope in this regard, but these are primarily online experiments posted by psychologists (for one notable example, visit http://www.cops.uni-sb.de/ronald/experim/).

VALIDITY AND RELIABILITY ISSUES IN ONLINE RESEARCH

Two of the most important issues in research design are control and validity (Pedhazur & Schmelkin, 1991). Although control is important for all types of research, Internet-based methods may be particularly adept at maximizing control (Stanton, 1998). For example, researchers can build in password controls so that respondent access is limited to those who have been pre-screened for the purpose of the study. Changes can be made in real time and research protocols can be made for more responses to the behavior of individual study participants, thus providing an unprecedented level of control in the matching of stimuli and respondents.

Perhaps the most pressing concern regarding control relates to the representativeness of the sample rather than the ability to manipulate or implement control mechanisms (Mehta & Sivadas, 1995). Some researchers have collected or recommend collecting comparison data using offline methods and have compared the validity of the responses as a means of ensuring representativeness (i.e., Dillman, 2000; Parker, 1992). Representativeness is particularly important for Internet-based research as the anonymity of respondents is very high owing to the very nature of the Internet and the potential for a user to create a "false identity." The most effective way to ensure representativeness is to select a group of study participants from the project's stated target population and to do so using reliable methods— sometimes through offline procedures prior to launching the online component of the research. Increasingly, however, there are consumer panels available to researchers that have been pre-recruited to be representative of the U.S. population, and it is likely that such will become increasingly available in other countries as the incidence of Internet access continues to grow.

Clearly, ineffective sampling may produce biased results regarding the effectiveness and impact of the study. As mentioned earlier, one of the disadvantages of using the Internet as a research vehicle stems from the population that uses it. Thus, if a researcher conducts an online study using an "open-access" Web site it is unclear how representative the sample will be of consumers in general, or even of consumers who have Internet access. As Yun and Trumbo (2000) noted, the social and economic representativeness of online samples may be skewed relative to the target population (historically Internet users have been more affluent, younger, and with a higher proportion of males than the general population).

A related concern—that also can result in nonrepresentative online samples— is differential dropout rate or mortality among participants. Technical problems because of different mail systems, server capabilities, and email survey attachments can all lead to high "mortality" rates that can bias final samples if, for example, the result is differential exclusion of those with less sophisticated computer systems (see, e.g., Couper, Blair, & Triplett, 1997). In one study using an email survey, 46.5% of 4,066 emails required some type of clerical intervention after they had been sent (see, e.g., Couper et al., 1997).

Other problems with representativeness may also arise when respondents assigned to a control group learn about a treatment and want to participate in the treatment group (sometimes referred to as the *diffusion* or *imitation of treatments*). This threat may be more likely to occur in research involving closely knit, online communities. Such was the experience of Walsh, Kiesler, Sproull, and Hesse (1992) during Internet-based surveys involving oceanographers participating in SCIENCENET. In this instance, oceanographers who were not part of the random survey sample contacted the researchers because they had heard about the study through a usenet group and wanted to participate.

Researchers must also work to ensure the internal validity of their measures. There are several threats to external validity. For example, a treatments-attributes interaction threat to external validity stems from an interaction between the variables under study and the people that are being studied. Although this threat can be a problem for both Internet-based and traditional approaches, in some instances Internet-based approaches may be more sensitive to a treatments-attributes interaction.

Other, relatively minor validity concerns involve the operationalization of the research methods given that an online environment is used for the research. For instance, the typical Web-survey respondent may be more likely to have different computer skills and higher levels of education than the general population (Yun & Trumbo, 2000); these individual differences could interact with the treatments being used. Similarly, threats to validity can arise from the environment within which the study is conducted (treatments-settings interaction). Internet-based data-collection approaches such as email or Web platforms can be accessed from almost anywhere. With the rise in handheld computers, wireless telephones capable of handling email, and the widespread use of laptop computers, Internet-based surveys can be accessed and completed at the participant's home or office or while traveling. The broad heterogeneity in the environment of the participant during his or her experience with the research protocol can potentially add variance to the results and if these differences vary systematically with treatments then confounding may also occur (see, e.g., Couper et al., 1997).

Another threat that researchers face using the online medium is that the experience level of participants may be higher with an online sample, leading to more opportunities for multiple-treatment interference. There are many chances for Internet users to participate in online surveys. Many of these surveys result in free products, cash, coupons, or drawings for prizes. In fact some researchers have commented that on-line participants expect more compensation that other participants (i.e., Sheehan & Hoy, 1999). To avoid this threat, some Internet panels have made efforts to exclude participation in multiple surveys.

Judging by the growth of research in the online environment and the scrutiny that such methods are receiving within the academic, practitioner, and legal communities it is likely that standards will begin to emerge to help guide researchers in selecting appropriate online research design and sampling methods. As Dillman (2000) noted, when controls are in place and the sample is representative of the population, online research may provide the richest type of platform for researchers because of the opportunities to use visual, audio, textual, and other types of stimuli. In the next section, we outline a general model of online Web-based research and then go on to describe a specific research application we have developed.

A "CLOSED-LOOP" MODEL FOR ONLINE RESEARCH

The basic idea of a "closed-loop" feedback system is not new to the online research environment, although online technologies may afford a novel set of tools to accomplish closed-loop research in real time and with unprecedented speed. At the heart of closed-loop systems is the output of a measurement system that is fed back directly into the underlying process and is used to modify the process itself. For example, consumer researchers interested in the effects of respondents' favorite popular music used as background in an advertisement could pretest to determine the musical tastes of a group of respondents and then use the top choice in the ads. Alternatively, the researchers could use individual feedback (each person's top choice) to construct ads tailored to each individual respondent (e.g., Englis & Pennell, 1994). The latter case is an example of a closed-loop procedure; this represents an increase in the sensitivity of the research operations in that interindividual variability in musical taste is more fully taken into account than in the former design.

Computer-mediated procedures generally, and in particular the Web-mediated methods, offer the potential to develop additional ways of "closing the research loop." Indeed, the Internet can be used to create a network of interactions among researcher(s), respondents, and even the users of the results.

This vision is not so different from the spirit that guided the original creation of the World Wide Web itself. The primary innovation of the Web was accomplished by Tim Berners-Lee, whose insight was to create hyperlinked documents whose links led from material stored on one computer (in today's parlance, a Web or file server) to documents stored on a physically distant computer system via the Internet. His development of the universal resource locator (url) protocol enabled the standardization of Internet addresses and the subsequent proliferatedtion of documents using hypertext mark-up languages (as platform-independent, browser-accessible documents) to create a Web of links among material stored on computers all over the world.

It is interesting to note that the original motivation behind these developments was to enable "big physics" projects to function more effectively and efficiently given that project teams were often comprised of members living in remote locations from one another and from the site at which their experiments would be conducted (e.g., Berners-Lee, 2000). These physicists were often faced with the need to design and build complex pieces of equipment within very close tolerances and then ship these components to the "experimental" site where they would be integrated with equipment built by other teams. By providing a means of document sharing that was platform independent as well as interactive, these scientists could work on a problem as a team, despite the fact that the team members were rarely physically in the same location. Similarly, as experiments were run the delivery of data by servers via the Internet provided an unparalleled degree of access by project team members as well as others having need or interest in the results.

The vision of these natural scientists in creating a set of tools that have resulted in the present-day World Wide Web is a powerful one. Yet this vision has been slow to enter the domains of social science research as well as in the realm of industry-driven marketing research. Given the original uses of the Internet as a defense department computer network and the use of the Web to share highly sensitive materials in connection with state-of-the-art nuclear physics, it is ironic that the resistance of industry researchers has often been grounded in the "questionable" security of serving up research protocols as well as findings over the World Wide Web!

Nonetheless, as noted earlier, we are seeing growing interest in fielding research protocols on the Web as well as the use of the Web as a medium in which to publish data. Although forecasting is always a risky business, we can offer a possible future direction for researchers who use Web-based methods to consider. As shown in Fig. 23.1, the Web makes possible a unique interactive process of research

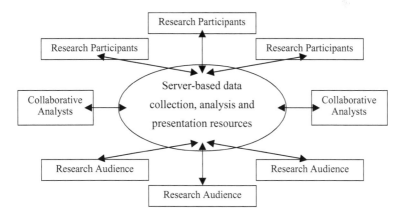

FIG. 23.1   The online "researchspace."

and analysis. This "researchspace" enables researchers to design procedures that are highly interactive and responsive to the behavior of study participants. These interactions might be limited to a single data-collection episode (as is typically the case in cross-sectional research designs) or these interactions might occur over an extended period of time as a series of discrete interactions over time. Thus, although an interview or other research process is conducted in as a virtual exchange it is possible for a researcher easily to follow up with participants over time.

Another dimension of online research has even more profound implications: The Web can enable an interactive process of data analysis and interpretation usually only found among an immediate team of collaborators. Rarely are original datasets made available to the research audience and even more rarely are the analyses conducted by the original investigators elaborated upon by those who read about the study in the literature. By publishing the analysis results as well as the data on the Web, researchers can engage in a dialog among a group of collaborative analysts, some of whom may enter the dialog only after the data have been collected and intial analyses are conducted and published.

MULTIMEDIA METHODS ONLINE

One of the unique features of the Web as a research medium is the ability to use multimedia stimuli—photograph-quality visuals, sketches, sounds, streaming video, and so on—with modest cost and the ability to reach large and/or geo-graphically dispersed populations. The emphasis in our online work to date has been on the integration of rich visual materials into the online research environment. Typically, the use of visual stimuli by consumer researchers is confined to small-sample qualitative studies that typically build on methodological traditions developed in disciplines such as clinical psychology, visual sociology, aesthetics, and anthropology. In the main, these techniques use visual material as part of a stimulus or response format and require "deep" interpretation as the analysis approach (Heisley & Levy, 1991).

For example, projective techniques such as autodriving and the TAT (Thematic Apperception Test) have been adapted to qualitative consumer research contexts (Heisley & Levy, 1991; Levy, 1981, 1985; Rook & Levy, 1983). Photographs and videos are routinely used in consumer ethnographies and naturalistic shop-ping and marketplace studies to document informants' reactions in vivo (Belk, Sherry, & Wallendorf, 1988; Belk, Wallendorf, & Sherry, 1989; Kozinets, 2001). A few isolated interpretive studies have employed images as a response format when subjects are asked to create collages expressing some underlying concept, as when respondents are asked to construct visual representations of the construct of "paradise" (Bamossy & Costa, 1997).

The Zaltman Metaphor Elicitation Technique (ZMET) developed by Zaltman and his colleagues (Zaltman, 1996, 1997; Zaltman & Coulter, 1995) represents a more systematic application of visually grounded research methods applied to both academic and industry research problems. As Zaltman (1996) noted, thought arises from images, not words, and two thirds of all stimuli reach the brain through the visual system. The ZMET system makes an important contribution as a corrective for the verbal bias in computer-mediated research. This methodology is superb for researchers wishing to conduct intensive qualitative research with a small sample to better understand how they metaphorically represent a brand personality in memory.

In contrast to the visually grounded approach represented by ZMET, one of our goals was to develop Web-based tools to manage the use of rich visual materials in order to generate data that can be quantitatively aggregated across respondents (see Englis & Solomon, 2000). Another goal was to create tools that would allow the respondent to "interact" with visual materials in a manner that would more closely allow them to express their perceptions, tastes, and other judgments and to provide those responses online via server-based software and databases. As noted by Holbrook and More (1981) and others, product evaluations are a gestalt phenomenon where design features must interact. Because pictorial information can be processed simultaneously, whereas verbal stimuli tend to be processed sequentially, the latter may hinder cognitive responses to gestalt-like phenomena. In addition, they argued that aesthetic, sensory, or symbolic benefits of products must be heard, tasted, or seen to be appreciated. Coupled with other findings indicating that pictures are more memorable than words and are more impactful stimulants of mental imagery (Pavio, 1969; Childers & Houston, 1984), the case for greater attention to visual stimuli by consumer researchers is clear.

A BROWSER-BASED, VISUALLY ORIENTED METHODOLOGY

At the core of our recent work on the development of online research tools is a Web-based interactive data-collection technique that allows respondents to manipulate visual images of products as a means of expressing their tastes and preferences. This tool is comprised of a browser-based software interface with an extensive database layer, which handles storage and retrieval of visual images (see also Englis & Solomon, 2000). One innovative feature of the software that generates the Web pages is that it is a form of dynamic html. Therefore, the large number of Web pages that might be required by a specific research application are not individually created html files, but are instead interactively created online in response to the behavior of the respondent. The specific pages, then, do not actually "exist" until the time of application when the program creates them "on the fly" on the basis of respondent behavior, research design parameters, and information in the database (visual and verbal).

These tools function on a remote server linked to the user's machine through an Internet connection. In this configuration, all Web-page components reside on the server and are assembled into Web pages as needed through the dynamic html interface and data are input to the server databases as a continuous tracking of respondent behavior at the browser. However, it is possible to use local storage systems in conjunction with a central Web server to administer research protocols. This flexibility allows researchers to solve several problems likely to be encountered in specific applications. For example, image loading times can be greatly reduced by storing the image database locally while allowing software and data streams to be controlled from the client server.

Because the software is browser based, it is platform independent and can be accessed by any standard computer system with Internet access. The dynamically created Web pages can be embedded in standard html pages or referred to by other browser-based software. In our present application, the research tools are embedded in a password-entry application that routes the respondent to the appropriate version of the application. Different "versions" constitute different experimental conditions or variations of a survey protocol. The password-entry application also serves to associate the respondent to the appropriate data record in the database, thereby permitting the interleaving of data necessary for repeated measurement protocols.

A Current Research Example: Life/Style OnLine ©

The application described here is part of a larger project concerning how consumers' lifestyle aspirations influence product evaluations (see also Englis & Solomon, 2000). This project builds on our previous work (e.g., Englis & Solomon, 1995; Solomon & Englis, 1997) in this area by examining how consumers' aspirations are expressed visually as they evaluate and select products across diverse product categories. This aspect of the research further develops our prior work in cross-category consumer decision making (Englis & Solomon, 1995, Englis & Solomon,1996; Solomon & Englis, 1994, 1997). There are three visual layers to the current data-collection paradigm: (a) an image-sorting tool (used here to allow respondent to sort images of people shown in their daily lives); (b) establishment of a social context in which product selection will occur; and (c) selection of an "ensemble" of products perceived to be ideally suited to each social context. Descriptive information pertaining to both the social images and the product images are included as the respondent navigates through the task.

The "Life" Layer of Life/Style OnLine ©

The task begins with the "Life" layer. A demonstration version of this portion of the software can be accessed at http://www.mind-share.net/portfolio.htm by following the links that lead to the Life/Style OnLine© demonstration. The first task is for respondents to sort a set of images of people shown in their daily lives—people engaged in leisure activities, at work, with their families, and so on. In the present application, respondents sort these photos into four categories—aspirational and avoidance categories, a category representing how they currently see themselves, and an irrelevant category. Once the respondent is satisfied with the image sorting she or he is then asked to confirm her or his choices and to select the one image most prototypic of each category. This prototype is later used as the stimulus image for a traditional questionnaire layer that collects data pertinent to the respondent's perceptions and evaluations of each social category. The prototype image (aspirational, avoidance, or current selves) is also used as a visual prompt (or avatar) for each social category in the "style" layer of the task, which is described in detail later.

Other Applications. We have developed a tool that is essentially a sorting task instrumented online. In the current application, the categories have been determined a priori to examine self-concept/product-congruence issues within the specific research application. However, the software can easily be modified to accommodate *any* research project requiring respondents to sort visual images into categories can be instrumented using this technology. The labeling of the categories as well as the specific number of categories can both be determined by the researcher, or the respondent can generate the number of categories he or she wishes to use and can provide their labels.

Once sorting is complete, using any of these task modalities the respondent can be asked to select a prototype image for each category, provide a label for each category, and she or he can then be sent to a questionnaire layer. The questionnaire layer can be created to contain questions common to all sorting categories or questions that are unique to selected ones. A sample of research questions that could be addressed by these sorting procedures includes:

- Stimulus discriminability and generalizability (e.g., sorting of logo or packaging options, confusion among trademark or logo designs)
- Aesthetics (e.g., sorting different options for product or package designs, retail store designs, ad executions, and so on)
- Typologies (e.g., beauty types research, product attribute typologies, Q-sorts)
- Perceptual mapping (e.g., MDS studies to understand dimensions underlying perceptions of product options)

The "Style" Layer of Life/Style OnLine©

The "Style" layer of Life/Style OnLine© asks the respondent to make product choices corresponding to one or more social scenarios. A demonstration version of this software can also be accessed at http://www.mind-share.net/portfolio.htm. Here the respondent metaphorically "moves" from room to room in the prototype individual's home and selects room-specific assortments of products that she believes are appropriate to a particular social context. Each social context is identified by a setting (e.g., a dinner party, backyard barbecue, or dinner at a restaurant), activities (e.g., dinner, a romantic encounter, leisure activities), and people present (e.g., friends, family, workmates). Information about each of these scenario features can be varied independently. For example, different groups of respondents may be presented with scenarios that vary in the formality of the setting in which the activity occurs (e.g., dinner at home versus at a restaurant) or the familiarity of the people involved (e.g., friends versus colleagues), and so on.

In the current phase of the project the respondent is asked to make selections from six discrete categories within each room on behalf of a fictional 20-something woman. For example, when the respondent is sent to the closet, she chooses within the following categories: outfits, shoes, perfumes, watches, hairstyles, and purses. She is asked to make a selection by clicking on the product image she desires. This process continues until a final selection is made for each of the six product categories.

Each scenario is mapped onto a set of rooms relevant to that scenario. For example, the respondent may first choose to visit the closet, where an outfit for the evening is chosen (e.g., an outfit, shoes, purse, and so on), followed by a visit to the kitchen for the selection of food and beverages. She might then go to the living room to choose furnishings (e.g., couches, carpeting, artwork, etc.) or to the dining room to select table-setting elements (flatware patterns, silverware, etc.). Because these physical "spaces" are virtual, the stylistic elements deemed ideally appropriate for a living room setting when a dinner party involves workmates might be changed for a different scenario involving the entertainment of friends.

The product assortments constitute a projective task in which visual (the person image from the life layer) and verbal (the scenario description) cues can be used as prompts. The collages are built up over time as the respondent moves between the contents of each product category to make a choice and then to the product categories associated with the room location in which selections are being made, where she sees the current status of her collage. The respondent can return to a product category as often as necessary and thus is free to modify her choices until she is fully satisfied with the resulting product assortment.

Following the creation of an assortment of consumption choices for a given scenario, the respondent is sent to a questionnaire layer where varying question formats are used to examine perceptions of the assortments (collages) as well as their constituent elements. In addition, respondents can be asked to provide input concerning what elements (i.e., products and/or product features) they might have preferred to include in the assortments but which were not included in the set of visual stimuli presented by the researcher.

Other Applications

- Consumer socialization/acculturation and rituals (e.g., bridal registry application with respondents picking ideal product assortments)

- Celebrity and endorser selections (e.g., perceived lifestyle elements associated with different celebrities with similar Q ratings)
- Product usage studies (e.g., the prompt is the product purchased, categories are steps associated with product usage, and within-category choices are options for product usage at each step)
- Conjoint analyses and other contingency tasks
- Qualitative studies (e.g., construction of collages, autodriving studies, visual projectives, etc.)
- Cross-cultural studies (e.g., incorporation of visual stimuli to overcome semantic barriers)

WEB-BASED REPORTS AND ANALYSIS

The typical process of data analysis and reportage in the literature represents a static "snapshot" of the research endeavor. Even the most rigorous applications of the scientific method may be fraught with subjectivity (Firat & Venkatesh, 1993; Solomon and Englis, 1997). This is particularly true in the social sciences, where inferential statistical methods are used to "interpret" findings. For this, and other reasons, several professional associations including the American Psychological Association require or recommend that the researcher maintain a full record of a data set underlying the reporting of original research. Another benefit of a Web-based research system is its potential to make available the findings of an empirical study with an unprecedented level of access to the details of the results.

One of the biggest complaints among industry consumers of market research—both custom and syndicated work—is that the reports often sit on the shelves of one or two members of the organization and are rarely consulted beyond the confines of those offices, if at all. Yet firms routinely invest large sums in commissioning research studies or in subscribing to omnibus data services. Web-based platforms for publishing the results of these research efforts offer a tremendous value-added for consumers of these research projects—and they do so at similar or lower costs than generating traditional paper reports. Security concerns can be readily addressed by placing online reports behind a password protected entry.

Static Web Reports

Web-based access to results that relies on static Web pages essentially takes an offline reporting method and translates it to the Internet. However, simply migrating an offline reporting method to a Web-based reporting method affords some immediate advantages. For example, the online report can be structured as a hypertext document, thereby providing the potential to allow the "reader" to navigate (by using hypertext links) through the report and to provide access to more of the raw content of the researcher/report writers process of analysis. Of course, a drawback of static Web reports is that the presentation of results is limited to the specific analyses used by the researcher who created the report.

Dynamic Web Reports

Static Web reports have the potential to offer a higher resolution view of the findings and analysis process in connection with empirical research. In contrast, dynamic Web reports provide a method to animate the view by providing online access to a changing database structure. The apparent structure of a dynamic report might match that of a static Web report in that a series of analysis are structured by the pages that make up the report. However, dynamic Web reports contain active links between the Web page being viewed and the database/s that contain the raw materials of the analyses shown as well as the analysis software that provides the underlying computations. Thus, dynamic Web reports can take two forms; these differ in terms of the mechanisms that trigger a refreshing of the data analysis as new data are posted:

1. One approach is to have the Web reports refreshed passively by using a time-based triggering mechanism. For example, a certain time of day can act as a server-based trigger of an analysis and Web report creating process on the server.
2. The alternative approach uses the behavior of the user to trigger an updating process that runs the analysis work in real time and then posts a new report page (or set of pages) for the user. One potential negative of this approach is that users may spend time waiting for computations to be completed and for new report pages to be posted. On the other hand, data can be accessed *ad lib*, a feature that might be valuable in extremely time-sensitive data-collection situations.

A group of academic researchers is currently using a dynamic Web-reporting system in connection with an online survey. The survey is part of an ongoing effort sponsored by researchers at Oregon State, The University of Memphis, and Berry College to improve the understanding of how business firms develop, manage, and implement their strategies in the Forest Products Industry. Participants enter the Web site using a preassigned password, complete the survey, and then are given the option of obtaining a unique identification number. Using their ID, number participants can view their own results and compare themselves to other respondents. Respondents may also return to the Web site any time after participating to view the real-time updates of the study's results.

Web-Based Data Analysis

A final method for presenting study results online provides Web-based tools for the user to construct his or her own analysis online. This approach also provides dynamic access to server-based database files but in addition uses server-based analysis software to conduct data analysis, tabulation, and report generation in real time. In this manner, the data are fully up to date and the final reports generated are customized to the needs of each individual analyst. One of the truly innovative aspects of this method is that it has the potential to transform the process of data analysis from a "lone" activity engaged in by the researcher and his immediate project collaborators into a broader collaborative effort among colleagues.

SPSS has recently made available a server-based tool that allows access to server-maintained datafiles and provides a security system as well. The goal is to expand access to data without having to duplicate and distribute the raw databases themselves. Data remain on the server in whatever formats the researcher wishes while a standard PC-based SPSS-11.0 interface is used to structure the analyses required. Data analysis is done on the server and results posted to the users machine.

Other solutions are more fully Web enabled in that a browser interface is created as the analysis design tool. For example, Web Elite, Inc. has a proprietary software system (http://www.proteusanswers.com/) that is customized on a client-by-client basis to provide a brower-based data analysis instrument. Their technology is similar to the approach used by SPSS in that database files are maintained and computations performed on a central server. However, no special software is required on the client machine. Instead, the analysis interface is accessed via a standard browser.

CONCLUSIONS

The creation of a highly interactive online researchspace enables the development of richer research designs that employ multimedia stimuli, wider geographic and temporal reach, and large reductions in research costs. Our own approach has been to develop tools that have an open architecture, permitting easy modification of functionalities and flexibility in the types of images employed and in the format of the feedback desired by the user. Adaptation to many research issues is advantageous because of the system's ability to integrate a broad range of stimuli, present these in comfortable and accessible environments in asynchronous time frames, aggregate responses across large numbers of respondents in multiple locations, and provide data to researchers almost instantly. These capabilities render the methodology ideally suited to a variety of research practitioner applications. Coupled with the structural flexibility of the system, this approach has the potential to accommodate the specific research needs of organizations spanning a wide spectrum of product categories ranging from soft goods and home furnishings to services such as tourism and entertainment. Some potential managerial applications include:

- New product development
- Packaging/logo/product design options
- Advertising pre- and posttesting using animatics, aided recall, and the life

- Pretesting of celebrity/endorser matchups
- Online consumer surveys
- Trend forecasting and diffusion studies
- Brand equity
- Simulations of store layout, tourism venues, and so on
- ecommerce/data mining
- Product bundling options for health care, financial services, and so forth
- Cross-category promotion and product placement decisions

Taken as a whole, the emerging Web-based data reporting and analysis solutions described here have the potential to impact the way the development of scientific knowledge by providing more widely disseminated and finer-grained reporting of results. These tools also provide a means of revisiting findings that might have been published years earlier and provide researchers with the possibility of testing alternative hypotheses or analysis models. Thus, the publication of a journal article need not be an endpoint to the analysis of the body of data that underlie a single researcher's (or research team's) view of the meaning of the findings. Instead, the publication of an article can be a stimulus to an ongoing dialog wherein each participant has direct access to the raw data as well as to previous analyses.

Future developments in the arena of online research tools are likely to include the development of intelligent agents that learn respondents' preferences and modify product options offered in subsequent iterations of the instrument, the creation of visual avatars by the respondent to assist in navigation through the site (and how these virtual reflections of the self can themselves be regarded as projectives), the comparison of designers' and consumers' conceptions of ideal products, the examination of contextual effects on product evaluation, and the study of individual differences in contextual sensitivity and visual versus verbal processing of research stimuli. Multimedia methods promise to be particularly useful for research populations such as teens, foreign consumers, or even illiterate respondents. We are just beginning to explore the promise of this methodology, and we hope our "vision" of the future is shared by many of our colleagues.

ACKNOWLEDGMENTS

This work was supported in part by a grant from the Department of Commerce/ National Textile Center (Grant No. A97-I11) and in part by the Richard Edgerton Fund at Berry College.

REFERENCES

Bamossy, G. J., & Costa, J. (1997). *Consuming paradise: A cultural construction.* Paper presented at the Association for Consumer Research Europe Conference, Stockholm, June.

Belk, R. W., Sherry Jr., J. F., & Wallendorf, M. (1988, March). A naturalistic inquiry into buyer and seller behavior at a swap meet. *Journal of Consumer Research, 14*, 449–470.

Belk, R. W., Wallendorf, M. & Sherry Jr., J. F. (1989, June). The sacred and the profane in consumer behavior: Theodicy on the odyssey. *Journal of Consumer Research, 16*, 1–38.

Berness-Lee, T. (2000). *Weaving the Web*. San Francisco, CA: Harper.

Bethlehem, J. G. (2000). The Routing Structure of Questionaires. *International Journal of Market Research 42*, 95–110.

Childers, T. L., & Houston, M. J. (1984, September). Conditions for a picture-superiority effect on consumer memory. *Journal of Consumer Research, 11*, 643–654.

Couper, M. P., Blair, J., & Triplett, T. (1997). A comparison of mail and e-mail for a survey of employes in federal statistical agencies. Paper presented at the American Association for Public Opinion Research. Norfolk, VA. Available on-line at: http://www.bsos.und.edu/src/papers.html.

Dillman, D. A. 2000. *Mail and Internat surveys: The tailored design method*. New York, NY. John Wiky Company.

Englis, B. G., & Pennell, G. E. (1994). "This note's for you...": Negative effects of the commercial use of popular music. *Advances in Consumer Research, 21*, 97.

Englis, B. G., & Solomon, M. R. (1995, Spring). To be *and* not to be?: Lifestyle imagery, reference groups, and the clustering of America. *Journal of Advertising, 24*, 13–28.

Englis, B. G., & Solomon, M. R. (1996). Using consumption constellation to develop integrated marketing communications. *Journal of Business Research 37*(8), 183–191.

Englis, B. G., & Solomon, M. R. (2000). *Life/Style OnLine©:* A web-based methodology for visually-oriented consumer research. *Journal of Interactive Marketing, 14* (1), 2–14.

Englis, B. G., Solomon, M. R. & Olofsson, A. (1993, December). Consumption imagery in music television: A bi-cultural perspective. *Journal of Advertising, 22*, 21–34.

Firat, A. F., & Venkatesh, A. (1993). Postmodernity: The age of marketing. International Journal of Research & Marketing, Vol. 10, 227–249.

Greguras, G. J., & Stanton, J. M. (1996). Three considerations for I/O graduate students seeking academic positions: Publish, publish, publish. *The Industrial/Organizational Psychologist, 33*(3), 92–98.

Grunert-Beckmann, S. C., & Askegaard, S. (1997). "Seeing with the mind's Eye": On the use of pictorial stimuli in values and lifestyle research. In L. R. Kahle & L. Chiagouris (Eds.), *Values, lifestyles, and psychographics*, (pp. 161–181). Mahwah, NJ: Lawerence Erlbaum Associates.

Hansen, F. (1981, June). Hemispheral lateralization: Implications for understanding consumer behavior. *Journal of Consumer Research, 8*, 23–36.

Heisley, D. D., & Levy, S. J. (1991, December). Autodriving: A photoelicitation technique. *Journal of Consumer Research, 18*, 257–272.

Hoffman, D. L., & Novak, T. P. (1996, July). Marketing in hypermedia computer-mediated environments: Conceptual foundations. *Journal of Marketing, 60*(3), 50–68.

Holbrook, M. B., & Moore, W. L. (1981, June). Feature interactions in consumer judgements of verbal versus pictorial presentations. *Journal of Consumer Research, 8*, 103–113.

Kehoe, C. M., & Pitkow, J. E. (1996). Surveying the territory: GVU's five WWW user surveys. *The World Wide Web Journal*, Retrieved January 14, 2001, From http://www.cc.gatech.edu/gvu/user_surveys/papers/w3j.html.

Kephart, P. (1998, June). Virtual testing: How interactive multimedia is changing the way research is done. *Marketing Tools*, pp. 32–35.

Kozinets, R. V. (2001). Utopian enterprise: Articulating the meanings of Star Trek's culture of consumption. *Journal of Consumer Research, 28*(1), 67–88.

Kuhnert, K., & McCauley, D. P. (1996). Applying alternative survey methods. In ed. A.I. Kraut, (Ed.), *Organizational surveys*, (pp. 233–254). San Francisco: Jossey-Bass.

Landis, C. (1995). An exploratory study of science educators' use of the Internet. *Journal of Science Education and Technology, 4*(3), 181–190.

Levy, S. J. (1981, Summer). Interpreting consumer mythology: A structural approach to consumer behavior. *Journal of Marketing, 45,* 49–63.

Levy, S. J. (1985, Summer). Dreams, fairy tales, animals and cars. *Psychology and Marketing, 2,* 49–63.

Mehta, R., & Sivadas, & (1995). Comparing response rates and response content in mail versus electronic mail surveys. *Journal of the Market Research Society, 17*(4): 429–440.

Pavio, A. (1969). Mental imagery in associative learning and memory. *Psychological Review, 76,* 241–263.

Pedhazur, E. J., & Schmelkin, C. P. (1991). *Measurement, design, and analysis: An integrated approach.* Hillsdale, NJ: Lawrence Erlbaum.

Reips, U.-D. (1997). Das psychologische experimentieren im internet [Psychological experimenting on the internet]. In B. Batinic (Ed.), *Internet für Psychologen* (pp. 245–265). Göttingen, Germany: Hogrefe. Retrieved December 4, 1998, from http://www.psy.unipd.it./.

Rook, D. W., & Levy, S. J. (1983). Psychosocial themes in consumer grooming rituals. In R. Bagozzi & A. Tybout (Eds.), *Advances in consumer research* (Vol. *10* pp. 328–333). Provo, UT: Association for Consumer Research.

Rosen E. F., & Petty, L. C. (1995). The internet and sexuality education: Tapping into the wild side. *Behavior Research Methods, Instruments and Computers, 27,* 281–284.

Schillewaert, N., Langerak, F., & Duhamel, T. (1998). Non probability sampling for WWW surveys: A comparison of methods. *Journal of the Market Research Society, 4*(40), 307–313.

Schmitt, C. H. (1997, March 2). Behind the wave: Consequences of the digital age. *San Jose Mercury News*, pp. IS–5S.

Schuldt, B. A., & Totten, J. W. (1994, Winter). Electronic mail vs. mail survey response rates. *Marketing Research*, 1–7.

Schwartz, J. (2001). New economy: A cyberlab for internet behavior. Retrieved January 14, 2001, from www.nytimes.com/2001/02/05/technology.

Sheehan, K. B., & Hoy, M. (1999). Flaming, complaining, abstaining: How online users respond to privacy concerned. *Journal of Advertings, 18*(3), 37–51.

Solomon, M. R., & Assael, H. (1987). The forest or the trees?: A gestalt approach to symbolic consumption." In J. Umiker-Sebeok (Ed.), *Marketing and semiotics: New directions in the study of signs for sale* (pp. 189–218). Berlin: Mouton de Gruyter.

Solomon, M. R., & Englis, B. G. (1994, January–February). The big picture: Product complementarity and integrated communications. *Journal of Advertising Research, 34,* 57–63.

Solomon, M. R., & Englis, B. G. (1997). Breaking out of the box: Is lifestyle a construct or a construction. In S. Brown & D. Turley (Eds.), *Consumer research: postcards from the edge* (pp. 322–349). London: Routledge.

Stanton, J. M. (1998, Automn). An empirical assessment of data collection using the internet. *Personnel psychology.* Retrieved October 13, 1998, from via proquest.umi.com.

Venkatesh, A., Dholakia, R. R., & Dholakia, N. (1996). New visions of information technology and postmodernism: Implications for advertising and marketing communications. In W. Brenner & L. Kolbe (Eds.), *The information superhighway and private households: Case studies of business impacts* (pp. 319–337). Heidelberg: Physical-Verlag.

Wall Street Journal Interactive Edition. (1998, November 16). Lands' End site will let users "Model" clothes on body type.

Walsh, S. P., Kiesler, S., Sproull, C. S., & Hesse, B. W. (1992). Self-selected and rendomly selected respondents in a computer network survey. *Public Opinion Quarterly* 56: 242–244.

Weible, R., & Wallace, J. (1998). The impact of the Internet on data collection. *Marketing Research 10*(3), 19–23.

Weimer, D. (1998, November 9). Can I try (click) that blouse (drag) in blue? *Business Week,* 86.

Yun, G. W., & Trumbo, C. W. (2000). Comparative response to a survey executed by post, e-mail, and web form. *Journal of Computer Mediated Communication.* Retrieved January 14, 2001, from http://www.ascusc.org/jcmc/vol6/issue1/yun.html

Zaltman, G. (1996). Metaphorically speaking. *Marketing Research, 8*(2), 13–20.

Zaltman, G. (1997, November) Rethinking market research: Putting people back in. *Journal of Marketing Research, XXXIV,* 424–437.

Zaltman, G., & Coulter, R. H. (1995). Seeing the voice of the customer: Metaphor-based advertising research. *Journal of Advertising Research, 35*(4), 35–51.

Author Index

Page numbers followed by f indicate a figure. Page numbers followed by t indicate a table.

Subject Index

Page numbers followed by f indicate a figure. Page numbers followed by t indicate a table.

An environmentally friendly book printed and bound in England by www.printondemand-worldwide.com

PEFC Certified

This product is
from sustainably
managed forests
and controlled
sources

www.pefc.org

This book is made entirely of chain-of-custody materials; FSC materials for the cover and PEFC materials for the text page

#0218 - 091012 - C0 - 229/152/30 - PB